T0389678

The Game of Contradictions

Historical Materialism
Book Series

The titles published in this series are listed at *brill.com/hm*

The Game of Contradictions

*The Philosophy of Friedrich Engels
and Nineteenth Century Science*

By

Sven-Eric Liedman

Translated by

J.N. Skinner

BRILL

LEIDEN | BOSTON

The translation of this volume was generously supported by the Riksbankens Jubileumsfond (RJ).

The Library of Congress Cataloging-in-Publication Data is available online at https://catalog.loc.gov
LC record available at https://lccn.loc.gov/2022050863

Typeface for the Latin, Greek, and Cyrillic scripts: "Brill". See and download: brill.com/brill-typeface.

ISSN 1570-1522
ISBN 978-90-04-52878-9 (hardback)
ISBN 978-90-04-52879-6 (e-book)

Contents

Preface to the English Translation

The first edition of this book, here available in English, was published in Swedish in 1977. That was decades ago; much has happened since then. At the time, the Soviet Union seemed to be a stable empire. The very idea that this colossus would disappear fourteen years later would have appeared to be divorced from reality. In China, Mao had died the year before, but his political programme was still unaltered. Vietnam had beaten the United States and become completely independent in a bloody war of liberation.

And in Europe a milder, more humane form of communism – Eurocommunism – had made some gains. In Sweden, we gladly spoke about democratic socialism.

Like all books, *The Game of Contradictions* bears deep traces of the time in which it was written. Anyone reading it well into the twenty-first century will be constantly reminded of this. A revision that would adapt it completely to the present would have required enormous effort and, moreover, deprived the book of its freshness. The publisher has chosen to publish the book in its original version, equipped with this introductory text from today.

The Game of Contradictions was an unexpected success upon publication. A second, abridged version came out in 1984, and was the one that most people referred to. An even more scaled-back version came out in German in 1986. Those times were not truly suitable for such a book. In what was then West Germany, it passed without a trace. In East Germany, it was kept a complete secret at first. Then came a dramatic change when the country began to come apart at the seams and people began to look for a more human version of Marxism. A large, positive review of my book was suddenly published in the leading journal *Deutsche Zeitschrift für Philosophie*. The author of the review had previously been shunted aside in his career as a dissident. Now he – and thereby also my book – were accepted, and I toured the country with my highly unorthodox interpretation of Engels. It was interesting, but at the same time obvious that the country was going downhill.

It collapsed a year later.

The unique aspect of *The Game of Contradictions* is that it puts Engels's philosophical writings – *Anti-Dühring*, *Dialectics of Nature*, and *Ludwig Feuerbach* – into a broad philosophical (and perhaps, in particular, scientific historical) perspective. In Part One, I follow in detail both Marx's and Engels's encounters with development in the natural sciences up to the breakthrough of Darwin's theories. They both primarily lie outside of the focus of the longer Part Two, which is a broad review of nineteenth-century scientific developments from physics to history. The philosophical problems that both researchers and philosophers encounter are constantly in the picture.

The task of Part Three, naturally, is to incorporate – or, rather, to embed – Engels's philosophical writings into this rich background. Only then do they become fully comprehensible. Like Marx, Engels wanted the theory that was developed above all in *Capital* (the first volume of which was published in 1867) to be a scientific theory on a par with its times. When – at first unwillingly – he wrote *Anti-Dühring*, it was a defence against the attack that the German philosopher Eugen Dühring had levelled against *Capital* specifically. This left its mark in part on the work and was also the foundation for its most singular feature, the theory of the laws of dialectics – about which more shortly.

Anti-Dühring, however, was actually a diversion from a larger project that Engels had been working on for some time. In fact, from the end of the 1850s he had been writing short paragraphs, particularly on ideas in natural philosophy that he clearly found interesting. But the real beginning was in 1873, when in a radiant letter to Marx he spoke about how he had found a number of dialectical contexts in both the natural sciences and history. This was the project he was compelled to break off to defend Marx; he resumed the work once *Anti-Dühring* was finished and completed a few longer sections.

But the project had to be abandoned again when Marx died in 1883 and it fell to Engels to complete the second and third volumes of *Capital*. This would be his chief task until his own death. But he also managed to write the long essay on Feuerbach – the most unified work he managed to write in general, and lacking the stumbling blocks (the dialectical laws, for example) that complicate the reading of both *Anti-Dühring* and *Dialectics of Nature*.

Part Three of my book elucidates the philosophical ideas Engels developed in his time. In the fourth and concluding part, the perspective is once again broadened. The chief task is to survey the problem of how science relates to ideology both in Engels's time and in Engels himself. Only thus do the elements characteristic of the times he lived in and the individual elements of Engels's philosophical writings become clear.

Anti-Dühring, *Dialectics of Nature* and *Ludwig Feuerbach* all played a crucial role in the development of what would soon come to be called Marxism. Above all, it was – as many of the pioneers of socialism and communism bore witness to – *Anti-Dühring* (like its abridged version, *Socialism: Scientific and Utopian*) alongside the *Communist Manifesto* that comprised the introduction to Marxism for the vast majority of its young advocates. In the often quite conventional introductions that were developed, the association with Engels was crucial. This tradition continued in the Soviet Union and the entire world Communist movement, especially after Stalin usurped power.

Everything became a dogmatic catechism. One of the versions of the dialect-ical laws found in *Dialectics of Nature* was turned into a guiding principle. In all the numberless introductory courses to Marxism – which soon became Marxism-Leninism – these three dialectical laws were repeated and laid out together with other similar material for memorisation. No effort was spared in the attempt to find applications for these laws. It went far too well, but for most it left a bitter aftertaste and the question: What did we actually learn from this?

In the 1970s, when I originally wrote my book, this was still a current exer-cise. That was why I decided to investigate its origins. I believe I succeeded and could thereby also show how temporary and fundamentally immaterial these laws were. But above all I was able to fish out the central elements of Engels's works, namely the attempt to place Marx's theoretical construction in a context of other emerging scientific theories.

I asserted in 1977, and I still assert in the 2020s, that there are important but easily ignored connections among various fields of research. In a time like our own of irrationalism and growing contempt for the sciences, elucidating these connections is important. Humanity's common sense does not really find the same expression in quantum physics as it does in the social sciences or his-torical research; but there is a connection there that Engels was on the trail of. Research today has changed fundamentally since Engels's time. There was no quantum physics then, and nothing was known of DNA. But the intricate connection between statements and critical questioning does – and must – continue, and be regarded not only in connection with the increasing number of finely branching specialisations but also in its greater human and historical context.

Since 1977, a tremendous amount of research has been devoted to the devel-opment of both science and philosophy from the nineteenth century onward and to Engels, Marx, and their intellectual environment. As regards the history of philosophy and science, I have not found it essential to update the results I presented in the original *Game of Contradictions*. Even though a tremendous amount of important philosophical – and in particular scientific historical – research has come out since 1977, I would like to assert that the panorama I painted in the 1970s is still essentially valid.

As regards Engels, however, I must take a position on what has happened after I completed the Swedish text. Here, namely, it is a question of the heart of the interpretation.

First, I must mention my own more current view on Engels – and above all Marx – is best shown in my 700-page biography *A World to Win: The Life and Works of Karl Marx* (London & New York: Verso, 2018). In the chapter that deals with Marx's and Engels's mutual relations, I briefly take up the subject that comprises the primary matter here.

In the literature on Engels, there is a book that not only provides its own contribution to the interpretation of Engels's philosophical writings but also stands out as a summary of earlier research, namely Kaan Kangal's *Friedrich Engels and the Dialectics of Nature*.[1] Kangal surveys large portions of earlier literature on Engels's philosophical works. Above all, it deals with the literature in English and Russian. The survey of the important Russian debate, primarily in the 1920s, is particularly valuable.

As regards German literature, the situation is worse. Presentations that are mentioned are treated unfairly as well. This becomes clear where the abridged German translation of this book is concerned. It is mentioned in a footnote among other ideas regarding when Engels's project began (my bid is 1858, with the earlier notes that would be included in *Dialectics of Nature*). The essential aspects of my study, on the other hand, are not mentioned.

Kangal primarily treats *Dialectics of Nature* as a completed totality, even if he touches in passing on the drastic changes the project underwent. He mentions, for example, that the number of dialectical laws changed in Engels's notes, but says nothing about their origins or their fateful role in the dogmatisation of Marxism. Any reader wishing to know something about this will need to turn to the book now in their hands.

Kangal's book is only one example among many of what was written about Engels after *The Game of Contradictions* was published. This also essentially applies to Elmar Altvater's monograph *Engels neu entdecken*.[2] Altvater does not mince words about the development of Engels's project over time, but this is in no way the subject of his book, which is instead relating Engels's work in an interesting way to the overshadowing problems of our time of the threats to the climate and the environment. Engels warned about humanity's belief in its omnipotence in nature. On the other hand, he did not speak as Marx did about the deepening rift between humanity and nature created by modern agriculture. Instead, Altvater seems more generally to emphasise Engels's great interest in natural science as exemplary for people of the twenty-first century as well.

Terrell Carver authored *Engels: A Very Short Introduction*, meritorious in itself but lacking scope for any more in-depth positioning of Engels's philosophical efforts.[3]

---

1   Kangal 2020.
2   Altvater 2015.
3   Carver 2003.

In connection with the hundredth anniversary of Engels's death, several conferences were arranged, the contributions to which were subsequently published. This concerns both a conference in Engels's birthplace, Wuppertal, and a conference in Paris. I myself provided contributions to both, in which I briefly summarised my studies of Engels. What I wrote there provides, at best, a hint of the results from *The Game of Contradictions*.[4]

It is striking that the name of Carl Schorlemmer occurs so rarely in the literature on Engels and Marx. Nevertheless, Schorlemmer was a close friend of both for many years, and as one of the leading chemists of the time he was a vital source of inspiration for Engels's philosophical works in particular.

In the last great Engels biography, Tristram Hunt's *Marx's General: The Revolutionary Life of Friedrich Engels*,[5] he appears twice, as a friend and inspirer. There is, on the other hand, no more detailed analysis.

There is, however, a longer article on Schorlemmer that examines him in more detail, namely Ian Angus's article 'Marx and Engels and the "Red Chemist"'.[6] It is an effective polemic against the idea that Marx was uninterested in the natural sciences, and it surveys a large part of the unfortunately relatively sparse material that exists on the intellectual exchange among Marx, Engels and Schorlemmer. It scarcely adds anything new in relation to my account from 1977.

In summary, it can thus be said that the rather comprehensive literature on Engels that has come out since 1977 does not render a new edition of *The Game of Contradictions* unwarranted. On the contrary, later studies lack both the broad philosophical and scientific historical framework and the more detailed study of how Engels's three philosophical works emerged. The dramatic interplay between Marx's and Engels's works in this field is especially absent.

It is therefore with particular pleasure that I leave this work to an English-speaking public.

Gothenburg, 31 January 2021
Sven-Eric Liedman

4   Bergmann et al. (eds) 1996; Labica and Delbraccio (eds) 1997.
5   Hunt 2009.
6   Angus 2017.

The Game of Contradictions

∵

Foreword

When I began planning the work that exists here as a large, heavy book, I thought I would produce something simple, easily understood and rather brief. It was not to be so. For that matter, there is no shame in demanding patience and attention from one's readers: simplicity is a virtue, but simplification is a nuisance. Some questions are terribly difficult and require time, space, reflection and verbosity. They can either be left alone or the effort they require can be devoted to them.

A number of problems having to do with Engels's philosophy have thus proven to be very intricate. But are they worth such great exertions? I think so, of course, otherwise I wouldn't have written all these pages. But I would like to devote the foreword to explaining why. I hope it will also be a simple introduction to the contents of this book.

The historical significance of Engels's philosophical writings is obvious. *Anti-Dühring*, at least, is one of the most translated and widely disseminated writings of world literature. Ideas and expressions from it, and from *Dialectics of Nature* and *Ludwig Feuerbach*, echo in nearly every textbook and handbook in the Soviet Union and Eastern Europe, in China, in Cuba and dozens of other countries and states. But these writings are also subject to a persistent controversy of a more global scope. It concerns their connection with Marxism in general and with Marx's theories in particular. A tremendous amount of literature comes out every year on this question, from Japan in the east to California in the west and from Tromsø in the north to Australia in the south. The scope and intensity are no coincidence: the understanding of what Marxism is – and by extension, what socialism and communism are – is highly dependent on how one views Engels's ideas on a general dialectic, including a dialectic of nature. These ideas serve as one of the major watersheds of Marxism.

But the overwhelming amount of literature on the subject should be an argument against every new book. A new book must at least be justified by the fact that it brings something that has not already been harped on and repeated in the many books that came before.

I do not intend to defend myself by providing an account of research that delves down to the smallest scraps of paper that Engels (and Marx) left behind on issues in philosophy and the natural sciences. This account is certainly important, particularly as the majority of previous literature bears troublesome, often devastating, traces of ignorance regarding what Engels (and Marx) actually said and occupied themselves with in these things. But a meticulous

© KONINKLIJKE BRILL NV, LEIDEN, 2023 | DOI:10.1163/9789004528796_002

study of the original sources has already been conducted. Its chief result has to date been published editions rather than dissertations. I would like to point out – since it appears to be unknown to most – that in the Soviet Union and Eastern Europe there is a tradition going back to David Riazanov's truly impressive work in the 1920s. Its foremost achievement to date is certainly the new second edition of the *Marx/Engels Gesamtausgabe*, the first volume of which came out in 1975, and which is distinguished by an exemplary, unrivalled exactitude, especially concerning commentaries and registers of every conceivable type. It is estimated that the edition will encompass 100 volumes accompanied by 100 volumes of *apparatus criticus*; it will be complete around the turn of the millennium. Accordingly, I could not wait for its completion, even if it would very much have facilitated my work.

There is also a large amount of carefully written monographs of various types that belong to this learned marxological tradition. East German writer Kurt Reiprich's book on Marx's and Engels's occupation with questions in the natural sciences is a substantial inventory; Russian author B.M. Kedrov's special study of Engels and chemistry lets nothing pass unnoticed. But at the same time, it must be said about these writings – like the vast majority of Soviet and Eastern European literature on Marx and Engels and on the history of Marxism – that they rarely open up interesting perspectives or pose worthwhile problems. They are anxiously eager to confirm what is already established and decreed. The image of Engels is thoroughly marked by the notion that he and Marx collaborated on every minute issue, and that the collaboration was distinguished by the most Olympian harmony. Engels's view of knowledge is described in the weakest and most evasive terms of reflection theory; his determination of the dialectic is very liberally sketched, and in the assurance that Engels never contradicted himself or Marx.

Let it thus be said that the thorough scrutiny of texts and manuscripts is itself not enough. It requires a judicious framework within which the details actually come to life and are given a context.

I regard the work on such frameworks as the substantial part of my work. The finished cabinet-work of the Soviet tradition is too narrow. The airy constructions – used, for example, in the Frankfurt School from Adorno onward – that exclude Engels because he does not square with the image of the philosopher that has been made of Marx are completely unsatisfactory.

The first, and narrower, framework I tried to construct pertains to the relationship between Marx's work and Engels's. Part One of the book is above all an attempt to determine Marx's scientific orientation. I assert that Marx's theories have *realistic* claims. He thus regards them not as temporary arrangements having a practical (i.e. revolutionary) basis but as images of a reality. The images are complex and complicated, to be sure, but they are intended to reveal the essential features of society.

This interpretation is crucial for all of the subsequent discussion. But I also wish to show how Marx, when he sat down to write what would at last become *Capital*, encountered a range of difficult issues regarding what kind of science he was actually on the way to developing. These issues concern firstly the relationship to classical liberal political economy, but by extension they also concern scientific work in general. Once again, Marx takes up Hegel. He also has a growing interest in scientific theories that occupy themselves with other areas of reality than his own (e.g. biology).

It is largely the same problem that will occupy Engels in his philosophical writings. It is here, in the general complex of problems, that the crucial similarity between Marx's and Engels's philosophical efforts lies. For the results – which in most cases are incomplete, and in Marx largely restrict themselves to isolated statements – many accidental circumstances come into play. I have taken note of these circumstances with a certain amount of completeness of detail.

But to determine the problems and to take stock of the accidental circumstances, it is not enough to keep to Marx's and Engels's own writings. Nor is it enough to put them in relation to the 'three sources of Marxism' (to use Lenin's expression) – that is, German idealistic philosophy with Hegel as its central figure, British political economy and early French socialism. These orientations certainly constitute the immediate conditions for Marx's and Engels's work. But the issues governing this work can in no way be understood only by looking for similarities and differences with traditions that were already passé in the 1860s and 1870s. It is the orientations that – like Marxism – are still in development or in embryo that comprise the most fruitful points of comparison. Hegel and Saint-Simon, Smith and Ricardo had already had their say when Marx was working on *Capital* or Engels on *Dialectics of Nature*, but a struggle with issues similar to theirs can be found in the discussions around conservation of energy, Darwinism, positivism versus German historicism, and so on.

To my knowledge, no one has to date established this broad scientific historical perspective in the tremendous amount of literature on the early history of Marxism. In the tradition of research that sought to erect high walls between Marx and Engels, the latter's late-developed philosophy is put in relation to Marx's very early statements on the world, nature, and humanity. So it is, for example, in Alfred Schmidt's *The Concept of Nature in Marx* (1971), which gained a great deal of influence, and among other things leaves its full mark on the image in the nearly manically agitated *The Tragic Deception: Marx contra Engels* (1975) by Norman Levine. This is a consequence of such factors as Marx's thought being thoroughly set in relation to its origins, the three sources, while Engels is left to swing freely in the air. The person who has perhaps done the most fundamental work in this spirit, Z.A. Jordan, has lifted his gaze a bit and caught sight of Comte's positivism in his work *The Evolution of Dialectical Materialism* (1967). However, he grapples with the simple issue of influence and finds – naturally – that Comte's teacher, Saint-Simon, was also one of the sources of Marxism. If he had instead lifted his gaze a little further, he would have found similarities between both Marx and Engels and the whole range of scientific and philosophical orientations of the age they lived in, and the issue would not have been solved with a bit of research into influence.

Part Two of my book is an attempt to sketch a panorama of the complex of scientific problems in the 1800s, or mainly the period from around 1840 to around 1890. This is no handbook presentation; on the contrary, it differs greatly from existing handbooks. I have left out, either entirely or to a great extent, disciplines that could provide me with excellent examples (e.g. linguistic research, geology and psychology). I have concentrated on the principle of conservation of energy, which touches on important areas of physics, chemistry and physiology; further, on Darwinism, a biological theory that is flooding far beyond its banks; and finally on the humanities and the social sciences, in particular on various historical disciplines: sociology and political economy, which at that time essentially had a common field of research.

I have attempted to establish a few distinct perspectives, of which I can only give a few insinuations here, on this extremely rich vein of material. One of them could be called *the antagonism between a scientific ideal based on theories that have already attained their (apparent, at least) final form and tendencies in new orientations in scientific research*. In one way, the antagonism is timeless: the image of what science should be is taken firstly from adopted theories. But the antagonism seems particularly powerful in the mid-1800s. The most complete, most imperative theory is Newtonian mechanics. Among the ideals that can be taken from it is strict determinism: every phenomenon is absolutely bound by law, and it is the task of science to formulate exactly these implacable laws. But most scientific disciplines were far from this ideal, and their advocates could react like the Romantics and Hegel earlier in the century, asserting that there was another, higher form of science originating in the spiritual life of humanity, in which mechanical determinism was said not to play a role. But they could also strive for the Newtonian ideal and try to approach it by tracking connections that genuinely seemed to be determined. It could be the relationship between stimulus and reflex, or the proportion of suicides in a community, which are thus brought out as the fixed building blocks of a future deterministic science.

But at the same time, a real scientific development was ongoing that did not square with the ideals of either the mechanical philosophy or romanticism. Let us take Darwin's theory of selection, for example. More recent Darwin research has shown that the theory of natural selection was subject to devastating criticism because it could not be formulated as an actual statement of laws. A law could only be shown to be completely valid if it could be applied in every individual case it commented on. The thesis that the individual who was better adapted to their environment superseded the individual who was less well adapted obviously did not fulfil that requirement. It was impossible to confirm the selection theory in each living organism in the way the law of gravity could be confirmed in every planet that moved and in every chunk of granite that fell to the ground. Most Darwinists reacted to the criticism by trying to link their theory to other more deterministic theories (e.g. organic chemistry).

But Darwin is not the only one on the trail of other, more complicated types of causality. Marx's theory of capital (and here I anticipate Part Three of this book) undoubtedly belongs to the same category. Marx sought to demonstrate a fundamental conformity to law in capitalism. But it was not a conformity of a mechanistic type: it could not be confirmed in every individual event in the development of capitalism. In that case, it would be refuted – as Eduard Bernstein and many others also believed – by every new small business that developed once the concentration of capital had gathered speed. Both Marx and Engels were aware of the problem, but like the Darwinists – and in general for everyone who is developing a new type of theory – it was not possible for them to clearly formulate it. The mechanistic ideal weighed heavily on them as well. Moreover, they would soon see Darwinism as the 'basis in natural history' (Marx) for their own theory. They also turned back to the Hegel of their youth, who had a number of important things to say on such subjects as the relationship between necessity (the general law) and chance (the individual case that fell outside the law). Nevertheless, their theory could not be expressed in the same terms as either mechanism, Darwin, or Hegelian idealism. There are central portions of text – and numerous individual statements – where they show themselves to be clearly aware of this and where they are trying to paint a new picture of the science they are developing. But this is not a matter of some coherent doctrine, and to be frank I do not believe that we will be able to develop it in its full breadth for some time to come. But that is another story.

Part Two also contains another perspective on the sciences of the nineteenth century. The problems of determinism, and other similar issues, were expansive: they pushed researchers outside the field of their own research to find similarities and differences with other disciplines. But at the same time science was becoming increasingly specialised. Specialisation is a process by which the scientists obtain increasingly limited and clearly delimited areas of competence. They can only comment with their own authority on matters that belong to their speciality. But a range of questions that belong to science cannot be limited to any such speciality – questions of scientific ideals, questions of the relationship between different areas of scientific theory and, naturally, questions of the uses of science, its 'benefit' – and a conflict thus arises between what I call *specialisation* and *system-building*. This conflict was extraordinarily strong during the period being discussed; Marx (and Engels in particular) were involved in it.

In the Introduction, I sought to construct a model for what fosters specialisation and interdisciplinary system-building; here I do not need to discuss this much. It is a simple schema that could apply to scientific development in general. Its originality lies in what I call the ideological determination of science. In discussions of how science is marked by the society in which it finds life, it has been consistently argued in this century that if science is at all bound to society, it is through its use for material benefits. It is forgotten that science was incessantly engaged in ideological battles about God and humanity, nation and nature, and that this linked it to society in the most tangible manner. This ideological use has consistently counteracted specialisation and encouraged system-building for the simple reason that a worldview or political orientation that seeks arguments in science cannot be satisfied with a limited technical field. It can be shown in detail how, for example, the ideological usefulness of Darwinism drove the original theory out into other areas. The question was continually pushed forward in the controversies between those faithful to the Bible and freethinkers and between liberals and socialists: Does the development of species also apply to humanity? Can human development and its various societies also be regarded as the expression of a struggle for existence? Darwinism also gained its own system-builders soon enough.

I ought to devote a few words to what I mean by 'system'. Each attempt to join two theories or to cross the boundaries between two specialities is the beginning of a system. But it is still not an actual system; it is a synthesis. The system-builder is trying not only to join the scientific theories into a whole, they are also trying above all to construct the total image of reality that the theories, taken together, are said to provide. In other words, they have an ontological claim with their overall image.

This type of system-building is extremely common in the latter half of the nineteenth century, and it comes more and more into irreconcilable opposition with increasing specialisation, which in due time would also invade the humanities, where one could otherwise romp freely (even the cautious Darwin did so). Over the short term, at least, specialisation has been victorious. It has natural support in the firmly organised and segmented research university, which in its Prussian model quickly showed its superior efficiency. It then became the pride and honour of the scientist to limit themselves and achieve certain results in their limited field. On the other hand, the conflict has in no way been resolved, and today it is obviously brewing once again. Many of the overall problems of the nineteenth century, particularly in the field of the humanities – where Marx's theories belong – have been pushed aside in the stable specialist knowledge that has developed. Now they are on the way back into focus.

Part Three begins with an inventory of Engels's complete and incomplete work on philosophy and the natural sciences, and their relation to Marx's theories as well as his own. Such work is necessary. The content of what Engels said cannot be understood without reference to origins, models and context. It is typical of the aforementioned works by Schmidt, Jordan and Levine that there is no mention of Carl Schorlemmer, the prominent chemist with whom Engels associated particularly intensely during the entire period being discussed. What Engels says about chemistry certainly appears to be mumbo-jumbo if the reader does not have the major standard work on chemistry, which Schorlemmer helped to author, before them.

I have therefore brought out Schorlemmer and others with whom Engels came into direct or purely literary contact, moving some pieces of the puzzle around and rearranging them. With the certainty that can generally be achieved in a historical account I have been able to show that it was neither Hegel nor Engels – as has always been said – but Marx who first coined the curious term 'dialectical law'. Engels made it his own only in *Anti-Dühring* when he defends it against Eugen Dühring's attacks, but subsequently it would also play a passing but fateful role in his philosophy. It can scarcely be illustrated more clearly than this that Marx was not ignorant of everything that would occupy Engels. The real relationship between their work has of course not been studied with such detail, but this detail shows that the question of the connection must be posed in a new way.

Part Three, however, also contains an attempt, in light of the preceding parts, to expose the various structures of thought in Engels's philosophical works. It is obvious that this is not a question of a single such structure: the various scientific ideals dragged Engels off in different directions. In certain of his statements, a positivist bent in the spirit of Comte can be traced: it concerns establishing extremely general laws that constitute compilations of a diversity of facts. Hegel occasionally also speaks through him. But there is also another – and more constant – tendency in his work that stands in fruitful and interesting relation to Marxist social theory. It contains a range of really original ideas about the relationship of knowledge to its object and, in particular, about the relation of the various scientific fields to one another.

In Engels, the opposition between specialisation and system-building is particularly noticeable. He can, with good reason, be called a specialist in a central field of the humanities. But the issues he encounters there compel him over the boundaries into other fields. He is well on the way to being a pure system-builder, but defends himself against it. When he comments on the natural sciences, he always refers to authoritative spokesmen, but at the same time he often notes that the scientific ideal and the worldview that are bound tightly up with their statements are foreign to him. He finds himself in a dilemma.

My interpretations of the central themes in his philosophy – his view of knowledge, his dialectics, his materialist ontology – speak, I hope, for themselves. I would like to state that his attempts here are interesting and original, but that they often remain just attempts. The speculations around 'quantity going over into quality' turn out to contain substantial ideas about the relationship between theories and fields of theory, and among the various levels of reality. The talk about the dialectic has not only a decorative function: there are relationships (e.g. between knowledge and its object, or among various theories) that appear as dialectical in Engels's view. The attempt to delimit the field of the humanities from that of biology is, in Engels, more nuanced than the 'either/or' solutions we are accustomed to ('either humans are biological beings, or biology has nothing to teach us about humanity').

I would like to emphasise that my interpretations intend to build exclusively on the materials Engels left behind. I have let obscurities that were eliminated in the later Marxist tradition remain as obscurities, and I hope that problems formulated only later – as well as knowledge and scientific ideas that belong to the twentieth century – have not left their mark on my interpretations.

The fourth and final part discusses the relationship between science and ideology. The power of ideologies over science is a central theme of the book, and of course Engels's work cannot be viewed in isolation from the ideology to whose foremost and most influential advocates he himself belonged: revolutionary socialism. The inclination of the entire second half of the nineteenth century for systems and overviews of science are intimately linked with the major ideological controversies. Essential elements in scientific development are also incomprehensible if the ideological charge of a range of theories is not taken into account.,

It should be noted that by 'ideology' I do not mean something misleading in and of itself – that is, not false consciousness or the like. In Marx and Engels, the word has various meanings (which I make a particular study of) but of interest in this context is, of course, that they are laying the foundation for a theory of ideologies while developing their own socialist ideology. From this perspective, Engels's attempt to develop what he at times calls a 'communist worldview' is particularly interesting. The theory of ideologies he himself is part of creating in *The German Ideology* says that people's ideas about themselves, society and the world originate in their concrete social roles. At the same time, he and Marx have an optimistic notion of the liberating power of knowledge: it is through knowledge of the real connections in society that the possibilities for a liberation from class rule open up. Both perspectives in no way exclude each other – real knowledge serves as a non-illusory ideology – but they can come into conflict where engaging actually existing science for one's own ideology is concerned. This conflict can be seen in Engels: it is his conviction that the world of human ideas originates in humanity's own existence, but when he looks for the guidelines for a world of communist ideas, he does not start from humanity's social existence but the world of atoms and molecules. He prepares the ground for the mistake that certain doctrines of the natural sciences from the nineteenth century should be the conditions for a revolutionary outlook. This is a mistake that turns up again and again in the history of Marxism.

The ideological significance of the natural sciences lies on another plane, however. Their first major – and still far from complete – ideological role was secularising the conception of the world. Only when humanity had liberated itself from the superior forces of heaven could they set to work at the superior forces on earth. But the natural sciences also yield much more concrete information on the frameworks for human existence. This is a viewpoint that has been obscured in Engels's writings since he was so keen on finding theories and facts in physics, chemistry and biology that in some way square with his own theories and facts regarding history and society.

To summarise, Engels's intent on building a worldview based on the Marxist theory of society and history is a good one, but his execution of that intent is inconsistent and obsolete. When he began *Anti-Dühring* and *Dialectics of Nature* in the natural sciences, where he was an amateur, he is not far too daring but far too cautious. He seeks protection in the authorities against the dangers of ignorance. Accordingly, he falls into the hands of the authorities.

The creation of this book has a long history, during which I was compelled to make use of many libraries and archives from Moscow in the east to

Manchester in the west, with the Internationall Institut voor Sociale Geschiedenis in Amsterdam lying somewhere at the heart of things. I have also tested
the patience of many seminars and other audiences with more or less unfinished theses and other isolated material that have now been included in this
work: sociologists, architects, philosophers, and lawyers have all listened patiently; historians of ideas – most of all those in Gothenburg – have been compelled to listen most patiently. Numerous people have read my manuscripts at
various stages of its creation and contributed valuable ideas. I thank them one
and all, none named and none forgotten.

4 July 1977, Gothenburg
Sven-Eric Liedman

Introduction

1 The Letter

'In bed this morning the following dialectical ideas on the natural sciences came into my head ...'

So began a letter by Friedrich Engels dated 30 May 1873.[1] The letter was addressed to Karl Marx. Engels had been living in London for three years; Marx was on a visit to Manchester to consult a doctor, and a few days later he would be returning to London.[2]

Clearly the message was an urgent one. Engels would soon enough be able to inform Marx of his new ideas in person.

It is obvious that he had not communicated any such ideas to Marx during their almost daily relations over the preceding years, or he would not have written this letter. The response he immediately received also indicated a certain amount of surprise, or at least uncertainty. The letter was greatly edifying, Marx wrote. But he would not venture any opinion until he had consulted the 'authorities' (the quotation marks are his own).[3]

By all appearances, the authorities are two Manchester residents: Samuel Moore, a lawyer and mathematician; and Carl Schorlemmer, the prominent chemist; both were close friends of Marx and Engels and shared their political opinions.

While Marx was writing his letter – one that dealt with everything except the dialectics of the natural sciences – Schorlemmer stopped by and was given Engels's ideas to study. 'He is essentially in agreement with you', Marx reported.[4]

Schorlemmer noted a few comments on Engels's letter. They were agreements such as 'Very good; my own view' and 'Quite right!'[5] It is not particularly surprising that Schorlemmer gave Engels his support. In the latter half of the 1860s, they had frequently visited each other in Manchester, and even after Engels had moved to London they met as often as the opportunity permitted. They were close friends, and Engels was the stronger, dominant party in their

---

1   MECW 44:500.
2   MECW 44:673; note 694.
3   MECW 44:504.
4   MECW 44:506.
5   MECW 44:500; notes *b*, *c*.

© KONINKLIJKE BRILL NV, LEIDEN, 2023 | DOI:10.1163/9789004528796_003

friendship. But Schorlemmer was also Engels's counsellor and guide in the natural sciences. They were also close to each other intellectually.[6]

At the same time, however, Schorlemmer's comments show that he was not aware of Engels's more far-reaching plans. He would otherwise not have had to make his position clear. Everything indicates that Engels had come quite suddenly upon the idea that would govern the majority of his activity in the period up until Marx's death in 1883.

2   The Philosophical Interest

The letter from Engels is dramatically padded out. Coming upon something new and epoch-making while lying in bed in the morning had a tradition behind it – it was how Descartes is said to have come up with analytical geometry.[7] Engels was also afraid of being robbed of his idea. He asked Marx and his natural scientist friends in Manchester not to pass the matter on.[8]

Naturally, however, the great project did not come out of thin air. Ever since the late 1850s, Engels and Marx had renewed their interest in philosophy and the natural sciences. Hegel had once again become of topical importance to them. Darwin and Darwinism had encroached on their world of ideas. The principle of conservation of energy (or the theory of the indestructibility of energy, as it was still often called) in particular occupied Engels's thoughts.

And at that exact time, the philosophical systems were on a triumphal march across Europe. A few years later, Engels would write in his foreword to *Anti-Dühring* that these systems had been springing up like mushrooms in Germany.[9] And not just in Germany! In Great Britain, in France, in the Nordic countries and in many other places, the proud and sincere attempt was being made to gather all current knowledge into a single whole. It was a process in which a great many renowned natural scientists – Huxley, Haeckel, Pasteur and others – played an essential role as inspirers and supporters.[10]

But there are other circumstances to keep in mind as well. The year was 1873; the Paris Commune was dead, the First International was dissolving. As was the

---

6   See below p. 346 et seq.

7   On the origins of the anecdote about Descartes, see Keeling 1968, p. 8.

8   MECW 44:504.

9   'For some time now in Germany systems of cosmogeny, of philosophy, of nature in general, of politics, of economics, etc., have been springing up by the dozen overnight, like mushrooms. The most insignificant *doctor philosophiae* and even a student will not go in for anything less than a complete "system"'. MECW 25:6.

10   This development will be dealt with in more detail in Part Two.

same later in the history of Marxism, a period when revolution was no longer at the door would be devoted to far-reaching, abstract work. Engels simply had the time for dialectics in the same way that Lenin, after the first Russian revolution of 1905, could concentrate on *Materialism and Empiriocriticism*. When another even more powerful revolutionary wave – the one after the First World War – had faded, the issues of Marxism and the dialectic, Marxism and philosophy, Marxism and the natural sciences returned to the fore. (There is much to indicate we are in a similar phase right now.)

For Engels, the period of relative calm – which could give rise to resignation in a revolutionary – became the conditions for a theoretical offensive. New areas of knowledge would be conquered by Marx's theories and his own. The scientific basis of socialism would be strengthened.

Engels was not alone in his efforts within the growing workers' movement. Eugen Dühring, whom he would soon come to regard as his main opponent, had come into his and Marx's field of vision back in 1868.[11] Even earlier, in 1865, Engels had received letters from Friedrich Albert Lange, the neo-Kantian philosopher, with a modest recommendation of the latter's *The Labor Question*.[12] In his response to Lange, and in a few letters to Marx, Engels expressed irritation and other sentiments over Lange's condescending manner in dealing with Hegel and unresisting transferral of Darwin's categories to human society. The questions of Hegel's significance and the areas of application for Darwinism would remain essential for him.

Towards the end of the 1860s, tanner and thinker Joseph Dietzgen had also sent Marx and Engels the manuscript for his *The Nature of Human Brainwork* to. In contrast to Dühring and Lange, Dietzgen considered himself an adherent and follower of Marx and Engels. He wanted to carry out their ideas – or, rather, provide a basis for them – in his own epistemological (in the broadest sense) work. 'The foundation of all science lies in knowledge of the thought process', he wrote in his first letter to Marx, who commented 'Bravo!' in the margins.[13]

---

11 Dühring reviewed the first volume of *Capital* in Dühring 1868. Cf. here the letters between Marx and Engels from 8 January 1868 onward (MECW 42:512 *ff*). Dühring reappears in the correspondence from 1876; see the letter of 24 May from Engels to Marx (MECW 45:118). In *Dialectics of Nature* (MECW 25) he plays a completely obscure role apart from the parts that comprised the preliminary work and omissions from *Anti-Dühring*.

12 Letter from Lange to Engels, 2 March 1865, *IISG Marx-Engels Nachlass*, L 3270. Cf. Engels's response, 29 March 1865, MECW 42:135 et seqq., and the letters between Marx and Engels regarding Lange, 6–11 March 1865, MECW 42:116 et seqq. Engels's letter to Lange was printed shortly after the turn of the twentieth century in *Die Neue Zeit*. Cf. here Vorländer 1911, p. 278. A modern edition of Lange's letter to Engels and others is Lange 1968.

13 Letter from Dietzgen to Marx, undated, *IISG Marx-Engels Nachlass*, D 1030; printed in Diet-

In a letter to Engels, however, Marx states that it was Dietzgen's bad luck that he had not studied Hegel.[14]

It has been questioned whether Marx and Engels really acquainted themselves with Dietzgen's thinking.[15] In any case, it appears likely that Dietzgen played a role when it came to focusing their attention – and Engels's in particular – on philosophical issues.

But there was also a more branched-off interest in theoretical issues within the workers' movement than what these three individual names in philosophy tell us. Events such as the trying battles around *Anti-Dühring* in the late 1870s bear witness to this. The controversies did not blaze up overnight; the conflicting standpoints had developed over several years. These worldviews were of interest to socialism. For Marxists, at least, they would remain so – though with varied intensity.

3   Engels's Philosophical Writings

In the letter from 1873, Engels develops several of the central lines of thought in his dialectics. He of course comes to a halt before the organic, before biology – but only 'until later' (*vorläufig*). As he does later, he asserts the indissoluble unity of material and movement, and he draws the conclusion that the difference between various natural sciences (later he would say: all sciences) lies in that they study different forms of material movement. He classifies the natural sciences in the same way as he would do, for the most part, from then on. The natural sciences form a hierarchy corresponding to the hierarchy of forms of movement. The path runs from the simpler to the more complex, from mechanics via 'physics proper' and chemistry to biology.[16]

These were the ideas he would cultivate and develop over the following decade. Over these years he substantially expanded his readings in the natural sciences in particular. It is possible to follow this activity in a fair amount of detail. In his letters, he disclosed much of what he was up to. More reliable information can be gained, however, from the certainly few but often exhaustive excerpts he left behind.[17] It would appear to be only his studies in chemistry

---

zgen 1911, III, p. 67 et seqq. and Dietzgen 1973, p. 119 et seqq. Cf. also letters between Marx and Engels regarding Dietzgen, 4 October 1868 and onward, MECW 43:120 et seqq.

14   Letter from Marx to Engels, 7 November 1868, MECW 43:154.
15   See for example Pannekoek p. 47.
16   MECW 44:500 et seq.
17   The excerpts are available in both *IISG* (Amsterdam) and in *IML-ZPA* (Moscow). The latter are recorded in a separate register in Reiprich 1969, p. 126 et seqq.

that he did not account for in this manner, but on that topic he had access to a living source of knowledge, namely Carl Schorlemmer.

Among the complete and half-finished chapters, drafts and paragraphs that were much later – only in 1925 – compiled and published under the title *Dialectics of Nature*, there are also a number of sections that can most closely be described as excerpts. Even in the more independently analytical sections, Engels gives a fairly exhaustive account of his sources.

Scrutinising the character or orientation in these learned studies is essential. Only through them can it be determined how *representative* Engels's ideas were of a time and a scientific and ideological situation. For example, it is striking that he sought support with greater confidence and feeling in the authorities of the natural sciences than among contemporary system-building philosophers. His philosophical inspiration is not contemporary; it is Hegel. Long before he devoted himself to his major philosophical project, he expressed the idea that Hegel's philosophy could find support in the new development of the natural sciences while simultaneously casting light on its intricate connections.[18] His ties to Hegel were and remained crucial for his work on a Marxist worldview.

But alongside Hegel he places such authorities in the natural sciences as Hermann von Helmholtz, Rudolf Clausius, Lord Kelvin, Charles Darwin and Ernst Haeckel.

Uniting such fundamentally different innovators is no easy task. In trying to assess the success of Engels's difficult enterprise, it must be remembered that he never came anywhere near to completing it. *Dialectics of Nature* is a torso. *Anti-Dühring* (or, to give its complete title, *Herr Eugen Dühring's Revolution in Science*) constitutes only a brief parenthesis in Engels's work. Marx knew what he was saying when, in a letter to Wilhelm Liebknecht, he stated that Engels was making a tremendous sacrifice in polemicising with Dühring. The work on Dühring compelled him, namely, to break off 'an incomparably more important piece of work'.[19] *Anti-Dühring* is of course an essential document. It is there that Engels, for the first time, is faced with the task of effectively uniting his ideas about the natural sciences with the Marxist understanding of society and history. In addition, the historical significance of the book is enormous – and that because through it, Engels's dialectical philosophy became known and gained influence until the publication of *Dialectics of Nature*.

But it is still first and foremost a polemical writing, and it has the necessary limitations of polemical writing. It is the subject of the polemic (i.e. Dühring's

---

18   As in the first letter where he told Marx about his newly awakened interest in both Hegel and the natural sciences, 14 July 1858; MECW 40:325 et seqq.

19   Letter from Marx to Wilhelm Liebknecht, 7 October 1876, MECW 45:154.

writings) that ultimately determine what is and is not essential to discuss. The militant intent of the book also provides the temptation of simplification and schematisation; it is a question of achieving a quick and resolute victory.

As is known, there is also a third work by Engels that is important in this context: *Ludwig Feuerbach and the End of Classical German Philosophy*. He wrote this only after Marx's death, and thus after editing the second and third volumes of *Capital* had become his chief literary task. It is a short book, only approximately 50 printed pages long, and its subject is largely the history of philosophy and ideas. At the same time, it contains numerous complete and rounded-off views on the connections between philosophy and science, ideas and observations, and systems of thought and society.

But neither *Anti-Dühring* nor *Ludwig Feuerbach* have the breadth of ideas hinted at and marked in the articles, excerpts and fragments now going by the name *Dialectics of Nature* (a title Engels, incidentally, did not actually sanction[20]). Trying to establish the principal lines of Engels's attempt at an all-encompassing dialectics therefore requires an effort at reconstruction. It is a matter of drawing out the lines he himself did not manage to.

4   Engels in the History of Marxism

An historical reconstruction of this kind is so much more essential since no thorough study, on the basis of either the history of science or of ideas, of the conditions for and principal lines in Engels's dialectics exists in the enormous literature on Marxism, on Engels, and on the dialectic. Nor, therefore, is there any proper explanation as to why this work became so overwhelmingly important for Engels himself and so controversial for the Marxists of his time and those that followed.

This is due in part to the refusal to a great extent to regard Marxism as one or more intellectual traditions that are accessible with the same means as any

---

20   Of the four folders with manuscripts and notes that formed the basis for the editions of *Dialectics of Nature*, the third bore the label '*Dialektik der Natur*'. Engels composed the table of contents of the various folders much later, and at least not before 1886 (MECW 25:685, note 512). In addition, Engels wrote 'Dialectics of Nature' as a sort of title on the various files that comprised the first folder (MEW 20:647 note 162). In the texts themselves, Engels did not use the phrase 'dialectics of nature'. When the manuscript was first published in Engels 1925, it was titled *Dialectics and Nature* (Russian and German parallel texts), as it still was in Engels 1927. Only in MEGA (1935) did the later normalised title *Dialektik der Natur* (Dialectics of Nature) turn up.

other theoretical or scientific tradition whatsoever.[21] The literature we will soon be confronted with concentrates primarily on a number of simple – but in isolation not completely meaningful – core questions of the type: What was Marx's attitude towards Engels's ideas? How can historical materialism, or the Marxist theory of society itself, be joined to the more comprehensive view? What practical significance (ideological and political) have the doctrines coming from Engels had for Marxism, socialism and communism?

I argue that it is possible to answer these questions only if they are places in a considerably much larger context than is customary. It is a matter of establishing the historical circumstances in detail, but it is also a matter of elucidating the connection with the later development of Marxist theory. There must be an explanation as to why the issue of a general dialectic – a dialectical materialism, as it gradually came to be called – became a watershed in the development of Marxism. There is a common perception that Marxist controversies over abstract matters always *concern something else*, that they are used as pieces in an ideological or political power game and that they themselves are of no importance.[22] A perception like this can always be tested: it is entirely possible to see whether a break in the tradition is answered and dictated by a break in political or ideological development.

But the issue thus expands to also apply to the rationality in the theory originating from Engels. Is it a theory that fulfils all the intellectual demands and theoretical requirements in the period when it is created? Does it pre-

---

21   The person in contemporary secondary literature who most closely had this intent was Yugoslavian philosopher Predrag Vranicki. With his history, he wanted to study the development of Marxist theory (Vranicki 1961, I, p. 9). Above all, however, he produced a number of (in most cases) penetrating and well-realised citations of the classics of Marxism. As regards his rather detailed treatment of Engels's later authorship (Vranicki 1961, I, pp. 211–48), he there expanded the traditional standpoint – fostered by the Praxis group, to which he belonged – that Engels's general dialectic had no intrinsic connection with historical materialism. He neglected placing it in its historical context entirely, nor did he succeed in explaining its great and controversy-causing significance in the history of Marxism. In more comprehensive overviews of the history of socialism, ideas regarding a development of theory in Marxism are almost entirely lacking; this process is obscured by political events and names in Cole (and even more so in the more superficial Landauer). *Histoire générale de socialisme* (published by J. Droz), the French counterpart that is more thorough and more oriented on essentials, had at the time of this book's writing published two out of the planned three volumes; it includes a number of valuable studies, none of which can be said to illuminate the development of Marxism in more than isolated spots.

22   This is especially common in presentations of the development of Soviet Marxism. Cf. the mutually very disparate ideas in Ahlberg and Negt 1969. Bochenski and Wetter go even further in the same direction.

serve its plausibility through all the fundamental scientific crises, philosophical upheavals, turns of the ideological tide and social convulsions that occurred after the 1870s and 1880s? Is it still plausible to as ontological questions (i.e. questions about what 'really' exists)? What kind of insights could the answers to similar questions provide?

The subject of this book, however, is Friedrich Engels's philosophy in its roots in the world of nineteenth-century science. By way of introduction, I will sketch in a few outlines of Marxism's subsequent development. This critical assessment will be provided in the concluding chapter. The primary task is historical, in a more limited meaning; it concerns the reconstruction of a world of ideas, a scientific environment, an ideological – and therefore social – field of force.

But every assessment of the context – or occasionally lack of context – in what Engels wrote assumes interpretations, and interpreting is also choosing among the traditions that lie between him and us. It would be ridiculous to demand some sort of loyalty to a tradition of this kind. What is important is to have some sort of idea of their various contents. Orientation in a landscape is possible only if something is known about the immediate location.

It is also necessary to subject Engels's doctrines to a thoroughly critical review to get at the lifeblood in them in general. From our own starting points, we must attempt to animate and experience Engels's struggle with the most far-reaching theoretical and ideological issues.

History is never virgin soil. We ourselves are always treading upon it.

5   The Watersheds in Marxism

The theoretical traditions of Marxism may appear chaotic, or at least as a number of incoherent zigzags among all the political and ideological controversies, national and international coalitions and oppositions, new theoretical and scientific orientations and fundamental social transformations. It is equally possible to find consistency in these traditions and in the conflicts among them.

We can put the questions of orthodoxy – of correct or essential Marxism – aside. That is an ideological issue, not a theoretical one. The theoretical question is: Which scientific positions, which theses on the world and humanity are not only compatible with the fundamental theory of the structure and development of human – and in particular capitalist – society but are also dedicated to providing it with richer content, stimulate it with new problems, bringing it greater and better knowledge and expanding its practical usefulness?

But this extremely difficult question can only be answered preliminarily and at the end of our study, and this preliminary answer will only apply to Engels's theses and the positions various orientations have taken on them during the development of Marxism.

Engels's writings in *Anti-Dühring*, *Dialectics of Nature* and *Ludwig Feuerbach*, however, remain leading controversial issues in Marxism. No method is better suited to structuring the various Marxist traditions than starting from their relationship to the fundamental statements in Engels. Drawing a boundary between revolutionaries and revisionists – as so often happens – is to look for the starting point in the political and ideological consequences of the theory. It is more expected, if also even more comfortable, to group the various orientations according to national affiliation.

The central theoretical antagonisms concern such aspects as the scope of the theory, its character, its relationship to ideology and to political practice. There are two questions – both even brought out emphatically by Engels – that are, if not the very foundation of the antagonisms, at least the most easily recognisable symptoms of them. They can serve as rules of thumb for how one Marxist orientation or another should be placed.

The first question concerns Hegel. It does not first and foremost concern what purely historical significance Hegel's philosophy had for the genesis and early development of Marxism. It concerns Hegel's current significance, or more precisely: whether study of Hegelian philosophy deepens insights into Marxism and promotes Marxist theoretical development.

It may seem peculiar that such an abstract question has been given such crucial significance. But the question contains more than it immediately seems to let on: the response is not primarily a position on Hegel but on the problem of the character of Marxism and its relationship to other scientific orientations.

The second question concerns the scope of the theoretical domain of Marxism. Is there a general Marxist dialectic, including a dialectic of nature? Is it possible, without botching and missing the historical materialist interpretation, to go beyond the field of human action and knowledge with the tools developed in Marxist social and historical research?

We can construct the following diagram in which '+' signifies a (for now unqualified) 'yes' and '–' a 'no' to the questions:

Dialectic of nature?

	+	–
+	1)	2)
–	3)	4)

Hegel?

By placing various Marxists in one of these four squares, we will of course not obtain any pure, clear categories: we will not reveal four clearly differentiated and coherent traditions at one stroke. But we will have a starting point for our clarifications.

In square 1, naturally, is Engels (I will let the controversial question of where Marx belongs wait), and here also are Kautsky, Lenin, most of Soviet, Chinese and Eastern European Marxism, and the majority of communist theoreticians in Western Europe and the rest of the world. Here is what is usually – often a bit sloppily – called 'orthodox Marxism'.

The second square, which thus contains those who embrace an all-encompassing dialectic but deny Hegel's current significance, houses two completely different orientations. On the one side, Stalin and those who carried out his ideas should be counted here.[23] On the other, the modern (primarily French) school with Louis Althusser as its most renowned representative ought to belong here.[24]

Square 3 is more homogeneous; a unified tradition in Marxism can be spoken of with certainty here. An essential work in this tradition is Georg Lukács's *History and Class Consciousness*, from which the threads run out to the Frankfurt School with Max Horkheimer, Theodor W. Adorno, Herbert Marcuse, Jürgen Habermas, Alfred Schmidt and many others. But in this same orientation there is also a more or less existentialist Marxism (Jean-Paul Sartre is its most renowned representative) and the Praxis School in Yugoslavia.

The last square, once again, may seem rather heterogeneous; it encompasses individual and solitary efforts rather than actual orientations. Here we will find, among many others, Eduard Bernstein's revisionism as well as late Karl Korsch (author of *Karl Marx*) and probably also C. Wright Mills, who wrote *The Marxists*. Enumerating more names here is unnecessary; what holds the group together is obvious enough. Here, there is an unwillingness to ascribe Marxism a kind of scientific exclusivity; there is thus a distance from the idea of a specific Marxist philosophy. In general, there is an intention to turn Marxism into

---

23   Concerning Stalin's position on Hegel, see Ballestrem 1968, p. 111 and the literature cited there, as well as Fetscher 1967, p. 46.

24   Althusser asserted, consistently and programmatically, that Hegel lacked relevance significant for fully developed Marxist theory; see Althusser 1968. His positions on the dialectics of nature, on the other hand, have scarcely emerged. Upon direct request (letter of 28 August 1972) he explained that: 1) the idea of a dialectic of nature had polemical value – history did not begin with humanity; 2) this did not prevent historical idealism; and 3) it could not be serviceable without a resolute cleansing of the positivist features in Engels, above all his concept of laws.

one social doctrine among many, fulfilling general demands for an orientation on empirical research. One could perhaps speak of 'empirical Marxism'.

This diagram could put us on the tracks of what is one of the major – all too seldom observed – boundaries within Marxism. Those who deny the general dialectic (including the dialectic of nature) regard Marxism as exclusively a more or less distinctive method of posing and solving problems. Those who are adherents, on the other hand, regard Marxism in addition and perhaps above all as a theory about reality (or a group of theories, or a system). According to the former, Marxism can preserve its identity even if it is gradually compelled to abandon all its original theses and theories of society and humanity, as long as it preserves its fundamental method;[25] according to the latter, there are at least some general theses that are indispensable for Marxism and in their opinion the Marxist ambition must always be to formulate as elaborate and comprehensive a theory as possible.

The issue of Hegel's topicality for Marxism does not reveal as clear a boundary, but it is essential for every attempt to assess the various interpretations of the distinctive theoretical character of Marxism.

6   The Determinations of Science

This diagram, however, notes only symptoms. It teaches us nothing about the conditions for the contradictory development of Marxism. In addition, a perspective and an apparatus of concepts are required that in principle must be useful in all scientific and general theoretical development. It is important not to ascribe any unique position to Marxism – in that case, the starting point would be that it is inexplicable.

Here, I will sketch out in passing some terminology that I have also used in other materials on the history of science and of ideas.[26] The terms will be of particular use in the more detailed scrutiny of Engels's work.

The inspiration for my terminology is Marxist as well. There does not need to be anything unfortunate in that. To be precise, I am attempting to apply and concretise certain features in the general Marxist conception of base and superstructure, insofar as that part can be used in the development of the sciences and of ideas. It is obvious that if this thesis is to have any value, it must also

---

25   Lukács 1968, p. 1 et seq.
26   In an as yet unpublished essay on traditions of research in the humanities and in a number of studies on the history of specialisation that are still works in progress.

be usable in Marxist theories; they of course appear there as theories among theories, related in different ways to the development of the social base.

To get at the question of what drives a theory or system of theories in one direction or another, it is necessary to distinguish a number of *determinations* (I use the term instead of the more customary *factors* or *functions*)[27] that characterise (determine) the theories in question in different ways and to various extents. Taken together, the determinations will constitute a rational whole, and it must be possible to concretise them.

First and foremost, the *internal* determinations must be distinguishable from the *external*. If what is intrinsic to the theory is allowed to flow into the use it can have, the needs it can feel or the forces outside science that could affect it, it is no longer regarded as a theory (i.e. as an attempt to explicitly express something essential about a larger or smaller part of reality).

Let us therefore, for a moment, ignore the external circumstances of the theories and the whole work of science. Taking the internal relationships into account in this manner, all theoretical or scientific development appears as the result of now harmonic, now contradictory relationships between problems and observations, large perspectives and small, theory and empiricism. I will

---

27   The term 'factor', which ought to be the most general, produces a semblance of exactness with its physical associations. In fact, entities both large and small – and often completely incompatible – are included in the 'factors' that influenced science in its course. The most common is the distinction between internal and external factors; cf. for example Kuhn 1970, pp. 69 and 75. Merton can distinguish 'economic factors' (1968, p. 664). The corresponding 'inner' or internal factors could be given various names. Horowitz (1961, p. 36) speaks about 'ideational factors'. Popper, who was otherwise not that prone to such vocabulary, could use the phrase 'human factor' (1961, p. 158). The term 'function' has a similar ambiguity. Horowitz (1961, p. 8) could distinguish between the 'truth functions' and 'ideological functions' of science and could also say that science, religion, myths and logic (!) had their functions in the genesis of human ideologues (p. 37 f). Merton (1968, p. 597) speaks of 'functions of norms of pure science'; the concept of function is otherwise central in the functionalist orientation in sociology, which had Merton as one of its leading representatives. Entirely regardless of the ambiguity in the terms 'factor' and 'function' in the context of the history of science, they are unusable in an analysis that starts from the Marxist model of base and superstructure. It is true that the term 'determination' is not accepted in the Marxist tradition; it occurs in places, for example Marx 1953, p. 7 et seq. (*Bestimmung*) and in Althusser 1965 and 1968 (above all in the phrase *surdétermination* [overdetermination] in passing). However, it is not from these sources that I took the term 'determination'. My reasons are, on the one hand, that the term is what could be called causally neutral (in other words, it lacks the mechanistic overtones of 'factor' and the biological ones of 'function') and on the other that the determinations constructed could be brought to the same general level. These are important conditions for an abstract model of an extremely complex sphere.

speak about the theoretical and empirical determinations, respectively, of the sciences.[28]

The history of the sciences is full of examples of speculative theories and orientations; the theoretical determination is strong there and the empirical weak. But there are also examples of collecting facts without any fixed theory in mind. Finally, there are cases in which both the theoretical and empirical determination are strong; these are theoretically advanced disciplines (with physics as the showpiece) in which theory and empiricism are normally in a harmonic relationship with each other.

The more advanced a science is, the more difficult it is to hear the echo of the society that surrounds and maintains it.

But this does not mean that the discipline in question needs to have isolated itself and lose every area of application. Quite the contrary. The usefulness of a science does not correspond to its internal qualities. There are two major areas of application outside of science to keep in mind. We are constantly reminded of one of them: *practical or material* application, the use that entails involving scientific knowledge in the development of the socioeconomic base. The other – in essential respects diametrically opposed – use is easier to ignore today. I will call this the *practical and ideal* application or, for brevity's sake, the *ideological* application. This entails using scientific results to confirm, strengthen or change humanity's ideas and values about the world and society or everything that could happen to them.[29]

Keeping the ideological application in mind will be of the utmost importance when studying Engels's philosophical works and the Marxist traditions that take various positions on them.

But establishing an area of application is not enough. It must also be asked: to what extent does the use of a theory or a conception mark the theory or conception itself? The question of whether the results of the scientific work are practical or materially or ideologically determined must be investigated.

If they are determined by their use, that does not at all mean that they are stained, distorted, or scientifically inferior. Both practical or material, and ideological, applications have often played an extraordinarily progressive role in the history of the sciences.

---

28   I use the term 'science' here in a neutral, descriptive sense; the boundaries with pure myth-making on the one side and the application of knowledge (technique) on the other are fluid.

29   In a more complete analysis, the knowledge used to secure or change the political and legal levels would naturally be taken into consideration; it would then be necessary to include a separate *practical and political* and *practical and legal* (*administrative*) use, primarily of the social sciences.

Two ways in which the external determinations characterise internal scientific relationships can be distinguished. On the one hand, we can speak of a quantitative determination. Generally speaking, this means that attention and resources are oriented on a definite, useful area and that this area is therefore brought into a more rapid rate of growth – perhaps at the cost of other scientific fields. The rapid development of certain biological disciplines in the late 1800s, for example, is incomprehensible if the ideological usefulness of Darwinism is not taken into account. Similarly, the approximately simultaneous expansion of chemistry cannot be understood if its rapidly growing significance for the development of agriculture and industry is ignored.

But the determinations can also be qualitative. All scientific work is then coloured by the external needs it has to fill. It is extremely easy to find examples of a qualitative ideological determination: science and ideology fit together like hand in glove. Not even a qualitative imprint of this kind, however, necessarily entails a distortion of the theoretical result. The reader only needs to recall the liberation and development that a long range of disciplines underwent when at one time they were invaded by new bourgeois conceptions. The significance a determination obtains for scientific development itself can generally only be determined on an internal path. The extent to which its use intervenes in the play between theory and empirical facts, marches off with theory or leaves important empirical facts behind must be seen.

I am therefore speaking of four types of determinations: two internal (theoretical and empirical) and two external (practical or material, and ideological).

I envision the relationships among these four as follows: by and large, the practical or material determination normally fosters the orientation of all research on the empirical, the concrete and the specialised. As regards the ideological determination, an ideological argument obtains greater cogency the larger the portion of the scientific hierarchy it can find support in (i.e. the broader and more comprehensive the theory or theories confirming a certain worldview, outlook on life, political ideology, moral doctrine or aesthetic are). This means that in contrast to the practical or material determination, the ideological strengthens the theoretical determination.

Without the ideological determination, the entire enterprise that Engels embarked upon well into middle age is entirely inexplicable.

The external determinations can be related to the base in a materialist schema of society. It is obvious that the material application belongs in the process of material production. But the ideologies – in the broad sense used here – can ultimately be connected with social classes, though in an indirect and abstract manner. We obtain the following model:

		internal determinations:	superstructure
superstructure		theoretical	ideological determination
base	practical and material determination	empirical	
			base

Of course, this picture is highly approximate. It illustrates a normal relationship between science and the environment that gives it life.

7   Marxism and Ideology

Every discussion of the origin and development of dialectical materialism assumes knowledge of the substantial ideological engagement in various sciences that is so striking at the end of the nineteenth century. In field after field, theory was set against theory and ideology against ideology. We must ask ourselves: What did this mean for the character and development of various disciplines? How did this mark all the prevalent attempts at syntheses and a 'scientifically based' worldview? What significance did this have in turn for the ideologies?

From the point of view of the history of science, the era in question is not only distinguished by ideological engagement. Internal scientific development is rapid. A range of new disciplines are engaged in material production in ways they never were before; it is now that we reach what is called 'the technology of physics and chemistry'[30] or the period in which the most advanced physics and chemistry can be transformed directly into technology. All this affected the views of science and strengthened its authority.

When physics underwent its well-known crisis of fundamentals early in the twentieth century, many came to the conclusion that science was not at all suitable as the foundation for worldviews. But there were also other circumstances that, relatively speaking, reduced ideological engagement in science. More and more philosophers abandoned the attempts to construct grandiose syntheses of human knowledge. In many scientific disciplines, the material orientation prevailed over the ideological: the useful field of genetics established

---

30   The term originates from Veblen (1923, Chapter x, 'The Technology of Physics and Chemistry'). Regarding this development, see also Landes (1965), Lilley (1965), Bernal (1969) and Andersson (1975).

itself and the great debates over Darwinism diminished. The ideologies themselves changed; in many cases, political opinions especially limited their field of interest to society.

It is obvious that this change affected the development of dialectical materialism. There were, of course, Marxists like Karl Kautsky and Georgi Plekhanov who in the first place attempted to guard the positions they regarded as essential in Marx's and Engels's Marxism. But they found themselves on the defensive. The offensive came from those attempting to revise Marxism and liberate it from what was perceived as passé and nineteenth-century. Hegel came under fire, and thereby also Engels's attempt at a materialist worldview, an ontology on the foundation of the sciences. In his well-known writing *The Preconditions of Socialism*, Bernstein spoke on the pitfalls of the Hegelian dialectic[31] and sought after a social-democratic Kant.[32] In fact, a number of Kantians turned up in Marxism at the turn of the twentieth century.[33] From a Kantian point of departure, they attempted to remove the ontological materialism, leaving only historical materialism behind. The entire question of a view of the world was repudiated as bad metaphysics. The theory of knowledge and science came into view. Whereas Engels devoted rather limited interest to the questions of the relationship between knowledge and its objects, attention was now being shifted to this field.

Lenin's *Materialism and Empiriocriticism*, which appears to posterity as an extraordinarily energetic attempt to maintain the influence from Engels in Marxism, also bears traces of this shift in perspective. Lenin was not addressing the Kantians in the first place, but the comrades in the Bolshevik party who were looking for new grounds in Ernst Mach's and Richard Avenarius's philosophies for the Marxist conception of history and theory of society. But what Lenin constantly brought to the fore was a realistic conception of knowledge, or the thesis that knowledge 'reflects' its object. He certainly did not lack support in Engels for this viewpoint. But it is striking that Engels's main problem – creating a coherent philosophy or theory of the world on the foundation of the current sciences – came in second for Lenin. There is nothing surprising in this,

---

31   Chapter 2a has the title *'Die Fallstricke der hegelianisch-dialektischen Methode'* (The Pitfalls of the Hegelian Dialectic Method); Bernstein 1899 and 1969.

32   Bernstein 1899, p. 256 et seq.

33   Vorländer, Staudinger and Stammler in Germany were among those who belonged to this circle; in Austria it flourished as 'Austro-Marxism', whose leading theoretician, Max Adler, made an ambitious attempt to unite Marx and Kant. Vorländer – who provides a rather detailed presentation of the Marxistically inclined discussions about Kant – and *Austromarxismus*, a volume of selected works, will have to suffice. Heintel and Weigand – Abendroth are special presentations of Adler's philosophy.

as the immediate struggle concerned these issues. But it shows how the ideolo-gical interest in specific scientific theories subsided, and how this relationship characterised the Marxist discussion in general. The general question was no longer 'What do the standpoints of the various sciences mean for a coherent conception of the world?' but 'What is scientific knowledge?'

It was only in the Soviet Union – and indirectly in the world communist movement – that the questions of the scientific hierarchy and the place of the Marxist conception of society in it returned to the fore. There were a great many conditions for this development. Unlike the 1870s and 1880s, in the 1920s and 1930s there was no longer a predominant interest in 'scientific conceptions of the world' throughout the scientific world. But the Soviet Union was suf-ficiently closed and independent to drive such a tradition forward on its own. The questions of what is real and consistent Marxism were ideologically crucial and were brought to the fore in all fields – in the sciences as well. It was also only then that the whole of Engels's far-reaching programme became gener-ally known – it was then that *Dialectics of Nature* came out in print. Similarly, Lenin's *Conspectus on Hegel's* Science of Logic, written in 1914 at the start of the First World War – was published, and here a Lenin with a focus of interest different than the one in *Materialism and Empiriocriticism*, a focus better har-monised with Engels's, shows through.

At the same time, however, the major discussions about Marxism and the dialectic in the Soviet Union bear witness to the fact that the inheritance from Engels and Lenin could be used in different ways. The conflicts between Abram Deborin and his adherents on the one side, and the 'mechanists' on the other, show this. The conflict especially concerned how coherent the scientific hier-archy is (i.e. the extent to which the organic sciences must differ from the inorganic sciences, the social sciences and humanities from biology, and so on). For Engels, this was the fateful issue itself, but it is characteristic that now in the 1920s he could be called to the defence of contrary and irreconcilable points of view.

The Soviet development would simultaneously be characterised by the cir-cumstance that in revolutionary socialism – indeed, in communism – orient-ations emerged that frankly denied the claims of dialectical materialism. In *History and Class* Consciousness, Georg Lukács stated that Engels had made a mistake when speaking about a specific dialectic of nature. This assertion would later be integrated into and developed in the Frankfurt School in Ger-many. Through the coincidence of the antagonisms regarding the dialectic of nature with concrete ideological and political differences of opinion, the entire discussion about dialectical materialism would be conducted with ideological overtones and governed by political means. The issues of what the development in a range of sciences since the days of Engels could mean for his ideas were neglected, or entire theories and orientations were also rejected as 'undialectical'. Einstein's theory of relativity, for example, suffered the latter fate, being branded as incompatible with Marxism until 1955.[34]

It was during the 1930s, after Stalin put an end to the discussion between Deborin and his opponents and staked out a general line in philosophy as well, that textbook Marxism reached its perfection in the Soviet Union. Dialectical materialism was codified into a number of superordinate and subordinate propositions. Theory and ideology became one. Scientific truth became the correct class standpoint.

Among those who want to remain Marxists but deny dialectical materialism, on the other hand, the question of the relationship of the Marxist conception of society to other scientific fields and theories moves completely into the background. It is often said – for example, among the representatives of the Frankfurt School – that there is a gap that has been established between the natural sciences and those dealing with humanity. The main issue, not only for Engels but for the entire late nineteenth century was thrown overboard.

By and large, both these main orientations have left their mark on the more theoretically oriented Marxist debate up to the present day. The standpoints of the Frankfurt School have developed in new but similar directions in existentially imprinted Marxism, in the oppositional Praxis School in the former Yugoslavia, and so on. Marxism in the Soviet Union and Eastern Europe can still be summarised in the handbook *Fundamentals of Marxism-Leninism*. This applies likewise on the same plane in China.

But the traditions have still changed and developed. As a doctrinal construction, dialectical materialism is no longer as closed off to new scientific orientations and theories. Today, scarcely any scientifically predominant theory is repudiated on the grounds that it is contrary to the fundamental principles of Marxism. At the same time, a new range of techniques and methods have been developed that aid in elucidating and developing dialectical materialism.[35] Uncertainty in general still prevails in the view of the area of application of dialectical materialism – an uncertainty that can actually be traced all the way back to Engels. On the one hand, dialectical materialism can be seen as only an aid in interpreting and finding the connections among various scientific results; but in addition it can be regarded as a supplier of heuristic principles that

---

34   Cf. here the extremely detailed Müller-Markus 1966.
35   Above all the abundant use of cybernetic models developed by Soviet researchers such as Vasily Parin and Alexander Spirkin can be included here. Also interesting in this context are the works of the East German Günther Klaus; see chiefly Klaus 1966 and 1972.

could be of use in scientific work itself. If the same theories that prevail in other quarters are accepted from dialectic points of view, the heuristic value must be at least extremely limited. (Naturally, the Marxist conception of history and society constitutes an exception – there are distinct and original theories here that differ from non-Marxist theories.) It thus seems that *de facto* acceptance of the fact that the process of research (at least in the natural sciences) is the same means either that one has a basic Marxist worldview, or that they do not but hesitate to openly draw this conclusion.

It could be said, purely generally, that the dialectical materialist tradition has essentially lost its exclusivity. But to the greatest extent it also promotes development in science and philosophy unaffected by Marxism. Interest in ontological questions, in questions dealing with the scientific conception of the world, is growing. Engels's major enterprise no longer seems as fantastic and unrealistic. It is bound up, in part at least, with the increase in ideological interest in science in general – and thus the ideological determination of science. The role of science in late capitalism as well as in the socialist world has become problematic. It is no longer possible to regard it as only a supplier of countless utilities; taken together, utilities can become dangers. One way or another, their use must be brought under control – but this is not possible if this is not understood in its internal and external connections.

Going back to Engels's incomplete – and in many respects, contradictory – works, studying their background and their use in later Marxism, is therefore in many respects an enterprise of immediate interest. Through it we will become acquainted with a piece of our own history, we will obtain clarity in what at least *could be* Marxism, and we will come in contact with a way of looking at the sciences that could, in part, be important and rewarding.

Let us give that a try.

PART ONE

CHAPTER 1

Back to Hegel

1 The Components of Marxism

The history of Marxism, over a century long, is criss-crossed by struggles over
the scope and limits of Marxist theory, its character and relation to other intellectual traditions.

Marxists have laid claim to scientific originality in at least four different
areas:

1. The theory of material production, in particular capitalist material production;
2. The theory of the relation between material production and other social
   phenomena (the materialist conception of history);
3. A general worldview founded on the specialised sciences; and
4. A theory of knowledge and of science.

The first two areas are usually put together under the heading of historical
materialism; the latter two, along with a phrase coined by Georgi Plekhanov,[1]
are classed under dialectical materialism.

From the days of Marx and Engels, it has been clear that a distinction must
be made between the specific theory of material production and the general
conception of history; Engels spoke with a particular liking of Marx's 'two great
discoveries'.[2] On the other hand, it is not at all as generally acknowledged that a
boundary should be drawn between a conception of the world, or ontology, and
a theory of knowledge and science. The distinction lacks any support whatsoever in the early tradition. Engels – as we will see later – used the word 'thinking'
alternately in its epistemological and ontological meanings, now signifying the
relation between knowledge and its object, now the physiological (and psychological) processes of the brain. A distinction is necessary to avoid ending up in
confusion.

---

1 The year is 1891; the place: *Die Neue Zeit*. It concerns a memorial article on Hegel; see
   Plekhanov 1891/92. Engels notified Kautsky that he found the article '*ausgezeichnet*' (excellent); letter of 3 December 1891 to Kautsky, MECW 49:317. Cf. Carew Hunt 1955, p. 5, Jordan
   1967, pp. 3 and 397, and Baron 1963, p. 287.
2 So, for example, in *Socialism: Utopian and Scientific*: 'These two great discoveries, the materialistic conception of history and the revelation of the secret of capitalistic production through
   surplus-value, we owe to Marx'. MECW 24:305.

One of the obvious major controversial issues regarding Marxism concerns the justification of dialectical materialism and of general ontology in particular. It concerns whether Marxism only becomes a complete and consistent materialist outlook with it, as Lenin asserts,[3] or whether – as Lukács says – it is only a simple mistake due to 'Engels – following Hegel's mistaken lead – extend[ing] the method to apply also to nature'.[4]

But the controversies over dialectical materialism are bound up with a range of other fiery issues. The most fundamental, theoretically speaking, are these: What distinguishes the materialist conception of history, and the theory of the capitalist method of production in particular? What differentiates it from other conceptions and theories of the same phenomena? Do these conditions also have consequences for other scientific fields?

2   Historical Materialism

If we were able to produce the distinct contours of historical materialism with a few swift cuts, the question of its character would not be so difficult. But the dispute applies to historical materialism as well. Indeed, that is where its actual foundation lies.

For the time being, we do not need to go into the various conceptions. Or, rather, we do not yet need to take them into account to the extent they entail different views in the historical question of how historical materialism appeared to Marx and Engels and how it was rooted in the intellectual age they lived in. This question leads to another question at the centre of this work, namely why the Marxist conception of history and theory of society came to be associated with a range of extensive problems concerning other sciences and theories, and the entire foundation of scientific activity. How rational was this connection? To what extent was it ideologically determined (i.e. determined by the ambition of creating a socialist worldview in competition with other worldviews)?

There are a few simple dates to keep in mind here. It is quite generally acknowledged that the materialist conception of history existed, at least in its essentials, in *The German Ideology*, the great and never-completed work that Marx and Engels wrote together in 1845–46.[5] It says there that 'consciousness'

---

3   LCW 14:336.
4   Lukács 1968, p. 24.
5   Cf. for example, the foreword, signed by the Institute for Marxism-Leninism in Moscow, to *The German Ideology*, MEW 3:VII, and Oiserman 1965, p. 379 et seqq. – in which the entirely

is determined by 'being', that it is thus humanity's practical material conditions that make history a coherent and intelligible process and form the foundation for their ideas.[6] The well-known distinction between base and superstructure that Marx made in the foreword to *A Contribution to the Critique of Political Economy*[7] is recognisable in these general formulations. It does not fundamentally differ from the general statement on human history that Engels makes in his more far-reaching works such as *Anti-Dühring*.[8] They can be read in Marx's and Engels's specialised historical studies such as *The Peasant War in Germany* (Engels) or *The Eighteenth Brumaire of Louis Bonaparte* (Marx). Generally, it could be said that class – or rather, the concept of class struggle – moved more to the fore from the *Communist Manifesto* onward, but with that nothing actually new is added.

But with that it is also said that neither Marx nor Engels depict the full range of their view of history. Their statements from the mid-1840s are highly consistent, but they are always satisfied with quite general assertions that leave the way open for differing interpretations of the relation between base and superstructure. As late as the 1890s, Engels was compelled to correct a number of misunderstandings regarding historical materialism – for example, in a letter to Joseph Bloch, a young student in Berlin. He explained that only '*in the final analysis*' was history 'the production and reproduction of actual life'. He admitted that in their polemic with an idealistic view of history, he and Marx often neglected to emphasise the active significance of the superstructure – of the political and legal forms and ideas.[9]

But the dispute over the character of the Marxist conception of history did not end with that. Differing perceptions of what the base-superstructure relation entailed, and its validity, are part of what essentially constitutes various Marxist orientations. It was so at the beginning of the twentieth century, it was so during the heated struggles of the 1920s, and it is so today. In Leninist Marxism, support can be found in Lenin's choppy assertions that 'social consciousness *reflects* social being'.[10] But it is also possible to resort to the strict division by Althusser and his group of society into different levels – socioeco-

---

dominant Soviet and East German conception of continuous and harmonic development of ideas and theories in Marx and Engels is palpable – with e.g. Althusser 1968, in particular p. 28 et seqq., where the main thesis is a radical rupture in Marx's scientific development.

6   MECW 5:43 et seqq.
7   MECW 29:263 et seqq.
8   MECW 25:135 et seqq.
9   Letter from Engels to Joseph Bloch, 21–22 September 1890, MECW 49:33.
10   LCW 14:323.

nomic, political and legal, and ideological – in which each develops relatively independently but one is predominant; the one that predominates is determined by the socioeconomic level, which holds its unique position only there.[11] The Frankfurt School, on the other hand, has turned completely away from all the talk of base and superstructure, or at the least declared that the distinction does not have general validity and, for example, has no application in late capitalist society.[12]

For the time being, we do not need to go deeper into this discussion, which of course has more conditions than the ambiguities in Marx's and Engels's statements on history. For now, we can be satisfied with the question of what Marx and Engels actually assert about the development of human society. In *The German Ideology* they were already emphasising that they were not aiming at 'a recipe or schema … for neatly trimming the epochs of history'. They only wanted to indicate some of the conditions that had to be taken into account in the concrete study of history.[13] Statements in the same spirit occur much later. In another of his corrective letters from 1890, to philosopher and social democrat Conrad Schmidt, Engels declares that Marx and his conception of history 'first and foremost a guide to study, not a tool for constructing objects after the Hegelian model'. The social formation of every epoch must be studied anew and in detail before its superstructure can be deduced from it. There was still a tremendous amount to do here![14]

The interpretation of these statements so that the thesis on base and superstructure is only a methodological recommendation to look for the conditions of the political, legal and spiritual life as much as possible in the socioeconomic base presents itself immediately. This recommendation promises that only along this path lie the greatest prospects for discovering connections among various historical phenomena. The thesis on base and superstructure would not mean, however, that Marx and Engels claimed to have established a really and continually existing relation between 'the production and reproduction of actual life' on the one hand and the political, legal and ideological conditions on the other.

But are Marx and Engels actually that modest? Do they not plainly say in *The German Ideology* that there is no history of politics, law, science, art or reli-

---

11   Cf. for example Althusser 1968, p. 96 et seqq. and Althusser 1973 [where is the ref in the bibliography?].

12   See primarily Árnason 1971, p. 94, p. 191 et seq. and Lichtheim 1971, p. viii.

13   MECW 5:37.

14   'Our view of history, however, is first and foremost a guide to study, not a tool for constructing objects after the Hegelian model'. MECW 49:8.

gion – that these phenomena in the superstructure cannot be understood in isolation from the history of the base?[15] Does this not mean that, in their opinion, there is a real and general connection between base and superstructure? Did Engels, in the aforementioned letter, not assume that the political, legal and ideological conditions can always be derived from the social formation? Is this not an assertion about the nature of historical reality?

Asserting that the materialist conception of history is only a method and not a theory is done with a thoroughly fixed idea of what a theory is – namely an arranged number of more or less general statements about reality in which the less general can be directly and unambiguously derived from the more general. What Marx and Engels say shows unequivocally that their conception of history cannot be formulated in a theory of this type.

But are theories of another type unimaginable? Can there not be statements about reality that are mutually related in another way?

In my opinion, the rational starting point for Marx's – and especially Engels's – digressions on issues of general philosophy, theories of science, and worldviews lies somewhere among these questions.

3   The Theory of Capitalism

It may seem as though historical materialism was fairly unproblematic for Marx and Engels. They only outlined it; they did not make it. Only when it became obvious that the outlines had given rise to misunderstanding did Engels make a few clear delimitations.

But then it must be remembered that for several decades after *The German Ideology*, the chief scientific task of Engels and especially Marx was the development of a theory about the capitalist mode of production. This is the theory developed in *Capital*, and the one Marx first sought his way towards in the immense collection of manuscripts from the late 1850s that now go under the name of *Grundrisse*.

Historical materialism in its full breadth does not manifest itself in these writings. It constitutes an assumption: only with it as a background and a landmark does the significance Marx and Engels ascribed to these studies become comprehensible. It serves as a guide for a number of connections Marx makes between material production and legislation, material production and social science.

---

15   MECW 5:92.

But it is only in the background. *Capital* is not a dissertation about the relation between the capitalist mode of production and bourgeois society, or the bourgeois world of ideas. Its subject, as Marx emphasised in the foreword to Volume One, is the capitalist mode of production and the relations of production and communication corresponding to it.[16] It is true that when he began the project that resulted in *Capital*, his intent was to analyse other modes of production than capitalism.[17] But it was always the base that was the main subject of his studies. *Capital* contains a theory of capitalism – a theory of the base.[18]

While Marx and Engels had developed the general principles of their historical materialism back in the 1840s, it was only over the course of the following decade that Marx arrived at the foundations of the theory of capitalism during renewed, deeper studies of the classics of economics, primarily Ricardo. It was at this point he made the distinction, so essential for his economic theory, between labour and labour power: the former a qualitative magnitude (use value) and the latter a quantity (exchange value). It is a distinction not found in the earlier economic literature, but it would become fundamental to Marx's work. In newer studies of the origins and early development of Marxism, this has been – with good reason – depicted as a turning point.[19]

But the theory of the capitalist mode of production will come under the purview of this study only to the extent that it cleared the way for Marx's and Engels's renewed interest in general questions of knowledge and science. The fact that it did so is beyond any doubt.

The theory of capital was developed as part of a distinct scientific tradition stemming from Adam Smith and David Ricardo. At the same time, however, it comprises a new stage in this trend. It starts from the same fundamental problems concerning the basis of economic value, the relation between production and economic prosperity, the principles for the distribution of the total wealth

---

16 'In this work I have to examine the capitalist mode of production, and the conditions of production and exchange corresponding to that mode'. MECW 35:8. Cf. p. 10: '... and it is the ultimate aim of this work, to lay bare the economic law of motion of modern society ...'.

17 'Formen, die der kapitalistische Produktion vorhergehn' (the form that precedes capitalist production), Marx 1953, pp. 375–413. A rewarding summary of the discussion concerning 'the Asiatic mode of production' and the precapitalist mode of production overall is Sofri [1975]. Godelier [1975] and Rodinson 1966 are also of great interest.

18 There are a number of trustworthy presentations in English about the economic theory in *Capital*, for example Mandel and Dencik.

19 The most detailed – and yet coherent – study of Marx's path to *Capital* is Rosdolsky 1969. Wygodski [1967] is also essential. The crucial importance of the concept of labour power is even more strongly emphasised in Nicolaus 1972.

among various social classes, and so on. In crucial passages, Marx corrects his predecessors. But above all he views the problems from another perspective; his entire view of the economic context in a capitalist economy is different.

This is bound up with the consequences of the economic doctrines being different for Marx than they had been for Smith and Ricardo. The differences emerged long before the theory of capital has been developed – indeed, back when Marx was a novice in economics. In the much-discussed 'Paris manuscripts' (the *Economic and Philosophical Manuscripts* of 1844), where Marx was largely satisfied with referring to and quoting the leading economists, he makes a number of statements that point toward his later, larger and more thorough reckoning with classical economics. He says that Smith, Ricardo et al. start from private property as a fact but do not attempt to explain it, that they lay out certain laws but do not comprehend – that is, they do not grasp the context around – these laws.[20] He comes even closer to the later, developed perspective when he declares that the difference between the primary economic categories (profit, ground rent, wages and so on) is 'not one which is grounded in the nature of things, it is a *historical* distinction'.[21]

The immediate and obvious reason for Marx already seeing the forms of capitalist economy here as historical and transitory is that, in contrast to his predecessors, he argues that the whole of capitalist society will fall into ruin. He is a socialist; he does not believe in Smith's 'stationary stage'.[22]

If the dispute stopped there, however, it would confine itself to ideology and would have no scientific significance.

The more Marx developed his own economic theory, however, the clearer it became that even on a plane fundamentally within the sphere of science, he was far from the point of view developed by Smith. He never attempted to formulate an exclusively economic theory; he did not believe in the possibility of abstracting a reality in which the economic categories emerged as pure and unadulterated. His own economics were at the same time a sociology, a doctrine of classes and the class struggle.

But even more: he attempted to show, in an increasingly elaborate manner, the transient character of capitalist relations. Its conformity to laws had not always been in force; there had been – and still were – modes of produc-

---

20   MECW 3:270.

21   Ibid., p. 285: 'The *distinction* between capital and land, between profit and rent, and between both and wages, and *industry*, and *agriculture*, and *immovable* and *movable* private property – this distinction is not rooted in the nature of things, but is a *historical* distinction ...'.

22   Smith 1950, I, p. 106 et seq.

tion that fundamentally differed from the capitalist one. And capitalism's own dynamic drove it towards its own dissolution; expansion was a vital necessity for the capitalist economy, but the antagonism between capital and labour meant that expansion would gradually be dampened down and shake the prevailing order in increasingly harder and ultimately unsustainable crises. The theory that Marx formulated has the inevitable ruin of capitalism as one of its most essential results.

All of this is fully developed in the *Grundrisse*. At its very beginning, Marx shows how the classical tradition of economics assumed that the fundamental relations of capitalism had always been valid, even if they were more primitive and plainer at the dawn of history. Starting from a shipwrecked Robinson Crusoe, it was assumed that the economic circumstances prevailing in a developed economy can be found in his living conditions, though in a simpler and thus clearer manner there.[23]

Quite contrary to this perception, Marx attempts to show how the capitalist economy becomes comprehensible only if it is regarded as different at heart from other economies. He wants to show how it grew out of the feudal economy but assumed a character that is essentially new. It has, as he says, its historical conditions that it later leaves behind and thus are not part of its constituent elements. Saving money and piling it up in the late Middle Ages is therefore a necessary condition for obtaining capital to invest; but the act itself of saving is *'non-capitalist'* since capitalism assumes that wealth and the results of production are thrown back into production to get the wheels spinning even faster. Capitalism is an expansive economy, which feudalism is not – but capitalism grew out of feudalism and has all its historical conditions in it.[24]

Marx therefore asserts, in contrast to his predecessors in economics, that history contains new creations – or rather qualitatively new conditions that thus cannot be derived from earlier conditions. The significance of this idea of his can scarcely be overemphasised. It is crucial; it constitutes the very starting point of his and Engels's renewed interest in the dialectic and the nature of knowledge.

The historical study of the origins of capitalism is in fact an important task in both the *Grundrisse* and *Capital*. It is primarily there that the thesis of the fundamental variability of history – or, for the time being, of economic history – can be substantiated. In *Capital* he therefore devotes a great deal of energy in showing how crucial it is for capitalist development that 'free' labourers appear

---

23   Marx 1953, p. 5 et seqq.
24   Ibid., p. 363 et seqq.

(i.e. people who can sell their labour power and are not bound to definite masters, towns or occupations). Only then can the capitalist production of surplus value begin.[25] He also asserts that the transition from handicraft to manufacture is gradual, or continuous: if handicraft occupies many labourers at once, it 'turns into' manufacture. But with that something qualitatively new also begins, a form emerges that follows completely different economic laws than the old handicraft. It is precisely at this point in *Capital* that Marx professes adherence to the Hegelian 'law' of quantity and quality, which applies here 'as in natural science'. It is a statement we will have to return to![26]

Still, Marx does not devote the greatest energy to the issue of the rise of capitalism but to its manner of functioning. By studying capitalism's unique conformity to laws, Marx also wants to affirm that capitalism must be moving towards its downfall, from which a qualitatively new economy will rise. Capitalism has both a beginning and an end.

To summarise:

Marx (and to a lesser extent, Engels) developed an economic theory on the basis of classical economics. It obtains its final form after many years of assiduous work with the older authorities. At crucial points, the Marxian theory differs from that of its predecessors. But the difference that stands out as the most essential and crucial, both for Marx and his fairly conscientious posterity, is that Marx wanted to show that capitalism is a changeable economic form.

This means, now, that economic history according to Marx contains crucial new developments, new conformities to laws, new forms whose conditions of emergence can certainly be traced in previous history but all the same cannot be reduced to these conditions.

The question immediately arises: What is it in classical economic theory that rules out the possibility of these kinds of new creations, and what is it in the new Marxian theory that differs from its predecessors?

Marx and Engels were not satisfied with referring to the ideological difference. They were not satisfied with referring to the fact that Smith, Ricardo and their ilk accept the capitalist system and regard its realisation as the absolute acme of history. With criticism like that alone they would have been no more than what they themselves scornfully called utopian socialists[27] – the difference between the bourgeois and the socialist ideas would have been simply a difference between different values, different ideals.

---

25   MECW 35:303 et seq.
26   Ibid., p. 313 et seq. Cf. below, p. 112 et seq.
27   In the *Communist Manifesto* (MECW 6:514 et seqq.), in Engels's *Socialism: Utopian and Scientific* (MECW 24: 287 et seqq.) and in many other places.

Ideology is important, of course. Extraordinarily important. But Marx and Engels did not simply, or even chiefly, assert that they had better, more humane values than their opponents. Above all, they asserted that the theory Marx had developed better explained economic and social reality – that it provides a better, more credible picture of it.

The difference then also had to be a theoretical difference.

Marx devoted an extraordinary amount of energy to studying the history of economic theory. He related it to the development of economic reality. He tried to show that a given abstract theory could see the light of day only in a fairly complex and developed economic reality. Aristotle could not regard labour as the only magnitude that creates value because a slave-owning society obstructed his view, Marx says in *Capital*.[28] Adam Smith could arrive at this abstraction since he had a richly differentiated economy as his object of study. For him, labour did not appear as a fixed type of labour, as agricultural labour or industrial labour, or anything else except as labour, pure and simple.[29]

For Marx, Adam Smith and Ricardo were great economists, but he waved off their immediate successors in his own time as 'vulgar economists'. Economic reality had developed since Smith and Ricardo; those who in Marx's time repeated what Smith and Ricardo said refused to draw the reasonable conclusions from the material of reality they had to start from.[30]

The limitations of the vulgar economists can be explained by their bourgeois point of view and desires, much as Smith's and Ricardo's limitations can be explained by the economic reality that surrounded them. But that does not settle the problem of the difference between Marx's theory and the others'. The external circumstances surrounding scientific theories is one thing; what constitutes them and makes them scientific theories is another.

But there is one important idea – widespread even among those who consider themselves Marxists – that Marx's theory should differ fundamentally from other theories. It should not be a theory of a kind that is comparable with Ricardo's or John Stuart Mill's, or for that matter with Darwin's or Newton's. It would be a mistake – that Marx, and in particular Engels, were guilty of now and then – to generally regard it as a fixed theory, expressible in a range of more or less general propositions.

---

28   MECW 35:70.

29   Marx 1953, p. 24.

30   Marx developed the concept of vulgar economy in *Theories of Surplus-Value* in particular, MECW 31. Vulgar opinions are ascribed to Malthus (32:213 et seqq., 273 et seqq.) but the most detailed treatment occurs in the reckoning with McCulloch (ibid., p. 353 et seqq.).

Taking a position on this idea is extremely important in this context, since it is crucial for the critique of Engels's dialectical efforts. Engels attempted to add the materialist conception of history, including the theory of capital, into a hierarchy of scientific theories from mechanism upward. Even there, it is said, he was mistaken about the theoretical orientation of Marxism.

We must test this idea carefully. For now, it is a question of a few preliminary remarks.

Often, this criticism has taken its starting point in the eleventh and last of Marx's *Theses on Feuerbach*: 'Philosophers have merely *interpreted* the world in various ways; the point is to *change* it'.[31] Marx wrote this ins 1845, just before he and Engels reckoned with the Young Hegelians in *The German Ideology* and developed the foundation for their historical materialism.

This thesis – and, for all that, much else that Marx wrote in his youth as well as in his later years – should be a sign that Marx had a conception of the theory that could not be joined with what Engels occupied himself with in the 1870s and 1880s. To make it add up, the representatives of this idea have often also been compelled to distance themselves from the older Marx – or, rather, from certain elements in him. So, for example, Jürgen Habermas – the most influential representative of the younger generation of the Frankfurt School – talks about the 'economic' Marx who saw the light of day in the late 1850s, showing such a 'peculiar theoretical laxity' towards the 'metaphysical' Engels that at times, including in *Capital*, he speaks as if he were on the same line with the latter.[32] To Habermas, it is obvious that the parallels Marx drew between his theory and certain theories of natural science are ill suited.

Of course, Habermas wrote this back in 1957, in a survey of some then relatively fresh German literature on Marx in which there was complete unity over Engels having distorted and adulterated Marxian theory. The idea he expresses, however, is nonetheless still representative. Marxism is a 'revolutionary humanism' and not a materialism in any prevalent philosophical meaning.[33] Historical materialism is 'essentially a revolutionary theory' – a theory only in the sense that it functions as a tool for changing society.[34]

---

31   MECW 5:5. The theses were first published in 1888 as an appendix to Engels's *Ludwig Feuerbach*.

32   Habermas 1971, p. 397.

33   Ibid., p. 394.

34   Ibid., p. 397. Here, Habermas is one example out of a possible one thousand: the image of a more or less revolutionary *humanist* Marx – profoundly distinct from a wildly spec-

In other words, the distinctive scientific and theoretical character of Marxism lies in its view of the relation between theory and praxis. It presents itself as a guide for action in changing society, but to be faithful to its self-imposed task it can do nothing but annihilate itself while claiming to reproduce a piece of social reality.

It seems as though this criticism of the 'metaphysical' Engels and the 'economic' Marx lets the thesis of the variable character of the mode of production – what constitutes the crucial difference between Marx's economic theory and Ricardo's – overflow all its banks: everything is in a constant flux that cannot be fixed in a few general assertions. In the most thorough and worthwhile reckoning with Engels's dialectic from the perspective of the Frankfurt School – Alfred Schmidt's *The Concept of Nature in Marx* – there is a criticism of Engels's ideas about time and space, which state that even these categories are historically determined.[35] The ultimate consequence of such a viewpoint would be that nothing that is historically changeable can even be provisionally determined; the only legitimate task for a Marxist would be relating all the statements made to the historical circumstances under which they came into being.

The idea of the fluid and difficult to determine is undoubtedly central to Marx's theoretical activities, but it is actually equally so in Engels. And here is one of the essential points of connection to Hegel and the sphere of Hegelian problems.

Hegel had his idealistic system, however. Those seeking to link Marxism to Hegel (i.e. the representatives of the Frankfurt School) have encountered difficulty there. Hegel spoke not only of constant change, he also sought a context in the entire enormous process of development, a beginning and an end.

But then, did Hegel not make the same mistake as the later Engels and – to some extent – Marx? Did Engels not simply follow Hegel's mistaken lead, as Lukács asserted in his book from 1923?[36] This is an idea that Adorno developed, with serious consequences, in *Negative Dialectics*. Hegel distinguishes between the spiritual and the material, arguing that the spiritual has primacy. Engels dis-

---

ulative or conventionally dogmatic Engels – is general fare, particularly in West German and Anglo-Saxon literature. See, for example, Hook 1933, p. 75 et seq.; Calvez 1956, p. 374 et seqq.; Sartre 1960, p. 129; Landgrebe 1965, p. 50 et seq. This viewpoint also recurs, with a better and more well thought out argument than anywhere else, in Jordan 1967, p. 13 et seqq. and *passim*, and in a manically agitated way in the recent Levine 1975, p. 1 et seqq. and *passim*. More level-headed but just as resolute is K. Hartmann 1970, for example p. 552 et seqq.

35   Schmidt 1971a, p. 55.

36   Above, p. 28.

tinguishes between the spiritual and the material, arguing that the material has primacy. According to Adorno, however, this is where the mistake of both lies. The dialectical method Hegel developed can never lead to a system, never to a closed totality of doctrines about the world. The spiritual and the material can in fact not be distinguished between; they are indissolubly united in the infinite chain of events.[37]

Here, Hegel (though deprived of his idealistic philosophy) has been brought into harmony with a Marxism that holds forth on the total unity between theory and praxis.

4   Theory and Praxis

We do not need to go any deeper into this kind of interpretation of Marxism, which can also be found far beyond the walls of the Frankfurt School. If the general philosophical and scientific theoretical conditions and implications of this interpretation are ignored, keeping to the narrowly historical questions, it is obvious that the interpretation assumes that much of what not only Engels but also Marx asserted starting in the late 1850s must be branded as un-Marxist. The real Marxism is to be found in their writings – or at least Marx's – from the 1840s.

But how could Marx and Engels embark upon such peculiarly un-Marxist speculations in their later years? It is not peculiar that they were inconsistent now and then, that they allowed themselves brief digressions from the basic idea they had. On the contrary, it is extremely natural and even easily supported by evidence in their writings. But how could they enter on a course, persistently and quite consistently, that would lead them far from any connection to what they actually stood for?

In the total historical interpretation of Marxism, the immediate historical circumstances in Engels's historical development – and Marx's in particular – have been distressingly forgotten.

When Marx and Engels wrote *The German Ideology* in the mid-1840s, both had obtained a solid knowledge of the new economics and a range of socialist theories. Their attack, however, concerned German idealist philosophy in its left Hegelian vintage. They also set to work on Feuerbach, who was of course materialist but lacked a historical perspective. Despite everything, it was this

---

37   Adorno 1966, p. 25 *et seqq.*, 31 et seqq., 102 et seqq., 195 et seq. Cf. also Lichtheim 1971, p. 22 et seqq.

German philosophy they had mastered best for the time being; in confronting it, they developed their materialist conception of history.

When in the late 1850s they both had another go at philosophy and Hegel, they had obtained a far more elaborate view on the issue of socialism and revolution. But above all, Marx had now developed his own theory on the socioeconomic context. That was his major gain in that decade.

When Marx and Engels emphasised the unity between theory and praxis, they did it in a polemic with German philosophy. It was, of course, the *philosophers* who only interpreted the world. It was the idealist philosophers in Germany who believed that a new society would shoot forth from their insights into the essence of Christianity. It was the philosopher Feuerbach who called himself communist only because he had realised that people needed each other. He thus 'like the other theorists, merely wants to produce a correct consciousness about an *existing* fact, whereas for the real Communist it is a question of overthrowing the existing state of things'.[38]

The same criticism could now be aimed at all socialists who believe that the world can be transformed with the mere insight of a good society. It was aimed, for example, at Pierre-Joseph Proudhon, whom Marx castigated in *The Poverty of Philosophy*.

But how did things now stand with the economists on the question of theory and praxis? This is a problem that, oddly enough, has been left out of the discussion. Nevertheless, it is a crucial one.

Neither Adam Smith, David Ricardo, Jean-Baptiste Say, Thomas Malthus nor John Stuart Mill were socialist revolutionaries. They could not be accused of wanting to realise socialism with the help of merely ideas and theories, since in general they did not want to realise any kind of socialism. By and large, they were adherents of a bourgeois and capitalist society.

They consequently lacked ideas about socialist praxis. But what attitude did they take to bourgeois praxis? What was their position on the issue of the relation between their economic theory and economic, social and political actions?

In many respects, classical economy is a child of the Enlightenment. It shares the optimistic cardinal idea of the Enlightenment that truth is useful, and use can only be reached via the path of knowledge.

Adam Smith himself was a typical man of the Enlightenment. He never questioned the connection between political economy and political benefit. How could he have done otherwise? He was a professor of moral philosophy. His

---

38   MECW 5:57; quoted text from p. 58.

economic theory grew out of his (entirely traditionally structured) studies in 'jurisprudence', which were divided into the four fields of 'justice, police, revenue and arms'. Revenue was the main question of economics.[39]

He posed the question of economics from the very beginning as a practical one: it was a matter of finding 'the most proper way of securing wealth and abundance'.[40] He was concerned about showing how insufficient knowledge of economic connections led to injurious political measures. The mercantilist thesis that wealth consists of money or precious metals had led to 'many prejudicial errors in practice'.[41]

The obvious connection itself between theory and practice is found throughout *On the Wealth of Nations*. Based on his fundamental insight that it is labour that, in one way or another,[42] creates exchange value, he draws his conclusions about how society should be organised in order to achieve the greatest possible wealth. He provides numerous examples of how insufficient insight into the fundamental economic connections led to imprudent policies.

For him, political economy was a practical science. In his expositions on education, he sided with the Aristotelian distinction between theoretical and practical disciplines; 'physics' and 'morals' were a division that 'seems perfectly agreeable to the nature of things'. In the Middle Ages, all knowledge was of course placed under the supremacy of theology, and morals degenerated into casuistry and asceticism. The objective of moral philosophy – to which economics thus belongs – was as systematic an order as possible.[43]

The systematic order, the developed theory, is thus necessary for practice. Separating theory from practice, however, and believing that if only the theory is there then practical life would soon put itself right – such a thought never crossed Adam Smith's mind.

Nor was it ever considered in the tradition after Smith that Marx worked through. With David Ricardo, the field of economic theory of course became narrower; scientific specialisation also left its mark on economics. His *Principles of Political Economy* deals with nowhere near as many social and historical phenomena as *The Wealth of Nations*, and at the same time its theoretical structure became more solid. Political economy had become more independent in relation to general moral philosophy.

---

39   Cf. Cannan 1950, p. xviii et seqq. and the quote from Smith.
40   Smith 1896, p. 157.
41   Ibid., p. 200.
42   On Smith's varied attempts at determining value, see for example Dobb 1973, p. 47 et seqq.
43   Smith 1950, II:290 et seqq.

This does not mean, however, that Ricardo essentially regarded the relation between theory, economics and political practice any differently than Smith. He was just as eager to draw the useful conclusions from his theses, and his dry prose became impassioned. When, for example, he spoke about wages, he railed against the Poor Laws, which did not help the poor at all but merely impoverished the rich. It was now understood why the Poor Laws had such an effect, however, and 'the remedy'[44] was thereby also at hand.

Ricardo's problem was a strictly theoretical one: it was a matter of finding the explanation for why the distribution of a society's wealth among the three dominant classes – landowners, capitalists and workers – was different at the various stages of development in society.[45] But his theory had practical implications, and he was concerned with indicating the paths by which the theory could be turned into action.

The same applies to the entire subsequent generation of English and French economists whom Marx had to take a stand on. They were no revolutionaries, since they saw no reason to revolutionise the bourgeois society to which they belonged. For them, it was not a question of revolutionising economic and social life but to administer it on the private and political path towards ever greater perfection.[46]

Marx realised this; he wrote thousands of pages on bourgeois economists in the *Grundrisse*, in *Capital*, in *Theories of Surplus Value* – but nowhere did he reproach them for not seeing the actual connection between theory and praxis. They were only aiming at a different praxis than he was, and they had a different theory. But they did not have a completely different type of theory; their theories and Marx's were comparable.

There is thus no specially ossified 'economic' Marx in contrast to the philosophical and revolutionary Marx, who together with Engels sketched out the materialist conception of history in *The German Ideology*. It remains to be seen whether there is a completely separate 'metaphysical' Engels.

---

44   Ricardo 1903, p. 82 et seqq.
45   Ibid., p. 1.
46   John Stuart Mill in fact attempted to go back to the broader, more practical perspective in Adam Smith; in the foreword to his *Principles of Political Economy* he also praised Smith for the latter's manner of always associating 'the principles with their applications'. Mill 1965, I, p. xci. Cf. also Bladen 1965, p. xxvii.

5   Renewed Interest in Hegel

A comparison between Marx's theory of capitalism and that of the classical economists is not unproblematic, however; nor was it for Marx.

The difference between the theories was not a matter of their being built on different empirical material. The most advance capitalist society – in England – was and remained the central object of study.[47] Marx of course used different sources than his predecessors did, above all official statistics. The sociological circumstances played a much more essential role for him: it was not simply an issue of 'the poor' or 'the workers', pure and simple.

This could not explain the differences, however. Nor could the general problems that were not posed for economic reality. For Marx as well, they concerned exchange value, production, distribution, conformity to laws in economic development, and so on.

Nor, as we have seen, could the deviations be simply and directly traced back to ideological differences or the differences between a bourgeois and a socialist world of ideas. Even there, there were plenty of socialists who stood closer to the bourgeois economists than they did to Marx on economic theory.

The issue was, to say the least, problematic.

Like Engels, Marx had apparently settled accounts with Hegel and the Hegelian inheritance once and for all in his early writings. He [Marx] had criticised the Hegelian philosophy of right and the state; Hegel had been repudiated in the *Paris Manuscripts*, the Left Hegelians had been castigated in *The Holy Family* and *The German Ideology*, and a Proudhon attired in Hegelian categories had been planed smooth in *The Poverty of Philosophy*.

During the years of political unrest in 1848 and after, the issues of philosophy and the scientific method were pushed into the background for both Marx and Engels. When the world settled down again, they took up other matters – economic theory for Marx and the concerns of practical life for Engels. Hegel and the issues of Hegelianism disappeared almost completely from their notes and letters.

But towards the end of the 1850s, it became time to sum up the experiences and knowledge they had gained. Then, if not before, it had become obvious that the distinctive and unique in the world of ideas that was theirs needed to be bound up with abstruse Hegelian philosophy. They had distanced themselves once and for all from Hegel and the Hegelians, but all the same Hegel was the foundation on which they had developed their way of thinking.

---

47   How essential it was for Marx to have the English environment in view is evident in such places as the foreword to *Capital*, MECW 35.

As regards Engels, his new interest in Hegel was also bound up with a growing curiosity in the natural sciences. This is in part a different story that we will
return to and is bound up with a radical transformation of the entire intellectual climate in England and in Europe. But in part it is also the same story: if
the question of the relation of the one scientific theory to the other theory has
been raised, it will soon grow to apply to more and more theories about more
and more areas of reality.

There is, however, a particular problem for Marx and Engels that always
appears acute to a modern-day observer but that they themselves did not formulate clearly and unambiguously. The theory of the capitalist mode of production that Marx developed is a theory of the base; it is a theory within the
framework of the materialist conception of history but it covers only a part of
the area of reality that this conception of history is intended to cover. It is thus
a question of a more general and a more special part of the same theoretical
conception.

The materialist conception of history, however, as it was formulated in *The
German Ideology* and then largely remained unchanged, is always formulated
in relation to and *in contrast to* Hegelian historical idealism. The theory of capital, on the other hand, is related to classical economic theory. The difference
between a philosophy of history such as the Hegelian and an elaborated special theory like Smith's or Ricardo's is not simply a difference in scope. It is a
difference in orientation, in problem, in area of application. It is quite simply
meaningful to ask whether Ricardo's or Smith's theories fit within an idealistic
or a materialistic conception of history; such questions are not posed within
the framework for the theory. We know, for example, that John Stuart Mill
regarded ideas as the driving force of history; we cannot, however, read this
from his economic theories but from his other theories and ideas (e.g. those
he developed in *On Liberty*).[48] It is no more immediately meaningful to link
Hegel's historical idealism with the economic ideas he expresses. Accordingly,
the conception of history and the theory of capital in Marx and Engels will face

---

48   Mill in fact developed two different theories on the driving forces of historical develop-
      ment. According to the one, expressed primarily in *Principles of Political Economy*, distri-
      bution comprised the flexible, active part of development; according to *On Liberty*, human
      advances depended on new ideas. In *On Liberty*, Mill declared frankly that freedom of
      opinion and economic freedom had no direct connection; both theories of development
      could consequently stand side by side. The reason that Mill allowed himself such an incon-
      sistency is that he demanded not society but the individual be regarded from a uniform
      perspective; the theory of distribution and the theory of ideas could thus be considered
      different abstractions of the psychology of the individual (human greed and – probably –
      intellectual capacity). See in more detail below, p. 257 et seqq.

in different directions, so to speak, at the same time as the conception of history must contain the theory of the base and have its origin there. The problem can be illustrated by the following figure:

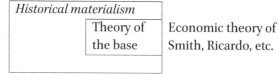

Idealist conception of history | *Historical materialism* / Theory of the base | Economic theory of Smith, Ricardo, etc.

Historical materialism and the theory of capitalism thus stand out in sharp relief against various backgrounds in Marx's and Engels's work. The thesis that being determines consciousness and not the other way around indicates the importance of developing knowledge about social being (i.e. the base), but it provides no instructions about how this knowledge is to be structured. It is extremely illuminating that Marx's main objection against the classical economists – their failure to comprehend the variable nature of the mode of production – plays no role in his and Engels's general works on historical materialism; the insight into the variability of history was deeply rooted in the Hegelian tradition.

The deficient correspondence between the design of the materialist conception of history and the theory of the base is important to anyone who wishes to understand the apparently exaggerated and partially arbitrary statements both Marx and Engels made about their relationship to Hegel. They wanted to find, somewhere in Hegelian philosophy, the foundation for the unique aspects of their theory of the base while it was Hegelian philosophy that they had at one time liberated themselves from.

They returned to a Hegel who was simultaneously *aufgehoben* (abolished) and *aufbewahrt* (preserved or sublated) in their own thinking – a Hegel they had turned their backs on but who had still not lost his power of attraction over them.

CHAPTER 2

The Rational Method

1   Grundrisse

Among all the schools and orientations fighting over the most correct and most reasonable interpretation of Marx, there is a great deal of agreement that the *Grundrisse* is central and crucial to understanding his work.[1]

The entirety of this tremendous manuscript – more than 700 printed pages – was completed between August 1857 and March 1858. The urgency was due not only to Marx considering himself essentially finished with his subject. He also thought that time was of the essence. A revolution might be at the door, and it was a question of being ready with a theory already worked out. After the events of 1848–49, he and Engels were convinced that a revolution could only be carried out in connection with a thorough capitalist crisis. In 1857, just such a crisis was in the offing. It had begun in the United States, and Marx was waiting for its arrival in England and on the Continent. He was keeping accounts of its spread.[2]

At the same time, he was spending his nights on the *Grundrisse*.[3]

The intimate connection between theory and practice in Marx is more clearly indicated by details of this kind than by various general assertions about his 'revolutionary humanism'.

It was during this work on the *Grundrisse* that that most abstract of abstracts – Hegel's philosophy – became an acute problem for him. He first set to work on an introduction, barely 30 pages long.[4] It is the document in which he comes closest to a real investigation of his own method. He also took a position, if briefly, on Hegel and the Hegelians. When it came to the point, however, he did not want the introduction to be printed. He gradually declared his plans to publish a single giant work and thought about publishing a number of instalments. Only the first half of *A Contribution to the Critique of Political Economy*

---

1 Here, in addition to Rosdolsky 1969, see Nicolaus 1973. McLellan 1971, p. 2 et seqq. and McLellan 1973, p. 290 et seqq. go even further – entirely too far. The *Grundrisse* played a prominent role in works such as Zelený 1970 and 1976, Althusser 1965 and 1968, and Rozental 1969.

2 Letter from Marx to Engels, 18 December 1857. MECW 40:224.

3 Cf. Foreword, signed by the Marx-Engels-Lenin Institute in Moscow 1939, in Marx 1953, p. vii et seq.

4 The work began on 23 August 1857 but was put aside in mid-September. Marx 1953, p. 4.

© KONINKLIJKE BRILL NV, LEIDEN, 2023 | DOI:10.1163/9789004528796_005

was completed. In the foreword, he explained that he had refrained from publishing 'a general introduction' he had written, since 'on further consideration it seems to me confusing to anticipate results which still have to be substantiated' and since his readers 'will have to decide to advance from the particular to the general'.[5] Instead, he provided a brief account of the path of his own intellectual development, and thus of the general principles that became a guide for his work. It is in this context that he introduced the terms that would become so well known later on: 'base' and 'superstructure'.

The introduction to the *Grundrisse* was finally published shortly after the turn of the twentieth century in Kautsky's *Die Neue Zeit*,[6] the leading journal of ideas in German social democracy. Ever since then, it has been extraordinarily significant for various orientations within Marxism. Max Adler, who tried to unify Marx with Kant, often took his starting point in it.[7] Lukács did likewise in *History and Class Consciousness* when he attempted to stake out a Marxism as far from Adler's as possible.[8] In newer and more influential works on Marxism, the introduction plays a thoroughly crucial role. It has, however, also remained the foundation for highly dissimilar and mutually incompatible interpretations. It is not a text that is easy to read.

It is of course correct, as Althusser says in *For Marx*, that the introduction to the *Grundrisse* is the closest Marx came to a presentation of his dialectical method.[9] But Marx himself wanted to write another such work. While working on the later parts of the *Grundrisse* in January 1858, he informed Engels in a letter that in his ongoing work he benefited greatly from having a few works of Hegel on hand 'by mere accident'. He added: 'If ever the time comes when such work is again possible, I should very much like to write 2 or 3 sheets making accessible to the common reader the *rational* aspect of the method which Hegel not only discovered but also mystified'.[10]

The time for such work clearly never came, but Marx never let the idea go. It came to the fore again when he became acquainted with the philosophical work of Joseph Dietzgen, whom he informed in a letter of his plans for a 'Dialectics'. He used nearly the same words in a letter to Engels a decade earlier.[11]

---

5   MECW 29:261.
6   Marx 1903.
7   M. Adler 1908, p. 6, p. 82 et seqq. The latter reference concerns the paper '*Marx und die Dialektik*' that was added to the rest of the text and is also reproduced in *Austromarxismus*.
8   Lukács 1968, p. 43 et seqq.
9   Althusser 1968, p. 187.
10   Letter from Marx to Engels, 16 January 1858. MECW 40:249.
11   Letter from Marx to Dietzgen, 9 May 1868. MECW 43:31.

When he died fifteen years later, the manuscript for such a work was the first thing Engels sought – in vain – among Marx's literary remains.[12]

What Marx would study during his final decades regarding his relation to Hegel is thus limited primarily to a long range of individual statements in the *Grundrisse*, in *Capital* and other places. Engels found the lack of a coherent work on the relation between Hegel's philosophy and Marxism troublesome. His *Ludwig Feuerbach* was a last attempt at filling the gap.[13]

But for us, turning immediately to Engels's book would be going down the wrong path. It is entirely possible to reconstruct, from Marx's manuscripts in the late 1850s, what could be called the Hegelian sphere of problems in his work on the theory of the base.

2   The Introduction

The introduction to the *Grundrisse* is primarily an attempt to explain the difference between the results the classical economists arrived at and Marx's own. The central section deals with the method of political economy, but Marx drifts into Hegel and the Hegelians. There are no actual economists among them; however, Marx has to demarcate and determine his method in relation to theirs as well.

From the beginning, Marx stressed that he was speaking about material production – that is, the base.[14] In a concluding section that exists primarily in the form of a few bare points, he would also get into the relation between base and superstructure.[15] These points do not provide much more than hints and pointers.

In his text, however, Marx immediately refers to the determinations of the materialist conception of history that he and Engels had made in *The German Ideology*. There is a similarity in the wording itself, and perhaps this is not chance, when he wrote the introduction to *A Contribution to the Critique of Political Economy* a few years later, at least, he had the yellowed, crumbling manuscript from the 1840s fresh in his memory.[16]

In *The German Ideology* it says that the conditions from which the authors proceeded are real conditions; it was 'real individuals, their activity and the

---

12   Letter from Engels to P.L. Lavrov, 2 April 1883. MECW 47:3.

13   MECW 26:353.

14   MECW 28:17.

15   Ibid., p. 45 et seq.

16   MECW 29:264.

material conditions of their life, both those which they find already existing and those produced by their activity'.[17] In the *Grundrisse*, Marx says: 'Individuals producing in a society – hence the socially determined production by individuals is of course the point of departure'.[18] The vaguer statements in the earlier text have been replaced with a single, much more determined concept: production. The term *Aktion* has no obvious connection to the base or to material production, and society is conspicuous by its absence in the older quote. It could be said that the developed theory of the base is what separates both statements.

The essential difference between the statements in *The German Ideology* and the *Grundrisse*, however, does not lie in their formulation but in who they address. *The German Ideology* was a reckoning with left Hegelian idealism. The *Grundrisse* is a reckoning with the individualism and atomism of the liberal economists.

According to Marx and Engels, the mistake of the Young Hegelians and the traditional German philosophers was that they started from what people asserted and imagined, and that for them people thus became the asserted and imagined person. The real starting point, however, had to be people bound to their practical circumstances, their material relations, their mundane activities. The philosophers had lowered themselves down from the heaven of ideas to earth. Marx and Engels wanted to rise from earth to heaven.[19]

The criticism of the economists does not concern their idealism. If they were idealists, it played no crucial role for their economic theory in a limited sense. The historical idealist John Stuart Mill is the subject of the main attack in the introduction to the *Grundrisse*. It is not his idealism, however, but the structure of his economic theory that is subject to criticism.

In their economic theory, the economists start from material circumstances and not, like the idealist philosophers, from ideas. But how do they attempt to determine what is essential in these material circumstances? They assume that the solitary individual – Robinson Crusoe on his island – provides the most lucid and abstract image of economic relations in general and in any society. A solitary producer and consumer follows the same economic laws as a collective.

Marx sees a manifestation of bourgeois individualism in this conception. With that, however, he has only determined the economists' approach *ideologically*. He has not elucidated their scientific method. He points out that of

---

17   MECW 5:31.
18   MECW 28:17.
19   MECW 5:36.

course the individual in bourgeois society appears as an independent unit – the social forms then appear as 'merely a means towards his private ends'. But in earlier types of society, the individual is part of different types of collectives, families, tribes and so on, and it is only in society – in a *fixed* and advanced type of society – that the individual can appear as independent.[20]

The bourgeois individualist view of history is thus unsustainable. But why is that so? What is it in the bourgeois economist approach that leads them straight to these unsustainable results?

For Marx, the answer lies in their way of making and using scientific abstractions. Abstractions are necessary for every kind of scientific work. Certain features or phenomena must be sifted out of the extravagance and diversity of empirical material and described as essential. The accidental must be overcome to find the shared, the connections, the crucial. But it does not follow from that how the various abstractions are to relate to one another or to the concrete material.

Economists have assumed that certain abstractions are always valid – and valid at every level. That is why they were able to move from one type of society to all types, and from society in general to the isolated individual.

But in that case, it must be possible to isolate the various abstractions from one another; they must be treated as independent agents that run through history, valid for individuals and groups and the whole of society. If the relation between the abstractions shifts from epoch to epoch, or if in general they can only be partially separated from one another, using them to draw straight lines upward and downward in history will not be possible.

Economic theoreticians have attempted this manoeuvre in various ways. The major difficulty lies in separating material *production* from *distribution* of the results of production among different social classes. Ricardo chose to regard production as something given, something that falls outside the actual sphere of economic problems. The major issues for economic theory is the shifting distribution among the three social classes: landowners, capitalists and workers.[21] John Stuart Mill developed a similar line of thought. Production developed with the necessity of a natural law. It is thus not subject to human will and human calculations. Nature provides the framework within which humans have to move. Distribution, on the other hand, can be influenced. Production determines the size of the cake, but humans can share it among themselves in various ways.[22]

---

20   MECW 28:17 et seq.
21   Cf. above, p. 51. See also Marx 1953, p. 17.
22   Mill 1965, in particular I:199 et seqq.

It is Mill's determination of the relation between production and distribution that forms the starting point for Marx's criticism. In that connection, it would have been fruitful if Marx had gone into Mill's *System of Logic*, or rather into Mill's view of scientific methods and formation of theory, which are closely bound up with his method of argument in economics. Marx, however, takes as little close notice as Engels of English empirical philosophy – the concrete outflow of this philosophy, economic theory, is set against Marx's own general philosophy of science.

For Marx, Mill's thesis of production was an attempt to raise the capitalist mode of production to eternal validity. It has always existed, though in more or less primitive forms, and it will always exist in a developed and advanced form. On a strictly theoretical level of economics, Marx differs from Ricardo and Mill in the understanding that production as well as distribution are subject to constant historical changes and that it is in fact production that is crucial for these changes.

The differences cannot, however, be reduced to differences in result; there are also differences in scientific approach. For Ricardo and Mill, the assumption that production and distribution can be isolated from each other is an obvious one. If, like Mill, the question of what people can do for the economy is posed, with his method it becomes necessary to isolate production as a constant in relation to human activity, while distribution is the variable around which these actions are to be concentrated. For Marx, production and distribution are mutually dependent variables.

To demonstrate the advantages of his point of view, Marx conducts a lengthy conceptual exercise with the primary economic categories of production, distribution, exchange and consumption.[23] These categories are continually interwoven with one another and can be made independent of one another only provisionally or in the abstract. Even purely logically, they are bound up with one another; production, for example, is always consumption (of raw materials) and consumption always production (e.g. of one's own body). In these respects, there is – as Marx says – an immediate identity between them. Production determines consumption – only that which is produced can be consumed – but consumption also determines production – what will not be consumed may in the long run not be produced, either.

Between production and consumption lie distribution and exchange. For that reason, the attempt to isolate distribution already seems futile. Marx also showed how the economists who tested this isolation were compelled to make

---

23   Marx 1953, pp. 10–21.

a number of duplicate determinations – of capital, for example – setting it in relation to production on one hand and to distribution on the other.

The structure of distribution, says Marx, is in fact determined by the structure of production. This does not mean, however, that distribution is entirely dependent on production. For example, it can be shown that a form of distribution could historically precede the corresponding form of production (such as mercantile capitalism preceding industrial capitalism). In addition, distribution is not simply the distribution of products; it does not begin only where production ends. There is also the distribution of the instruments of production, just as there is the distribution of the members of society among the various kinds of production.

Finally, Marx showed that the final link in the chain from production to distribution, economic exchange (and circulation) is similarly part of the economic totality.

3   Zelený's Interpretation

In relation to the classical economists, Marx thus asserts that the economic categories can be held separate even conceptually and in the abstract. Each mode of production constitutes a unique combination of the various categories. The classical economists were able to assume that capitalism was an eternal form of production because they did not place production in connection with the other economic categories. By not taking economic totalities into account, they were incapable of seeing the new and unique in different modes of production.

But how was the crucial difference between Ricardo's and Mill's approach on the one hand, and Marx's on the other, now to be determined?

A highly creditable attempt at such a determination is Czech philosopher Jindřich Zelený's *Logic of Marx*. In it, he sets Ricardo against Marx and draws a range of interesting conclusions from the comparison.

According to Zelený, Ricardo's analysis of capitalism is characterised by its differentiation of the empirical phenomenon and the underlying essence, and that this essence is conceived of as constant or unchanging. The essence can thus not undergo any qualitative changes, nor can it thus emerge in qualitatively different economies (i.e. economies with different 'essences') in history. In accordance with the starting point he chose, the issues Ricardo can take up are quantitative issues.[24]

---

24   Zelený 1970, p. 23 et seqq. and 1976, p. 14 et seqq.

But while Ricardo starts from 'the fixed essence' – that is, from an abstraction that is valid for all economic relations – Marx's starting point is of course also an abstraction, but one conceived of as a 'cell', the smallest changeable unit in a changeable organism. As is known, the commodity is the abstract unit he starts from in *Capital* and other places. According to Zelený, the commodity could thus be conceived of as the 'cell' of the capitalist mode of production.[25]

Zelený's interpretation has many subtle details that I will not go into here. But his general attempt at determining how Marx differs from Ricardo does not appear entirely successful. The image of the cell is not apt. Neither in Marx's time nor later have biologists attempted to determine a certain species of organisms by starting from their cells. Nor, seen from the history of development, is it changes in the cells that mark the transition from one species to another. The analogy is of course no better for Marx himself having used it.[26]

More essential than the 'commodity-cell' analogy is the perspective in which Zelený places Marx's method. Zelený stresses that Ricardo's conception of the fixed essence belongs in the mechanistic world of ideas.[27] In his economic theory, however, Marx would work in a tradition that was biologically oriented to a certain extent – or rather in the tradition that views human, historical and social relations in analogy with biological ones. It is a tradition most immediately from Hegel and the Romantic philosophers of nature headed by Schelling. Against the attempt to apply the basic principles of Newtonian mechanics in all areas, the organic, complex and changeable in all historical and human processes are asserted there.

Zelený's analogy is interesting because it can reveal a rational reason for Marx to expand his field of problems from economic theory in particular and history in general to also encompass a neighbouring science, namely biology. There should be an affinity between his own economic and historical method and that of biology.

However, let us first examine the question as a concrete issue of the significance of the organic models for Marx. He could have obtained these models from two places: German idealist philosophy on the one hand, and directly from biology on the other.

---

25   Ibid., p. 53 et seqq. and p. 39 et seqq., respectively.
26   For example, MECW 35:8.
27   Zelený 1970, p. 23, and 1976, p. 14.

4   The Concept of the Organism

We will study Marx's contacts with the natural sciences later on. But we can
start by mentioning one thing: the biological inspiration behind the expositions in the *Grundrisse* is minimal. It appears distinctly only once, when Marx
says that pre-capitalist economic systems can only be understood by starting
from the more complex capitalist system and drawing a parallel with comparative anatomy: 'The anatomy of man is a key to the anatomy of the ape'.[28] It is
an analogy that formed the starting point for a range of learned expositions
in the literature on Marx.[29] In reality it bears witness to Marx, so to speak,
being Romantically inspired in the 1840s in his view of comparative anatomy.
For a Romantic philosopher of nature such as Lorenz Oken it was obvious that
in its essence, humanity summarised the entire biological hierarchy and that
this hierarchy could be understood based on the human perspective.[30] Similar thoughts are also found in Hegel, for whom Spirit is the 'truth'[31] of all of
nature, and it can at least be traced in Feuerbach.[32] It was the thoughts of the
Romantic philosopher of natures, however, that guided actual research in comparative anatomy; it was these thoughts that constituted a tradition in biology
that was active and fruitful until the breakthrough of Darwinism.[33]

    It is obvious that this Romantic view has very little, if anything, to do with
the methodological reasoning Marx pursues in the *Grundrisse*. The idealistic
world of ideas hidden in the Romantics' anatomical studies lacks points of contact with Marx's comparisons among more or less advanced economic systems.
The analogy he makes is therefore superficial.

    In *Capital*, the parallels with the natural sciences and natural scientific
research play a relatively more prominent role; Marx's main interest has also
managed to change. Generally, however, there is no special emphasis on the
organic and the biological. The comparison between the cell and the body used
by Zelený is found in the foreword to the first edition; characteristically, it is
an image used to illustrate the relation between the simple and the complex
that was illustrated in the *Grundrisse* using Romantic biology. Marx had come

---

28   Marx 1953, p. 26.
29   Cf. for example, Schmidt 1971a, p. 34 et seq.
30   For example, Oken 1833–41, Vol. 4, Foreword.
31   So, for example, in *System of Philosophy*, Hegel 10:19. Comparative anatomy, however, occu-
      pies an obscure place in Hegel's world of ideas; cf. for example Hegel 9:676.
32   For example, in Feuerbach's *Grundsätze der Philosophie der Zukunft* (1843); cf. Feuerbach
      11:258 et seq.
33   Cf. Liedman 1966, p. 171 et seqq.

in contact with a more modern world of natural scientific ideas. But in itself, the new analogy does not say much more than the old one. This does not mean that there might be a direct connection between biologists' and social researchers' methods for approaching the problems. In the same context, Marx could otherwise draw parallels between the work he was pursuing and that of the physicist.[34] Only at the end of the foreword does he make an apparently more substantial comparison with the object of biology when he says that current society is not some 'solid crystal' but 'an organism capable of change'.[35] There is, of course, an actual rational connection to Darwinist biology: the problems of development do not apply to the historical conditions alone. On the other hand, his own view of historical development is in no way specified by such a statement. He only indicates, once again, what the crucial difference was between his conception and that of the classical economists: capitalism is not a permanent state of things.

It can quite easily be established that if Marx's ideas about complex totality had drawn any real support from an organism model, it was not through biology but through idealist philosophy. Or, rather: if, in comparison to the mechanistically inspired ideas of Ricardo, Mill et al. about the relations among various economic categories, Marx's assert an organic connection among them, it is not in the development of biological theory itself but in the philosophical speculations about the organic and the organism that the content of his viewpoint must be sought.

The boundary between biology and philosophical speculation in the early 1800s is of course often blurred, but making a distinction is essential for our main problem regarding the theoretical scientific conditions for Marx's work. In a philosophical context, the term 'organism' encompasses much more than living beings, the object of study for biology.

In the tradition that culminates with Hegel, there is a range of extremely precise ideas about what characterises an organism or – which was the same for the philosophers – an organised totality. In his *Critique of Judgement*, Kant enumerated some of the hallmarks of such organisms, and this enumeration would largely hold up to Schleiden's and Schwann's cell theory in the late 1830s, when the basic parts of organisms could no longer be identified with the various organs but with cells of a similar kind. Kant had distinguished the following characteristics:

---

34   MECW 35:8.
35   '... that the present society is no solid crystal, but an organism capable of change, and is constantly changing'. MECW 35:11.

1.   The parts of the organism are possible only in relation to one another.
2.   Each part must moreover be the cause and effect of the properties of the other parts.
3.   Each part must necessarily be thought of as existing for the sake of the whole and of the other parts (i.e. as a tool or organ).[36]

These characteristics were considered as being expressed in the processes, unique to the organisms, having to do with their generation, development and self-regulating equilibrium.[37] But as is known, the organic in idealist philosophy came to encompass far more than living beings: the nation and the state, legislation and language, art and morals and much more could be captured in terms of organic totalities. At almost every level, an organic ideal was set against the mechanistic ideal of the Enlightenment thinkers.

Hegel also contributed to this world of ideas. It is obvious, however, that the biological inspiration is relatively weaker in him than in the Romantic philosopher of natures.[38] He prefers to use words such as *Ganzes* ('whole') or *Totalität* ('totality') to represent a similar idea, but he could also go deeper into the biological world of expressions and speak of *Thier* ('animals') and *Pflanze* ('plants'). In such central texts as the foreword to *Phenomenology of Spirit*, he excels at words such as 'growth' and 'flowering'. Nonetheless, the ideas he associates with complex totalities – whatever names he gives them – are not as oriented on biology as, for example, Schelling's.

On the other hand, the characteristics Kant indicated for the organisms could largely be accepted by Hegel. His unities, totalities or organisms are complex quantities, the parts, elements or organs of which are subordinate to the totalities and can be understood only in relation to these totalities. It is the concept of the whole, not the concept of the more specific organism, that opens the path to understanding of Hegel's thinking. It is also the concept of the whole, and not the concept of any biologically rooted organism or cell, that marks the difference between Marx's theory on the one hand and that of Hegel and the classical economists on the other.

---

36   Kant 5: 373 et seq.
37   Ibid., p. 371 et seq. Schelling I:2, p. 29 et seq.
38   This can be seen in *Hegel-Lexikon* (= Hegel 26):1714 et seqq. under the headings 'Organik, Organisches' and 'Organismus'.

5   Hegel, Marx and Identity

Let us return to the *Grundrisse*. When Marx demarcated his conception from
Mill's and Ricardo's, he was particular about also rapidly marking it off from
Hegel's. After his exposition on the intricate relation between production and
consumption, he added: 'After this, nothing is simpler for a Hegelian than to
posit production and consumption as identical'.[39] Further on in the text, he
clarifies his own conception of the relation among the various economic categories – production, distribution, exchange and consumption – so that they
are not 'identical, but that they are all elements of a totality, differences within
a unity'.[40]

He shares the concept of totality with Hegel against the empirically-minded
economists. It is the concept of identity that he turns against Hegel.

We can immediately see how poorly his conception of the totality agrees
with the ideas about organisms that were developed in idealist philosophy.
There, each part is subordinate to the whole, each part serves the purpose of the
whole. In this world of ideas, the organism constitutes – however temporary –
a harmonic unity.

But Hegel's concept of the whole, which encompasses far more than the
organic (even in this extended sense), is also built on a significantly more complex and complicated conception of identity than hinted at by the organistic
lines of thought about the parts arranged into – or, rather, fused into – a totality. Marx's polemic against the Hegelian concepts of identity must be set in this
broader context.

As is known, Hegel has the general idea that everything is subject to change,
that everything is part of an unceasing process of development. In each such
process, totalities are formed of parts that are opposed to one another, but these
totalities are temporary and are burst asunder, to be replaced by new and more
complex totalities.

Marx's conception of the growth, establishment and dissolution of the various conditions of production seems to be a particular application of general Hegelian thought on development. Marx is not in agreement with Hegel,
however: Hegel understood the relation among the parts of totalities in a false
and speculative manner.

In his works, Hegel attempted to find a simple, uncomplicated starting point
that constituted the beginning of the infinite, increasingly complicated pro-

---

39   Marx 1953, p. 15.
40   Ibid., p. 20.

cesses of development. In *Phenomenology of Spirit*, where he follows the path of knowledge, he starts from 'sense-certainty';[41] in *Science of Logic* he starts from unqualified Being.[42] No matter which starting point is chosen, however, something is always left out; no matter which *etwas* (Something) is taken as the subject of investigation, *ein Anderes* (an Other) is ignored.[43] But then this Other becomes a problem, and above all the relation[44] between the first and the second becomes a problem. Both phenomena must be joined into a totality. This totality, however, further excludes other phenomena that must be included in turn. Among the parts included in the first totality there is still an opposition: they do not cease to be 'Something' and 'an Other' in their union.

This is a description of a theoretical process – a process of knowledge – but Hegel has his basic conception and asserts that every real development runs the same course. The path of knowledge is also the path of reality.

But for the time being, Marx's criticism of Hegel's conception does not apply to idealism but the conception of the relation among the parts in the whole, the moments of the totality. Here, we must grasp Hegel's conception before we can understand what Marx is criticising.

The antithetical pair of abstract and concrete plays a key role in Hegel, as it does in Marx. The simple starting point is always abstract because it excludes the 'an Other'. The unity of 'Something' and 'an Other' is concrete in relation to the moments included: the abstract means that the concrete is broken down into its components.[45] In principle, Marx's use of these terms does not differ from Hegel. In the *Grundrisse*, Marx says: 'The concrete is concrete because it is a synthesis of many determinations, thus a unity of the diverse'.[46] The wording is simpler, but the content is much the same.

The difference between Hegel's and Marx's view lies in the conception of the relation among the abstract determinations included in the concrete totality. To describe the relation among the moments in a temporarily stabilised totality, Hegel prefers a word that becomes extremely important in several different ways in the history of Marxism: Reflexion (reflection).[47] It is a word that emin-

---

41   Hegel 2:81 et seqq.

42   Ibid., 4:69 et seqq.

43   Ibid., 4:132 et seqq.

44   On the concept of relation in Hegel, see (the somewhat difficult to grasp) monograph by Wall.

45   The abstraction is 'a separation of the concrete, and an isolation of its determinations'. Hegel 5:61.

46   Marx 1953, p. 21.

47   The best investigation, in my opinion, of the concept of reflection in Hegel is Willem van Dooren 1965; see in particular p. 81 et seqq.

ently suits Hegel's purpose of showing the agreement between the ideal and the real, between idea and reality. Reflection is first a moment in the intellectual process: the analysis of a totality, and thus a process of abstraction. But it is not just any analysis. The one moment is regarded in its opposition to another moment; the totality is thus in view but still keeps the moments separate. In fact, Hegel distinguishes between several kinds of reflection,[48] but that is something we do not need to go into more detail here.

'Reflection', however, does not have only its everyday meaning of thinking something over but can also in ordinary language signify the phenomenon of light being reflected off a surface. Hegel makes use of this duality in the areas of application for the word. The moments in a totality can be broken down not only in reflection: they also reflect themselves and the other moments. It is in this reflection that the unity of the totality appears for reflection upon.

There is a close connection between reflection and totality in Hegel's thought. The law of identity in logic, $a = a$, constitutes the height of abstraction, with the use of which no change or process can generally be understood. It is the external (*äussere*) reflection that stops at this purely tautological thesis of identity. A higher form of reflection, however, understands that this identity is an identity between separate moments. This 'determinative' reflection determines a phenomenon by marking it off from an Other: this way, both 'Something' and 'an Other' are thus kept in view.[49]

But like abstraction, identity is not a phenomenon that applies only to thought processes. The concept of identity applies to real objects to the same extent. In any real totality whatsoever, the moments included are identical to one another and still separate.

6   Totality according to Marx

This is the concept of identity that Marx was opposed to.

Hegel, however, expresses himself in the contexts I cited about all-encompassing phenomena that are valid everywhere. Marx was working with a limited, specific theory. For Hegel, reason that creates unity raises itself over the various forms of reflections. With his philosophy, he wanted above all to resolve the major speculative issues formulated in the tradition of idealist philosophy. He wanted to find the unity between subject and object, between Spirit and

---

48   Hegel 4:492 et seqq.
49   Ibid., p. 508 et seqq.

Nature. His conceptions of identity were from the beginning formed in polemics with the 'philosophy of identity' of the Romantics and of Schelling in particular, in which the natural and the spiritual fused together unresistingly into a unity for philosophical thinking.[50]

The totality Marx spoke about is that of material production. In general, Hegel's totalities could be anything.

This difference is essential. By confronting his own conception with Hegel's, Marx – while commenting only on the study of material production – would come to face methodological and theoretical questions of an unlimited scope. In the introduction to the *Grundrisse*, this opposition is between the limited and the general is unexplained. He called the central section 'The Method of Political Economy', but he spoke as if what he was saying should apply to the scientific method as a whole. The totality whose structure he was studying was material production. But how does it relate to other totalities? The question was left half open. When, six months after having written his introduction,[51] he gets the urge to write about the Hegelian method in its full breadth, it can be imagined that it had more clearly arisen for him.

But even in the introduction, he took the key terms from Hegel: words such as 'determination', 'totality', 'moment' and so on are as little known – or at least meaningless – in the tradition of Smith, Mill and Ricardo as they are central for Hegel.

When Marx said that the parts in the totality of material production are not identical, he was of course referring to an identity in the higher, dialectical sense according to Hegel. Hegel defined 'moments' (i.e. moments in a totality) as something that was sublated or entered into a unity with its opposite, and thus something that was *ein Reflektiertes* (a reflected thing).[52] The moments in the totality thus reflect each other. They are subordinate to the higher unity of the totality.

The conception that Marx points out as his own is in all its details related to Hegel's. What Marx said about the totality of material production is as follows:

1. One of the moments – production – intervenes, marking both itself and the other moments (production *'greift über'* (dominates) itself and the other parts, it dominates the totality, it is 'dominant'). 'A definite [mode

50 The most detailed presentation on this topic is Schelling 1962, where the publisher, H. Fuhrmans, shows in detail how Hegel liberated himself from and soon turned against Schelling's philosophy. Ibid., p. 494 et seqq.
51 Above, p. 55.
52 Hegel 4:121.

of] production thus determines a definite [mode of] consumption, distribution, exchange and *definite relations of these different moments to one another*.[53] (We can assume that both these statements about the special position of production have the same content, and that the latter statement is thus simply a clarification of the former.)

2.   Production is determined '*in its one-sided form*' by the other moments. There is an interaction among all the moments.[54]

Marx added that the second characteristic, the interaction, applies to every organic entity. It is impossible to determine whether he was arguing that the first does not apply to similar entities. It can only be said that the traditional idealistic view of organisms did not permit any 'dominant' moment.

But with the term 'interaction' itself, Marx clarifies his relation to Hegel. According to Hegel, the conception of an interaction entails a further development of causality, pure and simple (*a* causes *b*, *b* is an effect of *a*). When causality is only taken into account, the various quantities are regarded as only 'external' in relation to one another (i.e. they are not part of the same entity or totality). Interaction, on the other hand, means they are no longer isolated from one another.

But mere interaction no more constitutes a totality for Hegel than it does for Marx. In the first part of his *Encyclopaedia*, Hegel declared that interaction 'stands on the threshold of the concept'. But it is thus insufficient to characterise a totality. In this connection, he cited an example that is of interest in our context not only because it attracted attention in the later Marxist tradition[55] but also because it is so concrete that it can be immediately compared with Marx's object, material production. The example deals with the relation between the character and customs of a people and legislation. Keeping solely to causality leads to the conclusion that the one is the cause of the other. But saying that both are part of the same entity and that they mutually mark one another comes closer to the truth.[56]

Marx was thus speaking about the question of the same type of interaction among moments in an entity. But there is a difference whose significance is difficult to assess. Marx asserted that there is an interaction among four different moments. Hegel generally never spoke about more than two quantities, always *Etwas* (Something) and *ein Anderes* (an Other). He defined *Verhältnis* (relation-

---

53   Marx 1953, p. 20.
54   Ibid., p. 20 et seq.
55   Lenin 38:154.
56   Hegel 8:346 et seq.

ship) as a mutual relation (*Beziehung*) between two sides,[57] and it is *Verhältnis* that was his technical term for the relation among the moments in a totality while the broader *Beziehung* played no role in his terminology.

The relationship between *Etwas* and *ein Anderes* in Hegel is the relation between the positive and its opposite; in the most general terms, the opposite is no more qualified as an opposite than just 'an Other'. This means that Hegel's determination of the 'relationship' as a relation between two, and only two, moments is of great significance for his dialectic.

But Marx was working here with an entity that had four moments. For that very reason his concept of totality is markedly much more complex than Hegel's.

We cannot determine whether Marx was deliberately distancing himself from Hegel here. On the other hand, it is certain that there is a definite intent in Hegel allowing only two moments: his logic would not permit more. This is bound up with his concept of identity – precisely the concept of identity Marx opposed.

Hegel argues that merely asserting the interaction between two moments (e.g. customs and laws) will not allow us to comprehend (or grasp the idea of) the totality in question. Using the concept, both the moments are arranged into an entity. The opposition between the one and the other is abolished; only by using the concept do they become a real totality together. It could equally be said that they only achieve synthesis through this; both 'sides' in the interaction are understood as 'moments in something third and higher ... which is the concept'.[58]

Since Marx's concept did not find this entity necessary or possible to achieve, he could incorporate four determinations into the same totality.

Marx was not looking for the point where the differences among the moments ended; instead, he was looking for a dominant moment, a moment that simultaneously determines the others (and itself) and interacts with them.

It would become a later task to specify what kind of relations Marx was hinting at with his rather scantily worded statements. No similar study exists in his later works, not even in *Capital*. Nor would he ever write the brief exposition on the rational in the Hegelian method. The statements on the totality of material production thus remain quite alone in his output.

---

57   Ibid., 3:125: The relation is '*eine Bezeihung von zwei Seiten aufeinander*'. Cf. also Wall 1966, p. 3.

58   Hegel 8:347: Both sides must '*als Momente eines Dritten, Höheren, erkannt warden, welches dann eben der Begriff ist*'.

7   The Economy of the Economists: Hegel's Entire Philosophy

Among Althusser's indubitable merits is his emphasis on the difference between Marx's and Hegel's dialectic being not only a difference between idealism and materialism but also a difference in views on the dialectical structure.[59]
On the other hand, Althusser's way of portraying Marx as some kind of notorious un-Hegelian is less convincing. The dynamic and tension in Marx's relation
to Hegel cannot be explained in such simple terms. It is neither whim nor
chance that drove Marx – like Engels – to take Hegel in hand again.

The introduction to the *Grundrisse* contains not only a reckoning with the
Hegelian concept of identity and system. Marx also investigated his relation
to Hegel's views on the relation between knowledge and its object. It is here
he reckoned with Hegelian idealism. I will attempt to show, however, that this
reckoning – which in the text immediately follows the study of the concept
of totality – is in fact built on the same idea of 'identity' and 'difference' that
deviates from Hegel.

Once again, Marx demarcated his idea against both the economists' and
Hegel's. He agreed with them all that in the scientific treatment of an object –
political economy, in the case in point – had to begin with the abstract. An
older economic theory could start from the obviously complex or concrete (e.g.
the population of a country) but no real knowledge of the economic connections could be achieved along that path. It was thus a major advance when
Smith instead ignored all concrete differences and disparities, taking labour
quite simply as the starting point of his theories.

Having found a valid abstraction, however, Smith and his imitators made the
mistake of believing that it would be similarly valid, regardless of all neighbouring relations throughout all of history. Marx did not use the term 'deductive' in
his criticism, it is true, but we can quite easily state that he reproaches Smith
et al. for holding a deductive view of science. Or, rather, he reproaches them
for assuming that if a few general economic relations could be demonstrated,
then these relations would be valid in the same way always and everywhere.
Having thus established that labour of any kind creates all value, they assumed
that labour always and everywhere has the same character as in capitalist
society. The threads could be drawn backwards directly from the present era
throughout all of history, and they would always run in the same order among
themselves.

It should be noted that Marx was no more trying to determine the economists' method as evidence of a general scientific ideal here than he was any-

---

59   Althusser 1968, p. 92.

where else. On the other hand, he took a position on the whole extent of Hegelian idealism.

Like Marx, Hegel regarded theoretical work as a path from the abstract to the concrete, and like Marx but in contrast to the economists he regarded this process not as a formally logical operation in which the particular is inferred from the universal but as a 'creative' development (i.e. a development in which continually new and varying content was added to the abstractions). The concrete results of a study cannot be predicted with a set of abstractions.

But Hegel also argued that since knowledge of reality could only be attained through a purely intellectual process, reality must also be intellectual – or, rather, ideal – in nature. This is where Marx raises his objections. The path from the abstract to the concrete is travelled through thinking, of course, while the concrete is what best corresponds to, and thus provides the best knowledge of, reality. But this does not mean, as Hegel argued, that the concrete as a result of scientific work *is* at the same time reality, or rather that the development from the abstract to the concrete in thinking corresponds to a real development from something abstract to something concrete. The concrete in knowledge is a 'conceptual totality', a 'mental concretum'.[60] It therefore cannot be identified with the concrete in external reality. Nor can one believe, like Hegel, that development from the abstractions to the complex is the path of reality. Marx devoted a great deal of energy – perhaps too much – to showing that economic development does not thoroughly develop from simple into more complex relations in any consistent manner. In other words, economic history in no way ran a course corresponding to or tallying with the path of developed economic theory from the abstract to the concrete.[61]

In fact, he faces in two directions in this demonstration: against both Hegel and the classical economists. The latter assumed that capitalist relations could be found throughout history – only simpler and more primitive the further back in time they went. Hegel assumed that every development, and thus historical developments as well, began in something simple and abstract in the same way thinking or theory does.

Marx, however, still directs his main attack against Hegel. Hegel was not only an idealist; he did not simply regard the real as an expression of thinking or the idea. His thinking on identity ultimately results in the concept of unity between thought and substance, the subjective and the objective, idea and reality. The limited criticism of Hegel's concept of identity that Marx offered in the

---

60   Marx 1953, p. 22.
61   Ibid., p. 22 et seqq.

Grundrisse is expanded here to apply to the cardinal thought itself, the identity between the theory and its object. Hegel claimed that every totality is a
unity (if temporary) of the moments included in it. Marx said that this did not
apply to the totality of material production. But now the perspective is suddenly broadened. What he stated about the relation between the concrete in
thought and the concrete in reality means that in principle, he aimed the same
criticism of Hegel's idea about the absolute fusion of the areas of the theory of
knowledge at he did at economic theory. He claimed that there is a correspondence between thought and reality but that this correspondence should not be
understood as an identity. Thought and its object are not one and the same.

Marx did not mobilise a materialist conception against Hegelian idealism.
We know from other places that he regarded the conception, the theory, and
the idea as derived and secondary. For him, the essential thing was to show
that knowledge and its object should not be identified with one another – and
thus not in any direction (neither Hegel's idealistic nor the opposite) in which
knowledge becomes only the immediate impression of its object.

The extraordinary significance of the introduction to the *Grundrisse* is in
respect to Marx not only setting his historical materialism against Hegel's historical idealism, as he did previously, but also confronting his theory of the base
with Hegelian methodology. His exposition, however, provided no answer to
an essential question, namely, the extent to which what he said about political
economy applies to *all* of the scientific method. Hegel, of course, ascribed universal validity to his statements on theoretical work. Marx, however, spoke on
the one hand about the method of studying a highly complex and specific piece
of reality, namely material production, and on the other hand used terms and
expressions in his criticism of Hegel that reasonably apply to all knowledge.

It seems as if the issue of the methodology of *other* sciences had not come
into his field of vision. But the issue is implicit in what he said. If he spoke about
political economy *as if* it applied to all knowledge, the problem of how political
economy relates to other disciplines must gradually emerge.

A comparison of the introduction to the *Grundrisse* with similar – though
more sporadic, accidental and scattered – statements in the first volume of
Capital shows that the specific issue of the relation between political economy
and such sciences as physics, chemistry and above all biology had become an
essential, crucial question for Marx. Finding the conditions for this change will
be an important task for us.

In our case, however, the introduction to the *Grundrisse* raises the question
of the relation between two areas of knowledge, one narrower and one broader,
both of equal interest to Marx. The one is material production (thus political
economy in the narrower sense) and the other is society and history in general

(i.e. the field of historical materialism). Unfortunately, Marx never finished his thoughts here; he only provided a few points. These points will give us a few highly valuable hints.

In one of the points – the sixth – Marx spoke about the unequal relation (*das unegale Verhältnis*) between material production and, for example, the development of art.[62] At first, it appears as if it concerned a rather banal problem that Marx took up only to protect himself against various common ideas that advancements in one field (e.g. material production) always entailed similar advancements in all other fields. According to one such idea, for example, Greek art was necessarily inferior to modern art. Marx claimed that no such baroque idea at all followed from belief in the primacy of material production.

Something more, however, lies in Marx's assertion than the simple rejection of the foolish thought that the degree of development of material production forms the foundation for appraising all cultural products. He also, and above all, spoke about an actual inequality in development. This statement is to be set against the idea of the unique position of material production. What Marx wanted above all to demonstrate is that even if material production determines historical development in general, this does not mean that all social phenomena are passively dependent on it.

These scanty and undeveloped statements cannot be hastily equated with what Engels claimed in his later correspondence from 1890.[63] There is substantial agreement, but more cannot be said. On the other hand, it is obvious that Marx's statements have a logical connection with what he said earlier in the introduction about the totality of material production and about the relation between knowledge and its object. 'Unequal relations' are continually in force in which *one* moment – production in the totality of material production, material production in society in general, the object of knowledge in the process of knowledge – is ascribed a unique position and identified as dominant but still not as the only crucial, independent or decisive one.[64]

There should thus be a structural similarity between these different fields. The issue of structural similarity itself is or will become the main overshadowing and problematic point in Engels's efforts with a dialectical materialism.

But in his introduction, however, Marx was far from the ambitions of creating a coherent view of the sciences. He even hesitated to call his conception of

---

62   Marx 1953, p. 29 et seqq.; quote, p. 29.
63   Cf. p. 344.
64   *Verhältnis* is Hegel's technical term for the relation between moments in a totality, he would not tolerate any 'uneven relation' in Marx's meaning.

history materialist and, in one of his incomplete points, spoke about realist (as opposed to idealist) historiography. In another point he announced his intention to take up accusations of his conception being characterised as materialist. We cannot determine what he meant by that; would he have rejected such accusations outright? He also intended to study the relation between his views and 'naturalistic materialism'. We cannot know what that would entail. The question had been raised for him, but he still did not have time to set to work on it.[65]

To clarify his point of view towards a naturalistic materialism, he needed to return to his and Engels's reckonings, above all with Feuerbach, from over a decade earlier. How remote various matters had been for him during the intervening period can be seen, for example, in his major reckoning with Carl Vogt.[66] For Marx, Vogt was only of interest as a political and ideological phenomenon; it was his political perfidy that captured all of Marx's attention. He did not devote a single line to Vogt as a leading representative of a naturalistic materialism.[67]

8   Relation to the Early Writings

So far, we have not put what Marx said about Hegel in the late 1850s into any relation with the much more detailed studies on the same subject that he achieved in the 1840s. This may seem peculiar. In the majority of the literature on Marx, the question of his relation to Hegel had its starting point in Marx's early writings. The immediate classical example is Herbert Marcuse's *Reason and Revolution*, in which Marx has a place in the Hegelian tradition[68] and where the 'Marxian dialectic' is determined starting from some of the statements in these early writings.[69] As a result, what Marx said about Hegel in his early years are infinitely more comprehensive and exhaustive than his offerings in the *Grundrisse*, in *Capital* and in other similar places. Moreover, Marx's early

---

65   Marx 1953, p. 29.
66   In 1859, Carl Vogt had published *Mein Prozess gegen de Allgemeine Zeitung* with attacks on targets including Marx; Marx's *Herr Vogt*, which was published in 1860, was essentially a response.
67   Vogt, alongside Ludwig Büchner and Jacob Moleschott, is regarded as the main representative of the materialist (or 'vulgar materialist') side in the materialism debate. Vogt's most important contribution here was his *Köhlerglaube und Wissenschaft*, 1854.
68   Marcuse 1960, pp. 273–322.
69   Ibid., p. 312 et seqq.

writings had the charm and pleasure of new discoveries when Marcuse wrote his magnum opus and for a few decades thereafter. There was, however, also a way of rationalising the method of distilling Marx's relation to Hegel in general from these early criticisms of Hegel. It was a question of finding Marx the philosopher outside, or under, Marx the economist and politician. The philosopher could be easily found in his writings before 1848. The later writings had to be viewed in light of the earlier ones.[70]

But the reason that a self-appointed philosopher can be found only in the young – or rather, perhaps, the very young – Marx is a superficial one. Here, in the spirit of the Young Hegelians and Feuerbach, Marx wished to devote himself to 'criticism' with a starting point in 'philosophy'. As he said in an article in *Rheinische Zeitung*, politics and religion are to be criticised based on the philosophy of the age.[71] Philosophy says what is essential and what is not. Feuerbach sought to reveal the essence of Christianity: he proceeded from his philosophical conception that the sensuous, the immediate and material always constitute the fundamental, whereas ideas and abstractions are derived and dependent. The Christian assertions about God and the hereafter must have their earthly content made clear; it turns out that God is nothing other than humanity's ideal image of itself.[72]

In the same spirit, Marx sought to criticise both Hegel's philosophy and economics and the politics in question. The terms 'philosophy' and 'criticism' were crucial for him.

But a new term comes into view early on: 'science'. Even in the *Paris Manuscripts*, in which he provided a serious account of his contact with classical economics, he spoke about economics as a science just as he spoke about the natural sciences.[73] The words characterise all research in a definite subject. A few years later, in *The Holy Family*, Marx and Engels spoke about science in both the general, neutral meaning and in a qualitative sense (i.e. in the sense of better or worse science, or of scientific and unscientific research).[74]

---

70   A classic example in this case is Thier. Even in directions where this type of reading of
      Marx is unknown, there are conceptions that in his early writings, Marx's dialectic had
      already been staked off in relation to Hegel's. Nicolaus 1973, in speaking about a few very
      early writings, asserts: 'All the elements of Marx's particular character as materialist *and*
      dialectician are present here, but the announced intent of focusing and systematizing the
      many points of difference with Hegel's *Logic* is not carried out'.
71   In an article of 14 July 1842; MECW 1:195 et seqq.
72   See above all Chapter 2, 'The Essence of Religion', in *The Essence of Christianity*. Feuerbach
      IV:14–40.
73   MECW 3:293 et seqq., 307 et seqq., 322 et seqq.
74   MECW 2, for example p. 31 (section written by Marx).

Science thus occupies the old position of philosophy, step by step. When Marx gave his later work the title or (as in *Capital*) the subtitle of *A Critique of Political Economy*, he thus took as the starting point of his criticism not what he called his philosophy but his own scientific theory.

Of course, this is not merely a difference in terminology between the younger and older Marx in relation to philosophy and science. The philosophy of his youth is quite general and abstract; his later economic theory and conception of history is concrete and well developed.

But this is exactly why it is important to keep the specific in mind when analysing his statements on Hegel in the *Grundrisse* and later on. It is not quite the same Hegel he was now interested in. In assuming that Marx was finished as a philosopher (i.e. he had already established his general starting points in his earlier works) can lead to serious mistakes. Let us take an example. Gerd Dicke wrote a scholarly dissertation, *The Identity Concept in Feuerbach and Marx*. Right in the foreword, he declared that above all, Marx must be understood as a philosopher. He therefore proceeds from Marx's early, openly philosophical works. The concept of identity in Marx becomes the concept of identity that emerges – or rather becomes discernible – in his early works. But that is precisely why Dicke does not discern Marx's new, specific criticism of the Hegelian concept of identity in the *Grundrisse*, which lacks a counterpart in the works from the 1840s but is indispensably important for understanding the relation between Marx's fully developed theory and Hegel's philosophy.

It is true that Marx never distanced himself from the main points of his early criticism of Hegel, as formulated in the major fragmentary manuscripts *A Contribution to the Critique of Hegel's Philosophy of Right* and the *Paris Manuscripts*. But he goes through several stages on the way to the *Grundrisse*. In his early writings, he attacks Hegel from Feuerbach's starting points. He 'everywhere makes the idea the subject'.[75] This meant that in his political philosophy, he turned the idea of the state into the driving force of development. Real people become merely expressions of the idea; they become its 'predicate' or its 'object'. In fact, they must relate to each other in the opposite manner. Hegel turns the predicate – what real people achieve – into the real agents of history and development.[76] This is bound up with the idealistic starting point of his philosophy. He sees abstract thought as the primary while nature is its alienation, its *Entäusserung*. Human history thus becomes the path of the idea from

---

75   'It is important that Hegel everywhere makes the idea the subject and turns the proper, the actual subject, such as "political conviction", into a predicate'. MECW 3:11.

76   MECW 3:23.

nature back to itself.[77] In *The Holy Family*, Marx still declares[78] that the essential characteristic of the Hegelian method is comprehending '*Substance*' as '*Subject*, as an *inner process*, as an *Absolute Person*'.[79] Of course, this is Hegel's manner of pointing out certain individuals – like certain nations or states – as expressions of the idea or as instruments for 'the stratagem of Reason' that provokes Marx's criticism here. But ultimately it is his entire idealism and anti-empiricism that Marx distanced himself from.

In his later works, Marx did not change his position in this respect: he did not doubt that the empirically given is the starting point for scientific work. Even if he later worded his assessment differently, he also held fast to the view he expressed in the *Manuscripts* that Hegel's great merit was his way of presenting history as a coherent process.[80]

But there are extremely substantial changes in his development that also affect his relation to Hegel. In the *Manuscripts* and other early reckonings with Hegel, he still sided with Feuerbach's idea of the *essence* of humanity that can be alienated or realised in society. It could be said that against Hegel's conceptions of various collective and abstract essences (state, people, class, etc.) he set the essence of the individual person.

Beginning with *The German Ideology* – or, rather, beginning with the brief *Theses on Feuerbach* – he transitioned from speaking about the person to speaking about humanity. The sixth thesis begins: 'Feuerbach resolves the essence of religion into the essence of *man*. But the essence of man is no abstraction inherent in each single individual. In its reality it is the ensemble of social relations'.[81] With this dissolution of Feuerbach's concept of essence, the materialist conception of history began. This meant not only that the historical perspective had been brought to the fore in a different manner than in Feuerbachian materialism. Above all, it meant that human individuals were not viewed in relation to an imagined human essence but directly, as marked by – and leaving their marks on – the prevailing material circumstances. The earlier Feuerbach-inspired criticism of Hegel had not lost its validity, but in a way, it had become of less immediate importance. There was a stroke of individualism in the earlier concept: the person, in the singular, was the starting point. In that respect, the

---

77   MECW 3:330 et seqq.
78   This written by Marx as well; cf. the division according to the table of contents, MECW 4:V et seqq.
79   'In the speculative way of speaking, this operation is called comprehending *Substance* as *Subject*, as an *inner process*, as an *Absolute Person*, and this comprehension constitutes the essential character of *Hegel's* method'. MECW 4:60.
80   MECW 3:332 et seq.
81   MECW 5:4.

criticism against Hegel's collective concepts such as state and nation gained particular clarity. Marx (and Engels) were now on the way to developing new collective concepts – above all, the concept of class – that was certainly not derived from any world of ideas like Hegel's but rooted in the practical circumstances of humanity, but nevertheless related to Hegel's philosophy of history in a different way than the concept of human essence.

Historical materialism, however, did not give Marx or Engels a reason to take up Hegel's philosophy again. With *The German Ideology*, they seem to have gotten a very safe distance from it. Hegel became relevant only when Marx was working out his specific economic theory. It must be remembered that what Marx now had to attempt to give shape to was not a general idealistic or materialistic background philosophy – a starting point for criticism – nor was it a broadly outlined conception of history. It was a complex, well designed theory of the base. That is why, in his second major confrontation with Hegel's philosophy, it was *other* matters that interested him than previously. He had not previously asserted the thesis of a non-identical relation, which he was now defending against Hegel's ideas about identity. Even more essentially: he had not spoken about any path from the abstract up to the concrete. He had reproached Hegel for not realising that knowledge had to have its start in the diversity, difficult to grasp, of the sensuous. He had not, however, taken a position on Hegel's thesis that scientific accounts had to start from a few abstractions. The reason is not difficult to find: the young Marx, who had taken a position on Hegel, had no abstract theory of his own corresponding to the one he now had to deal with.[82]

Thus, the essential result of the comparison between Marx's earlier and later criticisms of Hegel is that these are new pages in Hegel that are brought to the fore through Marx's own scientific development. His position on Hegel cannot be understood solely through studying his earlier and more detailed writings on the subject. Nor is it 'by mere accident' that he came up against Hegel again in the late 1850s.

9   The Scientific Method

Marx never completed his plans to develop the rational in the Hegelian method, however. To understand, or at least to divine, what he may have inten-

---

82   It is thus first in the *Grundrisse* that Marx speaks of abstraction as the starting point of
        scientific work. Marx 1953, p. 21 et seqq.

ded, we have the scanty statements in the introduction to the *Grundrisse*, and in part in *Capital*, at our disposal as well as a number of even more sporadic statements in his letters and the like.

One question that cannot be immediately answered using this material is quite central: What did Marx mean by 'method' in this context? As we have seen, he used the term in the introduction, where he spoke of 'the method of political economy'. He does not explicitly state what that means, however. He seems to have assumed that the world as such had such obvious content that it did not need to be studied.

As we have seen, however, the question of method is a decisive one in Marxism: one of the major subjects of dispute concerns whether or not the core of Marxism can be found exclusively in a method.

In other words: if he had managed to study the rational method at some point, would Marx have defined the core of his own doctrine?

One thing must be remembered, namely, that he promised only to describe what was rational in the *Hegelian* method. We do not know if he intended with that to arrive at a rational method in general. We only know that he – like Engels – almost exclusively related his own understanding to Hegel's in similar broad questions. This entails extraordinary difficulties: the differences and similarities with Hegel are insufficient to obtain a clear conception of his understanding.

A comparison between Hegel's and Marx's understanding of what a method entails must form the starting point, however. A substantial discrepancy between Hegel and Marx is then immediately detected, which Marx did not draw our attention to. Hegel spoke about the method of philosophy in contrast to the method of the specialised sciences. Marx spoke about (the rational in) this method applied to a specialised science – political economy. For Hegel, it was a matter of a philosophical interpretation of the results of the specialised sciences. For Marx, it was achieving results in a specialised science.

There is a way of resolving this difference by assuming that political economy for Marx had the same fundamental position that philosophy had for Hegel. The difference should consist simply of the difference that exists between Hegel's idealism and Marx's historical materialism.

On the other hand, political economy can only be fundamental for other social and historical disciplines which, moreover, Marx and Engels had asserted back in *The German Ideology*.[83] It can hardly be fundamental for physics or chemistry or biology. The issue of the applicability of the method in similar disciplines seems to cry out for an answer.

---

83   E.g. MECW 5:92.

Hegel defined his own method above all in relation to other philosophical methods (i.e. other methods that had come into use to create an overall picture of knowledge and the world). The fundamental error in the competing methods, according to Hegel, was that they had not been designed with reference to the absolutely unique position of philosophy in relation to other sciences, sometimes as if it concerned a question of experience. The empirical sciences have a method adapted to their subjects; for Hegel, this method meant above all 'the definition and classification of materials'.[84] Pure mathematics, which deals with pure quantities, was also resorted to. Against both of these approaches, Hegel now set a third that entailed adapting to a form corresponding to – or, rather, one with – the content's (i.e. the philosophical object's) own internal development. This was the dialectical method.[85]

Hegel thus hinted at a difference between formal disciplines (pure mathematics) and material or real ones (the empirical sciences); philosophy rose above them all, unifying form and content.

Naturally, Hegel rooted this understanding in his idealism: thinking – or rather higher, comprehensive, philosophical thinking – is identical with its object. Marx, however, wanted to liberate the Hegelian method from this idealistic assumption. He did not accept that thinking or knowledge (i.e. the form) should be identical with its object, but he wanted to assert that an optimal correspondence between them both is achieved with a dialectical method.

Hegel provided no consistent names for the methods he repudiated, or exiled to scientific spheres lower than that of philosophy. Sometimes, he referred closely to Kant's vocabulary, for example, when he declared that the philosophical method was simultaneously analytical and synthetic.[86] In this context, pure mathematics is to be regarded as an analytical discipline, whereas the empirical sciences are synthetic. Philosophy should therefore be both; it would abolish the opposition and unite analytical and synthetic at a higher level.

It is easier, however, to understand both Hegel and Marx (and later, Engels) if instead we speak about the inductive and deductive methods, and relate the dialectical method to them. What Hegel said about the inductive infer-

---

84   Hegel 4:50 (*Science of Logic*, Vol. 1): '*Erfarungswissenschaften haben für das, was sie sein sollen, ihre eigentümliche Methode, des Definierens und des Klassificierens ihres Stoffes, so gut es geht, gefunden*'.

85   Ibid., 4:50 et seqq.

86   Hegel 3:187 (*Philosophical Propadeutic*): '*Der Gang oder die Methode des absoluten Wissens is ebensosehr analytisch wie synthetisch*'. Cf. also Hegel 8:436 et seqq. (*System of Philosophy*, Vol. 1).

ence, moreover, agrees quite well with what he said about the empirical sciences.[87]

Here, the inductive method quite simply means going from what is provided by experience – from data or facts, or whatever it is called – and arriving at general statements or theories about reality by this *and only this* path. The deductive method, on the other hand, entails going from the general and drawing conclusions about the individual from this general.

It scarcely needs to be added that these descriptions are simplifications: the scientific method has rarely taken such pure forms. But this simplification exists even in Hegel, who spoke about pure empirical sciences on the one hand and pure mathematics on the other.

In all their makeshift simplification, the concepts 'inductive', 'deductive' and 'dialectical' can shed light on what Marx said about the method of political economy in his introduction to the *Grundrisse*. What we call an inductive method here would be represented by those starting directly from economic reality in all its diversity, difficult to grasp. This, Marx asserted, is the path the economists before Smith usually chose. Mercantilists and others thus took their starting point in a totality with many branches such as population, nation or state and from that attempted to distil a number of abstract relations such as value or division of labour.

The opposite path meant, on the contrary, letting the scientific description start from the abstract and seek diversity from there.[88]

The introduction to the *Grundrisse* could give the impression that this method is 'the right one', pure and simple. The same mistake presents itself immediately in that well-known section in the afterword to the second edition of *Capital* (Vol. 1) in which Marx spoke about the difference between the process of representation and the process of research.[89] The process of research entails assimilating the material in detail and discovering the essential and unifying; in other words, the path from the concrete to the abstract that is not expressed in the scientific description but precedes it. Instead, the description begins in the abstract and follows the path up to the concrete. It may then seem, Marx said, as if an *a priori* construction was concerned,[90] which makes it easy to believe that Marx – unlike Hegel – advocated

---

87   Hegel 5:152 et seqq.

88   Marx 1953, p. 21 et seqq.

89   The question of the method of presentation was current among many philosophers with whom Marx came in literary contact, e.g. Hegel and Comte. On this, in addition to Negt 1964, see also Schmidt 1971b, p. 121 et seqq.

90   MECW 35:19.

a purely deductive process.[91] In that case, however, the fundamental difference between his method and Smith's or Ricardo's would be incomprehensible.

The uncertainty depends, once again, on Marx not having related his general scientific ideal to anything other than Hegel's philosophy. The differences nonetheless become obvious if one studies the process of description he actually uses in the *Grundrisse* or in *Capital*, or gets into his criticism of the classical economists. In *Capital*, of course, he starts from a highly abstract category – the commodity – but the path he then follows does not run directly to the more concrete. In fact, abstract and concrete are mixed. So, for example, after the highly concrete eighth chapter on the working day comes the extraordinarily abstract chapter on surplus value. The same phenomenon can be observed in the various chapters, in the running description. The same applies to the *Grundrisse*, even though it is not a complete representation. The intentional demarcation of this zigzag path between abstract and concrete, between general theoretical assertions and empirical statements is obvious. In a letter from 1870, Marx spoke ironically about Friedrich Albert Lange's remark that in *Capital*, Marx made use of the empirical material 'with rare freedom'.[92] Lange did not understand that it was 'the *method* of dealing with matter – that is, the *dialectical method*'.[93] When, in the aforementioned afterword to the second edition of *Capital*, he spoke about 'treating Hegel as a dead dog', it was first of all Lange's statement on Hegel he was thinking of; the words were the exact same as in the letter from 1870.[94] But in the afterword, he did not take up the aims of his 'rare freedom'.

However, the dialectical method represented for Marx – like Hegel – a higher union of what we have called the inductive and deductive methods. His recurring, yet never essentially elaborated, criticism of the classical economists' manner of handling abstractions was a criticism of a deductive process. If it is assumed, namely, that a number of abstractions are valid for all reality of a certain type (e.g. economic reality), then reality will also appear as essentially similar, only more or less developed. Nothing qualitatively new can be imagined. The empirical material cannot be handled with any sort of freedom, since one can only attempt to recover the abstractions in the empirical material. No totalities in Marx's sense (or Hegel's, for that matter) can be imagined.

---

91   As Marx himself cites, ibid., p. 17, it was a misconception he encountered among his
      reviewers.
92   Lange 1875, p. 29.
93   Letter from Marx to Ludwig Kugelmann, 27 June 1870. MECW 43:528.
94   MECW 35:19, and the letter to Kugelmann, MECW 43:528.

There is a similar relation, expressible in stable statements of law, among the abstractions throughout all of history.

For Marx, the dialectical method thus certainly meant trying to achieve the same level of abstraction – or the same general theoretical validity – as if the deductive method were being followed, but always confronting the abstractions with the concrete material. Or, rather: the path from the abstract to the concrete is not a formal process but a creative one. The abstract is given, but its role in the concrete is not; it must be found again and again. In the totalities that the advocates of a deductive method refused to seek, the abstractions were part of continually new relations. It can never be verified that something new is being formed in history using these abstractions. The new is only seen in the concrete, the diverse.

Further on, we will return to these general statements about the method in order to gain greater clarity in them. Here, it was solely a matter of showing that Marx's new confrontation with Hegel had an internal connection with his work on developing a theory of the base. It is thus not an issue of a few temporary philosophical distractions.

But another relation has also become clear. What Marx called the method, or the rational method, was a highly general and far-reaching category, an issue of the relation between empiricism and theory, and this issue was placed in relation to far-reaching assumptions in knowledge theory about the relation between knowledge and its object. On the other hand, it did not concern any rules of thumb for scientific work, or detailed recommendations for how a scientist should work, gather material, develop their theories – and test them.

Nor can what Marx called the method be turned into an independent quantity, liberated from the theories Marx had laid out. When Lukács, in *History and Class Consciousness*, asserted that the Marxist method would endure even if all the individual theses laid out by Marx were disproved,[95] he ignored the fact that there is an internal connection between what, in this context, was called method and the theories laid out.[96] However 'the rational method' in Marx may be formulated, it will imply a number of statements about reality. It is inseparable from the assumption in knowledge theory about the primacy of the object in the knowledge process, as well as from the ontological assumption about the primacy of the material in history. It cannot be formulated without the thesis

---

95   Lukács 1968, p. 39 et seqq.
96   In this aspect, Hans Koch appears to be correct in relation to the young Lukács; cf. Koch, p. 194 et seqq. More dubious is the criticism Andras Gedö formulated in the same context, and which is based on Lukács having gone even more wrong than Stalin on the position of method; Gedö 1960, p. 36 et seqq.

that history contains qualitatively new relations. It could be imagined that the method Marx sketched out could be compatible with another view of what the capitalist phase of history means, or of the conditions under which capital would move toward its dissolution. But that would be the realm of pure speculation. With his talk of a 'method', Marx had rationalised his own theoretical results rather than provided hints for other scientists as to how they should work. It might perhaps be possible, entirely beside and largely independent of what Marx said, to fish out a method in a more specific sense from Marx's writings. This method, however, would not have any immediate connection with, and thus not entail a clarification of, his own assertions.

'Method' and 'theory' were not freestanding concepts for him, independent of each other. Like Hegel, he refused to see watertight bulkheads between 'form' and 'content', between 'process' and 'result'. Here, in fact, we are dealing with some of the ideas – in Marx as well as in Hegel – that are the most difficult to master but also the most central.

CHAPTER 3

Engels on Marx and Hegel

1 Marx and Engels

So far, we have spent our time almost exclusively on Marx's writings. Nevertheless, Engels should be our main character. It was Engels, not Marx, who wrote *Anti-Dühring*, *Dialectics of Nature* and *Ludwig Feuerbach*. It was Engels who attempted to indicate the place of the materialist conception of history in the hierarchy of the sciences.

But assessing these works of Engels is impossible without studying the general basis for Marx's theoretical works. We have seen that Marx, in the *Grundrisse*, faced problems that – so to speak – have their natural continuation in questions about the character of science – or, rather, of all sciences and all knowledge. The questions that Engels later asked thus had a connection with those theoretical works of Marx that culminated in *Capital* (I say questions, not answers). The search for a 'socialist world view' should thus not only be ideologically determined (i.e. springing from the need to find support for Marxism as a revolutionary ideology in science in general). It should also have its theoretical determination.

That is not to say, however, that *those exact problems* that Engels gradually tackled should have this inner connection with Marx's theory. That remains to be seen. We must carefully follow Engels's way of approaching the general questions of his time in philosophy, scientific theory, and the natural sciences. We must compare them with Marx's more limited efforts in the same field. But before we can go so far, we have another issue to take a position on, namely the extent to which Engels completely accepted the theoretical work that was first incompletely expressed in the *Grundrisse*. The chronology is helpful here: the *Grundrisse* was completed before Engels took up his studies in philosophy and the natural sciences in earnest. We thus have an opportunity to see where Engels stood in relation to Marx before the major philosophical issues again became of serious interest for him. We can subsequently follow how these studies affected his position.

The question of the relation between Marx and Engels is of course a notoriously heated one, and as it is often posed – 'Marx and Engels, or Marx alone?' – it is rather silly. When Lukács published *History and Class Consciousness*, he was immediately accused of wanting to play Marx off against Engels.[1] This is an

---

1 Cf. for example Deborin 1924, reprinted in Deborin and Bukharin 1969, p. 189. See also Korsch

unfair accusation; it would be more apposite for numerous later interpreters of the problem. George Lichtheim, for example, attains pure mendacity when – to show how uncontrollably far from Marx it was that Engels had developed his general dialectic – states that Engels took up this risky enterprise only *after* Marx's death.[2] In fact, Engels all but completely broke off his work on *Dialectics of Nature* when Marx died to tackle editing the second and third volumes of *Capital* instead.

But there are assuredly more ambitious ways of marking a boundary between Marx and Engels. In the context in question, it is of immediate interest. It has been developed in the greatest detail by Hermann Bollnow, and the drift of it is to show that from the very beginning and then throughout the whole long body of his work, Engels had a completely different fundamental outlook than Marx. The difference between Engels and Marx should not be restricted to Engels, with his general dialectic, entering into a field that Marx had left untouched. Engels had a different view of such central objects for Marxism as revolution and societal development in general. Bollnow took his starting point in Engels's *Principles of Communism* from 1847 – one of the models for the *Communist Manifesto*.[3] He claimed that Engels, in a way that is alien to Marx's entire view of society, regards the coming proletarian revolution by analogy with the industrial revolution. In other words, Engels had ignored the significance of politics and political action and regarded the development of society as something like a natural course of events fixed by law.[4] It is obvious that Bollnow compared the Engels of 1847 with an even earlier Marx: this 'philosophical' Marx who, according to the interpreters of Bollnow's tradition, is the only real and true one. If, instead, Bollnow had compared *Principles of Communism* with what Marx said about base and superstructure in *A Contribution to the Critique of Political Economy*, he would likely have come to the opposite conclusion, namely that Marx was more willing than Engels to regard the development of society by analogy with a natural process.

Naturally there are differences – crucial ones – between Marx's and Engels's entire intellectual presence. There is a difference in their main interests and a difference in their knowledge and reading. They did not express themselves in the same manner. Marx often wrote ponderously and laboriously; his sentences seem to have difficulty bearing the solid content of ideas. Engels formulated

---

1970, in particular the section 'The Present State of the Problem of "Marxism and Philosophy"', p. 98 et seqq.

2   Lichtheim 1970, p. 298.

3   MECW 6:341 et seqq. Engels took up the question of the industrial revolution, p. 345 et seqq.

4   Bollnow 1954, p. 77 et seqq.

himself more simply and easily. He had an aptitude for popularising, sometimes simplifying. Marx had a difficult but consistent conceptual apparatus;
Engels did not at all use as many technical terms but tried to bring out what
he meant with generally comprehensible but varied expressions. Marx's completed works are composed in an ingenious but not always transparent manner.
Engels followed plans in accordance with some simple principle, his chapters
stride forth in straight rows.

These differences are more substantial and fundamental than can be believed at first. In every comparison between Marx and Engels, it must be
remembered that they never really spoke the same language and that they had
background knowledge and frames of reference that did not coincide.

On the other hand, the dissimilarities were not so fundamental that they
could not collaborate in the most intense manner the whole time; in the 1840s
they wrote a number of works together. There is very little evidence that shared
authorship offered difficulties. After their first joint project, *The Holy Family*,
Engels wrote to Marx and complained that the sections the latter had written were far too exhaustive and difficult to read.[5] Nevertheless, this did not
frighten Engels away from immediately taking up a more comprehensive and
intense collaboration, the result of which was *The German Ideology*. Distinguishing Marx's and Engels's shares in the work is nearly impossible. It can
only be assumed that the tangible simplification in the manner of expression
compared with Marx's previous works had a great deal to do with Engels's participation.

The purely literary collaboration ended after they both ended up in England, and it is often difficult to determine how well informed the one was about
the other's writings. We have already seen how after Marx's death, Engels was
uncertain as to whether Marx had actually authored the dialectic he had promised. In this connection, Engels remarked that Marx had in many respects kept
secret how far he had gotten in his writing efforts.[6] Still, their mutual letters
bear witness to the fact that there had been an intense exchange of ideas and
opinions the whole time. After 1870, when Engels had also moved to London,
the correspondence naturally became markedly much thinner but there is no
reason to believe that the flow of information would have decreased for that
reason. Quite the contrary.

But that is not to say how far the actual accord went. They may have informed
each other of everything they were thinking, and they may have experienced

---

5   Letter from Engels to Marx, 17 March 1845. MECW 38:28.
6   Above, p. 56.

the greatest unanimity. They may have misunderstood each other, or inter-preted the consequences of what they stood for differently. It can also be assumed, like Habermas does,[7] that the friendship dampened their candour – or at least Marx's.

2   Engels's Review of Marx

The issue of the real or imagined agreement between their opinions will be taken up here in a limited, but crucial, context. As we have seen, Marx aban-doned his plans to publish the entire great work – of which the *Grundrisse* represented a model – in a single whole and instead expected to publish the work in instalments. Only the first instalment of this *Critique of Political Eco-nomy* came out. Marx was quite eager to have Engels review the work. Engels's review can be compared not only with the work reviewed but also with the entire *Grundrisse* and its introduction in particular, which Marx did not want to publish at the beginning of his work. We do not know how accurate Engels's knowledge of the *Grundrisse* was. Marx's letter to him is not especially inform-ative.[8] Nor do we know whether Engels had any idea of the content of the introduction. For the sake of our comparison, it is fortunate that Engels in his review took up a number of the general questions Marx dealt with in his intro-duction but not in the printed work. I can begin by mentioning that there are crucial differences between Marx's and Engels's approaches to the problems precisely here.

To grasp the relation between Marx the theoretician and Engels the theoreti-cian *at this exact point in time*, however, it is necessary to study the background behind Engels's review. It was Marx who insistently asked Engels to review *A Critique of Political Economy* in the radical newspaper *Das Volk*. The paper had already run the well-known introduction to the work, and it was to prevent a less knowledgeable reviewer who was less acquainted with Marx's works from writing an already-promised review that Marx asked Engels to immediately take up the pen. He provided some brief hints about what he wanted: '[b]riefly on the method and what is new in the content'.[9] Engels did not immediately respond to the challenge, and Marx wrote a reminder with further hints, includ-ing asking Engels to point out that the view of Proudhon and his followers had

---

7 Above, p. 45 et seq.
8 Cf. the letters from Marx to Engels, 8 December 1857, MECW 40:214; 18 December 1857, MECW 40:224; 11 January 1858, MECW 40:244; and 31 May 1858, MECW 40:317.
9 Letter from Marx to Engels, 19 July 1859; MECW 40:471.

been 'extirpate[d]'.[10] Engels replied that he would certainly write the review
but that it would not be immediate: namely, it required an *'undertaking'*.[11] A
few weeks later he was nevertheless ready with the first of the three planned
parts of the review and sent it to Marx to be read through. The accompany-
ing letter exudes an uncertainty that actually stands in sharp contrast to the
resolution with which he expressed himself a few decades later on the same
questions. He asked Marx:

> Take a good look at it, and if you don't like it *in toto*, tear it up and let me
> have your opinion. Through lack of practice I have grown so unused to this
> sort of writing that your wife will be greatly tickled by my awkwardness.
> If you can knock it into shape, do so. A few convincing examples of the
> materialistic viewpoint would not come amiss, in place of my indifferent
> reference to the February revolution.[12]

We do not know whether Marx actually made any changes, since the manuscript for the article has been lost. The example of the February revolution
remains in any case,[13] and it is at least a hint that Marx let the entire review
pass. There is, as we shall see, more that indicates this.

The remainder of the review was delayed,[14] however, and the extent to which
Marx checked it is not indicated in the correspondence. A second part was published in *Das Volk*, whereas the third – which would have dealt with Marx's
economic theories – was never printed because *Das Volk* shut down before
then. The manuscript for this conclusion has also been lost.[15]

It was thus a very hesitant and uncertain Engels who reviewed his friend's
work. None of that hesitancy is noticeable in the review itself, however. It is
written in Engels's usual straightforward style.

The first part of the review has as its main subject what Engels here called for
the first time the materialist conception of history[16] (in the Grundrisse, Marx
had not managed to elucidate his position on the term 'materialism' itself).[17]

---

10   Letter from Marx to Engels, 22 July 1859; MECW 40:473.
11   Letter from Engels to Marx, 25 July 1859; MECW 40:474.
12   Letter from Engels to Marx, 3 August 1859; MECW 40:478.
13   MECW 16:470.
14   Letter from Engels to Marx, 10 August 1859; MECW 40:481.
15   Cf. Note 310, MEW 13:696.
16   Previously, Marx and Engels had numerous times upheld a historically influenced mater-
      ialism in contrast to Feuerbach's naturalist, but the phrase 'materialist conception of his-
      tory' seems to occur here for the first time; MECW 16:469.
17   Cf. above, p. 74.

The obvious basis for determining it was Marx's own foreword to *A Contribution to the Critique of Political Economy*, which had previously been reproduced in *Das Volk* and from which Engels also took a longer quote. With that quote, Engels drew attention to Marx's conceptual pair of the base and superstructure. What he said in his own words scarcely differs from what Marx himself could have said. Here as well, like an echo from *The German Ideology*, we hear the admonition that the materialist conception of history cannot be used like some 'phrases' that can be applied vertically to everything in history; moreover, the historical material is gone over thoroughly.[18]

The second part of the review tells us much more. It deals with Marx's method in relation to the Hegelian dialectic. Now, the point is that Marx did not go into more detail on these questions in the published instalment of *Critique*. There is thus nothing corresponding to what he said in the *Grundrisse*. As he himself noted, his foreword gave only a few 'brief remarks' as to how his political and economic studies had developed.[19] Hegel is mentioned only in passing. He said nothing overall about totalities, about the unequal relation between the moments of the totalities and about other such things that play a crucial role in the introduction. The question of method has been pushed into the background.

But Engels commented in that much more detail. Even here, perspectives and points of view that would become central to his later, more thorough studies in the same subjects but are largely absent in Marx are recognisable here. Engels set the question of the Marxian method into a perspective of the history of ideas and the sciences. On the one hand he distinguished the idealist and dialectical tradition from Hegel, and on the other the materialist but undialectical tradition represented by the eighteenth-century materialists and their followers in the nineteenth century (Engels mentioned Vogt, Büchner and Moleschott). Whereas Hegelianism had completely degenerated in the hands of people who had only assimilated the 'most simple devices' of Hegel's, the materialists had constructed their philosophy directly upon the positive natural sciences. In criticising the latter, Engels was already using the term 'metaphysics' in the special meaning he would later excel at. A metaphysical conception is, according to this usage, a conception in accordance with which all scientific concepts can and should be fixed in absolute relation with one another. Engels argued that such a conceptual apparatus cannot be used to describe or explain a process. Engels made use of Hegel's term here; Hegel in

---

18   MECW 16:470.
19   MECW 29:261.

fact spoke of 'metaphysics of the understanding' as one of several species of metaphysics,[20] while Engels spoke of 'metaphysics' pure and simple. It is not difficult to understand why the word turned up just now in Engels's vocabulary. A year before he wrote his review of Marx, he had revealed an interest in Hegel's *Philosophy of Nature*, and he had also borrowed a copy of the book in question from Marx.[21] Marx's and Engels's renewed interest in Hegel did not have the exact same orientation; this is already evident on the terminological plane.

In his review, Engels asserted that the materialist conception of history unified dialectics and materialism. He did not yet have – as we soon will see – any plans to join together all knowledge and all the sciences under the joint protection of the dialectic and materialism. But a fundamental idea in the later major enterprise had nonetheless been formed (or, rather, survived) from his and Marx's writings in the 1840s in which the ideas about a new type of materialism are found developed but without the concept of the dialectic playing any role in the context.[22] What Engels said here about a 'more materialist'[23] conception than the old mechanical materialism has a clear logical connection both with his and Marx's reckonings with Feuerbach in the 1840s and with his own later all-encompassing dialectic. Nonetheless, there is a substantial difference. What Engels devoted himself to in his review was primarily an explication of the method in Marx's work. His sense of uncertainty and unfamiliarity prevented him from coming forward with a claim to independence. He was thus not trying to draw conclusions beyond what Marx said in his book.

It is this cautiousness, however, that makes a real comparison with Marx easier. Engels said what he thought Marx also would have said.

According to Engels, what distinguishes Hegel is the endeavour to 'develop any branch of science in its specific inner coherence'.[24] The description differs in its wording from what Marx said in the *Grundrisse*, but the content would seem to be the same. It refers to Hegel's unwillingness to distinguish between the form and content of knowledge. It would thus be impossible to single out

---

20   See above all *System of Logic* II (Natural Philosophy), Hegel 9:255 et seqq.
21   Letter from Engels to Marx, 14 July 1858, MECW 40:326; and letter from Marx to Engels, 15 July 1858, MECW 40:331. Cf. below, p. 108.
22   In the *Economic and Philosophical Manuscripts*, for example, Feuerbach's ideas about a materialist science dominate Marx's thinking. '*Sense-perception* (see Feuerbach) must be the basis of all science'. MECW 3:303. In *The German Ideology*, where Feuerbach is accused of keeping history and materialism separate (MECW 5:41), the new materialism is presented as '*practical* materialist' or '*communist*'; ibid., p. 38.
23   MECW 16:473.
24   MECW 16:472.

a given scientific form – Newtonian mechanics, for example – as the only scientific one. Every scientific content, and thus every type of knowledge object, has a certain form – that is, a certain type of method, of theory, and so on.

But Hegel was an idealist, and his concept of the unity between thought and its object has idealism as its condition. Since Marx, in *Critique*, did not take up the question of method in a more general sense, he did not need to take a position on Hegel's philosophical points of departure. On the other hand, this was what he did in the *Grundrisse*, and it was what Engels was compelled to do in his review.

According to Hegel, the object of thought corresponds to thought itself (or logic, as he preferred to call it), which is why at heart, the object – indeed, all of reality – *is* thought. At heart, thought, logic, and the real are the same. Human history – the field that Marx and Engels were commenting on in the texts in question – is thus essentially a logical process in which the starting point, as in thought, is abstract and simple and development means that increasingly complex and concrete forms are established.

In the introduction to the *Grundrisse*, Marx agreed with Hegel that the basis for scientific representation is the abstraction, and that the path then runs toward the concrete. Engels thought about that himself when he said in his review that a critique of political economy could either be historical or logical. By historical, he meant here an approach starting from the swarm of events, from the diversity of accidental occurrences and disorderly courses of events. It is the same thing Marx meant by a theory in which the concrete (e.g. a population or a nation) in its raw diversity constitutes the basis for the representation. When Engels said that the logical representation was the preferable one, he thus said in principle the same thing Marx said when he asserted that one had to start from the abstract. It is only the terms that differ; they selected different words out of Hegel's extravagantly rich vocabulary.

So far, then, the agreement is total. The difference lies in the manner of avoiding Hegel's idealism and still asserting that real knowledge is attained by starting from what is in fact a construction in thought – that is, the abstract.

In his introduction, Marx unhesitatingly declared that 'the method of advancing from the abstract to the concrete is simply the way in which thinking assimilates the concrete … This is, however, by no means the process by which the concrete itself originates'.[25] It thus does not appear that – as Hegel assumed – the abstract relations also must chronologically be *earlier* than the concrete relations.

---

25   Marx 1953, p. 22.

We already know how exceedingly central this line of thought itself is in the introduction to the *Grundrisse*. It has to do with the entire polemic against the Hegelian identity concept; it contains the thesis on the unequal relation.

But Engels, just as clearly and unambiguously, expresses another opinion. What he calls the logical representation (i.e. the one starting from the abstract) 'is indeed nothing but the historical method, only stripped of the historical form and of interfering contingencies. The point where this history begins must also be the starting point of the train of thought, and its further progress will be simply the reflection, in abstract and theoretically consistent form, of the course of history ...'.[26]

Engels thus regarded thought and its object – logic and actual history – as essentially identical. He differed from Hegel in his view of what is reflected and what is the mirror. He differed from Marx, however, by generally assuming that a reflection, a correspondence, was concerned.

And that is an important difference!

In other respects, it is not easy to immediately compare Marx's text from 1857 and Engels's from 1859. There are scattered words and statements that could also indicate that Engels stood closer to Hegel than Marx did. Quite simply, Marx could take into account a totality with four different moments.[27] Engels, on the other hand, established a relation (*Verhältnis*) here in the strict Hegelian manner as a relation between 'two aspects'.[28] But it is impossible to determine if there is thus a real difference between Marx's and Engels's approaches.

---

26   MECW 16:475. Remarkably enough, the simple yet extraordinarily fundamental fact that Engels *at that time* was so unfamiliar with the main point in Marx's reckoning with Hegel in the *Grundrisse* seems not to have been noticed in the abundant literature. The traditions that look for an unfathomable gap between Marx and Engels have, like Bollnow and Habermas – to say nothing of Lichtheim! – sought to substantiate the differences through sweeping comparisons among writings from widely different periods in Marx's and Engels's development. Reichelt 1970, p. 133, touches on Engels's review but draws no conclusions from it. Other traditions that imagine an unbroken and harmonic collaboration between Marx and Engels are no more scrupulous in arranging comparisons. The greatest study of Engels's economic thinking, namely Russian economist Lev A. Leontyev's 500-plus-page work on Engels and Marxism's economic theory, belongs here. Engels's review from 1859 was treated in detail there without notice being taken of any difference between Marx's and Engels's positions; Leontyev 1970, p. 279 et seqq., in particular p. 282. Cf. also Zelený 1970, p. 57 et seq., and 1976, p. 43 et seq. In the major biographies of Engels, the silence is even more awkward; G. Mayer 1934, II, Gemkow et al. 1970, and Henderson 1976, II.

27   Above, p. 69 et seqq.

28   MECW 16:475.

But the obvious dissimilarity in the approaches to the relation between theory and its object raises a number of questions that belong to the field of historical contingency rather than to the field of logical development. It is not certain, but it is highly likely that Engels also sent the second part of his review – the one in question here – to Marx for approval.[29] Why did Marx not correct such approaches that obviously conflicted with what he himself laid out in a text, though unpublished, that nonetheless was his own thoroughgoing attempt at placing his own method in relation to Hegel's? Was Hegel's deviation from his own standpoint not that crucial to him? Or did he silently let Engels have his own opinion – in an article that all the same alleged to lay out Marx's, and only Marx's, method?

There is also another possibility, namely that Marx in fact no longer stood for the opinions he had expressed in the introduction. This appears extremely unlikely, however; the comments Marx devoted to his introduction in the preface to *Critique* indicate no such thing. Even more importantly, what Marx said even in his afterword to *Capital* about the relation between method of representation and method of research can be regarded as a brief expression of the same ideas he devoted a more thorough study to in the *Grundrisse*.

The only explanation that seems at all reasonable is that despite everything, Marx regarded the study of his method as an unimportant matter in comparison to the development of his economic theories. The work on the latter also continually came before the elaboration of the long-planned presentation of the rational kernel in the dialectic. This explanation, however, does not seem really plausible. When Marx requested his review from Engels, he emphasised that it was precisely the method that attention should be drawn to!

The coincidences seem to remain coincidences in this question. If we do not wish to go into risky psychological interpretations, we will have to be satisfied with stating that it is peculiar that Marx had no objections to Engels's manner of identifying 'logic' with 'history'.

The obvious discrepancy between Marx and Engels in the writings in question cannot simply lead to the conclusion that their understanding of the fundamental questions of theory are notoriously incompatible. Engels's review was not a natural stage in his own theoretical development: his study of the Marxian method was at Marx's request and not spontaneous. Quite simply, Engels felt unprepared to author such a demanding summary.

---

29   In the letter of 13 August 1859, Marx wrote that he wanted Engels's second article 'by Wednesday' – this obviously assumes that he would read through it before it was sent on to *Das Volk*. MECW 40:482.

Still, this is an issue of an important document. It gives a hint – indeed, for now just a hint – of Engels's relation to Hegel and to Marx. It also shows that, faced with the more limited issues of method, he – like Marx – was forced out into large, comprehensive problems of the kind that would fully capture his attention fifteen years later. It bears witness to the fact that here, he had already regarded the question of the relation between materialism and the dialectic as the major, crucial one as regards establishing the characteristics of Marxist theory.

CHAPTER 4

The Encounter with the Natural Sciences

1   Theoretical and Ideological Determination

When Marx designed and characterised his theory of the base, or material production, he was compelled to take a position on a range of issues having to do with knowledge or science in general. This is no arbitrary manner of playing philosopher. It has to do with the very nerves of his theoretical work.

When Engels reluctantly took up the task of describing Marx's theory, he faced the same problem. He was still a long way away from his ambitions of creating a general dialectic.

In other words, this meant that the expansive questions that both he and Marx took up in the late 1850s were *theoretically determined*. They sprang from the very theoretical work Marx was occupied with. Marx designed a scientific theory that was not only new, but also of a new type for its field. It is a well-known phenomenon of the history of science that such work raises questions that are of a general knowledge and scientific theoretical nature.[1]

But it is not equally obvious – or not equally unequivocally determined by the very theory Marx was developing – that it was precisely Hegel's philosophy that would constitute the point of comparison for him and for Engels. It is not enough to point out here that the well-known circumstance that they both were brought up in the Hegelian manner of thinking. That is not reason enough for Hegel to again become of topical interest to them. On the other hand, the circumstance that the general conception of history – historical materialism, into which the theory of material production was integrated – was designed from the beginning in opposition to Hegel, Young Hegelianism and Feuerbach is a crucial one. Either historical materialism as it was formulated in *The German Ideology* was shaped and delimited in relation to conceptions other than the Hegelian, or the theory of material production must also be placed in relation to Hegel.

Hegel thus becomes a problem to work on, as long as historical materialism is materialist in opposition primarily to Hegelian idealism. But for now, the perspective will be rather narrow. Hegel's philosophy is all-encompassing. Marx vacillated between talking about the method of political economy and all sci-

---

1   Cf. for example Kuhn 1970, p. 111 et seqq.

entific methods. Engels brought the materialism that proceeds from the natural sciences into view. But he also demarcated it from application of the Marxian method, which in light of his later statements may seem surprising. In his review of Marx's *Critique* he declared, namely, that Marx's materialistic view is not only of importance for political economy but also for all historical sciences. In a parenthesis he added: '*und alle Wissenschaften sind historisch, welche nicht Naturwissenschaften sind*'[2] (and all branches of science which are not natural sciences are historical). A few months later – on his first encounter with Darwin's *On the Origin of Species* – he would change his opinion. But he still left the natural sciences out of the equation with a hasty gesture, a parenthesis.

In the end, however, neither he nor Marx would be satisfied with this reticence when facing other scientific fields. Hegel's philosophy had already tempted them with diversions into the natural sciences. And more importantly: at that time, in the mid-1800s, a tremendous increase in interest was being witnessed in how various scientific theories related to each other and in how they could be put together into entities or systems. The question of the day became the extent to which one theory could find support or guidance in another. Darwinism, for example, which had come into the limelight at that time (1859) claimed to deal with all species – but what was its significance for the disciplines that dealt with humanity, its societies, its history? There was thus, even in this search for the relations between different areas of knowledge, a theoretical determination internal to science. The ideological, however, was no less important! The natural sciences were dragged into the ideological battle: liberals sought support in it, various socialists modelled their views of society on it. The battle for ideological support from all sciences, especially the natural sciences, had long been in full swing when Engels gradually entered into it.

We will study this course of events in detail later.

Marx and Engels, however, were not blank pages when they got involved in this overheated ideological and theoretical atmosphere. They were already in their forties. They had lives full of changes as revolutionaries, as journalists and as authors of scientific texts behind them. They both had a thorough philosophical schooling in the wake of the Hegelian Spirit. They both (not just Marx) were extraordinarily at home in economic theory. Marx in particular had a solid humanistic education.

They must have come into contact with the natural sciences as well before 1859, and their idea of them must have been marked by all their other insights and activities.

---

2   MECW 16:469.

Nonetheless, the history of the natural sciences in Marx's and Engels's lives before 1859 may seem peculiarly short and incomplete. Therein may lie one reason that they first hesitated and then sought to set their own research in relation to what was current in the natural scientific disciplines.

2 Previous Contact with Natural Philosophy and the Natural Sciences

We have seen how, in the *Grundrisse*, Marx gave an example of how comparative anatomists work that unmistakably belongs in the world of ideas of Romantic natural philosophy.[3] There is nothing surprising in this. The contacts he had in previous years concerned natural philosophy rather than the empirical natural sciences. He had given up all idea of his plans to study physics and chemistry in Bonn.[4] In Berlin during the winter term of 1836–37, he had followed the lectures of the Romantic Steffens in anthropology – 'assiduously',[5] according to the transcript. In a long, much-discussed letter he wrote to his father in 1837, he stated that, in order to arrive at philosophical clarity, he had studied 'natural science, Schelling, and history' – we do not know which natural science it was.[6] When he was writing his doctoral thesis on the relation between the natural philosophies of Democritus and Epicurus, he also studied Hegel's natural philosophy as a preparatory measure.[7]

These details do not say much in and of themselves, but if we turn to his early writings it becomes immediately more than obvious that natural scientific issues in a literal sense occupied his attention to a rather small extent. This is not surprising. Natural philosophy played a relatively large role in Hegel's

---

3 Cf. above, p. 62.

4 Cf. Cornu 1955–70, I, p. 68.

5 For Steffens at the time, anthropology – by which he meant the science of humanity in all its aspects – was the basis of all science. Its foundation was the Romantic natural philosophical doctrine about the unity of spirit and nature. Even the emotion of religious faith would guide the good anthropologist. See Steffens 1822, p. 8 and p. 14 et seqq. On Marx at Steffens's lectures, see Cornu 1955–70, I, pp. 81 *n* and 89 et seq. As Cornu points out, Marx could not possibly have been influenced by Steffens. Another Romantic scientist whom Marx listened to was geographer Carl Ritter, who according to Cornu was a Schellingian and was not without significance for Marx's development in a materialist direction; Cornu 1955–70, I, p. 131. Both statements are dubious with regard to what Ritter actually wrote. Ritter did not accept the Schellingian theory of a unity of nature and spirit (Ritter 1852, p. 23 et seqq., p. 41, p. 183), and his position can in no respect be described as materialistic (ibid., p. 12, p. 103 et seq. and others).

6 MECW 1:18.

7 MECW 1:439, 491 *n* and others.

system – though not comparable to the role it played for Schelling and the other Romantics – whereas the later Hegelians devoted themselves nearly exclusively to 'spiritual philosophy' and then, primarily, to the philosophy of religion and of right.[8] Even Feuerbach, who regarded nature as primary, had a highly negligible interest in that same nature as an object of natural philosophy or the natural sciences. It is possible to read the whole of his main work, *The Essence of Christianity*, without encountering any statements at all that immediately concern the sphere of problems in the natural sciences.[9] It was actually the sober-mindedness and empiricism of the natural *scientists* that interested him.

By and large, the same applies to the young Marx. We can choose an example from the *Economic and Philosophical Manuscripts*. One important statement there is that human history is a part of natural history.[10] The glimmer of descendance theory can be imagined here; it can be seen in light of Marx's initial judgement of *Origin* that 'on the basis of natural history, [it] provides the basis for our views'.[11] When Marx asked himself the question, however, of whether humans nonetheless had not been created, he argued in a manner that shows he was quite far from even pre-Darwinist ideas. He took up a few objections against the belief in creation that at the time in question were being championed by natural philosophers but more rarely by empirically-minded scientists. Among other things, he said that the theory of spontaneous generation was the only practical refutation of the belief in creation. This statement, which returns in *The German Ideology*,[12] throws a certain light over Marx's (and through *The German Ideology*, Engels's as well) relation to the natural sciences and natural philosophy of his time. The theory of spontaneous generation (*generatio aequivoca*) meant that organic bodies could arise directly from decomposing organic material, or even from inorganic material. The theory was fostered by the Romantic natural philosophers as well as by other researchers who cannot be considered as belonging to Romantic natural philosophy

---

8   The absence of natural philosophy in the modern monograph by Brazill (1970) is striking.

9   'Nature' occurs, in addition to the phrase 'humanity's (unchanging) nature', above all in the meaning 'non-human reality with which humanity must be in close contact and cannot liberate itself from' (food, drink and other necessities of life that religion seeks to depreciate). Cf. Feuerbach VI: 222, 225, 333 et seqq. Feuerbach spoke about the scientific method above all in *Vorläufige Thesen zur Reform der Philosophie* and in the previously cited *Grundsätze der Philosophie*, Feuerbach II:244, 258 et seqq. and others. On this, cf. Schmidt 1973, p. 131 et seqq. Schmidt argues – rightly, of course – that Feuerbach here overestimates 'the specific scientific basis of his philosophy'.

10   MECW 3:305.

11   MECW 41:232.

12   MECW 5:40.

(e.g. G.R. Treviranus and Friedrich Tiedemann).[13] The interesting thing about the latter two is that they also assumed an actual development of species long before Darwin, and unlike the Romantics – and Hegel – did not regard the relation among various species as simply 'ideal' (i.e. differentiated among more or less developed species without assuming that they had developed over time).[14]

But the ideas around spontaneous generation met with strong criticism in the 1830s and 1840s from successful empirical research. Marx was clearly unaffected by such criticism, which was particularly keen in Berlin during his years there. The foremost advocates of this criticism were the well-known physiologist and anatomist Johannes Müller and his pupil at the time, Theodor Schwann – one of the authors of cell theory.[15]

But Marx put forward the argument on spontaneous generation more in passing. Whether he also assumed with this argument that a development of the entire diversity of species took place after an initial spontaneous generation is impossible to determine. With his continued reasoning, he threw the whole problem over. He employed a fictitious argument between a believer in divine creation at the dawn of time and someone who wanted to regard humanity itself as the only creator. The former claimed that following the succession of generations upward would gradually come to a point where divine creation must have occurred.

But his opponent objected that humans had always created (i.e. bred) humans. Marx's formulation ran as follows: the fact of the matter is that 'der Mensch in der Zeugung sich selbst wiederholt, also der *Mensch* immer Subjekt bleibt' (humanity repeats itself in procreation, *humanity* thus always remaining the subject). The argument is interesting because it in fact contains one of the three characteristics of the organism that were regarded as self-evident in all biological discussions in the early nineteenth century until Schwann laid out the thesis that all living beings were made up of cells.[16] The argument was usually formulated as 'species create themselves'; with Marx it was not a question of any species at all, but of humanity.

This argument, however, played a subordinate role for Marx. In conclusion, he argued that the question of an original creation was distorted and incorrectly posed. In asking how humans once arose, humans must first be imagined as not existing; for some reason, that was impossible. Marx reinforced this somewhat sophistic argument with the assurance that for socialism, the history

---

13   Liedman 1966, p. 183 et seqq.
14   Tiedemann 1830, p. 95 et seqq.; Treviranus 1831, p. 45 et seqq.
15   Cf. J. Müller 1838, p. 10 et seqq. and the research reported there.
16   Section *'Theorie der Zellen'* in Schwann. Cf. below, p. 162 et seq.

of the world was thoroughly a product of human labour and thus that further explanation was unnecessary. Humanity's own history is the irrefutable proof that everything came into being and was developed through humanity.[17]

The argument in the *Manuscripts* is interesting because it shows that Marx was pushing aside the exact questions that would be of central significance for him after his encounter with Darwinism. The main reason for this cannot be sought either in the insufficient general interest in issues of natural science among young philosophers in the more or less Hegelian tradition, or in Marx's own obviously rather sporadic orientation on the contemporary natural sciences. First and foremost, there was still no scientifically sanctioned theory of the development of species, nor would there be until Darwin's breakthrough. The question of creation and of biological evolution, for the time being, was a rather awkward subject for a non-biologist with materialist inclinations.

Engels's earlier contacts with the natural sciences appear to be of the same kind as Marx's. He was not uninterested, of course; he acquired a great deal of general knowledge.[18] But it did not become the main question. There were matters he quickly informed himself about, such as Justus von Liebig's ideas on the uses of chemistry in agriculture.[19] No attempts at the later assiduous interest in the general questions of the natural sciences can be seen. For him, as for Marx, the natural philosophers including Hegel have no attraction of the kind that would incline someone to deeper study and further development. When, in some of his early works, he defended Hegel against Schelling during the charged times when Schelling was holding lectures in Berlin, he passed in silence by the natural philosophy that was quite important in the context.[20]

From the perspective of the fully developed materialist conception of history, research into nature would also come into a new light for Marx and Engels. This manifests itself with all desirable clarity in *The German Ideology*. The world view aspects fade entirely into the background; the connection of the nat-

---

17   MECW 3:305.
18   It stopped at the mere mention of names and general theories. Reiprich (1969, p. 18) attached great importance to Engels, in *Schelling and Revelation* (MECW 2:222), citing a statement by Cuvier aimed at Schelling's natural philosophy. For Reiprich, this became a sign of Engels's early orientation in science. The mere mention by Engels of names such as Newton, Black and Lavoisier in *The Condition of England* (MECW 3:470) for Reiprich became further testimony of his insights!
19   In *Outlines of a Critique of Political Economy* (MECW 3:440). Engels wrote this in 1844; the first edition of Liebig's epoch-making work on the subject, *Organic Chemistry in its Application to Agriculture and Physiology*, was published in 1840.
20   The only exception is the quote from Cuvier (note 18 above), but it played no role whatsoever in his general criticism of Schelling.

ural sciences to industry and trade absorb all interest. Marx and Engels accuse Feuerbach of seeing nature as unchanging – an eternal object to the sensuous way of thinking. The nature that humanity comes in contact with, Marx and Engels claimed, is just as changeable as humanity itself; it is continually transformed through its own activities. Nature in Manchester now consisted only of factories and machines, while previously it was strewn with spinning wheels and looms. In the Roman *campagna*, only pastures and tree stumps can be seen where there once were vineyards and rich men's villas. Feuerbach spoke of the world that was revealed to the eye of the natural scientist. But, Marx and Engels asked, what would the natural sciences be without industry? Even the 'pure' natural sciences (the quotation marks are their own) obtain their materials and their purpose through practical human activity.[21]

It is obvious that these statements contain several different points of view on nature and the natural sciences that are not inevitably bound up together. The nature being spoken about is very much a sensuous, empirical nature, a chaos of changes and accidental occurrences that are due to the ravages of humanity. It is a nature that in no way eliminates the nature of the natural sciences with its invariances and constancies. The changes to a landscape have nothing to do with the law of gravity. If we are to interpret Marx's and Engels's statements rationally, it must mean that the knowledge of nature that the natural sciences provide us do not – as Feuerbach believed – immediately teach us anything about human societies and history; the nature that humanity had to and has to grapple with has changed with them.

But the text also contains another point of view having to do with the historical development of the natural sciences. It involves the development of the natural sciences continuously being tied to the development of the base, that its advances follow advances in trade and industry, and that trade and industry provide scientists with instruments and objects of research. Quite simply, we are dealing with a special application of the historical materialist thesis of the supremacy of the base – here, as so often elsewhere in Marx and Engels, only hinted at in a few short sentences.

It would be very unfortunate if it were to be assumed that these statements contained everything there is to say from a historical materialist point of view about nature and the natural sciences. The theories of the natural sciences would thereby be reduced to history and historical circumstances, and their claim to contain truths about nature would openly be left aside. Nonetheless, it became the ultimate consequence of interpretations, for example, such

21   MECW 5:40.

as Alfred Schmidt's in *The Concept of Nature in Marx*. According to Marx, he [Schmidt] says, nature can never be separated from the forms of humanity's 'social labour'.[22] Nature cannot be determined 'speculatively or physically' but only 'economically and materially'.[23]

However, this manner of presenting the historical materialist position as the only true, absolute theory – or at least the knowledge that contains all other knowledge in itself – has no support in *The German Ideology* or other similar texts. What Marx and Engels objected to is not the claim to truth in any natural science but the view of society and history in Feuerbach as it was expressed in the latter's statements about nature, in particular human nature. They took no position on what the natural scientists perchance had to say about reality (i.e. about that part of reality the natural scientists have as their object of study).

3   The Natural Sciences and Historical Materialism

When Marx and Engels were formulating their historical materialism, it also involved limiting the field for their studies. The wide-embracing philosophical categories that previously played so great a role, particularly in Marx's earlier works – the essence or nature of humanity, alienation and so on – lost their far-reaching philosophical content and would signify limited historical and societal relations.[24] Historical materialism therefore resulted in a *specialisation* in Marx's and Engels's development: they were of course still commenting on an extraordinarily comprehensive field, but nonetheless one that was more limited than previously.

---

22   'In Marx, nature only appears through the forms of social labour'. Schmidt 1971a, p. 58.

23   Ibid., p. 61.

24   Both humanity's 'essence' and its 'estrangement' (*Entfremdung, Entäusserung*) from this essence play a prominent role in the *Economic and Philosophical Manuscripts of 1844*. MECW 3:229 et seqq. In the sixth thesis on Feuerbach, the entire idea of a human essence is dissolved: 'Feuerbach resolves the essence of religion into the essence of man. But the essence of man is no abstraction inherent in each single individual. In its reality it is the ensemble of social relations'. MECW 3:4. The earlier concept of estrangement (regarding humanity's estrangement from its essence) must thus also change. In *The German Ideology* the word itself is mentioned only once, with an ironic reservation: 'This "estrangement" (to use a term which will be comprehensible to the philosophers) ...' MECW 5:48. Later, when in the *Grundrisse* the words 'estrangement' and 'alienation' cross Marx's lips the connection with the old ideas of essence (humanity's *fixed* essence) has completely disappeared, and it becomes a question of the definite circumstances that apply to humanity's roles in material production. See for example Marx 1953, p. 715 et seqq.

Marx's work on a developed theory of the base in the 1850s can be regarded as a further step in this process of specialisation. He did not occupy himself with society and history across the field but only with what, according to his materialist view, was the fundamental creator of context in societies: the base.

The natural sciences are of interest from such a perspective primarily in immediate relation to the development of the base: it is their practical, technological use that comes into view. In the 1850s, Marx studied a number of works dealing with the application of the natural sciences. He read and copied excerpts from Justus von Liebig's *Organic Chemistry in its Application to Agriculture and Physiology*[25] and a long range of writings on the history of the technology and its discoverers.[26]

What Marx said about the natural sciences in the *Grundrisse* deals throughout with their connection to the development of the base – and in particular of the capitalist base. It was therefore not the theoretical assertions about reality that interested him in this context. He expressed a number of historical statements about the development of the sciences and of the technology. Wage labour, he claimed, is a condition for the usefulness of science in material production.[27] On the other hand, it is the use of science that constitutes one of the crucial differences between manufacture and modern large industry. The division of labour prevails in manufacture, he claimed, whereas industry is marked by the combination of many similar tasks and through science.[28] In manufacture, each worker is skilled within an extremely limited trade; with the development of more complicated machinery, however, these specialised tasks were abolished one after another. The worker became a steward of the machinery instead. But the development of the machinery presupposed the development of science at the same time as it was one side of capitalism's necessary development from a lesser to a greater share of fixed capital (the machine represents precisely such capital). The development of capitalism is

---

25   *IISG Marx-Engels Nachlass*, B 49 (Heft XLIVm 1851), p. 34 et seqq., B 59 (Heft LIII, p. 1 et seqq.), and B 106 (Vol. XCVIII). The latter was written as late as 1865–66, that is, in the final push for the first volume of *Capital*. Marx also excerpted other writings of Liebig there.

26   Ibid., B 51 (Heft LXI, prob. Oct 1851): excerpts from J.H.M. Poppe's *Lehrbuch der allgemeinen Technologie* (1809), *Die Physik vorzüglich in Anwendung auf Künste* (1830), *Geschichte der Mathematik* (1828), and *Geschichte der Technologie* (I–II, 1807–11); A. Ure's *Technisches Wörterbuch* (I–III, 1843–44); and J. Beckmann's *Beiträge zur Geschichte der Erfindungen* (I–V, 1780–1805). In B 59 (Heft LIII, 1851) there are also excerpts from J.F.W. Johnston, *Lectures on Agricultural Chemistry and Geology* (1847).

27   Marx 1953, p. 188.

28   Ibid., p. 479 et seq.

thus not possible without the development of science, which is why capitalism must engage science. Discovery becomes a business, Marx said. But he warned against the idea that the discoveries constituted a driving force in the development of capitalism. Instead, the condition is the division of labour, which entailed breaking down labour into ever smaller, ever more mechanical components that could then be transferred to the machines.[29] The development of the material process of labour is thus primary, the development of knowledge secondary.

Here, Marx in fact conducts a kind of model argument for his entire materialist conception of history. The path from the strict division of labour in manufacture to the standardised labour around 'the great machinery' is a coherent development, and to the development of technology appears accidental. If the development of production and technology is regarded as a totality, the former constitutes the dominant, or all-embracing, moment. There is interplay between the moments, however: the development of science is not only marked by, but also in turn leaves its mark on the development of production.[30]

Similar lines of thought reappear in *Capital*. Among the circumstances that determine the productive power of labour, Marx also mentioned 'the state of science, and the degree of its practical application'.[31] One of the most comprehensive chapters in the first volume of *Capital*, Chapter Fifteen, concerns 'Machinery and Modern Industry'.[32] We can recognise lines of thought from the *Grundrisse* there, though the statements about the development of science are not as prominent[33] and the detailed documentation of the character of modern industry, on the other hand, much more detailed.

The natural sciences thus stand out in two closely related ways in Marx's developed theory of capitalism. On the one hand, it concerns their technical use in production. On the other, it concerns their modern historical development in general, which is regarded as crucially determined precisely by their practical application.

In the *Grundrisse*, however, a perspective on the natural sciences from within science is entirely absent. In other words, there is no comparison whatsoever between the natural scientific and the social scientific methods and theory.

---

29   Ibid., p. 591 et seq.
30   Ibid., p. 592.
31   MECW 35:50.
32   Ibid., pp. 374–508.
33   See primarily ibid., p. 389 et seqq.

4   Engels, Darwin and Grove

Characteristically enough, it was Darwin's *Origin of Species* that roused Marx's interest in a natural scientific theory – not for the sake of its practical application but for its theoretical implications.

Engels came into contact with Darwin's book even earlier, and its significance for him would be no less. He had, however, already revealed an interest in the new natural sciences before this. It occurred above all in a letter from 1858[34] in which he told Marx that he was pursuing studies in physiology that he intended to combine with comparative anatomy.[35] What he was reading is impossible to establish. He explained that immense progress had taken place in the natural sciences over the preceding thirty years of which '[o]ne has no idea, by the way'.[36] This anonymous 'one' could hardly be just Engels (before he began his physiological studies) but most assuredly alluded to most generally educated people who were not scientists. Engels had been gripped by a suspicion that what was happening in the natural sciences was of great significance for people's ideas and way of thinking, but that it had not yet reached anyone other than specialists. This very idea about the partially hidden significance of the natural sciences would henceforth inspire him and give his studies a touch of restless curiosity and impatience.

In the letter, he also hastened to establish what was determining the advances in physiology. First, he mentioned the developments in organic chemistry, and second the use of the microscope. The microscope, he said, had only been properly used over the preceding twenty years, and it had paved the way for results that were even more important for physiology than those that organic chemistry had made possible. Here, he cited the 'discovery of the cell', made by Schleiden for plants and by Schwann for animals. He dated the discovery to 'about 1836' and this insignificant misdating[37] shows, if nothing else, that he wrote the letter with no physiology textbooks within reach.

He had not only found matters of interest in physiology, however, but in physics as well. Here, he spoke about 'the correlation of forces in physics, or the law whereby mechanical motion, i.e. mechanical force ... is ... converted

---

34   Cf. above, p. 91.

35   'I am presently doing a little physiology which I shall combine with comparative anatomy'. Letter from Engels to Marx, 14 July 1858, MECW 40:326.

36   'One has no idea, by the way ...' Ibid.

37   M.J. Schleiden published his 'Beiträge zur Phytogenesis' in *Müllers Archiv* 1838; Schleiden announced his findings that same year and summarised them later in *Mikroskopische Untersuchungen* (1839).

into heat, heat into light, light into chemical affinity' and so on. It was thus what was still being called the law of indestructability of force, which later was called the law of conservation of energy,[38] that had become of interest to Engels. He had learned that an Englishman, whose name he had forgotten, had 'now' shown that the transition from one type of force to another could be determined purely quantitatively. The person he was thinking of was James Joule, residing in Salford only a few kilometres from Manchester, where Engels was staying, and if the word 'now' was intended to signify a recent occurrence, it was poorly chosen: the work Engels was alluding to was sixteen years old at the time.

We can with a great deal of certainty say that the work from which Engels obtained his information about physics – whether he read it or only had it presented to him – was William Robert Grove's *On the Correlation of Physical Forces*. The way he stated the content of this new theory – indeed, the designation 'correlation of forces' – was extraordinarily closely bound up with Grove's manner of expression and world of ideas. We will see that Grove's work was also crucially significant for Engels later and that it would initiate Marx into the mysteries of the new physics.

On the other hand, it is rather futile to look for the external circumstances that roused Engels's interest in such material as physiology and physics, which until then had been quite distant to him. There were numerous paths along which the impulses could have reached him: newspapers and periodicals, books, friends and acquaintances. Samuel Moore and Carl Schorlemmer, the two 'authorities'[39] who would later enrich his interests in the natural sciences in different ways, had not yet turned up in his circle of acquaintances.

It is obvious, however, that Engels's interest had an accent all its own. From the very beginning, he set the new natural sciences in connection with Hegel's natural philosophy. The purpose of his letter was to ask to borrow Marx's copy of *Philosophy of Nature*. He explained that there were 'highly speculative things' in modern physiology and that he was curious whether 'the old man' had said anything about it. He was already attempting to translate these new modes of thought into Hegel's language. The cell is Hegel's 'being in itself' that then developed in accordance with the Hegelian pattern into its idea, which is the complete organism. The theory in physics of how forces transition into one another is striking *material* evidence of Hegel's thesis that the reflex categories dissolve into one another. In every field, the same structure can be recog-

---

38   Cf. below, p. 145 et seqq.
39   Cf. above, p. 13.

nised – what Hegel said about the relation between quality and quantity is being confirmed everywhere. For the time being, Engels did not speak – in an un-Hegelian manner – about the *law* of quantity and quality, but the later quite dominant idea about the structural similarity between different objects of knowledge and fields of knowledge was already to hand.[40]

It was an extraordinarily essential circumstance that Engels, in his studies in the new natural sciences, was guided by the question of how they related to Hegel's philosophy. The usual, and mostly horribly maltreated, problem of the differences between Marx's and Engels's views of the dialectic and the natural sciences is only manageable when starting from their respective ways of approaching the natural sciences. When Marx – a few years later than Engels – was also captured by the interest in the theoretical results of research into nature (and not only for its technical applications), the important problem for him became how these results related to historical materialism and his own theory of capital. Not so for Engels! It is obvious that this kind of question occupied him, especially when he came into contact with Darwin, but it still remained of secondary importance. In general, he did not take it up in earnest until – with the greatest distaste – tackled his polemical pamphlet against Dühring in 1876, which dealt entirely with refuting the latter's attack on Marx's theory in *Capital*. Nevertheless, in 1873, when he sketched out his plans for a dialectic of nature, he did not even hint at the connecting link with the specific Marxist theory of society and history.[41]

We already know that the methodological and theoretical problems that Marx faced when he attempted to elaborate his scientific conception should fully logically and consistently lead to comparisons with the theories and methodology of other scientists – especially the natural scientists. For now, however, Marx did not employ these comparisons. What inspired Engels at roughly the same time when he tackled the natural sciences were very general questions dealing with the natural sciences in their entirety, the philosophy of nature in its entirety, and finally Hegelian philosophy from A to Z. For the time being, Engels was thus not prepared to rush in where Marx feared to tread. His efforts were in no way, or at the least only highly indirectly, determined by Marxist theory. Nor (and this is an equally important circumstance) were they ideologically determined – that is, they were not motivated by a desire or a need to sketch out a consistent socialist world view.

Engels's review of Marx's *Critique*, which we have already gone through thoroughly, also shows that he had not yet engaged his newly gained insights into

---

40   MECW 40:326 et seqq.

41   Cf. above, p. 16.

the natural sciences for Marxian theory. Instead, he swept the natural sciences aside as un-historical sciences.[42]

5   The Reaction to Darwin

Marx was not yet prepared for any reactions to Engels's thoughts on Hegel and the new theories, in his response to Engels's initial letter on the subject, he only said that he would send what Engels had requested (Hegel's *Philosophy of Nature*), but dwelt in greater detail on his own permanent economic crisis.[43] After that, there was silence about the natural sciences in their correspondence until December 1859. Engels then announced, almost in passing, that he was reading Darwin, which he found to be 'absolutely splendid'. Then, with a steady hand, he brings up two crucial aspects of *Origin of Species*. On the one hand, Darwin had put an end to teleology with his book, which until that point had not received a deathblow. Engels was thus breathing a sigh of relief. Like Marx, he had been compelled until then to avoid the awkward issue of the development of species, quite simply because there was no convincing theory of it. On the other hand, Darwin had made the greatest attempt to date to demonstrate historical development in nature. We know how crucial these words were for Engels. Only a few months earlier he had declared that the natural sciences were not historical sciences. Darwin had bridged the gap between the sciences of humanity and the sciences of nature for him. Through Darwin, he took the first step toward the idea that would later become absolutely central for him, namely, that all sciences are historical.[44]

Italian philosopher Valentino Gerratana thus got it completely wrong in believing that for Engels, Darwin's book only confirmed the ideas about the history of nature that he had already been harbouring earlier.[45] The interest in the natural sciences that Engels had revealed up to that point did not concern any historical aspects in them at all.

As far as we can follow it, Engels's interest had been completely dominated by Hegel's philosophy of nature. The conclusions he immediately drew from Darwin's book would crucially change his relations with Hegelian philosophy. However correct it may be to describe Hegel as the philosopher of development before all others, but one of his main ideas was that it was only humanity

---

42   Cf. above, p. 98.
43   Letter from Marx to Engels, 15 July 1858, MECW 40:328 et seqq.
44   Letter from Engels to Marx, 11 or 12 December 1859, MECW 40:551 et seqq.
45   Gerratana 1973, p. 62.

that developed over time, and thus developed historically.[46] Engels was speaking completely in the spirit of Hegel when he excluded the natural sciences from the historical sphere. With Darwin, he went over and above Hegel: there was a history before humanity. The circle of problems had expanded, no longer encompassing only the formation of concepts in the natural sciences but also the development of natural phenomena over time. The road between the natural sciences and historical materialism lay open, even if it would still be some time before Engels would walk it.

In his letter, he made another observation that would recur in both his and Marx's statements on Darwin. He said that the 'crude English method' had to be put up with into the bargain.[47] When, a year later, Marx first commented on *Origin of Species*, he said that the book was in the 'crude English fashion',[48] an assessment he would later repeat.[49] It is possible that both Marx and Engels were referring in general with their simplified assessment to Darwin's cautious empiricism, which compelled him to hesitation or silence in the face of a number of substantial problems. Unfortunately, they drew no parallels with the 'English' method they knew best: classical economics. But both reacted all the more vehemently to Darwin's way of using Malthus's theories of overpopulation; it is possible that here was where the 'crudeness' and 'clumsiness', in their opinion, was expressed. In that case, in their criticism of the Darwinian method they were touching on something that was extremely important to them both – so important that we will return to it in a later, more systematic context, namely, the question of the relation between theories of society and biological theories.

Nonetheless, both Marx and Engels received Darwin's book with a sense of relief and satisfaction.[50] But that relief and satisfaction, at least to begin with, did not have quite the same basis. For Engels, Darwin filled a gap in the world-

---

46   Hegel summarises his conception with the words: *'Nur in den Veränderungen, die auf de geistigen Boden vorgehen, kommt Neues hervor'*; only here is there a *'Prinzip der Entwicklung'* (principle of development). Hegel 11:89 et seqq. (Philosophy of history).

47   'One does, of course, have to put up with the crude English method'. Letter from Engels to Marx, 11 or 12 December 1858, MECW 40:551.

48   Letter from Marx to Engels, 19 December 1860, MECW 41:232.

49   Letter from Marx to Ferdinand Lassalle, 16 January 1861, MECW 41:247.

50   A number of special studies have been written on the relation between Marx, Engels, and Darwin; see e.g. Lucas, Colp, Heyer and the aforementioned Gerratana (note 45). They are distinguished by insufficient knowledge either of Marxism, or of Darwinism, or of both. The curious idea that Engels was some kind of vulgar Darwinist is a shared feature. It even appears with full force in Lichtheim 1961, p. 234. In that connection, the starting point is usually Engels's words from Marx's funeral, in which Marx and Darwin are compared

view he was busy developing. For Marx, the descendance theory meant first and foremost that the materialist conception of history had gained a foundation in biology to rest upon. To Engels, he wrote that *Origin of Species* contained 'in the field of natural history, the basis for our views';[51] to Ferdinand Lassalle he wrote that 'it suits my purpose in that it provides a basis in natural science for the historical class struggle'.[52]

Marx's interest in Darwin was, at least at that point in time, more specific and more mundane. At the same time, however, he ran a greater risk of assessing Darwin and the entire Darwinian complex of problems completely from the outside: descendance theory only had its value in relation to his theory of history. On at least one occasion he was also prepared to discard Darwin for another descendance theory that immediately seemed to constitute a better 'foundation' for his own field. In 1866, he informed Engels that he had read French biologist Pierre Trémaux's *Origine et transformation de l'homme et des autres êtres* and declared that this work entailed a significant advance in comparison with Darwin. Trémaux claimed that it is not selection that determines the different species and variations but the external environment, the 'soil formations'. Trémaux's chief interest was explaining the differences between the races in this way; the different races were formed by different geographical conditions.[53] Marx noted with some satisfaction – which, considering his own theory, may seem surprising – that Trémaux could use his scheme of interpretation in a more full and varied manner in historical and political conditions than Darwin could. Trémaux had found, for example, 'a basis in nature' for nationality.[54] With that, however, biology would also penetrate into the field of the social sciences and severely restrict the field for Marx's and Engels's theory of class struggle.

---

    on the issue of scientific pre-eminence (MECW 24:463). The comparison between Darwin's 'law[s] of development' of the species and Marx's 'law[s] of development' for capitalism is roughly as prominent in Marx's *Capital* as it is in Engels's writings and statements.

51   Letter from Marx to Engels, 19 December 1860, MECW 41:232.

52   Letter from Marx to Ferdinand Lassalle, 16 January 1861, MECW 41:247.

53   Pierre Trémaux arrived at his results during various anthropological field studies in Sudan and elsewhere; his primary interest was the origins of the human race, and not of species. His *Origine et transformation* is also built on extremely limited biological material. The discussion of the theories of earlier evolutionary biologists, including Darwin's, is threadbare (see e.g. Trémaux 1865, pp. 13, 129, 160 et seqq.). With great pride, he declares that he has laid down a 'great natural law': 'the law of the coincidence of soil and types' (p. 11). The law is formulated in the following, not particularly clear manner: 'The perfection of beings is or becomes proportional to the degree of elaboration of the soil on which they live' (p. 17).

54   Letter from Marx to Engels, 7 August 1866, MECW 42:305.

Marx's enthusiasm was not to Engels's taste. They both usually agreed on most things, but they had very different perceptions of Trémaux. Engels declared that Trémaux could not be taken seriously for the very reason that he lacked insight into geology and did not have the least idea about criticism of sources.[55] Marx responded, evidently hurt but still obviously subdued in his enthusiasm, that whatever errors Trémaux may have committed, his fundamental idea about the influence of the soil was worth taking seriously.[56] Engels replied frankly that the environment was certainly worth taking into consideration – but Darwin and others had already done that. Apart from this unoriginal idea, what Trémaux had put forward was pure nonsense.[57]

With that, the discussion was concluded, and Marx seems to have capitulated unconditionally. The disagreement shows not only that Marx judged the descendance theories from a narrower viewpoint. It also shows that Engels, at least at that time, had a significantly more certain assessment – and was markedly more widely read – in the subjects in question than Marx. Trémaux's book quickly met with well-deserved oblivion; the racist overtones in it are what stand out most clearly today. Objectively speaking, it has nothing to do with Marx's theory of society.

6   Continued Studies

During the 1860s, Marx would also pursue scattered studies in the natural sciences that had no immediate connection with his own field of research. They concerned above all the law of conservation of energy, on which he – like Engels – took his knowledge from Grove's *On the Correlation of Physical Forces* and on which the general viewpoints he expressed in his letters are also strikingly reminiscent of Engels's earlier formulations. He was, however, also concerned about emphasising the accidental nature of his studies: in two different letters, he wrote that he 'had an opportunity of looking at' Grove's book.[58]

He could also pursue such accidental diversions into fields where Engels had not gone before him; during a period of illness in 1865, for example, he would become interested in a few novelties in astronomy.[59]

---

55   Letter from Engels to Marx, 2 October 1866, MECW 42:320.
56   Letter from Marx to Engels, 3 October 1866, MECW 42:322 et seq.
57   Letter from Engels to Marx, 5 October 1866, MECW 42: 323 et seq.
58   Letter from Marx to Engels, 31 August 1864, MECW 41:553; and letter from Marx to L. Philips, 17 August 1864, ECW 41:551.
59   It was American astronomer David Kirkwood who, starting from Laplace's nebular hypo-

Earlier that same year, both he and Engels had exchanged views on the well-known solar radiation experiment[60] that John Tyndall had performed.[61] It is obvious that the two of them were now looking around in the world of the natural sciences with amused curiosity. But it is also obvious that Engels had gone further in general orientation and, especially, at that time he had obtained better personal guidance. Precisely in 1865, and in one of the letters dealing with Tyndall, he mentions for the first time a new acquaintance that would soon come to be his closest friend after Marx: Carl Schorlemmer, still only mentioned as a 'chemist' who explained the content of Tyndall's experiment to Engels.[62] Soon enough he would appear by name and as a full-length figure in Engels's correspondence.

It is therefore not surprising that chemistry would soon be a favourite field of Engels. But not only for him! Marx had earlier harboured an interest in chemistry – or, more precisely, its practical applications; as we have seen, he had read such authors as Liebig at a very early stage. Now he would also attempt to familiarise himself with the new theories in chemistry. Like so many others thirsty for learning, he attended the lectures of German chemist August Wilhelm von Hofmann – who was a professor in London at the time – and these lectures would even leave their mark on *Capital* (to be precise, in the controversial section where Marx – earlier than Engels ever did – spoke about the Hegelian law of the relation between quality and quantity, which would find expression in both the natural sciences and in history).[63] Marx announced the news that the natural sciences would be dragged into *Capital* in this way in a letter to Engels that dealt specifically with Hofmann. Marx explained, however, that he would not apostrophise Hoffman, who had not contributed

---

thesis, sought to lay down a law on the relation between the rotational period of the planets and attraction. During a period of illness, Marx had familiarised himself with Kirkwood's theory; cf. letter from Marx to Engels, 19 August 1865, MECW 42:184. Engels was a little sceptical in his reply (21 August 1865, MECW 42:186). Marx attempted to allay some of his doubtfulness in his letter of 22 August 1865 (MECW 42:187) but thereafter the entire history disappears forever from their correspondence.

60   The experiment was one of the many with which Tyndall sought to illustrate the mechanical theory of heat (heat as a form of movement). Cf. Tyndall 1870, p. 413 et seqq.

61   Letters from Marx to Engels, 25 January 1865, MECW 42:67, and from Marx to Engels, 12 February 1865, MECW 42:91. In both these letters Marx describes the experiment in almost exactly the same words. See also letters from Engels to Marx, 5 March 1865, MECW 42:117, and 4 January 1866, MECW 42:212. In the latter, Engels recommends Tyndall's *Heat Considered as a Mode of Motion*.

62   Letter from Engels to Marx, 6 March 1865, MECW 42:117.

63   MECW 35:313.

anything original in the context, but Laurent, Gerhardt and Wurtz, among whom the latter was 'the real man'.[64]

Curiously enough, in his response Engels did not comment on Marx's completely sensational introduction of the concept of *dialectical law* but instead commented only on the names Marx cited. Schorlemmer the authority had informed Engels that Wurtz had only popularised the molecular theory; the big names were instead Gerhardt and Kekulé.[65] Marx clearly took note of the remark about Wurtz, since his name disappears from the note in question in *Capital*. Laurent on the other hand, remains with Gerhardt; Kekulé is not mentioned. In the postscript Engels made to the third edition, he explained quite frankly that Marx had overestimated Laurent's and Gerhardt's importance to molecular theory.[66]

We thus see how Marx, at the time he was busy with a final revision of the first volume of *Capital*, was actively occupied with the newest discoveries not only of biology but also of chemistry and physics. He was not on the hunt for a world view in these quick studies. Nor, however, did he seem to be satisfied with the 'basis in natural history' for his theory, but was also interested in similarities in laws and theories among various sciences. It appeared as if he were occupied with broadening the methodological perspective he had set up in the introduction to the *Grundrisse*, but had not actually managed to develop it fully in *Capital*, which was already nearly ready for print. The criticism of the first edition of *Capital* also shows that what he said about the scientific method, Hegel, dialectics, quantity and quality and the negation of the negation was not fully intelligible.[67] Much later, it would be the task of Engels, in the polemic with Dühring, to attempt to analyse what Marx meant. Once we have gotten that far, we will see the extraordinary significance Marx's scattered statement had for Engels's way of developing the dialectic. In some peculiar way, it has been forgotten in the literature on dialectical materialism that it was Marx, and not Engels, who first spoke about a dialectical law. The discussion has been so entirely caught up in the question of whether or not Marx accepted what Engels was doing that Marx's own activities have been completely ignored. The simple circumstance that *Capital* came out in 1867 while Engels began in earnest to work out a kind of general world view only in 1873, has fallen out of the account.

---

64   Letter from Marx to Engels, 22 June 1867, MECW 42:385.
65   Letter from Engels to Marx, 24 June 1867, MECW 42:387 et seq.
66   MECW 35:313, note 2.
67   Cf. 'Afterword to the Second German Edition', MECW 35:11 et seqq.

Marx did not give up his studies in the natural sciences when he put the finishing touches on *Capital*; nor, however, did he pursue them more systematically. Through Schorlemmer he attempted at least to learn the basics of the new chemistry. Engels promised that Schorlemmer would send him a textbook: Henry Roscoe's *Lessons in Elementary Chemistry*, which Schorlemmer had revised and translated into German. After various delays that made Marx impatient (to say the least),[68] the book finally arrived. Marx was enthusiastic.[69] He copied excerpts from it – an interesting circumstance, since he rarely did this with anything he did not intend to make active use of (not even Darwin or Trémaux were the subject of such notes). The excerpts are extremely scrupulous and do not ignore even very elementary matters. But they broke off quickly; Marx had clearly precipitately switched to other books and subjects.[70] A decade later, Marx copied excerpts from a much larger work by Roscoe and Schorlemmer, their *Treatise on Chemistry*[71] – but he was now oriented on the mineralogical sections and his excerpts were unambiguously bound up with his interest in agrarian chemistry.[72]

On the other hand, his study of the earlier, shorter textbook obviously had to do with his interest in dialectical matters in chemistry. We have every right to suppose that he intended to develop in more detail the lines of thought that were only given space in a note in *Capital*. The year was 1868 – and now, in a letter to Joseph Dietzgen, Marx once again announced his intent to author a brief presentation of the dialectic.[73]

But other, more immediately important matters came between. The subsequent volumes of *Capital* remained to be written, and the political work in the International demanded time and attention. The remote and the abstract had to yield to the concrete and close at hand. The interest in the general theories of chemistry once again paled in comparison to the interest in practical agrochemistry. Schorlemmer's knowledge was put to use for studies in the chemistry of agriculture, not the molecular theory.[74]

---

68   Cf. letters from Engels to Marx, 24 June 1867, MECW 42:387; from Marx to Engels, 2 November 1867, MECW 42:458, from Marx to Engels, 27 November 1867, MECW 42:476 et seq.; and from Engels to Marx, 28 November 1867, MECW 42:479.

69   Letter from Marx to Engels, 30 November 1867, MECW 42:485, and from Marx to Engels, 7 December 1867, MECW 42:495.

70   Excerpts 'Chemistry', *IISG Marx-Engels Nachlass*, B 108 p. 2 et seqq. The notes were made in 1868, that is, after the enthusiastic letters in November 1867 (Note 69).

71   The first volume of *A Treatise on Chemistry* was published in 1877 and the German counterpart, *Ausführliches Lehrbuch der Chemie*, that same year.

72   *IISG Marx-Engels Nachlass*, B 145 p. 111 et seqq.

73   Cf. above, p. 55 et seq.

74   Cf. letter from Marx to Engels, 3 January 1868, MECW 42:507; from Engels to Marx, 6 Janu-

In general, it appears as if Schorlemmer played a very important role for both Marx and Engels during these years. Engels carefully followed Schorlemmer's research in organic chemistry and talked about them with palpable pride in letters to Marx.[75] These reports, however, always concerned highly concrete matters that Schorlemmer had carried out in his laboratory. It appears as if both Marx and Engels, towards the end of the 1860s, were occupying themselves significantly less with the more spectacular and wide-embracing results in the natural sciences than they had done in the middle of the century.

At that time, Friedrich Albert Lange and Joseph Dietzgen were certainly calling their attention to general philosophical issues.[76] The natural sciences were not engaged to any great extent, however.

Only in 1873, when Engels arrived at the idea of developing a proper philosophy of the natural sciences, did these matters again become of interest in a way that left an imprint in letters, excerpts and manuscripts. That, however, is a later story.

ary 1868, MECW 42:510; and from Schorlemmer to Marx, undated (1868), *IISG Marx-Engels Nachlass*, D 3986.

75   Cf. for example, letter from Engels to Marx, 29 March 1868, MECW 42:560, and from Engels to Marx, 10 May 1868, MECW 43:33. On Schorlemmer's research, which Engels provided an account of here, see further below, p. 352 et seqq.

76   Cf. above, p. 15 et seq.

PART TWO

CHAPTER 5

The Return of the Systems

1   The Nineteenth-Century Undulation

In the preceding chapters, we kept almost exclusively to Marx's and Engels's own writings, letters and excerpts. We saw how the problems and interests that – fully developed – would determine Engels's activities over the ten-year period from 1873 to 1883 were emerging, slowly and at first only in rough outline.

Now we must broaden our perspective. Engels's general dialectic had its inner connections with the materialist conception of history and the specific theory of the base, of course. At the same time, however, it was an expression of the late nineteenth century's powerfully increasing interest in scientific syntheses and systems, worldviews and all-encompassing philosophies. Marx and Engels were not alone during the 1860s in expanding the sphere of their problems, under the influence of Darwinism and the law of conservation of energy, far beyond their own scientific fields of specialisation. They were in the midst of a mighty current.

Systems were springing up like mushrooms out of the ground in Germany, Engels wrote in the preface to *Anti-Dühring*.[1] This was correct, but the systematic fervour was strong in England and France as well. Germany had its unique philosophical traditions from Romanticism and Hegel. There were plenty of system-builders, however, in nineteenth-century Europe. France had Comte, England had Spencer, and many of the most renowned scientists – Helmholtz, Tyndall, T.H. Huxley and Pasteur, to name just a few – were giving talks and writing papers about the possibilities of creating a unity out of current knowledge. These were talks and papers that animated Engels.

In fact, one can speak of an undulation in system creation in the nineteenth century. Early on, systems were legion. Most of them came into existence in Germany, of course, but they represented attractive alternatives across nearly all of Europe. The idealist Romantic systems were, in a sense, responses to the older mechanistic systems that sought to arrange all knowledge in accordance with Newtonian principles. Syntheses were thus set against syntheses.

A few decades into the century, the systematic fervour had in general toned down. The specialised sciences were advancing victoriously. The change was

---

1   MECW 25:6.

© KONINKLIJKE BRILL NV, LEIDEN, 2023 | DOI:10.1163/9789004528796_008

most dramatic in Germany, where all-encompassing philosophising had developed the most and the speculative philosophers had left a stronger mark on research in the individual disciplines than in England or France. Later in the century, it was often said that a line could be drawn by around 1830: it was then that empirically oriented specialised research took the seat of honour. In his *History of Materialism*,[2] Friedrich Albert Lange argued that the most important cause of the change in the scientific ideal was the shift from generally theoretical to more practical interests. He found the influx around chemistry as a utilitarian science to be significant.[3] Like Lange, Ernst Haeckel asserted that the philosophical syntheses had fallen into disrepute 'particularly since 1830'; within the natural sciences, at least, knowledge of the individual had become the only real goal of research. Haeckel also argued, however, that by arranging endless numbers of uncoordinated details, specialised research of this kind must again raise the questions of connections and systems. The theory that he pointed out as the one that could bring a new order to the empirical chaos was, naturally, Darwinism. From around 1860 it was also possible, he said to speak of a new period of system-building.[4]

In itself, this attempt at dating events does not say much, but it nevertheless indicates an extremely important circumstance. Regarded in general, the unity of knowledge appears as a principal goal for the scientific endeavour at the century's start, while its exactitude, empirical content and practical application were ranked higher in the middle years. In the latter half, the issue of unity once again became attractive, but it was no longer a question of the same unity. The various specialised sciences had undergone powerful development and were only marginally influenced by the new systems. The systems, for their part, were not laid out with the same dictatorial claims against the specialised sciences as previously; above all, it was a matter of drawing out and coordinating the tendencies that, the system-builders argued, existed in various disciplines.

These general – very general – features of nineteenth-century development are, however, neither particularly interesting nor apprehensible if their general determinations cannot be found.

---

2   Lange 1876, Vol. 2, p. 72, p. 81 et seq.
3   Ibid., p. 83.
4   Haeckel 1873, p. 71 et seq.

2   Specialisation and System-Building

The dynamic in this course of events can be traced back to the contradiction between *specialisation* and *system-building*. There is an obvious tension between specialties and systems that can be tracked far back in the history of science. During the period in question here, it is continually discernible.

Specialisation finds its expression above all in the fact that the individual scientist's field of work and knowledge covers an ever-smaller part of the scientific hierarchy from mathematics to the human sciences. If specialisation is non-existent, a person who has been admitted as a valid member in the scientific community[5] can comment on any field of human knowledge whatsoever without being labelled a charlatan for it. This completely neutral position has likely never been achieved, but the classical universities placed few obstacles in the path (specialist training was required for at least the judicial and medical professions, but this limitation accordingly applied to the practical profession and not scientific activities). Anyone who had gained recognition in the fraternity of the learned was, in principle, competent to work in any branch of science whatsoever.

But in and of themselves, the institutional determinations do not say whether or not an actual specialisation is under way. Specialisation means that the field of a certain profession is being screened off and is becoming accessible only to those who have specialised knowledge in it. This is also not to say that specialisation affects all disciplines simultaneously or equally as hard. When, at the beginning of the nineteenth century, most physicists indignantly rejected the comments of the Romantic philosophers of nature about their subject, it was a sign that physics had become a specialised field. A number of disciplines in biology, on the other hand, were invaded by Romantic ideas. In other words, specialisation had gone further in physics than in biology.

It is obvious, however, that the institutions – universities, scientific academies, colleges or whatever you like – influence the course of specialisation to a great extent. We will soon return to this.

System building does not immediately depend on the degree of scientific specialisation. A system, in the meaning the term is being used here, is a con-

---

5   The term 'scientific community' is found in a pleasantly broad sense in Kuhn 1970 and then in the literature oriented on the science of sociology that took Kuhn's work as its starting point. On this, see Kuhn's own 'Postscript', Kuhn 1970, p. 176 et seqq. The concept of scientific community is not institutionally determined; the community in question does not need to limit itself to certain types of institutions. Instead, what keeps the community together and defines it is different types of (scientific) consensus.

sistent attempt at finding connections, general features and differences among different areas of knowledge. Systems therefore do not assume any completed specialisation; Thomas Aquinas left a system behind him. Specialisation, on the other hand, means that system-building becomes problematic and usually controversial; the systematist has to move in several different spheres of authority. It is possible to speak of systems that do not contain the entire scientific hierarchy (e.g. systems of natural sciences), but systems can also contain moral, religious and political ideas and thus not be limited to the field of science.

What is it, though, that drives the systems forward, and what forces set the specialisation process in motion?

Let me refer to the conceptual apparatus I introduced earlier.[6] In it, I distinguished two external and two internal determinations of science. The external were the practical and material, and the ideological; the internal were the empirical and the theoretical. It is obvious that the empirical determination favours specialisation. The more intensely observations and experiments are employed, the more exact data becomes accessible, and the scientific field in which empirical expertise can be claimed becomes that much smaller. It is obvious that the tremendous increase in the mass of knowledge in the eighteenth and nineteenth centuries drove specialisation forward.

The theoretical determination is not as unambiguous in its relation to specialisation and system-building. On the one hand, it is clear that theoretical development itself – that is, the development of exact and advanced theories – in a number of natural sciences made them unapproachable for non-specialists. On the other hand, the theoretical problems do not come to a halt at the boundaries that the specialisation process has set. Questions about the relations between physics and chemistry, chemistry and biology, biology and the social sciences and so on are eminently theoretical. In the nineteenth century, they came to the fore again and again through the new, epoch-making theories. The step from the great theoretical questions to systems is not a long one; the law of conservation of energy and Darwin's theory of natural selection are splendid examples of this.

Of the external determinations, the practical and material normally – and at least to a remarkable degree, in the nineteenth century – fostered specialisation. The knowledge that could be of use in material production had to be detailed empirical knowledge. Those who could develop it and procure it for production had to have specially oriented professional knowledge. Only at a later stage – or when environmental issues had become acute – did the lack of

---

6   Above, p. 23 et seqq.

coordination among various fields of knowledge become a real practical and material problem. But that did not occur until long after the end of the century.

The ideological determination works in the opposite direction. Since scientific results are to be used to confirm, reinforce or change moral, political, religious or aesthetic ideas, it is important that they encompass as much of the scientific hierarchy as possible. Later, we will experience the intimate connection between the assiduous system-building of the late nineteenth century and the involvement of science in various controversial ideological issues.

There are thus driving forces both within and beyond science for both specialisation and system-building. Estimating their mutual strength during a given period must take the dominant situation of the problem into account, as well as the various social forces that take the knowledge into their employ.

Scientific institutions in the broadest sense can be said to *bring about* the various determinations. They are established to meet certain requirements and fulfil certain expectations; they are reformed and restored when new requirements and expectations are imposed. They change with the general development of society. But they are no passive instruments. They are not only influenced by the historical situation of the sciences; they influence it as well. As long as the classic corporatist form of the university exists it puts a brake on specialisation, whereas the specialised colleges of the eighteenth and nineteenth centuries accelerate it.

3   The System-Builders

But what does this mean, concretely?

What we are seeking to explain is how Comte, Spencer, Haeckel, Dühring, von Hartmann and, finally, Frederick Engels found it both possible and important to comment on a long range of disciplines that seemed to lie far beyond their own fields of work and skills.

We know that they had a tradition of system-building to fall back on; the all-encompassing system was in fact the classical manner of presenting the sciences, and it had been brought powerfully to the fore by Schelling, Hegel and many others.

But we also know that there was an opposing tradition – more scientifically respected at the time – in which the specialist stood out as the only one who could accomplish anything of value. And this was more than an ideal: a number of disciplines had already *de facto* been specialised, difficult for outsiders to access and pursued almost solely by people with an exclusive orientation on them. These specialties rapidly multiplied. The dream of surveying all knowledge and creating a real unity from it must have appeared increasingly utopian.

But how did the various system-builders think this unity would be achieved? There was, in fact, a broad spectrum of opinion here that can be traced back to various positions in epistemology. Finding a point of unification among the various branches of knowledge can be regarded as a more or less active process: the work of the system-builders in interpreting or re-interpreting the given in the specialised sciences can, in other words, be regarded as more or less radical. With that, there are also different ideas about the relation between the specialised scientist and the systematist. The more active the systematist, the less the specialist's authority becomes for him. If the systematist regards themselves primarily as someone who is only coordinating the results from various disciplines, the word of the specialist also becomes law for them.

The Romantics, with Schelling at their head, had taken an extreme point of view. Schelling declared that his goal was to create a philosophical natural science; his philosophy of nature was in fact the real natural science. Chemistry, physics and mathematics presented him with material to build his philosophy from, but it was he alone, the philosopher, who could give meaning to the whole.[7] Namely, it was only the philosopher who could see the entirety of all knowledge and resolve the contradictions that exist among various fields of knowledge.[8]

Hegel's view of the relation between philosophy and the specialised sciences was more complex. The object of philosophy was not, as it was for Schelling, the sum total of the *specialised* sciences; each specialised science had its special object to study, while philosophy – according to Hegel – lacked such a fixed object. At the same time, however, philosophy was to study all knowledge and lift it to a higher level, so to speak. According to Hegel as well, philosophy was thus highly active in relation to the knowledge that the various sciences presented to it.[9]

For Comte, the increasing specialisation was a problem, a difficulty that the system-builder had to overcome. The growing *division du travail intellectual* was a necessary feature of scientific development, he claimed in the first volume

---

7 'Mein Zweck ist vielmehr, die Naturwissenschaft selbst erst philosophisch entstehen *zu lassen, und meine Philosophie is selbst nicht anders als Naturwissenschaft. Es ist wahr, dass uns Chemie die* Elemente, *Physik die* Sylben, *Mathematik die* Nature lessen *lehrt; aber man darf nicht vergessen, dass es der Philosophie zusteht, das Gelesene* auszulegen'. Schelling 1:2, p. 6.

8 Cf. in particular Schelling 1:5, p. 266 et seqq., p. 305 et seq.

9 The most easily comprehensible account of this in Hegel ought to be his 'Foreword' to *Science of Logic*, Vol. 1; Hegel 4, 13–19.

of his *Course of Positive Philosophy*. But the split had its risks; the human spirit could get lost in the details. A new type of specialist was therefore needed, who would devote themselves to the study of *généralités scientifiques* or the 'spirit' of the various sciences, their principles and their connections.[10] The goal, which the positive sciences were always approaching but, according to Comte, could never completely achieve, was to arrange all knowledge under a single principle.[11]

On the other hand, Comte viewed positively the possibilities of building a system on the basis of the specialised sciences. The task of philosophy was rather passive: the connecting principles existed – if not manifestly, then latent – in the various disciplines, and it was the task of the philosopher to bring these principles to light.

Spencer would later come to advocate a similar idea.[12] In and of itself, it was obvious that the system-builder, who had a more or less expressly empirical view of knowledge, had to regard system-building itself as a primarily passive process. It was, after all, the specialised sciences that were closest to the empirical material and possessed and provided real knowledge. The system-builder's most important active and critical contribution would consist of ruling out the specialised scientific results that conflicted with proper empirical principles.

Similarly, rationalist ideas – or, rather, the idea that higher, homogeneous knowledge is something humanity creates with its reason – are found in the background to the Romantic's and Hegel's idea that the philosopher re-creates what is given by the specialised sciences in their philosophy.

As a fully logical consequence, a systematist such as William Whewell is on the spectrum between empiricists and rationalists in his view of the relations between system and specialised science. His thesis – first put forth in *Philosophy of the Inductive Sciences* – is that all scientific, inductive knowledge assumes a number of ideas such as space, time, force and so on, which cannot be derived from experience. Summarising this inductive knowledge thereby assumes that these ideas and their significance can be established; that becomes the active task of the philosopher.[13]

When the great zeal for system-building spread after the middle of the century, the question of what the system actually meant in relation to the specialised knowledge became central but also surrounded by a great deal of con-

---

10   Comte 1:22 et seqq.
11   Ibid., p. 4, p. 43 et seq.
12   Cf. Spencer's definition of philosophy in Part II:1 of *First Principles*; Spencer 1862.
13   Whewell 1967, p. 74 *ff* and *passim*.

fusion. We will see later how notoriously difficult this would be for Engels to master, torn as he was between Hegel and contemporary authorities in the natural sciences.

But with this, we have only seen how a few influential systematists considered that the relation between specialty and system was or should be constructed. What they actually did with the knowledge they obtained from the various disciplines when incorporating it into their overall picture is another question.

If the various sciences formed an entirely harmonic unity, the task of bringing them together would have been simple – so simple that it would almost seem unnecessary. But the relation among the branches is in fact problematic. Even among the specialists, there are irreconcilable ideas about the relation between physics and chemistry, chemistry and biology, biology and the sciences of humanity. In nearly every discipline, there are different traditions and orientations advocated by eminent specialists. There are irreconcilable theories and hypotheses. There are conflicting scientific ideals. Nineteenth-century physics and chemistry were filled with theoretical conflicts: vitalists and mechanists fought in biology, and Darwinism gave rise to new antagonisms.

Every system-builder is thus compelled to choose sides against their will. In field after field, they must join with one group of specialists against another. They must put more faith in the expertise of one than in another.

This was the actual situation in the nineteenth-century sciences, which compelled the system-builder to actively pick and choose in the various specialised fields. They could then follow various rules of thumb. If they were empirically inclined, they could consistently choose the ideas and theories that seemed more satisfactory from an empirical perspective. But they assuredly had to follow other rules for their consistency. Empirical support for vitalist and mechanist ideas, for example, changed rapidly during the century. Careful experiments in the 1830s and 1840s showed that spontaneous generation, in the form it had been imagined until then, was empirically unthinkable; it gave vitalism the winning cards.[14] On the other hand, the roughly contemporary cell theory – empirically well substantiated – suited the mechanistic conception better. In chemistry, the older ideas about special organic compounds was found to be unsustainable – once again, support for mechanism. But further on in the century, Pasteur enjoyed brief but brilliant success in giving impetus to vitalist ideas about chemical products that belonged solely to the organic world.

---

14   Cf. above, p. 101.

He would soon be refuted by new experiments and new theories[15] – but it is clear and obvious that the system-builder who would only give proper empiricism their support had to re-examine their understanding often, with little time to rest, and additionally – as a non-specialist – having to do so on flimsy grounds.

Instead, they could – and this was usual – assert, for example, that the vitalist assumption of a special, unique field for organic life was a dubious one. But in that case, they were adding another, reductionist, principle to their empirical principle. They thus assumed that all learning, all knowledge, must constitute a whole and that scientific development must primarily be moving toward a greater uniformity (this is an assumption we have already met in Comte). They were hurrying empirical specialised research on ahead.

In fact, this is what all system-builders were doing. They were sifting out tendencies in the current sciences and extrapolating complete, final scientific knowledge. They also had to be able to trace lines backward in time to see how knowledge had developed. Their ideas about the history of science thus also played a role in their system-building.

4   The Institutions of Science

With the development of specialised sciences, however, presenting overall views of science becomes a more hazardous enterprise. Whatever the systematist's starting point, they have to collect information from an ever greater, ever more differentiated field of learning.

They also face greater difficulties in being heard, believed and appreciated. A horde of specialists stand at the ready to criticise and correct them. How could they overcome such criticism? It depends to a great extent, of course, on who they turn to. If they are out to provide guidelines and perspectives for the specialists – as Schelling, and to some extent Hegel, were – they naturally need to have arguments against the initial criticism they are exposed to. But if their business is above all to popularise learning and draw ideological conclusions from it, being at a loss for any answers toward the specialists is not as catastrophic; they attain their main goal if they succeed in convincing a public that is generally thirsty for knowledge.

The relation of the system-builder to the specialist cannot be elucidated if aspects of the sociology of knowledge, and more specifically the sociology of

---

15   On this, see Dagognet 1967.

science, are not constructed on the system-builder's activities. The developments during the nineteenth century are bound up with the development of
the institutions of learning and of scientific communication. The role of the
systematist changes in this scholarly context; their place does not remain the
same. Their authority is different.

At first glance, we can see that the more influential system-builders had a different position in society and the intellectual towards the end of the century
than they did at its beginning. There is also a clear difference among various
European countries[16] – Germany and England form the extremes, after a fashion – and the difference is most striking in the earlier period. In Germany,
Romantic philosophy and Hegelianism were inseparably bound up with the
universities. They came from a scholarly environment where philosophy was
regarded as the crown and summary of all the other disciplines.

In England, the universities did not occupy a position comparable to the one
they had in Germany. Intellectual life pulsed more freely in many places other
than Oxford and Cambridge. There were no Hegels or Schellings there. The few
contemporary English equivalents – among whom the poet and philosopher
Samuel Taylor Coleridge should chiefly be named – got along in the world as
free men of literature. But even the most outstanding scientists – men like
Dalton and Davy, Faraday and Tyndall and Joule, made a living as private tutors
or had professorships at the Royal Institution in London.[17] Out in the country
towns, clubs and societies flourished with scientific experiments, discussions
on the philosophy of nature and questions about the practical applications
of science on the programme.[18] In these unfettered environments there were

---

16   A lucid presentation of the relations of sociological science in various European countries
      is provided in Ben-David 1971. Developments in the nineteenth century, with the emphasis
      in Germany, is provided in Chapter 7, p. 108 et seqq.
17   The standard modern work on Coleridge and German idealist philosophy is Orsini 1969.
      Clearly exaggerating, George Haines declares that scientists in Victorian England 'were,
      for the most part, isolated individuals, inquiring into the secrets of nature for their private
      edification, pride, or wealth'; Haines 1957, p. x. These recluses, however, often gathered
      together in more or less informal assemblies and organisations, and the debates about the
      social uses of science and its institutional relations were lively throughout the nineteenth
      century. The standard work on this is Cardwell 1972. MacDonagh 1975 also provides some
      interesting aspects, and also takes up the difficulties the Royal Institution encountered.
      There is a great deal of literature on the Royal Institution; see in particular the monographs
      by M. Jones 1974 and B. Jones 1971. The task of the Royal Institution was more to educate
      the masses than to devote itself to 'pure' science. On this, see Elkana 1974, p. 151 et seq.
18   On the most famous of these societies, the Lunar Society in Birmingham, see the mono-
      graph by Schofield. Its counterpart in Manchester was the Manchester Literary & Philo-
      sophical Society, on which more in, for example, Caldwell 1968, p. 3 et seqq., and Clow 1968,

at least efforts at system-building, though very different to what Schelling or Hegel – or Coleridge – devoted themselves to. An esteemed member of the Lunar Society in Birmingham was one Erasmus Darwin, grandfather to Charles and author of the remarkable work *Zoonomia*, which came out in the late 1790s. The most important scientific institution remained the Royal Society, even if its lustre faded palpably during the nineteenth century. Oxford and Cambridge were thoroughly exclusive and orthodox facilities of learning, and the conglomerate in London that developed in the first half of the century and became the University of London differed from the accepted universities primarily through its political and religious liberalism.[19] The universities did not reach the very front lines of research until the end of the century, when new and practically oriented universities were also founded in Manchester, Liverpool, Leeds, Birmingham, Sheffield and Bristol.[20] But they never became the seat for any system-building.

In France, scholarly life had been reshaped from the ground up during the French Revolution and the Napoleonic era. Many of the pre-revolutionary universities had been closed while specialised colleges, oriented on strict professional education, gained a stronger position. Under Napoleon, higher education and research was placed entirely in the hands of the state.[21] These changes were bound to thoroughly alter the conditions for the sciences.

The tradition of the *philosophe* from the Enlightenment had been exclusively a tradition of system-building; it culminated in *La grande Encyclopédie*, the summary of all human knowledge.[22] The tradition did not die out with

---

p. 127 et seqq. There were also assemblies of an even more private and unofficial character that would come to play a significant role. Here above all belongs the X Club, whose members lived in London and included Spencer, Huxley, Tyndall, the chemist Frankland and the natural scientific Jack-of-all-trades John Lubbock (Lord Avebury). On this remarkable brain trust see, for example, Frankland 1902, p. 148 et seqq., Spencer 1904, Vol. II, p. 115 et seqq., L. Huxley, Vol. I, p. 368 et seqq. and Peel 1971, p. 18.

19   D'Irsay 1932, p. 245 et seqq. and Cardwell 1972, p. 92 et seqq. Naturally, there were numerous prominent scientists at Oxford and Cambridge as well. Among all those of interest in our – very extensive – context, however, there is only one who had a professorship at any of the classical English universities: William Whewell, who was a professor first of mineralogy, then of moral philosophy, at Cambridge.

20   Regarding the ideas behind these new seats of learning, see in addition to Cardwell 1972, p. 136 et seqq., also Roscoe 1906, p. 96 et seqq., and Thompson 1886.

21   D'Irsay 1932, p. 139 et seqq., 148 et seqq., 168 et seqq. A number of interesting viewpoints – though quite one-sided – on the French development from the revolution to Comte can be found in Hayek 1952, p. 105 et seqq. A special study regarding the professionalisation of science in France has been carried out by Crosland.

22   The tremendous amount of literature on the French Enlightenment, the *Encyclopédie* and

the revolution and Napoleon, but it sought out entirely new forms. Romantic and Hegelian ideas did not gain any overwhelming circulation in France, which can be partly explained by the remaining force of Enlightenment thinking. The single outstanding advocate of Schelling's and Hegel's ideas, Victor Cousin, was associated with the Sorbonne during his philosophically more active period but had no possibility of gaining influence over the advocates of other subjects compared to what Schelling and Hegel had gained in Jena, Munich or Berlin.[23] The French system-builder who went furthest in both originality and influence in the nineteenth century, August Comte, was shut out from all higher facilities of learning for his materialist opinions and completed his colossal six-volume *Course of Positive Philosophy* in impoverished isolation.

Comte began as a socialist in the spirit of Saint-Simon, and in his system the ideological motivation for system-building remains stronger, or at least more obvious, than in the German Romantics and Hegelians. In that respect, he resembles his privately tutored English counterpart, Herbert Spencer, and he heralded the intellectual climate from which Engels's ideas about scientific socialism came. The systems began to liberate themselves more and more from scholarly organisations. The system-builders of the late nineteenth century more rarely had any firm connections to any scientific institution. This applied not only to England and France, but to Germany as well.

The development of scholarly life in Germany is worth particular attention. It was there that the all-encompassing philosophies were the most numerous and powerful. It was also there, however, that the universities became the earliest strongholds of specialised research, thereby providing models for the trend in other countries.[24] The antagonism between specialist and system-builder was thus also strongest in Germany.

---

the tradition of the *philosophe* is superbly summarised in Gay 1967–70. Regarding philosophy, see also Goyard-Fahre 1972.

23   On Victor Cousin, see the aged but still useful biography by Janet 1887 and the small work (79 pages) by Cornelius 1958.

24   The university ideology that long prevailed in England was expressed by the well-known cardinal John Henry Newman. The universities should supply education of an ethical and aesthetic type, and moreover provide its adepts with the necessary knowledge for their future professions; they would not be research facilities. Cf. Newman 1947, *passim*. Whewell also took a very active part in these discussions. In his university ideology he was very close to Newman, even though he emphasised the significance of purely scientific – and in particular mathematical – education at the universities more strongly. Cf. Whewell 1838, above all p. 45 et seqq. The German university system, however, would be brought out as an ideal by those who looked after both the advances of pure research and its material benefits. On this, cf. Haines 1957. The antagonism between the English and the German

It was in Prussia, first and foremost, that the sciences would be organised in a new way; the most striking example of this change was the new university in Berlin, which was founded in 1810.

The development of Berlin University may seem paradoxical.[25] It was a university planned in accordance with Romantic ideas about the unity of education and the supremacy of philosophy; in other words, it was to be a university that would produce nothing but systems. The ideal of the supremacy of philosophy was realised to such an extent that the philosophical faculty, in all its breadth, gained a dominant position – where the lower faculties were kept in good order – that would have been unthinkable in the older universities. It was not, however, the subject of philosophy – as Fichte or Schleiermacher[26] had intended – that would naturally sit at the top of the hierarchy. Philosophy became, at least from the 1830s, only one discipline among many.

The university in Berlin thus became the seat of theoretically oriented, highly specialised research. For that matter, it did not lack ideological determination; it only became a different one than in the old universities. In centralist Prussia (and later the German Reich) the traditional corporative freedom of the universities in relation to the state was unthinkable. Scientists fulfilled their duties toward the state as industrious and loyal specialists. A special code of honour for specialists developed that proved highly useful in the struggles against Darwinism and socialism, for example, in the 1870s.[27]

Scientists would thus justify the existence of their relatively favourable position by producing knowledge in a limited field that could be of use, both ideologically and in a practical material fashion, to the state. Learning could thus be used both to influence citizens' ideas and to be put into material production.

There is thus one side of the nineteenth-century process of specialisation that we could easily forget in our admiration of what specialised research meant on a purely scientific plane. Specialists are efficient for the production of knowledge, but they are also ideologically easy to handle and benign when

ideals became even more palpable in the United States. American students flocked to Germany to enjoy the *Lehrfreiheit*; cf. for example Herbst 1965, pp. 1–22 and the literature cited there. These ideas took root in the United States; they were given their most thorough expression in Flexner 1968. The background is also drawn up in the introduction to the latest edition of Flexner; cf. Kerr 1968.

25   On the background to and early development of the University of Berlin, see Deiters 1960, p. 15 et seqq., Schnabel 1964, p. 205 et seqq., Weischedel 1960, p. xi et seqq., and R. König 1935, p. 20 et seqq. Also important are the essays Kessel 1955 and Kessel 1963.

26   Fichte 1910, p. 1 et seqq., or Fichte 1960, p. 30 et seqq., and Schleiermacher 1910, p. 147 et seqq., or Schleiermacher 1960, p. 141 et seqq.

27   Cf. below, p. 503 et seqq.

they limit themselves to their fields of specialisation. They can be incorporated into a context they have no influence over; and this context is not only the sum total of the sciences but also the society in which they live.

This is why, in the nineteenth century, system-builders risked not only appearing as charlatans. They could also have been stamped as politically or morally suspect – or dangerous.

The antagonism between specialist and system-builder was doubly critical in late nineteenth-century Germany. The German system-builders risked harsher, more merciless criticism than their English colleagues, who had a solid tradition of privately tutored individuals and amateurs behind them. Hegel and Schelling could successfully act unhindered at their universities, but their counterparts fifty years later usually had to keep themselves outside of the entire scholarly apparatus.

Eugen Dühring's fate was a typical one: he was a private lecturer (*Privatdozent*) at the university of Berlin but lost his teaching rights in 1877. He had aimed criticism at the conditions in the university, but it is obvious that it was his zeal in commenting on and drawing ideological conclusions from all knowledge that made his position untenable. Moreover, the action against him was led by perhaps the university's most celebrated specialist, Hermann von Helmholtz.[28] Dühring was subsequently forced to live as a freelance writer: a significantly less enviable situation in Germany than in England.

There were certainly those who succeeded in defending systems and still remaining at the universities: Ernst Haeckel is the foremost example. There were two reasons Haeckel accomplished this feat. First, he was a respected specialist in biology. Second, he denied all dangerous, socially disruptive teachings.[29]

But most of those who moved about the commons of science were outsiders to the German universities. So it was with Ludwig Büchner, one of the leading forces in the extremely ideologically inflamed *Materialismusstreit*, or materialistic controversy,[30] when he published *Force and Matter* in 1855. His comrade in arms, Carl Vogt, lost his professorship in Giessen after the revolution of 1848 but then took an academic position in Switzerland. The third materialist in the controversy, Dutch physiologist Jacob Moleschott, was ejected from the German university system but accepted by the Swiss.

---

28   The spark that ignited was a lecture that Dühring gave on women's opportunities for higher education (Dühring 1877). The best account of the Dühring affair should be Biermann 1973, p. 89 et seqq.

29   Haeckel 1878, p. 3 et seq. and below, p. 503 et seq.

30   The best account of *der Materialismusstreit* should still be Lange 1876, Vol. II, p. 88 et seqq.

The system-builders who emerged later in the century sought their livelihood in the free literary market. Eduard von Hartmann had no academic training in general but rather a military one. He made a virtue out of his position
outside all regular scholarly contexts, scorning the *Zunftphilosophie* or *Profess-
orenphilosophie* (craft guild or academic philosophy) being carried out at the
universities.[31] In his own way, he stands out as the most typical system-builder
at the end of the century.

In the attempt to assess Engels's work from the 1870s and 1880s, we cannot
forget that by standing outside the regular scientific and scholarly organisations, he is consistent – so to speak – with the ideal image of the system builder
of the time. He was working in England, of course, but he wrote in German and
his works were first published in German for a German-speaking audience. His
ideas were not disseminated through any official channels. The German Social
Democrats were busy building up an informational network for the dissemination of theoretical ideas as well, through publishing houses, newspapers
and journals. *Anti-Dühring* was published – under protest[32] – in the Social-
Democratic organ *Vorwärts*, and *Ludwig Feuerbach* originally came out in the
new theoretically and ideologically oriented journal *Die Neue Zeit*.

Both Marx and Engels were thus outside institutionalised science. In a pinch,
Marx could be accepted by German academics as a specialist in economic theory, which the reviews of *Capital* show.[33] But when Engels spoke about philosophy, physics, chemistry and biology, he shared the same conditions as the
free-floating system builders in Germany, however unwilling he was to have
something in common with them.[34]

Official institutions, universities and academies and the like have at least a
pretext of impartiality. By being precisely official, they represent all interests –
or, rather, they abolish the antagonisms between these interests in complete

---

31 Cf. '*Mein Entwicklungsgang*' in Hartmann 1876, p. 35 et seq., '*Die Schicksale meiner Philo-
    sophie in ihrem ersten Jahrzent (1869–1979)*' in Hartmann 1885, p. 10, and in the polemic
    against Darwinism Hartmann 1875, p. 1. Even Dühring expressed his contempt for 'guild
    philosophers', for example, in Dühring 1903, p. 125.

32 Cf. below, p. 516 et seqq.

33 In the Afterword to the second German edition of *Capital*, Marx explained: 'The learned
    and unlearned spokesmen of the German bourgeoisie tried at first to kill *Das Kapital* by
    silence ... As soon as they found that these tactics no longer fitted in with the conditions
    of the time, they wrote, under pretence of criticising my book, prescriptions for "the tran-
    quillisation of the bourgeois mind" ...' MECW 35:16.

34 Outside the workers' press and reactions from Dühring and his supporters, nothing was
    heard about *Anti-Dühring* and *Ludwig Feuerbach*; in German scientific periodicals and the
    like, the silence was complete.

objectivity. Their failure to do so in nineteenth-century class society is another matter. They would nonetheless stand out as the bearers of actual science. Free organisations with their independent forms of communication openly appeared as advocates for partisan interests; their ideological determination was obvious. The self-evident task of the socialist organ in which Engels appeared was to work for an ideology, a network of values and assertions held to be true. When Engels brought the modern natural sciences into the debate, he engaged them for the cause of socialism in the same way Spencer engaged them for liberalism, or von Hartmann for pessimistically minded conservatism.

The system-building of the late nineteenth century was thus, to a considerable extent, a way of bringing accepted science into the battle between world views, political ideologies and moral systems. The specialists, who in their specialised research appeared as sitting above the antagonisms, could contribute material to the fight; as long as the specialists remained specialists, they had a kind of immunity. But when – like Huxley or Haeckel – they drew far-reaching conclusions from their specialist knowledge, they lost that immunity. For Engels, as we shall see, it was extremely important to distinguish between what the specialist said within their domain and what they stated out in the commons of knowledge and ideas.

But since all those – specialist or not – who wanted to draw conclusions about the knowledge in question intended to influence and convince an audience well beyond the circle of specialists, popularising knowledge, making it accessible for to as many as possible, became an important task for them. This was not an unproblematic process. It was a matter of translating theories and hypotheses from one language into another, from one world of concepts into another. In particular, where the exact sciences were concerned it was also necessary to drop from a higher level of precision to a lower one, and to represent in pictures and analogies what the sciences expressed in formulas. And which world of ideas would the populariser refer to? What could they assume was known and comprehensible for the audience they were addressing?

To this difficulty of an internal nature can be added an external, primarily social one. For the specialists, there is a range of generally accepted signs that make them specialists: positions at scientific academies or universities, the possibility of publishing in specialised journals, the willingness of their colleagues to accept, or at least discuss, their results. As I have previously pointed out, the specialist has an official status. But for a populariser, there are no similar signs that they have obtained a secure position precisely as a populariser. Expounding on what the knowledge means is a freer and riskier occupation. The populariser does not have a circle of other popularisers to confirm their position; rather it is the public successes – the success among others, the recipients – that clearly state whether or not they have succeeded. But these successes immediately say more about how nimble the populariser is than it does about their objectivity.

The popularisation of science, however, was a strong current in the nineteenth century. Of all this popularisation, the portion dealing with system-building was small, though important. Making knowledge accessible to many was a necessity if the knowledge was to be put to practical use in industry. For liberals and socialists, it was moreover a condition for people's political activity that they possessed as broad an orientation on life and society as possible. Popular science from nearly every discipline also became a weapon in the struggle against Christianity.

It is self-evident that even the most easily accessible popular version of science requires systematisation; it must provide an image of the context of the knowledge. But only a small part of popular science can have the heavy, pretentious form of the fully developed system. In all the educational associations and workers' institutes that emerged in the nineteenth century, the sciences were brought together in simpler ways. But the systems' connections with the broad popularisation movement is obvious; in them and through them, the authors of the systems reached their audience.

Not only system-builders, but also specialists took part in popularisation. Disseminating the latest truths of knowledge was regarded as an important task by many scientists during the latter half of the nineteenth century. They devoted time and energy to authoring easily accessible textbooks, travelling on lecture tours and at times organising adult education themselves. Especially in England, where the specialist was much freer in relation to state institutions than in Germany or France, these activities directed at the general public assumed unimaginable dimensions. Leading scientists became popular speakers who drew enormous crowds. Darwinism – rapidly developed by its followers into a world view and already armed with important consequences for Christianity and faith in the Bible – played a major role, but a great deal of other knowledge also attracted large crowds. We have a vivid depiction by Jenny Marx, Karl's wife, of how St. Martin's Hall in London was filled with huge, enthusiastic crowds, burning with passion, who listened to 'the top men in science, Huxley (Darwin's school) at the head, with Sir Charles Lyell, Bowring, Carpenter, etc.'. Since these lectures were held on non-working days they encountered bans by the authorities but in general these activities could nevertheless not be stopped.[35]

---

35   Letter from Jenny Marx to J.P. Becker, 29 January 1866, MECW 42:568 et seqq.

So it went in the metropolis of London, but similar lectures roused similar enthusiasm in other places around England. Henry Enfield Roscoe, the great chemist and liberal politician, wrote in his memoirs about how he, stirred up by a famine in the workers' districts in Manchester in 1862, took part in organising a relief effort that gradually resulted in an adult education organisation – a 'workers' college'. His and his colleagues' popular scientific activities were feverish; Huxley, Tyndall and many others came to Manchester. And Roscoe himself went on tour.[36] Roscoe also provided other information showing that it was indeed not just Darwinism and the battles around it that roused public interest. His own popular readers in chemistry, he asserted, sold 335,000 copies. Other, less demanding, books he wrote also achieved tremendous success in sales.[37]

There were also other channels through which scientists sought to bring their problems and ideas out. *Nature*, founded in 1869, was a journal that reported regularly from the research areas of general interest, and the reporters were primarily the most renowned natural scientists. Huxley, Wallace, Carpenter and many others appeared in its pages.[38] Spencer was able to publish a letter to the editor explaining what he actually meant by the famous phrase 'survival of the fittest'.[39] For Engels and others who were in need of expert news from the world of science, *Nature* was a goldmine.

English scientists (and British in general) were also busy organising themselves in various free societies, all of which lacked the high official mark of the Royal Society. These associations placed the practical (material, and also ideological) use of science high on the agenda, unless they had the character of loosely organised trade unions intended for the professional reputation and security of a special group.[40]

---

36   Roscoe 1906, p. 124 et seqq.

37   Ibid., p. 149 et seqq.

38   Wallace was particularly active, writing a number of articles and reviews on the subject such as 'The Last Attack on Darwinism' (Wallace 1872a) and 'The Beginnings of Life' (Wallace 1872b). Huxley contributed such studies as 'On the Hypothesis that Animals are Automats, and its History' (T.H. Huxley 1874), and William Carpenter reproduced his powerful philosophical 'Inaugural Address' to the meeting of natural scientists in Brighton in 1872 (Carpenter 1872).

39   In his small letter to the press, Spencer declared that those who believed 'survival of the fittest' could just as well be replaced by 'preservation of the fittest' were wrong. Like Darwin's 'natural selection', the latter expression presumes a selector – in other words, it has teleological content (Spencer here thus has occasion to take a shot at Darwin), whereas Spencer's own 'survival' lacks any such trace. Spencer 1872, p. 263 et seq.

40   A superb account with historical examples, above all from the nineteenth century, is the chapter on 'Scientific Organization' by Blume 1974, pp. 99–130. See also Cardwell 1972, p. 59 et seqq., p. 72 et seqq.

In Germany, the popularisation of science took partially different forms. There were educational institutions for workers here and craftsmen of various types as well; it was here that many of socialism's pioneers – August Bebel ahead of the others – received their first schooling beyond general adult education.[41] But the most renowned specialists were scarcely involved in this activity. This did not mean that they did not try to convey their insights and knowledge. Many did so along official – to say nothing of ceremonial – paths, at speeches in honour of formal occasions at the universities, celebrations of royal or noble name days and birthdays, and so on. The public they addressed with the speeches themselves were more festively dressed than great. But the speeches then went to print and were often published in large numbers. One of the classics of popular science, Hermann von Helmholtz's *Popular Scientific Lectures*, consists largely of similar ceremonial lectures.[42] The introductory lectures at the conferences of the *Versammlung deutscher Naturforscher und Aertze*[43] (Conference of German Scientists and Doctors) also played an important role.

---

41   See, for example, Schraepler 1966, p. 12 et seqq.

42   The important essay '*Über das Verhältniss der Naturwissenschaften zur Gesammtheit der Wissenschaft*' (Helmholtz 1876, Vol. I, p. 1 et seqq.) was thus originally an *Akademische Festrede* (academic ceremonial speech) given in Heidelberg in 1862, while '*Über das Ziel und die Fortschritte der Naturwissenschaft*' (ibid., Vol. II, p. 137 et seqq.) was the inaugural address of the congress of natural scientists at Innsbruck in 1869. Only the lecture '*Über die Wechselwirkung der Naturkräfte und die darauf bezüglichen neueren Ermittelungen der Physik*' (ibid., Vol. II, p. 99 et seqq.) was directly labelled 'popular' from the beginning; it was given in Königsberg in 1854. The speeches that Emil du Bois-Reymond collected in two volumes, *Reden*, are mostly ceremonial speeches given at the meetings of the Academy of Sciences in Berlin. Some of them were given in his capacity as the rector of the University of Berlin. The officious character is noticeable everywhere. A third great German speaker, the historian Heinrich von Sybel, could give speeches to industrial workers in Barmen on '*Die Lehren des heutigen Sozialismus und Kommunismus*' but zealously emphasised his academic position (Sybel 1885, p. 83). Otherwise his speeches were largely official orations.

43   These addresses often played a crucial role in the general scientific debate; in what follows, we will encounter such addresses by du Bois-Reymond, Virchow and many others. The *Versammlung deutscher Naturforscher und Ärzte*, which met for the first time in 1822, has been the subject of an exhaustive study by Pfetsch 1860, pp. 252–313; it is the most interesting part of a work that is otherwise filled with trivial figures and tables. This congress was the direct model for the British Association for the Advancement of Science; the man who conveyed the impulse from Germany was above all the mathematician Charles Babbage, who reported his impressions from the meeting of natural scientists in Berlin in 1828 in an article, 'Account of the Great Congress of Philosophers in Berlin' in the *Edinburgh Journal of Science* (his translation of the German name of the congress says a great

Among other things, the differences between the German and English conditions meant that the step from the specialists' popularisation to the system-builders' more or less popular summaries was a longer one in Germany; even as a populariser, the German specialist was wrapped up in the ceremonial costumes of official science.

But be that as it may, it is obvious that system-building as it turned out had an important driving force in popularisation and especially in the use of popularised science in ideological battles. Most systems that blossomed during Engels's most active period appeared with clear ideological terms and claims. Both the system-builder and the more specialised populariser submitted material and contributions to a continuing – or, rather, intensified – struggle between religious, political and ethical views.

5   Theories and Systems

So far, we have only viewed the systems from an external perspective. If, however, system creation had been only an extra-scientific matter and the increasing specialisation had been the only direction of internal development, the gap between nineteenth-century science and its outflow into the systems would have rapidly become abysmal.

Internally, however – in what I have called its theoretical determination – there is a drift toward, or a need of, maximally far-reaching theories. The power of this drift or need depends above all on the predominant situation in the sciences. Even a quick glance at the development of a range of sciences in the nineteenth century shows how the need of far-reaching theories (to say nothing of systems) was bound up with the arrival of revolutionary new theories or with the intensified antagonisms between competing theories within the same discipline. We have already seen one example in Marx's theory of society. There are, however, other similar cases that have drawn more attention: the principle of the conservation of energy, Darwinism, and so on.

In other words, this meant that under certain conditions in the history of science, the antagonism between specialisation and system-building also appeared as an *internal* antagonism. Continued specialisation was regarded as a threat to theoretical development. Many of the century's leading scientists expressed their distress over the fact that their areas of competence were so

---

deal about the differences in German and English vocabularies); Babbage 1829. Cf. also Babbage 1864 and Cardwell 1972, p. 59 et seqq.

limited. Hermann von Helmholtz – who nonetheless had an unusually broad range at his disposal – complained in a lecture from 1862 that not even the greatest polymath could master more than 'a small branch' (*ein kleines Theilgebiet*) since professional field after professional field had become specialties.[44] In the same spirit Rudolf Virchow, the originator of cellular pathology, declared fifteen years later that the competent scientist was a dilettante (*Halbwisser*) the moment they stepped outside their own branch.[45]

The risk thus lay in no longer being able to create more general theories, or to even grasp the connection between different areas of theory. No solution was seen in the collaboration between various groups of specialists – nor was any effort put into similar tasks in the various associations of scientists that already existed or were being inaugurated.

On the other hand, there were many who divulged hopes that progress could be made by studying what was called the philosophy that lay hidden in the various specialised theories. What was meant by that, rather, was the general conditions of the theories of knowledge and of science. Physiologist and populariser William Carpenter came forward with a great idea about how humanity interpreted nature; he regarded the unity among various branches of knowledge from a perspective of biological development.[46] T.H. Huxley studied the history of philosophy in depth and wrote essays on such figures and Hume and Berkeley in order to correctly grasp the sciences of his age.[47] Helmholtz turned to Kant.[48] Physicist John Tyndall formulated the philosophy that, in his opinion, lay hidden in the new branch of thermodynamics.[49]

The examples are numerous. The tendency is already clear: a philosophical, or rather an epistemological, platform was being sought from which, it was hoped, the diversity of the theories could be surveyed.

But why was help so rarely sought among the contemporary expert philosophers? The preference was for the history of philosophy. The expert philosophers, the university professors, had also come to appear as a type of specialist. It is true, of course, that many of them still spoke about all knowledge as Kant or Hegel once had. In Germany – and, moreover, in Berlin itself – the great standard-bearer of Hegelian philosophy, Karl Ludwig Michelet, was still

---

44   Helmholtz 1876, Vol. 1, p. 1.

45   Virchow 1877, p. 13.

46   Carpenter 1860, p. 366 et seqq.

47   T.H. Huxley 1897. Huxley gladly proclaims in the foreword: 'If you will lay your mind alongside the works of these great writers ... you will have had as much sound philosophical training as is good for any one but an expert'. Ibid., p. xii.

48   Cf. below, p. 168 et seqq.

49   See above all Tyndall 1870, p. xiv et seqq.

active. He was occupied with laying out his philosophical system well into old age; between 1876 and 1881 he published *Das System der Philosophie als exacter Wissenschaft* in five volumes. It seems to have had no effect outside the circle of expert philosophers. Philosophers close to Hegel turned up even in England, at the old English universities; it became a dominant orientation towards the end of the century through men such as T.H. Green, Herbert Bradley, Bernard Bosanquet and others.[50] They were able to exercise influence on research in the human sciences and the social sciences, but not in the natural sciences. Few, if any, seem to have sought a point of unity among all knowledge in their systematic commentaries.

Philosophy had thus become a specialty, and a different philosophy was being sought that was interspersed in research and the formation of theories.

With posterity's view from afar of the history of nineteenth-century science, it can be seen that the search for the philosophical foundation of the sciences was a meaningful and sound occupation. Many of the predominant controversies within and between the disciplines were largely dependent on incompatible conceptions of what constituted knowledge and good science, how theory related to empiricism and how the various theories were bound up or ought to have been.

In physics, the orthodox Newtonians asserted that every force had to have a corresponding type of matter; that was what the theory allowed and entailed. Their opponents, with Michael Faraday at the head, abandoned this notion – force was something real, something indestructible; it was linked to matter but not to a specific type of matter. Faraday could thus imagine something such as vibrations without vibrating matter. He also assumed that every kind of force could be converted to every other kind of force.[51]

The break from the thesis of the unambiguous connection between force and matter was a condition for getting rid of such hypothetical substances as heat matter, electric matter and so on, and thus for achieving the full theory of the indestructibility of force. But the difference between the older and the newer conception was not immediately dependent on new observations or experiments – on the other hand, the new conception made them possible – but on different interpretations of far-reaching categories such as 'force' and 'matter'.

The same would later apply to the transition from the concept of *force* to the concept of *energy* as the most general physical category (through which

---

50   On this topic, see the lucid account in Passmore 1957, pp. 46–94.
51   On this topic, see Agassi 1971, in particular p. 109 et seqq.

the theory of the indestructibility of force changed its name to the principle of conservation of energy).[52]

As we will see later, however, these discussions of the fundamental concepts of physics would be of great significance for the development of chemistry; for biologists, who prefer to express themselves in terms of matter and energy, they would have consequences as well. In other words, the path to the traditional problems in philosophy, whether they were materialist or idealist, empiricist or rational, always lay open.

In the discussions of these general matters, one of course often encounters an optimistic conception that the old questions that had previously only been speculated on were now on the way to being solved with sound empirical methods. W.R. Grove, who made such a strong impression on Marx and Engels, thus declared that modern science proceeded without exception from the facts and that it was new facts that would give rise to new solutions for old problems.[53] He thus assumed that the more facts that were gathered, the closer we would come to the definitive solution. Helmholtz was more sophisticated, but even he asserted that it was through increasing experience that we would come ever closer to an exact understanding of natural processes.[54]

But such statements – which naturally were legion in this period of optimism over development – were bound up with a conception that seemed to predominate throughout the nineteenth century without exception, namely that established, theoretically developed sciences could not undergo what would later (from the beginning of the twentieth century) be called fundamental crises – revolutions in the theoretical foundation itself. This meant that the more theoretically advanced a science was, the more certain it was that its foundations would remain for all time. Development must thus also mean that more and more disciplines would attain this secure position.

Later, we will see how essential the very absence of suspicion of possible fundamental crises was for the system-builders' profession. For the scientific specialists, this absence (which we can detect only with the benefit of hindsight) meant that the issues of epistemology and scientific theory appeared as implicit in existing science: it was only a matter of discovering them, bringing them to light and discussing them with the support of competent and reliable experiments and observations.

---

52   The most modern – and very illustrative – account on this topic is Elkana 1974. See in particular p. 8 et seqq.

53   Grove 1855, p. 1 et seq.

54   Helmholtz 1876, Vol. I, p. 9 et seqq.

These philosophical efforts by the scientists thus often bore the mark of chance and unresolved contradictions. At the same time, however, they brought to the fore the issues that were the centre of attention for the system-builders. There was thus a connecting path between specialists and systematists that made the systematists, if not reliable, then of interest to the specialists. Numerous specialists certainly hoped that the issue of the connections among all the branches of science would solve itself – or, rather, through the positive development of science. But for the time being, they had to take a position on problems that were still unsolved and controversial.

In the chapter immediately following, we will illuminate in more detail how the system-builders' questions about unity and connection would appear in some of the most controversial domains of nineteenth-century science. It is important to see, from the beginning, what foundation the many varied systems had in the science in question. It is almost trivially self-evident that they had *some* foundation, for the reason that every theoretical scientific work has a trace of systematics (i.e. an attempt at compiling knowledge into hypotheses and theories). But it is a matter of studying this foundation in more detail. It is a matter of seeing how the foundation has actually been laid, and it is a matter of testing whether, in the sciences – or at least in some central sciences – there are crucial conditions for the tremendous increase in system-building that occurred starting in the 1860s and was succeeded by a dramatic downturn only a few decades later.

The systems cannot be regarded only as ideological elaborations of loosely assembled knowledge, even less as poor repetitions of philosophies whose time had passed. Their ideological significance and imprint, their connections with older philosophical traditions, are obvious. But they also have support in the specialised sciences.

CHAPTER 6

Conservation of Energy, and Systems

1 The Problem

The principle of conservation of energy is a concept with many names. It is also called the first law of thermodynamics. There were physicists and philosophers who preferred the designation 'principle of the constancy of work'. Others preferred to speak of the constancy of movement. In the early history of the principle, people spoke of the law or theory of the indestructibility of force.

Prior to the theory of relativity, the principle of conservation of energy was expressed as energy being constant: it could neither be created nor destroyed. There were different forms of energy: mechanical movement, heat, electricity and magnetism; commonly, a special chemical energy or force – affinity – was also distinguished. Other divisions were also made: what they were is not the main point. The main point is that the forms of energy could pass into each other: heat could be converted into mechanical movement, such as in a steam engine; mechanical movement could be converted into electricity, such as in an electric motor; and so on. But *the sum total of energy remained the same.*

Modern physics words the same insight differently. Energy is not said to be constant; the sum total of mass and energy is constant. Energy has a certain mass, mass a certain energy, and mass can be converted to energy and vice versa. But the sum total of mass and energy is always the same.

The complicated and contradictory history of the principle of conservation of energy has been the subject of a number of accounts of the history of science. Many of them are distinguished by pronounced expertise and learning, from Ernst Mach's famous little monograph[1] to later studies by Hiebert,[2] Kuhn,[3] and Elkana.[4] Related subjects such as the concepts of force and fields and the development of thermodynamics, have also received detailed presentations; here, the names of Mary B. Hesse[5] and D.S.L. Cardwell[6] above all deserve mention.

---

1 *Die Geschichte und die Wurzel des Satzes von der Erhaltung der Arbeit* (Mach 1872). On its significance for Engels, see below, p. 413 et seq.
2 *The Historical Roots of the Principle of the Conservation of Energy* (Hiebert 1962).
3 'Energy Conservation as an Example of Simultaneous Discovery' (Kuhn 1955).
4 *The Discovery of the Conservation of Energy* (Elkana 1974).
5 *Forces and Fields* (Hesse 1966).
6 *From Watt to Clausius. The Rise of Thermodynamics in the Early Industrial Age* (Cardwell 1971).

© KONINKLIJKE BRILL NV, LEIDEN, 2023 | DOI:10.1163/9789004528796_009

Providing an account of this development once again, in rougher outline, would be superfluous. Attempting to overcome the irreconcilable ideas and opinions that emerge in the works in question would also be futile. My perspective is more limited: I want to see how the antagonism between specialisation and system-building emerges in and is influenced by the principle of conservation of energy. The formulation of this principle is not simply one of the great events of nineteenth-century physics; its significance for the development of the scientific conception of the world is enormous. In what follows, I will place the expressions and statements of the specialists and the system-builders alongside one another. I will provide examples of how the specialists, by keeping to their specialties, left loose threads hanging that the system-builders could seize hold of. I would, however, also like to show how some of the specialists were busy with developing what could be called partial systems, or theories of such scope that they became bits and pieces of entire worldviews. Beyond the theories and the empirical research, philosophical assumptions can be traced that were more rarely brought to light by the specialists themselves. The development of the principle of conservation of energy not only has a place in the history of a few successful scientists; its conditions also lie in the history of philosophy and it penetrated into the philosophies on its own beginning in the mid-nineteenth century.

2   Physics and Chemistry

The principle of conservation of energy touches immediately upon three fields of research: physics (mechanics included), chemistry and physiology. In this sense, it is interdisciplinary.

But during the early development of this principle, these fields were not three firmly demarcated specialties, fit into the same scholarly organisation and firmly marked off in relation to one another. The relation between them was particularly intricate. It would thus appear from Lavoisier onward, a former specialisation was being *conquered*, or rather the chasm that earlier had been established in the eighteenth century between the fields of physics and chemistry was being bridged.

But that is a separate history. It was extremely rare for the leading chemists of the eighteenth century to also be physicists, but the distinction between the fields of work was not due to any strict division of intellectual labour. Chemistry and physics developed in separate theoretical and practical contexts, and their institutional positions were not comparable. Chemistry was not, strictly speaking, a scientific specialty. It led an uncertain life in the universities as a sub-discipline in the medical faculties, where pharmacology gave it its *raison d'être*. But the field lay open for many more than just medics. The men of practical action – mining engineers and others – were making substantial contributions. In other words, its practical and material determination was strong: what was practicable also had to be theoretically plausible.

The predominant theory in chemistry – phlogiston theory – must be viewed in this light. It was not formulated in relation to Newton's theory of gravitation, the predominant theory in physics; at times it was determined in a manner that directly contradicted Newton's fundamental assumption, namely, that phlogiston was assumed to weigh less than nothing. The essential thing, however, is that chemistry had its own, relatively independent development for a time, when Lagrange, d'Alembert and many others were developing a mechanics that was mathematically complete.[7]

With Lavoisier's new, quantitatively determined theory of combustion, and more so with the developments in chemistry that had their basis in this theory, chemistry would join the scientific hierarchy in which mechanics constituted its foundation and starting point. The relation between chemistry and the various parts of physics became a theoretical issue of extreme importance. It would, however, also become a problematic relation that would occupy physicists and chemists throughout the nineteenth century.

The boundaries between both fields were constantly shifting. Heat played a key role here. As long as it was assumed that each force corresponded to a certain type of matter, a particular heat matter had also been assumed. Lavoisier regarded heat as a special element, and that conception did not lose followers until the mechanical theory of heat – with its close association to the principle of conservation of energy – broke through in the 1840s and 1850s. Heat had thus first been an object of study for chemists, and this was far more natural since the heat phenomena that were being more systematically studied were those that could be noted in connection with chemical reactions. It was thus a long

---

7   The relatively independent development of chemistry in the days of phlogiston theory is evident from the abundantly rich collection of examples in Partington 1962–64, Vol. III, *passim*. In a literature that is more focused on discussion or on directly posing problems, the question is often asked whether phlogiston theory accelerated or delayed the development of chemistry. Among popular accounts, Meyer, for example, gives the former answer (Meyer 1905, p. 139 et seq.) and Butterfield the latter (Butterfield 1957, Chap. XI). It is possible here to talk about a hypothetical question in the worst sense of the phrase. Lavoisier's theory is unthinkable without phlogiston theory, but it is equally unthinkable without the development of mechanics. A chemistry that developed directly out of the principles of Newtonian mechanics on the foundation of empirical material that chemists had in the eighteenth century could only be imagined with difficulty.

time before serious attention was paid to heat as a 'cosmic phenomenon'.[8] In its general content, however, heat was an object of study more for physicists than for chemists.

In the early nineteenth century, however, there was no strict division of labour between physicists and chemists to speak of. For this very reason, it was impossible for essential objects of study (for example the study of gases, which played as crucial a role in the development of the atomic theory in chemistry as it did for the mechanical theory of heat in physics) to be held in common. When scientists such as John Dalton or Joseph Louis Gay-Lussac are characterised as both physicists and chemists in textbooks, this means primarily that their main fields constituted a shared domain for the physics and chemistry at the time.

This scientific development, however, also meant that the areas traditionally and unambiguously assigned to physics and chemistry respectively turned out to interlock with each other. Electricity was a sub-domain of physics just as surely as the theory of elemental compounds belonged to chemistry. With electrolysis – as it was developed by Luigi Galvani and Alessandro Volta in the late eighteenth century – and a range of efforts up through Michael Faraday (known as both a physicist and a chemist), the intimate connection between electrical and chemical phenomena became clear. This was a development that was parallel in part to the one through which electricity and magnetism, two of the main fields of physics, were put in relation to each other. But the course of events is only parallel, not identical. The difference can be explained, at least to some extent, by the specialisation between physics and chemistry that was now in full swing. The results of studies by Hans Christian Ørsted, Faraday and others of the relation between electricity and magnetism became a theory for both: the electromagnetic theory.[9] A similar result in chemistry was Jöns Jakob Berzelius' electrochemical theory, in which he was in no way attempting to unify electricity and chemical reactions but was looking for an explanation of the chemical reactions in electricity (or, rather, in the electrical charges of the elements and radicals).[10] The difference is an essential one. No one was trying to reduce the theory of electricity to the theory of magnetism (or vice versa), but the chemists were trying to reduce the theory of chemical reactions to the

---

8   Cardwell 1971, p. 187.
9   Ørsted's discovery of electromagnetism has been the subject of particular interest through Joseph Agassi's well-known 'reconstruction' in Agassi 1963, p. 67 et seqq. On Faraday, see also Agassi 1971.
10   One modern monograph is Levere 1971. For a detailed account of research and discussions see also Partington 1962–64, Vol. IV, p. 168 et seqq.

theory of electricity. It can be seen how a scientific hierarchy was beginning to be established in which chemistry was assumed to sit at a higher (i.e. less fundamental) level than physics.

Berzelius was of course laying out his theory at a point in time when many stood out as both physicists and chemists (though not Berzelius himself).[11] But during the vehement discussions about electrochemical theory in the 1840s and 1850s it was almost exclusively a matter for chemists, who related it in part to the field of chemistry, where they commented as experts, and in part to the theory of electricity, which they assumed as given and developed in another field of research. Nothing similar ever happened during physicists' discussions of the relation between electricity and magnetism.[12]

We can find a striking example here of what could happen during a process of specialisation, when the two fields that develop into independent specialties are not based on a shared theory (as physics and chemistry became in the twentieth century).[13] The great discussions among the ageing Berzelius, Frankland in England, Dumas, Laurent, Gerhardt and Wurtz in France and many others regarding the plausibility of the electrochemical theory almost never concerned what electricity was – that fell outside their fields of expertise and work – while the results of the discussion were an extraordinary contribution to the theoretical development of chemistry. Berzelius's once quite advanced theory of radicals, which would prove that even organic compounds could be understood based on electrochemical theory, was discussed here, and the molecular theory, later so crucial for chemistry, was developed against it. According to Berzelius, the radicals in organic compounds corresponded to the elements in inorganic compounds: in other words, they constituted the fixed building blocks of the organic compounds and their electric charges determined how they could bond with other substances. Back in the 1830s, Dumas had shown that the positively charged hydrogen atom in certain organic compounds could be replaced with a negatively charged chlorine atom without changing the chemical properties, thus developing his own type theory.[14] From this gradually emerged molecular theory, which was the only way the concept

---

11   Berzelius received his education in the faculty of medicine, and worked within it (at Karolinska institutet) throughout his working life. On Berzelius's life and habits, see Jorpes 1970.

12   This naturally does not mean that everyone who regarded themselves – and were regarded – as competent physicists accepted electromagnetism completely. In some of the earlier interpretations of the constancy of energy (or, more precisely, of force), electricity and magnetism were regarded as two distinct 'forces' alongside mechanical force, heat and so on. See for example Grove 1855, p. 7 et seqq.

13   Levere 1971, p. vii.

14   On this topic, cf. Partington 1962–64, Vol. IV, p. 364 et seqq. and Levere 1971, p. 158 et seqq.

of *molecule* could consistently be distinguished from the concept of *atom*.[15] The radical could also be defined in relation to the molecule: the radical was a 'remnant' of the molecule.[16]

The electrochemical theory was thus rejected in the form it had taken with Berzelius. This entire dramatic course of events took place with electricity as a kind of sleeping partner. Against electrochemical theory were placed others that took their inspiration and models from other fields of physics: Laurent's *Méthode de chymie* thus drew attention to the 'number and structure' of atoms, and the model Laurent used – though without developing it into a full theory – was undoubtedly taken from mechanicism.[17]

The issue of the reduction of chemistry to physics was in fact just as controversial as it was difficult to grasp for a large part of the nineteenth century. The whole question of chemical affinity revolved around this problem – which was, however, often formulated in an extraordinarily elusive manner and could thus also be deferred by many advocates of infallible empiricism to the domains of a more speculative natural science or (perhaps preferably) of a future, more advanced chemistry. We have an excellent example of this in André Wurtz's four-volume *Dictionnaire de chimie pure et appliqué* (1868–78), which is a magnificent and, moreover, extremely influential attempt at compiling the results of chemistry at that time. As regards the issue of how the course of events in chemistry is ultimately to be explained, on the other hand, a marked restraint is displayed. The introduction to the article on affinity, authored by George Salet, stated with characteristic uncertainty that affinity – whatever it is – is the cause of chemical compounds.[18] Further on in the article, Salet went through various hypotheses about the nature of affinity. He concluded that every theory of affinity would be premature at the stage the research was in at the time. The connection with electricity was obvious, and it was equally clear that heat could be converted into electrical current and chemical force. In due time, therefore, a mechanical theory of electricity and of affinity could be laid out

---

15   For quite a long time, it was possible to speak of a 'molecule' as synonymous with a 'compound atom' and assume that the atom worked in the same way whether it was 'simple' or 'compound'. See for example Regnault and Strecker 1853, Vol. I, p. 668. In Vol. 2, however, a more modern concept of the molecule was introduced (Regnault and Strecker 1863, Vol. 2, p. 31).

16   An extraordinarily lucid contemporary depiction of this development can be found in Roscoe and Schorlemmer 1877–84, Vol. III, pp. 1–35.

17   Laurent 1854, p. 321 et seq.

18   'On appelle *affinité* la cause quelle qu'elle soit des combinations chimiques'. G.S. (George Salet), *'Affinité'*, in Wurtz, Vol. I:1, p. 69.

just as a mechanical theory of heat already had been. But one great difficulty remained: *'c'est le fait de l'attraction'* (the fact of attraction). With the optimism typical of his time, however, Salet believed that the question could gradually become the subject of experimental verification.[19]

The general world of ideas that can be continually glimpsed in Salet's argument has to do with the principle of conservation of energy, which has an obvious applicability in chemistry. In the original theory of the indestructibility of force, 'chemical force' was one of those included in the great balance sheet. But in a way, it occupied an exceptional position. This was bound up with the specialisation of chemistry; ascertaining the nature of chemical force or affinity was the task of the chemists, and – as we have seen – chemists were deeply divided. Nor did the heated discussions they held really fit into the pattern that the thesis of the indestructibility of force entailed. The chemists discussed whether electricity was the *cause* of affinity, but according to the general theory affinity, like electricity, was one of the forces that could be converted into the other forces.

We can see the latter train of thought most clearly in W.R. Grove, the first successful populariser of the principle of conservation of energy. Grove did not speak about forces or energy but about the various 'affections' of matter; this was bound up with his heavily pursued empirical – or, perhaps, almost positivist – ideal that prevented him from speaking about causes, but only about relations among facts.[20] In this matter, however, this did not change his interpretation. He counted six different 'affections': mechanical (movement), heat, light, electricity, magnetism and chemical affinity, each of which was exchangeable with each of the others.[21] He thus did not assume that affinity would have any special place in the theory. On the other hand, he saw it as the problem child among the six in the sense that they had 'the least definite idea' about it. Its effects differed so strongly from the effects of the other 'affections' that a boundary was drawn – perhaps not fully logically, according to Grove – between the physical and the chemical. It could be imagined vaguely as 'a molecular motion'. Its close connection with electricity was known, but affinity and electricity were nonetheless separate magnitudes.[22]

---

19   Ibid., p. 77 et seq. For similar lines of thought, see the articles *'Atomicité'* by A.W. (André Wurtz), ibid., Vol. I:1, p. 448 et seqq. and *'Chaleur'* by G.S. (George Salet), ibid., Vol. I:2, p. 813 et seqq.

20   Grove 1855, p. 5 et seqq.

21   Ibid., p. 42.

22   Ibid., p. 37 et seq.

Grove's argument shows, in all its vagueness, that the general theory he advocated was not immediately compatible with the primary problem of chemistry. For chemists, affinity never stood out as one of six similar 'affections'.

If Grove were to have granted any of these 'affections' a unique position, it would have been mechanistic movement. He was very cautious, but he assumed that all forces could be shown to be different types of movement. In other words, he outlined a strictly mechanistic programme.

For Hermann von Helmholtz, a reduction of this kind was the main point. It was the primary task of theoretical physics to show that all the forces of the natural sciences could be reduced to the force of Newtonian mechanics.[23] The relation of chemical affinity to the physical forces did not thereby change. According to Helmholtz, *Verwandtschaft* (affinity) was only the chemists' technical term for a particular type of attractive force.[24]

For the time being, however, we do not need to go deeper into these questions. The examples from chemistry and physics ought to be enough to show that, at least from the 1840s and several decades following, there was an asymmetrical relationship between the disciplines of physics and chemistry. Physics was at the service of a universal theory that also included chemistry. But the problems that dominated chemistry were not simply compatible with this universal theory – the theory of the indestructibility of force – but concerned primarily the relation between affinity and various physical forces, particularly electricity.

It is thus not the process of specialisation as such – the distinction between the physicists' and chemists' fields of competence and of work – that caused the asymmetry between the theories and problems of physics and chemistry. Specialisation reinforced the asymmetry and was simultaneously accelerated by it, but its actual foundation was that physics and chemistry did not have a properly functioning shared theory. For the time being, chemistry could not be unresistingly incorporated into the domains of the principle of conservation of energy, as long as the relation of chemical reactions to physical forces were so fundamentally and notoriously unclear as they actually were. The uncertainty was reinforced by the fact that chemists were more and more rarely familiar with the secrets of contemporary physics.

In this regard, the relation between physics and chemistry, through its own ambiguity, could tempt system-builders into looking for the point of unity.

---

23   See for example *Über die Erhaltung der Kraft*, reprinted in Helmholtz 1882, p. 16. See also
       Helmholtz 1876, p. 111. For a more detailed investigation, cf. Elkana 1974, p. 114 et seqq. and
       in particular p. 129.
24   Helmholtz 1876, p. 109.

This is also what happened. One of the many tasks of all the systems that were rapidly constructed on the grounds of the principle of conservation of energy was to show that chemical affinity could be incorporated into the hierarchy of forces. For the system-builders, the harmony itself was a necessary requirement: as chemistry interlocked with physics, so would biology interlock with chemistry. However, this unity could be achieved through rather peculiar detours. We see, for example, how Ludwig Büchner, who so assiduously chose examples from chemistry when arguing about organic life, let affinity be absorbed into and disappear among the forces of physics – which, according to his unusually generous treatment, were eight in number – but nonetheless later in the same account spoke about a particular *'chemische Thätigkeit'* (chemical motion), a term that is not found in the technical language of professional chemists and that Büchner left hanging in midair.[25] This is an example of poor system-building.

When Herbert Spencer faced the same task, he went about it more cautiously. He referred completely to the authority of W.R. Grove, asserting that he was only reproducing the viewpoints in the aforementioned work by Grove. As regards chemistry, however, there is an interesting difference. As we have seen, Grove had depicted chemical affinity as the problem child among the forces, one still relatively unknown. For Spencer, on the other hand, it was completely obvious; its connections with the other forces scarcely needed even to be pointed out![26]

A somewhat later system-builder, Eugen Dühring, incorporated chemistry into the desired unity in another, equally simple manner. The indestructibility of forces became an issue for physics; chemistry, on the other hand, presumes the indestructibility of *matter*.[27] Since force and matter are assumed to be inseparable magnitudes, physics and chemistry would if anything come to be regarded as different but complementary perspectives on the same object.

What these system-builders said differed on crucial points, but nonetheless not definitively, from what contemporary physicists were saying about chemistry. But they lacked the physicists' professional position, and it was against them and not the physicists that the professional chemists directed their criticism. From a scientific viewpoint, it would have been more fruitful if, for example, Justus von Liebig had taken up the standpoints on the chemical force

---

25 Büchner 1876, p. 23 et seqq. In earlier editions, for example, Büchner 1855, Büchner had not yet gotten on to the question of the different forces of the principle of conservation of energy.
26 Spencer 1862, Vol. 1 (First Principles), p. 263.
27 Dühring 1878, p. 4 et seq.

that Grove or Helmholtz had constructed instead of responding to the opinions of Jacob Moleschott and Ludwig Büchner.[28] But the latter had much more far-reaching intents – they wanted to bring materialism to a successful close – and they were not speaking to an audience of specialists.

Nor, for Liebig, was placing what he called the chemical force among the physical forces the main issue, but distinguishing it from the vital force. He brought out his argument before the theory of the indestructibility of force had become generally known (though he himself published the pioneering work, Robert Mayer's *Bemerkungen über die Kräfte der unbelebten Natur* in his journal in 1842) but its dissemination and development did not lead him to later change his manner of expression. It was above all in *Animal Chemistry, or, Organic Chemistry in Its Applications to Physiology and Pathology* and the popular and extraordinarily influential *Chemical Letters* that he laid out his ideas on the chemical force as against the vital force. His comments are especially interesting because they so clearly developed the perspective of the pure chemist, as yet incompatible with that of the physicist and a poor foundation for the system-builders' passion for unity.

In a simple and radical manner, Liebig distinguished between external and internal relations in bodies. It was a distinction that had previously been cultivated by the Romantic natural philosophers, among others.[29] Only in later editions of *Chemical Letters* would he supplement the determination of 'the external form' with 'the mechanical course'.[30] Internal conditions, however, are explained using only two different forces: the chemical force and the vital force. Though Liebig may have been discussing organisms here, his perspective lacks all connection with what the physicists of the time usually established. The chemical force and the vital force were thus regarded as working upon contact (and not over distances) – on the other hand, he did not utter a word on other direct forces. The chemical force and the vital force, he said, lie closer to each other than any other causes or forces in nature.[31]

---

28   It was certainly not Liebig who took up the fight; it was Jacob Moleschott, whose *Der Kreislauf des Lebens* was a polemic against *Chemische Briefe*. Büchner also came later with views on Liebig's popular account, and Liebig devoted a great deal of attention to the criticism in later editions of his work.

29   Exemplary here were Schelling's early natural philosophical works; see for example Schelling 1/2: 185 et seq.

30   In the fourth edition (Liebig 1859, Vol. I, p. 17) the sentence from the first edition (Liebig 1844, p. 16) '... *die Kenntniss der äusseren Formen befriedigt sie /die Physiologen/ nicht mehr* ...' was supplemented thus: '... *die Kenntniss der äusseren Formen und der mechanischen Vorgänge befriedigt sie die Physiologen in unserer Zeit nicht mehr* ...'.

31   Liebig 1844, p. 22.

The vital force is interesting in another context, one we will soon investigate. The chemical force as Liebig depicts it is not related to the forces of physics. This is an extraordinarily important condition.

The asymmetry, however, between physics and chemistry, between physical and chemical forces, did not remain unchanged in the decades after Liebig first made his statements. As we have seen, the discussions of electrochemical theory and the development of a solid molecular theory did not create the asymmetry, but the attempt at rationally demarcating chemistry from physics can be said to have been an important result. It is striking that physicists, chemists – and system-builders – long avoided drawing any real boundary between physics and chemistry, though they seem to have presumed a more than temporary difference between the fields. They could argue, as John Tyndall did in his 1854 Royal Institution lecture 'On the Study of Physics', where he said that what we call physics is in fact the part of physics lying between astronomy and chemistry. Whereas astronomy is physics that deals with 'masses of enormous weight' and chemistry is physics that deals with atoms and molecules, physics in a limited sense has what lies between the world of the great and the world of the small as its object of study.[32] This very simple division according to the size of the object is of course completely unsatisfactory. Among the genuinely physical phenomena Tyndall names are, for example, light and heat – phenomena Tyndall really would not have wanted to explain as processes in medium-sized objects.

Once the concept of the molecule had developed in chemistry, it entailed a possibility of rationally determining physics and chemistry for each other. The concept of the molecule had been secured in physics – especially through the mechanical theory of heat – and the relation between atoms and molecules had thus been demonstrated in chemistry. Physics could now be determined as the science of molecules, and chemistry as the science of atoms, as for example August Kekulé von Stradonitz did.[33] This division was evidently in no way derived from the principle of conservation of energy – that is, it did not have its origin in the thesis on chemical force or affinity – but it was bound up with the idea that the real object of study for chemistry was the force or forces that determined the atomic composition of the molecules. This division also presumed that mechanics was regarded as a fundamental discipline separate not only from chemistry but also from molecular physics.

---

32   Tyndall 1879, Vol. I, p. 334.
33   Kekulé 1878, p. 12.

We have therefore arrived at what looks, at least, like a real scientific hierarchy with mechanics at the bottom followed by physics and chemistry, perhaps co-lateral, perhaps with physics lower (the latter point is notoriously unclear).

Engels, who devoted particular attention to the question of the relation between physics and chemistry, concurred with this division. We will see later what consequences this had for his interpretation.

3   The Vital Force: Mechanism, Chemistry or Biology?

Studying the relations between physics and chemistry (which are difficult to grasp, to say the least) moreover as two separate problem areas and two emerging specialties is of particular interest because the question, as far as I can see, is in no way ideologically controversial. All the external influences having to do with commitment to one worldview or another can thus be ignored.

At the same time, on the other hand, all the other, more central boundary issues in nineteenth-century science were controversial questions between competing ideologies, which could concern the relation between organic and inorganic chemistry, chemistry and biology, biology and the human sciences.

Nor did the interest, with all its ramifications, in the principle of conservation of energy – or, to use the older term, the indestructibility of force – have anything to do with the relation of chemical force to physical forces. On the other hand, it was intimately bound up with the question of the relation of biology, and physiology in particular, to physics and chemistry.

Yehuda Elkana asserted that the principle of conservation of energy in the general theoretical formulation it received from Helmholtz has its conditions in the problem of vital force. He found it important that both Robert Mayer and Helmholtz had medical training and thus focused their attention on the question of the relation between the organic and the inorganic as it was being discussed with inexhaustible energy among German physicians in the 1830s and 1840s. Through its very broad content, the ambiguous, somewhat nebulous word *Kraft* led Helmholtz into the universal problem that made the development of the concept of *energy* possible.[34]

Without a doubt, the question of vital force was a crucial and central one for everyone who used the principle of the conservation of energy in an ideological context. But it would also have played a crucial role for theoretical development.

---

34   Elkana 1974, p. 97 et seqq., p. 122 et seqq.

In the perspective of system versus specialisation, the relation between biology on the one hand and physics and chemistry on the other appears as one of
the most essential and simultaneously the most intricate. Studying the boundary between the living and the dead was a theoretical task of the greatest dignity, and for most of the system-builders of the nineteenth century it was also
crucial for the entire structure of their systems. If the living were regarded as
something new in principle – that is, a field that could not be explained in the
terms used in physics and chemistry – the scientific hierarchy also had to be
depicted as split and nature as heterogeneous. For a large part of the nineteenth century, the universal problem of the reduction of theories focused on
the special problem of reducing biological theories to physical and chemical
ones.

In fact, however, this special problem contained a number of partial problems that belonged to various areas of research that would also soon develop
into specialties. This meant that the question of the relation between the
organic and the inorganic appeared differently depending on the area of competence from which it was viewed. It also meant that the degree of its difficulty – indeed, its very complexity – was determined by the perspective one
held through their expertise.

The battle over vitalism and mechanicism concerned two extremely different, coherent yet still distinct and separate problems. On the one hand it
was what for the sake of simplicity we will call the *chemical problem*, which
concerned the relation between organic and inorganic compounds, and the
relation between chemical processes inside and outside the organism. On the
other hand, it concerned the *mechanical problem*: could organic processes
be regarded as complex expressions for the force mechanicism was speaking
about? The asymmetry between physics and chemistry in the nineteenth century appears more clearly in the discussions about vital force than anywhere
else.

In the specialist perspective, there is a substantial difference between the
chemical and the mechanical problem. The major specialists in the former
were chemists: scientists such as Berzelius and Liebig, Pasteur and Berthelot.
When the biologists – or the physiologists, who are primarily the subject here –
took up the chemical problem, they referred to the chemists as authorities. The
mechanical problem was to a much greater extent the biologists' own affair.
Despite everything there were not many who, like Helmholtz, could act as
sovereign authorities in both physics and physiology. Physicists who had no
physiological training could not comment on organic versus inorganic without
going outside their field and joining the band of system-builders (which some,
for example John Tyndall, actually did). The mechanistic debate was thus to

a great extent the biologists' own debate. Mechanicism played the same role there as the theory of electricity did for the chemists in the controversy surrounding the electrochemical theory: it was assumed to be a given mass of knowledge that was to be related to their own field of specialisation. The fact that numerous biologists were particularly at home in physics did not change this.

The reason for the difference is not difficult to find. The distance between biology and chemistry was, despite everything, markedly shorter than the distance between biology and mechanics; moreover, organic chemistry was undergoing a restless, and in part contradictory, development at the time: there was no predominant and settled opinion in the field to refer to as there was in significant parts of mechanics.

In all other respects, organic chemistry developed into its own specialisation soon after the middle of the century. Berzelius and Liebig had commented on all the problems of chemistry with self-evident authority, but in the generation after Liebig there were more who regarded themselves as either entirely or to a great extent specialised in organic or inorganic chemistry. August Kekulé von Stradonitz emerged only as an organic chemist (it was he, as well, who marked off organic chemistry as 'the chemistry of carbon compounds') in works such as his great and incomplete *Lehrbuch der organ-ischen Chemie oder Chemie der Kohlenstoffverbindungen*. Professorial chairs of organic chemistry also began to be established. The first holder of such a professorship in the United Kingdom was Carl Schorlemmer. When he and his colleague in Manchester, H.E. Roscoe, authored the colossal six-volume *A Treatise of Chemistry*, it was natural that Roscoe – a specialist in inorganic chemistry – would be responsible for the earlier parts and Schorlemmer for the later.[35]

This specialisation would have no immediate significance for the discussion on vital force, but it marked who were experts on the chemical problem. The chemical problem was the problem of the chemists, and of the organic chemists in particular; it remained for the physiologists to evaluate what significance the chemists' conclusions could have for the entire complex of problems in the vital force.

In this complex of problems, the chemical problem itself played a subordinate role. If it is believed that the concept of vital force is primarily linked to organic chemistry, then the development in which Schwann's cell theory and Helmholtz's *On the Conservation of Force* played such a crucial role cannot be

---

35   On this topic, cf. Roscoe 1892, p. viii, and Roscoe 1895, p. 395.

understood. At the same time, however, the chemical problem is the more concrete one. Later on in the century, it obtained a more dominant position due to the great development of organic chemistry: it was then that the idea of laboratory demonstrations of the basis of life in the proteins began to be played with in earnest.

But the view of the organism had also thoroughly changed by then. We have already seen how the predominant understanding looked at the beginning of the century.[36] The parts of the organism are thus possible only in relation to the whole; each part is both the cause and effect of the properties in the other parts, and each part is the organ or tool for the whole and the other parts. On a more concretely biological level, this understanding meant that a quantity for the organisms' wholly unique processes and conditions was assumed. This concerned heredity and the whole of development from seed or egg to complete organism, and it concerned all the complicated processes that hold the organism in balance.[37]

As long as this perspective was held, the question of the chemical composition of organisms naturally appeared essential but not crucial. It was actually only the chemists themselves – Berzelius, Liebig, and others – who placed primary importance on organic chemistry in the debate around vital force.

In this way, it can be understood why the early syntheses of organic compounds attracted so little attention from biologists.[38] Friedrich Wöhler's synthesis of urea in 1828 – the first of its kind generally acknowledged – had a long wait for commentary. Johannes Müller, one of the absolutely central figures of the debate, was responsible for one of the earliest when in a *Jahresbericht* (annual report) on advances in anatomy and physiology for 1833 declared that Wöhler's synthesis was of 'immense significance' for physiology.[39] Müller, however, did not imagine that the demonstrated possibility of synthesising compounds that otherwise only occurred in organisms would change the view of the relation between organic and inorganic at a stroke. When, in his influential *Elements of Physiology*, he analysed his approach, he carefully distinguished between the questions of organic matter and of the functions of the organism.[40] Only the former question, of course, was directly affected by Wöhler's synthesis. Müller asserted – and sought support in Berzelius here – that the difference between organic and inorganic compounds had not been eliminated.

---

36   Above, p. 63 et seqq.
37   For earlier formulations, see Kant 5:286 et seqq. and Blumenbach 1788, p. 2.
38   Cf. Liedman 1966, p. 206 et seqq.
39   J. Müller 1834, p. 4.
40   J. Müller 1838, p. 1 et seq.

Urea 'can be scarcely considered as organic matter, being rather an excretion than a component of the animal body'.[41]

These biologists thus held fast to the thesis that there was a difference in principle between organic (or genuinely organic) and inorganic compounds.[42] They sought support for this thesis above all in Berzelius – they did not declare themselves to be authorities – but they thereby succeeded in thoroughly turning the question of the relation between organic and inorganic into a question of the unique functioning of organisms.[43] The fact that organic compounds can only be produced in the organism must be due to the fact that the organism functions differently than inorganic matter.

We can clearly see this in Müller's textbook when he proceeds to the question of the nature of the organism and of life. Organic processes are unique primarily through their teleological character: it is thus the seemingly goal-oriented interaction between the organs and the organic unity he has in mind. The chemical processes in the organism are thereby also subordinate to the organic whole. In inorganic nature, all chemical processes take place in accordance with the laws of affinity, but in the organism *'noch etwas Anderes'* (something else) comes about that changes the combinations.[44]

Müller wrote this at a time when his belief in 'imponderables' – special heat matter, electric matter and so on – was still unshaken. The theory of the indestructibility of force was yet unborn, and Müller could thus assume that the specific teleological character of the organic processes was due either to a particular imponderable (some kind of special life material) or to a unique force, a vital force. To bring some order into his argument, it must be assumed that he was saying that the potential force would be immaterial as opposed to the hypothetically assumed materiality of life matter.[45]

Müller's line of thought, as representative as it was influential, clearly shows that for biologists the question of the relation between organic and inorganic compounds was a subordinate one. The overriding problem concerned the relation between the organism and its parts, the organs.

For the chemists who joined the discussion, the relations appeared otherwise: it was a natural, almost trivial result of their specialisation.

We have already encountered Liebig's argument. For Liebig, it was the relation between chemical force and vital force that constituted the core of the

---

41   Ibid., p. 3.
42   Tiedemann 1830, p. 91 et seq.
43   Treviranus 1831, p. 4305 et seq.
44   J. Müller 1838, p. 4.
45   Ibid., p. 24.

complex of problems. If a clear picture could be gotten of the relation, it would be possible to get to grips with the question of the relation between organic and inorganic. In other words, for Liebig, it was the state of research in organic chemistry that determined the situation in the discussion of vital force.

This is why Liebig defined the question as concerning which chemical processes within the organism could be identified with processes outside it, and which appeared unique in principle. The former could be regarded as effects of chemical force, the latter of vital force. We can understand the role of oxygen in respiration or of hydrochloric acid in digestion with our knowledge of the properties of oxygen and hydrochloric acid outside the living organism. The same must also apply to the compounds that are of course only found within organisms but that could be synthesised in modern chemistry (by that time, Wöhler's synthesis had gained numerous successors).[46]

There are, however, processes within the organism that not only lack counterparts in inorganic nature but could never be imitated in the laboratory. 'Chemistry will never be in a position to produce an eye, a hair, or a leaf'.[47]

It appears here as if Liebig – like Müller – came to a halt before the teleological character of the processes of life. He did not, however, bring teleological reflections into the argument but kept strictly to his aspect as a chemist. On the whole, he asserted that it was the vital force that regulated the chemical processes in the organism. The chemical force, as we know it from inorganic nature, is of course also active in the organism – the cause of two bodies with similar composition combining is always the chemical force – but in the organism it is subordinate to the vital force.[48]

In *Animal Chemistry*, Liebig – like Müller earlier – took up the question of the materiality of the vital force. The problem of vital force would be simplified if we regarded it as the property of a certain kind of matter.[49] In *Chemical Letters*, he did not discuss this problem at all. It is far too risky to assume that it was the theory of the indestructibility of force that made Liebig avoid it. Rather, he let it come out in its later and more popular representation.

---

46   Liebig 1844, p. 22 et seq.
47   Ibid., p. 24.
48   Ibid., above all p. 135 et seq., p. 145 et seqq.
49   Liebig 1842, p. 282.

4   Organisms and Teleology

The fully developed theory of the indestructibility of force would, however, soon enough have effects on the chemical problem as Liebig formulated it. But these effects were indirect rather than direct. The entire question of vital force was changing. Prior to that, the understanding of what constituted and distinguished the organism had undergone substantial development.

Theodor Schwann's thesis that all living beings are constructed of cells entailed much more for the complex of problems around vital force than the early syntheses in organic chemistry. Namely, this simple thesis itself was associated with a new perspective on the functioning of organisms. Against the predominant idea that the organism must ultimately be regarded as a complex system of dissimilar organs that act together, Schwann set the thesis that the nature of the organism is determined by the diversity of similar cells. First and foremost, the problem of the relation between organic and inorganic was thus greatly simplified. The starting point was no longer the body's complex and specific tools but its seemingly undifferentiated smallest components. The relation between the parts and the whole no longer had an immediately teleological character – the part serving the whole – and all questions concerning the relation between organic and inorganic, including those of organic chemistry, became primarily questions of the relation between simple cells and inorganic matter.

Schwann set forth his idea in *Microscopical Researches into the Accordance in the Structure and Growth of Animals and Plants*, where he developed what he called the 'Theory of Cells'. Its task was to demonstrate a shared principle of development (*Bildungsprinzip*) for the elementary parts, or cells, of all plants and animals.[50] Previously there had been a strict differentiation between various parts of the organism, and in particular the animal body – external tissues, muscles, nerves and so on had thus been treated as different magnitudes in principle – and one consequence, according to Schwann, had been the assumption that it was the organism that joined all the 'molecules' together into a differentiated unity in a manner that met the demands of the physiological functions.[51]

This understanding easily led to what Schwann called 'the teleological view': the organism is formed and functions through a mystical force that directs and regulates all organic processes towards a definite goal, namely the continued

---

50   Schwann 1839, p. 191. On cell theory, cf. Klein 1936 for historical data; see further also Canguilhem 1967, p. 43 et seqq. and Duchesneau 1975, p. 404 et seqq.

51   Schwann 1839, p. 192.

existence and development of the organism. The alternative was 'the physical view', according to which the 'basic forces' were essentially the same as that of inorganic nature – to be precise, in that they operate blindly and in accordance with necessity (i.e. mechanically) and that like 'the physical forces' they were determined by matter.[52]

When Schwann subsequently attempted to argue for the physical view, he concentrated on the issue of cell formation itself and cellular function. He drew parallels with the formation of crystals with the intent to show that the cell could be explained in principally the same way as the inorganic crystal. He saw the cause of cell formation in a particularly plastic force that, in a strictly mechanistic fashion, he classified as a form of the force of attraction. Crystal formation was also the result of attraction; behind both the cells of biology and the crystals of chemistry the same basic mechanical force could thus be glimpsed.[53]

The homogeneous cells, however, were joined together into differentiated organisms. Schwann treated this greater, more complicated issue in more vague terms; he pointed out that there were striking similarities between organisms and aggregates of crystals.[54]

What Schwann had developed with this was less a complete *Theorie der Zellen* (theory of the cell) than a mechanistic perspective of the organism, which meant that he clearly and unambiguously subordinated the chemical problem to the mechanical in the same way that Johannes Müller and other vitalists viewed the chemical problem in the light of teleology. The opposition between mechanical and teleological was, without exception, the primary opposition for the biologists; the chemical problem was the secondary one. It is therefore completely reasonable to view Liebig's approach to the problems of the vital force as essentially a function of his specialisation in chemistry, whereas on the other hand the rather tepid estimation by most biologists of Wöhler's synthesis can largely be explained by the fact that as biologists, they did not regard the nature of organic compounds as a primary issue.

The mildly surprising result was thus that in the discussion that preceded (and in part conditioned) the development of the principle of conservation of energy, like the discussion that immediately followed it, the connection

---

52   Ibid., p. 221 et seq. Schwann in fact says that organic force, like physical ones, is determined *'mit der Existenz der Materie'*. It is thus not a statement that the *chemical composition* of matter determines the organic forces but a more general and vague one in which chemistry is left out of the account.

53   Ibid., p. 239 et seqq.

54   Ibid., p. 253 et seqq.

between biology (or, rather, physiology) and physics was more immediate and vivid than the one between biology and chemistry.

Elkana drew attention to the fact that the close connection between physiology and physics was a condition for the development of the principle of conservation of energy in the form it obtained through Helmholtz. Like Schwann, Helmholtz had belonged to the circle around Johannes Müller in Berlin for several years, and years of study of the problem of the vital force lay behind his work *Über die Erhaltung der Kraft* (On the Conservation of Force). Müller the vitalist thus assembled around him a number of researchers not only with a fundamental mechanistic conception but also – and this is no less important – solid insights into physics.[55]

Even though this combination of knowledge was not typical – in England and France, it occurred hardly at all – it had far-reaching consequences for the entire discussion around vital force.

Against Schwann's mechanistic perspective stood Müller's vitalism; the discussion was thus between two viewpoints that were clearly distinct but nonetheless belonged to the same relatively isolated tradition of research. Müller's conception was developed above all by another of his most outstanding students, Jacob Henle. In important parts of his *Allgemeine Anatomie* (General Anatomy), Henle took Schwann's *Mikroskopische Untersuchungen* (Microscopic Studies) as his starting point. Even though he sought to correct Schwann's account on a number of points, he nevertheless accepted in substance the theory of the cell that Schwann had outlined.[56] On the other hand, he polemicised against Schwann's main thesis, namely that the crucial characteristics of life could be found in the simple cell. In the organism, the cell was subordinate to the whole: 'The sum of cells is an *organism*, and the organism *lives* as long as the parts serve the whole'. This relation of cell to organism showed that it was futile to explain the organic using physical forces. It is true that Henle also took support for his thesis from the idea that organic compounds differed from inorganic ones, but the essential point in his argument was nonetheless that he sought to develop Müller's teleological perspective based on the new understanding of the cell. He asserted, therefore, that the individual cell was always an incidental quantity in relation to the organism. The cells could multiply and the organism grow without the signs of life diminishing. The cells were consumed and replaced after a period of time. The organism was thus more than

---

55   Elkana 1974, p. 97 et seqq. Elkana, however, did not devote enough attention to Liebig's unique position as a chemist; see p. 103 et seqq.
56   Henle 1844, pp. 150–216. The criticism in particular is formulated on p. 209 et seq.

a conglomerate of cells, and the order of the cells in the organism was not a result of their own activity but of the organism's overall effect in accordance with a plan to which functions such as the replacement of cells belonged.

Henle therefore started from Müller's position; he sought to adapt it to the new conditions of research in physiology. In developing the vitalist standpoint, however, he went further than Müller. He unhesitatingly asserted that what he called the organic 'idea' was independent of matter – a question Müller in general did not want to take a position on.[57]

The question of the materiality of the vital force was not crucial to vitalism, however; it could be claimed or rejected without its position within biology changing. This was an essential position. A system-builder could not be content without a clear answer to such a question, since it played a role in their entire system. On the other hand, a biologist within a relatively isolated tradition of research was not guided in their work by this question; in other words, Henle did not do things differently than Müller simply because he assumed the immateriality of the vital force or of the idea.

But the vitalist tradition was not the strongest one among Müller's colleagues and successors. The mechanistic perspective was represented with extraordinary vigour by Helmholtz, Emil du Bois-Reymond and – to a certain extent – Rudolf Virchow. It was developed from another direction by Rudolf Hermann Lotze, one of the most consistent mechanists.

All of them came forth with an accomplished reductionist programme. The forces at work in the organism could be traced back to the force of mechanics. A reduction to chemistry or to such physical fields as the theory of electricity were therefore not enough. It was assumed that these fields, in turn, could be reduced to mechanics.

Elkana has shown how this programme guided Helmholtz, who assumed that the Newtonian concept of force (mass × acceleration) was a fundamental concept in mechanics and that physics could be reduced to mechanics. He also assumed that the concept of *vital force* – in the sense it was given in the Müllerian tradition – was fundamental to physiology. A crucial task for him, therefore, was showing that this vital force was reducible to the forces of physics and thus ultimately to the fundamental force of mechanics.[58]

---

57 'Die Summe der Zellen ist ein Organismus, und der Organismus lebt, so lange die Theil eim Dienste des Ganzen tätig sind'. Henle 1844, p. 216.

58 In *Über die Erhaltung der Kraft*, Helmholtz formulates the goal thus: 'Die Naturerscheinungen sollen zurückgeführt warden auf Bewegungen von Materien mit unveränderlichen Bewegungskraften, welche nur von den räumlichen Verhältnissen abhängig sind'. Helmholtz 1882, Vol. I, p. 15. For a more detailed study, see Elkana 1974, p. 129.

The German word *Kraft*, which Helmholtz used, is certainly extremely rich in content, and there was thus a range of partially quite diffuse complexes of problems that Helmholtz wanted to solve with his theory of the indestructibility of force. But the traces of reductionism are clear and unambiguous.

One of those who most quickly accepted Helmholtz's theses and, moreover, made them one of the main points in his physiological research was another of Müller's assistants, Emil du Bois-Reymond.[59] His orientation is already unmistakable in the choice of subject for his magnum opus: *Untersuchungen über thierische Electricität*. In a long introduction, du Bois-Reymond expounds on his principal position. He rejects all talk of organisms being fitted for purpose. It was, he said incisively, just as reasonable to speak about the solar system being fitted for purpose as it was about living beings. Biology would remain in an undeveloped state for as long as the teleological reflections within it were used as a starting point.[60]

Helmholtz's and du Bois-Reymond's conceptions are mechanistic in the strictest sense. Not only was every teleological aspect declared anathema, but all the forces of nature could be traced back to the fundamental force of Newtonian mechanics.

There is, however, another orientation that could be called mechanistic without containing this strict reductionist component. It also had advocates within the Müllerian tradition. In a paper from 1856, *Alter und neuer Vitalismus*, Rudolf Virchow attempted to find a point of unity between the vitalist and the mechanist conceptions. In contrast to du Bois-Reymond, he allowed himself to speak of the 'functional processes of life' (*doch so zweckmässigen Vorgänge des Lebens*),[61] but he rejected vitalism's customary attempt to explain this fitness for purpose using a force that is particularly teleologically active.[62] He did, however, want to be regarded as being a kind of more modern vitalist since he found a distinct difference between living and dead; we can, he argued, only understand this difference if we assume a particular organic force distinguished from 'the molecular force'.[63] But even this force was mechanical (i.e. non-teleological in nature).[64]

---

59   Elkana 1974, p. 142.
60   Du Bois-Reymond 1848, p. lxviii.
61   Virchow 1856, p. 9. Virchow's biographer Ackerknecht called Virchow's opinion 'Neovitalismus', which is extremely misleading; Ackerknecht 1953, p. 40.
62   Virchow 1856, p. 10.
63   Ibid., p. 20.
64   *Ibid.*, p. 11 et seqq.

It is therefore possible to distinguish between a reductive and an irreductive orientation in the mechanistic tradition. According to the former, a scientific explanation is not complete until every phenomenon, organic and inorganic, can be traced back to the explanatory models of the most fundamental science: mechanics. According to the latter, the goal is only to demonstrate a strict causality in nature; we must be content with taking several fundamental forces into account.

In light of Engels's later efforts to create an irreductive materialism, the mere existence of such an irreductive orientation in biology is of interest.

On the other hand, Virchow's paper is not much more than a hint, a quickly outlined programme, and it scarcely gave rise to any orientation for research in biology. The principal lines in physiological research remained strict mechanicism on the one hand and a teleologically imprinted vitalism on the other.

A reductive orientation with a great deal of impact was advocated by Rudolf Hermann Lotze, who stood out as a respected specialist in both medicine and philosophy. He developed his conception in a number of comprehensive textbooks.[65] His 1843 essay *Leben, Lebenskraft* had a strongly standardising influence.[66] It had perhaps its greatest strength in its analysis of concepts; the fundamental discussions among biologists – and especially German biologists – were marked by a not insignificant confusion of concepts. He pointed out, among other things, that concepts that were being contrasted with each other out of hand as causality and teleology might very well be different aspects of the same thing. The fully developed teleological aspect, in which every moment on the path towards the alleged goal was known, was only a reversion of the causal. If we say that d is a goal for a and we also know the intervening moments b and c, we have both the causal chain a-b-c-d and the teleological chain d-c-b-a at the same time. Lotze's conclusion was that the teleological aspect only has a provisional value in the natural sciences, namely so long as we do not know the entire context of causes.[67]

---

65 So, for example, in *Allgemeine Pathologie und Therapie der medinischen Naturwissenschaft*, 1842, and *Medicinische Psychologie oder Physiologie der Seele*, 1882.

66 On this, see for example Virchow 1856, p. 66, and Lange 1876, Vol. II, p. 106 et seqq.

67 Lotze 1843, p. x et seqq. The article was included in R. Wagner's *Handwörterbuch der Physiologie*, which was first published in instalments; Lotze's article was included in the sixth instalment. Wagner's *Handwörterbuch* played a major role in the general biological and medical discussion. The publisher himself was a vitalist and would later throw himself with gusto into the materialist debate (R. Wagner 1854), but in the great anthology he published, advocates of a strictly mechanistic view such as Lotze and Helmholtz also contributed.

Lotze also attacked the concept of force, prevalent among biologists, in which 'force' was quite simply synonymous with 'cause'. According to Lotze, saying that the cause of the unique phenomenon of life was a special vital force was an improper use of the concept of force itself: an attempt to explain a diversity of different phenomena, unrelated to each other, using a single force. It would also lead to absurd conclusions, for example, that this vital force would be linked to a definite substance, a vital matter or similar.[68]

Lotze wrote the paper unaware of the theory of the indestructibility of force, but the impulse it contained could be developed without difficulty in the direction where the new concept of force belonged. The assumption was only that the indestructible force would be understood in a reductionist spirit – that is, as Helmholtz and Grove had done.[69]

5   Reductive Mechanicism

Reductive mechanicism,[70] which played an important role in nearly all branches of the natural sciences, may appear to be a fully worked out system. It contains relatively definite principles for how the natural sciences are related to one another and, implicitly, also for how the different levels of nature are bound up together.

But it is among the most characteristic elements of this reductive mechanicism in the form it took with Helmholtz, du Bois-Reymond, Lotze – or Schwann, for that matter – that it was always asserted with reservations; it was relativised or subordinated to some higher point of view. What this higher point of view was changes from advocate to advocate; it is, however, consistent. Schwann, an active Catholic, let his 'physical view' end in a belief in the divine origin of all of nature.[71] Helmholtz, who professed himself an adherent of a Kantian type of epistemology and science, distinguished between the natural sciences and the human sciences and let the natural sciences in their

---

68   Lotze 1843, p. xx et seqq.

69   Above, p. 151 et seq.

70   By 'mechanicism' – which is the term generally used in the literature – I mean a generally non-teleological view of the phenomena of life entirely in accordance with the prevalent vocabulary. 'Reductive mechanicism' is my term for the far more specific conception advocated by Helmholtz, Grove, Schwann, Lotze, du Bois-Reymond, John Herschel and many others among their contemporaries, which entailed all 'forces' in inorganic and organic nature can, or in future science will, be expressed in terms of the concept of force in Newtonian mechanics (mass × acceleration).

71   Schwann 1839, p. 221 et seqq.

mechanistic formulation be merely the representative of one of two possible perspectives on reality; like Kant, he found the conditions for the exact natural sciences in human reason.[72] In his 'ignoramus et ignoramibus' address, du Bois-Reymond went even further and asserted that all external processes are strictly determined and that we could therefore predict every future event, but that with this knowledge we would not reach any real insight about the nature of reality.[73] For his part, Lotze let his mechanicism end in an idealistic metaphysics.[74]

It is therefore obvious that in this tradition there was a willingness to limit the breadth of the natural scientific perspective. To be precise, there were attempts to get away from, or at least circumscribe, the implications it had for a worldview, and with that to allow less scope for the ideological use of the theories.

Later, we will examine this entire outlook, which gained considerable significance for the system-builders of the late nineteenth century, more closely. It developed against the background of the systems of the Romantics and Hegel, in open opposition to the universal declarations based on the principle of conservation of energy and in a materialistic spirit advocated by Büchner, Vogt and many others. It had a personal basis in the ideologies of the various scientists, but in general it also had to do with their positions as specialists, specialised in a definite field and thereby – precisely in their specialisation – prevented from commenting on anything lying outside their specialty. Specialisation is one of the conditions for their willingness to express their general theses with reservations. Büchner, Vogt and a number of real system-builders who followed them lacked this condition.

For specialists who were occupied with such broad categories as the forces of nature and their mutual relations, the demarcation that they were themselves assigned by other specialists with a less theoretical and more empirical orientation was so much more important. Helmholtz's *Über die Erhaltung der Kraft* was repudiated by many physicists at first because it was considered to be too speculatively inclined.[75] It can thus be said that the antagonism between the

---

72   See Helmholtz 1876, Vol. I, p. 1 et seqq., in particular under the heading '*Erkenntnisstheorie*' in Helmholtz 1882, pp. 591–660. A selection of Helmholtz's epistemological writings can be found in Helmholtz 1976.

73   Du Bois-Reymond 1872 and 1886, Vol. I, p. 105 et seqq. On du Bois-Reymond and his conception, see Herneck 1960.

74   Lotze's ambitions are most clearly seen in the great, in part quite popularly written work *Mikrokosmus* (Vols. I–III, 1856–64).

75   Cf. Helmholtz's own later comments on his early work in Helmholtz 1882, p. 68. See also Elkana 1974, p. 169.

theoretical and empirical determination of the science gained its significance for the theoretically minded specialists' attempt to limit the breadth of their theories.

In a theory such as the one on the indestructibility of force, there are no definite limits in the theory itself for its area of application. The term 'force', so vague and ambiguous outside of mechanics, was used in all fields of knowledge, so the theory could easily be developed into a universal theory. Anyone seeking to avoid that was reduced to the determinations of the field of application of the theory by epistemology and scientific theory. In order to avoid entirely too far-reaching statements about reality, they turned to far-reaching questions about knowledge. They could not rid themselves of philosophy.

The slow, and not completely peaceful, transition from looser theory of the indestructibility of force to the more consistent principle of conservation of energy entails nothing fundamentally new here. The principle could also form the foundation for one or another far-reaching system, the most well-known of which being the one Wilhelm Ostwald created.[76] But the primary direction of development lay elsewhere; it moved away from systems. This course of events will be touched upon later in our account.[77]

6   Summary

The antagonism between specialisation and system-building expressed itself in multiple ways in nineteenth-century physics, chemistry and physiology. The principle of the conservation of energy was above all an attempt to bring together the various fields of knowledge into a shared theory. The principle, as it was formulated, entailed a synthesis; for system-builders it provided immediately unlimited opportunities to construct new, scientifically based explanations for the world. They encountered resistance, however, from a number of specialists in the natural sciences. The principle did not abolish the antagonism that existed among the various disciplines. It provided a broad general perspective, nothing more. The asymmetry between physics and chemistry remained, and was strengthened, through specialisation. In physiology, vitalism endured as a potential alternative. The conclusions drawn by the system-

---

76   Ostwald's great natural philosophical work, which was primarily published after he had made a name for himself in physical chemistry, actually contained a system – 'energetics' – that, in the style of the classical systems, resulted in an ethics. Cf. above all *Die Energie* (Ostwald 1908) and *Energetische Grundlagen der Kulturwissenschaft* (Ostwald 1909).

77   Cf. below, p. 510 et seq.

builders assumed both a unity and a unanimity within the natural sciences that in fact did not exist. At the same time, however, the principle of conservation of energy pointed in the direction of the system-builders; through it, there was a basis for their activities in the actual internal developments.

The ideological cogency of the new principle is no less essential. Ideological and theoretical determinations hook into each other. For ideological and other reasons, however, many specialists hesitate before the ideological use of their specialties.

We can already understand why the concepts of force and energy exercised such an almost magnetic attraction on Engels. In their general and popular formulation, they crossed boundaries and seemed to be applicable to all kinds of reality. They therefore raised ontological questions. Precisely through their general character, however, they faced the problems of epistemology and scientific theory; the same difficulties concerning 'the scientific method' that Marx and Engels wrestled with in their own area of specialisation can be met in another domain.

CHAPTER 7

Darwinism: Hypothesis or Worldview?

1   Darwin's Theory

No theory that came to light in the nineteenth century attracted the system-builders as much as Darwin's theory of natural selection.[1] Darwin himself detested systems; he wanted to appear as a solid specialist.

But there were strong reasons for bringing the theory of natural selection into the struggle among different conceptions of the world and of science. Its explosive ideological effect was obvious: here the Christian belief in creation was being thrown into question, and here was an image of the world of nature that – with a few strokes of the pen – could be an image of humanity's world of struggle and competition.

From an internal perspective, Darwin's theory was equally as problematic, both upwards and downwards in the scientific hierarchy. The theory as Darwin formulated it lacked connection with physics and chemistry, and it thus squared poorly with the principal orientation in the discussion within physiology that we acquainted ourselves with in the preceding chapter. It was nonetheless a theory at a high general level: it encompassed the development of every living thing. Quite simply, it did not suit the leading scientific ideals of the nineteenth century; it was neither mechanistic nor vitalistic, neither reductionist nor irreductionist. Nonetheless it filled a yawning gap, and it corresponded to another of the major nineteenth-century categories of thought: it was a theory of development, a historical theory in the very broadest sense of the word. It dealt with changes in time in the same way as the Kant-Laplace nebular hypothesis or (on an even more abstract plane) the new discipline of thermodynamics did.

But it was also problematic in its relation to the disciplines sitting above it in the scientific hierarchy, the disciplines concerning humanity and society. For its most unhesitating adherents – to which Darwin himself did not belong – it constituted the bridge between dead nature and humanity.

I will return to the significance of Darwinism for social theory and conceptions of history in the following chapter. Here, it is a question of its relation to general scientific ideals and more fundamental natural scientific theories.

---

1   As is known, what was new and original in Darwin's creation was not the idea of descendance of the variability of species but the explanation of the changes in species (i.e., the theory of natural selection).

2   Problems Raised by the Theory

A great deal of attention has been paid to the intense scientific theoretical debate around Darwinism in a large and rapidly growing amount of literature. There is a rewarding collection of reviews and other standpoints on *The Origin of Species*[2] in *Darwin and His Critics*, edited by David L. Hull, for which he provided an equally rewarding introduction. Standard works that have Darwin's scientific profile in view are Gavin de Beers's *Charles Darwin. A Scientific Biography* and Michael Ghiselin's *The Triumph of the Darwinian Method*. Likewise of interest are Peter Vorzimmer's *Charles Darwin. The Years of Controversy* and Gertrude Himmelfarb's *Darwin and the Darwinian Revolution*. C.C. Gillispie and J.C. Greene put Darwin in a broader perspective in the history of ideas in *Genesis and Geology* and *Darwin and the Modern World View*, respectively. This same Greene also authored *The Death of Adam*, well worth the read. An extremely useful study of the spread of Darwinism is Alvar Ellegård's *Darwin and the General Reader*. Among the minor studies aimed at the relations between the theory of natural selection and philosophical currents are Ellegård's 'The Darwinian Revolution and Nineteenth-Century Philosophy of Science',[3] John Passmore's 'Darwin's Impact on British Metaphysics'[4] and J.H. Randall's 'The Changing Impact of Darwin on Philosophy'.[5]

The theory of natural selection was quickly drawn into the century's major debates on the scientific method. Darwin was anxious to design his theory in accordance with the prevailing ideals. Nevertheless, his approach in *Origin* would be rejected by the most renowned scientific philosophers of his home country. John Herschel, the astronomer who presented the ideas of reductive mechanicism[6] in *Preliminary Discourse on the Study of Natural Philosophy* – a book that made a strong impression on the young Darwin – not only claimed that every natural phenomenon could be explained in terms of Newton's mechanics; like Lotze and Schwann, he also wanted the great machine of nature to be regarded from a teleological perspective, and thus as a construction of a divine being. Darwin's thesis that the variation within a species was random therefore conflicted with Herschel's mechanistic ideal, while the absence of an extremely teleological explanation disrupted his worldview.

---

2   Henceforth referred to solely as *Origin*.
3   In *Journal of the History of Ideas*, 18, 1957, pp. 362–93.
4   In *Victorian Studies*, 3, 1959, pp. 41–54.
5   In *Journal of the History of Ideas*, 22, 1961, pp. 435–62. An extremely rewarding overview of the ongoing intense research into Darwin and Darwinism can be found in Greene 1975.
6   Cf. above, p. 168 et seq.

The main combatants in one of the major disputes over the scientific method, William Whewell and John Stuart Mill, also directed criticism at Darwin's work from their different points of departure. Darwin did not satisfy Mill's empirical ideal, while he wounded Whewell's belief in creation.[7]

From our perspective, Herschel's repudiation is interesting; it concerned immediately the connection of the Darwinian theory to other natural scientific theories. We will later see examples of similar criticisms directed by biologists. We will also see how a range of Darwinists – Ernst Haeckel and August Weismann above all – sought to expand the theory itself in conformity with the mechanistic ideal. Out of the limited theory of natural selection would come a system.

But here as well in the background, of course, there are general epistemological and scientific theoretical views that were the primary issue for Mill. The questions of induction and deduction played a crucial role. Empirical and rationalist ideals were set against each other.

It is crucial for the discussion of Darwinism that most of those in the debate regarded all scientific – or at least all natural scientific – theories as essentially of the same type. The same relation would prevail between individual cases and general conditions. Using Newton's law of gravity, every individual case that fell under the law could be exactly calculated (within the limits held to for the time being). Every individual case thus confirmed the law. The requirements of induction as they had been determined were thereby also fulfilled.

The same was now being demanded of Darwin's theory. The general statements Darwin made about the development of all species should be confirmed with regard to each individual example. It did not matter that Darwin's theory was a theory of development while Newton's was not. From mechanist quarters, in fact, a universal theory was often demanded that would contain a general law for the development of the entire universe. Laplace's celebrated spirit[8] hovered over the nineteenth century. The goal of science was to be able to determine every past event and predict every future one. The history of the entire universe was regarded as determined down to the details.

As we have seen, other laws of development besides Darwin's had been brought to the fore in the nineteenth-century natural sciences. In most cases, they were regarded from the same deterministic perspective as Darwinism.

---

7   An outstanding summary of Herschel's, Mill's and Whewell's criticism is Hull 1973, p. 7 et seq., p. 22 et seqq.

8   That is, Laplace's assumption that a superhuman intelligent being (*ésprit*) could calculate every past and future event in the universe, if it only had access to a complete mechanistic theory. Laplace developed this line of thought in *Essai philosophique sur les probabilités* (1814).

James Clerk Maxwell's statistical concepts did not change the world of ideas; according to David L. Hull, C.S. Peirce was one of the very few who drew more far-reaching conclusions from Maxwell's ideas and thus saw the affinity between these and Darwin's theory.[9] According to Peirce, both cases had to do with laws that commented on tendencies and were therefore not applicable in every individual case that the law commented on.[10]

Otherwise, however, predominant opinion was that Darwin's theory was incomplete, or purely objectionable, as long as it did not have the form of a deterministic theory of development.

Even for nineteenth-century social theories, which to a great extent had the goal of elucidating the motion and rhythm of social development, the general scientific ideal – in which tendencies were viewed in the light of the law of gravity – was of great significance. To an extent, this was of course bound up with the fact that several of them were closely related to Darwinism. But this in itself was a difficulty that was their own. It was not only Spencer's synthetic philosophy, but also to a great degree Comte's and Buckle's positivist theories of history that bore traces of a superior scientific ideal. For Marx – and for Engels in particular – determining the relation between their theory of history and society and the general idea of what a law of development was or should be also became an acute problem.

3   Darwin the Specialist

We will gradually examine in more detail the mechanistic criticism of the theory of natural selection. There is, however, another aspect that has come into view. When demands were raised that the theory of the development of species should be combined with and perhaps subordinated to more fundamental theories of nature, these demands came into conflict with the demands for specialisation or, more precisely, for exhaustive expertise within a limited field. The Darwinists could – like Haeckel – set out into the wilderness of the great philosophical questions, but they could also – like Darwin himself – keep timidly to the specialties they had staked out.

The process of specialisation therefore has significance even where Darwinism is concerned: the development of Darwinism is in fact incomprehensible if the increasingly more stringent demands for scientific competence are not

9   Hull 1973, p. 33.
10   Peirce 1877, p. 1 et seqq.

taken into account. On the one hand, Darwinism had to appear as a solid theory in the scientific world, developed and tested by specialists; on the other, it was demanded that the Darwinists themselves comment on other scientific theories. Moreover, Darwinism was immediately engaged in the ideological struggle, and for that it was required to either develop into or adopt a conception of the world. The dilemma was a difficult one.

As a scientific specialty, the theory of natural selection was comprehensive enough. Above all, it assumed a regrouping of the traditional arrangement. Taxonomy, which dominated botany and zoology, played a key role; a crucial point of contention was the concept of species, its delimitation and stability.[11] Comparative anatomy, with its roots in an earlier – often highly speculative – thinking on development, was also brought into the picture here.[12] Physiology, which through its rapid development had become the central discipline of biology (a position that Darwinism would upset after a fashion), had obvious significance; Darwin himself brought physiology into the very heart of his theory when, after the example of German biologist Karl Ernst von Baer, he defined the difference between more and less developed species as the difference between a greater and lesser degree of physiological differentiation.[13]

Naturally, the extraordinarily intimate connection between Darwin's theory and the new Lyellian geology should not be forgotten, either. Geology formed a crucial basis for the entire theory of the development of species. An expert in the problems of Darwinism thus also had to be familiar with geology.[14]

In particular, after Haeckel formulated his biogenetic law ('ontogeny recapitulates phylogeny' – the individual repeats the development of the entire species), embryology entered the inner domains of the theory.[15] But genetics, Darwinism's problem child, also very much belonged to these inner domains. In *Origin*, Darwin attempted to avoid every more definite statement about the mechanisms of heredity; for his theory, he believed he only had to assume that

---

11   On this topic, see Ghiselin 1969, in particular pp. 89–102, and the literature cited there.

12   Cf. above, p. 62.

13   Darwin 1872, p. 127. Naturally, the more far-reaching Haeckel went more resolutely into these domains; in his chief scientific work, *Generelle Morphologie*, he dealt with Darwinist theory in its relation to anatomy (Haeckel 1866, Vol. I, p. 22 et seqq.) and in relation to physiology (ibid., p. 17 et seqq.).

14   Regarding the connection between geology and Darwinism, see the special works by Gillispie and Greene 1959.

15   Haeckel develops the fundamental law of biogenetics in Haeckel 1866, Vol. II, p. 3 et seqq. The connection with embryology is emphasised in particular on p. 20 et seqq. It is emphasised even more – indeed, it becomes the '*Grundgesetz*' of organic development – in Haeckel 1874, p. 3 *ff* and *passim*.

variation within the species was random, but without leaps or mutations.[16] Later, he developed his complicated theory of pangenesis, according to which heredity was constituted of small seeds or germs that developed in the various parts of the parent organism.[17] Here, as with other Darwinists, genetics was formed as a single large supplementary hypothesis for the thesis that heredity was continual and did not occur in leaps and bounds. The theories of mutation that gained popularity towards the end of the century were vehemently rejected, and when Mendelian genetics finally broke through around 1900, it would spell a death sentence for the theory of selection to many biologists well into the 1930s.[18]

Organic chemistry was also brought into the field of problems for Darwinism, though only just a corner of it. This was unavoidable: if it was asserted that the entire diversity of species had its origin in one or a few extremely simple species, the question immediately arose how these species – and thereby organic life – arose out of inorganic matter. An assiduous search took place for ever simpler organisms – organisms that stood precisely on the boundary with the inorganic. At the same time, chemists were working on the questions, still difficult to grasp, of the relation between proteins and life; chemists and biologists met in their endeavours, and for biologists the chemists' assertions about the chemical basis of life were of great importance.[19]

---

16   'The laws governing inheritance are for the most part unknown'; Darwin 1872, p. 13.

17   A lucid account of this is given in Himmelfarb 1959, p. 265 et seqq.

18   An illustrative example of the wane of Darwinism among biologists can be found in Volume III of Erik Nordekskiöld's *The History of Biology*, where Darwin's theory of natural selection is treated exclusively as a disproven theory whose time has passed. The later synthesis between the theory of natural selection and modern genetics is summarised in Julian Huxley's (1942) *Evolution: The Modern Synthesis*, which also contains many interesting backward looks at the varied assessments of Darwinism.

19   Here as well, Haeckel was one of the most zealous boundary-crossers. He sets forth his programme in *Generelle Morphologie* (Haeckel 1866, Vol. I, p. 12 et seqq.) and devotes a great deal of attention to the questions of the relation between organic and inorganic (ibid., pp. 111–66). See also below, p. 200 et seqq. Darwinism provides us with one of the most beautiful examples showing that the process of specialisation in science is not unidirectional: a far-reaching theory can demolish the boundaries between already established specialisations. Even Darwinism's opponents in biology followed in this disciplinary expansion. It is worthwhile to compare, for example, the first and second editions of Albert Kölliker's embryological lectures (Kölliker 1861 and 1879). The crucial new elements in the second edition are the chapter '*Allgemeine Betrachtungen*' (pp. 377–99), in which Kölliker takes up broad biological connections in relation to both Haeckel's fundamental law of biogenetics and to the strictly mechanistic ideal in biology in general; Kölliker's field of work has thus also grown.

There was thus a long range of professions that together constituted a motley collection of profiles as regards scientific orientations and levels of development but were of immediate significance for Darwin's theory. Those who took it upon themselves to develop the whole of Darwinism into a solid scientific specialty – and there were many, in fact – were faced here with a task that was superhuman in the later nineteenth century. At the same time, Darwinism was bombarded with accusations that it did not view the development of species from an even broader natural scientific perspective, and in the ideological battles answers to nearly every question were demanded from it.

Nowhere can the dilemma of Darwinism in the face of the demands of specialisation be seen more clearly than in Charles Darwin himself. The image of Darwin has become so difficult in the extreme to define not only because Darwin has been – and remains – controversial, but also because he himself spoke with two voices: now with greater certainty, now with extraordinary caution and restraint. For that reason he could be depicted in the tremendous volume of literature devoted to him and his work now as a Newton of the biological sciences, thought more significant as a theoretician and summariser than the latter,[20] now as an insignificant epigone without his own opinions.[21] He has been portrayed as completely unphilosophical;[22] his problems are said to have been above all metaphysical and religious;[23] he has been portrayed as a prominent figure in the mechanistic sciences;[24] he has been depicted as entirely too speculative and with a poor sense of the significance of empiricism.[25]

All these incompatible statements on Darwin reflect not only the positions of the various authors on Darwin but also Darwin's own ambivalence in relation to philosophy and far-reaching theories, empiricism and detailed knowledge.

---

20 Haeckel 1873, p. 23 et seqq. Cf. also J. Huxley 1924, p. 247 et seq.
21 Darlington 1959, p. 1 et seqq.
22 Schaxel 1918, p. 8; Wyss 1958, p. 178.
23 Himmelfarb 1959, p. 130 et seq.
24 Dewey 1910, p. 24.
25 All these irreconcilable statements are bound up not only with the changing ideas of the various sources; they also have their basis in Darwin's method of casting around small statements about science and research work. In newer literature, Darwin's relation to modern scientific views has been exhaustively discussed. Ghiselin, for example, traces in Darwin's difficulties with the inductivist scientific ideal an inclination for modern hypothetical and deductive explanatory models. Undoubtedly there are statements by Darwin that could be interpreted in that direction; at the same time, however, there is a striving to adapt to the demands of the inductivists. If Darwin is a pioneer in this field of scientific theory as well, he is at least very unaware of it.

Darwin had started from an extremely definite perspective of nature, and his much-discussed development up until he laid out the theory of natural selection is the history of how this general, philosophical and religiously anchored perspective gradually proved unsustainable. In his youth, he had learned to regard nature as a perfect teleological system. His teacher had above all been the theologian William Paley,[26] for whom he harboured unreserved admiration.[27]

Darwin thus started out from the assumption that every plant and animal species had a function in the great totality of nature, just as every organ, every instinct and reflex in an organism served the organic totality. During his journey around the world on the *Beagle*, he obtained evidence that there were troublesome exceptions to the rule.[28] When he gradually began to accept a variability of the species, he had a tendency to save at least parts of the teleological perspective by seeing examples of cruelty, a lack of suitability and the like as natural elements in an enormous process of development that was largely adapted to its purpose.[29] In the fully developed theory in *Origin*, such viewpoints had almost completely faded away. It was only on the final page that he suggested something like it when – to placate potential critics, as it were – he spoke about his conception of the development of life: 'There is a grandeur in this view of life, with its several powers, having been originally breathed into a few forms or into one'.[30] In later editions he clarified his piety in the final chord he struck by adding 'by the Creator'.[31]

But in itself, the theory he presented has nothing to do with the final sentence. The entire theory of natural selection is based on showing that the development of species is an immanent development; it comes about by itself.

---

26   William Paley's foremost work, *Natural Theology or Evidences of the Existence and Attributes of the Deity* (1803), comprises a splendid example of the mode of argument in 'natural' theology. In the first chapter, Paley attempts to show that the purposefulness of nature must be explained in the same way as that of the clock: an intelligent creator must be assumed. It is striking that Paley's reasoning here is of essentially the same type as the one that one of Darwin's most important critics, John Herschel, used; the emphasis is only elsewhere. Herschel emphasised mechanics more, and Paley more the purposefulness of the mechanics.

27   Darwin wrote to John Lubbock on 15 November 1859: 'I do not think I hardly ever admired a book more than Paley's *Natural Theology*. I could almost formerly have said it by heart'. Darwin 1887, Vol. ii, p. 229.

28   Darwin 1959, Vol. ii, p. 279, p. 377 et seqq.

29   Cf. above all his 'Sketch' from 1842, reproduced in Himmelfarb, p. 164 and elsewhere.

30   Darwin 1859, p. 490.

31   Darwin 1872. p. 560.

The teleological perspective has thus fallen away. It could be expected that Darwin would have developed an opposing naturalist, or perhaps more distinctly materialist, perspective. But this did not happen. The one view of totality was not replaced by another more explicit and thought out conception. Instead, Darwin tried to avoid, or simply answer evasively, questions that he did not find standing in a clear and unambiguous relation to known facts.

This uncertainty was bound up with his understanding of the relationship between science and philosophy. A good scientific theory could not smell of speculation. In his opinion, older descendance theories lacked empirical concretion. Early on, he described Lamarck's method of explaining the development of species as 'nonsense',[32] and he found the reason in Lamarck's building his theories on a minimum of facts; it possessed instead 'the prophetic spirit in science'.[33] Equally harsh was his judgement of Robert Chambers's *Vestiges of Creation*.[34]

It should not be concluded from this that Darwin openly rejected all far-reaching philosophy. Instead, it must be assumed that he – in a way he never successfully elucidated – distinguished between philosophy and scientific theory, both of which had their legitimate fields but mixed together gave rise to nonsense and superficiality. This position emerges most clearly in Darwin's assessment of Herbert Spencer. Spencer – who incorporated Darwin's theory of natural selection with ease into his great theory of development, and moreover supplied some of Darwin's key terms[35] – was of course an extraordinarily important phenomenon for Darwin. But Darwin's position was ambiguous. He thought highly of Spencer the philosopher: 'I suspect that hereafter he will be looked at as by far the greatest living philosopher in England; perhaps equal to any that have lived'.[36] This did not mean that he regarded Spencer as a sound guide in the sciences. In his autobiography he declared that Spencer's 'deductive manner of treating every subject' was deeply foreign to him. Spencer's conclusions never convinced him. The fundamental generalisations in synthetic philosophy 'may be very valuable under a philosophical point of view', but they did not seem to have 'any strictly scientific use'.[37]

---

32   Cf. letter to J.D. Hooker, 11 January 1884; Darwin 1887, Vol. II. p. 23.
33   Himmelfarb 1959, p. 149.
34   Ibid., p. 180 et seq.
35   Darwin admitted his debt of obligation here, as always, with great willingness; see, for example, regarding the expression 'survival of the fittest' and Spencer, Darwin 1872, p. 63; and regarding 'differentiation', ibid., p. 130 et seq.
36   Darwin 1887, Vol. III, p. 120.
37   Darwin 1958, p. 109.

Darwin here distinguished very sharply between philosophy and science. The philosophy he alluded to was the philosophy of the system-builder; science was the solid scientific specialty.

He certainly was not arguing that philosophy à la Spencer completely lacked value for science; it could provide the scientist with ideas for sound empirical work. Darwin did not believe that scientists began from a *tabula rasa*, or rather from a number of pure facts that they then piled into general theories.[38] But the philosophical theses were of value for science only if they could lead the researcher along the trail of facts; for that, they are obliged to use their philosophical sphere. In *Origin*, Darwin referred to Spencer's law of differentiation – that all development is moving toward ever greater differentiation[39] – but added 'But as we have no facts to guide us, speculation on the subject is almost useless'.[40] 'We' and 'us' are the members of the scientific community – for the time being, 'we' will stay away from the law of differentiation.

No matter how carefully Darwin wanted to keep himself away from philosophical speculations in his scientific work, it was nonetheless a large and diffuse philosophical question that constituted a powerful driving force in almost all of his scientific work. It was, as we have seen, the question of teleology. Darwin's manner of handling this question was determined to a great extent by his intellectual starting points – it was the simple, firm and not very sophisticated teleology of Paley, rather than the wide, more complex problems in the debates around vitalism and mechanicism that we previously became acquainted with, that staked out the path of his research. His goal was to reject teleology à la Paley. The theory of natural selection was to be an empirically supported, non-teleological theory.

It was thus a matter of explaining the suitability for purpose in organic nature – but also the purposeless or antithetical to purpose. 'Being suited for purpose' is therefore a description, a descriptive expression: an organ, an instinct or an entire species can have a purpose in relation to the individual, species or the entire organic environment. It was a matter of explaining this suitability for purpose without assuming any final causes. It was also a matter of explaining deficiencies in suitability, and the same explanatory model had to be applicable in both cases.

---

38   On this topic, cf. son Francis's clarifying investigation in Darwin 1887, Vol. I, p. 149. Cf. also Darwin's letter to H. Fawcett, 18 September 1861; Darwin 1903, Vol. I. p. 196.

39   Spencer 1862, Vol. I, Chap. xv contains the general presentation of the law of differentiation.

40   Darwin 1872, p. 130 et seq.

For Darwin, suitability for purpose was a relative concept: the degree of suitability is synonymous with the degree of adaptation to the environment. It was natural selection – supplemented with sexual selection[41] – that achieved this adaptation, and therefore this suitability. Darwin had a clear view of the descriptive character of the concept of suitability. If, based only on the condition that a biological phenomenon is suitable or functional, it is assumed that it must be part of a great plan or the like, this explains nothing: 'It is easy to hide our ignorance under such expressions as 'the plan of creation', 'unity of design', &c., and to think that we give an explanation when we only re-state a fact'.[42] Suitability thus stood out as a fact for Darwin, and it was a question of explaining this fact without bringing unprovable assertions into it.

Darwin's viewpoint can be summarised thus: an organ, an instinct or an entire species could possess or could lack a function in its context (the organism or the environment). If the phenomenon in question lacks a function, it must be assumed that it had such a function at one time but then lost it through some change or another in the organism or the environment. Through natural selection, the phenomenon tends to regress (become rudimentary) and gradually disappear completely. Every unit in the organic world tends to gradually adapt itself to the totality it is a part of.

It is therefore this general statement about tendencies that constitutes the core of the theory of natural selection. That is why it may seem peculiar that Darwin was constantly compelled to repel accusations of nonetheless having applied a teleological perspective despite his explicit statements. He avoided technical, well defined scientific language, preferring to express himself in images and analogies. Even the term 'natural selection' was a rather risky metaphor: did not selection assume that someone was selecting? Who was selecting? Nature? Darwin exculpated himself:

> Every one knows what is meant and is implied by such metaphorical expressions; and they are almost necessary for brevity. So again it is dif-

---

41   In *Origin*, Darwin speaks relatively little about sexual selection (cf. Darwin 1872, p. 89 et seqq.), whereas it plays a crucial role in his *The Descent of Man*, where it is regarded as the most important cause in the emergence of the various human races (Darwin 1871, Vol. II, p. 384). From the perspective in question, sexual selection entails nothing new; it is no more teleologically tinged than natural selection. By and large, it means that not the organism's entire environment – as it is with natural selection – but only a small part of it (namely, representatives of the opposite sex) is defined as the deciding selective factor.

42   Darwin 1872, p. 552.

ficult to avoid personifying the word Nature; but I mean by Nature only the aggregate action and product of many natural laws, and by laws the sequence of events as ascertained by us.[43]

This expression, however, is only partially explanatory. What the various laws of nature are cannot be known, only that Darwin grasps them in David Hume's empirical sense.[44] Certainly, Darwin wanted to see his own law of tendencies as one of these laws, but it squared rather poorly with Hume's definition. The gradual adaptation of species to their environment cannot be perceived as 'the sequence of events as ascertained by us'.

This much is clear, however: Darwin's theory of natural selection did not make any teleological assumptions. But for that matter Darwin did not rid himself of the teleological problem; for him, it was not solved in one stroke with the theory of natural selection.

Some of his general statements about teleology may fall in the sphere of speculative philosophy, where he so unwillingly dwelled.[45] What he said, however, nonetheless forms a contribution to the contemporary debate in the sciences over teleology and mechanism. The statement that he could not imagine that the totality of the universe came about by chance[46] – a notion that is full of doubts[47] – can safely be attributed to a sphere of private metaphysical opinions that he did not vouch for with his scientific authority. But when these statements were combined with the thesis that not every event in the universe could be planned or aim towards a higher purpose,[48],[49] it immediately became a contribution to the ongoing contest over the scientific ideal. There was, as we have seen, a lively current – in England represented above all by John Herschel – that asserted that the universe was strictly determined and

---

43   Ibid., p. 82. On the attacks on Darwin for a hidden theology, see Darwin 1903, Vol. I, p. 267 et seqq. Similar accusations emerged in modern times as well (e.g., in Darlington 1959, p. 26).

44   David Hume's interpretation of causality as the invariant relation between observation of *a* and observation of *b* (*b* always follows *a*) played the role of a constant aiming point for empirical British natural scientists; cf. T.H. Huxley 1897, *passim*.

45   Cf. here also the statements in the letter to Julia Wedgwood, 11 November 1861, Darwin 1887, Vol. I, p. 311; and to W. Graham, 7 August 1881, ibid., p. 316.

46   Ibid., p. 313 et seq. and 316, respectively, and in letters to A. Gray, 26 November 1860, ibid., Vol. II, p. 353; and to Lord Farrer, 28 September 1881, Darwin 1903, Vol. I, p. 395.

47   Darwin 1958, p. 92 et seqq.

48   Cf. in particular the letter to A. Gray, 26 November 1880; Darwin 1887, Vol. II, p. 353.

49   Cf. the statements 'I met him by chance' (i.e., it was not my intent to meet him) and 'It is by chance which side of the die lands face up' (i.e., there is no law that will help us predict which side of the die will land face up).

that this deterministic system required an extraphysical explanation. Darwin, on the other hand, asserted that there were at least some events that were accidental.

The concept of chance itself has a troublesome ambiguity that would soon come to twist and distort the entire discussion around Darwinism. Something happening by chance could mean either that it happens unintentionally or that it happens irregularly. Obviously, the theory of natural selection implied that natural selection was unintentional, but Darwin also assumed at the start that the spread of genes was irregular (i.e. that no law for how it takes place could be drawn up). The latter statement does not belong to the law itself of the tendency for organisms to gradually adapt to their environment but to the rudimentary theory of heredity that formed part of Darwin's understanding of biological totality. The combination of unintentional and irregular chance, however, says much about his scientific ideal.

We can see that it is traces of the same patterns of thought that could have made him assume both that there was a kind of – undefinable – intent behind the universe as a whole and that there were unintentional events in the universe. If, namely, the universe was both intentionally brought about and thoroughly determinate, then every event must also be intentional. If intent is assumed, then every unintentional event is also irregular.

Many Darwinists after Darwin sought to express an idea that tallied better with the contemporary deterministic ideal. Even the scientist closest to him, T.H. Huxley, expressed himself in this direction. When he dealt with the relation between Darwinism and teleology, he declared openly that Darwinism excluded teleology in the sense of conscious planning but that, on the other hand, squared with a different kind of teleology. Science believed in an order in nature and thus in the possibility of absolute predictions.[50] Huxley thus rejected every element of intent and planning in his teleology, and what remained was only the reversion of a strict causality: teleology starts from the end of a chain of causality, not the beginning. Naturally, it could be said that such an idea about teleology only leaves 'a verbal sack'[51] behind. For Huxley, it was a way of adapting Darwinism to a predominant scientific ideal that is decidedly not Darwin's.

---

50   T.H. Huxley 1887, p. 179 et seqq.
51   Ellegård 1958, p. 140.

4   Criticism towards Darwin

As soon as *Origin* was published, it was subjected to furious criticism from different sides. Here, we will ignore the external criticism, aimed primarily from the religious side. Religious viewpoints and considerations would, of course, also leave their mark on the positions of various scientists in important respects. From our perspective, however, it is the scientists' manner of criticising the theory of natural selection as a scientific theory that is of greatest interest. This criticism influenced Darwin's attempts, and even more so those of the subsequent Darwinists, to change and develop the original theory further. It also left its mark on the efforts of the system-builders. It tore Darwinism between the certainty of specialisation and the fascination of the major syntheses.

To be precise, we will shed light upon five different types of criticism aimed at Darwin:

1.   Darwin had insufficient empirical support for his far-reaching conclusions. He broke sound methodical rules.
2.   He was deeply teleologically inclined.
3.   He denied the existence (or possibility) of general, necessary natural laws.
4.   His theory of the directionless variation of organisms did not hold true.
5.   He ignored the issues of the detailed structure of organisms, just as he did the physical and chemical problems.

These points are related to one another in an intricate fashion. I will, however, go through them one by one, also showing how they left their mark on the Darwinists' attempts to adapt to the criticism.

The first type of criticism is common, and appears in the most varied contexts. It could be aimed from varied scientific ideals and has a certain amount of support in Darwin's own style in which a cautious empiricism constitutes the basis for far-reaching conclusions. Even those who largely accepted the theory of natural selection could complain about Darwin jumping too quickly to general statements. The physiologist William Benjamin Carpenter – one of the most important popularisers of the time – thus asserted that Darwin should either simply have presented his great thesis or gone into much more detail than he did in *Origin*. He relied, however, on Darwin's promise that he would soon set out his results in a larger volume than *Origin*.[52]

---

52   Carpenter 1860, reproduced in Hull 1973, p. 92 et seqq. Cf. also the review – if not agreeable, then at least understanding – of Pictet, reproduced in Hull 1973, in particular p. 143. On Darwinism's reception in France, see Farley 1974 and above all the great Conry 1974.

But for the most part, this criticism was based on showing that the theory of natural selection was unscientific, either wholly or in part. Darwin violated the proper inductive method; English-speaking critics often formulated their accusation as Darwin violating 'the true Baconian method'.[53] As we have seen, methodological objections of this type[54] were levelled by both Mill and Whewell, the leading authorities on scientific theory in England. But it was just as characteristic of the criticism levelled by various types of professional scientists. The most vociferous contributions in this direction came – at least in England – from physicists and mathematicians.[55] They referred to the high standards achieved by the exact sciences. They pointe to both the lack of exactness and to the relatively insignificant foundation of facts in Darwin's theory. One of the most ambitious critics, mathematician William Hopkins, attempted to formulate the core of Darwin's theory that could be subjected to direct testing.[56] He assumed, however, that biology had far to go before it could reach the level of theories in physics. He also doubted that Darwin had taken his science in the right direction; in *Origin*, he found 'a want of strict adherence to philosophical and logical modes of thought and reasoning'.[57]

The theory of natural selection was thus both methodologically uncertain and deficient in its design. This verdict, however, applied to more than the purely scientific theoretical weaknesses; it also irritated this type of critic that Darwin had not sought any connection to more fundamental theories of the natural sciences. We will return to this point.

In Germany, where reductive mechanicism had attained a very prominent position among physiologists and pathologists, the theory of natural selection was subjected to similar treatment by a number of representatives of the subject. The veterans of Johannes Müller's laboratory found Darwinism unsatisfactory. Rudolf Virchow asserted that as a hypothesis, it was so uncertain that it ought not to be offered to the public yet.[58] Emil du Bois-Reymond, who was an adherent of an exaggeratedly mechanistic ideal,[59] did not regard the theory of natural selection as a fully important contribution to the great general theory of nature he had been dreaming of.[60]

----

53   Cf. H. Fawcett's repudiation of such criticism, also reproduced in Hull 1973, p. 231.
54   Above, p. 182.
55   On this topic, cf. Hull's comments in Hull 1973, p. 228, p. 349 et seq.
56   Hopkins, reproduced in Hull 1973, p. 257.
57   Ibid., p. 267.
58   Cf. below p. 506 et seq. On the reactions of German biologists to Darwinism, see Montgomery 1975.
59   Above, p. 174 et seq.
60   Du Bois-Reymond distanced himself from Darwinism's claim to have developed a sound

The uncertainty and the alleged methodological deficiencies in Darwin were also criticised in one of the most substantial negative criticisms, physiologist Albert Kölliker's *Über die Darwinsche Schöpfungstheorie*.[61]

All criticism of this type, however, was bound up with the major weaknesses that most of the critics had: determining what kind of theory and what kind of adherence to laws Darwin was working with. Now and then, an insight was discernible that the thesis itself of natural selection did not criticise an adherence to law of the same kind as the one Newton had demonstrated. So, for example, Carpenter could speak – in passing – of 'the modifying tendency of Natural Selection'.[62] It would not become more than an attempt, however: nearly the whole scientific community was caught up in the idea that all laws that could be set out in the natural sciences were of the same type.

Darwin's tentative and cautious manner of expressing himself led to further misunderstandings. There was, for example, a palpable confusion regarding Darwin's relation to teleology. The ambiguity in the term 'teleology' itself contributed to this. Descriptive suitability for purpose and explanatory teleology were not often distinguished; merely the statement that something is fit for purpose in relation to something else could give rise to the observation that it had to do with a teleological viewpoint. It was thus in this spirit that Kölliker attacked Darwin, based on Darwin's statement – vague as it was – that each part of an animal served the best interests of the animal in question.[63] Another opponent, however, Swiss botanist Carl von Nägeli – to whom Darwin otherwise ascribed great significance – rejected Kölliker's hasty conclusion, arguing that Darwin was only starting from a *'Nützlichkeitsprincip'* (principle of utility).[64]

A significantly more important criticism was based on the fact that Darwin was not attempting to lay out or supplement any general law of nature with his

---

natural scientific theory in an address titled 'Darwin versus Galiani' given in Berlin in 1876 (du Bois-Reymond 1886, Vol. I, p. 211 et seqq.). The morphological laws are not laws in the theoretical natural scientific sense but rather 'rules' (p. 219). He did, however, harbour respect for Darwin's scientific contribution, as evidenced in his commemorative speech 'Darwin and Copernicus' (ibid., Vol. II, p. 496 et seqq.) Cf. also Haeckel 1905, p. 28 et seq.

61 Kölliker 1864, p. 4 et seqq. On Kölliker, see Zuppinger 1974.

62 Carpenter 1860, in Hull 1973, p. 108.

63 *'Mit Bezug auf seine* Grundanschauung *ist erstens hervorzuheben, dass* Darwin *im vollsten Sinne des Wortes* Teleolog *ist. Ganz bestimmt sagt er ... dass jede Einzelheit im Baue eines Tieres zum Besten desselben erschaffen worden sei und fasst er die ganze Formenreihe der Tiere nur von diesem Gesichtspunkte auf ...'* Kölliker 1864, p. 4.

64 Nägeli 1865, p. 24.

theory. As we have seen, at the heart of this objection lay the idea that the theory of natural selection itself conflicted with both general deterministic ideas and the more specific reductivist and mechanistic scientific ideals.

There were great difficulties, however, in stating what exactly was wrong from a deterministic and mechanistic aspect. William Hopkins was on the trail of the difference between a law of invariance and a law of development[65] when he spoke about the difference between continuity and discontinuity. But the terms themselves that he used produced odd associations. Hopkins was clear about Darwin claiming that the development of species is continuous,[66] but at the same time he regarded the entire theory of biological development as an attempt at describing a discontinuity. By continuity, however, he meant unchangeability: the movement of the planets is continuous in the sense that they are continually repeated, whereas in Darwin's conception species would undergo changes. When Darwin – like Lamarck did earlier – sought to explain this changeability, he was certainly attempting to preserve continuity by assuming that the same natural causes always influenced the change.[67] But – to summarise Hopkins's problem – how could a set of constant causes result in a change?

Natural selection is, of course, not a 'natural cause' in this sense; for the critics, it was an obvious shortcoming in Darwin's theory as it was first presented, that an attempt was never made there to specify these natural causes. It looked, at least, as if Darwin did not assume any conformity to laws in nature.

For numerous opponents, it stood to reason that a theory of the development of species would have the form of a necessary law of development, in which biological development was linked to, and viewed as a continuation of, the development of inorganic nature. Kölliker declared that Darwin did not believe in '*allgemeine Naturgesetze*' (general laws of nature) that found expres-

---

65   The laws of invariance thus establish a constant, the laws of development account for regularities in the development of a system (e.g., the system of living beings, of human societies). In the debate in question, no distinction is made between the one and the other. In twentieth-century scientific theoretical debates, the great controversial question was whether the laws of development could really be designated laws and not as individual statements. Figures such as Karl Popper advocated the latter conception; cf. Popper 1957, p. 36 et seqq. A lucid but nonetheless penetrating portrayal of the argument is given in Schuon 1975, p. 75 et seqq. The question is of crucial significance for the interpretation of the theories of Marxism. It is equally as crucial for evolutionary biology. On the latter, cf. Simpson 1949, pp. 37, 43 et al. and Bertalanffy 1952, p. 153 et seqq.

66   Hull 1973, p. 253.

67   Hull 1973, p. 242 et seqq.

sion in the same manner in nature; that was why, Kölliker argued, that he could attribute a crucial role to natural selection.[68]

Nägeli also regarded explaining the development of species as a necessary development resulting from the interaction of necessary natural laws as an ideal. In his conception, there was moreover a teleological element: species changed from lower to higher species and were therefore characterised by '*eine notwendige Vervollkommenung*'[69] (a necessary improvement). Determinism and teleology were united in him, as they were in many others in the debate in question.

The view than Darwin did not assume any necessary laws of nature was closely bound up with the criticism of his original thesis that variation within the species is directionless. It was important for Darwin to reject the idea that there should be any necessary line of development from simpler to more complex species – a line that could be explained, for example, so that the variations within each species tended towards more complex forms. Instead, Darwin assumed that variation occurred in all directions. The assumption can be interpreted thus: If we could describe the characteristics of a parent pair – which one doesn't matter – numerically with values between, say, 1 and 100, and the parent pair in question had the values 45 and 55, then according to Darwin the characteristics of its offspring would spread outside these limits – say, between 40 and 60, but with the highest probabilities for the values around 50.

The primary aim of the assumption is thus to avoid the idea that the species change towards greater complexity from some internal cause; or, to reuse the numerical example, that the values of the offspring would deviate upwards from their parents' or that the average would be above 50. But this assumption of Darwin's was now being combined with diverse statements that the variation was accidental also in the sense that it had no observable cause.[70] It was therefore entirely irregular.

One important criticism of Darwin's concept of chance was levelled by professor of technology Fleeming Jenkin. Jenkin showed how variability itself among species stood out as an unproven assumption in Darwin; the theory assumed it but said nothing about its limits or determinations.[71] It has been assumed that Jenkin's criticism was a crucial reason for Darwin's attempt in the fifth edition of *Origin* to support his concept of variation with diverse assump-

---

68   Kölliker 1864, p. 13.
69   Nägeli 1865, p. 24.
70   Hull's commentary, Hull 1973, p. 344 et seq.
71   Jenkin, reproduced in Hull 1973, p. 305 et seqq.

tions about which mechanisms determined variation. Peter Vorzimmer has shown that the assumption is not plausible purely for reasons of time – Darwin had made the corrections before he learned of Jenkin's criticism[72] – but it is nonetheless correct that Jenkin had summarised a criticism that presented itself immediately in the scientific community of the time.

There are critical contributions in which deterministic and teleological elements work together in the condemnation of Darwin's thesis of directionless variation. Carl von Nägeli is a case in point. He attempted to show in empirical detail that Darwin's theory of natural selection was unable to explain a range of morphological phenomena. It could thus not account for why physiologically similar organs could be morphologically different.[73] Organs such as the ears of a hare did no good: they could not be explained even by the history of the species, as a rudimentary organ. In a letter to Nägeli, Darwin conceded that he could not explain such functionless phenomena 'and only hope to see that they may be explained'.[74] In *Origin*, he asserted his general conception more firmly and warned against rash assumptions about 'what structures now are, or have formerly been, of use to each species'.[75]

With his critical views, however, Nägeli wanted to clear more space for a conformity to laws in the development of species itself. Against Darwin's *'Nützlichkeitstheorie'* (theory of utility) he set, as we have seen, his own *'Vervollkommnenungsgesetz'* (law of improvement) – *'ein Gesetz notwendiger Vervollkommenung'* (a law of necessary improvement). He did not argue, however, that development was determined by intent; it was teleology in the sense of reverse causality that he embraced. He emphatically rejected the assumption of intent and intervention in the process of development.[76] He claimed that organic development followed a fixed plan and that organisms had a tendency to develop towards more complicated structures. He found the same tendency in inorganic nature, where simpler compounds became absorbed in more complex ones. According to Nägeli, Darwin's theory of natural selection could certainly explain the development of physiological functions, but not morphology. Nägeli thus regarded nature thoroughly as a tremendous hierarchy of more or less complex forms, where the more complex developed out of the less complex in accordance with necessary natural laws.[77]

---

72   Vorzimmer 1963, p. 371 et seqq.; on Jenkin and his review, p. 386 et seqq.
73   Nägeli 1877, p. 27.
74   Darwin 1887, Vol. III, p. 50 et seq.
75   Darwin 1872, p. 221 et seqq.
76   Nägeli 1877, p. 18, p. 29.
77   Ibid., p. 29 et seq.

Like Nägeli, Kölliker harboured the idea of the great deterministic universal law. He rejected Darwin's natural selection (or 'the principle of beneficial varieties', as he phrased it) and instead assumed a 'great plan of development' that 'forms the basis for the entire organised world'.[78]

Darwin's thesis that variation was not directed towards more complex forms was therefore criticised by Kölliker, who also refused to accept the idea that variation should be continuous, assuming instead that it took place 'by leaps'. Kölliker himself did not attach any great importance to this criticism to begin with,[79] but we know from later reckonings with Darwinism that it touched the core of Darwin's theory. In purely general terms it can be said that in every theory of development – whether they concern physical, biological or historical phenomena – are of greatest importance if the development (that is, the transition from one stage to another) is determined as essentially continuous or discontinuous. In the latter case, distinct causes of the transition must be assumed (whatever they may be) and a more complex theory from a causal perspective is thereby obtained. Even though Darwin himself gradually gave up the idea that the causes of the variation could not be determined, he held fast to his thesis on continuity. It spared his theory a range of difficult problems but simultaneously made it immune to both Mendel's genetics, which asserted that heredity was discrete or discontinuous (*either* red *or* white flowers) and to the mutation theories that were asserted with ever greater force towards the end of the century.

What distinguished Darwin's original theory was that variation, like the mechanisms of heredity themselves, appeared unproblematic: they required no particular explanation, as long as they appeared as passive material that natural selection had worked upon. In its economic form, however, the theory came to lack any connection with the surrounding natural scientific theories and with that would violate one of the predominant scientific ideals of the time. Darwin's attempt at his own theory of heredity scarcely filled the void: it was natural selection, and thus external circumstances or the environment, that retained its role as agent and independent variable.

---

78   *Meine Hypothese der Schöpfung der Organismen ... underscheidet sich jedoch sehr wesentlich von der* Darwin'sche *durch den gänzlichen Wegfall des Principes der nützlichen Varietäten und der natürlichen Züchtung derselben, und ist mein Grundgedanke der, dass der Entstehung der gesammten organisirten Welt* ein grosser Entwicklungsplan zu Grunde liegt, der die einfacheren Formen zu immer mannichfaltigeren Entfaltungen treibt'. Kölliker 1864, p. 13.

79   Ibid., p. 13. Kölliker returns to the question with greater clarity in his work *Morphologie und Entwicklungsgeschichte des Pennatulidenstammes nebst allgemeinen Betrachtungen zur Deszendenstheorie.*

The critics often formulated their criticism as Darwin only accounting for the 'external' and not the 'internal' causes of the development of species. This viewpoint is found in both Nägeli and Kölliker, and it was presented with particular force by the botanist Albert Wigand. Like his German-speaking colleagues, Wigand was looking for a universal law of development under which the development of species could be subsumed.[80] In this universal law, all processes – external and internal – appeared as strictly determined but simultaneously part of the same great plan of creation: we are thus once again dealing with a combination of mechanism and teleology.

As regards descendance itself, the critics demanded that all the knowledge of causal contexts that had been assembled in physiology and anatomy, embryology and genetics – indeed, ultimately chemistry and physics as well – be put to use in explaining the development of species. They therefore had another, more far-reaching research programme than Darwin, but this research programme also led them to concrete standpoints that were irreconcilable with Darwin's. The intrinsic properties of organisms were presumed to be of significance for the very changes in species. The difference can be clarified if we assume an ideal case. According to Darwin, in an environment without overpopulation and without changes to external circumstances such as climate, soil and the like, no change in species would take place. According to his opponents, on the other hand, the species would nonetheless develop because even their intrinsic properties constituted causes for descendance.

This is why, for example, mutation theory – or the theory of '*die heterogene Zeugung*' (heterogeneous reproduction), as Kölliker phrased it – could be regarded as a characteristic manifestation of the anti-Darwinian research programme, namely to the extent mutation was assumed to depend on nonaccidental factors in the organism. For his part, Kölliker saw the reason for mutations in changes to the 'embryonic rudiment', changes that according to his own basic assumption of the 'great plan of development' were strictly predetermined.[81]

Naturally, it could be said that Kölliker and his peers ended up on flimsy terrain when they attempted to reach their scientific ideal. What the embryonic rudiment was lay shrouded in darkness. The great botanist Wilhelm Hofmeister, who also actively took part in the discussion of the internal causes of the development of species,[82] had already suspected or inferred the existence of chromosomes, but it was only in 1885 – long after Kölliker's statements –

---

80   Wigand 1874–75, in particular Vol. I, p. 336.
81   Kölliker 1864, p. 10 et seqq.
82   Hofmeister 1867, p. 563 et seq.

that the material basis of heredity could be localised with any certainty in the cellular nucleus with its chromosomes.[83]

On the other hand, these later successes show that Kölliker was on a navigable path. The criticism of Darwin's theory that concerned its deficient connection with other, more fundamental biological and other natural scientific theories would also exercise a thorough influence, if not on Darwin himself, then on his most renowned followers. Huxley, as we have already seen, embraced the ideal of universal determinism.[84] Both of the most famous Darwinists in Germany, Ernst Haeckel and August Weismann, would be influenced by the criticism in different ways.

But the criticism that Huxley, Haeckel and Weismann took as their starting point was not only the one levelled by biologists of various shades of opinion. They did not share Darwin's cautious abstinence towards philosophers and other free-floating intellectuals.

In Haeckel's case in particular, the ambition was to turn Darwin's theory into a universal theory among universal theories, original and programmatic. When he introduced his master to a German audience in his article on the 1863 conference of natural researchers, he proclaimed, full of faith, his leading idea that *'Darwin bedeutet eine Weltanschauung'*[85] (Darwin signifies a worldview). He was a warm friend of various older and contemporary worldviews of a natural philosophical vintage (e.g. Goethe's[86] and Ludwig Büchner's[87]). In his eyes, Darwin had launched a new era in natural philosophy.[88] Haeckel himself had been schooled by some of the leading representatives of a non-speculative natural science: Johannes Müller, Rudolf Virchow and Albert Kölliker,[89] but he did not share his masters' strict distinction between philosophical speculation and true science. On the contrary, the distinction for him was abominable; contemporary scientific thinking suffered from living *'in diesem dualistischen Zwiespalt'* (in this dualistic schism).[90] Separating science from philosophy did violence to what, according to Haeckel, was entirely crucial to scientific work. The operations of philosophical thought began namely in the most elementary formation of theory and was therefore of significance for the entire hierarchy

---

83   Cf. Darlington 1959, p. 83 et seqq.
84   Above, p. 183 et seq.
85   Bölsche 1920, p. 105.
86   Haeckel 1873, p. 73 et seqq.
87   Ibid., p. 98.
88   Ibid., p. 72.
89   Bölsche 1920, p. 32 et seqq. Cf. Haeckel's own grandiloquent phrasing in Haeckel 1866, Vol. I, p. 18.
90   Haeckel 1866, Vol. I, p. 94.

of theories. For the sake of consistency, every theory from the highest or most general – the worldview itself – to the lowest was the same, philosophically speaking. According to Haeckel, there were two types of theories:

1. Monistic, or mechanistic, or causal, or natural theories.

2. Dualistic, or teleological, or vitalistic, or supernatural theories.[91]

The theories of physics, which according to Haeckel were without a doubt fundamental, were now of type 1. But even biology had to adapt itself to the same mechanistic worldview. This had previously been impossible, since suitability for purpose in organic nature could not be explained. Now, Darwin had come with the solution. His theory – of natural selection – was such a high-level theory that it could be called a (natural) philosophical theory. It provided, in fact, a mechanistic explanation for one of the greatest philosophical questions, namely how phenomena that were fit for purpose could arise without 'zwecktätige Ursachen' (a purposeful cause).[92] This differed from earlier explanations – mechanistic and vitalistic – of biological phenomena in that it was a truly general theory that left no facts unexplained. The *dysteleological*, or antithetical to purpose (e.g. rudimentary organs or maladjusted instincts) do not remain unexplained as in a vitalistic theory. Not only phylogeny, or the development of species, but also the geographic propagation of species, the geographic allocation of extinct species and (through Haeckel's own fundamental law of biogenetics)[93] ontogeny, or the development of the individual organism, obtained a satisfactory explanation through the theory of natural selection.[94]

This theory is thus a mechanistic theory, according to Haeckel. But with that, it must be a theory in the same spirit as the theories in physics and chemistry. In Haeckel's sweeping argument, this now meant that the theory of natural selection not only had the similarity with the other theories of lacking teleological features. It was built directly on the same foundation that physics and chemistry had laid. Haeckel's reasoning was as follows:

---

91 Haeckel 1873, pp. 16, 19, 30 et seq., 67 and several other places.

92 This specific expression was used only in later editions of *Natürliche Schöpfungsgeschichte*, e.g., the tenth, Haeckel 1902, p. 258. Similar expressions and the same lines of thought also occur earlier; cf. for example Haeckel 1873, pp. 17, 31 and 67. Like Darwin, Haeckel used 'purposeful' (*zweckmässig*) in a purely descriptive sense. Being purposeful is to have a function, and the main question according to Haeckel is whether the purposefulness of an organism can be explained causally or if 'final causes' (*causae finales*) must be assumed, ibid., p. 67.

93 Above, p. 177.

94 Haeckel 1873, p. 24.

1. The operating causes in Darwin's theory are adaptation and inheritance.[95]

2. These are physiologically determined.

3. According to the science of the time, physiological phenomena were '*durch physikalisch-chemische oder mechanische Ursachen bedingt*' (determined through physical and chemical, or mechanical, causes).[96]

With such general reasoning, Haeckel sought to escape the criticism that the theory of natural selection related to other, more established natural scientific theories in a free-floating manner. One determination for his generally arguing as he did was, of course, that he kept to his high philosophical plane where Darwinism appeared as a worldview. He had joined the ranks of the system-builders, and Haeckel the system-builder should be examined in the context where he belongs.[97]

It was not only Haeckel, however, who went in for or was influenced by the discussion of Darwinism outside biology. In temperament and pretensions, August Weismann was quite different from him; but he as well also sought to place the theory of natural selection among the truly great wide-embracing questions. It is typical that Weismann – as Haeckel otherwise did[98] – attached great importance to the criticism that one of the most pronounced system-builders of the time, Eduard von Hartmann, levelled at the theory of natural selection.[99] No circumstance is better suited to illuminating how Darwinism – in Weismann's case, held forth by a fastidious expert – had grown beyond the narrow framework of biological specialisation.

Weismann, in contrast to Haeckel, made a clear and sharp distinction between philosophy and Naturforschung (natural science). The task of philosophy was to lay out a '*vollständige, geschlossense Weltanschauung*' (complete, consistent worldview) on the basis of the knowledge gathered at a certain point in time. Philosophy was thus strongly synthetic in character, but it also had to draw lines from what was known with certainty into the probably and partially yet unknown – in other words, it provided a temporary worldview. In contrast, the natural sciences that gathered the knowledge that was to construct the philosophy did not need to have any sort of conclusive character; indeed, it had to always remain inconclusive since not every problem could arrive at any

---

95   Cf. the ninth and tenth lectures in Haeckel 1873, pp. 157–224.

96   Ibid., p. 27.

97   Below, p. 279 et seqq.

98   Below, p. 284.

99   Weismann (1876) set forth his criticism in the second part of *Studien der Descendenz-Theorie*, which bore the title of *Über die letzten Ursachen der Transmutation*.

definitive solution. On the other hand, it had to have a firm foundation, and this foundation could not be obtained in philosophy. Philosophical speculation could not guide it. In its search for new truths it could orient itself in accordance with the knowledge already established. For biology, it was a matter of accommodation to physics and chemistry: biological research had to strive as much as possible for a total reduction of the organic to physical and chemical entities.[100]

Even if such a reduction had not yet been achieved, according to Weismann it was necessary for research to attempt to established more and more connections. It thus also ought to assume total conformity to laws in nature (to which a critic could rightly object that it thereby also became a philosophy in Weismann's sense). For Weismann, the ideal of reductive mechanicism was fully alive.

His own efforts with the theory of natural selection would thus also be influenced by the basic ambition to develop or partially transform it in accordance with the scientific ideal. The criticism that Darwinism did not occupy itself with the 'intrinsic' factors and thus the physical and chemical basis of organisms had to be shown to be unfounded. The concept of chance, which played a role in the earlier formation of Darwin's theory, had to be eliminated.

Weismann solved the dilemma in a rather simple but nonetheless effective manner. He extended the principle of selection to apply to the interior of organisms as well. There was thus also a 'struggle for existence' among the organs of an organism and among the cells within the organ. Indeed, he went so far that he wanted to see a struggle between the various tendencies in the cell so that the 'stronger' tendencies stifled the 'weaker' ones and were thus inherited. In his influential theory of heredity, he polemicised ardently against the belief in the heredity of acquired characteristics and thus arrived at a standpoint opposed to both Darwin's and Haeckel's.[101] The changes in heredity were not determined by the destiny of the individual organism but by changes in the gene pool itself. But these changes could be explained using the theory of natural selection.[102]

Weismann was not alone in seeking the influences of natural selection in the interior. The developmental mechanists, with Wilhelm Roux at their head, did so as well – one of Roux's central works, by the way, was titled *Der Kampf der Teile in Organismus*[103] (*The Struggle of the Parts in Organisms*).

---

100   Weismann 1876, p. 279 et seqq.
101   Darlington 1959, p. 80 et seqq.
102   Weismann lays these thoughts out clearly and lucidly in Weismann 1902.
103   Published 1881.

Expanding the area of application for the concept of selection in this manner did not avoid the one thing that tortured mechanistically inclined Darwinists more than anything, namely that the core of Darwinism was not a deterministic law but a law of tendencies. The tendency for adaptation would apply within organisms as well.

But Weismann was not aware of this dilemma, probably because – like many of his contemporaries – he immediately believed he recognised cold determinism in the chance that entails an absence of purpose and thereby forgot the chance that signifies a non-determined context. Instead, he swept aside the remains of a further concept of chance from the theory of natural selection. In *Studien der Descendenztheorie* (Studies of Descendance Theory), he objected against Hartmann that directionless variation was in no way postulated in Darwinism. He claimed that Hartmann regarded variation as something the organism added and not – as should be done in the natural sciences – as something belonging to the innermost nature of the organism. For his part, he argued that the limits of an organism's variability depended on a number of intrinsic, and not extrinsic, factors.[104]

In contrast, Weismann refused to depart from the central thesis of Darwinism that variation was continuous and thus did not occur by leaps and bounds.[105] He thus did not deviate from a pattern that could be regarded as fundamental in nineteenth-century Darwinism.

5   Darwinism and Worldviews

The image of Darwinism and its position in the scientific community would be very incomplete if it were presented solely as a specialised theory that was developed into a much more general conception, or a 'worldview' outright, under pressure from physicists and various biologists with a broader, firmer scientific ideal. From the hour of its birth, it ceased to be simply a matter for the sciences alone; ideological viewpoints – religious, ethical, political – invaded its field and determined its development in essential respects. The ideologically dominant issue was whether human development also fell within the domains of the theory of natural selection. Theoretically speaking, the question was evident in advance and not particularly perplexing: the idea that every species except humanity would be subject to biological development would simply be

---

104   Weismann 1876, p. 285 et seq.
105   Weismann 1902, in particular Vol. II, pp. 258–371.

bizarre. But Darwin – not for theoretical, but ideological, reasons – avoided saying anything about the descent of humanity in *Origin*. Later, he and Huxley and
Haeckel would devote attention to the issue that may seem disproportionately
large from the viewpoint of the theory of natural selection but was justified
by popular interest.[106] To an equivalent extent, questions of heredity that were
theoretically speaking fundamental and crucial but less essential from the public's point of view were neglected or fobbed off with *ad hoc* theories. Therein
probably lies the most general explanation that Mendel's genetics, or rather the
type of studies in genetics he represented, completely escaped public attention.[107]

Scientific theoretical and ideological ideas, natural scientific theories and
religious and political ideas would engage with each other in ways that were
difficult to grasp in the great public clash over Darwinism. It is obvious that
even the scientific specialists were influenced by extrascientific ideas in their
evaluations of the theory of natural selection. Taking a position *for* or *against*
Darwin became a thoroughly significant personal decision. When John Herschel, Rudolf Virchow or Emil du Bois-Reymond distanced themselves from
the theory of natural selection, it was entirely consistent with their scientific
ideal. But their positions were influenced by much more than their scientific
ideal, whether it had to do with religious ideas, metaphysical requirements or
quite simply views on the function of science in society.[108]

The theory of natural selection could in fact be combined with the scientific
ideal that was theirs, if at the same time it got help from external ideas and
ideals. The best example of such a combination can be found in John Tyndall,
who stood unhesitatingly on the side of the theory. Among the physicists of
the time, he was quite alone in such a resolute position (for the sake of comparison, it can be mentioned that Helmholtz did not find it worth the effort to
mention Darwin even once in his nearly 2,500-page *Wissenschaftliche Abhandlungen*).[109] It could perhaps be said that there was a number of external circumstances that predestined Tyndall to positions that were unusual for physicists
of the time. He was Irish – already unique among British scientists of greater

---

106 Cf. below, p. 243 et seqq.
107 Gasking 1959, p. 71, explains the silence around Mendel by the fact that no other leading
      biologist was occupied with the same type of problem that he was. The reason for this,
      as far as I can understand, lies on an ideological plan external to science rather than – as
      Gasking seems to argue – one internal to science.
108 Cf. above, p. 173 et seq., and below, 503 et seqq.
109 On the other hand, in ceremonial contexts Helmholtz could make so bold as to mention
      Darwin; see for example Helmholtz 1878, p. 26. He did not take a position of his own on
      Darwin.

renown[110] – and anti-Catholic; against Catholicism he wanted to set another worldview coloured by the natural sciences. A generally liberal position made him positively inclined toward the view of humanity and of society that Herbert Spencer represented. He also became close to Spencer personally through the informal yet lively 'X Club', to which Huxley and the chemist Frankland – some of the other most active and influential scientific popularisers during the nineteenth century – also belonged.[111] Tyndall's interest in worldviews may seem much more peculiar since at the same time he recommended specialisation in scientific education that was extreme as measured not only by the very modest British standards of the time but also compared with all the ideals of specialisation in our time.[112]

In the theory of natural selection, Tyndall did not see a fledgling hypothesis about the development of species but a solid and essential part of a worldview based in the natural sciences. In his controversial Belfast Address[113] he masterfully developed the principles of Darwin's *Origin*.[114] In this account, there is no point at which it could be said that he overinterprets or changes *Origin* in the direction of his own deterministic ideal. Later in the Address, he goes far beyond Darwin in his zeal to find a worldview, instead seeking support in Spencer:[115] for Tyndall there, it was a question of arranging humanity's mental life and, above all, its intellectual capacity in the same overall perspective.

But the most interesting thing in our context is his attempt at combining the theory of natural selection with his own deterministic ideal. He declared that Darwin's theory was one of the major 'generalisations' of modern science. He added, however, that there was another, even more general theory of even more 'radical significance': the principle of the conservation of energy. He interpreted the principle in a strictly deterministic spirit: all phenomena, physical as well as vital, were connected in a single inexorable causal connection. Organic and inorganic were part of the same totality, fixed by law. The organic – what

---

110   Cf. Cardwell 1972, p. 7.

111   Above, Chapter 5, note 18. See also special accounts by MacLeod 1970 and Jensen 1970.

112   Cardwell 1972, p. 93 et seq.

113   The 'Belfast Address' was delivered first before the British Association for the Advancement of Science and is reproduced in its entirety in Tyndall 1879, Vol. II, pp. 137–203. Tyndall then had to assiduously defend his theses; cf. 'Apology for the Belfast Address', ibid., pp. 204–25, and 'The Rev. James Martineau and the Belfast Address', ibid., pp. 226–52. Tyndall also took a position on Rudolf Virchow's attack on Darwinism; cf. below, p. 504 et seq.

114   Tyndall 1879, p. 175 et seqq.

115   Ibid., p. 184 et seqq.

Mr. Darwin occupied himself with – fell doubtless under the domains of the principle of conservation of energy. The mental, to which Mr. Spencer devoted his attention, was included on the same balance sheet.[116]

The crucial thing for Tyndall was therefore that the theory of natural selection did not *violate* the principle of conservation of energy. He certainly could not assert that the principle of natural selection constituted an application of the principle of conservation of energy: it pertained to a field that also belonged to the domain of the principle of conservation of energy but it sought an explanation for the phenomena through which the principle of conservation of energy expressed itself, namely the development of species over time, and it thus made use of occurrences, variation and natural selection, which cannot usually be regarded as applications of the principle of conservation of energy.

Tyndall's argument is therefore unobjectionable after a fashion; on the other hand, however, he passed over the circumstance that the theory of natural selection is not a deterministic theory in silence. He confined himself to the remark that the more general conception, the principle of conservation of energy, was deterministic.

His scientific ideal was largely the same as Herschel's, Virchow's or du Bois-Reymond's. The reason that his position on the theory of natural selection was diametrically opposed to theirs lies not on the plane of the sciences, but on one that is ideological in the broadest sense.

The example of Tyndall is interesting because it shows how strong the ideological determination was where Darwinism was concerned. The ideological determination often went hand in hand with the theoretical: ideology required large areas of reality for its support. Tyndall set the principle of conservation of energy on the side of Darwinism with the same resoluteness that other physicists mobilised it against Darwinism. Tyndall had no great interest in – rather, it was a polite admiration for – the tremendous amount of empirical material that formed the basis of the theory of natural selection; on the other hand, he had a burning interest in the consequences it had that related to worldviews.

116   Ibid., p. 182 et seqq.

CHAPTER 8

The Human Sciences

1   The Human Sciences and the Nineteenth Century

The great discussions of the nineteenth century around the principle of conservation of energy and around Darwinism revealed a range of thorough and
fundamental antagonisms. The same antagonisms appeared in acute form in
the tug of war over what the study of humanity and its historical development
can and ought to be. The ideal of determinism was asserted here as well: if
humanity was at all to be the subject of scientific treatment, the conformity
without exception to law in all human relations must be assumed and investigated. Reductionism was constantly under discussion: could social relations be
regarded as complex expressions of biological relations? But to these general
questions, so well known from the debates on the principle of conservation of
energy and on Darwinism, still others were added: is it of any importance here
that humanity is studying itself, its own relations and behaviour and thoughts?
What role do the facts that humanity has consciousness, that it considers its
actions, that it potentially has free will all play? What do individual deviations
among people entail? Can the influence of one's own values on the scientific
results be avoided in the study of humanity?

All these problems and more were in focus in the continual exchange of
views on the extent to which the disciplines that occupied themselves with
humanity and human culture could be ranked as sciences and, if so, whether
they are or could be sciences of the same type as the natural sciences. To understand the various positions in the debate, the highly changeable institutional
conditions under which these disciplines were pursued in different environments and countries – and thereby the various intellectual traditions rever-
berating in the diverse and often mutually incompatible methods of studying
humanity – must be taken into account.

From our modern-day outlook, there is one thing we must keep in mind. The
radical distinction between the social sciences and the human sciences we now
make is foreign to almost the entire nineteenth century. In essential respects,
the modern distinction is more administratively than rationally determined.
What we call the social sciences are not held together by a synchronic way
of looking at things; historical and genetic perspectives manifest themselves
nearly everywhere, while in some essential parts, the human sciences (in linguistic research, some aesthetic disciplines and so on) construct synchronic

© KONINKLIJKE BRILL NV, LEIDEN, 2023 | DOI:10.1163/9789004528796_011

views.[1] Nor did the difference that Wilhelm Windelband and Heinrich Rickert[2] saw between nomothetic and idiographic disciplines (in which the former
aimed at laying out general statements of law and the latter at presenting the
unique) form the real boundary. There are studies in the human sciences that
are pursued with nomothetic goals in view, and studies in the social sciences
that undoubtedly have an idiographic purpose.

But even if in many respects the boundary between the human sciences
and the social sciences bears the mark of the accidental, it has still been of
unprecedented significance for modern developments. There is no doubt that
synchronic and nomothetic ideals are strongest in the social disciplines, and
diachronism and idiographic ideals in the humanistic disciplines. The ambition of attaining a theoretical character of the type found in the natural sciences, in other words, is stronger in the social sciences. To put things concisely
and simply, it could be said that the great conflict in the nineteenth-century
human sciences was resolved in so far as the tradition that obtained its ideals
from the natural sciences came to dominate one block of subjects while the
other tradition, which asserted that humanity had to be studied with methods
entirely their own, gained an advantageous (though continually questioned)
position in another block of subjects. What had been a unified field of problems for the philosophers, historians, sociologists and economists whose ideas
we will study below, had been split in two.

For this reason, the world of ideas of the nineteenth century will be difficult
for us to grasp. For most, labelling Marx as a social scientist is obvious – economics, sociology and economic history are of course the branches he moved
among, above all – but we then forget that a boundary between the social sciences and the human sciences would have appeared purely nonsensical to him;
his materialist conception of history applied to the entire field of humanity.
Comte stood out just as obviously as a social scientist – he was, at least in
name, the father of sociology – while it was in fact the intellectual history of
humanity, an extremely humanistic field under the modern classification, that
formed the backbone of his accounts of social development. Regarding historians such as Droysen and Treitschke or a philosopher such as Dilthey, on the

---

1   According to the Swedish division, economic history belongs to the social sciences whereas,
    for example, literary history in recent times became literary science in that it had to be liber-
    ated from a purely historical orientation.
2   The terms *idiographic* and *nomothetic* in the meaning 'emphasis on the individual' and
    'emphasis on conformity to law' originates from Windelband; the corresponding distinction
    in Heinrich Rickert is *historical and natural scientific*. Cf. Windelband's *Geschichte und Natur-
    wissenschaft* (1894) and Rickert's *Die Grenzen der naturwissenschaftlichen Begriffsbildung*
    (1902).

other hand, we would undoubtedly designate them as humanists if we forgot that they occupied themselves with problems that belong equally as much to the modern social sciences.

It would be thus highly misleading to speak about nineteenth-century social sciences and human sciences as two separate entities. There was certainly talk about the 'social sciences' (in German at least: *Gesellschaftswissenschaft*)[3] in the nineteenth century, but it referred either to a special discipline clearly distinguished from political economy or economics, for example, and distinct in contrast to the prevalent political science, or also to a uniform outlook that included the humanist subjects.

The attempts to find a common designation for what we now sum up under both categories of social sciences and human sciences are legion. In his *System of Logic*, Mill uses the term 'moral sciences'.[4] In the German translation, this became '*Geisteswissenschaften*', a name that Wilhelm Dilthey used after some hesitation in his *Einleitung in die Geisteswissenschaften*. Dilthey, as he himself pointed out, also could have chosen such designations as '*Kulturwissenschaften*', '*Soziologie*' or '*Gesellschaftswissenschaft*' as Comte used it, or '*moralische*' or '*geschichtswissenschaft*'.[5] For his part, Comte primarily used the designation '*physique sociale*'; '*sociologie*' was a synonym to begin with but later obtained a more independent meaning.[6]

We must therefore remember that these names – including *Geisteswissenschaft* – signified both human sciences and social sciences in their current meanings. No designation had a monopoly; there was no counterpart to the generally accepted 'natural sciences'. One important reason was certainly that the various proposals for names were biased. Whereas *Geisteswissenschaften* more or less clearly implied the idea of a scientific sphere clearly distinguished from that of the natural sciences,[7] names such as *physique sociale* and *sociologie* bore traces of the opposite idea. The name 'moral science' might possibly seem more neutral, and moreover it had tradition on its side: from the old distinction

---

3 '*Gesellschaftswissenschaft*' could thus both refer to a discipline about social conditions in contrast to the political (see Treitschke 1859) and to a general discipline about the entirety of human development in Comte's meaning (cf. below, note 5).

4 Mill 1851, Vol. 11, p. 401 *ff*, or Mill 1973, Vol. 11, p. 833 et seqq.

5 Dilthey 1922, Vol. 1, p. 5 et seq.

6 '*Physique sociale*' is the joint title of volumes 4–5 of Comte's *Cours*. According to Comte, 'sociology' was an identical term, Comte 4:201 *n*. The reason Comte allowed 'sociology' to push out '*physique sociale*' was that Adolphe Quetelet used the latter term for his first great statistical work (Quetelet 1869, 1st ed. 1835), about which Comte otherwise seemed not to know much more than the title, cf. Lottin 1912, p. 366 et seq.

7 So it is even today; cf. for example Habermas 1971, p. 19.

between natural philosophy and moral philosophy there would appear a more modern one between the natural and the moral sciences. On the other hand, the word 'moral' itself became increasingly restricted in meaning and, perhaps for that reason, unsuitable.

In what follows, I will use the term *human sciences* for the disciplines that are occupied with humanity in all aspects except the immediately biological. It is a name that bears the stamp of neutrality, at least.

2   The Specialisation of the Human Sciences

There is no modern literature dealing with the full breadth of the complex of problems of the nineteenth-century human sciences. The more pretentious surveys usually start from the philosophers' tug of war regarding empirical and rationalist or purely speculative scientific ideals. This applies, for example, to Maurice Mandelbaum's *History, Man & Reason* which, as many of the monographs on nineteenth-century positivism did, divulges the simplification that the crucial difference between Comte's positivism and Spencer's synthetic philosophy is not observed: positivism ultimately became a general empiricism, and Spencer could thus be accommodated in it.[8] The copious literature on historicism[9] suffers from the same deficiencies. Hegel, reputed to be a highly speculative philosopher, cannot be considered as belonging to historicism according to several authors since the majority of historicists worked with concrete historical material. In fact the crucial distinction between empirical material and empiricism often seems to be lost here: the historicists were

---

8   Mandelbaum 1971, p. 10 et seqq. Cf. also Charlton 1959, p. 3 et seq. and Kolakowski 1968, p. 108 et seqq. On the other hand, W.M. Simon 1963, p. 217 et seqq. has clearly recognised the crucial differences between Comte and Spencer. In the anthology *Positivismus*, the connection between twentieth-century neopositivism was particularly marked, and naturally Spencer thus became a positivist as well, cf. for example p. 3 et seq. On the opposition between Spencer and Comtesian positivism, cf. below, note 48.

9   Rothacker carried out a separate study of the word *Historismus* in German. Rand has written a valuable paper concerning the ambiguity of the word. In German, the word has obtained such an accent that it is primarily idiographical historiography that is referred to; the essential connections between philosophy and concrete historical research are thereby obscured. Cf. accounts by Heussi 1932, Engel-Janosi 1944, and Iggers [1972]. Popper's 'historicism' (in Popper 1961 et al.) has a diametrically opposite content: historicism entails an idea that various laws of development can be drawn up; Comte and Spencer are typical 'historicists'. One historicism also encompassed Hegelianism, but by 1910 Eisler defined historicism so that Hegel, but not Comte and Spencer, were included in the concept. In Italian philosophy, the word has had this content ever since Croce, cf. Rossi 1960.

not empiricists, but they were usually better versed in the empirical material than their empiricist opponents Comte and Spencer.

The crucial issue in nineteenth-century human sciences was not empiricism or speculation but the issue of the relation of the human sciences to the natural sciences. This was not an unambiguous issue; the very conceptions of what constituted the natural sciences was shifting. The standpoints scientists took were additionally highly dependent on the insights they had into the natural sciences and the human sciences, respectively. A great many of those who dominated the nineteenth-century discussion had their principal education and field of activity in one of the natural sciences. Others such as Comte, Mill and Spencer were scarcely specialised in any field; at the least, they did not take any specialist positions in the discussions. Others, on the other hand, stood out as experts in one or another of the human sciences. They looked at the human sciences from within, and the natural sciences from without.

The position and problems of the human sciences during the nineteenth century were connected with the process of scientific specialisation.[10] The specialisation did not take place in a uniform manner, and the relations between one discipline that constituted an area of specialisation (in other words, a limited and more or less screened-off field of work and competence) and a discipline that had not attained the same position are extremely intricate and significant. The specialised field normally had greater prestige (which, on the other hand, was bound up with the tendency for theoretically more advanced fields to specialise earlier). If discipline A was specialised and discipline B unspecialised, it meant that the representative of A could comment on B without appearing to be a charlatan, whereas the representative for B avoided that fate when commenting on A only if he cited some authoritative representative of A.

Among the natural sciences, mechanics specialised the earliest, followed by a range of other fields within physics. Chemistry became a real specialty well into the nineteenth century; organic chemistry separated from inorganic chemistry after the century's midpoint. Physiology became its own field of work and competence in Johannes Müller's school during the 1830s and 1840s. Darwin's theory of natural selection resulted in part in a regrouping of the biological specialties; comparative anatomy, taxonomy and a range of other disciplines were brought together into one field. On the other hand, the ideo-

---

10   The fruitfulness of the perspective emerges in all clarity when it concerns the historiography of Higham, in particular the exhaustive paper 'European and American Historiography' by Gilbert 1965.

logical determination of the theory of natural selection soon became so strong that the Darwinist biologist was pushed beyond the borders of this field as well, creating Darwinist worldviews or at least making their way well into the fields of the human sciences. Even though this expansion was short lived and barely survived the nineteenth century, it constituted one of the most striking examples showing that the process of specialisation was not one-sided. The development could, at least temporarily, move in the opposite direction when a conception emerged that was theoretically far-reaching and ideologically controversial.

The course taken by the specialisation of the human sciences was extremely complex. It is not just that the various disciplines became real fields at highly different times. Specialisation did not occur simultaneously in the great scientific powers of the nineteenth century (France, the United Kingdom, Germany) and it had highly variable theoretical, ideological and institutional conditions. Germany occupied a unique position: the human sciences were already truly specialised there by the mid-nineteenth century or perhaps even earlier. The comparison between Germany on one side and France – and above all the United Kingdom – on the other provides us with the insight that it was not only the specialisation itself of a scientific field that was of importance for the position of the field. It was also a matter of having an identity in the scientific hierarchy, general acceptance as a science among sciences with certain characteristics (either these characteristics were now regarded as being unique to the field in question or not) and thus being given space in a more or less differentiated concept of science. The German scientist Helmholtz could unhesitatingly ascribe an independent position[11] to what he, like Dilthey, called the moral sciences; his English colleagues Herschel and Tyndall would never have dreamed of such a thing. It was not just that Germany had a number of specialisations in the human sciences earlier than other places. In substance, the human sciences were regarded as sciences held together by a certain type (and a type through which no full unity prevailed) of scholarliness, and not as attempts at sciences or the embryo of future sciences.

Of course, the traditional sharp distinction between natural and moral philosophy played a role in the demarcation of a particular field of the human sciences. But moral philosophy had not been a specialisation in the older university – on the contrary, it would have been available to anyone belonging to the fraternity of the learned – nor had it obtained any clear profile. It was composed of a number of disparate elements, and thus lacked the cognitive iden-

---

11   Helmholtz 1876, Vol. I, p. 16 et seqq., p. 23.

tity[12] (i.e. the relative unity of perspective, approach to problems and formation of theory) that constituted a necessary condition not only for specialisation but also for the type of connection among disciplines that was typical of the German or German-inspired human sciences of the nineteenth century.[13]

On the other hand, it was from the old moral philosophy that the oldest specialisation in the human sciences emerged: political economy. Adam Smith was a professor of moral philosophy, and one of his many official responsibilities was lecturing in economics.[14] Economic theory certainly had a long tradition that could be developed in a coherent history of the doctrine all the way back to antiquity,[15] and in many essentials this tradition had continued outside moral philosophy and the universities. A motley collection of politicians and civil servants, merchants and private bankers, philosophers and free-thinking literary men had developed the theories of mercantilism and physiocracy. It may thus appear as an accident that it was precisely a professor of moral philosophy who gave it its initial modern form. Nor would the tradition that Smith began find its primary home in the universities – or at least for close to a century. His followers made their way along the most varied paths: Ricardo was a banker; Malthus a vicar before he became a teacher of history and economics at the East India Company's newly inaugurated college in Hertford;[16] Say was a politician before he received a professorship at the Collège de France; Sismondi was at first a merchant, then a landowner; and in the fullness of the tradition is John Stuart Mill, civil servant with the East India Company but above all an encyclopaedically multifaceted free-thinking literary man.

Political economy thus obtained no professional identity through Smith. It did, on the other hand, gain a stronger cognitive identity than it previously had, and in essential respects it developed into a specialisation accessible only

---

12 The term is used by Thackeray and Merton 1972, p. 473, in contrast to 'professional identity'. A discipline obtains cognitive identity through 'a set of shifts that a field of learning experiences as it changes from a diffuse, unfocused area of inquiry ... to being a conceptually discrete discipline, able to command its own tools, techniques, methodologies, intellectual orientations, and problematics', whereas professional identity largely entails that the subject obtains special experts. A discipline with cognitive identity is thus largely what I call here a specialised discipline.

13 On the term 'moral philosophy', see Diemer 1968a or b.

14 Cf. above, p. 49.

15 Review works are legion; the most used are probably Schumpeter 1954 and, for a more elementary stage, Roll 1973. The aspects emphasised here peek out only temporarily in a brief passage in Schumpeter, see ibid. p. 380 et seq.

16 On Malthus's career, see Bonar 1924.

to those who had been schooled in Smith's or Ricardo's world of ideas. As a specialisation, it long remained relatively independent in relation to the other human sciences.

Political economy in its classical form had nothing to do with the independent block of human sciences that formed in nineteenth-century Germany. From the beginning, this block included another economic theory linked to the organic conception of state and society.[17] Political economy in Smith's vintage had primarily a problematic and unclear position in the prevailing scientific hierarchy. Nor had it been defined in relation to the natural sciences; in other words, it did not constitute a conscious attempt to conquer a part of social reality in the name of the natural scientific method or theory. It is particularly significant that the early nineteenth-century natural scientists paid relatively modest attention to economics[18] and that the economists, on their part, rarely had an education in the natural sciences or a specific interest in them.

In this respect, the conditions were diametrically opposed in another discipline that well into the nineteenth century partially assumed the character of a true specialisation and would soon come to transform large and essential parts of the field of the human sciences including political economy. We speak here of statistics. Social statistics of various types had been gathered for ages; Sweden was first with official statistics in 1749 with the Tabellverket parish records.[19] Statistics as a uniform theory, however, did not see the light of day until the statistical material began to be scrutinised from the perspective of probability calculations. This did not take place until several decades into the nineteenth century, and as we will later see it had revolutionary significance for the views of the relation between the natural sciences and the human sciences.

Anyone seeking the date when modern statistics first constituted itself as a discipline would do well to select the year 1833. At the annual meeting the British Association for the Advancement of Science held that year in Cambridge, an informal (for the time being) group met to discuss the possibilities of

---

17   On this topic, see for example Roll 1973, pp. 211–31 and p. 326 et seqq.; Schumpeter 1954, p. 503 et seqq. Unfortunately, these authors of history of economic ideas are not familiar with the historicist world of ideas.

18   The exception really consists only of those who were fostered in the older tradition where there was a close connection between botany and (practical) economy; Swedish botanist Carl Adolph Agardh, who would become an outstanding economic theoretician, chiefly deserves mention.

19   Cf. Sköld 2004.

statistics.[20] The group's composition is striking. It included, for example, John Herschel – the physicist who served as the high priest of the scientific ideal of mechanicism in the United Kingdom – and Charles Babbage, the mathematician who so assiduously preached the beneficial application of science (and especially mathematics) and who himself was best known for the blueprints of a complex calculator.[21] Here was also the Belgian astronomer and meteorologist Adolphe Quetelet, who would soon stand out as the integral name in statistics. The group also included Malthus, whose theory of overpopulation was essentially a statistical theory, and William Whewell, the philosopher who began his scientific career as a mineralogist.[22]

This example provides a hint that at the start, modern statistics was no more a professional unity than political economy. But in contrast to political economy, it had strong support in the natural sciences and it emerged with a claim to be able to create knowledge about humanity in all its aspects using statistical methods. It was perceived as a mortal threat or a shining promise by nearly all thinking representatives of the natural sciences in the latter half of the nineteenth century.

3   German Historism

Political economy and statistics thus attained a relatively high degree of specialisation long before they became true professions. Their early development ran through the primarily Anglophone and Francophone spheres, however, and not through Germany.

The human sciences that emerged in Germany and would soon establish themselves as a uniform group of specialisations had a completely different character that – like the German natural sciences – was linked to the universities. It was highly professional: particular scientific careers led toward each of the specialisations. It had a range of fixed ideological and theoretical conditions that clearly differed from those of classical Smithian economics or of statistics.

---

20   On this topic, see *Reports*, p. 481 et seqq., and Quetelet 1869, Vol. 1, p. 11 et seqq. On the role of the British Association, cf. also Howrath 1931.

21   On Babbage as the driving force behind the British Association, see in addition to Howrath also Blume 1974, p. 220.

22   Babbage's multifarious activities have been the subject of a major dissertation by Bell (unpublished). Of great interest is Babbage's *Reflections on the Decline of Science in England* (1969 [1830]).

The differences between the German traditions on the one hand and the British and French on the other can be illustrated using the different meanings of the word *science* that emerges. As long as philosophy, in particular in the structures of natural philosophy and moral philosophy, remained the dominant term in a theoretically designed and coherent knowledge, then the differences in meaning between *science* and *Wissenschaft* were insignificant and fairly temporary: there was no particular German development of the word to speak of. For Kant, *Wissenschaft* was synonymous with exact natural science.[23] Only when the Romantic and Hegelian traditions were established in Germany and the term *philosophy* began to be pushed aside by the term *science*[24] did a clear difference emerge. The word *science* in English and French had the basic meaning of the natural sciences; in order for a discipline that did not have nature as its object to be ranked as a science, it had to adapt itself to natural scientific theories and methodology. For Mill, it was natural that his 'moral sciences' were not real sciences until they could set forth statements of law in the natural scientific style.[25] Buckle's idea was to rank history as a science; the same had already been done for disciplines such as political economy and statistics. However, said Buckle, a science must – like the natural sciences – look for 'regularities'.[26] Comte had earlier formulated the same idea. His *physique sociale* was an attempt to create a new, true science that linked directly to the natural sciences.[27] The group that assembled around statistics in Cambridge in 1833 also intended, as Quetelet so eloquently explained, to create a new science in the style of and on a level with the natural sciences.[28]

In Germany, on the other hand, the word *Wissenschaft* came to be used in all the disciplines that were cultivated at the German universities, regardless of orientation. The foundation of not only this linguistic usage but also of the entire world of ideas this usage implied can be found in the Romantic ideas

---

23   Cf. for example his *Metaphysische Anfangsgründe der Naturwissenschaft*, Kant 7:190 et seqq. On the term 'science' and its complex history (*scientia*, also *scientiae*, occasionally also in the phrase *scientiae humanae*) see Diemer 1968a and 1968b, it can be emphasised that the meaning 'exact natural science' in no way enjoyed a monopoly in Kant's time.

24   The word 'scientist' was coined by Whewell. Agassi wanted to show that Faraday harboured philosophical ambitions by preferring to call himself a 'philosopher' rather than a 'scientist'; in fact, Faraday was defending himself against a new-fangled idea, Agassi 1971, p. 3. Soon enough the term 'scientist' would catch on in pace with 'science' pushing out 'natural philosophy'.

25   Mill 1851, Vol. II, p. 402, or Mill 1973, Vol. II, p. 834.

26   Buckle 1857–61, Vol. I, p. 2 et seqq., in particular p. 5.

27   Comte 4:11 et seqq.

28   Quetelet 1869, Vol. I. p. 109. Cf. also *Reports*, p. 483.

about science, whereas the emergence itself of a number of independent specialised sciences – so foreign to the Romantics – can if anything be related to
the development of the character of the universities.

For Schelling, the leading Romantic, it was natural to speak of a number
of *Einzelwissenschaften* (individual sciences) all the way from mathematics to
'*die Wissenschaft der Kunst*' (the science of art). But none of these disciplines
could retain their scientific rank and position if they did not allow themselves
to be incorporated into an organic whole, the unity and structure of which was
determined by philosophy, '*die Wissenschaft der Wissenschaften*' (the science
of sciences). It was thus philosophy that gave the disciplines their scientific
character. History research that was 'pragmatic' (i.e. that demonstrated causal
connections in the past with the intent of thus providing the present with practical recommendations) was unscientific; for Schelling it was simply *Geschichte*
(a narrative) whereas scientific history was *Historie*.[29]

Similar, but not fully as extreme ideas can be found in Hegel.[30]

According to the Romantics and Hegel, all areas of research could therefore
be ranked as sciences. In fact, it would be extremely peculiar if they had singled
out the study of humanity for discrimination; as is known, a leading idea among
them was that any true explanation had to begin from the more complex and
join the simpler – or, in other words, to move downwards from above in the
scientific hierarchy. History had revealed a broader and more essential part of
this truth, which was the goal of the sciences, than the natural sciences themselves.

Their ideas on coherent knowledge, however, had a relatively brief life in
Germany as well. There were few physicists and chemists who wanted their
disciplines to be incorporated into the great unified science, and the Romantic
(and to some extent Hegelian) influence on biology and medicine did not span
very many decades.[31] The significance of Romanticism for the history of science
is not exhausted there, however. It was from the complex world of Romanticism's ideas that the independent human sciences in Germany sprouted forth.
Despite all the Romantics' intentions, Romanticism thus came to contribute to
the split in the sciences – and the very concept of science – in Germany and

---

29   Schelling, *Vorlesungen über die Methode des akademischen Studiums*, Schelling 1:5, p. 307
      et seqq.
30   On the unique position of philosophy, see primarily '*Einleitung*' to *Wissenschaft der Logik*,
      Hegel 4:36 et seqq. Schelling's '*Historie*' does not recur in Hegel, but he speaks in similar
      phrases about a higher '*philosophische Geschichte*' in his *Geschichtsphilosophie*, Hegel 11:33
      et seqq.
31   Cf. Liedman 1966, p. 142 et seqq.

in countries and environments where German influence reached. A block of natural sciences was obtained on the one hand, and a block of human sciences on the other.

Romanticism provided a programme for research in the human sciences – a programme that was intended for all the sciences but became dominant in subjects such as philosophy, philology and history of various types. The programme could be developed – and did develop – in various directions, and it underwent a number of sweeping changes; as we will soon see, this contained conflicting elements. The original programme can, at least, be traced in an overwhelming amount of research throughout the nineteenth century and up to the present day.

Its characteristics can hardly be deduced from the writings of the Romantic philosophers such as Schelling.[32] A few general ideas can be said to be fundamental, above all the one that at every level encompassed by science there is a more or less complex organic connection and that it is a matter of laying out the (ideal or real)[33] laws of development for these various connections, whether it concerns biological species, states or forms of art.

These lines of thought, however, were developed much more concretely and moreover used on empirical material in the human sciences by a number of Schelling's younger and older contemporaries. Ideas on organic development had deep roots in the tradition; Herder had blazed the trail for the Romantics with his four-volume *Ideen zur Philosophie der Geschichte der Menschheit* (*Ideas upon Philosophy and the History of Mankind*). Prior to Herder, ideas of a similar character had been developed by figures such as Vico, who could in turn be linked to a type of thinking that had varied throughout the Christian Middle Ages back to antiquity and Aristotle. What allows us to speak of a new tradition in the human sciences from Romanticism forward is not the fact that any new fundamental idea emerged but rather that there was a unique combination of general ideas, theories, empirical processes, ideological assumptions and especially institutional conditions, and that this combination was determined in contrast to contemporary and immediately preceding phenomena such as Enlightenment philosophy, the mechanistic scientific ideal, the actually existing natural sciences and so on. The programme of the human sciences, which kept the tradition together, can more or less clearly and more or less completely

---

32   Here, I am referring primarily to earlier Schelling, Schelling before 1810 (i.e., the Schelling who published himself).

33   A real development is a development in time; an ideal development is a development only in the idea (i.e., as the Romantics and Hegel usually imagined organic development: species were unchanging, but they expressed a coherent sequence of ideas).

be traced and reconstructed in the works of a long range of historians, philologists and philosophers. It is found in Wilhelm von Humboldt's writings on history, language and philosophy; it shines through in jurist and historian Karl von Savigny's *Vom Beruf unserer Zeit für Gesetzgebung und Rechtswissenschaft* (Of the Vocation of our Age for Legislation and Legal Science); it developed into general principles in Hegel's philosophy of spirit. It is not tied to any special orientation in the various disciplines; it was represented by antiquarians such as B.G. Niebuhr and Johann Gustav Droysen, and by historians such as Leopold von Ranke and Heinrich von Sybel who were primarily occupied with later periods. Even though most among these historians were occupied with the history of states, laws and ideas, there were also those who devoted significant attention to economic history. Best known among these was Wilhelm Roscher, and the great philologist and historian August Böckh had written an epoch-making two-volume work, *Die Staatshaushaltung der Athener*, back in 1817.

Among all the representatives of regenerated human sciences, there was at the start no idea that the disciplines in the human sciences would constitute a block of subjects entirely independent of or outright opposed to the natural sciences. Moreover, the romantic ideas about the universal science were entirely predominant. In his paper *Über die Aufgabe des Geschichtsschreibers*, Humboldt could distinguish between mathematics, the natural sciences and the human sciences, all of which were occupied with 'ideas'; these ideas appeared as concepts in mathematics, as forms in the natural sciences, and as expressions of the human psyche in the human sciences. They thus constituted different parts of the same fundamental scientific totality.[34] It was only when Romantic philosophy released its grip in earnest over the natural sciences that the differences between the natural sciences and the human sciences that Humboldt – like Schelling and Hegel – perceived as relative began to be regarded as absolute. Humboldt's ideas about history recur, for example, in Johann Gustav Droysen's *Grundriss der Historik* (Outline of the Principles of History), but with the crucial difference that for Droysen, the gulf between the human sciences and the natural sciences appeared to be unbridgeable. Droysen certainly had other natural sciences in mind than Humboldt did.[35]

---

34   Humboldt 1822, p. 228.
35   Droysen's *Grundrisse* was printed first for his own students' needs (1858 and 1862); the first edition offered for sale was published in 1868. The last and best edition, which contains Droysen's complete writings on the philosophy of history, is Droysen 1937, published by R. Hübner. A worthwhile character study of Droysen is Meinecke 1929, p. 249 et seqq. An ambitious work that contains *inter alia* an unusually clear account of Hegel the historicist, is Rüsen 1969, see above all pp. 16–21. On his view of the relationship between natural sci-

Nor were the human sciences specialised among themselves to begin with. The humanists roamed rather unhindered over large fields – but this was no accident. Philosophical ideas were present everywhere; there was a close intrinsic connection between philology and various parts of historical research. The regeneration of philology consisted in the character of languages being perceived as essentially a problem of development; this was the main idea of comparative linguistics.[36] On the other hand, the regeneration of historical research depended significantly on putting philological methods to use in the study of the historical source material.[37] There was thus an intimate connection that also appeared in such a way that a number of representatives of the human sciences stood out as both philologists and historians: this applies to Jacob Grimm, August Böckh and others. When this personal union between the disciplines was severed, it was not due to any new ideas about how philology and history should be pursued but rather to the quantitative increase in materials and the ongoing specialisation of methods internal to the disciplines.

It is also important to remember that to begin with – and not until the boundaries with the natural sciences had become impossible to cross – the representatives of the new human sciences perceived their common enterprise as homogeneous and uniform. The mutual differences were more striking to them. One only need think of the bitter feud between the historical school, with Savigny at their head, and Hegel.[38] The dividing line between them was truly significant: according to the former, it was not possible to distil any of the general principles of historical development – much less any of their goals – from the multiplicity of historical data, whereas Hegel and his followers regarded knowledge of the past as the foundation of a theory of the rhythm, orienta-

---

ence and history, see 'Einleitung', § 1 et seqq., Droysen 1937, p. 325 et seqq.

36   A stimulating, well-informed and self-willed work in which the development of linguistics is compared with that of biology and political economy, is Foucault 1966, see in particular p. 292 et seqq.

37   On this topic cf. for example Gooch 1959, p. 25 et seqq.

38   The 'historical school' in fact refers to a broader and a narrower phenomenon (i.e., historical research of the type Niebuhr, Grimm and others devoted themselves to on the one hand, and the definite orientation in the history of law that Savigny, Puchta and others represented). However the term is defined, the main scientific orientation is the same and conflicts with Hegel's philosophy of history. Hegel is no more a representative of the historical school than he is an advocate of natural law; the major difference is instead that he sought the fundamental context of history in its goal – the fully developed state – whereas his opponents ascribed its origin – the 'people' – an equivalent historical and philosophical significance. Hegel is thus more teleological and thereby also more constructive; the contradiction remains even when considering less 'democratic' historians such as Ranke. Cf. E. Simon 1928, p. 102 et seqq.

tion and connections of historical development. It is of course wrong to trace a more general antagonism between empirical science and speculative philosophy in this particular antagonism;[39] the philosophical elements are, if not as expressly set off, equally as fundamental for Savigny and his closest followers.[40] If philosophy was later pushed into the background in general, it was not due to a new anti-speculative orientation – Droysen, and later Dilthey, also based their opinions on a philosophy – but on the ongoing specialisation. Specialisation and empirical material, as we have seen, have an affinity.

It is therefore possible to find a unifying band between the range of representatives of the human sciences that dominated the German universities during almost the entire nineteenth century and later spread unevenly across Europe and North America. There is a customary name for this highly complex and differentiated unity: *historism*. Even though it is a severely ambiguous designation,[41] it will be used here as well for lack of a better one.

The hallmark of historism is the thesis that true, or scientific, knowledge of a phenomenon is achieved only by studying its development. This historist thesis can have various dimensions: for Schelling and Hegel and other advocates of a belief in an all-knowing, comprehensive philosophy, the category of development is all-encompassing. There is nonetheless a difference between humanity's historical development and the development of nature; only humanity, Hegel said, has a history.[42] By that he meant, in fact, two different yet related things: both that only humanity develops over time, and that humanity alone has self-awareness, which means humanity alone acts intentionally, actions that affect its development.

The view of nature and its development plays a subordinate role for the core of this historist conception. The historist orientation also consists of claiming that the category of development plays no role in nature or that nature –

---

39   This mistake is found in works such as Herbst 1965, p. 102 et seqq.

40   All these ideas about 'peoples' and 'organic totalities' and other material from the Romantic world of ideas are naturally not the result of empirical research but philosophical ideas of the same type as Hegel's 'Spirit' and 'state' (and, for that matter, 'peoples' and 'organic totalities'; much, perhaps most, is common to Hegel and the historicist school).

41   Cf. above, note 9. Other important literature of an earlier date is Ernst Troeltsch's *Der Historismus und seine Probleme* (1922) and above all Friedrich Meinecke's *Die Entstehung des Historismus* (1936). On these, see Iggers 1972, p. 245 *ff* and p. 282 *ff* respectively. Mandelbaum 1971, p. 41 *ff* provides a particularly broad use of 'historicism'. In short, it encompasses all thinking on development in the nineteenth century, thus also Comte's, Spencer's, and indeed even Marx's. The name that in this case should be used for the tradition based in Romanticism and Hegel is an issue that Mandelbaum does not take up. Cf. also Mandelbaum 1967 with its detailed overview of the literature.

42   Cf. above, p. 110.

like humanity – develops over time. The crucial item in the second part lies in Hegel's determination: no scientific knowledge of humanity's development can be achieved if intentional human action is not taken into account. As we have seen, Wilhelm von Humboldt argued that the historian had to trace 'ideas' as an expression of the human psyche. The philosophically less well-versed Leopold von Ranke expressed similar ideas.[43] In his *Grundriss der Historik*, Johann Gustav Droysen went so far as to declare that every historical fact was composed of many acts of will, and that it was the task of the historist critic to determine the relation between the source material and the acts of will to which it bears witness.[44] Wilhelm Dilthey, the man who most clearly and most profoundly summarised historism's research orientation and views on science, proclaimed that what distinguished humanity from nature was its self-awareness and that the fundamental discipline of the spiritual sciences therefore had to be a 'descriptive and analytical philosophy'. Humanity, its ideas and the development of its social institutions could therefore only be understood with a fundamental knowledge of humanity's intellectual life.[45]

There certainly were few among the advocates of historism who gave psychology such a key role among the human sciences. The idea that historical study – and all the human sciences were perceived as historical – should be aimed at deciphering human intents, thoughts and feelings was nonetheless fundamental to all their work. It would be hasty and misleading to say that they were united in an idealistic view of history. Their shared assumption was of a less general nature: to obtain knowledge of history, the psyches of the people involved in the historical process must always be taken into account.

---

43   See further F. Wagner 1951, p. 207.

44   Droysen 1937, p. 335 f (§ 28 f).

45   Dilthey 1922, Vol. I, p. 28 et seqq. Dilthey developed his ideas about a fundamental science of psychology in *Ideen über eine beschreibende und zergliedernde Psychologie*, Dilthey 1922, Vol. V, p. 139 et seqq. Against his own 'descriptive and analytical' psychology, he set Wilhelm Wundt's 'explanatory' version, oriented on the natural sciences. The literature on Dilthey is immense. A large part – perhaps the largest – starts with the 'Lebensphilosophie' that Dilthey developed rather late and has important points of contact with modern existential philosophy; here see, for example, O.F. Bollnow 1955, Acham 1964 and Hodges 1952. It is also in this increasingly irrational world of ideas that Lukács took his starting point in his virulent criticism of Dilthey in *Die Zerstörung der Vernunft* (Lukács 1960, p. 363 et seqq.). The accounts that provide the clearest explanation of Dilthey's development, in which the ideas he developed early on about the human sciences are also thoroughly analysed, are Suter 1960 and Johach 1974. Makreel 1975 provides a broad account, somewhat lacking in concentration, of the entire Dilthey phenomenon. Ineichen 1975 provides an overview of contemporary research into Dilthey.

This was the principle that distinguished historism from, for example, Comte's and Buckle's perception; a developmental approach, though with another orientation, could be found among the positivists as well.

We have thus been able to establish two principles in historism:

1. Achieving knowledge of a phenomenon entails, at least in the human sciences, achieving knowledge of its history: its origin, development and eventual ruin.

2. This knowledge must include insights into the mental processes that have a connection with the phenomenon in question.

But these determinations are insufficient. Otherwise, both Herbert Spencer and John Stuart Mill would be historists. In his *The Study of Sociology*,[46] Spencer declared that 'psychological truths underlie sociological truths, and must therefore be studied by the sociologist'.[47] This statement was aimed at Comte and the positivists.[48] Even Mill attacked Comte for the opinion that history and

---

46 'Sociology' is Spencer's name for the discipline that studies human societies in general, that is, also (and primarily, it could be said) their historical development. Sociology comes in where psychology ends; what we here call the human sciences are thus psychology plus sociology, according to Spencer's terminology. On this topic in more detail, see Spencer's important *Classification of the Sciences*, reprinted in Spencer 1966, Vol. XIV, table facing p. 92.

47 Spencer 1880, p. 92.

48 In addition to *Classification of the Sciences*, Spencer also polemicised with Comte in the appendix to the first edition, titled 'Reasons for Dissenting from Comte' (Spencer 1966, pp. 117–144 with later additions). It is not out of conceit that Spencer wanted to mark his independence. The difference between Comte's and Spencer's systems is thoroughly fundamental and concerns not only their views on the significance of (individual) psychology for the explanation of social events. The driving forces of history for Comte are *rational* (the growth of knowledge), and for Spencer primarily *irrational* (or instinctive and biologically rooted). Against Comte's assertion that political and moral disorder are grounded in intellectual disorder and that salvation can only lie in a true science, Spencer sets his main thesis: 'Ideas do not govern and overthrow the world: the world is governed or overthrown by feelings ... The social mechanisms do not rest finally on opinions; but almost wholly on character ... All social phenomena are produced by the totality of human emotions and beliefs; of which the emotions are mainly pre-determined, while the beliefs are post-determined'. Spencer 1966, p. 128. There is thus no counterpart in Spencer to Comte's trisection of history in accordance with intellectual capacity (theological, metaphysical and scientific); there is no counterpart in Comte to Spencer's general laws of development (integration, differentiation, etc.). Comte's and Spencer's views on knowledge, on the context and development of the sciences are irreconcilable. Et cetera, et cetera. Spencer built his understanding of Comte above all on the great linguist Gustave Littré's (1863) *Auguste Comte et la philosophie positive*, which seems to have given him a picture that was simplified in some respects. It thus appears as a mystery that posterity so often sees crucial similarities beyond system-building and an extremely general empiricism between Comte and Spencer; cf. above, p. 204.

society could be understood and explained without taking the human psyche into account.[49]

The difference between the historists on one side, and Mill and Spencer on the other, consists in the latter taking a generalised psychology into account. It was therefore knowledge of certain regularities in the human psyche that formed the basis for the study of history and of society. To the extent the historists took a position at all on similar ideas – and it was actually only Dilthey who did so – they did not accept the idea that any insight into the historical process could be arrived at using such psychological laws. For them, history comprised an extremely complex tissue of opinions, ideas, political and other institutions, economic conditions, geographical and biological (racial) circumstances and so on. They could call attention to one type of circumstance or another as more crucial, or at least central, in a historical study. We know how Hegel emphasised the significance of ideas at the expense of external conditions, and of the state at the expense of 'civil society' (i.e. the social economy); we know how Schelling, the Schlegel brothers and Schleiermacher placed art or religion at the centre. A long range of historians from Ranke and other advocates of the historical school up through the representatives of the 'Prussian' school – Heinrich von Treitschke above all – placed an emphasis on political relations. This partiality for one type of history or another can, but does not need to, be the expression of a fully realised philosophy of history; there were more than just Ranke who cherished a dream of a 'universal history' in which all types of historical factors would be included in a harmonic totality but no general principles, no statements of law could be winnowed from the plentiful material.[50]

A negative perception of generalisations in the fields of the human sciences could be said to unite the historists. This did not mean that they would not acknowledge certain types of historical laws – which we will return to – but that they denied that history could be reduced to a number of general statements. A crucial moment in each historical process is the unique and the individual, and thus above all the unique intents associated with the unique personalities. For historians, these unique intents and people appear only in the close study of historical sources; it is therefore there, and only there, that the knowledge necessary for their science can be obtained.

---

49   Cf. Mill 1865. Mill was well aware that he was closer to Comte than Spencer was; cf. for example the letter from Mill to Spencer, 3 April 1864, Mill 1972, Vol. II, p. 934: 'No Englishman who has read both you and Comte, can suppose that you have derived much from him ... I myself owe much more to Comte than you ...'.

50   Ranke's ideas on a universal history are at the centre of attention in Laue. Regarding a universal history, see also Butterfield 1955, p. 44 et seqq.

It is in this latter consequence rather than the general assertions about the human sciences where we have the core of historism. The good historist, properly enveloped in a strong tradition, did not need to be aware of the general assertions; on the other hand, they worked consistently in accordance with the norm that *in historical study, unknown material could not be concluded from known material using generalisations obtained from the study of the known material.* Each piece of historical material therefore had to be presumed unique.

In their historical writings, historists could – and often did – break with the norm; it was nevertheless their guiding light and they assessed historical works using it. Even for Hegel, the most constructively inclined among the historists, it was obvious that the truth about history emerged only from the hard-to-grasp confusion of events, persons, intents and thoughts.[51]

If we keep the historists' norm in mind, we can fully understand the dynamic in the development of the nineteenth-century human sciences. The norm differed from the research norms of empiricism, but it nonetheless had empirical consequences: it justified a strong orientation on the empirical material, on the multiplicity of facts. The idea that every piece of material bore witness to unique events and contained details that were indispensable to understanding the organic totality of historical development became a spur to assiduous and tireless detailed studies of historical documents. We only reach the truth, the young Ranke declared, through the study of concrete individual cases; we do not have the right to append even the tiniest detail.[52]

In classical empiricism from Francis Bacon onward, the truth was regarded as manifest; that is, the truth emerged directly from the empirical material for the unbiased observer.[53] For the historist, on the other hand, the truth was latent: it was a pattern that lay under the material and that emerged only if the entire material was within sight.

The marked orientation on the factual and documentary was therefore not a chance ingredient in the scientific programme of historism; there were not two opposite sides, one speculative and one grounded and oriented on the facts, in historism. The most comprehensive and scrupulous enterprise in the

---

51   See here above all *Vorlesungen über die Philosophie der Geschichte* (published posthumously), in which Hegel declares that world history, from the perspective *it must be viewed from*, appears as '*ein unendliches Gemälde menschlicher Lebendigkeit, Tätigkeit under den mannigfaltigsten Umständen, Zwecken aller Art, der verschiedenartigsten Ergebungen und Schicksale*', i.e., a mass of '*Begebenheiten und Zufällen*'. Only from this swarm of '*Einzelheiten*' does the activity of the Spirit emerge. Hegel 11:111 et seqq.

52   Ranke 1824, p. 28.

53   Popper 1972, p. 13 et seqq.

nineteenth-century human sciences in general, the publication of medieval written sources in *Monumenta Germaniae historica*, which began in 1826 and would thereafter occupy a large section of Germany's leading historians,[54] is a typical expression of historism. Criticism of sources and documentarism could be united – and also gradually were united – with other worlds of ideas than that of historism. But historism constituted an integrating moment …

What we call historism here is a name of the entire tradition of research based on Romanticism and Hegel that dominated large parts of research in the human sciences in the nineteenth century. Its crucial achievement consists of giving the human sciences a position as sciences and, to be precise, as sciences of the same rank as but a different orientation than the natural sciences.

This development, however – which led to the professionalisation of the human sciences – cannot be understood if only the general ideas and norms of historism are taken into account. The independent human sciences developed in a highly fixed and distinctive scientific organisation: the German university.[55] The University of Berlin and its successors were not only the strongholds of professionalisation: *it was there that research became an exclusive occupation.* The universities' task with the greatest status was the training of researchers, not of morally outstanding citizens.[56] It was a matter of imparting professional skills as researchers to the best adepts.

As we have seen, this development has nothing to do with the Romantic world of ideas; just the opposite, it was contrary to their intentions.[57] But in the human sciences, however, ideas that had their modern origins in Romanticism would provide an orientation for professionalisation and accelerate specialisation.

In fact, the natural sciences and the human sciences professionalised in parallel. Most of the natural sciences – to the extent they did not allow themselves to be governed by Romantic ideas about unified science – were far more specialised than their counterparts in the human sciences. Mechanicism assumed a range of knowledge in mathematics; parts of physics and chemistry experimental accomplishments. This was a strong breeding ground for true professionalisation. Certain institutional conditions that were not a given, however, were required for professionalisation; there was still space for learned amateurs. Pursuing the advanced natural sciences required specialisation (i.e.

---

54   On the significance of *Monumenta*, see Knowles 1963, pp. 65–97.
55   Above, p. 133 et seq.
56   For general views on this development, see Ben-David 1971, p. 123 et seqq. Zloczower 1966 is a specialised study.
57   Above, p. 133.

acquiring a considerable amount of exact knowledge and skills), but one did not need to be – or could not be – a natural scientist by profession. In his *Reflections on the Decline of Science in England*, mathematician Charles Babbage declared that all the sciences except mathematics could be pursued by people with other occupations; it was thus a matter of ensuring that vocational education at the universities left time and room for studies in the natural sciences. The best students in England were moving towards jurisprudence, Babbage said; but there were also natural scientific talents to cultivate among future doctors and priests.[58] Babbage spoke from experience. John Herschel, one of his closest friends, certainly had a fundamental schooling in mathematics and the natural sciences, but his primary university studies concerned jurisprudence. Through fortunate financial circumstances Herschel could make a living as a private tutor, whereas W.R. Grove, for example, made his living as a lawyer.[59]

The professionalisation of a range of natural sciences was on the way, however; it had already been partially realised in the French university and college system.[60] Creating the professional natural scientist did not require any institutional reorganisations. It occurred, it could be said, when practical work in the research laboratory became an indispensable part of university education in the natural sciences. The future specialists learned their occupational skills there, and there was no other way open to them to the pinnacles of research.[61]

The laboratory was therefore integrated into the German university system. But the professionalisation of the human sciences – not at all as given in light of the earlier tradition – required a new institution that became the analogue of the laboratory: the seminar. The history of the seminar remains to be written.[62] This much nevertheless remains clear: the seminar form gained decisive significance for the development of the human sciences and later for

---

58   Babbage 1830, p. 10 et seqq.

59   See Partridge, 'Introduction' to Merschel 1966, p. viii et seqq.

60   See for example Cardwell 1972, p. 27 et seq.

61   Johannes Müller's physiological laboratory in Berlin and Justus von Liebig's chemical laboratory in Giessen were exemplary.

62   'Seminar' referred not only to the form of education itself; it was also the name of what we now call an 'institution' with a library, etc. No distinction was made between humanistic 'seminars' and natural scientific 'laboratories'; both could be called 'seminars', but here I use the word for the form of education in which experiments were not conducted. Typical viewpoints on the seminar are provided by authors such as Paulsen, who also provides valuable information about its history; p. 266 et seqq., 400 et seqq. Herbst 1965, p. 34 et seqq. 105 et seqq. provides a good picture of the significance of the seminar form in particular for the development of historical research.

the specialisation of various human sciences. The older university education had been concentrated primarily in lectures, and secondarily in the private colleges,[63] which were the models for the seminars. The seminars, however, required much more active participation from students. There, they would not primarily provide accounts of knowledge or acquaint themselves with the teacher's knowledge; they were to take on and demonstrate a range of occupational skills. Special proseminars gradually developed where the emphasis was completely on technical proficiency and proficiency in a number of supplementary disciplines. Apprenticeship examinations in excerpting and abstracts, handling of and references to sources had to be passed there; proficiency in palaeography or numismatics or other collateral branches of knowledge that were of benefit to the study in question were to be demonstrated.[64] The journeyman years followed in the upper seminar, where the students developed into professional researchers; they were expected not only to deal critically with their source material but also to present scientifically valid reports. They were also under the more personal influence of their instructors here. The craftsmanship that was taught at the proseminar was to be refined into true science.

There is no end of evidence of the significance of the seminars. Among this evidence there is one aspect that is particularly emphasised, namely the influence of the instructor – that is, the leader of the seminar – over the participants. The seminar became the breeding ground for schooling; the instructors left their mark on the entire orientation of the students. It need only be remembered how Ranke's school of history was formed in the history seminar he held from 1833 onward.[65] This aspect is naturally important: the instructors had the opportunity to influence their adepts like never before.

There are other aspects, however, that are equally as important to emphasise. Norms for the seminar system were developed that nearly everyone who made use of this form of education submitted to. These norms applied not only to the methods of research but also to the methods of reporting. Unwritten rules developed for how a human sciences text should look: how sources and literature should be reported, how the account should be outlined and reviewed,

---

63   On the forms of education in older universities, see Lindroth, p. 29 et seqq.

64   Herbst 1965, p. 105; Paulsen 1902, p. 271. An interesting, though rather late document is E. Bernheim's *Entwurf eines Studienplans für das Fach der Geschichte* (1901). Of even more interest is, for all its brevity, G. Waitz 1867, a small tribute in pamphlet form to Ranke in which Waitz describes how professional historians were trained under his tutelage; he realised fully that this professionalisation being implemented ruled out taking needs external to science (e.g., the need of high-school teachers of history) into account.

65   Gooch 1959, p. 107.

and so on. A number of external characteristics thus developed for how a professional account should look. Norms developed for how it was to be reviewed, criticised and evaluated. The systems of norms, along with increasing specialisation, became increasingly separate within the various human sciences. It became increasingly difficult to attain this professional character for those who had not been coached at the seminars.

But the regular seminar operations also contributed to an extraordinarily large increase in productivity among the human sciences. From the very beginning, the students had to be productive: gathering sources, publishing editions, writing commentaries and gradually independent papers and dissertations. One important task was to be at the professor's service with material – and, occasionally, perhaps more than that.[66] Gigantic multi-volume works grew out of seminar activities. Specialist journals – open only to those who could demonstrate their professionalism in their writing style – increased in number, becoming more voluminous and more specialised.[67] Being the editor of such a journal meant possessing power and influence. Heinrich von Sybel obtained just such a position of power through *Historische Zeitschrift*, which he founded in 1859.[68] Another important organ – though with a broader choice of subject and a more open ideological tinge – was *Preussische Jahrbücher*, which first came out in 1858. Through it, Heinrich von Treitschke obtained a central position during his over twenty years as its editor.

The specialisation of the human sciences was not born out of the programme of historical research, but out of the development of more – and more elaborate – methods and techniques and out of the increase in material, dissertations, journals and so on within the various disciplines. Even philosophy evolved toward specialisation. Lotze stood out for many as the only philosopher associated with a university who pursued the old system-builder tradition.[69] In the discussions about the mutual connections of the sciences and about worldviews and view on life, the professional philosophers rarely made names for themselves; in the materialism battles around 1850 they were already on the outside.[70] It was, on the other hand, the great age of the historians of philosophy: Adolf Trendelenburg in Berlin looked back to classical philosophy –

---

66   With a touching lack of suspicion, Dilthey's favourite disciple Georg Misch tells how the students around Dilthey noted how they rose in their teacher's esteem when 'whole pages' of their research appeared in the teacher's work, Misch 1947, p. 42 et seq.

67   For general viewpoints, see Gilbert 1965, p. 329 f. and Herbst 1965, p. 39 et seq.

68   Here, see Oestreich 1969.

69   See for example Hartmann 1888, p. 1. Vaihinger mentions a further 15 older system-builders, most with university connections (1876, p. 4 et seq).

70   Lotze's name was brought into the conflict by Vogt 1859; cf. Lange 1876, Vol. II, p. 106.

in particular Aristotle – to get rid of the idealist system-builders; Kuno Fischer in Heidelberg, who in his earlier years professed himself an advocate of Hegelianism, developed a method of his own for the history of philosophy[71] that he applied primarily in his enormous nine-volume *Geschichte der neueren Philosophie*; and Friedrich Überweg in Königsberg developed his historical programme in his three-volume *Grundriss der Geschichte der Philosophie*. It was typical that the history of philosophy was now being treated with more uniform methods. Philology, especially classical philology, became an important adjunct science; accounts of sources, problems of interpretation and so on assumed central importance. The historical perspective also dominated in the abundant literature on logic and epistemology. The first thesis of historism – that a phenomenon can only be known by following its historical development – could apply to human thinking as well.

As time went on, the human sciences thus appeared in this tradition as a range of independent disciplines with a common orientation. Wilhelm Dilthey viewed them in this light. According to him, each of the moral sciences, or the sciences of 'historical and social reality' (*die geschichtlich-gesellschaftliche Wirklichkeit*), developed individually. The increase in our knowledge of the world of humanity depended entirely on advances in the individual disciplines. The task Dilthey assigned himself in his *Einleitung in die Geisteswissenschaften* was to demonstrate the shared foundation of the moral sciences in epistemology.[72] In other words, he wanted to elucidate the methods that the representatives of the individual moral sciences were practicing but not giving accounts of. He complained that the representatives of the 'historical school' – a term he undoubtedly used broadly, comparable to what we have called historism – had not designed the theoretical principles for their work and that a certain amount of vacillation had arisen in the face of the attempt to model the human sciences according to the natural scientific template made by 'Comte, St. Mill, [and] Buckle'.[73] Dilthey thus regarded it as his primary task to stake out the boundaries with the natural sciences within which most representatives of the human sciences in Germany stayed more through intuition than perspicacity. He himself followed the programme of historism in his attempts to draw the boundaries to such an extent that he tried to define the human sciences by

---

71   Falkenheim 1892. A detailed work about the relation of the history of philosophy to philosophy is Geldsetzer 1968, who emphasises the development from Kant to Hegel but also depicts in great richness of detail the lively debate about the philosophy of history in the late nineteenth century.

72   Dilthey 1922, Vol. I, p. 116.

73   Ibid., p. xvi.

depicting their development from antiquity forward; a second, systematic portion of his *Einleitung* was never completed.

It may seem as if Dilthey had succeeded extremely well in his intention. No one investigated the leading principles in the human sciences that had now become independent as clearly as he did during the high tide of historism. His perspective is, of course, that of the history of philosophy and of ideas: it was obvious to him that the disciplines that were occupied with what he called '*die Systeme der Kultur*' (the systems of culture) were more fundamental in the hierarchy of the human sciences than the sciences of '*die äussere Organisation der Gesellschaft*' (the external organisation of society, i.e. the development of the state, law, the economy and so on).[74] It was an opinion that, for example, the historians of the Prussian state hardly shared.[75] There was nonetheless no one among the representatives of the disciplines of the 'external organisation' who accounted as clearly for the fundamental principles of their own working methods as Dilthey.

The expression of the three main components of historism that we have so far called attention to can be found in Dilthey: the orientation on the aspect of development, on the mental and on the individual or unique.[76] Dilthey, however, clarified that there were more components to keep in mind. The motive for treating human history in a specific manner lay not only in the fact that it dealt with beings who act intentionally and who often have unique intentions. The fact of the matter is also that researchers themselves are intellectual beings; while natural scientists have to create knowledge about phenomena they cannot identify with, humanists are occupied with objects of the same kind as they. They understand their objects through understanding themselves; they understand actions and the motives behind them through knowing that motives of various types lie behind their own actions. This naturally does not mean that they identify themselves with every historical person: they could equally perceive them as strange, odious, and so on. The essential thing is that each individual must be perceived 'from within' and not 'from without', as with the objects of the natural sciences.[77]

It is possible to derive a general subjectivism from these viewpoints. In the *Lebensphilosophie* (philosophy of life) that Dilthey later developed and

---

74   Ibid., p. 40, p. 52 et seq.
75   Treitschke's and Sybel's world of ideas in its political and ideological context has been developed in a furious work by Schleier 1965. Treitschke can also be read about in Dorpladen 1965.
76   See for example Dilthey 1922, Vol. I, p. 28 et seqq., p. 101 et seqq.
77   Ibid., p. 109.

was primarily what made him known to posterity,[78] this subjectivist element is unmistakeable; and it is an element that hardly made him representative of the entire tradition of historism.[79] In the general form, however, as Dilthey expressed his intention in the *Einleitung*, he could be said to have put a more generally accepted principle into words. The general result of the argument was namely that individuals, not groups or classes, were accessible to understanding 'from within'. The individual as a 'mental and physical living entity'[80] was the starting point of all the human sciences; it was through understanding individuals that the humanist could understand the entities in which individuals could be included: families, states, classes and so on.

It was therefore not a question of individualism in the sense used by liberalism; Dilthey's view was in fact compatible with the view that it was various organic totalities in society – the family, the corporation and the state, for example – that constituted the natural entities in society (potentially personified in their leaders, heads of families, the king and so on). Instead, the crucial element was that such natural totalities were only fully accessible and comprehensible in their manifestations in the individuals included in them.

The individuals, however, only found expression in the concrete, individual source material. The practical conclusion was therefore that 'historical and social reality' could not be understood in any of its aspects without working with this source material. This conclusion is reminiscent of the one that was acquired from the conception of the irregularity of human intentions and the human psyche:[81] history and society could not be exhaustively described in a number of generalisations. But there, it was a question of an ontological statement, a statement about the nature of the historical and social reality. Here, the conclusion was reinforced with an argument from scientific theory: it was primarily not an issue of history but of the historian. Anyone who did not occupy themselves with the individual in history – devoting themselves only to the abstract and the general – was no real historian. According to Dilthey, the crucial shortcoming in Comte, Mill and Spencer was that they worked without 'the intimate feeling for historical reality that can only develop from years of study of its particulars'.[82]

---

78   Cf. above, note 45. The philosophy of life is fully developed in works such as Dilthey's *Die Typen der Weltanschauung und ihre Ausbildung in den metaphysischen Systemen.*

79   Cf. for example Ranke's much-discussed objectivism (*wie es eigentlich gewesen*).

80   Dilthey 1922, Vol. I, p. 28 et seqq.

81   Above, p. 218 et seqq.

82   Dilthey 1922, Vol. 1, p. 23.

It was in this conclusion, and not the long argument that led to it, that Dilthey could be said to speak for all of historism. He provided a well thought out argument for one of its dominant norms for research in the human sciences. A scientist could make a contribution without devoting his research efforts (though part of his training) to empirical studies: this was of course the case, for example, in theoretical mechanics, and it could be so – according to the predominant inductivist view of the natural sciences – in all the fields of the natural sciences where a firm empirical foundation had been laid. According to Comte and Buckle, Mill and Spencer, it could also be so in the human sciences. The assiduous collection of sources and their detailed study in papers and dissertations could lay the foundation for generalisations made by more far-reaching spirits than the source critics. Dilthey formulated historism's counterattack: *No one could make an independent contribution to the fields of the human sciences who had not devoted a significant portion of their research efforts to humanist empirical studies.*

Dilthey formulated yet another – broader and vaguer, but just as central – norm of historism, having to do with the significance of value judgements for the human sciences. In this area his arguments may seem looser than elsewhere, but it is bound up with the fact that the issue was still surrounded by a certain amount of obscurity. The idea of value-free science had not yet been formulated.[83] Throughout almost all of the nineteenth century there was, as we shall later see in more detail, a generally embraced idea about the significance of the sciences – and the human sciences in particular – for assessments, but there was no similar idea, either uniform or clearly expressed, about the significance of value judgements for the sciences. Dilthey, however, could be said to have spoken in the spirit of historism when he asserted that the human sciences also differed from the natural sciences in the respect that value judgements had a significance for the work itself in the human sciences. According to his own definition, this work essentially consisted of the judgement by individual people (i.e. the researchers) of other people and their actions. This judgement would involve not only an explanation of why the actors of history acted in one way or another; since researchers were not only beings who thought but also wanted and felt, marked by the values of their own time and their own society, their own values would mark their accounts. For Dilthey, this did not mean the green light had been given for value judgements in the work in the human sci-

---

83   The actual originator of the idea is Max Weber, though it has deep roots elsewhere, such as in the tradition that Dilthey represents (and to which Weber belongs in part). For a critical evaluation of Weber's idea, see Elzinga 1973, p. 20 et seqq. In our context, Weber's view of history has its particular interest; on this topic see Abramowski 1966.

ences. He could, in fact, sharply criticise the bias of a number of contemporary historians (e.g. Treitschke).[84] What he had in mind, rather, was that the world of the human sciences was a moral world – a *'sittliche Welt'*, as Droysen said[85] – and that its development was thus essentially a moral development, the stages of which could only be judged in accordance with the moral yardsticks that were given in the humanist's own time.

Dilthey thus distinguished between three types of components that were inevitable in the humanist account: facts, generalisations (or 'abstractions', as he preferred to say) and 'value judgments and rules'. Among these, facts and generalisations formed a group by themselves; they were indissolubly linked. Value judgements and rules were 'from the bottom up' separate from facts and generalisations in that they were neither true nor false but correct or incorrect. Nevertheless, they belonged to the humanist account.[86]

4   Comparisons with France and England

The independent humanistic and historist tradition that emerged from the German universities had numerous consequences that are worthy of consideration. In particular, it made life more difficult for the system-builder, who wanted to create a unity of all knowledge. Historism provided no clues as to how the natural and the human were bound up; for its representatives, the question was usually given in advance, obvious and thus rather uninteresting. The natural sciences were treated as a dead block just beyond the horizon. Not even Dilthey, who displayed such zeal in bringing disparate knowledge together into a unity and, moreover, pursued a number of studies in the natural sciences in his later years,[87] had more than a few words to say about the natural sciences. Like many others, he sought inspiration in Emil du Bois-Reymond's statements on the boundaries of the natural sciences and in them found strong support against Ernst Haeckel's limitless worldview,[88] and he provided arguments that if the human sciences were to be built on the natural sciences, then the fun-

---

84   See for example Dilthey 1960, p. 290 *ff* with letter from Dilthey to Treitschke (June 1870) and response from Treitschke (11 July 1870).

85   Droysen 1937, p. 326 (§ 3).

86   Dilthey 1922, Vol. I, p. 26 et seq.

87   Dilthey 1960, pp. 243, 261, 283. It was as a 35-year-old professor of philosophy in Basel that Dilthey followed a few series of lectures, primarily in physiology; he also familiarised himself with the writings of Johannes Müller and Helmholtz.

88   Dilthey 1922, Vol. I, p. 9 *f*, 12 et seq.

damental problems of the natural sciences – the questions of space, of movement, and so on – were of immediate interest to the human sciences, which they were not.[89] According to Dilthey, the natural sciences and the human sciences formed two different worlds. The standpoint he formulated theoretically could be said to have been followed by nearly all historists in practice after Schelling's and Hegel's universal philosophies had released their grip on the natural sciences.

Historism as a fully developed phenomenon assumed professionalised, specialised human sciences. Professionalised, specialised human sciences, on the other hand, can give rise to other views than historism; the development of the twentieth century bears witness to this. Historism also assumed a living, unbroken tradition reaching back to the Romantics and to Hegel.

Even if the German universities were the first to form research in the human sciences into an occupation with professional skills and professional secrets, there were strong starting points for a similar development in France by the early part of the century. There was a strongly organised and state-run college system there as well; in fact, it was there where the system first saw the light of day. There as well, documents and source collections began to be published in the nation's interest. Some of those who took part the most diligently in this enterprise and made the most use of it, Augustin Thierry and Jules Michelet, were moreover deeply influenced by German Romantic ideas and thus – like Niebuhr and Ranke and all their followers – combined an organic view of history with a burning interest in the documentary and the factual. They did not stand outside these learned organisations; Michelet even became a professor at the Collège de France. The conditions for a process similar to that in Germany appeared good, at least for historical research.[90]

But developments took another path in France. The world of Romantic ideas faded away, and there would be no talk of professionalisation in the German sense for decades yet. The reason for the former can be sought in the Enlightenment tradition becoming the stronger one despite everything. As regards the latter, it must be remembered that the institutional conditions long remained different in France. Research studies in historical and philosophical subjects only became available in 1868 as a result of the inauguration of the École Pratique des Hautes Études.[91] Professionalisation proceeded rapidly after that;

89   Ibid., p. 4 et seqq.

90   The best account of these matters is still probably Gabriel Monod's well-known biography *La vie et la pensée de Jules Michelet* (1923). On the publication of the document see also Gilbert 1965, p. 323 et seqq.

91   On the liberal Enlightenment tradition in French historiography, see Stadler 1958. On the

its definitive document is C.V. Langlois's and Charles Seignobos's *Introduction aux études historiques*, a textbook that breathes the same reverence for the factual and documentary as the most fact-oriented German historism; however, it lacks the superstructure of historism, the idea of the great hidden context that would emerge from the multiplicity of details.[92]

In the middle of the nineteenth century and for a few decades after, August Comte's anything but professional analyses of the human sciences and their connections with the natural sciences were able to play a key role in France. When the ideas of Comteian positivism at long last and after difficult battles sank roots into the German human sciences, it first had to be professionalised. It was thus Karl Lamprecht – a professional historian, partially schooled in Paris – who succeeded in breaching the walls of historism. Against the general programme of historism, he set the general programme of positivism. He thus aimed at generalisations, laws of historical development, connections to the natural sciences. But he did not share Comte's contempt for historism's search for facts. He attempted to connect with the tradition from Ranke but simultaneously broaden the perspective: even the individual and the distinctive would form the basis for the great laws of humanity's development.[93]

The United Kingdom professionalised even more slowly than France. There were chairs in history at the old universities, but the intent behind them was openly moral and ideological: to contribute to 'the better education of the gentry'. Having anything to do with research or research studies was long unthinkable. The work with sources and editions of sources did not become a universal concern until William Stubbs, who was influenced by Ranke's ideal, became a professor at Oxford in the 1860s. Similar developments at Cambridge were initiated by Lord Acton. Characteristically enough it was in the new, partially German-inspired university in Manchester that true research studies began in the 1890s. At the turn of the twentieth century there was also a major

---

significance of the *École pratique* for the professionalisation of historiography, see for example Marwick 1970, p. 37.

92   'Without documents, no history', both authors declare. Historiography cannot borrow methods from other sciences: it must itself begin from the beginning. Among the meaningless questions are those such as what historiography is to be used for. Langlois and Seignobos are thus adherents of a view of science that belongs more to the twentieth century than the nineteenth; they represent neither Ranke's historicism nor Comte's utilitarian positivism (aimed at general statements of law) but are closer to Mach's neopositivism and Weber's value-free science. On their orientation and significance, see Marwick 1970, p. 50 *f* and Gilbert 1965, p. 346 et seq.

93   Lamprecht 1896, p. 72 *ff*, and – in more resolute form – Lamprecht 1902, p. x et seqq. On his struggle, see for example Schönebaum 1931, p. 217 et seqq.

discussion among professional historians about what kind of science the sub-ject of history was and what its scientific character consisted of.[94]

The most influential and normative historians in the mid-nineteenth cen-tury and the decades following had been amateurs: Thomas Babington Macau-lay and Thomas Carlyle, brilliant authors with insufficient – and for their his-tory writings, almost fully meaningless – academic education behind them; and Henry Thomas Buckle, an autodidact. For Carlyle and Macaulay, the historical account was beautiful art and moral edification: 'facts are but the dross of his-tory', Macaulay said.[95] We have already seen Buckle express the same contempt for the assiduous gathering of facts.[96] Buckle, however, wanted to refine history into a natural science where Carlyle wanted to let it be governed by ethical and aesthetic norms. There was very little regarding ideals and values that united the three historians. One thing did unite them, however: they were amateurs, and they were amateurs with good consciences.

5   Summary

The human sciences presented a varied and contradictory image in the nine-teenth century. Some of them closed themselves off outwardly and became specialisations at an early stage: this applied to political economy and the new discipline of statistics. They were excluded or were transformed into unrecog-nizability in the scholarly environment where devoting oneself to research in the human sciences became a profession the earliest, namely at German universities. Professionalisation preceded specialisation there: the individual specialisations emerged from professional activities and especially from voca-tional training.

It is obvious that the relationship of the human sciences to the natural sciences had to be problematic, whatever degree of professionalisation and specialisation they presented. No matter how humanity and its historical devel-opment were defined, it was obvious that from certain aspects it was a being of nature and an object of study by anatomists, physiologists and evolutionary biologists. In its relationship to the law of gravity, it was no different from stones or planets, and the new principle of conservation of energy that attracted such

94   Marwick 1970, p. 46 et seqq.
95   Macaulay cited according to Marwick 1970, p. 44. On Macaulay's value-free method of dealing with the historical baggage, see for example Crump 1928, p. 161 et seqq. On the increasing professionalisation of historiography in England as well, see Southern 1961.
96   See above, p. 210.

keen attention could scarcely come to a halt before it. With Darwinism, the problems increased tenfold. Like all other species, humans had undergone evolution. But how did this evolution of a species relate to its historical development, to the development of societies and states? The question demanded answers.

Historism did not provide any constructive solutions. It had developed out of the determinations of the relation between natural and spiritual that Schelling and Hegel had provided, but these determinations were now out of date. Relating the human sciences to the natural sciences was not, so to speak, part of the programme of historism.

In the traditions that stood free in relation to historism, however, the issue of the human sciences was no less troubling and distressing. In the following chapters we will see how the opposing standpoints in a number of key questions bore the traces either of a fundamental uncertainty or a desire to simplify the questions to what was manageable and easy to understand – and nonetheless let them constitute answers to sweeping, grandiose problems.

Facts and Laws about Humanity

1   Between Theory and Reality

All attempts at bridging between various fields of science and at overarching theories or systems during the late nineteenth century have their background and conditions in rapidly increasing specialisation.

But the attempts could have highly changeable purposes and character. We can imagine two extreme cases. In one, there is the attempt to only demonstrate or achieve a *theoretical* agreement among the fields. It is pointed out that the same scientific ideal exists or should exist internally; it is asserted that they are the same type of problems, theories and methods that are put to use or at least should be put to use. What can scientifically be stated or predicted or explained is of the same type in both places.[1]

In the other extreme case, it is only the *actual* connection between the objects of two or more scientific disciplines that is to be demonstrated or assumed. The objects of different spheres – atoms and molecules, animals and humans, physiological and psychological processes, or societal institutions and ideas – are said to actually be of the same type or nature, entirely regardless of whether or not the scientific theories about them are similar. An *ontological* statement in the broadest sense is thus being made.

Both extreme cases can be perceived as two poles, between which all discussion about the relation among scientific fields takes place.

The distinction between theoretical and actual connections is extremely important for the reason that it often lies as a hidden assumption or, rather, as a forgotten complication in the struggle between the contexts of science and of reality. It is not an unconscious one, of course: ultimately, it applies to the general issue of the relation between knowledge and its object. But in the concrete interpretations it is often forgotten whether a theoretical or a real connection is to be demonstrated. The argumentation will therefore oscillate imperceptibly between similarities or differences in scientific theories and similarities or differences between areas of reality.

---

1   As already indicated by my mode of expression, the theoretical concordance could both be asserted in a description of whether a science actually is – and is put forth as – a norm (the science *should* be or become such); the theoretical connection or lack thereof could be seen as already existing or as something that better future research would achieve.

Certain tendencies are nonetheless clearly visible. Among those who assert the ideal of *reductive mechanicism*, and who thus argue that all science – or at least all the natural sciences – can and should be reduced to Newtonian mechanics, there is a palpable inclination to place emphasis on the *theoretical* connection. For a Herschel, a Lotze or a du Bois-Reymond, the closed hierarchy of mechanist disciplines they strove for did not provide a total picture of reality. For Herschel and Lotze, the true reality was something beyond that, accessible only with the help of religious experience or metaphysical thought. According to du Bois-Reymond, it was not possible to reach the very reality that humanity primarily desired: the one through which the universe could be understood.[2]

The strictness in the assessment of scientific theories that characterise reductive mechanicism is thus thoroughly paired with a striking leniency in relation to unscientific explanations and an interest in external knowledge. The reductive mechanists were of course not arguing that such theories as satisfied their demands for exactness and precision would not reveal essential aspects of reality. But they suspected, or tracked, or hinted at another reality beyond it as well, and this extrascientific reality became more self-assertive and important the more complex the area of reality it applied to (i.e. the less the strictly mechanistic theories were applicable). The image of the world that they asserted was thus not an extrapolation based on mechanistic theories.

On the other hand, there was a long range of more or less philosophical minds who sought support in the security in the certainty of mechanistic theories but built an ontology on their foundations. This is what the representatives of mechanistic materialism – people such as Büchner and Vogt – did; Haeckel also belongs to their circle in essential respects.[3] Here, however, it can be observed how they were less interested in scientific theories and methodology, and that much more in the statements of the theories about reality. At

---

2 Cf. above, p. 168 et seqq.

3 Haeckel's view is a bit more complicated, since he asserted that all scientific research, even at the lowest empirical level, is associated with certain philosophical assumptions about the nature of reality; cf. for example Haeckel 1866, Vol. I, p. 63 et seqq. He did not, however, doubt that the connections that his own monistic philosophy presented among various scientific spheres were also real connections among spheres of reality; the similarities he found led him immediately to the conclusion that inorganic and organic nature were in reality of the same type; ibid., pp. 111–66; see in particular his interpretations of Schwann 1839, p. 161 et seqq., where Schwann's assumptions about a religious reality beyond the reach of science dissolve into nothingness.

most, Büchner and Haeckel were only slightly interested in the issue of how a proper scientific explanation should look, or how one scientific theory could be reduced to another. Their dominant idea was that the object of scientific study was all of reality. They left no room for any extrascientific explanations of reality.

There were numerous variations between the poles of scientific categories and ontology, however. Herbert Spencer, who was more interested in the reality behind the scientific theories than in the scientific theories as such, would not have accepted the idea that the more complex (i.e. the organic) was less accessible to knowledge than the less complex; the same general laws of development applied everywhere and to the same extent. At the same time, however, he reserved an area for the scientifically unexplainable such as the more or less divine foundation for all of reality. Spencer's view of science and reality can be illustrated as follows:[4]

The unknowable
Science:

Inorganic development	Organic development	Supraorganic (societal) development

There were also thinkers who were occupied with the relations among various scientific disciplines who pushed the ontological issue entirely into the background. This applied, for example, to John Stuart Mill, who devoted no attention to the relation of humanity to the rest of nature when discussing the relation between 'moral sciences' and 'natural sciences'.[5]

The relations between the theoretical and the actual became more complicated in fully developed historism, which as we have seen started from total explanations of reality of Schelling's or Hegel's model in which the relation

---

4 The wavy line in the figure therefore corresponds to the boundary between the first and second part of *First Principles*; in the first part, Spencer develops his well-known agnosticism. Important remarks about the architecture of the system can also be found in *The Principles of Sociology*, Vol. I (Spencer 1862, Vol. VI, p. 4 *ff*), regarding in particular the 'superorganisms' and their structural similarity with organisms. Spencer's classification system is naturally also of crucial significance, Spencer 1966, p. 76 et seqq.

5 Mill 1851, Vol. II, in particular p. 405 *ff*, or Mill 1973, Vol. II, p. 836 et seqq.

between spirit and nature had been carefully investigated and the moral and natural sciences incorporated into the same totality:[6]

Reason (the absolute)	
Nature and the natural sciences	Spirit and the moral sciences

When historism had developed and stabilised, the philosophical superstructure tended to crumble away. In Dilthey we can see the process in its completion. Dilthey represented an extremely dualistic view of the sciences: there was a group of natural sciences, another of moral sciences, and there was no natural connection between them.

There was also, however, another feature in fully developed historism that deserves attention. Dilthey spoke about the theoretical relation among the scientific blocks, but only very indirectly about the actual relation among the corresponding areas of reality. His primary contribution consisted of *rationalising the actual differences between two traditions of research that the universities Dilthey had in view shared among themselves.*[7]

A reason can be seen here why Darwinist evolutionary biology – which claimed to have knowledge to provide not only about the development of the human species but also of the human psyche – seemed to trouble Dilthey and his peers to such an insignificant extent. It was a long time before Dilthey took a position on Darwinism in general in his scientific writings; by then he had long ago invaded the human sciences.[8] Nonetheless Dilthey seemed to have received the theory with sympathy; he accepted a biological perspect-

---

6 The rising line thus marks that the spiritual, and thereby the sciences concerning it, house a larger part of common sense or the absolute: the natural sciences can be understood through them, but not the other way around. The scientific explanation moves from the more complicated to the less complicated.

7 In his fully developed philosophy of life, Dilthey sought to incorporate a world view rooted in science into his schema of world views; it would become an exponent of '*der Naturalismus*'. Dilthey 1911, p. 31 et seqq. Here, both research traditions are given a shared basis of 'world views' external to the sciences (historicism points in the direction of another world view, '*der objective Idealismus*', with which Dilthey sympathises); the important difference between them, which Dilthey more than anyone sought to determine, is trivialised here into becoming a difference among various personal sympathies, moods, preferences and such.

8 This occurs above all in a part of *Beiträge zur Studien der Individualität* not published by Dilthey (the rest was published in 1895) that is now found in his collected works: Dilthey 1922, p. 303 et seqq.

ive on humanity so long as this perspective was not regarded as the only scientific one.[9]

It could be said, somewhat incisively, that Dilthey accepted the biological foundation in the actual but not in the theoretical. The same phenomenon could be observed on a less fundamental plane in Trietschke, who found no guidelines whatsoever for his own historical work in the theories of natural science, but when it suited him – as when speaking of socialism – he could say that Darwinism provided arguments for the prevailing class divisions in society.[10]

2   The New Anthropology

These examples are however not enough to fully elucidate the relations between historism and Darwinism. Many historists, through their practical activities, were already so firmly bound to their type of science that natural scientific theories of various kinds appeared as an undifferentiated unity to them. There were, however, also important points of contact between historism and Darwinism, points of contact that the historists themselves perhaps did not see but undoubtedly paved the way for Darwinist thinking in the human sciences. In many essentials, Darwin shared the first maxim of historism, namely that a phenomenon obtained its scientific explanation if its origin and development could be elucidated. It was this orientation on mere change, rather than the fixed context of causes, that was the immediate reason so many natural scientists quickly distanced themselves from the theory of natural selection.[11] Darwin did his best to meet this criticism. When he drew close to the sphere of the human sciences – as in *The Descent of Man* – he was not afraid of any such criticism and he formulated there, as we will see later, all central questions as issues of origin and change.

Darwin was not alone in this; in *The Descent of Man* he could refer to a tremendous amount of literature in anthropology, ethnology and the history of religion that were distinguished by the same perspective. It was literature that in many important aspects had already been influenced by Darwin's evolutionary biology. But its character cannot be explained, solely or even primarily, by Darwinian influence; it was from the start the child of the same spirit as the theory of natural selection.

The study of 'primitive' humans, societies, customs and religions experienced a tremendous expansion at that time. Societies were formed: The An-

---

9   Cf. Suter 1960, p. 77 et seq.
10   Treitschke 1875, p. 22.
11   Cf. above, p. 188 et seqq.

thropological Society of London in 1863, the *Berliner Gesellschaft für Anthropologie, Ethnologie und Urgeschichte* in 1869, and so on. The writings flowed. The renowned biologist Sir John Lubbock, later Baron Avebury, published *Prehistoric Times* and *The Origin of Civilisation*. Adolf Bastian, who had medical training, assembled a tremendous amount of ethnographic material during his many long expeditions; the first compilation he made of his results was titled *Der Mensch in der Geschichte*. Lawyer Henry Maine studied non-European, particularly Indian, conceptions of justice; his most influential work was called *Ancient Law*. E.B. Tylor's works *Researches in the Early History of Mankind and the Development of Civilization* and the two-volume *Primitive Culture* were epoch-making.[12]

The ideological determination in this abundant activity was strong. Classical imperialism would soon reach its zenith. The anthropological literature piled up arguments for imperialist policies. Racialist ideas, notions of the infinite superiority of European civilisation, and deprecating judgements of all other cultures permeated the writings.

Let us adopt an internal perspective here. Anthropology[13] had become a boundary discipline between the human sciences and the natural sciences. It included physical anthropology through its interest in races, but the study of societies, legal systems, religions and so on brought it into the sphere of the human sciences. Its key terms were 'history' – preferably in the synthesis 'prehistory' – 'civilisation' and 'culture'. Its predominant ambition was finding the connecting link between biological development and historical development. It thus sought an actual connection between two areas of reality. On the other hand, the theoretical ambition was much more modest; anthropologists in general appeared not to have regarded bringing natural scientific and humanist theories in line with each other as a problem. Darwinist biology, which soon became their guiding light, in general became an exponent

---

12   Probably the best presentation of these matters to date is J.W. Burrow's *Evolution and Society*, particularly Chapters 3–7. Beuchelt 1974 provides a large, weighty, but not very systematised presentation of the history of 'folk psychology'; the new anthropology here comprises 'prehistory'. On Bastian and the German variant, see p. 9 *ff* and on Darwin, Tylor et al. see p. 67 et seqq.

13   Here, I use 'anthropology' as an umbrella term for physical and social anthropology, ethnography and ethnology, substantial parts of the history of religion ('primitive religion') and historical linguistics ('the languages of primitive peoples') as well as the studies of prehistory in this connection, and so on. It is a simplification of the terminology that lacks immediate support in the vocabulary of that time, according to which anthropology, ethnology, ancient history and so on stood side by side. The reason for introducing a single term here is solely practical: what I am endeavouring to do is demonstrate the common features in all the sporadic labours being discussed here.

of the predominant natural scientific ideal only when it had arrayed itself in ceremonial costume. Most likely they came only fleetingly in contact with the more developed humanist programme of research in the form of historism.

In contrast to the historists, anthropologists also lacked the advantages and problems of specialisation and professionalisation. The leading anthropologists possessed a variegated mixture of background knowledge, proficiencies and experiences. Darwin, who was anxiously concerned about his position (and limitations) as a specialist when he moved about the commons of the natural sciences, set out freely and easily in anthropology. Huxley, Haeckel and Lubbock carried on even less unhesitatingly there. The fixed research techniques, the scrupulous management of sources and facts, the strict standardisation of the scientific method of accounting that were so characteristic of the human sciences that were dominated by historism were conspicuously absent in anthropology. Professional anthropology was long in coming. Adolf Bastian partially obtained a position as a professional anthropologist when he was given a place in the Berlin educational system. But even in Germany there were examples of non-professional anthropological research. Rudolf Virchow, the great pathologist, devoted himself to anthropological studies, naturally with all the prim caution he was capable of. Tylor obtained a position – the first of its kind – as a reader in anthropology at Oxford in 1884, becoming a professor in 1896. By then it was quite late.

But this did not mean that anthropology lacked an orientation in research. I have already called attention to the orientation on the category of development, or more precisely the norm that a phenomenon is explained if its origin and development are elucidated. But another norm can also be distinguished – one for the even more precise historism. It denied generalisations, or at least generalisations applicable to human nature. The programme was summarised by J.G. Frazer, a disciple of Tylor, in *Early History of the Kingship* where he said that what anthropology primarily needed was 'not so much theories as facts'.[14] Maine was more to the point when he said that certain relations were more 'natural' (i.e. in better concordance with human nature) than others. The economic conditions in India were thus just as much (and just as little) an expression of a shared nature for all humanity as those in western Europe.[15]

It may be objected that anthropologists certainly made generalisations – if not about humanity, then about races, primitive societies and so on. This is correct. However, the orientation on the factual and thus on the distinctive and

---

14 Frazer 1905, p. 5.
15 Maine 1875, p. 24.

unique is nonetheless palpable: it was the distinct race, the distinct culture and so on that they were trying to capture in the broad sweep of facts.

The significance of this orientation, however inconsistent it may appear in the work of the anthropologists, emerges only if it is compared with a view of 'primitive' humanity that had previously been dominant. This view cannot be completely summarised in the phrase 'noble savage' – it was expressed by many others than those who argued that the savage was noble and good.[16] The crucial element was instead the idea that humans revealed their true nature, the one slumbering inside everyone else, outside of all societies and institutions – and thus outside of 'primitive' society as well. It was thus the idea of bourgeois individualism clothed in theoretical terms. It was this idea that formed a governing element in Thomas Hobbes's and John Locke's political thinking. It was an idea that played a crucial role in eighteenth- and nineteenth-century moral philosophy. Through Adam Smith it became constitutive for the earliest of the specialised human sciences, political economy. Smith started from the notion that there was a uniform human nature, just as there was a fixed amount of resources in nature outside humanity. These were the assumptions for his theory of economic development. There was a 'natural' development, a 'natural' allocation, a 'natural' freedom.[17] The same assumptions are found, though less explicit, in Ricardo.[18] It still played a crucial role in Mill, for whom it was obvious that the general 'laws of Mind' formed the foundation for the laws of 'Society'.[19]

Marx called all these notions about original human nature, common to all, 'Robinsonades'.[20] Humanity and its conditions were elucidated with thought experiments about the solitary Robinson Crusoe. As Crusoe arranged his life on his island, unaffected by other people and laws and institutions, so would all people in the same situation order their lives; and so – according to the optimistic credo of the political economists – would life actually be ordered in a future, natural and perfect society. For Marx, the crucial error in these notions lay not only in the theory of universal human nature but also in the notion that historical development constituted a uniform and unbroken process in which the perfect capitalist society emerged in more or less rudimentary forms. The same economic relations, the same laws would prevail at all levels.

It is precisely these notions that the new anthropologists questioned. They looked around at the world and could not find the common 'natural' patterns

---

16   On the noble savage see Fairchild 1928, *passim* and Burrow 1966, p. 4 et seqq.
17   Cf. Smith 1950, Vol. I, pp. 18, 33 et seqq., 157; Vol. II, p. 37 et seq.
18   On this topic, cf. Marx in *Capital*, MECW 35:87 n.
19   For example, Mill 1851, Vol. II, p. 402 or Mill 1973, Vol. II, p. 834.
20   MECW 35: 87 et seqq., Marx 1953, p. 5 et seq.

that moral philosophers and political economists assumed. Not even Smith's and Ricardo's followers remained unaffected by doubt. Walter Bagehot, who occupied a real position of power in both the worlds of finance and scholarship through *The Economist*, attempted to unite Ricardo's theories with Darwin's theory of development. His book, *Physics and Politics*, was a barely sophist-icated attempt at creating the worldview of liberal politics and economics.[21] An element of historist relativism had crept into Bagehot's world of ideas, however. He noted – with mild surprise – that not even optimism in progress was shared by all people and cultures, and Darwin quoted him with enthusi-asm.[22]

For the real head of neoclassical economics, Alfred Marshall, the new sig-nals meant above all that greater attention had to be paid to economic and historical development. He sought support in Darwin for the thesis that all eco-nomic development was continuous[23] – his economic theory did not acknow-ledge mutations any more than Darwin's theory of natural selection did – but he also asserted that the connections among various social phenomena were 'organic'[24] and placed the superior discipline of the human sciences, which he called 'social science', on an equal footing with 'reasoned history'.[25]

3   The Origins of Humanity

The anthropology that was developing thus bore traces of the same historical relativism that was typical of historism. On the other hand, anthropology com-pletely lacked the interest of the historists in the individual person, the great individual, the singular mental life.

The direct connecting links between historism and anthropology were few and temporary. There was at least one personal intermediary: philologist and historian of religion Max Müller (or Muller), who was schooled in Germany but moved to England as a youth in 1847. He advocated the entire programme of historism but came to be a relatively important name in the new anthro-pology. It was characteristic of him that he quickly accepted the Darwinist thesis about natural selection and attempted to apply it to language: in every language there was a struggle for existence between words and grammatical

---

21   *Physics and Politics* was first published as a series of articles in *Fortnightly Review*, 1867–69.

22   Darwin 1871, Vol. I, p. 166.

23   Marshall 1890, p. xiv. Cf. Meier and Baldwin 1957, p. 70 et seq.

24   Marshall 1925, p. 317.

25   Marshall 1897, p. 121.

forms.[26] There were others who came into literary contact with historism. Henry Maine deserves mention here above all; Savigny's school had a lasting influence on him in his view of law and the history of law. J.W. Burrow probably expressed Maine's relation to historism correctly when he said in *Evolution and Society* that Maine accepted 'the historical bias of the German School' but left its 'epistemology' aside.[27]

Like historism, the entire movement that I have brought together under the designation 'new anthropology' generally did not have its primary significance through a programme of research or a set of norms for research work. Its significance and its power lay instead in that the synthesis could fill the gap between humanity and biology, between known historical development and the development of the species.

One of the most characteristic and influential exponents of new anthropology was Darwin's *The Descent of Man*. This was another Darwin than the one who spoke in *Origin*. Since the image of Darwin as the cautious and scrupulous observer has become so predominant in the modern literature, it may be of interest to see him comment on the development of humanity and societies with significantly less caution. To be sure, the fact that he took so long in fully drawing the rather obvious conclusion that the development of species included humanity as well is usually regarded as an extreme manifestation of his restraint. He was then attacked by both Huxley, who published *Man's Place in Nature*, and Haeckel, who in a number of writings (*The History of Creation, Über die Entstehung und den Stammbaum des Menschengeschlechts*, and *Anthropogeny*) laid out the descent of humanity. In the introduction to *The Descent of Man*, Darwin declared that if he had read *The History of Creation* before writing his own work, 'I should probably never have completed it'.[28] This statement may seem a little puzzling. Only two of the thirty lectures that comprise *The History of Creation* concerned humanity. Most are extremely briefly presented, and the attention Darwin devoted to the history of human development has no counterpart here.

It is true that Darwin entered the sphere of the human sciences only in certain parts of *The Descent of Man*. This primarily concerns the chapter on

---

26   Darwin calls attention to this bold application of the principle of natural selection with satisfaction; cf. Darwin 1871, Vol. I, p. 60.

27   Burrow 1966, p. 145. Burrow, however, seems to see this 'epistemology' as something 'mystic', which is not apposite. The person in Germany who partially united anthropology and historicism was Theodor Waitz, the brother of the historian. Waitz collaborated on works including *Historische Zeitschrift* but constructed purely historical viewpoints on prehistory there; cf. T. Waitz 1861.

28   Darwin 1871, Vol. I, p. 4.

humanity's 'mental powers' in comparison with the lower animals (Part 1, Chapters 2–3) and the chapter 'On the Development of the Intellectual and Moral Faculties' (Part 1, Chapter 5). There, Darwin was moving about in fields where he had not pursued any research. Instead, he used information and theses from others. The literature he made use of was of a strikingly popular type: to a great extent it involved articles in journals such as *Quarterly Review*, *Fortnightly Review*, *Fraser's Magazine* and *Nature*. His most important authorities were a number of researchers we have already encountered: Maine and Lubbock, Müller and Bagehot. He also referred a good deal to Wallace, who devoted great attention to anthropology.[29] A highly advanced position was occupied by Francis Galton, whose newly published *Hereditary Genius* provided Darwin with numerous ideas about the genetic character and roles of various social classes and peoples in the struggle for existence.

As regards modern society, Darwin found interest in a paper by the prominent statistician William Farr.[30] The involvement of a statistical way of looking at things – so distant from the methods prevalent in the works Darwin otherwise used – may seem perplexing but was in fact quite typical. It was modern society, Western and Central European society of the nineteenth and to some extent the eighteenth century, that occupied modern statistics. There was thus rapidly growing and rather well cultivated empirical material here, so different by nature from the accumulation of isolated observations and facts about prehistoric and 'primitive' cultures that Darwin could take from the anthropologists. For Darwin, modern society could thus be captured in the quantitative terms of statistics, while its most distant prehistory could be sketched using scattered details. For the history lying in between, he showed no interest in general; he made only a few individual observations about Greek high culture and the fall of the Spanish empire.[31]

Darwin had more sources of inspiration, however, than he mentioned in texts and notes. Some opinions were perhaps so natural to him that he counted them among the public property of the time. So, for example, he had an argument about economic development in which he spoke completely in his own name and on his own authority. He thus declared that 'without the accumulation of capital the arts could not progress' – it was thus the classical economic

---

29 See Burrow 1966, pp. 126 and 131. In two recent writings on Wallace by McKinney 1972 and Williams-Ellis 1966, Wallace's anthropological interests are generally not discussed.

30 William Farr began as a doctor, devoting himself primarily to population and disease statistics. His more important articles were published posthumously in 1885 under the title *Vital Statistics*.

31 Darwin 1871, Vol. I, p. 177 et seqq.

thesis that capital is a universal economic category and the ultimate driving force of social development. He also asserted that the disparity between rich and poor that capital accumulation led to did not eliminate natural selection. The children of the rich went into careers where merciless competition prevailed. That in addition there were people who could live without thinking about their daily bread was an absolute condition for all progress. All intellectual work was pushed further by such people: 'and on such work material progress of all kinds mainly depends, not to mention other and higher advantages'.[32]

Here, Darwin was speaking with the words of an amateur but the certainty of a specialist. He would never go in for anything similar in any field of the natural sciences.

Darwin's primary task, however, was not to provide an image of the society in which he lived. He was after the origins of humanity, and the backbone of his account was a range of rather simple explanations of those origins.[33] He took it for granted that *if* two phenomena had the same genesis, the difference between them was insignificant or not crucial; and conversely *if* two phenomena appeared essentially different, then that indicated they did not have the same origin. These were assumptions that could very much be called into ques-

---

32   Ibid., p. 169. Oddly enough, Darwin's highly authoritative statements about society and human history were not the subject of any great amount of attention. His debt of obligation to Malthus for the ideas about selection have been pointed out (e.g. Ghiselin 1969, p. 60), as have naturally his epoch-making studies of emotions in *The Expressions of the Emotions in Man and Animals* (Ghiselin 1969, p. 187 et seqq.). On the other hand, he denies 'social Darwinism' (ibid., p. 70; Burrow 1966, p. 20), which naturally is correct in so far as this doctrine has much more to with Spencer's fully developed social theory than with Darwin's sporadic statements. (On social Darwinism, see Hofstadter 1955; on Darwin's relation to it, also McConnaughey 1950 and above all M. Jones 1974. On the development of Darwin's own opinions, see Mirzoyan 1961 [in Russian].) What was *not* subject to attention, however, were his sweeping judgements about society and history, where his demands on his own expert knowledge and meticulousness were so infinitely far less than when he was moving about in his specialised field – something that naturally had nothing to do with any personal variety but with a view, then prevalent in England, of what history and knowledge of society required for competence. Cf. below, p. 295 et seqq.

33   Jon Elster makes an important distinction, though modelled on modern economic historiography, among three historical types of explanation: the genealogical, which only inquires into origins (Elster [1971], p. 17 et seqq.); the functionalist, in which every change is seen as a function of the change in all the other parts (p. 23 et seqq.); and the genetic, which like the functional inquires into the interaction among the various parts but also seeks to define the change in a more profound way than 'everything changes with everything' (p. 36 et seqq.). It is obvious that Darwin only sought to provide a genealogical explanation for the origins of humanity.

tion, but in the discussion that Darwin intervened in they were obvious. Darwin was therefore attempting to show on the one hand that the same principles of selection applied to human societies as everywhere in organic nature in general, and on the other that there were no crucial differences between humans and other animals.

The first ambition influenced his views on the times he lived in. Civilised races were in the midst of pushing out less civilised ones; this was natural selection in action.[34] Imperialism not only found brilliant support in the theory of natural selection; in turn, it confirmed this theory.

On the other hand, the second ambition influenced his image of humanity. He saw it as his task to show that there was no 'fundamental difference between man and the higher mammals in their mental faculties';[35] the difference was 'one of degree and not of kind'.[36] Darwin went through the range of attributes that were considered to grant humanity its unique position: language, the ability to form abstractions, the use of tools and so on. In each of these areas he found analogues among the animals. Humanity's most exclusive property, however, was its 'moral sense'. Explaining its origins in animal behaviour thus required particular effort. Darwin entered into a moral philosophical discussion with fresh courage. He declared that the topic had certainly been the subject of numerous studies but that so far no one had set about doing so 'exclusively from the side of natural history'.[37]

Darwin's solution to the issue was a very simple one. Humans are gregarious animals. Like other gregarious animals, they needed to develop certain 'social instincts' in order to survive. Morals had their origins not only in these social instincts; morals were also 'fundamentally identical' with them. Darwin attached entirely crucial significance for moral philosophy to this thesis; in other words, its reach was in no way limited to any domain of the natural sciences. It rejected or corrected other derivations of morals. The moral sense could thus not have its origins in egoism or selfishness, nor did it suffice to say that it could be derived from the principle of the greatest possible happiness.[38] What for Hobbes or Bentham was primarily a logical question (i.e. a question of the connection between different moral values and norms) and secondarily a normative one (that is, a question of the best system of morals) was thus

---

34   Darwin 1871, Vol I, p. 169.

35   Ibid., p. 35.

36   Ibid., p. 105.

37   Ibid., p. 71.

38   Here, Darwin names neither Hobbes nor Bentham, both the leading representatives of their respective ideas.

for Darwin exclusively an issue of a developmental and historical origin. Once morals had been attributed to social instinct and this in turn to flock behaviour, it was thereby also proven that the difference between human morals and the flock behaviour of other animals was 'one of degree and not of kind'.

4   Development and Determinism

Like a number of other anthropologists and biologists in the later nineteenth century, the Darwin that entered the sphere of the human sciences could be said to have embraced the *principle of simple development*. It is essential to distinguish this from other principles of development that flourished during the nineteenth century. Development was just as central a category in Spencer, but for Spencer it was a question not only of substantiating an origin and a change but also, and above all, investigating how complex phenomena such as organisms and societies ('superorganisms') developed and what conformity to laws this development produced. In this respect, Spencer was on the same side as the historists from Schelling and Hegel onward who certainly sought no conformity to laws, but rather complex patterns and hidden connections in complicated entities such as cultures and states.

It is also important, however, to differentiate the type of explanation that Darwin represented from the *linear* conceptions of development that played such a central role in, for example, classical political economy. According to these linear conceptions, there were a number of constant properties and regularities in nature and humanity, and the central task was to obtain knowledge of these properties and regularities in their complete, unrestrained or 'natural' form and then to extrapolate them backwards in historical development (and forward, in predictions). These conceptions were expressions of the same mechanistic view that dominated in large parts of the natural sciences. Darwin's conception of development did not spring from such ideals, nor did that of historism.

Even if it can rightly be said that the thinking around development played a dominant role in the nineteenth-century world of ideas, and that it all but reigned supreme as regards its views of humanity and society, it is equally important to point out that there were a number of different conceptions of development that were compatible with widely different ideas of what science was. In fact, it is here in the range of different conceptions of development – and thereby in the conceptions of what causes changes or stability – that the field of tension in which the various humanist traditions found themselves can be most clearly discerned. Questions of causal connections, of the relative significance of different (economic, social, political, ideological and so on) factors, of the role of the individual and the collective were transformed into questions of historical development. There was a fundamental unity in the midst of the fundamental disagreement.

One dominant problem concerned the relation between development and determinism. As it was in the natural sciences, so it was in the human sciences. Another related problem, as we have already seen, concerned the actual relation between humanity and nature, and a third (often interwoven with the second to the point of confusion) the relation between the natural sciences and the human sciences.

If we wish to study the changing positions on these questions, we cannot be satisfied with looking at what various authors claimed they wanted to do; we also need to look at what they actually did. The distinctive character of historism stands out better in the laborious assembly of facts into complex totalities than in the open declarations. Darwin's indeterminacy appears vaguely or not at all in what he stated he wanted to do, but conversely it is clear and unmistakeable in his way of arguing for a connection between the development of species and the historical development of humanity.

This is also to say that it is rather in tendencies than in clear statements and remarks that we can distinguish the various primary orientations in the human sciences. It is a matter of seeing which working tasks lie closes to one or another orientation, which questions were prioritised and thus also what type of material became the most important object of investigation.

Let us sketch out a few such primary orientations during the late nineteenth century:

I. *Main problem:* The theoretical relation between the natural sciences and the human sciences.
    Crucial question: Can humanity be studied in essentially the same way as (the rest of) nature?
    a. *If 'yes': The main task* is to develop the methods that have proven successful in the natural sciences (or certain of the natural sciences). *Model disciplines:* Statistics, or alternately political economy.
    b. *If 'no': The main task* is to develop unique humanist methods. *Model disciplines:* Universal history, in which the organic connection between established facts is investigated.
II. *Main problem*: The actual relation between humanity and (the rest of) nature.
    Crucial question: Does humanity differ crucially from other beings?
    a. *If 'no': The main task* is to demonstrate how it is essentially similar to other beings and that it has a common origin with them. *Model disciplines:* Evolutionary biology, including racial biology.

b.   *If 'yes': The main task* is to demonstrate the fundamental differences in characteristics and origins. *Model disciplines*: Theology, speculative anthropology.

Here, it is a matter of general tendencies and preferences, not clearly distinctive orientations. Anyone working from standpoint ia could very well adopt standpoint iia, and ib could be joined with iia, and so on. Many of those working in the human sciences could perhaps not be classified among one group or another at all – the nature of their work is not articulated in any of the orientations. Nonetheless, the essential point is that the schema of analysis gives us the possibility of specifying some of the central and influential standpoints in the human sciences of the nineteenth century.

The more straightforward advocates of the fourth standpoint (iib) will not occupy us further here. This is the long range of Christian critics of Darwinism from Bishop Wilberforce onward; their standpoint has been analysed in a number of works,[39] and their stubborn defence of the Biblical belief in creation played a large role in how the advocates of the diametrically opposed standpoint (iia) pled their case. Since their fundamentalism falls outside the sphere of problems that interest us, we will pass them over in silence.

Otherwise, it is primarily a matter of finding striking examples of how the varied starting points in the views of the relation between nature and humanity, and between the human sciences and the natural sciences, come through. The main task is to demonstrate that equating humanity and nature, and equating the human sciences and the natural sciences, are not the same thing.

Standpoints ia and ib represent what I call a *theoretical tendency*, and iia (likewise iib, of course) a *realistic tendency*. The theoretical tendency was strong in August Comte and John Stuart Mill, Adolphe Quetelet and Henry Thomas Buckle. It was also predominant in historism. The realistic tendency was predominant in Darwin and the Darwinists, and among all the anthropologists of various orientations who were occupied with the prehistory of humanity and with primitive cultures. It was also promoted by a number of historians and other humanists who sought to apply the principles of evolutionary biology in their respective branches.

The representatives of the theoretical tendency were primarily interested in the hierarchy of the sciences; the representatives of the realistic tendency were primarily interested in the hierarchy of reality – the ontological hierarchy.

---

39   For an analysis of the specifically religiously tinged discussion of Darwinism, see Simonsson 1958. Cf. also Ellegård 1958. Turner 1974 provides viewpoints on the relation between natural science and religion.

Let us now see what the differences between the tendencies could concretely involve.

Those who put the main stress on the theoretical relation between sciences concentrated their attention on similarities and differences in methods, problems and theories among different sciences; they asked above all what kind of facts could be established, what kind of generalisations could be made and what kind of theories could be laid out in one discipline or another. Those who put the main stress on the actual relation between areas of reality asked about the real connecting links between them; the theoretical similarity or difference between various sciences played a lesser role for them.

Those who asserted that the human sciences were or could become the same kind as the natural sciences also asserted that above all the same kind of theories could be laid out there as in the natural sciences. Their theory of natural scientific patterns was normally mechanism; the hierarchy of the natural sciences followed after in decreasing levels of perfection. The representatives of the realistic tendency, on the other hand, were immediately most interested in the field of biology, which most closely bordered on their own fields of study.

It is therefore not difficult to understand why statistics (and more rarely political economy) could become the model discipline for those who asserted a fundamental concordance between the natural sciences and the human sciences. With the new statistics, honed by probability calculations, a way opened up to treating humanity and its societies with mathematical methods and thus with a precision that had previously been unthinkable. For the pioneers of modern statistics, men with a primarily natural scientific orientation,[40] transforming the human sciences was perhaps not an explicit ambition; this was a conclusion the humanists themselves had to draw. On the other hand, it was obvious that statistics, with or without explicit ambitions, would have revolutionary significance if they were really taken seriously.

From a present-day perspective it would be easy to believe that what was new about statistics lay in the concept of probability. In fact, it was the other way around: it gave the deterministic conceptions the strongest possible support. It should be recalled that the very emblem of determinism, Laplace's calculating intellect, had been presented in his *Essai philosophique sur les probabilités*. Probability calculus was intertwined with determinism from its roots, and would long remain so. When it began to be used in the human sciences, the intent was to demonstrate unbroken conformity with laws there as well.

---

40   Cf. above, p. 208.

The concept of probability was used in an ambiguous manner (as it has been down to our time).[41] The probability of a theory and the probability in a theory were not distinguished. Or, in other words: there was no distinction made between statements, for example, that a certain generalisation ('All swans are white') had a certain probability, depending on how many observations had been made, and statements that there was a certain probability that one thing or another would be the case ('80 % of all swans are white'). Laplace expressed this ambiguity as probability being linked to both our ignorance and our knowledge at the same time.[42]

The question of probability thus constantly became also a question of the certainty of knowledge. It was associated with the simple insight that every induction was incomplete and thus that the induction was more certain, the larger amount of empirical material it was based on.

The ambiguity could be seen with all desirable clarity in Adolphe Quetelet's writings: *Sur l'homme et le développement de ses facultés* (published as an expanded edition under the title *Physique sociale ou Essai sur le développement des facultés de l'homme*) and *Letters ... on the Theory of Probabilities*. In both works, Quetelet started from the degree of certainty we achieve when we verify the same phenomenon a number of times and subsequently transition to speaking about the probability *within* theories. It can be imagined that the use of the concept of probability in inductive logic could create associations with uncertainty: there, it means that uncertainty is inherent in every generalisation. But this is not so. On the contrary, the grip of determinism hardens.

There is an argument in Quetelet that can be regarded here as symptomatic. In brief, it runs: If we observe that the same event occurs a number of times, we can with a certain amount of probability assume that it will occur yet again. If we have made the observation 10 times, the probability of a reoccurrence according to Quetelet is $\frac{11}{12}$. But the probability that the event has a cause and thus did not occur by chance is infinitely greater! If we say that the probability of something new occurring is $\frac{1}{12}$, then the probability of the ten observed cases being due to chance is $\frac{1}{2^{12}}$. The probability of a reoccurrence thus increases with arithmetically, the probability that the conformity is determined by a cause increases geometrically.

Determinism could hardly have stronger support. Quetelet took his 'rule' from English mathematician Thomas Bayes,[43] and his conclusions were sup-

---

41   Cf. Popper's distinction between 'probability of events' and 'probability of hypotheses', Popper 1968, p. 146, and his criticism of the confusion, ibid., p. 254 et seqq.

42   Laplace 1959, p. 898 et seq.

43   Quetelet 1846, p. 23 et seqq., 368 et seqq. On Bayes, see the article by Hacking. We must

ported by such figures as John Herschel, who reviewed the English translation of *Letters*. In the review, he said that probability calculus could be regarded as a supplementary discipline for 'inductive philosophy': with its help, the regularities and constant causes could be seen behind the temporary deviations.[44]

Quetelet's reasoning on the probability of an unambiguous cause, however, naturally does not need to be limited to a course of events in which the same thing occurs. The consistent further development – which he did not make explicit, but was surely implicit – is that as soon as a statistical regularity can be shown, we have the right to assume a causal connection behind this regularity. If it can be shown in a large number of cases that, for example, event a occurs in 30 cases out of 100, event b 50 cases and event c in 20, it can be said with a probability that stands in relation to the number of observations made that there is a definite causal connection, or a network of definite causes, behind this exact distribution. Similarly, if a change in the proportions is observed, a change in the causes can be assumed: the chances of accidental changes are extraordinarily small.

Quetelet's main ambition was, as the titles of his most well-known works show, to apply probability calculus to the human sciences – or, rather, to humanity in all its physical, mental and social aspects. His most well-known concept was the concept of *l'homme moyen*, or the average man – the simulated person who demonstrates a statistically average value in all their characteristics. This was the person that interested him in the construction of his theories. He was well aware that his bold enterprise met with protests from humanists of a different temperament. 'I have seen more than one historian revolt at the idea of ranging the suicide of Demosthenes amongst the number of probabilities', he wrote in *Letters*.[45]

He was unwilling, however, to deprive any human sphere of its mathematical treatment. Statistics opened the way for an 'entirely new mechanics'. Up to then, all the forces that defined humanity and its world had been neglected, with humanity's free will being pleaded as the excuse. Statistics had been collected without making more than short-term practical use of them. The great men of mathematics from Pascal to Gauss had devoted attention to probability calculus but had left aside the material that could be used on humanity. This was primarily due to the fact that there was no proper training in how

---

notice that what Quetelet says is *not* the probability that a certain conformity to law will arise (e.g. that a die will land on six a given number of times) is thus and so; he is talking about the probability that the conformity to law *will have a cause.*

44   Herschel 1850, in Quetelet 1869, Vol. I, p. 44 et seqq.
45   Quetelet 1846, p. 3.

the material of experience was to be handled. Analytical mechanics could be developed without observing reality – but not celestial mechanics, and human mechanics even less so. The same regularity in nature – or even greater – could nonetheless be verified in human relations.

The mechanistic ideal was thus alive and central for Quetelet.[46] Nevertheless, he did not stand out as an advocate of *reductive mechanicism*; he discerned specific moral forces that influence humanity, and he declared that these moral forces had a nature that we would probably never make out. This did not prevent them from becoming the subjects of statistical calculations.[47] Quetelet also declared that humanity's own effect on the world was infinitely smaller than that of the forces of nature, and as regards the individual person, their significance in the greater context was inestimably small (*'sensiblement nulle'*).[48]

Of course, Quetelet did not mean that the statistical average would be applicable to every separate individual and in every individual case: knowing the average age at death does not mean knowing anything about your age at your death. On the other hand, the individual – however remarkable or distinctive they may be – seems not to have offered anything of scientific interest to Quetelet. The philosopher and the lawmaker, he said (and by 'philosopher' he meant the scientist according to the older vocabulary), were not greatly interested in the particulars. Deviations should instead be eliminated, and it remained for the authors and the artists to make the most of these extremes that endowed a society with its picturesque elements.[49]

5   Comte, Buckle and Mill

Quetelet stands out as one of the most important, most consistent – and perhaps the most ignored[50] – innovators in the nineteenth-century human sci-

---

46   Quetelet 1869, Vol. I, p. 106 et seqq.

47   Ibid., p. 146.

48   Ibid., p. 108.

49   Ibid., p. 127 et seq.

50   It is typical that he is not even mentioned in a large, pretentious survey such as Mandelbaum 1971. Even in the historiographic literature he is conspicuous – despite his extraordinary significance for Buckle and indirectly for Lamprecht and all statistically oriented historiography – by his absence. W.M. Simon mentions him in two lines as a parallel phenomenon to Comte (1963, p. 142 et seq). One has to turn to Lange 1876, Vol. II, p. 402 et seqq. for a plausible evaluation of Quetelet's significance. Marx takes up Quetelet's statistical theories in passing (e.g. in MECW 37:847). The best monograph on his statistics and efforts is still Lottin from 1912. The little article by Freudental 1975 provides a good modern introduction.

ences. He certainly deviated from his strict programme, for example when he was intrigued by the old homunculus concept (the idea that individual people pass through the development of all of humanity in their lives).[51] He worked largely without distractions, however, and his direct and indirect influence was enormous.

Quetelet's approach to the problem of the relation between humanity and nature was extremely theoretically oriented. While Darwin was satisfied with successfully deriving the origins of human morals, Quetelet declared that morals as such were unexplainable; the only thing that interested him was that the effects of this incomprehensible force could become the subject of calculations.

Quetelet placed the traditional problems in the human sciences of the relation between the individual and the general (and thus between individuals and groups, people and humanity, facts and generalisations) in a new light. One of the people who was the most irresistibly captivated by his theses was Henry Thomas Buckle, who reverently referred to Quetelet in his *History of Civilization in England*[52] (for which Quetelet thanked him with lengthy quotes from Buckle in *Physique sociale*).[53] Buckle used statistical material in his account for a very definite purpose, however. He wanted to show that individual decisions – individual acts of will – did not affect the total amount of human actions in a society. The number of murders was quite constant from one year to the next, as was the number of suicides, the number of marriages and so on. One did thus not have to look into individual emotional lives to find the real causes of similar actions that were customarily regarded as highly individual decisions. The meaningful occupation for a historian was thus to track 'regularities' in each social process. The fact that regularity also characterises human actions emerges from the statistical evidence and can be expressed mathematically, Buckle declared.[54]

There were crucial differences between Quetelet and Buckle, however. Without exception, Quetelet moved only in fields where statistical material existed. Buckle described a historical development that with respect to statistics was almost entirely unworked. He used statistics as an argument for seeking 'regularities' everywhere, whether or not they emerged with the exactness of figures.

---

51   Quetelet 1869, Vol. II, p. 90 et seq.
52   Buckle 1857–61, Vol. I, p. 25 et al.
53   Quetelet 1869, Vol. I, p. 139 et seqq.
54   Buckle 1857–61, Vol. I, p. 20 et seqq.

For the very reason that Quetelet bound his accounts up with statistics, he was prevented from drawing up any major guidelines for a history of humanity. Moreover, he had his suspicions that the unexplainable 'moral forces' had something to do with historical progress[55] – and therefore the history of progress that Buckle wrote would go even further beyond his own reach.

Buckle was not only influenced by Quetelet, however; Auguste Comte also belongs among his spiritual fathers. As we have seen, he shared Comte's contempt for a history that only gathered facts.[56] He also shared Comte's ambition for writing the complete history of civilisation.

Comte gave no indication of the significance of statistics; in general, concrete references are extremely few in his uncontrollably flowing, long-winded and unwieldy prose. But he expressed the same fundamental ideas as Quetelet and Buckle, namely that it was not individual events or people, and even less so the unique actions and personalities, that gave us insights into any social or historical process whatsoever. On the contrary, Comte said, we can almost always ignore such things. The essential thing is the common, the regular and the constant, occurring everywhere.[57]

But Comte and Buckle wrote history, which Quetelet did not. For Comte and Buckle, the living material of statistics – the mathematically treated material – played no role. They were satisfied with endowing their accounts with a more superficial similarity with the natural sciences. Comte distinguished between the static and the dynamic in social physics. The terms are prestigious, but the distinction is important. The static describes the social condition as a condition in balance; it is an account of the main components and their mutual relations.[58] The dynamic describes the same condition as a condition in development; it is a matter of finding the laws for its 'natural progress'.[59] John Stuart Mill took over the distinction in his *Principles of Political Economy*, in which he devoted the three first volumes to the static in economics and the fourth to the dynamic. For Mill, the static was the study of 'the field of eco-

---

55   Quetelet 1869, Vol. 1, p. 146.
56   Above, p. 210.
57   'Dans la recherche des véritables lois de la sociabilité, tous les événements exceptionnels ou tous les details trop minutieux, si puérilement recherchés par la curiosité irrationelle des aveugles compilateurs d'anecdotes stériles, doivent être presque toujours élagués [removed] comme essentiellement insignifiants: tandis que la science doit surtout s'attacher aux phénomènes les plus vulgaires, que chacun de ceux qui y participent pourrait spontanément apercevoir autour de soi, comme constituent le fonds principal de la vie sociale habituelle'. Comte 5:9.
58   Comte 4:430 et seqq.
59   Ibid., p. 498 et seqq.

nomic facts' and the causal relations among these facts; the dynamic became the laws of economic change (which for Mill, just as obviously as for Comte, were synonymous with economic progress) and the extreme tendencies of change.[60]

Comte, Buckle and Mill borrowed all their power and confidence from the vocabulary of physics in their attempts to go from the accidental and the individual in the historical and social course of events to conformity with law. They found it in the development of human knowledge. From the beginning, humanity was completely at the mercy of external circumstances, of their biological constitution and the environment in which they lived. Step by step, however, they obtained knowledge of their world, and this knowledge gave them above all the possibility of mastering and changing it.[61]

The essential thing for both Comte and Buckle was therefore that this entire process could be described and explained without reference to the individual. Buckle, who was more concrete in his historical writing, described the factors that determined humanity's world from the beginning but also – if they were favourable – gave them the possibility of changing it. This was what he called 'physical agents': climate, food, soil and also 'the General Aspect of Nature', or the various ways in which nature leaves its mark on human experiences and thinking. Different natural environments provided humanity with different possibilities for developing its ingenuity – the most fertile environments prepared the ground for passivity – but they also left their mark on its intellectual and moral orientations. National character – or 'national thought', as Buckle phrased it – had its origins in 'the General Aspect of Nature'.[62]

The physical agents, or driving forces, thus formed the starting point for all of historical development; from them developed humanity's moral conceptions, and they constituted the basis for its knowledge. In different environments, the physical agents could be differently advantageous for humanity's gradual liberation from the rule of those same agents.

Like Comte, Buckle emphasised that advances in the historical process depended on intellectual, not moral, advances. Moral systems were largely the same from era to era, and intellectual ones varied, Buckle said.[63] The 'moral forces' that Quetelet found so distinctive and significant, the 'moral sense' that for Darwin was humanity's foremost characteristic, was according to Comte and Buckle without actual significance for historical development. They were

---

60   Mill 1965, Vol. II, p. 705.
61   For example, Comte 4:36 et seq. and Buckle 1857–61, Vol. I, p. 18 et seq.
62   Buckle 1857–61, Vol. I, p. 36 et seqq., p. 109 et seqq.
63   Ibid., p. 166 et seqq.

pure intellectualists. There was a connection, or rather an affinity, between this intellectualism and their belief that everything could be explained by scientific and theoretical means. Quetelet, the exponent of a scientific ideal similar to that of Herschel or Lotze, gladly left a field open for 'another world'. Darwin's motive in emphasising the significance of morals was of another type. His primary goal was to demonstrate the actual link between the biological and the nearly instinctual and affective. The path from animal to human was easiest to substantiate in the development of emotions and of the will. This line of thought was fully and consistently developed in Herbert Spencer. Spencer's central criticism of Comte concerned the latter's intellectualism. The central line of development in history was not that of the intellect but of the emotions, Spencer said.[64]

Let us return to Buckle and Comte, however. There was despite everything an important difference between them. Comte sought to move away from the individual by simply leaving psychology entirely aside. The human psyche generally did not need to be taken into account when regarding historical and social development. To strengthen this kind of conclusion, Comte proclaimed that the mental could completely be reduced to the physiological: the mental development that could be traced in the historical could be described entirely in physiological terms. The development from the instinctual to the intellectual could be described as a development from one condition in which the rear part of the brain constituted the centre to a condition in which humans regulated their lives from the front part of the brain.[65]

When Buckle was defining his historical determinism, however, he took up psychological terms; he spoke about motives for actions. An action being causally determined meant that it was performed in accordance with one or more motives, and that the motives had their fixed determinations. If, Buckle said, we have complete knowledge of the determinations, we can also predict the action with complete certainty. It was a definition that in its essentials resembled the one Mill gave in *A System of Logic*. The similarity in part concerns the wording itself; even if Buckle did not refer to Mill, it can rightly be assumed that he took his inspiration from Mill. Buckle spoke only of 'motives', and Mill about 'motives which are present to the individual's mind'. And, more importantly: Mill said that the knowledge of the 'character and disposition' of the person in question was significant. Individuality, the individual distinctive character was thus a factor to be taken into account. For Buckle, such an assumption

---

64   Cf. above, Chapter 8, note 48.
65   Comte 5:37.

would complicate the calculation. He would have yet another variable, or range of variables, to include.[66]

We are thus dealing here with a scale of viewpoints ranging from Comte's (which completely eliminated the mental) through Buckle's (in which the differences between various mental constitutions were ignored) to Mill's (according to which differences in character and mental dispositions played a role regardless of how broad a perspective we construct). With that, Mill was arguing entirely as a consequence of his opinion that the conformity to law in society was built on the conformity to law in the individual psyche.[67]

Comte, Buckle and Mill, however, were united in the ambition to create human sciences in accordance with the norms of the natural sciences, a 'social physics'. They essentially represented a theoretical tendency: the starting point for their arguments was the relation among sciences, not between spheres of reality.

6 Mill's Individualism

Mill's programme for the human sciences deserves somewhat closer scrutiny. Mill was a specialist in a discipline of the human sciences – political economy. While statistics, with its mathematical methods and its air of exactness became the model of the human sciences for Buckle, political economy played a similar role for Mill. By Mill's time, political economy had only been invaded by mathematical methods to a very insignificant extent; the statistical material being used was also of limited range. On the other hand, it spoke assiduously of laws and legal contexts. To a great degree, classical economy was a nomothetic discipline.

Mill's view of the range of the laws of political economy was determined by his basic conception that every study of society had to start from the study of the individual. Political economy was based only on the side of the human

---

66   Buckle says 'That when we perform an action, we perform it in consequence of some motive or motives; that those motives are the results of some antecedents; and that, therefore, if we are acquainted with the whole of the antecedents, and with all the laws of their movements, we could with unerring certainty predict the whole of their immediate results'. Buckle 1857–61, Vol. I, p. 17. Mill says 'that, given the motives which are present to an individual's mind, and given likewise the character and disposition of the individual, the manner in which he will act may be unerringly inferred ...' Mill 1851, Vol. II. p. 406 or Mill 1973, Vol. II, p. 836 et seq.

67   Mill 1851, Vol. II. p. 449 et seqq. or Mill 1973, Vol. II, p. 875 et seqq.

psyche that had to do with its desire for gain. It was therefore an abstraction from a broader mental context, and with that also an abstraction from a broader social context: it ignored all circumstances that were significant for a society that were not economic – including its economy.[68]

When Mill, in his own political economy, thus spoke about the static and the dynamic in economic conditions, it was an issue of the static and the dynamic for a limited sector of society. But there were more possible abstractions than the economy; there were several disciplines in the human sciences that could strive for the status of physics. Just as the economy was built on the psychology of greed, so were other sciences built on society in equivalent psychological disciplines. Mill was highly consistent in his individualistic principle, which thus served as a kind of rule of thumb for his theories and could be formulated as: *There is nothing in society that does not have its equivalent and its basis in the individual.*

But Mill did not distinguish solely between fundamental humanist disciplines that dealt with the individual and the derived human sciences that dealt with society. He also distinguished between inductive and deductive disciplines – a distinction applicable to the entire scientific hierarchy. It was thus not a question of different sciences with different subjects, but of complementary methods of creating knowledge. According to Mill's epistemology, the inductive process had to precede the deductive. There was an inductive psychology, in which 'the Laws of Mind' were laid out on the basis of experiential material. But there was also a corresponding deductive discipline. Mill called it 'Ethology, or the science of the formation of character'. It was a name that would not be adopted; the term 'ethology', as is known, would much later be used for an entirely different discipline. What Mill meant by 'ethology' was, if the object of study is considered, what others called anthropology: it had all of humanity (and not just its psyche) as its subject. In its scientific character, it differs substantially from later, relatively atheoretical anthropology and is in fact a typical representative of the traditional doctrine of 'human nature'. But Mill had a rather complicated view of the relation between the general assertions about what humanity is and the concrete human material the assertions were commenting on. Every generalisation is an abstraction, and it was possible to make a range of different abstractions about the individual that would be put together into various disciplines about the individual. As regards applying the ranges of abstractions in the deduction, it would turn out that the empirical material would not arrange itself in accordance with them. No reliable state-

---

68   Ibid., p. 481 et seqq. and 901 et seqq. respectively.

ments could thus be made about the real person, and thus no exact predictions, even though there may be a collection of reliable laws about humanity available. Statements only about *tendencies* could be made. One could say what normally is the case, one could say what was likely to take place.[69]

Mill imagined an analogous deductive science of society: a political ethology[70] in which the same relation between abstract and concrete prevailed. In this connection he turned to Comte – for whom he otherwise cherished a pronounced and deep respect – when the latter argued that reliable predictions in sociology were imaginable. One could only speak of tendencies, Mill objected; it could be asserted that 'a particular cause will operate in a certain manner unless counteracted' but one could never be assured 'to what extent or amount it will so operate' or that 'it will not be counteracted'.[71]

If we look at Mill's concrete statements about society and historical development, we find that these statements of principle have their counterpart in his view of society. We may be content with one example. In his well-known *On Liberty*, Mill depicts the role of political liberties at various stages of historical development. He did not, however, relate them in any way to economic conditions, and only in passing pointed out that political freedoms had nothing to do with economic ones.[72] It was thus not possible to relate political and economic conditions to each other in any exact manner; their mutual significance could not be established with any certainty.

The idea presents itself immediately of associating Mill's statements on tendencies with certain ideas of probability – in other words, his argument was that in the human sciences, only statements that one thing or the other would be the case *with a certain amount of statistical probability* could be achieved. But that would be a gross misinterpretation. For Mill, as for Buckle, statistics provided extraordinary support for the thesis that human actions were determined.[73] Using statistics, however, only empirical generalisations could be achieved.[74] It was thus an inductive discipline, and was of no help for deductive ethology.

Mill's standpoint is extraordinarily interesting not because it displayed any great pervasive force but because it involved an original way of solving the

---

69   Ibid., p. 432 et seqq. and 861 et seqq. respectively.

70   Ibid., p. 486 et seqq. and 904 et seqq. respectively.

71   Ibid., p. 476 et seq. and 897 respectively.

72   Mill 1859, p. 130.

73   Buckle gave Mill this conviction; the expression thus appears in editions of *A System of Logic* after 1865 and when Buckle specifically is being discussed. See Mill 1973, Vol. II, p. 933.

74   Ibid., p. 935.

dilemma that pressed such large parts of nineteenth-century science. Mill sought to unite strict determinism with an idea that science could never be completely deterministic. Total conformity to law was its condition but not its goal – or, rather, a goal that was far too high for it.

Mill's standpoint reflects the tension between the 'social static' and the 'social dynamic'. Conformity to law was accessible in the static but not in the dynamic, in change: there, only tendencies could be achieved.[75]

7   Dilthey

The idea that different fields of the human sciences constituted abstractions of a totality that was more complex than the sum of these abstractions was something Mill had in common with the great spokesman of historism, Wilhelm Dilthey.[76] But the important similarities end there.

Dilthey acknowledged that Mill displayed greater understanding than, for example, Comte of the distinctive character of the human sciences. Mill nonetheless sought to adapt the human sciences according to a pattern alien to the natural sciences. For Dilthey, Mill's endless talk about the relation between induction and deduction appeared to be 'monotonous and tiring rattling'. Mill had not realised that the object of the human sciences had to be understood 'from within' and not 'from without' like those of the natural sciences.[77]

Even though both Mill and Dilthey proceeded from the idea that there were a number of distinct disciplines within the human sciences, their views on the mutual relations between these various disciplines were completely distinct. Mill regarded it rather as an advantage if a discipline developed in an independent direction. According to Dilthey, on the other hand, the disciplines had to be held together in a strict organic totality. Otherwise, the image of the entire 'historical and social reality' would be distorted. This had happened: Dilthey cited, for example, the theories of natural rights and natural religion, and in addition political economy. Similar abstract and liberated disciplines had vitiated science and damaged society.[78]

---

75   Mill distinguishes between 'physical, or concrete deductive, method' (Mill 1851, Vol. II, p. 474 et seqq. and 1973, Vol. II, p. 895 et seqq. respectively) and 'inverse deductive, or historical method' (ibid., p. 494 et seqq. and 911 et seqq. respectively).

76   See for example Dilthey 1922, Vol. I, p. 91 et seqq.

77   Ibid., p. 108 et seq.

78   Ibid., p. 113.

The very idea of introducing a distinction between 'static' and 'dynamic' into the human sciences was naturally completely foreign to him. But he could not escape the problem hiding behind the distinction. According to the fundamental position of historism, every object of study in the human sciences comprised an organic totality in development. Investigating both the relations among the moments included in that totality and the changes in that totality had to be essential. Dilthey distinguished between constant and changing relations in history. There were thus certain elements that always characterised cultural systems, states, societies and so on, others that changed and gave every epoch or orientation or particular state its distinctive features. True to his fundamental position, Dilthey argued that both the constants and the changes were based in the mental and 'psychophysical' characteristics of humanity. Constants and variations could thus be distinguished there as well. There were essential characteristics that united all humanity and were expressed in their creations – cultures, states, and so on – but at the same time all people were different. There were also various human characteristics that found expression in different epochs, in different societies and so on: the totalities left their mark on individuals as much as individuals did on the totalities.[79]

Dilthey therefore by no means ruled out generalisations from the sphere of the human sciences: demonstrating constant features of history was nothing other that expressing generalisations about it. But the generalisations in no way exhausted historical reality: there were infinitely many variations.

Mill and Dilthey were united in their view of the relation between abstract theory and concrete human reality. Theory could not capture this entire reality. But the difference in their positions was nonetheless entirely crucial. According to Mill, knowledge itself of the concrete deviations provided no new scientific insights. The human sciences, fully fledged, would comprise a number of highly abstract or general statements that nevertheless could not indicate more than the general tendencies in reality. Our knowledge would not increase if we surveyed the individual deviations – such deviations would not lead to changes in the statements of law. According to Dilthey, everything that could not be subsumed under laws comprised the results of research in the human sciences just as must as the laws themselves did. The human sciences evolved to the same extent through establishing new, unique facts as it did through formulating new statements of law.[80]

---

79   Ibid., p. 114 et seq. Cf. also p. 30 et seq. on the relation between individual and society.
80   Ibid., p. 113.

When Dilthey spoke about laws in the moral sciences, however, he did not primarily intend general statements about constant relations but laws of development (i.e. laws about regularities in a complex process). He mentioned, for example, Grimm's law in linguistics,[81] Thünen's in political economy[82] and even what he called 'Comte's law of the relation between the internal logical connections of the sciences and their historical sequence'.[83] These laws naturally assumed certain constants, but they ended in general statements about how the relations among these constants resulted in regularities in development. When Dilthey contrasted laws with facts, he was thus contrasting primarily the regular with the irregular in a process of development.

Dilthey represented a fundamental indeterminism in the same way Mill represented a fundamental determinism. Dilthey's indeterminism, however, did not prevent him from assuming that human affairs of whatever type conformed to laws up to a certain, clearly undefinable[84] limit. Every attempt at eliminating the deviation, the individual or the spontaneous was foreign to him; at the same time, however, he was strikingly tolerant toward all kinds of statements of law regarding historical processes *provided that they were not ascribed universal validity*. Comte's law of the natural sequence of the development of the sciences – or, rather, the natural sciences – was therefore acceptable as long as it did not reach the rank of a law of universal historical development.

Dilthey displayed a similar tolerance in relation to methods and approaches that were used in the human sciences. He even gave a nod to statistics, declaring that it would be possible to calculate exactly the intensity of spiritual movements by subjecting book publishing and libraries from various eras to statistical investigation.[85] In a way, he thus anticipated an orientation in modern

---

81   By that, Dilthey meant the laws of sound shift that Grimm laid out in the 2nd edition of his *Deutsche Grammatik*, Vol. I (1821).

82   'Thünen's Law' can be understood as both a normative law that makes a statement about the *best* allocation of the product of labour between workers and capital, and a law of development that says which allocation societal development is tending towards (if it is not heading toward pure chaos, that is – in Thünen's meaning – towards violent antagonisms between workers and capitalists). The law is formulated as $\sqrt{a \times p}$, where a signifies the worker's traditional standard of living and p the product of labour per worker. Thünen presents his research in *Der isolierte Staat in Beziehung auf Landwirtschaft und Nationalökonomie* (1826–63, Vols. I–III). See further the biography by H. Schumacher 1883.

83   Dilthey thus accepts Comte's thesis of the three stages (religious – metaphysical – positive) as a law of development for the *natural* sciences; however, he denies the general validity Comte ascribes to it. Dilthey 1922, Vol. I, p. 111.

84   Its indeterminacy emerges from the fact that the possibility cannot be ruled out that new empirical material will contain deviations.

85   Dilthey 1922, Vol. I, p. 115.

literary sociology.[86] The significance he attached to such statistical studies was naturally infinitely limited compared to Quetelet's or Buckle's expectations. For Dilthey, it was not a matter of eliminating the mental or the individual, nor was it a matter of providing the human sciences in general with an air of quantitative precision.

When he acknowledged statistical methods, as when he ascribed validity (though limited) to 'Comte's law', he was giving expression to *methodological pluralism*, which was also among the hallmarks of historism. It was not a pluralism without reservations: it meant that many different types of methods, quantitative and qualitative, generalised and individualised, could be of use in the human sciences if they were only incorporated into a uniform, organic context. From the starting points of historism it seemed impossible to delimit and define the breadth of one method or another other than in relation to concrete research material. The relative significance of quantities and qualities, of laws and facts had to be determined case by case. The decision-making instance was ultimately the individual researcher; their intuition, their craftsmanship, their knowledge of the distinctive features of the material, their general scholarship decided things. This did not mean *carte blanche* for subjectivism. The unwritten norms for craftsmanship and scholarship, indeed for the scope of intuition, were as definite as they were inexorable.

For this reason, the reactions of historists to Comte, Mill or Buckle were not unambiguously negative. When Johann Gustav Droysen reviewed Buckle in Sybel's *Historische Zeitschrift* (the review later appeared in Droysen's *Grundriss*) he admitted, like Dilthey, that statistical methods were of value to the human sciences. He did not deny that human actions could be subject to generalisations; they could, he said, be expressed in the formula $a+x$ where a signified the common that conformed to laws and x signified the individual and the unique. The value of a could simply be assumed to be quite large, and the value of x negligibly small. But this did not mean that x, the individual, could be left aside. It had the same scientific value and interest as the general.[87]

Even when the historist programme was expressed in this rather modest wording, the universal ambitions were palpable. The human sciences had to study the human in all its diversity. Nothing was too large, nor was anything

---

86   Chartier and Roche 1974 provide an excellent summary of the quantitative studies of the book and library system, p. 115 et seqq.

87   The review bears the ironic title '*Die Erhebung der Geschichte zum Rang einer Wissenschaft*' (Droysen 1863) and can be found later in Droysen 1868 and 1937; on statistics and the individual, see Droysen 1863, p. 13 et seq., corresponding to Droysen 1868, pp. 60 and 1937, p. 397 et seq.

too small for research. It is impossible to understand this ambition of historism without placing historism in its ideological context. The question of scientific currents and ideologies, however, will be treated in a different context.[88]

8   History and Biology

As I have already indicated, Comte, Buckle and Mill as well as the historists were primarily interested in the relation among various sciences, theories and methods. Their first question did not concern the relation between humanity and nature but between the human sciences and the natural sciences. (It hardly needs to be added that their general ideas about nature and humanity influenced their views of the respective sciences. Their arguments, however, would have had a completely different design and character if they had been *based on* these ideas.)

We have also seen how, in other traditions, the sights were set on the actual relation between biological development and humanity's historical development. In the anthropological research that flourished at the end of the nineteenth century, interest in scientific theory was normally very slight and interest in the facts that illustrated human history from a biological perspective very great.

Points of conflict between the more theoretical and the more realistic orientation were not immediately to hand. They were occupied primarily with different fields and thus with different types of material. The anthropologists' theses about a distant 'prehistory', like their studies of 'primitive' societies, did not come into direct opposition either with what the historists, or a Mill or a Buckle, were occupied with. Historism had its given orientation on 'the great cultures' (Western in particular) while those who had political economy or statistics as their model sciences obtained their crucial material from modern society.

The opposing perspectives, however, also gradually had to come to light. We can see this most clearly in the views of the significance of the biological *races*. For the historists in general, the biological differences between humans was of extremely secondary interest, and 'race' according to the historist programme had to be defined in terms of 'people', 'culture', 'nation' and so on (i.e. in terms that belonged to the sphere of the human sciences). A good historist could thus

---

88   Below, p. 467 et seqq.

very well harbour racist ideas, but he saw the differences in the races ultimately as differences among various cultural traditions.[89]

Similarly, a Mill or Buckle rejected the idea that the concept of race had any significance in explaining the historical development of humanity. 'Of all vulgar modes of escaping from the consideration of the effect of social and moral influences on the human mind, the most vulgar is that of attributing the differences of conduct and character to inherent natural differences', Mill said in *Political Economy*,[90] and Buckle quoted him approvingly. The races having any original significance for historical development, Buckle added, was 'altogether hypothetical'.[91] Tellingly, Comte was also among the authorities he used for such a position.[92] For Comte, Mill and Buckle, the concept of race had no explanatory value.

But by contrast, race became the fundamental historical category for the representatives of the tradition that sought primarily the actual connection between humanity and nature. This was entirely logical; in seeking above all to determine the extent to which human development was a continuation of biological development, the concept of race and its kinship with the concepts of variation and variety was – or had been, while Darwinism was at its peak – immediately available. The various races became the foundation for the various lines of historical development; and the historical process of advancement depended ultimately on racial changes. Humanity had developed as a biological creature, and thus had also developed as a social and cultural creature. New societies or major social changes had their biological counterparts. Herbert Spencer saw a special North American white race take form, and he awaited a similar Australian race with excitement.[93]

---

89   Biological racism entails explaining cultural, class and other differences among groups of humans by their different physical (racial) characteristics. The biological differences thus become fundamental to the cultural, political, and social. For the historicists, it was the other way around. Hermann von Treitschke, among the better-known historicists who clung most to antisemitism, declared at the same time that the 'better' among the Jews could be integrated with the German people; their willingness for usury and other evils that Treitschke ascribed to them could thus be abolished in a new political and cultural community with the German 'people'. Cf. Mosse 1966, p. 200 et seqq. Theodor Waitz, who most closely applied historicist viewpoints to anthropology, declared that humanity comprised a (biological) unity; the differences between various peoples and cultures depended on *whether* the respective people or culture *had* a history, and if so *which*; T. Waitz 1861, p. 289 et seqq.

90   Mill 1965, Vol. I, p. 367.

91   Buckle 1857–61, Vol. I, p. 37.

92   Comte 3:355.

93   Spencer 1862, Vol. I, p. 202.

When this view of human development found expression in ideas that concerned not only prehistory or primitive societies, it came into open conflict with the views of a Mill or a Buckle. A telling example is Friedrich von Hellwald's two-volume *Kulturgeschichte in ihrer natürlichen Entwicklung bis zur Gegenwart*. As a historian, Hellwald was a complete amateur but he had acquired a tremendous amount of reading in a number of areas and he was influenced above all by Darwinist thinking. He dedicated his work to *'Ernst Haeckel in Verehrung und Freundschaft'*[94] (in admiration and friendship).

Hellwald vehemently attacked Buckle and Mill (though his references indicate he had only read Buckle). The concept of race was absolutely fundamental for cultural history, he asserted. Disregarding it was due either to ignorance of contemporary ethnological insights or to the inability to push into the heart of the matter. It was, namely, racial abilities that determined how a people would react to all the external influences that got in their way.[95]

It can safely be said that Hellwald did not really succeed in putting history right with his concept of race. Moreover, his account is entirely unruly, bearing the marks of a compiler and full of whim.[96] Even here, something symptomatic can be seen: in the tradition where he was active, consistency was not a cardinal virtue.

9   Spencer

There was, however, at least one representative of the realistic tendency who devoted great attention to the theoretical side of the human sciences: Herbert Spencer. Spencer attempted not only to bridge the natural and the human. He also strove to sketch the outlines of a science of the 'superorganic'. In contrast to numerous of his like-minded colleagues, all of his scientific ambitions were not placed in biology and the biological; in many respects, his social theory and his sociology had an independent role in his 'synthetic philosophy'.[97]

Spencer was a faithful advocate of the thesis that a phenomenon could not be understood if its origin and development were not understood.[98] But as we

---

94   In addition to his cultural history, Hellwald also wrote a large number of relatively popularly held works on geography and racial biology.

95   Hellwald 1883, Vol. I, p. 46.

96   On his concrete use of the concept of race, see above all Vol. I, pp. 50 et seqq., 332. 450.

97   See for example Peel 1971, p. 131 et seqq.

98   See for example *The Principles of Sociology*, Vol. I; Spencer 1862, Vol. VI, pp. 456 et seq., 621.

have seen, he did not practice *the principle of simple development*.[99] In other words, he was not content to lay out the simple genealogy of social phenomena but sought to investigate their connections. He did not speak, like Comte or Mill, about social static versus social dynamic, but there was a similar distinction in his work.

His sociology had a rather easily comprehensible structure. He began with 'the Data of Sociology', which was primarily an analysis of the fundamental factors in all social development. He did not, however, argue that this 'data' would be lying bare and easily accessible for the observer. It could be distilled out only when a concept of the totality had been obtained.[100]

Typically, he believed he had reached analytical clarity by looking back to the primeval state of the social superorganism. He drew pictures of 'Original External Factors'[101] and 'the Primitive Man'.[102] Like many others, he thus distinguished between external and internal factors here. The external was humanity's environment – soil, climate, flora and fauna – and the internal were its physical and original mental characteristics.[103] One could say that he was depicting the static image of primitive society here. Humanity's physical and mental characteristics were adapted to its environment; a condition of balance prevailed.

But Spencer immediately sought to prove that a static condition in society was inconceivable: there was a tension, a dynamic in the condition of society itself. Spencer was speaking of secondary, or derived, factors here. As soon as society existed, it constituted an active force that changed the environment it had emerged from. Society also grew (Spencer did not account for *why* it had to grow), and therefore differentiated: the division of labour increased. Society as a whole influenced its parts, and the parts in turn influenced the whole. Society left its mark on, and was marked by, other neighbouring societies. This produced various phenomena ranging from language to tools, from towns to theology, and these products determined in part their development.[104]

Spencer was naturally anxious to show that social development observed the same general laws of development that he had traced in organic and inorganic nature: the process led to increased differentiation and integration. The higher

---

99   Above, p. 246.
100 Spencer 1862, Vol. VI, p. 454 et seq.
101 Ibid., p. 16 et seqq.
102 Ibid., p. 41 et seqq.
103 Ibid., p. 10 et seq.
104 Ibid., p. 11 et seqq.

state of society differs from the lower in the same way as the higher organism from the lower, and a fully developed planetary system from the nebula in that it consists of several parts, that these parts are more distinct and that at the same time they are mutually bound by stronger causal bonds.[105] He did not explain why these specific laws of development had general validity: the facts that reality constituted a uniform context and that this context of reality was in uninterrupted development were self-evident conditions for him. What lay beyond that, he gladly left to the Unknowable.[106]

Spencer carefully distinguished between the structure and functions of society (as he differentiated between the structural and functional aspects of organisms, i.e. their anatomy and physiology). He also regarded the products of society – in the broad sense just given – as a particular group of factors. The ultimate task of sociology was to 'consider the interdependence of structures, and functions, and products, taken in their totality'.[107] The structural properties of society influences its functions but is in turn influenced by the functions; both structure and functions determine and are determined by production. A condition of interaction prevails.

The concept of functions played a central role for Spencer, and he used it in his sociology in the original biological content (a certain part of a society has a function in the same way as an organ has a function in an organism). An important consequence of his way of looking at the matter was that his theory of society contained no actual *causal hierarchy*. It was not just that he did not indicate the unique position of the structural conditions in relation to the functional, or vice versa. His general theory meant that all types of factors could in principle be regarded as equally important: they were part of the same great context in which everything influenced everything. While Comte and Buckle emphasised intellectual development and Marx material production, Spencer allowed a range of external and internal, original and secondary, material and ideal factors to sink into the same totality.

In concrete cases, he could depart from this general principle, such as when in a polemic with Comte he asserted emotions at the expense of the intellect.[108] This is one example of how his realistic tendency came into conflict with his

---

105   Cf. Spencer 1862, Vol. I, (*First Principles*), for example p. 175 et seqq.
106   Cf. above, p. 247.
107   Spencer 1862, Vol. VI, p. 466.
108   Cf. Chapter 8, note 48. Here, perhaps, it is still not a question of a direct departure; even in this polemic, Spencer refers to social totality. Emotions, the instinctual, have precedence over in that they have their inertia and their biological context; the intellectual sphere, understood as habits of thought rather than distinct ideas, could be equated with them.

general theory: it was easier to draw the biological background in the development of emotional life than in the development of the intellect.

By refraining in general from a causal hierarchy, Spencer escaped the problems of determinism that complicated nineteenth-century thinking around development to a great degree. Satisfaction with saying that everything changed everything meant not needing to ask the question of how cause is distinguished from effect and how cause determines effect: according to the starting point, everything was equally cause and effect, and the one cannot be distinguished from the other.

10 The Concept of Development

We have now seen how the accumulated weight of the problems of scientific theory that had built up in the mid-nineteenth century bore down on the human sciences. The difficulties that the principle of conservation of energy had roused, and the difficulties that evolutionary biology had brought to the fore, echoed in the discussions of the human sciences.

We have also seen how degrees and types of specialisation and professionalisation influenced not only the work in the human sciences but also the views on their relation with the natural sciences. We have seen how the latter inevitable issue was determined by whether someone was primarily interested in the relation among various theories or among different spheres of reality.

The most intractable result, however, concerns the concept of development itself. The concept is especially complicated, and no matter how it is formulated it leads to a number of difficulties concerning 'static' versus 'dynamic', definite processes versus tendencies and so on. Anyone who wished to develop a complete concept of development toward the end of the nineteenth century had at least seven different alternatives to choose from. (If it had been possible to combine these alternatives freely, there would have been more than a hundred different theories of development to deal with. It is not a question of this many, however; there is a natural kinship among a great many of the alternatives.) It can thus be stated that development is either:

1. *ideal or real.* When the Romantics or Hegel spoke about, for example, the development of species, they were not thinking of a development over time. In a somewhat analogous manner, those who asserted that chemical processes, for example, had developed out of mechanical ones could have in mind a reduction in the theory and not likewise a real development.

2. *teleological or non-teleological.* Calling the other alternatives 'causal' or 'deterministic' development would be misleading; teleology and strict determinism were often united, as we have seen.

3. *linear or non-linear.* If development is linear, its continued or its previous development can be extrapolated by knowing its starting position (e.g. primitive society) *or* its end result (e.g. a fully-fledged capitalist society).

4. *simple or complex.* Anyone attempting to substantiate a simple development can be satisfied with demonstrating that a phenomenon has undergone a change (in other words, that it had different properties at one point in time, t_0, than it did at t_1) and thus disregards the factors that had determined this change.

5. *determined or non-determined.* There is in fact a scale of interim positions between these alternatives: certain phenomena can be regarded as determined and others not; the development can be presented as accidental or its main features could be depicted using certain laws of tendency, and so on.

6. *continuous or discontinuous.* This alternative is closely related to alternatives 3 and 5. It could be asserted, for example, that development was linear and/or determined between certain crucial 'breaks' or 'leaps'.

7. *Comprehensible from the start or the end point.* Each of these alternatives unite a long range of ideas. Those seeking the content and orientation of history in a primitive prehistory or in the biological origins of humanity select the first option, just as much as those who, in imitating Herder, were on the hunt for the 'people's' original customs; on the other hand, the classical political economists – as well as Hegel and Marx – asserted that it was only in the fully developed economic or moral system that the preceding development was comprehensible. In strict determinism, the antagonism is overcome if it is assumed that the development can be calculated in any direction whatsoever; Laplace's spirit moves freely both forward and backward in time.

There was thus an abundance of concepts of development, and what is more, many of these concepts could with good reason be called scientific (i.e. they played a clear and constructive role in various disciplines and orientations). The thinking around development was more than just a fad, and in fact also more than a powerful current of ideas that permeated field after field of research. There were (and are) purely internal reasons to ask questions about development as soon as there were processes, transformations, and changes to make – and new processes, transformations, and changes were continuously coming into the reach of the sciences. It was thus not only patterns of thought obtained from without, from ideologies, that would leave their mark on research. Research had to ask questions on its own terms about what one or another type of development meant and how it could be studied.

There was ground for the system-builders here. Their problems were of interest to the specialists as well. Paradoxically enough, it was the split in the sciences and the ideals of the sciences, rather than their unity, that gave meaning to the many attempts at systems 'on scientific grounds'.

But the split was also fertile ground for the diversity of systems. There were many possible sciences. There were many possible syntheses of knowledge. There were many different ideological consequences that could be drawn from various disciplines and orientations. It was almost an issue of distinguishing different primary types of systems and seeing which type of scientific rationality they had or were striving for.

Since the system-builders' problems were also those of the various sciences to such a great extent, however, the question of where the boundary between systems and non-systems should be drawn became the first that had to be asked. We can assume from the start that it is not a fixed boundary. There is no definite point where Spencer the system-builder is replaced by Spencer the sociologist. We can, on the other hand, hope to find a number of simple and practical rules with which the *typical* systematic accounts can be distinguished from the *typical* specialised scientific accounts.

CHAPTER 10

Texts, Structures and Systems

1   Studying Texts and Systems

It is now a matter of setting the systems in relating to the various nineteenth-century scientific traditions. For the time being, we will disregard the *ideological determination* of the systems and keep to the sphere internal to the sciences (or rather, perhaps, internal to theories).

There are two paths by which we will attempt to circumscribe some of the characteristics of the systems. One, which will only be sketched out here, entails an analysis of the style or text itself. There are many different types of technical texts that are intended to provide scientific insights. Much can be learned about their address, their claims and authority by studying their external characteristics. We are going beyond the conscious intentions and explicit ambitions of the various authors here. Just by adapting themselves to a certain form of presentation, the respective authors make a number of choices the consequences of which do not need to be comprehensible to themselves but need only to be perceived as conventions or simple matters of course. If we were to be formal, we could say that I am attempting to conduct a semiotic analysis of nineteenth-century technical texts – that is, a type of analysis that to date has been exclusively devoted to literary texts.[1] Here, however, it is a question of only a few extremely general characteristics and distinctive features in an overwhelmingly large amount of material. A more detailed study of certain types of texts would certainly yield a much more differentiated result.[2] The purpose of the current presentation is limited to the very general, to symptoms and tendencies.

The other path is intended to lead to insights about the structures of the systems. Different syntheses of knowledge and the sciences at a certain point in

---

1   On semiotics, cf. Eco 1984. Obviously, the scientific text could also be the subject of analyses of the same kind. Among thinkers such as Lévi-Strauss – whose main field of work was not pure literature, but the myth – there are valuable accounts along this line; see for example his interesting and challenging investigations of history in *The Savage Mind* (1971, p. 224 et seqq). See also further, note 2.

2   Interesting efforts in *another* direction can be found in Hayden V. White's essay 'Historicism, History, and the Figurative Imagination' (1975), which studies the historical scientific text with regard to its rhetorical character and is based directly on Roman Jakobson's and Lévi-Strauss's lines of thought.

time could consist of different elements, and these elements could be related to each other in distinct ways. The various scientific disciplines – which comprise the building blocks of the systems – may change in number and scope among different systems. As we have seen, they are changes that have their counterpart in science itself: drawing boundaries between disciplines and fields of theory is problematic and controversial. Even more controversial is the question of what the boundaries consist of: it concerns quite generally the problem of whether one theory can be reduced to another and if so, what this *reduction* entails. Different systems can also have different main points of emphasis; in other words, they could contain different key disciplines from which the systems obtain their character. Finally, the systems are either 'ascending' (*concretising*) or 'descending' (*abstracting*). In the former case it is assumed that a scientific explanation is always based on the simple and moves toward the complex; for the system this means starting from the simplest (e.g. mechanics) and finding the way upward in the scientific hierarchy. An abstracting system, on the other hand, starts from the most complex and complicated. The universal pattern of explanation is obtained in the human psyche or human products such as art, religion or philosophy.

Let us see where both paths can lead us.

2   The Mysteries of the References

In a richly differentiated scientific culture, there are a large number of different types of texts. These can be roughly divided according to *format* – everything from the brief paper to the large multi-volume work. The can also be divided according to their intended or natural *addressees* – from pure technical prose addressed to a group of specialists to the popular account that demands the attention of the educated public or is to be put in the hands of schoolchildren. Another related but not coincident basis for division aims at the *use*. The abstract, theoretically oriented text intervenes in the theoretical development of science, the empirically charged presentation intends to provide the discipline with new observations. In both cases the use is internal. But there are also texts that are intended primarily for a practical or material use: there are dissertations about the art of constructing manure pits. There are also texts that openly offer themselves for ideological use, that thus attempt to influence people's thoughts and beliefs with scientific arguments. The same text can naturally unite two or more of these uses. There is, however, a palpable tendency toward specialising the texts of a discipline for the various uses the more specialised that discipline becomes.

The *publication forms* of the texts also have tremendous significance. If a paper or a review is published in a journal, it must normally subject itself to certain norms and limitations. Journals can be more or less fixed on a topical orientation, or be addressed to a larger or smaller audience. Similar will apply to series of various types, of collections and reference works and so on. A single author of an independent work can, through a certain type of title, bind themselves to a certain type of presentation, for example, through having the title begin with words such as *Handbuch, Manual, Introduction, Einleitung* or *System.*

There are, however, characteristics of the scientific text itself that more clearly and unmistakably reveal its character. Above all, we can take as our starting point the *references* in the broad sense – that is, the manner in which the author of a text seeks to substantiate that what they are asserting is correct.

One classic type of reference we can call *reference to pure authority*. We rarely meet it in its unadulterated form in nineteenth-century literature with scientific pretensions; in those cases, it is in fundamentalist theology and the like. It exists much more abundantly in the learned prose of previous centuries, especially in dissertations of all kinds. To find a really authoritative example, we can turn to the writings of Thomas Aquinas. When he argued for one standpoint or another – in *Summa Theologica,* for example – he began with one or more citations. The citations were firstly from the Bible, secondly from Aristotle and thirdly from church fathers and Christian theologists or philosophers other than Aristotle. He indicated quite carefully where the citations had been taken from; as regards the Bible, he provided the source literally chapter and verse.

Without exception, it concerned references to witnesses to the truth. Their words deserved to be taken seriously. But there was authority, and then there was authority. Uppermost in the hierarchy of authorities was the Bible. This was what constituted pure authority for Thomas; everything else – Aristotle included – was further down on the scale. The Bible could thus not be guilty of any errors whatsoever.

But it was a matter of interpreting the Bible and the other authorities. Their truths had to be incorporated into a greater, rational context. To begin with, the authorities appeared to contradict each other; there were even places in the Bible that seemed to point in opposite directions.[3] It was a matter of finding the correct solution, which consisted of showing that the opposition between the authoritative sources was illusory.

---

3   Thomas Aquinas, for example, *Prima secundae,* qq. 91, Art. 4 (with objections from Sirach and the Book of Psalms).

Quoting an authority did not simply mean placing complete confidence in the authority; appeal was made to those that held the same position. Whatever one Bible quote or another may have been based on, it was assumed that *the condition that it was taken from the Bible was reason enough for all the readers that the author wanted to reach and influence to regard it as true.* It was not a matter of discussing veracity; it was a matter of laying out what the truth entailed.

Not only the Bible, but also many other sources have been treated this way in scholarly Western literature. A number of philosophers and scholars of antiquity, numerous Church fathers and theologists up through the Reformation and later, and a number of medieval commentators achieved the rank of pure authorities in varying types of literature and within different schools of thought. This is not the place to go into the determinations for or the changing content of presentations of that sort. It is the formal side that is of interest. A reference to a pure authority means that the citation itself of the source – that is, of one document or another – is enough to indicate the truth of the text cited. What the author leaves to themselves is nothing more that the interpretation of the text. Since they appeal to those with similar opinions – that is, to people who embrace the same authority – they do not need to emphasise the infallibility of the authority. The quote (or abstract) and citation of source are sufficient.

When the author in question enters into a polemic with those who do not embrace *the same* authority, they cannot be satisfied with such references. When the Aristotelians in the seventeenth century were faced with the awkward task of polemicising against the Cartesians and others who differed, they could not quote what Aristotle said but had to go in for other types of argumentation. Above all, they asserted that all the new theories, all novelty was dangerous and subversive.[4]

The opposite of references to pure authority is *references to pure experience.* This is a type of reference that was typical of the entire strictly empirical tradition from Francis Bacon onward. According to this view, nature (and perhaps all of reality) was an 'open book' that everyone who had a minimal level of literacy – that is, a normal ability to understand – could read.[5] It was therefore completely irrelevant *who* had made an observation; any observation worth the name could be made by anyone at all. What was important in the scientific text was that not only the result of the observation but also the determinations

---

4 Cf. Lindborg 1965.
5 Popper 1972, p. 13 et seqq. Cf. above, p. 226.

under which the observation was made are reported. Anyone wanting to test the content of the text could thus, in principle, duplicate the observation.

In an experimental discipline, this meant describing the apparatus used as well as all the measurements and steps taken to arrive at an exact result. Once the apparatus had been normalised, its description moved to the textbooks that comprised the literary introduction to the subject; in the scientific texts themselves only new apparatuses or new uses of traditional apparatuses were described. In subjects where the experimental development was rapid or generally chaotic, descriptions of this kind could take up a large portion of the scientific text; such was the case in nineteenth-century chemistry and twentieth-century experimental psychology.[6]

But references to pure experience existed not only in experimental disciplines. Nor were they limited to the natural sciences. A similar tradition emerged in the human sciences, and it reached its full power in nineteenth-century historism. Here, it was a matter of a complete account of the historical source. The sources became material for experience, accessible to anyone who had learned to interpret them. In their own way, every source reference became a reference to pure experience. *Monumenta Germaniae historica* and other source editions became worlds of easily accessible experience.

Strict empiricism never dominated in this tradition, however; it was therefore not assumed that the entire humanist account could be derived from observations. Other sources of knowledge were also assumed: insights, 'erudition' and so on.[7] Georg Waitz, one of the most outstanding and typical representatives of the *Monumenta* school, declared that complete knowledge of the sources was not sufficient for the work of the historian. Knowledge of previous interpretations – that is, the secondary literature – was also required. This kind of statement reveals an opinion that the conclusions are not given as a result of the material of experience itself; there are different reasonable interpretations, a considerable portion of which can be found in the secondary literature. Purely in general, it could be said that a connection is assumed between facts that do not emerge from a study of the facts in the source material.[8]

---

6 No more detailed study of these matters exists, but I can refer to the overwhelming impression that the perusal of any nineteenth-century chemical journal or twentieth-century psychological journal would provide.

7 This was particularly clear at the time of the breakthrough of strict source-critical historical research around the turn of the twentieth century.

8 'Es ist mir bei dieser Darstellung darauf angekommen, wie die Quellen in möglichster Vollständigkeit zu benutzen, so doch auf die früheren Bearbeitungen eine ausgedehnte Rücksicht zu

We can also distinguish a third type of reference that covers a rather broad group. These are references to consistency and logic, to theoretical connections and common sense – in a word, *references to rationality*.

When Thomas Aquinas was constructing his philosophy, he did not make use only of quotes from authorities. The argument that an idea was consistent with what he had previously arrived it in his presentation was an extremely common one, as was the argument that something squared with common sense in general. These therefore concerned references to rationality.

In a rationalist tradition, such references played an extraordinarily central role. We can see how conclusive evidence and absolute certainty becomes the highest criterion of truth in Descartes and others.[9] Referring to common sense in general meant referring to the common sense of each and every reader. If the argument was valid and the reader equipped with a normal human intellect, they would perceive the same conclusive evidence as the author. The same criterion of evidence could also be reshaped in a more exclusive direction: only the true genius could behold the truth. This became a central line of thought in the young Schelling and his successors. Anyone who did not understand, and thereby did not perceive certainty – they were not a genius and could consequently not penetrate the innermost connections of existence.[10]

But references to rationality had a much broader use than this in different kinds of scientific texts. It was at hand as soon as it was pointed out that something was consistent with a way of thinking or a theory. It was thus not bound to any special epistemological conception of common sense but could and had to exist even when the purest empiricist took up the pen. On the other hand, it was self-evident that they were more central in abstract, theoretically oriented texts. They were as dominant in eighteenth-century analytical mechanics as they were hidden away in the experimental chemistry of the same era.

---

nehmen. Nichts scheint mir verkehrter bei aller historischer Arbeit, als die Meinung, es genüge auf die Quellen selbst zuruückzugehen, und aus ihnen das bild der Dinge, auf die es ankommt, zu gewinnen'. Quoted according to review of K. Hegel 1861, p. 224 et seq., from a declaration by Waitz in *Göttinger gelehrten Anzeigen 1860.*

9   On this topic, cf. Halbfass 1968, p. 41 et seqq.

10   Cf. Schelling, *Aphorismen zur Einleitung in die Naturphilosophie*: anyone who would understand his system must have *'den Geist ... es zu beleben'* (Schelling 1/7, p. 184 n.); in *Ideen zu einer Philosophie der Natur*, he explains that his philosophy is based on axioms that are irrefutable to the insightful (Schelling 1/2, p. 60). The same line of thought is found in Fichte, for example in *Erste Einleitung in die Wissenschaftslehre*; Fichte 1845, p. 439 et seqq.

3   The Authorities of the Texts

In a world where no person could obtain any knowledge whatsoever on their own, all references would be references to pure authority. In contrast, in a world where everyone was equally intellectually equipped, having the same possibilities of making observations and experiments, and where knowledge in principle could be housed in every human brain, all references could be references to pure experience or to rationality. But the world in which scientific texts are produced is a cross between them, and the scientific text has to adapt itself accordingly.

Presentations in analytical mechanics are available to everyone, provided that they have mastered the mathematics used. Experiments in physics and chemistry can be performed by everybody – who has access to and knows how to operate the apparatus and can draw reasonable conclusions from the experiment. And further: if a scientific author has mastered the entire scientific field, they would not need to cite any other scientists as authorities.

In reality, however, all scientific texts from any era whatsoever must assume a particular level of education among their readers that is not limited to literacy, the general capacity for observation and the power to reason. With scientific specialisation, authors have to deal with more groups of readers with specific skills and knowledge. This would leave its mark on scientific texts. Certain insights are taken for granted: the authors of seventeenth-century dissertations did not explain who Aristotle was or what his philosophy in general was based on; eighteenth-century presentations of mechanics assumed a general knowledge of Newton's theory of gravity. A complete account was therefore not required; the reader was assumed to have obtained such an account before tackling these texts.

But with expanding specialisation, this assumed background knowledge became increasingly different in the various specialised disciplines. If the text touched on a field of specialisation where it did not itself belong, it could not assume the fundamental orientation of its natural readers in the field: the text therefore became elementary.

But it underwent another, perhaps even more important change. If its author was himself not a specialist in the field in question – and the further specialisation had gone, the less likely it was that they were a specialist in one area while writing a scientific presentation in another – they could not act as their own authority in it. They could therefore not claim to have mastered its theories and methods; they could neither refer to their own pure experience nor investigate the rational operations carried out in the discipline in question. They had to cite an authority or an authoritative presentation in the field in question.

With that, the reference to authority came back into scientific texts. It was now a question of references to scientific authorities in a strict sense: by making such references when entering a field other than one's own, there is *de facto* acceptance that it concerns a specialised field – that is a field that requires specific insights and knowledge beyond that of general education.

A careful distinction must be made between references to secondary literature in an unfamiliar field of specialisation and references to secondary literature that falls within the sphere of the author's own skills and work. There is a purely formal difference that is worth a great deal of attention. As soon as another scientific work is mentioned with an agreement, a condemnation or a correction, this means that the author of the text considers themselves competent to judge the work; they indicate that they themselves could have written the same work (and perhaps, if they have serious remarks, done better). Naturally, their comments could also concern only a part of the work, and it could be that it is also only this part that the author considers as their own field. When, on the other hand, another work is only cited as a witness to the truth, the conclusion cannot immediately be drawn that the work in question is regarded as an authoritative representative of another field of research. As is known, there are 'great names' that have become natural authorities for their colleagues in the subject, and there are also reasons of convenience and space to mention only in passing the results that other scientists have arrived at. More than the unannotated reference is thus required to substantiate that a certain author in a certain text is being treated as an unfamiliar authority.

The treatment of a given discipline as a specialised field depends in part on *conventions*; these are conventions that especially find expression in the scientific texts. Certain kinds of knowledge and skills – often, but not necessarily, acquired in a certain kind of education – are regarded as necessary conditions for presenting independent results and for commenting on other's efforts in the field. But all observers do not need to be unanimous. There are numerous examples of how one group of scientists, without gaining a hearing, attempted to screen off a domain and make it the exclusive possession of their own type of expert knowledge. There are also examples of how authors of varying temperaments and types have refused to accept the boundaries of specialised fields that have already been established.

Romantic natural philosophy in the spirit of Schelling is a good example of both phenomena. Schelling and his adherents asserted that certain general philosophical issues pertaining to nature could only be treated with the type of thinking they devoted themselves to. It was a question of mastering an extremely complex and complicated conceptual apparatus, having knowledge of a number of changing natural scientific theories and a specific Schellingian interpretation of them, and of demonstrating the capability of laying out and solving problems of a very definite type. Producing a Romantic text of natural philosophy thus required no mean amount of schooling, and all clearly divergent methods of treating similar issues were dismissed by Schellingites as 'unscientific'.[11]

At the same time, however, the Romantic natural philosophers refused to accept any specialisations of the natural sciences. Even though they lacked the mathematical schooling that was assumed in Newtonian mechanics or the methodological skills that were developed in various parts of physics and chemistry, they commented unreservedly on these disciplines. Schelling himself had attempted to justify this sovereign attitude.[12] It was extraordinarily striking in his presentations and those of his peers. Here, there were no references to authorities for unfamiliar specialised fields; here, the authors were sovereign in their judgements.[13] The great witness to truth was their own sense of the conclusive evidence.

The natural philosophers paid for their reckless advances with the sharp accusations of incompetence and quackery of the offended specialists.[14] The attempt to create a particular specialised field of the natural sciences met with a brief – and during its years of success not even partial – response.

It is therefore important to keep in mind that a real scientific specialisation assumes assent not only among those who want to practice the specialisation but also among their colleagues in other scientific fields. Ultimately, it also requires the assent of the authorities providing grants and assignments and of the more articulate general public: a really successful and enduring specialisation requires a broad response; it must obtain an independent place in the scholarly organisation and a general recognition of representing the only expert knowledge within a limited technical field. The specialisation must therefore create a fixed identity for itself, and an identity that is so complex that

---

11   This perhaps most clearly emerges in Schelling's *Vorlesungen über die Methods des akademischen Studiums*, in particular 'Erste Vorlesung', Schelling I/4, p. 211 et seqq. Most challenging is 'Zwölfte Vorlesung', which deals with physics and chemistry (ibid., p. 327 et seqq.).

12   For example, Schelling I/2, p. 6: '*Mein Zweck is vielmehr, die Naturwissenschaft erst philosophisch entstehen zu lassen, und meine Philosophie ist selbst nicht anders als Naturwissenschaft*'.

13   In the writings of Schelling, Oken, Steffens and other natural philosophers, the 'lower' empirical treatment is happily left to others, but the assessment of the empirical material is sovereign: there are no other authorities in theoretical work.

14   Among the sharpest critics were Berzelius, Liebig and Helmholtz: examples of vigorous attacks can be found in Liebig 1859, Vol. I, p. 372 et seq. and Helmholtz 1876, Vol. I, p. 8 et seq. respectively.

it can be recognised by both amateurs in the subject and colleagues as well as external instances that are nevertheless important for the advancement and independence of the sciences. One of the most important aids is therefore the codification of the scientific text. It is highly probable that the space for individual divergences in the design of the texts shrinks, the more specialised a discipline becomes. More – and more limited – types of texts appear: articles and other accounts of the scientific theoretical and methodological conditions of the discipline, introductory textbooks, popularisations, reviews of technical literature (with well-standardised criteria of assessment) – and moreover a weighty core of reports, papers and books that inform the highly limited technical audience of the results of research.

It is in this last literary group that the standardisation is at its greatest. Strict norms are developed for what can occur in literature of this type (without needing to be verbalised). The norms can be rigid in the face of the new and untested. Hermann von Helmholtz's epoch-making *On the Conservation of Force* was refused by tone-setting journals because it contained 'philosophy' – that is, it touched on a field that was considered harmful to the sound, secure presentation of physics.[15] Helmholtz covered himself in the beginning by saying that the dissertation was intended primarily for physicists and that he had not developed the philosophical foundations. At the same time, however, he asserted that the theoretical – in contrast to experimental – physics had to look for the hidden causes behind the regularities the experiments demonstrated;[16] in the eyes of the journal editors, he was already out in deep water with a statement like that. Much later, Helmholtz partially distanced himself from similar statements and ambitions – in a note to the paper he declared that in his introductory remarks he had been more influenced by Kant than he had been aware of, and that the search for hidden causes was not a practicable scientific task.[17]

In fact, Helmholtz soon became a standard-setter and a model through his scientific texts, whether he was in the sphere of physics or physiology or at the theoretical or experimental level. A formal study of the texts in the three hefty volumes of *Wissenschaftliche Abhandlungen* would yield a great deal; these

---

15   Above, p. 169 et seq. It is relevant here that German physicists, out of antipathy towards philosophical speculation, sought to make physics a pure 'experiential science'; they thereby also developed a mistrust of theoretical physics in general. So it was with figures including Johan Christian Poggendorff, from whose *Annalen der Physik und Chemie* Helmholtz's article had been rejected. On this topic cf. Wiedemann 1895, p. xiii et seq. and xxvi.

16   Helmholtz 1882, Vol. I, p. 12 et seq.

17   Ibid., p. 68.

texts could well be compared with Helmholtz's own *Popular Lectures on Scientific Subjects*. Here is not the place for such a study; I will provide only a few viewpoints.

First, it can be noted that in his internal presentations, Helmholtz thoroughly avoided references to disciplines and authorities that did not belong to his own sphere of competence. Even when, in a somewhat more popular account – an overview of modern theories of electricity – he came to Berzelius's electrochemical theories, he carefully avoided taking a position on their value as a chemical theory.[18] More distant fields generally did not come into his field of vision; while he could talk about the human sciences in his popular accounts,[19] he did not mention a single word about the field in his specialised papers. Darwinism and the entire complex of problems associated with it were, as we have seen,[20] also conspicuous in their absence.

In contrast, he conducted a detailed discussion with authorities from his own fields. He often gave only a name, which he assumed the reader would be well familiar with. If he went into a more detailed review, he also indicated the source, page number and all: the interested reader was invited to check the correctness of the reference. Helmholtz's references breathed a spirit of collegiality and affinity – or cliquishness, if you like. The world of physicists, like the world of mechanistically inclined physiologists, comprised a unity. Everyone who belonged to those worlds could, in principle, have the same experiences and make the same calculations. 'The astounding sensitivity of a cylindrical jet of air that is impregnated with smoke to sound has already been described by Tyndall; I have confirmed the same thing'.[21] Even in the heat of polemics, he assumed that all competent scientists could achieve unanimity if they only devoted sufficient care and attention to the matters at issue. When he expressed himself so sharply that his opponents were insulted, he quickly became repentant. He concluded an exchange of opinions with French mathematician and physicist Joseph Bertrand with a brief assurance that he did not doubt *monsieur* Bertrand's honesty and expert knowledge.[22]

It would of course be worth a separate study to see what is required in general for an author to be brought into scientific discussion and thereby into

---

18   The lecture was nevertheless held for members of the Chemical Society in London and
      published first in its *Journal*: 'On the Modern Development of Faraday's Conception of
      Electricity', later in Helmholtz 1882, Vol. III. See there above all p. 61 et seqq.

19   For example, in the already frequently mentioned '*Über das Verhältniss der Naturwis-
      senschaften zur Gesammtheit der Wissenschaft*', Helmholtz 1876, Vol. I. p. 1 et seqq.

20   Above, p. 198.

21   Helmholtz 1882, Vol. I, p. 152.

22   Helmholtz 1882, Vol. I, p. 145.

collegiality. Far from every contribution in a scientific debate comes up for discussion. Factors such as the author's position and reputation among professionals, the manner in which their contribution is published (e.g. in a more or less respected journal) and the purely formal features of their presentation certainly play a role. It is not enough to be innovative and brilliant. There are other things that govern and sift attention. There are, for example, good reasons to assume that Helmholtz did not notice Robert Mayer's pioneering work on the indestructibility of force because it was published in Liebig's *Annalen* – a journal of chemistry that fell outside the fields Helmholtz specialised in and monitored.[23]

4   Text and Specialisation

I therefore assert that a study of the scientific text itself could provide a measure of the degree of specialisation of various disciplines. Helmholtz's papers, like the journals and other publications in which he published them, provide clear ideas of how groups of scientists marked off their fields of specialisation through their way of writing, of arguing, of making references. The same applies to the specialised human sciences. Going through, for example, Heinrich von Sybel's *Historische Zeitschrift* would reveal a similar character. It was a special forum for historians of the historist school and spirit. Of course, it had features in its orientation that do not seem to have sprung directly from the historist programme itself (e.g. favouring recent history and German history). Here, it could be said that the ideological determination outflanked the internal one.[24] In all other respects, the universal historist ambitions were carried out with a great degree of consistency. The technical field was not limited to political history: it was history in all its relevant aspects that was to be treated.[25] The special technique of historical writing was demonstrated in nearly all contribu-

---

23   Wiedemann 1895, p. xxvi.

24   Sybel introduced the first number of the journal with a striking foreword, in which he also declared that the science the journal represented excluded 'feudalism', 'radicalism' and 'ultramontanism'. Sybel 1859, p. III et seq. It had to be constantly emphasised that according to historicism, science was not only compatible with certain values but indissolubly associated with definite values in an ideological totality; cf. for example G. Waitz 1859b, p. 1 et seq. on the relation between objectivity and patriotism.

25   This was not only Sybel's explicit programme; it is discernible if one looks at the breadth of subjects that were taken up in essays and reviews. The orientation on 'the state' is noticeable, but at that time the state was not only understood as a political machine but also as the bearer of cultural, social, and economic relations.

tions and papers. Papers at the lowest empirical level (i.e. detailed reviews of sources) rarely appeared in *Historische Zeitschrift*, of course. The papers had a broader empirical base, but on the other hand their connection to the specialised studies and thereby to the sources was clear and accounted for.[26]

The specialised character of the journals manifested itself most clearly in the treatment of secondary historical literature. The reckoning with non-specialised historical writing is telling; for example, Droysen's review of Buckle's history of civilisation is found here.[27] Droysen was obviously appealing to an audience whose agreement he assumed; for him, it was therefore not a question of convincing his readers that Buckle's approach was objectionable but of working up a condemnation that for the readers was self-explanatory from the start. The extensive sections for shorter reviews that claimed to report on and assess all historical literature of scientific value in Germany are also telling. The crucial grounds for assessment were given and regarded as indisputable. It was a matter of providing a coherent and homogeneous audience information, the use and general orientation of which was self-evident for that audience.[28]

Historische Zeitschrift thus assumed through its entire character a circle of readers who agreed that historical research constituted a specialised discipline and that there were thus fixed grounds for assessment of what was good historical research.

But what happened when this consensus did not exist? What happened when it was not assumed that a certain field was only available to a definite type of theory, method and manner of presentation, all of which assumed the specialised schooling of their practitioner?

We have already seen examples of this in the attempts to link biological development and human history that were legion towards the end of the nineteenth century. They were particularly numerous in the United Kingdom, where the specialised human sciences were much weaker than in Germany

---

26   The synthetic ambitions are dominant: the journal summarised and evaluated concrete historical research.

27   Droysen 1863. Droysen's antipathy towards 'dilettantism' was as great as Waitz's; in another programmatic declaration for the journal, Waitz said: '*Vielleicht keine Wissenschaft hat mehr von den Dilettantismus zu leiden als die Geschichte*'; G. Waitz 1859a, p. 20. The same spirit characterises L. Häusser's detailed criticism of both the British amateurs Macaulay's and Carlyle's monographs on Frederick the Great; Häusser 1859, p. 43 et seqq.

28   The reviews take up a great deal of space. One part of them comprises largely only bibliographical items, while others shape themselves into enormous surveys over hundreds of pages. The spirit is extremely uniform; despite assiduously searching, I have not found a single review that breaks with the historicist programme (as I have defined it) in the first twenty volumes.

or France. They would also soon gain their natural association to Darwinism with its veneration for authorities in the natural sciences and their relative contempt – or, rather, indifference – for expert knowledge in the human sciences.

One of the classical cases of a text that through its very character denied the scientific character of the human sciences is Darwin's *Descent of Man*. The parts that dealt with humanity's historical development contain numerous vague references to diverse authors. These references did not distinguish between one author and another – scientific backgrounds and types of specialised knowledge played no role – nor were there any open or latent ideas that the observations forming the basis for a solid understanding of humanity's development would require any particular type of method. A chaotic world of experiences was opening up, from which anyone at all could take what they liked.

We can illustrate this with an extreme case, namely Darwin's treatment of the question of whether humanity's religious ideas had any counterparts among the other species. The reason he took up this question in general was naturally that the thesis of belief in God was so unique for humanity that it could not generally be imagined that it could have developed from something non-human. Darwin's attention was concentrated here, as elsewhere in *Descent of Man*, on the issue of origins. It was a matter of finding some animal counterpart to religion.

He first pointed out that belief in a single god did not unify humanity. Ideas about hidden, spiritual forces, on the other hand, did. Darwin cited a few statements about the beliefs of 'savages'. Among his authorities, tellingly enough, was Herbert Spencer – a man whose fervour for synthesis frightened Darwin when he was working on his own solid specialisation in the natural sciences but who now thus had to suffice.[29]

But the crucial task itself for Darwin was therefore to find the counterpart in the animal world to the rich flora of religious ideas. The beliefs of the 'savages' that natural objects and forces were animate had to have some sort of correlation. Here, Darwin cited *one single* reason for his idea about the biological origins of religion; he did so with reservations such as 'perhaps' and 'a little fact'. In fact, he only related an anecdote about his dog. The dog was laying on the lawn one warm day, a short distance from a parasol. A breeze blew up and the parasol began to move; the dog began growling and barking. Darwin drew the conclusion:

---

29   Darwin 1871, Vol. I, p. 66 n. On Darwin's position on Spencer, cf. above, p. 188.

He must, I think, have reasoned to himself in a rapid and unconscious manner, that movement without any apparent cause indicated the presence of some strange living agent, and no stranger had a right to be on his territory.[30]

It is thus the same Darwin who in his technical biological works showed such remarkable exactitude and caution in handling empirical material and in argumentation, that brushes aside a complicated problem here with a droll anecdote. He may have been completely right in his conclusion, or rather, he may have had good reason to shrug off an intricate problem that had nothing or very little to do with the main issue – the biological origins of humanity. Darwin was obviously arguing, however, that the origin of religion was a real problem and he did not intend to produce a joke or a good story. The fact of the matter was that on questions having to do with religion or other human affairs, he did not acknowledge any fixed scientific norms and thus no strict expert knowledge. It rubbed off onto his presentation. While he devoted decades to studying the mechanisms of artificial selection in animal breeding and the like, and endless pages full of text to reporting his results for a discriminating technical audience, he built his conclusion here on a single, completely accidental and unsystematic observation for which he provided a daring anthropocentric interpretation and surrounded in the text with 'perhaps' and 'I think'.

Darwin was a serious authority, however, and for many even his dog provided the answer to the origin of religion. Herbert Spencer called it as a witness to the truth in *The Principles of Sociology*, characteristically without indicating where Darwin related the anecdote. He decorated Darwin's tale with a few details and interpretations as if to deprive it somewhat of its character of a chance occurrence binding it to nothing.[31]

5   The System-Builders' Texts

It is thus of crucial significance for a presentation whether or its author considers it to be dealing with a specialisation. The difference is of the same kind for those who, like Darwin, kept to limited scientific fields as it is for those who, like Spencer, sought to construct a system of all knowledge.

---

30   Darwin 1871, Vol. I, p. 67.
31   Spencer 1862, Vol. VI, p. 140 et seq.

The system text – that is, the presentation that seeks to create a unity of all or large parts of knowledge – naturally seeks to emulate the scientific text as much as possible. In a scientific culture where knowledge is still closely connected, it will in all essentials achieve the rank of scientific text *de preference* by itself. Thomas Aquinas's *Summa Theologica* is a system, but it is also the most sublime expression of the method of scientific presentation of the era. As soon as a specialisation emerges and becomes generally accepted in the scientific community, the conditions change for each system that wishes to include the specialisation in question. If the system-builder themselves is not a specialist, they have to support themselves on that specialisation's own authorities and they have to be ready to allow themselves to be corrected by those authorities if they do not want to be singled out as a charlatan. Whether or not they themselves are a specialist, they cannot make use of the specialised method of presentation that has been adapted to an audience of specialists. They thus have to *popularise*. The extent of this popularisation depends on what audience the system-builder is appealing to; but it can safely be maintained that the smallest imaginable audience the system-builder could conceive of comprises scientists in the various disciplines the unity and connections of which they wish to demonstrate. If any of these disciplines are specialised, the system-builder has to popularise it to the point that the representatives of the other disciplines can understand his account.

It can thus be established as a universal norm that every system claiming to encompass a specialisation must contain an element of popularisation if it is to achieve its goal at all. But conversely, it is also true that the system-builder does not need to feel obligated to popularise such disciplines that for one reason or another they do not regard as a specialisation (if they are striving for a popularisation, it means they are appealing to more than those who received what could be called a general scientific education). They may themselves act as an authority in the field. They can refer to other authors as colleagues of equal merit whose theses and results can be critically reviewed.

That is not to say that every system involves popularisation. Popularisation becomes necessary only when a specialisation has emerged and become accepted.

But popularisation can serve many purposes other than that of the system-builder. Popularisations have existed for as long as there has been organised knowledge. Plato and Aristotle appealed to a broader audience with their dialogues than with their lectures for their disciples at the Academy and the Lyceum. The wandering preachers of the Middle Ages popularised theological knowledge for their listeners. In all elementary education, no matter which society, knowledge had to be simplified. Every insight considered to be of value, even for those who had not received the schooling that the independent treatment of the insight assumes, is digested the same way. The process of digestion would be worth a study on its own.[32] Studying successful popularisations from one era to another would be studying the changing images of the world and attitudes to life in their living relations to classes and groups.

But here, it is a question of the relation between scientific discipline, system and popularisation in the nineteenth century. Science has not always claimed to produce new knowledge: in many epochs and orientations it has instead regarded its primary task as reviving forgotten or hidden knowledge; laying out the knowledge of antiquity or mystical prehistory for contemporaries; or bringing the true Aristotle, the true Hippocrates or the true Hermes Trimegistus to life. Only when the idea becomes generally accepted that knowledge can be developed and continually achieve new triumphs in earnest does the idea that scientific activity is an activity through which *new knowledge is created* become predominant. The highest, most prestigious occupation for a scientist is to expand accumulated knowledge. Advances can be won in many ways: through conquering and charting new areas of reality, through new theories, through new interpretations and connections.

The scientific text is influenced by the demand for incessantly innovative science. The author must account for what they are bringing that no one has brought before. They must, though in an extremely concise manner, account for the prevailing situation in science (i.e. provide a picture of how much is known before they bring their innovative contribution). They must provide an idea of what they have to add – moreover so that his evaluators and critics can assess his contribution.

It is not only those who keep to definite, well demarcated subjects, however, who are animated by the ambition to renew. System-builders are as well. The system-builders must be popularisers the moment they handle a specialised discipline; at the same time, however, they are more than just popularisers the moment they attempt to establish an order among theories and disciplines and areas of reality they do not consider to be already scientifically distinct.

Now, these claims of innovative activity are something than unite all of the nineteenth-century system-builders we have any reason to take into account, be it Schelling or Hegel, Comte or Spencer, Dühring or Hartmann, Büchner or Haeckel. There is nothing remarkable in that. What these system-builders laid

---

32   Viewpoints on the history of popularisation can be found in Gregory and Miller.

claim to was creating a unity or demonstrating a connection in what had been split, or unexpectedly or seemingly contradictory.

It was characteristic of nineteenth-century systems, however, that they contained the same claims to originality and creativity as the large number of more specially oriented scientific presentations.

So far, we have found a number of features that are crucial to the systems and also had to leave their mark on the system text itself. They concern:

1.   attitudes to specialised and non-specialised disciplines;
2.   degree and type of popularisation; and
3.   claim to scientific innovation.

These categories, however, have their inevitable connection with the position of the systems within society – or, to be precise, within the sociology of knowledge. The system-builder must somehow acquire authority, which means they become a reliable populariser of various scientific disciplines for the groups they wish to reach and influence; they must justify their demands for innovation; they must incessantly battle the spectre of charlatanism. The representative of a generally accepted specialisation has many opportunities to convince themselves and those around them of their expert knowledge. They have a more or less normalised schooling in their branch, they can continually demonstrate their skills in the techniques that are considered necessary for the specialisation, they can demonstrate their ability to meet the thousand requirements for a scientific presentation that have emerged in their field. Not least, they have the reactions of a definite and limited audience – colleagues in the subject – to deal with, whether they like it or not.

The system-builder lacks all or most of this security. Or, rather: in Schelling's and Hegel's time, when the systems held a strong position at numerous universities and other scholarly contexts, the system-builder still had a good portion of it but lost it almost completely over the course of the nineteenth century. Their only support from the accepted sciences – which nevertheless was not support intended specifically for them – was the persistent declarations of the specialists that the time was ripe for major syntheses, for revision of the philosophical foundations of the sciences, for worldviews and explanations of the world.

Since the system-builders did not have any associations, no specialist journals or any seats of learning specially intended for them, their activities were not normalised, either: they attempted to write as best they could, substantiate as best they could, convince as best they could. They went at each other with fresh spirit. Spencer attacked Comte, Hartmann attacked Haeckel, and Dühring swore his independence from everyone and everything that had to do with systems. In general, it was typical that no single system-builder of any significance at the time conceded anything to their contemporary system-builders; at the very most, significantly older and long-dead colleagues – perhaps Hegel, perhaps Leibniz – might be good enough.[33]

The system builders thus did not look to each other for support. They sought to create their authority in other ways.

Some of them had a scientific background that gave them some stamina. Ernst Haeckel was an indubitable authority in essential parts of biology. Since the majority of his expositions – even in his broadest works on worldviews – dealt with biological questions, he could speak on his own behalf on many points. His security perhaps made him a little more nonchalant than most when he entered unfamiliar territory; as we have seen, his proof that Darwinist biology had a natural connection with mechanistic physics and chemistry was of a looser type.[34] When, on the other hand, he went in for the most general philosophical questions, he looked backward in time for his authority. Goethe was his idol above all others.[35]

Ludwig Büchner had medical training, but he had no respected position as a scientist. This influenced his method of presentation: he spoke outwardly with the authority of science, and attacked religious and other opponents in the name of science.[36] When a real scientific authority was quoted against him, on the other hand, he became uncertain and resorted to other types of argumentation. Justus von Liebig mounted assaults on the type of materialism that Büchner advocated, and this was noted with satisfaction in various newspapers. Liebig even defended the concept of vital force, which for Bücher was the very culmination of an unscientific approach. Büchner chose not to refute Liebig directly, but the popular instances that sought to take advantage of Liebig's statements. He declared, on the one hand (and rightly so) that the problem of vital force was not simply a problem that chemistry and the chemists could solve. 'Physics and mechanics' also had to have a say in the matter, and the deciding point itself fell to 'physiology and medicine'. On the other hand, he admitted that Liebig was a great chemist (*'ein grosser Chemiker'*) but that no single person, no matter how great, could alone constitute the authoritative instance on a scientific question.[37]

---

33   Engels can be incorporated into this pattern as well; he held the system-builders of his time in contempt, and Hegel was his system-building authority. Cf below, 11: 29 et seqq.

34   Above, p. 194 et seqq.

35   See above all Haeckel 1873, p. xvii *f* and 65 et seqq.

36   Foreword, Büchner 1855, p. ix et seqq., and more markedly in later editions, e.g. the 14th; Büchner 1876, p. xxi et seqq.

37   Büchner 1876, p. liii et seqq., in particular p. lviii.

Bücher's dilemma was the same that every system-builder encountered if they accepted specialised scientific fields and nonetheless attempted to bring unity to the multitude of incompatible ideas among specialists. They had to set authority against authority, specialisation against specialisation.

Büchner did not cherish any great hope of converting the specialists themselves, the reason being that – like many other system-builders – he did not acknowledge a separate 'philosophical' sphere, a region for specialists in the general from which the particulars could be surveyed and the connection between the specialists' patches of ground and small allotments could be mapped. He threw himself upon the multitude of authorities.

This left its mark on his entire manner of presentation. He flooded his readers with quotes from the great personages in the various natural sciences. Even in the formal clothing of the quotations, we can see he was not appealing to the specialists. He indicated names and book titles, but almost never page references: he did not intend for the readers themselves to go to the source and form their own opinion. The name of the author was to guarantee the reliability of the quotation; the author was to speak, and the reader to listen without interrupting.

But a system-builder can partially escape Büchner's dilemma if they assert that they possess a particular ability to draw far-reaching conclusions about the details (the difficulty instead becomes convincing the readers that there is such a synthetic ability in general). Eugen Dühring, who was one of the most headstrong synthesisers, sought to draw his power both from his philosophical schooling and from being at home in various individual sciences. In his memoirs, which bore the expressive title *Sache, Leben und Feinde* (Acts, Life and Enemies), he declared that a mathematical schooling was a good prerequisite for an all-embracing philosopher[38] and that the 'higher' (i.e. more exact) natural sciences – astronomy in particular – were the natural starting point for anyone trying to create a worldview.[39] He was also careful to emphasise that he had studied law, with which he intended to endow his economic writings with greater dignity.[40] In *Natürliche Dialektik*, the first work where he attempted to create unity in the diversity of the sciences, he swore to his almost complete philosophical originality but declared in the same breath that most of all, he wanted approval from the representatives of the exact natural sciences.[41] It was thus neither the general public, thirsty for learning, nor the philosophers who would be his witnesses to the truth.

---

38   Dühring 1903, p. 110 et seq.
39   Ibid., p. 18.
40   Ibid., p. 58 et seqq.
41   Dühring 1865, p. v et seqq.

At the same time, he imagined that precisely through some sort of philosophical or synthetic capacity he could say something that the representatives of the exact natural sciences could not arrive at on their own. In his dialectics of nature, he also incorporated a social theory – or more precisely a theory of right – in which the concept of right was derived from the concept of revenge (*Rache*).[42] Biology, in contrast, played a highly obscure role, and Darwin figured only with a statement that in Dühring's opinion was inconsistent and showed that logic and a schooling in logic was needed in the sciences.[43]

Dühring's accounts thus contained very few references to authorities. In the fields that were central to his system, he named himself as his own authority. The innovations he saw himself as bringing had to do with what he called the dialectic (not to be confused with Hegel's). In contrast to normal logic, the dialectic had '*zeugende Kraft*' (creative power); it was therefore constructive, and with its help new connections between knowledge and spheres of knowledge could be developed.[44]

Obviously, Dühring failed almost completely in his ambitions to win the favour of the exact natural sciences. Their most authoritative representative in Germany, Helmholtz, was one of those who drove the dangerous system-builder out of the university of Berlin.[45] Dühring did not, as he had hoped, influence the internal development of the sciences; on the other hand, however, he briefly became a power factor in the ideological struggle.[46]

Dühring's contradictory opposite was Eduard von Hartmann. He lacked all formal schooling, and could not make his audience respect him by pointing to his degree qualifications. He and Dühring agreed on one point along, and that was their contempt for 'craft guild professors' and 'trade guild philosophy' – that is, for a science (and in particular a philosophy) that neither wished nor dared to move beyond the narrow boundaries of its territory.

Unlike Hartmann, Dühring did not feel at all compelled to demonstrate an ability to produce a professional scientific text. With Hartmann, this ambition occasionally reached sublime heights. The crucial point in his activities was producing a philosophical, or more precisely a speculative, interpretation of biology, in particular Darwinist biology. His *Philosophy of the Unconscious* was above all an attempt to provide descendance theory with a teleological interpretation: the development of species was no more blind and unpremeditated

---

42   Ibid., p. xi.
43   Ibid., p. 15. Cf. further below, II:127 et seqq.
44   Ibid., p. 1 et seqq.
45   Above, p. 134 et seq.
46   Cf. below, p. 511 et seqq.

than historical development, and all organic phenomena demonstrated a suitability for purpose that necessitated taking final causes into account.[47]

Hartmann had to weather criticism from the biologists because he was a
charlatan who was unable to interpret biological contexts with any expert
knowledge. Hartmann's response to the criticism reveals, in all its brilliant simplicity, what expert knowledge was in his eyes. He published his own polemical
pamphlet against *Philosophy of the Unconscious* titled *The Unconscious from
the Standpoint of Physiology and Descendance Theory*, naturally without revealing his identity. Five years later, in 1877, Hartmann published a second edition
where he informed an astonished public that he had attacked his own work.
His foreword to the second edition exuded triumph. Few had suspected the
document's secret.[48]

One of the goals of his anonymous polemic was, he declared, to show that
he 'theoretically (*gedanklich*) had completely mastered the standpoint of the
modern natural sciences' while in contrast his adversaries in the natural sciences had not even mastered his own philosophy and its general assumptions.[49]

For Hartmann, the ability to write a scientific text *as if* a specialist had taken
up the pen (i.e. complying with its norms and conventions) was therefore the
decisive sign that he could comment with full authority on the theoretical problems of the specialisation in question. It is relevant to the point that the general
discussion about Darwinism was being conducted on a quite abstract plane
with sweeping arguments *pro et contra*. Even the biologists often conducted
the discussion with a limited and partially standardised selection of empirical
examples; the exchange of opinions therefore did not require coming out with
one's own experiences of biological phenomena. In his anonymous book, Hartmann showed that he could handle the usual examples and turn them in the
direction of a non-teleological explanation. His text thus did not differ in principle from the texts on biological questions he produced in *Philosophy of the
Unconscious*; only the conclusions were the opposite.

Hartmann enjoyed no success among the biologists with the proof of his
expertise. It can certainly be said that his standpoints were the subject of their
criticism to an astounding extent: not only Haeckel and Oscar Schmidt,[50] who

---

47   Cf. for example Dühring 1902, p. 125; Hartmann 1875, p. 1; Hartmann 1876, p. 35 et seq. and
      Hartmann 1885, p. 10.
48   '*Vorwort zur zweiten Auflage*', Hartmann 1877.
49   Ibid.
50   Oscar Schmidt wrote a specific polemic against Hartmann, *Die naturlichen wissenschaft-
      lichen Grundlagen der Philosophie des Unbewussten*.

usually kept to the commons and half-philosophical outlands of the discussion, but also fastidious specialists such as August Weismann[51] discussed his opinions in earnest. Teleology as such, however, was retreating into biology. It was only when the tendency changed (though temporarily) at the turn of the twentieth century that Hartmann gained the support of professional biologists (i.e. the 'neo-vitalists' with Hans Driesch at their head).[52] Hartmann now truly felt the wind in his sails. For several decades he had been on the defensive, but in *Problem des Lebens* he went on the attack against a biological conception he now dared describe as scientifically obsolete.[53]

Hartmann sought to authorise his philosophy both through proving his expertise, primarily in the field of biology, and through arguing for the existence of a particularly speculative field of philosophy – a philosophical specialisation, if you will. Comparing his presentations with one of Spencer's or one of Comte's soon reveals that he perceived his situation as a system-builder as more precarious than they did. This was bound up in part with the fact that he was active in an intellectual environment that held the specialisations in a firmer grip. For Comte and Spencer, however, the joining of the sciences (and in part precisely because of this) was also a much simpler affair. The connection among the disciplines and therefore among the theories was latent in them. The philosopher did not need any profound reinterpretation; they only needed to draw a few definite, though hidden, conclusions.

Comte and Spencer also had it considerably easier for the reason that they did not take any specialised human sciences into account. When we say that Comte and Spencer made original contributions to sociology, it may be correct in the sense that they developed certain general lines of thought here that influenced the later social sciences. It is not correct, however, if with that we imagine that they would have worked any differently in the human sciences – with richer expert knowledge, a greater amount of their own experiential material, and so on – than they did in the natural sciences. They were certainly more audacious: they ascribed an active, innovative capacity to themselves here. But their approach and their manner of presentation were essentially the same. They drew out the threads from the natural sciences that they regarded as standard for all the sciences. Their type of argumentation was the same. In all fields, they stood outside the specialists' discussion. They sought to adapt themselves after those specialists whose absolute expertise they did not ques-

---

51   Above, p. 195. A bibliography of the literature on Hartmann and the unconscious is found
      in Plümacher 1881, p. 117 et seqq.
52   On this topic, see Driesch 1905 and Haller 1968.
53   Hartmann 1901, p. 1 et seqq.

tion; they only sought to supplement the viewpoints of the latter with their own broader perspective. Spencer could – not without reason – point out that he had brough a number of general viewpoints to evolutionary biology. His verbal imagination had at least given Darwin and his followers a number of general and effective phrases: 'struggle for existence', 'survival of the fittest' and so on.[54] He did not regard himself as a professional biologist, however. In the foreword to *Principles of Biology* he thanked T.H. Huxley and J.D. Hooker for putting their expertise at his disposal, but at the same time he emphasised that the general doctrines were his own.[55] He wanted to appear as his own specialist in the general.

He would never have admitted to similar help from specialists in *Principles of Sociology*, for example. In the foreword, he only discussed the suitability of the designation 'sociology'; the scientific field itself had not yet been constituted.[56] Spencer recognised no group of experts (i.e. any type of specialist that could guide and correct him) here.

But Spencer's presentations – like Comte's – are formally similar; he moves about in either a specialised or non-specialised field. The unity in the immense synthesis emerges from the very style of writing. Both Comte and Spencer are strikingly parsimonious with references and substantiations. References to other literature are rare, as are accounts of how one or another result had been arrived at in science. Anyone keeping within the framework of a specialisation is careful to account for the entire scientific discussion and demonstrate how they themselves arrived at their results so that their colleagues in the subject could in principle duplicate the work. Comte and Spencer – and all the nineteenth-century system-builders in general – had no reason to offer up their texts for such inspection. The ones who were closest to being their inspectors were their fellow system-builders, but as we have already seen the system-builders did not regard themselves as being engaged in any noble competition for the best system. Each and every one of them were sovereign.

The system-builders' natural audiences changed, of course; their popular and ideological ambitions were differently marked. Spencer is relatively easy to read, and Comte somewhat more difficult; Dühring is definitely not 'popular'. There are features, however, that unite all system-builders in their approaches to different groups. To name a few:

---

54   Canguilhem conducted a small special study of Darwinism's catchphrases; ibid., p. 1 et
       seqq. The expression 'struggle for existence' originally comes from Malthus.
55   Spencer 1862, Vol. 11 (*Principles of Biology*, Vol. 1), Preface.
56   Spencer 1862, Vol. v, p. v.

a)   In relation to specialisations that they accepted but could not themselves
     claim to have mastered:
     1.   they were willing to take corrections from the specialists' criticism
           on anything that was obviously regarded as belonging to the special-
           isation; and
     2.   they considered themselves capable of giving the specialists know-
           ledge about the position of the specialisation in the scientific hier-
           archy, and also potentially about the most general theoretical guide-
           lines of the specialisation.
b)   In relation to scientific fields that they did not regard as specialisations,
     they moved about with their own authority and were not willing to simply
     be corrected by those who were conducting detailed research in the field;
     in their synthetic presentations, at least, they nevertheless did not go into
     any particulars but approached the field in the same way they approached
     the specialisations.
c)   In relation to the non-scientific audience, they spoke with the authority
     of science as a whole.

These approaches, which therefore emerged in the system texts themselves,
were entirely natural in a partially specialised scientific culture.

6   The Structure of the Systems

There are other formal features of nineteenth-century systems that could be
pointed out. There were system-builders who through the format itself of their
presentations sought to demonstrate their versatility and expertise: this was
the case in particular with the thousands of pages of Spencer's and Comte's
works. There were also system-builders who created their own terminology and
thereby attained an analogue to technical vocabulary. Comte's verbal imagination in this connection is remarkably vast: 'sociology', 'social physics', 'social
static' and so on are all his creations. Spencer used more customary terminology but gave them his own definite content: 'differentiation', 'integration' and
so on.

We will not enter deeply into these matters, but pass over to another perspective on systems from which their relations to the individual sciences stand
out even more clearly. This concerns the structures of the systems – that is,
the parts from which they are constructed and the mutual relations of these
parts.

The parts are the various scientific fields that according to the system-
builder comprise the natural – or at least plausible – units that together con-

stitute the scientific hierarchy. Every system-builder kept to a classification of the sciences.

But the classification as such was not particularly enlightening or interesting. What was interesting and significant was how the various elements were united with each other. In dividing the sciences, the system-builders were at the mercy of the same relative confusion as the representatives of the individual sciences. There was a number of divisions and proposals for names and boundaries in the nineteenth century that were difficult to grasp. The classifications at various scientific academies and research associations, the division of subjects at university philosophical departments and the division of professional fields that the scientific journals spontaneously produced presented a map that was equally as variegated as the system-builders' own proposals.

There are many different traditions and several bases for division that appear in this extravagance. We need only study a few examples to understand how difficult it could be to organise the various disciplines into a uniform context. The traditional significance of the word 'physics' was the natural sciences, or more precisely natural philosophy (i.e. theoretical science) in general.[57] Mechanics liberated itself in many quarters, however, and was regarded as a separate discipline. Chemistry had its partly unique traditions from the eighteenth century and earlier, and would also without exception be placed in opposition to what was called 'physics' during the nineteenth century. Physics became more frequently the name of the area thought to lie between mechanics and chemistry – theories of electricity and magnetism, optics and acoustics and theories of heat (thermodynamics).[58] But where did astronomy, one of the old key disciplines of physics, belong? Its most advanced portion was celestial mechanics. Did astronomy belong to mechanics or to physics, or was it something else, an independent or plainly superior discipline?

There were similar difficulties concerning the sciences that were occupied with living beings. The former strict division between zoology and botany was questioned; the joint designation of 'biology' was introduced by Burdach, Lamarck and Treviranus around the turn of the nineteenth century.[59] But there were also a number of traditional disciplines that dealt with living beings from

---

57   Cf. Diemer 1968a or b, p. 177 et seqq.

58   Cf. for example Tyndall's essay 'On the Study of Physics' in Tyndall 1879, Vol. I, p. 333 et seqq., and the various classifications presented in *Die Klassifikation der Wissenschaften als philosophisches System* (pub. R. Rochhausen). Cf. also such different authors as Hegel 8:23 et seq. (classification of natural philosophy); Spencer 1966, p. 78; Whewell 1968, p. 190.

59   According to earlier understanding, Lamarck and Treviranus were the first to use the word 'biology'; both did so in 1802. But Schmid has shown that C.F. Burdach spoke about biology in 1800. Cf. also Ballauff 1971.

different aspects: anatomy, physiology, pathology and so on. How did they relate to biology? And where in the hierarchy did the new branches – histology,[60] cytology, cellular pathology, and so on – belong? Even more troublesome (and even more controversial) was how organic chemistry related to the various fields of biology. The antagonisms between vitalism and mechanicism echoed in the battle over this issue.

The multitude of classifications in fact reflected a long range of conditions that determined the entirety of scientific activity in various ways. Shifting theoretical ideas can be read here: new and old, current and obsolete. A strict distinction between botany and zoology corresponds to the theory that plants and animals are fundamentally separate entities and comprise their own 'kingdoms' in nature.[61] In contrast, a uniform biology (i.e. a theory of living beings) assumes a theory in which plants and animals are united by the same type of life.[62]

Naturally, these theoretical assumptions could be of absolutely no significance for scientific activity itself – nonetheless, they endure in various demarcations of the branches.

A division, however, could also be determined by old or new areas of experience. What kept astronomy together was the area of experience of 'the heavenly bodies'. New experimental techniques could open new areas of experience; histology is a classic example of how microscopy provided research with a new type of object: organic microstructures.

But the external uses of the sciences could also influence the classification. The distinction between applied and theoretical sciences originated with Aristotle.[63] When increasing numbers of disciplines can be put to practical use, an increasingly strict distinction between pure and applied branches also emerges. The grouping of disciplines, however, is also more thoroughly marked by external circumstances. The old departmental divisions at the universities constitute perhaps the most striking example here. What kept the changing fields of medical study together was not a theory; it was more or less well-founded ideas about what a physician should be able to do to successfully

---

60   Histology, or microscopic anatomy, first appeared as a distinct discipline in Henle's *Allgemeine Anatomie*.

61   Nature's three kingdoms were animal, vegetable and mineral, corresponding to the three distinct disciplines of zoology, botany, and mineralogy.

62   On the other hand, the Aristotelian doctrine of the three 'souls' – plant, animal, and human – that dominated thinking up until the late eighteenth century and beyond entailed a clear distinction between the lives of plants and animals.

63   Aristotle distinguished between theoretical, practical, and poetic 'episteme'; cf. for example Ross 1949, pp. 20, 187.

practice their profession. The theological disciplines obtained their structure in part from the Christian outlook – an ideological determination – and in part from various practical considerations, among which training in the priesthood gained decisive significance only at a later stage.[64]

The divisions at the various scholarly organisations – in themselves justified by various practical and theoretical arguments – could also play a role, however. The fact that in many places – Sweden, for example – the subject of economics long had a position in the university organisation as a subdivision of botany would undoubtedly influence its academic orientation; economics went together with the natural sciences, and the reasons for this were in part purely administrative.[65]

All that has just been said seems to indicate that scientific specialisation had its significance for the division of the sciences. Mechanics distinguishing itself as a separate field in relation to physics had to do with the fact that from Newton onward, there was a truly specialised theory practiced by specialists. On the other hand, the dividing line between physics and chemistry had no material basis in its own specialisation from the start; it actually became so only over the course of the nineteenth century.

But the professionalisation of a subject – that is, the process by which the practice of a given discipline became an occupation – also had a significance that did not need to coincide with that of specialisation. In the German universities of the nineteenth century, professionalisation and specialisation took place in the human sciences in particular; the range of professions influenced the classification of the sciences.[66]

The system-builders were thus faced with an enormous number of potential scientific hierarchies. Their various divisions bore the mark of a diversity of shifting conditions in older and contemporary science. For the system-builder, it was a self-evident and inevitable task to try to decide in favour of a single hierarchy, a hierarchy they had to defend as the one that best elucidated the connections among the different parts of knowledge.

---

64   On the theological faculty, see Lindborg 1965.

65   On this topic, cf. for example Liedman 1986.

66   A subject is not a professional matter only as a result of its being a livelihood for a professor; it also requires that professors cannot – as they could in older universities – change subjects relatively freely. As long as they are able to, it is academic teaching that is the profession, not the specific discipline. No study of the decreasing mobility among subjects in nineteenth-century universities has yet been published; I can only plead that I am working on one myself, which in time will be published and will confirm what has been said.

Similar hierarchies were laid out wholesale and retail throughout the nineteenth century.[67] In comparing them, one is struck primarily by their diversity. There was an abundance of proposals as to the best, most natural or most practical division. Going deeper into the differences would be going too far; a few general features and a number of examples will have to suffice.

It was not only pronounced system philosophers such as Hegel, Comte and Spencer who painted immense tableaus of all the parts of knowledge. French economist and mathematician A.A. Cournot produced his own division,[68] as did his countryman, the renowned physicist A.M. Ampère.[69] Jeremy Bentham appended an investigation of the division of the sciences to his *Chrestomathia*.[70]

A comparison of these systems soon reveals that there was a range of similar problems that the classifiers faced. They had to investigate the relation between formal sciences such as mathematics and logic, and the real disciplines. They had to explain how more theoretically oriented branches related to branches of a more empirical character. They also had to differentiate between areas of more practical and more theoretical research, between a 'theoretical' and a 'practical series' of sciences, as Cournot described it.[71]

Most interesting – at least for those wanting to acquaint themselves with the character of the system-builders – is the differences between the divisions that appeared entirely or almost entirely instinctive to their originators.

In the division of subjects that applied in university faculties, academies and so on without all claims of being systems, there was a competition between two bases for division that could be called the methodological and the ontological. The distinction between the 'three kingdoms' of nature or between physics and biology has in view *primarily* the differences between different spheres of reality. On the other hand, the distinction between static and dynamic in mechanics or between anatomy and physiology in biology does not claim that there is are static and dynamic parts of reality or that organisms can be divided into an anatomical and a physiological part. The basis of the distinction is methodological in the broadest sense.

The relation between methodologically separate disciplines was discussed quite assiduously in the nineteenth century. The study of the 'form', or 'struc-

---

67   One outstanding presentation here is *Die Klassifikation der Wissenschaften als philosophisches Problem* (cf. above, Note 58). See also Diemer 1968a or b.

68   Cournot 1851. New edition 1912.

69   Ampère 1838.

70   Bentham 1841.

71   Cournot 1912, p. 510 et seq. Cournot also discerns a '*série cosmologique et historique*'.

ture', of a phenomenon and its 'function' should complement each other. Biologist and system-builder Ernst Haeckel distinguished between three areas of study in biology, corresponding to three aspects that could be applied to living beings. One was the 'theory of matter, or chemistry' (*die Stofflehre oder Chemie*), another was the 'theory of form, or morphology' (*die Formlehre oder Morphologie*), and the third and final was the 'theory of force, or physics' (*die Kraftlehre oder Physik*).[72] The term 'physics' may be confusing, since at the same time Haeckel called morphology the biological static, and physics the dynamic. His line of thought is nonetheless clear: like inorganic nature, organic nature could be studied from three perspectives: chemistry, static, and dynamic. There was thus a kind of methodological symmetry that, for Haeckel, was a sign of the essential affinity of the respective areas of research.

The distinction between a 'static' and a 'dynamic' aspect is, as we have seen,[73] customary in a number of different contexts. Comte's distinction in particular between social static and social dynamic displayed great penetrating power. A classification of the sciences needed go no further than noting the different methods of research and commenting more generally on how they complemented each other. Authors who above all aimed at investigating the epistemological conditions for the various disciplines had to investigate more closely how the different perspectives related to each other and what type of knowledge they could provide. The pronounced system-builders, on the other hand, went a determined step further. They did not stop on the methodological plane but went further to ontology. Their classification was ultimately not a classification of scientific fields but moreover a classification of spheres of reality.

Naturally, it is not a question here of any absolute or razor-sharp difference. Authors such as William Whewell, John Stuart Mill or Wilhelm Dilthey were not system-builders in the same sense as Spencer or Haeckel, but there were many ontological assumptions and hints in their presentations. Whewell's Kant-inspired theory that different sciences were based on different 'ideas' was connected with his belief in a divine being;[74] Mill's attempt at adapting the methodology in the human sciences to that of the natural sciences was based on the reasoning that humanity basically did not differ from other

---

72   Haeckel 1866, Vol. I, p. 10 et seqq. Haeckel's schema becomes even more complex over the course of his account; see for example his tableau on the various parts of zoology, ibid., p. 238. See also the account of biological classification in *Klassifikation*, p. 105 *ff* and in particular p. 111 et seqq.

73   Above, pp. 258 and 268.

74   On this topic, cf. Butts 1968, p. 4 et seqq.

objects of study[75] while Dilthey by contrast assumed the unique character of the human.[76]

For none of them, however, was the goal of their presentations to arrive at an ontology. On the other hand, the system-builders were system-builders in their ambition, with the help of science – or more precisely the sciences assembled together – to reveal reality. The methodological relations between static and dynamic, physiology and anatomy, synchronic and diachronic historical writing may have been important to them; they may have devoted great attention to the question of reducing biological theories to physical ones; the results, however, of their discussions of these and similar questions was always statements about how the various parts of reality related to each other in accordance with the understanding of science.

This would also leave its mark on their classification. When Hegel divided the sciences into natural sciences and human sciences, the natural sciences into mechanics, physics, and organic physics, and the human sciences into anthropology, phenomenology and so on, he certainly devoted great attention to the methodological questions; his primary task was nonetheless separating different parts of reality (and thereby both subjective and objective reality) from one another. The difference between mechanics and physics is, to be sure, a difference between different ways of looking at a physical reality according to Hegel. At the same time, however, mechanics is the sphere of reality that spreads *between* inorganic bodies, and physics (which includes chemistry) the reality that *also* encompasses the intrinsic qualities of those bodies.[77] The same applies to Spencer's and Comte's classifications. Apart from purely formal mathematics, Comte distinguished the primary disciplines of astronomy, physics, chemistry, physiology and social physics (or sociology). They corresponded to various real stages in the development of reality.[78] Spencer, who devoted a great deal of writing to polemicising with Comte's division, was off on the same errand: explaining, on the basis of a discussion of the assumptions and results of science, what reality was and how it coheres.[79]

---

75   Mill 1851, Vol. I, p. 414 et seqq. or Mill 1973, Vol. II, p. 844 et seqq. The object of study, to be precise, is 'human nature'.
76   Dilthey 1922, Vol. I, p. 28 et seqq.
77   Cf. for example Hegel 8:66 *ff*, 150.
78   Comte 1:19 et seqq.
79   Spencer distinguishes between abstract, abstract-concrete, and concrete sciences (logic/ mathematics – mechanics/physics/chemistry – astronomy/geology/biology/psychology/ sociology); it is the third group, which deals with *totalities*, that simultaneously corresponds to the ontological hierarchy (with the reservations that the doctrine of 'the unconscious' entails). Spencer 1966, p. 78 et seqq.

But in many places, the difference between a methodological and an onto-logical investigation of the context of the sciences was scarcely noticed, or not at all. The crucial change in this case did not come until neo-Kantianism and in particular with Friedrich Albert Lange's two-volume *History of Materialism* with its strict distinction between the methodological materialism of the nat-ural sciences and a metaphysical materialism.[80]

The reasons that so little attention was otherwise paid to the difference between methodological and ontological hierarchies of the sciences are not difficult to understand. In specialised research there was a similar, and just as little noticed, difference between what I have called a theoretical and a realistic tendency.[81] With a bit of simplification, it could be said that the methodological classifiers extrapolated the theoretical tendency to apply to all knowledge, whereas the pronounced system-builders drew extreme conclu-sions from the realistic tendency. But it is also important to remember that the difference between theoretical and realistic tendencies and between ontolo-gical and methodological statements did not become apparent in concrete sci-entific research or presentations. In the scientific discussion of vitalism versus mechanicism, the argument had immediate – and to the same extent both methodological and ontological – consequences. When Helmholtz advocated a reduction of vital force to the forces of mechanics, when Müller sought to demonstrate experimentally that the theory of spontaneous generation was untenable, or when Schwann explained that organisms were constructed of cells in the same way that crystal aggregates were formed from crystals, it was not evident from their arguments whether they were striving for methodolo-gical or ontological connections or differences, respectively, between living and dead, between biology and physics. Every concrete scientific result simultan-eously implied a statement about *how reality should or could be studied* and a statement about *how it is constructed*. There was an obvious link between the one and the other: reality appears thus and so, provided that it is stud-ied with such-and-such methods. It was a later, or rather broader, question of how the reach of the results was determined. In many (perhaps most) con-texts they remained indeterminate. Many of the nineteenth-century natural

---

80   Lange 1876, Vol. 2, p. 139 et seqq. Lange quite correctly places the cleft in connection with increasing specialisation: being occupied with an ever-smaller portion of reality makes it more difficult to comment on reality as such. '*Specialforschung macht also vorsichtig; sie macht aber auch bisweilen engherzig und arrogant*'. Ibid., p. 140. It was, however, from a philosophical perspective that Lange wanted to criticise the inferences from science to ontology.

81   Above, p. 233 et seqq.

scientists excelled at comprehensive scientific statements in which methodological and ontological claims remained undecided. This applies, for example,
to John Tyndall's comments on the relation between the principle of conservation of energy and Darwinism.[82] Other scientists revealed their understanding
in contexts that lay far beyond their stricter scientific activities. Emil du Bois-
Reymond's *Ignoramibus* address is a striking example.[83]

To understand the temptations and successes of the system-builders, it must
be remembered – as we have already seen several times – that what they were
occupied with was closely linked to the discussions and problems of the specialised sciences. The most common argument that could be directed *against*
systems was that the system-builders were not specialists in all the areas they
moved around in. This was a comment that could just as equally be levelled
at those who sought to construct primarily methodological hierarchies. The
system-builders were subjected to the more general argument that they misunderstood the nature of scientific theories by making ontological statements
about reality only late in the century. Mill and Spencer still obviously saw no
crucial difference in general between each other's way of writing about the sciences.[84] William Whewell[85] and John Herschel[86] drew no boundaries in principle against ontology, and Helmholtz only did so in his epistemological and
popular writings.[87]

7   Types of Systems: Spencer and Hartmann

If we said that the system-builders ultimately strove for a classification of reality, that naturally would not mean that in general they would not pay a great
deal of attention to methodological questions. Most of them were actively
occupied with the problems that dominated large parts of the nineteenth cen-

---

82   Above, p. 198 et seqq.
83   Above, p. 169.
84   See for example, Spencer's essay 'Mill versus Hamilton – The Test of Truth' in Spencer 1966,
      p. 188 et seqq. and in particular p. 200 et seqq., and Mill's letter to Spencer of 11 March 1865,
      Vol. II, p. 1010 et seq.
85   Whewell 1968, e.g. p. 186 et seqq. (where the issue appears as definitively unsettled).
86   Herschel 1966, e.g. p. 75 et seqq.
87   Here, for example, the most Kantian of Helmholtz's writings can be studied: his senior
      researcher lecture from 1852, *Über de Natur der menschlichen Sinnesempfindungen*, Helm-
      holtz 1882, Vol. II, p. 591 et seqq. A special study of Helmholtz's epistemology has been
      conducted by Lenzen 1947. Cf. also the study of Helmholtz's and Mach's concept of sci-
      ence done by G. König 1968.

tury debate around scientific theory and were subject to the consideration of the more theoretically minded and reflective scientific specialists. They took a position in this discussion, and their viewpoints emerged clearly from the very structures of their systems.

Here, we will distinguish two such partially related questions. The one concerns scientific explanations, or more precisely the orientation of scientific explanations. The other concerns the relations among various theories, or more precisely the problem of whether, and if so how, a scientific theory could be reduced to another scientific theory.

Four different main types of systems can in fact be distinguished, all according to their relation to these general questions. These four main types – among which there are a considerable number of intermediary forms – correspond to four positions in both scientific theoretical and internal debates.

First, we have the standpoint that a scientific explanation means that the more complex is traced back to the simpler, is explained through the simpler. This means, for example, that mechanics provides the basis of explanation for physics and chemistry, these in turn for biology, and so on. It also means (and in fact this is a more fundamental relation) that more complex phenomena in a given field of science ought to be explained by simpler phenomena in the same field. So according to this conception, for example, complex phenomena such as reflexes and instincts ought to be explained as far as possible in terms of simpler biological phenomena, physiological by anatomical, and so on.

The systems (like scientific ideas in general) that adopted this idea we can call 'ascending' or 'concretising' (the path runs from the more abstract to the more concrete).

The opposite standpoint means, on the contrary, that the complete explanation must be sought in the more complex; the inorganic becomes comprehensible only in relation to the organic, the biological in relation to the mental, and so on. Consistent 'descending' or 'abstracting' systems are found in various types of idealism, in which the spiritual is regarded as the foundation of the material.

Both ascending and descending systems, however, can in turn be divided into reductive and irreductive.[88] A fully reductive system is a system in which every theory (and thereby every field of science) can be expressed in terms of the closest lying more fundamental theory. If the system is also ascending, reductionism thus means that all theories can ultimately be expressed in the

---

88   There is a great deal of modern scientific theoretical literature on reductionism and irreductionism. On this topic, see for example Gillet 2016.

most abstract language of the sciences: mechanics. If it is descending, on the other hand, it is the discipline at the other end of the hierarchy – whether it is called philosophy, or something else – that provides the key to all other theories.

If the system is irreductive, on the other hand, the hierarchy is regarded as clearly segmented into the various fields of science, where each field displays unique features in relation to its neighbours. It could be said, purely in general, that most real system-builders strove for reductive systems; it was in the very idea of system-building, so to speak, to demonstrate as great a unity as possible in knowledge. But there were many notable exceptions. The foremost of them in the nineteenth century were Hegel's and Engels's systems. Their irreductive character was the primary reason behind the frequently recurring question of whether they constituted real systems – a question we will have reason to return to.[89]

But for now, let us work on the assumption that there were primarily four types of systems, namely:

Ia.   *Abstracting and reductive*;
Ib.   *Abstracting and irreductive*;
IIa.   *Concretising and reductive*; and
IIb.   *Concretising and irreductive*.

The first type is represented by the vast majority of systems in the late nineteenth century; it was the type that was represented in many variants and variations by Spencer, Büchner, Haeckel, Dühring and so on. They had general support in the ideal of reductive mechanicism, but they involved something different and more than this ideal as it was advocated by Herschel, Helmholtz and others. The assumptions about scientific theory were developed into ontological statements: everything real that we could obtain knowledge about was matter in movement, and all forms of movement or development – even the most complex – were expressions of the same fundamental mechanical movement.

The only one who, to my knowledge, tried to develop the second type of system in the nineteenth century was Engels. He strove to unite the dominant mechanical materialism of the time with Hegel; that is what the originality of his contribution comprises.

The third type of system was represented by the entire band of Romantic philosophers from Schelling onward, while the last had its great representative in Hegel. When Hegel settled accounts with Schelling, his first crucial point

89   See below, p. 373 et seqq.

of attack was the Schellingites' striving for a total identity in which the differences among various fields of science and spheres of reality were abolished. 'It was the night in which all cows are black', Hegel said in a famous phrase from his Foreword to his *Phenomenology of Spirit*.[90] Instead, Hegel imagined a much more complex process of development in which the transition from one stage to another – and thus from one science to another, from one sphere of reality to another – was marked by 'leaps' (i.e. by changes that were not only quantitative but qualitative as well).[91]

We can demonstrate the different types of systems with the following simple table:

	reductive	irreductive
concretising	Comte Spencer Büchner Haeckel ...	Engels
abstracting	Schelling ...	Hegel

All these systems were defended with ontological claims, but the standpoints they contained about the nature of the fields of science (and thereby of scientific explanations) had their support in different orientations in the sciences that were oriented on specialisation. The question of reduction or not was, as we have seen multiple times, one of the dominant issues in scientific controversies and debates in the nineteenth century. The leading ambition in Helmholtz's early works on the indestructibility of force was to reduce all the forces of nature, including the vital force, to a fundamental mechanical force.[92] In chemistry, the question of whether there was a fundamental physical theory with which chemical crosses could be explained was a frequently recurring question; another controversial question concerned the relation between organic and inorganic chemistry.[93]

The great protracted reckoning between mechanism and vitalism in biology was essentially a question of reducing the living to the dead. In that dis-

---

90   Hegel 2:22.
91   Ibid., p. 22 et seqq.
92   Above, p. 151.
93   Above, p. 148 et seqq.

cussion we can also find the counterpart to the difference between ascending, concretising systems and descending, abstracting ones. The mechanists sought to explain the phenomenon of life by starting from the simplest occurrences of life, from organic matter, organic structures (cells) and so on. The vitalists found the characteristic and decisive organic phenomena in far more complicated areas. While Theodor Schwann explained life using an analogy between cell and crystal formation, his mentor Johannes Müller's standpoint was dominated by such complex phenomena as instincts and reflexes.[94] Darwinism was primarily a concretising theory in which it was a matter of deriving more complex forms of life from simpler ones. Against its explanatory schema, its critics – especially Eduard von Hartmann – cited organic phenomena that were most obviously suited to the purpose, complex and seemingly intelligently designed.[95]

The same applied to the great discussion on the relation of the human sciences to the natural sciences. Those who sought a direct link started from such human relations as could be regarded as more 'natural' (i.e. from simple mental phenomena closely linked to physiology) or from what was perceived as primitive and original types of humans and societies. In the historist tradition, on the other hand, the most complex human activities, such as the arts or sciences, and the most complex types of societies such as modern Western European society were the natural starting point – or, rather, the point from which everything human could be surveyed. External relations, more easily accessible for quantification, were usually regarded as secondary or as the outflow of a human creative force that lay behind them. For Dilthey, it was self-evident that the sciences of culture were fundamental in relation to the sciences of the external organisation of society.[96]

We do not need to expand this collection of examples any further. The tendency is clear enough: to an enormous extent, the systems constituted extrapolations of perspectives, problems and theories that flourished in the individual disciplines. In a differentiated and contradictory scientific environment, however, it was not obvious which perspectives, problems or theories should be brought into the system; in the nineteenth-century world of theories, the accepted sciences provided support for all four types of systems I have mentioned. Whatever the system-builder chose, they had to come in conflict with currents that could claim to be scientific.

---

94   Cf. Watermann 1960.
95   Here, see above all *Wahrheit und Irrthum im Darwinismus* (Hartmann 1975).
96   Above, p. 224.

This conflict, however, could find expression in widely different ways among different system-builders. We can illustrate this with examples from Herbert Spencer and Eduard von Hartmann, who in this respect stood so far apart from each other as can be imagined. As system-builders they had only one thing in common: both were scientific amateurs. They therefore had no scientific authority of their own to securely lean on. In all other respects they were the antitheses of each other. The one regarded his system as a simple further development of the dominant tendencies in contemporary science, the other claimed to possess a particular philosophical insight that provided the possibility of seeing farther and deeper than ordinary scientists. The one chose ascending explanations without exception; he moved from the simpler to the more complex. The other asserted that all of reality could be put in order only if it were assumed that the ultimate driving force was a spiritual phenomenon, called The Unconscious.

There was another difference, however, that from the perspective now in question was more important. In his great *System of Synthetic Philosophy*, Spencer never got into discussions with scientists, he never reported any divergent opinions, he cited no examples of authorities whose perceptions did not square with his own. Science was there only to provide examples that confirmed his own views.

Hartmann, in contrast, incessantly feuded with large parts of the established scientific community. He got into discussions with nearly all the leading representatives of Darwinism. He freely and openly picked and chose among every type of theory and hypothesis.

For Spencer, scientific development was a clear, unambiguous and one-sided process. The specialised sciences added bit by bit to the great scientific explanation of the world. Fully fledged science was indeed a long way away and could never be completely achieved. But developments were always moving towards that great goal. The Spencerian laws of development were being confirmed piece by piece. The merit Spencer ascribed to himself was that he had mapped out where the sciences were going and thus the tendencies in the sciences that were progressive.[97]

Hartmann, in contrast, regarded scientific development as an extremely complex and complicated process that was closely connected with (speculative) philosophical development. Science, like philosophy, progressed in a spiral: in one era Kantian perspectives predominated, followed necessarily by Fichtean, Schellingian and Hegelian. Hartmann regarded neo-Kantianism with

---

97   Spencer, *First Principles*, Spencer 1862, Vol. I, p. 487 et seqq.

its view of the sciences as a harbinger of neo-Fichteanism, a neo-Schellingia-nism and so forth. The same questions continually recurred, only on a higher plane, and the questions gave rise to other questions that had been asked earlier and were now being asked under different and better conditions.[98]

Hartmann's viewpoint of course assumes a relatively independent sphere for philosophical speculation, or metaphysics as he called it. It may therefore seem paradoxical at first that in fact he was far more receptive than Spencer to new impulses from the individual sciences. Once Spencer had laid out his main lines, he would only be influenced marginally by what was happening. Nor did he budge an inch when new philosophical and scientific currents made them-selves felt in the United Kingdom in the 1870s, threatening to make essential parts of Spencerian edifice of thought obsolete.[99] Throughout his literary life, however – which stretched over four decades – Hartmann was extraordinarily receptive to new currents, especially in the specialised sciences.

In a general – if also rather superficial – sense, Hartmann was thus less dog-matic and more flexible than Spencer. In another just as general and just as superficial sense, Spencer was more consistent and principled than Hartmann.

The crucial difference, however, lay in their disparate relations to scientific development. For Spencer, this development – no matter how much of an empiricist he may have been – hardly offered any surprises. He followed it to the extent it could provide additional details that could be incorporated into his synthetic philosophy. For Hartmann, on the other hand, it was an extremely dramatic development full of contradictions and constantly new tendencies. Even if he could assert that he had largely remained faithful to his earlier under-standing in *Philosophy of the Unconscious*,[100] it was obvious that he allowed himself to be influenced by new currents.

While the relation between philosophy and specialised science was unprob-lematic for Spencer,[101] it was distressing for Hartmann. Clearly without noticing it, he vacillated among a range of different conceptions, each of which reflec-ted predominant tendencies in the contemporary scientific and philosophical debate. It is of interest to examine more closely these conceptions, which more clearly than most in the genre illuminate the dilemma of the system-builder.

The common starting point for all of Hartmann's various approaches to the question is the thesis that all knowledge was to be brought into total unity in

---

98   Cf. in particular Hartmann 1910, p. 22 et seqq.
99   On this topic, cf. Peel 1971, p. 224 et seqq.
100   See, for example, 'Vorwort' to Hartmann 1907, p. iii.
101   Cf. above, p. 267 et seqq.

philosophy. The changes and vacillations were greatest in his earlier works but never disappeared completely.

One of these conceptions can be summarised in the phrase 'inductive metaphysics'.[102] Hartmann outlined it above all in *On the Dialectical Method* and *Naturforschung und Philosophie* (*Natural History and Philosophy*).[103] It recurred in *Philosophy of the Unconscious*, though in less tangible form. It comprised a daring, if also highly incomplete, attempt to unite speculation and empiricism. Philosophy should be empirical, which according to Hartmann was the same as following an inductive method. New knowledge could thus only be gained through inferences from the less to the more general; through deduction only the validity of the knowledge could be tested. Induction, however, is not a mechanical process through which observations are added together but a creative process – indeed, it is the fundamental process of thought.[104]

Hartmann's reasoning here greatly resembles Ernst Haeckel's on the same question.[105] According to both, there was both an empirical and a philosophical element in science all the way from pure observation to the total generalisation. But in contrast to Haeckel, Hartmann argued that there was a sphere that *for the time being* lay beyond the reach of empirical science – and that was metaphysics. Good metaphysics, however, consisted of a number of inferences from what had already been established scientifically; it also was therefore inductive in its method.[106] From this the conclusion can thus be drawn that the boundary of metaphysics with the positive sciences was receding, provided that sciences were advancing (which Hartmann assumed). On the other hand, it remained entirely unclear where the boundary lay between those generalisations that belonged to the sphere of the sciences and those that belonged to metaphysics. Without admitting to it, Hartmann seems to have distinguished between

---

102   Hartmann took his thoughts on this topic primarily from Schopenhauer. In *Die Welt als Wille und Vorstellung*, Schopenhauer declares that metaphysics is the science of '*die Erfahrung überhaupt*' (Schopenhauer 1922, p. 201). Hartmann sets what he regards as his own and Schopenhauer's inductivist conception against Hegel's and Schelling's; cf. for example Hartmann 1876, p. 90. Among the monographs on Hartmann's epistemology, with regard to his metaphysics, Caldwell and Schmitt can be mentioned.

103   Cf. Hartmann's own information in 'Mein Entwickelungsgang', Hartmann 1876, p. 37. The essay 'Naturforschung und Philosophie' is included in Hartmann 1876.

104   Hartmann 1868, p. 111 et seq.

105   Cf. for example Haeckel 1873, p. 71 et seqq. Any direct influence between Hartmann and Haeckel is extremely unlikely. There is nothing to indicate that the either was familiar with the other's writings when they were forming their similar lines of thought. Cf. also Hartmann 1906, p. 12.

106   Hartmann 1876, p. 424 et seqq.

two types of inductions: one that led to general scientific theories and one that reached all the way into metaphysics.

The second conception of philosophy that emerged in Hartmann's writings was entirely incompatible with the first. According to it, the most comprehensive results of philosophy – its principles – were the result of a mystical impulse. The results could not be completely justified via an inductive method. Induction was the scientific method, of course, and in probability calculus – a discovery Hartmann greatly respected – it reached perfection. But the philosophy built solely on induction could not attain '*einem einheitlichen System der Wissenschaft*'[107] (a coherent system of science). This was the same Hartmann who asserted that metaphysics as the temporary arrangement of a unified science is only induction based on existing science, in which the ideas had been '*zu Ende gedacht*'[108] (thought through to the end).

We do not need to go deeper here into the question of what Hartmann meant by 'mystical'.[109] What is nevertheless obvious is that he sought to save an independent sphere for metaphysical thinking. He drew the inspiration from Romantic philosophy with its theory of the sovereign genius, but he also had support from the new, more or less speculative, psychology in which the concept of the unconscious – of such decisive importance for him – played a central role.[110] Truly brilliant thoughts were the result of unconscious impulses and not of conscious calculations.

There was, however, a third conception that gradually became dominant in Hartmann's writings. What determined it was a strict distinction between the natural and what Hartmann, like many others, called *Geisteswissenschaften*. The distinction made itself felt in Hartmann's writings from the 1870s; it is one of many examples of how he was influenced by currents in contemporary science. In his paper *Anfänge naturwissenschaftlicher Selbsterkenntnis* (Origins of Scientific Self-Knowledge), he distinguished between philosophical and historical *Geisteswissenschaften*.[111] This distinction between philosophy and history

---

107   Hartmann 1869, p. 9.

108   Hartmann 1876, p. 429 et seqq.

109   Hartmann devotes an entire chapter (B IX) of *Philosophie des Unbewussten* to the question of 'Das Unbewusste in der Mystik', where he also takes up the question of the innovative philosopher as mystic. In the copious literature on Hartmann, proper attention has scarcely been devoted to the contradiction between his metaphysics of induction and his ideas about mysticism. Cf. however Drews 1902 (the most exhaustive biography), p. 93 et seqq.; Koeber 1884, p. 108 et seqq.; Braun 1909, p. 4; Ziegler 1910, p. 21 et seqq. and Bertallanffy 1936, p. 153 et seqq.

110   The major works by Fortlage 1855 and Ulrici 1873 played a significant role here.

111   Hartmann 1876, p. 456 et seq.

played no role in his general reasoning, however. The essential thing is that the natural sciences and the *Geisteswissenschaften* each have their metaphysics.[112] Between the positive sciences and their metaphysics lie natural and moral philosophy. To unite both complexes of knowledge in a single, uniform metaphysics it must be assumed that the knowledge comprises a totality. This is only possible if the *Geisteswissenschaften* are taken as the starting point.[113]

We thus see how Hartmann, using the concept of spiritual sciences, succeeded in expression an assumption that was latent in all his system-building, namely that the definitive explanation was a descending or abstracting explanation that cast light over the less complex, less intelligently arranged, less 'spiritual' by presenting it as reflections of the more complex, more intelligently arranged, more 'spiritual'. The explanatory model can be found everywhere in his writings, above all in his vitalist reckonings with Darwinism.

But in Hartmann's third conception, the path from positive science to uniform metaphysics is an exceedingly long one. The reduction of various disciplines, philosophies and metaphysics takes place only on the highest plane. The total abstracting explanation belongs in a sphere far above ordinary assiduous scientific work.

His complicated hierarchy of specialised sciences, philosophies and metaphysics thus expressed the system-builder's dilemma in a considerably specialised scientific environment. Only by adding layer upon layer of syntheses did he overcome all the boundaries between branches and achieve his goal: a unified science and the makeshift explanation of the world.

8   Summary

The first difficulty faced by the system-builder was the difficulty in making themselves credible. Once a number of sciences had become specialised and their status as specialisations had been accepted in the scientific community, the system-builder occupied a precarious position outside the circle of authorities. They could not meet the increasingly fixed norms of the various specialisations for training, theoretical proficiency, and practical experience. They did not have the specialist's thoroughly initiated audience.

---

112 Ibid., p. 457 and Hartmann 1877, p. 30.
113 Cf. 'Allgemeine Vorbemerkungen' to Hartmann 1877, pp. 18–45, and Hartmann 1876, p. 456 et seqq. This line of thought is fully developed only in *Kategorienlehre*, Hartmann's main philosophical work.

At the same time, they had to take over the theoretical problems of the individual disciplines, summed up over the entire scientific field. The specialised scientist could simply avoid the problems of the mutual relations of theories, of explanations and reductions if they unresistingly followed a prevailing tradition. For the system-builder, these problems were entirely crucial for their systems. Only if these problems were solved would the system have structure.

These were the difficulties of the kind Engels brought on himself when he decided to attempt to create a unity of all current knowledge. Our immediate task is to study his efforts in more detail in light of the variegated world that was nineteenth-century science.

PART THREE

CHAPTER 11

Engels's Four Periods

1   Introduction

The most important task in the first part of this book was to see how Marx's and Engels's interest in general questions about the basis of and connection between various scientific theories emerged from their theoretical work. We saw that Marx's interest in the hierarchy of the sciences was much more closely related to his own theory of history and society, whereas since the late 1850s Engels was above all on the hunt for a scientifically based but Hegelian worldview.

The most surprising result of the study was certainly that it was Marx, and not Engels, who first conceived of the term 'dialectical law'. The authorship itself does not say much, however: it is now a question of examining more closely what significance this new category had for Marx and Engels. As regards Marx, in the last decade of his life he devoted himself relatively little to questions that had a direct point of contact with the theses he put forward in *Capital*. Engels, on the other hand, would be influenced even more by them and occupied himself with them. Our immediate task is to more closely follow Marx's and Engels's work on the relevant questions from 1873. After that, however, is a larger and more difficult task, namely to rationally reconstruct the content of these assiduous efforts – that is, to present their fundamental (often contradictory) elements and thereby to draw conclusions from the incomplete, often fragmentary work that Marx, and above all Engels, left behind. Naturally, this reconstruction cannot stop in 1873 – which was when Engels had the idea of developing his own scientific worldview – but has to cover the entire period from the end of the 1850s (and indirectly their early writings from the 1840s).

In the second part just completed, I sought to sketch the outlines of the complex and dramatic world of science that both Marx and Engels belonged to in their own way. It was an attempt at a double exposure. On the one hand, the various scientific lines of development were put in relation to the uneven and in no way one-sided trend towards increased specialisation and professionalisation. On the other, I sought to demonstrate how a range of similar problems were painfully relevant in various scientific theories ranging from physics to the human sciences. One important result was that there was a tension that often developed into open opposition between specialisation and general theoretical problems. In many cases, the work of the system-builders appeared to be attempts to go beyond the strictly specialised sciences to thus get at the problems they had in common. On the other hand, it was a risky path. Those who did not recognise specialisations risked not only the disfavour of the specialists but also – even worse – producing accounts of less scientific value.

It is crucial for the study of the early history of Marxism to realise that even Marxist theory had to grapple with theoretical difficulties and problems as its neighbouring and related theories in the then-current world of the sciences. To become a valid theory, it had to be put in relation to all the difficult questions that played such a crucial role in contemporary scientific debates: the questions of determinism, development, tendencies and so on. We will soon see how these questions would determine important parts of Engels's work on a scientific worldview. All his sporadic but constantly recurring statements on 'chance and necessity', on the constantly changing categories of thought and reality, in the 'last instance', on facts and theories and laws are at once characteristic and original contributions to the then-abundant discussion.

On the other hand, Engels's path towards a general dialectic was lined with accidental occurrences, among which the biggest and most important was that for an external reason – Marx's death – he never got the opportunity to complete his far-reaching plans.

2   The Four Periods

Back in the introduction[1] we acquainted ourselves with the letter of 30 May 1873 in which Engels first announced his ideas on a dialectic of the natural sciences. With that letter, a new phase in Engels's relevant studies could be said to have its beginning.

It is very important to distinguish between the different phases in Engels's work. Only when we have a clear idea that he did not always have the same ambitions or the same ideas can we understand what he was accomplishing.

The *first phase* lasted from the end of the 1850s to 1873. During this phase, there was nothing to indicate he intended to develop his own dialectical philosophy. He read the natural scientific and philosophical literature he came across. He commented on them in his letters. He made no significant excerpts.[2]

---

1   Above, p. 13 *et seq.*
2   He made notes on J. Beete Jukes's *The Student's Manual of Geology* in 1869 or 1870 (*IISG Marx-Engels Nachlass*), for Rudolf Clausius's *Über den 2. Hauptsatz der mechanischen Wärmetheorie* (*IML-ZPA* 1:1:4042) in 1870 or possibly as early as 1867, and he began a number of excerpts

He displayed a general interest in the relation between the new theories and Hegel's philosophy.

The *second phase* properly began with the previously mentioned letter from May 1873. By all appearances, however, Engels had had plans for another less comprehensive work concerning Ludwig Büchner's materialistic philosophy earlier that same year. A few pages under the title *Büchner*, which are included in the folders that comprise *Dialectics of Nature*, seem to have been written earlier that spring.[3] It appears possible, at least, that Engels had informed William Liebknecht somewhat about a planned polemic.[4] What he says about Büchner in the notes are at least of double interest, both in light of the statements about Büchner that first Marx and later he himself made,[5] and because in them he so unambiguously trained his guns on mechanical materialism. We will return to this.

What makes the letter to Marx so significant is that Engels for the first time claimed an original view of the dialectic in the natural sciences. It was thus his own conception, and not Hegel's or Marx's, that he sought to develop.

The crucial difference between Engels's working method before and after the letter, however, lies in his very intention to develop a dialectic of the natural sciences. It was then than he began systematising his studies; it was then that he attempted to sum up his ideas and impulses. There was, on the other hand, nothing to indicate that entirely new lines of thought had seized him. His primary perspective remained the same as it was before 1873; the crucial issue was still the extent to which essential parts of Hegel's natural philosophy was confirmed by the new natural sciences.

No decisive change and no definitive expansion of perspective took place before 1876, when Engels unwillingly took on the task of writing a polemic against Eugen Dühring. It was then that the *third phase* began.

How can we establish this with any certainty, however? It does not seem possible from reading the manuscripts, fragments and short paragraphs that together constitute what is now called *Dialectics of Nature* in the order they have been given in modern editions. The pattern emerges only if they are studied in chronological order.[6]

---

regarding the works of Helmholtz, Thomson and Tait and others in 1870 without completing them, however, before 1880 (*IISG* J 41; *IML-ZPA* 1:1:3930).

3   MEW 25:689.

4   MECW 25:673, note 223.

5   Below, p. 336.

6   62 of the 181 articles and paragraphs in *Dialectics of Nature* cannot be reliably dated, but most of these 62 were probably made after 1878. MECW 25:689.

The majority of the 92 sections of *Dialectics of Nature*, which were without doubt written before May 1876 – when Engels began writing *Anti-Dühring* – consists of short paragraphs. They provide us with a good idea of the orientation of his studies. Hegel was a constant presence in them. At the start of the period, Engels was occupied in particular with Hegel's *Encyclopedia*.[7] He had also brought to the fore Grove's *Correlation of Physical Forces*,[8] one of the books that had wakened his interest in the questions that now dominated his work. One name that constantly recurred in these early fragments is Ernst Haeckel.[9]

During this second phase, there were two partially bound up lines of thought that completely predominated. The one, and more general – continuously related to Hegel – was that there are no fixed categories; what the new natural sciences had shown was that phenomena previously regarded as incompatible and clearly separate flowed into and mixed with one another. In the manuscript on Ludwig Büchner, which most likely was the earliest of them all, Engels distinguished between a metaphysical[10] and a dialectical orientation, which was of crucial significance for his entire way of thinking. The former involved the use of absolute pairs of opposites that excluded each other, the latter that 'these fixed opposites of basis and consequence, cause and effect, identity and difference, appearance and essence' were considered untenable; the antitheses merged into each other.[11] The dialectic, however, did not only abolish the concepts with which thought worked; it also showed us that what appeared invariable in objective reality transitioned into something else, and developed into something new. A note from 1875 states that there were no 'hard and fast lines'. Engels took the most significant example from evolutionary biology with its theory on the variability of species.[12] From the very beginning, Engels thus assumed a parallelism between thought and objective reality. It was ultimately the disappearing and changing nature of reality

7   See for example several notes in MECW 25:494 et seq. and 520 et seq., all of which are from 1874. Hegel's *Science of Logic* figures in another note from 1874; ibid. p. 521. The fact that at this time, Engels was engaged in intensive study of Hegel is shown in a letter to Marx dated 21 September 1874 in which he declared: 'I am deeply immersed in the doctrine of essence'. MECW 45:50.

8   See for example MECW 25:525 and 527. On Grove's significance for Engels, cf. above, p. 108.

9   See for example MECW 25:487, 488 et seq. and 530. Clausius appears 1874–75, 562 et seqq.; the problems of mathematics in particular in 1875, 25:536 et seq., 541, 542 and so on.

10   He took the word from Hegel – who uses it, however, in several meanings: Engels's 'metaphysics' most closely corresponds to Hegel's *Verstandes-Metaphysik*; cf. Hegel 9:255 et seqq. and above, p. 91.

11   MECW 25:482 et seq.

12   MECW 20:493.

that made it necessary for thought to work with opposing concepts that none-theless did not exclude each other.[13]

Reality, however, can be the object of real knowledge, and the categories of thought can be adapted to it. The natural order is changeable, but the order exists. It is here that the second, more particular line of thought in Engels's early notes comes in. This is the theme that he primarily dwelled on in the letter to Marx about the new ideas he had had.[14] Everything that exists is matter in motion, but there are different forms of motion. The new natural sciences can show how the different forms of motion pass into one another. Mechanical motion, heat, electricity and so on are thus not thoroughly separate entities; they represent different qualities, it is true, but the transition from one quality to another can be determined quantitatively.[15]

When Engels first presented his ideas, he stopped at the transition from inorganic to organic nature.[16] For the time being, it was the principle of conservation of energy as laid out by Grove that primarily comprised the foundation in the natural sciences for his reasoning. But his perspective can be broadened without difficulty to cover the entire hierarchy of the natural sciences. In his early paragraphs, he would soon also take a number of examples from biology.[17]

On the other hand, human history turns up surprisingly late in this context. It was not until a paragraph from 1876[18] that the subject of humanity came up. It was precisely in this paragraph that Engels for the first time sketched out in earnest the main idea in his *non-reductive materialism*.[19] The universe comprises a totality in that it consists of matter in motion. This does not, however, concern the *same* motion but a number of different forms of motion from mechanical to motion that is expressed in human history. The transition from one form of motion to another can in principle be defined and calculated, but each of these forms develop unique 'phenomenal forms'.[20]

---

13   Cf. for example the important section 'Abstract identity'; MECW 25:495 et seq. (Written 1874).

14   The central statements of the letter are also included in *Dialectics of Nature*; MECW 25:527 et seq.

15   Engels does not use the words 'quantity' and 'quality' here, but it is entirely certain what he otherwise usually refers to with these terms.

16   MECW 44:503: 'Organism – for the present I shall not indulge in any dialectical speculations on the subject'. Schorlemmer comments in the margin: 'Nor shall I'.

17   As evidenced by his frequent references to Haeckel; cf. above, Note 9.

18   Though *before* Engels set about the polemic against Dühring.

19   The term was previously used for Engels's understanding by authors including Alfred Schmidt; cf. A Schmidt 1971a, p. 49.

20   MECW 25:517 et seq.

Like the main elements in non-reductive materialism, the thesis of the fluid character of all categories remained a cornerstone of Engels's world of ideas. But what was it that came into being during the third phase of his development?

In short: it was the theory of dialectical laws and what they entailed, both directly and indirectly.

There is no trace of these laws before *Anti-Dühring*. When Engels attempted to draw up his view of the dialectic, he still had no idea that he would do so with the help of any general laws.[21] He could speak of 'both of the main oppositions' (*die beiden Hauptgegensätze*) and mention 'identity and difference'[22] and then add (without changing the word 'both') 'cause and effect'.[23] Thus it was not only a concept of law that was absent, but also categories in the three dialectical laws that are being discussed here.[24]

The first time Engels spoke about dialectical laws was in *Anti-Dühring* – to be precise, in the context where he *defended Marx's statements in* Capital *on the law of quantity and quality against Dühring's criticism*.[25] The circumstance that it was Marx, and not Engels, who introduced the concept of dialectical law can scarcely be more clearly demonstrated than here. But as if to further emphasise this, Engels – who otherwise was scrupulous in stressing his own originality in the field[26] – explained that Marx was the first to realise that the laws were in conformity with the new science.[27]

Engels went a step further in *Anti-Dühring* than Marx did in *Capital*, however. Marx had spoken about the negation of the negation but without singling it out as a dialectical law.[28] Eugen Dühring had also gone on the attack against this concession to Hegelian vocabulary. In his lengthy defence of Marx, Engels also raised the negation of the negation to the rank of dialectical law.[29]

---

21 See for example, 'Dialectics, so-called *objective* dialectics ...' written in 1875; MECW 25:492 et seq.

22 The fact that here, as he did in the 'Introduction' (written in 1876), he placed such great importance on the pair of opposites, chance and necessity, makes it likely that the crucial section on 'Chance and Necessity' (MECW 25:498 et seq.) – which cannot otherwise be dated – was written in the period *before Anti-Dühring*.

23 MECW 25:497 (written in 1875).

24 Naturally, Engels had already been speaking about quantity and quality, but without their forming a law. Even the negation of the negation shows up in one spot (MECW 25:472, note from 1875).

25 MECW 25:111 et seq.; the passage itself is on p. 117.

26 This unease appears even in the 1873 letter to Marx; MECW 25:504. Cf. further below, p. 52et seq.

27 MECW 25:118.

28 MECW 35:750.

29 MECW 25:130.

The road thus lay open for a whole number of dialectical laws. But it was not a road without difficulties. When in 1878 Engels resumed the work on *Dialectics of Nature*, he first worked out a plan for the entire work. The introduction he had written before setting to work on *Anti-Dühring* remained. After that introduction, however, a whole new section was added – a section on the universal validity of the dialectical laws. These laws had suddenly become *four* in number. The law of quantity and quality was the first, followed by a law of the unity of opposites. This second law had been under discussion in *Anti-Dühring* as well, but it had not been singled out as a dialectical law there. It had figured in connection with both of the laws Engels spoke about there – the negation of the negation, and quantity and quality – but had, if anything, taken a position as a dialectical principle superior to all else.[30] Now, it had thus obtained a co-lateral position. The law of the negation of the negation was the third law, but there was also a fourth: the '*Spirale Form der Entwicklung*'[31] (spiral form of development).

The following year, 1879, when Engels was developing the ideas from this outline in more detail, he spoke only of three laws. The law of spiral development had disappeared without comment, and with that we have arrived at the enumeration of dialectical laws that became – and has remained – the standard for large parts of Marxism ever since *Dialectics of Nature* was published in 1925. Here, Engels attempted to show that the three laws were firmly anchored in Hegel's philosophy, or more precisely in the various parts of *Science of Logic*.[32] Engels took no more note of the fact that the very idea of a dialectical *law* was foreign to Hegel than the early Marx did.

Here, before we subject the question to a more analytical treatment, we can confirm that the connection among Engels's three laws is rather curious. The second – the law of the unity of opposites – is reasonably more comprehensive than the others; it expresses everything that Engels had always regarded as the main principle of dialectics. The relation between quantity

---

30   MECW 25:111 et seq.

31   MECW 25:313. It is possible that Engels, on thinking it over, was arguing that the law of the negation of the negation covered the law of spiral development (i.e. the idea that similar configurations recur at continually higher, more complex levels).

32   MECW 25:356. According to Engels, the first law was developed in the first book of Hegel's *Science of Logic* ('The Doctrine of Being'), the second in the second book ('The Doctrine of Essence') and the third in the third book ('The Doctrine of the Concept'). Apart from the fact that Hegel did not speak about any laws, the statement has a certain amount of legitimacy as regards both of the first two laws but not as regards the third. Nor is the relation between the three laws comparable with the relation between being, essence and concept in Hegel.

and quality constitutes a special case of the unity of opposites: it says that a pair of opposites, quantity and quality, stand in a reciprocal relation to each other. As regards the negation of the negation, Engels did not develop what he meant by that in this unfinished text. It became fully clear, however, from the examples he provided earlier in *Anti-Dühring* that it was not applicable to all processes; its primary fields seemed to have been certain parts of biology and history.[33]

To understand the grounds for this – though temporary – division in Engels, we must later also consider the concept of *laws of thought*.[34] The laws of dialectics must also apply to thought, and the three laws correspond (though somewhat incompletely) to the three laws of thought that were usually employed in traditional logic.[35]

Engels, however, never completed the section on the laws of dialectics. He completed other chapters between 1880 and 1883, and after Marx's death he largely abandoned his great project. Instead, his main task was to edit and publish *Capital*. In another work, *The Origins of Family, Private Property and the State*, which he finished in 1884, he kept closely to what Marx had been working on in the last years of his life. As he himself mentioned,[36] he started from Marx's notes on the research of American ethnologist Lewis H. Morgan.[37] Marx and Engels thus took a position on the tradition of research that we have called the new anthropology, the primary goal of which was to link biological and human history.

But Engels would also return, if temporarily, to the more far-reaching philosophical questions. This occurred above all in *Ludwig Feuerbach and the End of Classical German Philosophy*. He wrote this little document in 1886, and it was published that same year in the German Social Democrats' new theoretical journal *Die Neue Zeit*. Two years later, it came out in book form. Its primary task, Engels said in the foreword, was to provide a comprehensive account of

---

33   In addition, he also provides examples from mathematics; MECW 37:116 et seq. Explaining (to take Engels's example of quantity and quality) a series of chemical compounds using the law of the negation of the negation seems impossible; in this case, would the third compound in the series (e.g. the methane series) comprise the negation of the negation of the first? The claim that the dialectical laws are universally valid thus seems unsustainable from the start.

34   Engels otherwise uses the phrase 'laws of thought'; MECW 25:356.

35   Cf. below, p. 377.

36   MECW 26:131.

37   Marx's excerpts from Morgan, Phear et al. have been published with an introduction by Lawrence Krader: *The Ethnological Notebooks of Karl Marx* (Marx 1972). On these and Engels's treatment of them, see below, p. 142 et seq.

the relation between Marx's and Engels's view, and Hegel's philosophy.[38] Engels criticised Hegel for building a system. Hegel's method, as Engels understood it, in fact excluded all systems: it taught that everything that took fixed form must soon be broken down again. The system became a concession to the demands of the times. The method that Hegel developed was revolutionary, but the system was conservative.[39]

It can be regarded as an irony of history that the criticism of Hegel the system-builder Engels levelled here was repeated by many who also argued that Engels had committed Hegel's mistake and only replaced Hegel's idealistic system with a materialist one.[40]

In general, it could be said that by experimenting with a set of dialectical laws, Engels approached a system in the classical sense, in which all knowledge and all reality is subsumed under a number of general statements. On the other hand, it was only for a brief period and in a number of rather limited places in his texts that he brought up the dialectical laws for discussion at all. The concept of dialectical law has nearly as temporary and transitory a significance in his authorship as it does in Marx's. It is an extraordinarily interesting circumstance that in *Feuerbach*, Engels on the whole did not speak about any dialectical laws. This does not give us the right to conclude that he would consciously have abandoned his earlier positions on the question. What we can say with certainty is that the idea itself was not at all as central as it had been in the late 1870s. We can also say that the entire kind of criticism he levelled at Hegel is difficult to immediately reconcile with the thesis that the dialectical laws are found in Hegel's idealist philosophy (that is, his idealist system) and that it was only a matter of giving them their materialist content (which could very easily be interpreted as a challenge to construct a materialist system).

It should be added that the question of the system was and remained problematic for Engels. In *Anti-Dühring* he had already let the system-builders, with Dühring at their head, have it with both barrels.[41] As we have seen, most of the system-builders at the end of the nineteenth century were afraid of mixing with other system-builders; in that sense, Engels was typical. Through his irreductionism, on the other hand – an irreductionism that was, most significantly, the consequence of the thesis that all categories are fluid and changeable – Engels found himself in a problematic relation to the systems.[42] One can reas-

---

38   MECW 26:519.
39   Ibid., p. 357 et seq.
40   So, for example, Adorno and Lichtheim (see above, p. 46 and 87).
41   MECW 25:6 et seq.
42   Cf. below, p. 373.

onably speak of several different and irreconcilable tendencies in Engels. He did not have a coherent picture of what his work with different sciences and their theoretical assumptions should result in.

If we are to be precise, we can distinguish a *fourth phase* in Engels's work, one that began with Marx's death. It was, however, not a particularly uniform phase: in addition to *Capital*, Engels worked on various matters such as *Origins* and *Ludwig Feuerbach*, and additionally there were the comments in his letters on the core of historical materialism. What constituted this phase, if anything, was that Engels had now abandoned, or was compelled to abandon, his ambition of creating a great general work on the dialectic.

We can therefore speak of four phases:

1. The period from ca. 1858 to 1873, when Engels harboured a general interest in the question of the relation between new theories in the natural sciences (particularly the principle of conservation of energy and Darwinism) and Hegel's philosophy.
2. The period from 1873 to 1876, during which he prepared a major work whose supporting elements would be the ideas he had on the fluid nature of all categories.
3. The period from 1876 to 1883, when through *Anti-Dühring* he was compelled to take a position in earnest on the question of the place of Marxist social theory in the scientific hierarchy, and when he took over and developed Marx's concept of dialectical law without abandoning his fundamental ideas.
4. The period after 1883, when he was compelled to abandon his major project but in a few minor works sought to investigate his and Marx's relations to Hegel's philosophy, the new anthropology, and so on.

3   Unity

It is important to keep these individual periods in mind, since through them the changing and partially mutually contradictory tendencies in his work will be easier to understand. But this division into periods should only be understood as a temporary aid. They must not obscure the circumstance that the whole time, Engels was dealing *on the whole* with the same problems and that he did so *on the whole* from similar starting points. Hegel's philosophy, and thus the dialectic, the new natural sciences and thus what he understood as scientifically supported materialism was always at the centre of his attention. Even if he came relatively late – or in *Anti-Dühring*, directly – to the question of the link between the natural sciences and Marx's and his social theory, it was naturally a constant presence in his world of ideas. It can be completely ruled out that he would have begun developing his general philosophy without any thought as to its significance for the theory that was the main point in Marx's theoretical work and was equally intended to play a leading role in the socialist movement that was beginning to take form.

It is also given that Engels had an idea the whole time of the *ideological significance* of his enterprise (that is, its significance for the development of the workers' movement and socialism). It is, however, a problem that we will return to in the concluding ideological analysis.

Other questions that just as thoroughly left their mark on Engels's enterprise, on the other hand, will be dealt with in this third part. They are questions we became acquainted with in the analysis of the general scientific situation in the nineteenth century. We saw there that scientific specialisation created a new *problem of authority*, widely different from what had been of immediate interest when the Bible, Aristotle or some other great figure was regarded as the norm of the sciences. Once a science became specialised and its position as a specialisation was accepted, it meant that only whose who qualified as a specialist in the science in question could comment in its domains in their own name and on their own authority. For those on the outside, it was a question of citing the specialists' assertions. If the specialists disagreed with one another, the outsider would have to choose. If they wanted to create a unity from several different specialisations that were not united by some shared, generally accepted theory, they have to find the point of unity themselves. But the question then became on which authority they would do so (i.e. which particular insights they could point to).

Naturally, these were difficulties that would get in Engels's way just as much as they did for Spencer, Comte or Hartmann. We will see how he – often indirectly, through his method of argument – selected his own authoritative fields. Terms such as 'theory' and 'philosophy' thus played a considerable role: general conceptions that were raised over the specialisations and also elucidated the connection between various disciplines. But the boundary between specialisation and interpreting a specialisation was always fluid, and difficult to draw: where did the specialist – whether Helmholtz, Tyndall or Darwin – cease to be a specialist? Where did their word cease to be authoritative?

Engels could rightly claim to be a specialist in important parts of the human sciences. Behind him, he had Marx's even greater authority in the same field. But how did that influence Engels's arguments once he entered into these domains? We will also find that he claimed other specialisations for himself; he was not only a 'specialist of the general' in Comte's meaning but also spoke on his own authority, for example, about Hegel's philosophy. This influences his method of presentation.

One difficulty in common for Marx and Engels was that they had no scientific organisation behind them; in other words, they did not have a scientific community where their words would naturally be brought up for discussion. It proved difficult to find even a serious assessment of *Capital*, which nonetheless – whatever perspective it was assessed from – is one of the nineteenth century's weightiest contributions to economics in any category.[43] Engels published *Anti-Dühring* and *Feuerbach* in *Vorwärts* and *Die Neue Zeit*, both organs of the German Social-Democratic Party. We do not know what form he imagined for the publication of a completed *Dialectics of Nature*. In any case, he stood outside the forms of publication that could be said to have been accepted by the leading sciences. Building an alternative organ that was also open to serious theoretical discussion was important to him and his comrades in the party and in the struggle. It is in contexts like this that Engels's claims to a particular *scientific socialism* that he raised in *Anti-Dühring* and later should be judged. These claims have deep roots in his and Marx's world of ideas, from the early reckonings with what they called utopian socialism. The main thrust, however, was not against other types of socialism but against competing conceptions of science and scholarship.[44]

But the general features of Engels's bold enterprise do not apply only to its external circumstances. They also apply in the greatest degree to the complex of theoretical problems itself. What Engels was attempting to do was closely connected with the difficult questions that were raised in field after field of the sciences in the nineteenth century. What was truly interesting about his incomplete work only emerges if it is placed in relation to the entire dominant world of problems in which the principle of conservation of energy, Darwinism and various humanist orientations were developing. We have already become acquainted with this world, in which the main issue was not the relation between the sciences pure and simple but the relation between the treatment of causality (and thus determinism, finality and so on) and of development by the various sciences. The key issue became the question of the scientific treatment of *systems in development*, whether it was the solar system, living beings or human societies. It was a question that Marx faced in the *Grundrisse*, and there for Marx – as for many others – it had also developed into a question

---

43   Cf. above, p. 89 et seqq.
44   Below, p. 434.

of the relation between a scientific theory and the reality it dealt with. This question, in turn, was the most important *theoretical* reason that Marx renewed his study of Hegel and sought inspiration in Hegel's determination of 'totality', 'moment' and so on for a solution that made his own theory scientifically possible.

We will find that Engels's initially tentative effort has its clear connections with precisely this world of problems, but also that the connection constantly threatened to become clouded by temporary impulses first from one direction, then from another.

4   The Various Sources of Inspiration

The most elementary question that can be asked in the face of Engels's work concerns his contacts with the multifaceted scientific world of his time. In the chapters immediately following we will account for his *literary* and *direct sources of inspiration*. The former are the various kinds of publications he read; it is thus a question of also tracing the manner in which he chose his literature and how he processed it and transformed it for his own purposes. The direct sources of inspiration are the people with whom he exchanged ideas, either verbally or by letter. Marx is in a class by himself here; he unceasingly influenced Engels. Also of particular interest, however, is Carl Schorlemmer, the chemist and communist who was Engels's close friend. We must ask the question of the manner in which he could have influenced Engels. Engels also came in contact with a number of other great personages whose significance for his world of ideas we will need to investigate.

After that, however, it is a question of providing a more systematic account of Engels's thoughts. First, the study will deal with his view of the relation between philosophy and theory on the one hand, and specialised science and empiricism on the other. The result will be an attempt to clarify both his and Marx's epistemology and phenomenology. With that, it will also become an attempt to show what the dialectic is, or more precisely what could reasonably be called dialectic in their understanding of knowledge and science.

Only after that will there follow a reconstruction of Engels's view of various sciences and thus of his ontology, or interpretation of reality. The final chapters will deal with ideologies and their significance for science and the understanding of science. Only from that perspective will Engels's syntheses of the knowledge of his time be fully comprehensible.

CHAPTER 12

The Literary Sources

1 The Material

First of all, it is a question of seeing how Engels obtained knowledge of and insights into the various disciplines that he intended to join in his philosophical work. It is obvious that this work here must have taken a more definite direction after having decided in 1873 to work out a particular general theory or philosophy. What he read in the relevant subjects had to be brought together in his overall plan; and he must reasonably have had an ambition to look for the literature that would provide him with the best information about the prevailing situation in various sciences.

We must therefore attempt to reconstruct this working process. Any such reconstruction, however, must necessarily be makeshift and incomplete. The material we have to work with is Engels's written comments of various types: excerpts, letters, paragraphs and more comprehensive presentations. We cannot determine exactly how representative these written documents are of his real work. His note may be more or less random; crucial impulses may have left no traces while careful notes turned out not to lead to any results of value for his work. Of course, we also have only highly indirect knowledge of what he himself said and what he was verbally informed of.

After these necessary reservations, however, we can nonetheless establish that the various types of notes he left behind provide certain definite accounts of how he searched for, selected and processed his literary sources of inspiration.

As regards these various types of notes, the pure *excerpts* do not nearly cover the scope of Engels's readings. In general, Engels did not make excerpts at all as assiduously as Marx; even in physics, chemistry and biology, for example, Marx left behind more – and more elaborate – excerpts than Engels.[1] There is nothing to indicate that Engels would have thrown out old notes when their contents were merged into more complete presentations. The excerpts that form the foundation of one of the fully elaborated sections in *Dialectics of Nature*, the chapter on electricity, are preserved in this manner.[2] There is every reason to

---

1 Marx left approximately thirty excerpts behind, a number of which concern the practical application of the discipline in question.

2 IISG *Marx-Engels Nachlass*, J 32 and IML-ZPA 1:1:4299 (excerpts of Wiedemann's *Die Lehre von Galvanismus*).

© KONINKLIJKE BRILL NV, LEIDEN, 2023 | DOI:10.1163/9789004528796_015

assume that Engels more rarely began working up a book or a paper with carefully reported presentations of them. More often, he seems to have selected striking quotes or texts for briefer comments and paragraphs of the type that appear so frequently in *Dialectics of Nature*. Similar paragraphs with brief references were, as we have seen, very common during the second phase (1873–1876) of his development, when his work was in a more preparatory stage. This way of immediately selecting the essential and significant without first forming a picture of a presentation in its entirety may indicate an excellent relation with the texts. Engels moved more lightly in the literature than Marx did.

The elaborated excerpts are therefore few in number, and cover only an insignificant portion of Engels's reading. Calculating generously, it could be said that ten excerpts from nine different works are involved. But this figure includes a few short extracts from Hegel's *Logic* that cover only a single page.[3] This page says very little about Engels's relation to Hegel's writings, which were a constant presence in his notes.

A few other excerpts are of limited, if any, significance for *Anti-Dühring* or *Dialectics of Nature*. Back in 1869 or 1870, Engels had extracted a few items from an elementary textbook on geology[4] that left no noticeable traces in his later writings. The paragraphs from Carl Fraas's *Klima und Pflanzenwelt in der Zeit*[5] were somewhat more significant. It is relevant here that Marx had previously taken excerpts from the same work[6] and that he had brought Engels's attention to this in his letters. It was above all Fraas's theses of how humanity had historically influenced and changed their external environment that awakened Marx's, and later Engels's, interest.[7] Engels also made some use of Fraas in *Dialectics of Nature*.[8]

Inspiration from Marx can probably also be taken into account behind Engels's notes on d'Alembert's *Traité de dynamique* from 1743.[9] These excerpts are, however, typical as regards the orientation on the subject: it was in the fields where Engels felt the most uncertain – various parts of mechanics and physics – that he sought to confirm his reading in excerpts. This is not to say

---

3 *IISG Marx-Engels Nachlass*, J 54.
4 By J.B. Jukes; *IISG Marx-Engels Nachlass*, J 16, p. 10 et seq.
5 Ibid., J 42, p. 17 et seq.
6 Ibid., B 112, p. 48 et seqq.
7 See in particular the letter from Marx to Engels, 25 March 1868; MECW 42:557 et seq.
8 MECW 25:460. Engels does not mention Fraas by name here.
9 Marx analysed d'Alembert in his mathematical manuscript: cf. Marx 1974, p. 146 et seq. Engels's excerpts, *IISG Marx-Engels Nachlass*, J 42, p. 20 et seq.

that this was any sort of general behaviour in him; as far as we know, he did not take excerpts from Rudolf Clausius's writings, which nonetheless played an important role in *Dialectics of Nature*.[10] Nonetheless, it is a question of a palpable tendency. He thus read a few works by Helmholtz – both *On the Conservation of Force*[11] and *Popular Lectures on Scientific* Subjects (second series)[12] with pen in hand. Both later played an important role in his work. In 1873, he took excerpts from Ernst Mach's later celebrated *History and Root of the Principle of the Conservation of Energy*.[13] He did not mention the work later, but it can be assumed to have been of some significance for him.[14] Moreover, he excerpted William Thompson's (Lord Kelvin's) and Peter Guthrie Tait's *Treatise on Natural Philosophy* (Vol. 1).[15] It was often quoted in *Dialectics of Nature*, usually as an example of un-philosophical natural science.[16]

A unique position among the excerpts is held by those he took from Gustave Wiedemann's *Lehre von Galvanismus und Elektromagnetismus* (Vols. 1–2, 2nd ed.).[17] They were done in two batches, and are extremely detailed. Engels thus wanted to leave nothing to chance or to let anything be forgotten here. He also acknowledged in a note to the chapter on electricity in *Dialectics of Nature* that the presentation as regards 'the real' (*das Tatsächliche*) was built on Wiedemann's major work.[18]

The few excerpts Engels left behind mutually differ as regards scope and orientation. Being able to speak in general about 'excerpts' in these ten cases depends on the fact that without exception they concern references and extracts from publications and not treatments of some kind. At the very most, Engels allowed himself an extra exclamation point or two. He reproduced long citations and was careful to indicate chapter headings and page references. If the excerpted works were in English or French, Engels switched between these languages and his native German in the excerpts.

---

10   MECW 25:390.
11   *IISG Marx-Engels Nachlass*, J 42, p. 18 et seq.
12   *IML-ZPA* 1:1:6488.
13   Ibid., 1:1:3521.
14   Cf. below, p. 413 et seq.
15   *IISG Marx-Engels Nachlass*, J 42, p. 2 et seq.
16   For example MECW 25:382 et seq., 392 et seq.
17   Cf. above, Note 2.
18   MECW 25:402.

2   Engels's Authorities

Several of the excerpts – all few in number – that Engels made can thus be regarded as safety measures on his part. He wanted to learn, he wanted to be sure of his subject; he therefore extracted carefully from these publications.

The great majority of the works that he found reason to quote in *Anti-Dühring* or *Dialectics of Nature*, however, were not dealt with in similarly scrupulous notes. They turn up in quotes or only by mention of their name in his articles and fragments. It is difficult to determine how carefully he studied them.

Among the more difficult, more technically designed works on physics this actually applies only to Clausius's work; otherwise it is simpler, more popular presentations of the type such as Grove's *On the Correlation of Physical Forces* that, so to speak, flow directly into Engels's writings. Chemistry and chemical literature occupy a unique position, since Engels constantly had Carl Schorlemmer's eminent expertise at hand;[19] it is striking that in general, Engels extremely rarely referred to the literature in chemistry though examples from chemistry often played a key role in his arguments. He had a living textbook in the subject available.

On biological questions, on the other hand, he poured abundantly from the most recent literature; he made use of Haeckel's writings in particular. Here he took no excerpts; he took immediate hold of what was of interest and significance for his own context. For him, Darwinist biology was a storehouse of the newest exciting knowledge in which he could move relatively freely.

If we move over to the sphere of the human sciences, we will easily note a substantial change in attitude. Engels was on his home territory here. In the second and third sections of *Anti-Dühring*, which deal with political economy and socialism, respectively, Engels argued entirely from his own – or rather, his and Marx's own – standpoint. He did not turn to the literature in the human sciences to seek support for his standpoint. He cited it, but only to accept or reject it on his own authority. This was the simple, natural consequence of his dealing here with his own *special theory*, which he could assume he had mastered top to bottom and with its use could assess the types of statements that fell within the sphere of the theory. We will soon see what he considered himself able to assess on the subject of special theories in other fields. Whatever it may have concerned – and in fact, it concerns significant parts of the theories – it did not concern the fundamental authority of the theories. He had

---

19   Cf. p. 346

to assume that these theories – whether it was thermodynamics, molecular theory or evolutionary theory – were for the time being the best representatives of their respective scientific fields, that they provided the best empirical ('factual') information from the fields in question and that moreover they also provided the best fundamental scientific explanation of this empirical material. Similarly, he assumed that his and Marx's own theory of society was the best representative of the sphere of the human sciences. As far as it was concerned, however, he did not need to rely on anyone else's authority. This altered his method of argument. It was assessed in accordance with the yardsticks that Marxian theory provided.

There is thus an obvious consistency in Engels's manner of using scientific authorities in accordance with which field they represented. There is, however, one area of literature remaining to be mentioned that to some extent occupies a place apart. This is philosophy in the broadest sense – with the emphasis on all-encompassing, systematic philosophy. We have already seen that Engels did not ascribe any authority whatsoever[20] to the system-builders of his time – Büchner, Dühring and so on. He treated the great personages of history with far greater reverence. This was partially bound up with his thinking that philosophy, in certain respects, could anticipate scientific development. He accorded this honour to both Aristotle and Descartes.[21] Kant also received a portion, though less for the sake of his critical philosophy than his nebular theory.[22] Hegel naturally occupies a special position; Engels's interest was from the beginning linked to the issue of the extent to which Hegel had anticipated later developments in natural science. It would be incorrect, however, to state that Hegel had natural authority for him. His question concerned whether what Hegel said *was consistent* with what had later been arrived at. The test thus concerned whether Hegel was right, and what was judged as obviously correct were the new natural scientific theories – and, perhaps, rather, the general philosophical conclusions that Engels drew from these theories.

The authoritative sources were thus the new theories on the one hand, and Engels's philosophical interpretation on the other. The latter authority was first announced in the repeatedly mentioned letter to Marx in 1873, in which Engels first announced the idea that he had his own philosophy, or overall theory. It was this idea that spurred him to write a major philosophical work.

---

20   Cf above, p. 135.
21   MECW 25:325.
22   Ibid., p. 323 et seq.

3   The Selection of Literature

But how did Engels select his literature? How did he attempt to obtain an overview of the various fields he was dealing with?

For three fields – chemistry, the human sciences, and philosophy – the
answer is simple: he didn't look at all. As regards chemistry, there was his friendship with Schorlemmer. We will return to this in the next chapter. Engels did
not go into the human sciences in general in the work under discussion until he
defended Marx against Dühring; there, Marx's *Capital* was the obvious authoritative starting point not only for his defence but also for his entire investigation
of the sphere of the human sciences. He thus did not attempt to substantiate
anything with the use of other literature in the human sciences. Posterity could
naturally complain that Engels never assessed any other humanist tradition.
Marxian theory, it is true, was clearly profiled in relation to classical economics
and what it stood for. On the other hand, the relation to the historicist tradition – with which it had more than a purely genetic connection – would have
been worth investigating. The category of development, like the problematisa-
tion of the relation between individual and general, between fact and law, was
central to both. But Engels appears never to have harboured any interest in historicism, and even Marx's interest seems to have been of the more sporadic
type.[23]

Once again, as regards philosophy, Engels had an early schooling in older literature on the subject to fall back on; he could continue approximately from
where he left off in the mid-1840s. He did not doubt for a moment his ability to
orient himself in, for example, Hegel's philosophy. He sought no guidance for
his study.

As we have seen, Engels believed there was nothing to be obtained from
newer philosophy. He selected the writings he studied in depth entirely accord-

---

23   Marx mentions Mommsen, for example, in *Capital*, but it concerns Mommsen's concept
      of capital and thus something that has an immediate connection to Marx's own object
      of study; MECW 35:178, 181. Niebuhr earns a sarcastic mention in one note; ibid., p. 243.
      Sybel and Treitschke come into their field of view only through their attacks on *Cap-
      ital* and socialism, respectively; cf. letter from Engels to Adolf Hepner, 30 December 1872
      (MECW 44:462) where he praises a reckoning with Sybel by Schramm in passing (on Sybel's
      criticism of Marx, cf. above, Chapter 5, note 42), and the letter from Marx to Engels,
      1 August 1877 (MECW 45:258 et seq.), where Mehring's anonymous brochure against Treit-
      schke 1875, *Herr von Treitschke, der Sozialistentödter und die Endziele des Liberalismus* is
      described as 'most boringly and superficially written' but not entirely without interest.
      Neither Marx nor Engels showed any interest in the programme of historicism after Hegel
      and the Young Hegelians.

ing to principles other than their philosophical or scientific informational value. He thus did not familiarise himself with Spencer's works – in his three main philosophical writings, Spencer is mentioned only once, and that in passing with no reference to the literature.[24] He devoted only slightly more attention to Comte. In an outline from 1878 he promised to deal with some of Comte's view of the context of the sciences, but nothing came of it.[25] Hartmann was castigated in passing in a deleted foreword to *Anti-Dühring* (the so-called 'Old Foreword').[26] In general, we cannot determine how much Engels acquainted himself with the works of these philosophers. On the other hand, he made a penetrating study of Büchner, and of Dühring in particular. Why? It can safely be said that his conception lay closer to Spencer's and Comte's than to Dühring's, at least. The reason for his choice obviously lies on the ideological plane. Engels did not study Büchner and Dühring to take something of theoretical value but to combat the ideological conclusions that could be drawn from their systems and could directly and abruptly threaten the ideological conclusions of Marxism.

In other scientific fields, Engels was on the hunt for all the objective information he could find. For as long as he did not intend to write his own philosophical work, it was chance that determined what he came in contact with. We do not know what gave him the impulse to read, for example, Grove's little work on the physical forces. As regards Darwin's *Origin* and other central representatives of the new field of evolutionary biology, no active search was required – only a general interest – to have one's eyes opened to them. This applied, at least, to the literature in English. Marx and Engels had information on German Darwinism that was equally as available. They were informed about it primarily through Ludwig Büchner's *Sechs Vorlesungen über die Darwin'sche Theorie*. Büchner sent it to Marx, who found it rather worthless and saw its only value in that it provided information about the work of Haeckel and other German Darwinists.[27] It was only after this that Haeckel made his entry into Engels's letters and notes.

When Engels made up his mind to develop his thinking on the natural sciences, his reading took on a more definite orientation. It is not difficult to find his entryway into the relevant literature: it was the journal *Nature*, which began

---

24   'Spencer is right in as much as what thus appears to us to be the *self-evidence* of these
        axioms is *inherited*'. MECW 25:536.
25   MECW 25:313.
26   Ibid., p. 340.
27   Letter from Marx to Engels, 14 November 1868, MECW 43:158 et seq., and 18 November 1868,
        ibid., p. 161.

publication in 1869. The articles in *Nature* provided him with a large amount of ideas, and they comprised a significant portion of the literature he cited in *Dialectics of Nature*. They provided him with information about other books of interest and significance.

Nature possessed a great deal of authority for Engels. When he justified constructing the chapter on electricity on Gustav Wiedemann's great work, he quoted a statement from *Nature*.[28] He did this as late as 1882, when he had nonetheless obtained a great deal of reading on his own. The bond to *Nature* was stronger than ever.

There was above all one type of article in *Nature* that captured his attention: investigations by prominent natural scientists into the general – or philosophical, if you will – foundations of and conclusions from their sciences. The more spectacular speeches given at the annual meetings for the British Association for the Advancement of Science, for example, were printed in *Nature*. At the meeting in Belfast in 1874, John Tyndall gave the lecture that later became known as the 'Belfast Address'.[29] He spoke on 19 August, and could be read in *Nature* the following day.[30] A lecture given by T.H. Huxley at the same congress on the theory that animals were automata was run fourteen days later.[31] Both lectures roused Engels's enthusiasm: they showed that the natural scientists were on the hunt for a philosophy. No philosophy had more to teach them than Hegel's.[32]

It is true that Engels made no great use of these speeches in *Dialectics of Nature*; what Tyndall said about religion – that its affairs were not those of science, but belonged to the domain of emotions – became the subject of a brief ironic comment written in 1874.[33] Also to the point is that religious and teleological questions, which played such a great role in the English debate, interested Engels to an extraordinarily small extent. There were, however, other matters in Tyndall's address that in all likelihood strengthened Engels in his understanding of the new natural science. Tyndall's manner of linking the principle of conservation of energy and Darwinism – which we have already acquainted ourselves with[34] – quite likely attracted his positive attention. It became one of many substantiations that the specialists themselves in the natural sciences were searching for a path towards a new unitary science.

---

28   MECW 25:402, footnote.
29   Tyndall 1879, Vol. II, p. 137 et seq.
30   *Nature*, 20 August 1874, Vol. X, p. 309 et seq.
31   T.H. Huxley 1874.
32   Letter from Engels to Marx, 21 September 1874, MECW 45:48 et seq.
33   MECW 25:481.
34   Above, p. 199.

Nature thus became at once a source of knowledge and of inspiration for Engels. He could, for example, in a paragraph with the header '*Naturdialektik* – references' provide references to three articles in *Nature* on such different matters as unicellular animals, the Ice Age and spontaneous generation.[35] Here, it was a matter of sources of pure knowledge for him: the articles would form the foundation of his own conclusions on the natural dialectic. In another case, he took up an article by P.G. Tait on 'Force' to show that Tait – whose philosophical ability he otherwise distrusted – could regard potential energy as a special case of motion.[36]

It is obvious that *Nature* was the most vivid and multifarious source for Engels. His path toward larger monographs and textbooks often seems to have run through mentions and reviews in *Nature*. The names that were significant for him – Helmholtz, Thomson (Lord Kelvin), Darwin, Huxley and so on – continually recurred in the journal. Books that were reviewed were often included in Engels's readings. James Clerk Maxwell's *Theory of Heat* was the subject of an enthusiastic report,[37] and Engels was soon ready to consult it.[38] The often-lively debates that took place on the pages of *Nature* likely also gave him ideas about where the current problems and contradictions in natural science lay. It can be assumed, for example, that the controversies concerning the physical concepts of force and energy made a certain impression on Engels; much of what he would write about physics concerned related issues, though he sought refuge in the weightier textbook literature. In *Nature* there were lively and rather easily understandable articles such as Charles Brooke's 'Force and Energy. The Conservation of Energy a Fact, not a Heresy of Science'[39] and John Moore's sharp response, 'The Conservation of Energy not a Fact, but a Heresy of Science'.[40] Whatever active use Engels may have made of these articles, they had in any case strengthened him in his understanding that even the specialists were occupied with fundamental philosophical questions and that natural science as such did not automatically produce any unity.

But *Nature* was not Engels's entire frame of reference for natural science. He turned to a number of the more significant standard works in physics and biology, whether because of impulses from *Nature* or otherwise. He read, as we

---

35   MECW 25:579. One of the essays is a lecture by Tyndall on optics; Tyndall 1876.
36   MECW 25:387 et seq. Even the essay by Tait dates back to a lecture; cf. Tait 1876.
37   Stewart 1872, p. 319 et seq.
38   MECW 25:389, footnote; 390, 565.
39   Brooke 1872, p. 122 et seq.
40   J. Moore 1872, p. 180 et seq.

have seen, monographs and textbooks by Helmholtz, Thomson and Tait, Maxwell, Darwin and Haeckel. He thus oriented himself in a significant portion of the literature that could be said to have comprised the standard repertoire in the science of his time. We do not need to go into the question of how deeply he went into these works here: for the time being we can be content with stating that he sought and found inspiration in them. He also gradually experienced greater certainty. When he was busy with *Anti-Dühring*, he could inform Marx with some satisfaction:

> Natural science, in particular, is a field in which I feel very much more at home and one in which I am able to move about with a fair amount of freedom and assurance, albeit with considerable caution.[41]

Even later, in 1882, he was so sure of himself that he claimed to have formulated a 'universal natural law of motion'.[42]

It is natural that the many years of intensive study thus lulled him into a sense of security. It should however, be immediately stressed that his reading had a highly definite limit. It is therefore striking that, as far as can be seen, he never consulted any of the specialist journals in any branch of natural science, nor did he therefore keep informed of the continual discussion among specialists. He became aware of it through popular presentations and through the textbooks, but he lacked contact with the process of immediate research itself. The results of the research were transformed immediately into general philosophical questions for him.

There is nothing surprising in this: he always looked at natural science from the outside, as an inquiring and critical observer. What he was interested in was not the earthbound empirical or detailed theoretical problems but the grand conclusions. The front lines of research were continually moving in the specialist journals. The general theoretical issues displayed much greater stability. For the specialist, all literature quickly goes out of date. For those who – like Engels – were occupied with the general conclusions, the changes were nowhere near as rapid. He used Grove's *Correlation of Physical Forces*, whose third edition was published in 1855, or Helmholtz's *On the Conservation of Force* from 1847 with the same amount of satisfaction as fresh copies of the second edition of Gustav kirchhoff's *Lectures on Mathematical Physics* from 1877 or the fourth edition of Maxwell's *Theory of Heat* from 1875. He did not treat d'Alem-

---

41   Letter from Engels to Marx, 28 May 1876, MECW 45:124.
42   Letter from Engels to Marx, 23 November 1882, MECW 46:384.

bert's *Traité de dynamique* from 1743 as a historical document but as a relevant contribution to the ongoing scientific debate.[43]

This was entirely natural in the lofty expanse he was travelling in. On the other hand, natural science at the time often moved in the same expanse, beset by the great questions, eager to create great general theories and eager to bring the knowledge of natural science to a larger audience and the ideological debate. Engels felt a great deal of support for his enterprise in the literature he came in contact with.

43   MECW 25:379 et seq.

CHAPTER 13

The Direct Inspirations

1 The Contacts

Engels did not get suggestions and ideas and information only from the literature he read. Naturally, he also got it from the contacts he had and thus through the environments he was active in. But these influences are much more subtle and difficult to determine than the literary ones. We have few tangible facts to go by, and on this narrow basis we can only arrive at a number of conjectures and probabilities.

We know that a number of people were in close contact with Engels during the years he was developing his general dialectic. We also have a number of substantiations – above all in letter form – that they were familiar with and interested in Engels's enterprise. We can conclude in different ways that in various respects they influenced and inspired him.

The difficulties are bound up in part with the fact that Engels was an outsider to all scholarly organisations and institutions. He cannot be regarded as an exponent of an institutionalised tradition; his activities cannot be included in a definite pattern of conventions and personal relations of dependence; he had no mentor and no crowd of students. Those who were primarily ready to learn from him were on the other side of the sea, in Germany. His personal contacts with them were sporadic, despite everything. He never succeeded in preventing even the most intellectually skilled among them – Wilhelm Liebknecht, Karl Kautsky and Eduard Bernstein – from misconstruing and vulgarising his theses.

Engels thus carried out his work in relative isolation, or rather without organised, immediate contacts. We know that some people influenced him, but as it appears their influences were of a spontaneous type: Engels and his friends exchanged thoughts and gave each other ideas in an informal manner.

Among these people, Marx is in a class by himself. We have already seen that he likely influenced Engels in the latter's philosophical labours more than anyone so far has been prepared to assume. On many points it is in fact difficult to distinguish Engels's activities from Marx's. This means that we must again and again take into account not only what Engels, but also Marx, wrote. In this chapter I will only provide the external framework for their collaboration.

On the other hand, it will be necessary to investigate the relationship between Engels and Carl Schorlemmer in more detail. Schorlemmer's life and work must be presented. Schorlemmer was, after all, Engels's only direct contact with advanced institutionalised natural science.

There were also other people who were of more or less direct significance for Engels's philosophical activities. Lawyer, mathematician and socialist Samuel Moore is often mentioned in Marx's and Engels's letters in the same breath as Schorlemmer; together, they comprised the 'authorities' in Manchester.[1] Marxist philosopher Joseph Dietzgen could also have provided Engels with certain suggestions. By all appearances, the politically and ideologically active socialists in Germany – Wilhelm Liebknecht, August Bebel and so on – neither gave Engels any impulses nor tried to. Their influence can generally be said to have consisted of calling Engels's attention in various ways to the *ideological need* of a particularly socialist and Marxistically grounded worldview, which is why they will be dealt with in the concluding section on ideology.

Other individual representatives of international socialism, on the other hand, may have influenced Engels as regards different parts of the theoretical content in his work. This concerns primarily French socialist Paul Lafargue, physician and Marx's son-in-law, with whom he exchanged a number of ideas on biological matters.

2   The Partnership with Marx

As regards Engels's relations with Marx, it is obvious that most of them – and the most essential aspects in them – are only indirectly accessible to posterity. The significance, for example, that Marx's ideas about a dialectical law had for Engels's work after 1876 can only be determined by confirming the shift in Engels's worldview after he took up the defence of *Capital*. There was thus no explicit statement in which Engels declared that from then on, he accepted Marx's idea.

We find direct substantiation of the influences primarily in their mutual correspondence. But the exchange of letters between them diminished rapidly and drastically after Engels moved to London and the need for written correspondence was reduced to a minimum. This drastic decrease in the number of reciprocal letters can be confirmed in clear, simple figures. Dividing the correspondence into five-year periods, the following number of preserved letters is obtained:

---

1   Cf. the letter from Marx to Engels, 31 May 1873, MECW 44:506.

Year: 1855–59   288
       1860–64   249
       1865–69   446
       1870–74   109
       1875–79   52

During Marx's final years, from 1880 to 1883, he and Engels exchanged 75 letters. This was during a period when Marx, owing to his illnesses, had to travel to various health resorts. As regards the period from 1870 to 1874, 77 of the 109 letters were written before 20 September 1870, the day Engels moved from Manchester to London.[2] Everything that is preserved in general from this – entirely crucial, from our perspective – period consists of letters from various short trips, vacation jaunts and the like. With a few brilliant exceptions – for example, the letter about Engels's new ideas on a natural dialectic from 1873 – they deal with sporadic signs of life and greetings and not, as previously, lengthy analytical and argumentative epistles in essay form.

From this aspect, highly limited as it is, it may seem unfortunate that Engels – as he himself expressed it in the foreword to the 1885 edition of *Anti-Dühring* – withdrew from '*dem kaufmännischen Geschäft und Umzug*' in Manchester and settled down in London a short distance from Marx's residence,[3] there to devote his time and energy to scientific studies.[4] On the other hand, it is obvious that his liberation from the boring, time-consuming office duties at the firm of Ermen & Engels in Manchester[5] was an absolute condition for Engels to be able to devote the time that he did to questions of philosophy and natural science. There is also every reason to suppose that the exchange of ideas, knowledge and experiences between him and Marx, so abundant prior to 1870 as the many letters bear witness to, intensified even more when they lived in the same city.

But we can only indirectly, and rather uncertainly, establish the content of this exchange. Moreover, we know more about how familiar Engels was with Marx's work than the other way around. Namely, we have quite certain insights into the surprises Marx's literary remains had to offer Engels. We have

---

2 Cf. MECW 25:648.

3 See notes in MECW 44:76.

4 MECW 25:10.

5 Engels's conditions of employment at the family firm and his final liberation from his book-keeping position – his occupation was in fact no more lavish than that – is examined in detail in the major Engels biographies; cf. G. Mayer 1934, Vol. II, p. 10 et seq. and Henderson 1976, Vol. II, p. 196 et seq. See also Stepanova 1958 and Jenkins 1951, *passim*.

already seen that Engels was not sure that Marx had not worked out the brief presentation of the dialectic that he had promised.[6] The fact that Marx had not informed his friend of this – particularly since it dealt with a subject Engels had very much at heart – indicates a certain reticence. We also know that the condition that the manuscripts for the second and third volumes of *Capital* were in was an unpleasant surprise for Engels.[7] We cannot determine whether he knew before Marx's death about the ethnological excerpts that formed the basis of his *Origin of Family, Private Property and the State.*[8]

But the insights and hints we thereby have deal entirely with what Marx did and did not write. The fact that he did not give Engels full insight into the condition of the manuscripts is not to say that he would not have debated with Engels the ideas and insights he attempted to express in his manuscript.

In one specific area, moreover, he gave Engels immediate access to his notes: mathematics. A letter from Engels to Marx with a detailed discussion of essential parts of this manuscript show that Engels borrowed them and now, to his delight, found that he could understand Marx's train of thought.[9]

As regards Marx's insight into Engels's writings from the 1870s and early 1880s, we know even less. We thus have no idea of the extent to which he read the sparce manuscripts that comprise *Dialectics of Nature*. His reaction to the letter in which Engels first announced his ideas is brief and rather uninteresting.[10] When, several years later, Engels wrote to him and explained that during his studies of electricity theory he had first succeeded in formulating a 'universal natural law of motion',[11] Marx congratulated him on the splendid result but had nothing more to say about it.[12]

It would have been even more important for our knowledge of Marx-Engels intellectual relations if we had had a few simple, unambiguous substantiations of Marx's familiarity with *Anti-Dühring*. It is not just that *Anti-Dühring* was Engels's first major attempt at relating his own ideas on the natural dialectic to historical materialism and thereby Marx's theory of capital. It is also there that we can trace how Marx's sporadically expressed ideal of a dialectical conformity to law influences Engels's entire world of ideas.

---

6   Above, p. 55.

7   Engels's various reactions to the manuscripts for the still unfinished volumes of *Capital* that Marx left behind can be well be studied in the omnibus Marx and Engels 1954, pp. 277–380.

8   On this topic, see p. 446 et seq.

9   Letter from Engels to Marx, 18 August 1881, MECW 46:130.

10   Letter from Marx to Engels, 31 May 1873, MECW 44:506.

11   Letter from Engels to Marx, 23 November 1882, MECW 46:384.

12   Letter from Marx to Engels, 27 November 1882, MECW 46:385.

These simple, resolute substantiations are absent. We know that it was Marx, and not Engels, who was behind one chapter in *Anti-Dühring*, namely the primarily doctrinaire historical 'From the 'Critical History'' in the second part, which was included in a shortened version in the first editions of *Anti-Dühring* but later in a more detailed vintage.[13] Marx being able to contribute in this manner with a section in a running presentation indicates that he was quite familiar with the orientation and character of the book.

Engels was naturally eager to stress that Marx agreed with *Anti-Dühring* in detail. 'I read the whole manuscript to him before it was printed', he declared.[14]

There is no reason to doubt Engels's disclosure. *Anti-Dühring* is from first to last a defence of Marx against Dühring. In many respects, moreover, it was a work commissioned by Marx's and Engels's closest advocates in Germany, Wilhelm Liebknecht above all.[15] It was not given from the start that it was Engels, and not Marx, who would bring up Dühring's system for discussion; at least among the German Social Democrats it was believed that Marx would handle the attack.[16] The letters between Marx and Engels also bear witness to the fact that it was after some hesitation and a sense of laying a more important work – *Dialectics of Nature* – aside that Engels took up the task of attacking Dühring.[17]

Anti-Dühring thus appeared from the start to be a shared concern for Marx and Engels. It would also have been extremely remarkable if Marx had not involved himself in what Engels wrote: the book is essentially a popularisation of *Capital*, written with the intent of correcting other popularisations.[18]

But even if we can assume with good reason that Marx had read *Anti-Dühring* in manuscript form, we cannot determine thereby how carefully Marx thought through the broader theoretical consequences of the work. It would have been peculiar, for example, if Marx had not been informed of Engels's defence of his theses on quantity and quality and the negation of the negation, but the mere awareness of these studies is not the same as a careful review of what these theses *could lead to*.

---

13   MECW 25:9 and 15.
14   MECW 25:9.
15   On this topic, cf. Liebknecht 1963, pp. 190 and 195 et seq. Cf. also Engels's 'Old Preface' to
       Anti-Dühring, MECW 25:336.
16   Cf. the letter from Marx to W. Liebknecht, 7 October 1876, MECW 45:154 et seq. The information could be read in an (anonymous) report by Motteler from the Socialist Congress in
       Gotha, 1876.
17   Cf. the letters from Engels to Marx, 24 May 1876, MECW 45:118; from Marx to Engels, 25 May
       1876, MECW 45:119; from Engels to Marx, 28 May 1876, MECW 45:122; and 25 July 1876,
       MECW 45:131.
18   Cf. below, p. 514 *et seq.*

It is otherwise striking how Engels commented on *Anti-Dühring* with a certain nonchalance; it is as if he wanted to ascribe less weight to the theoretical content of the work. In a letter to Eduard Bernstein, he thus declared that did not intend to let his big project be interrupted by such 'journalistic activity' (*journalistische Tätigkeit*).[19] Later, when he had more or less given up the hope of completing *Dialectics of Nature*, he could of course speak more respectfully of his work.[20] As long as he had the greater work in front of him, he regarded the polemic against Dühring as a minor diversion, and it is entirely possible that Marx shared that perception. But we know nothing of this with certainty.

As regards the intellectual relations between Marx and Engels, we in fact obtain the most certain – and most interesting – information by comparing their writings. It is there that not only the individual ideas but the context of those ideas emerges. These changing but mutually comparable patterns of thought, however, will be compared in the following chapters.

3   Schorlemmer

Among those who directly and personally influenced Engels's philosophical work, Carl Schorlemmer occupies a unique position. He was a major internationally recognised authority in organic chemistry, and at the same time he was a member of the First International and the German Social Democratic Party. After Marx, he was Engels's closest friend.

We know surprisingly little about him.[21] The literature on him is quite comprehensive but highly irregular. He played a role in the accounts of the history of chemistry,[22] and he is often mentioned in works dealing with the early history of socialism and of Marxism.[23] But the pictures of Schorlemmer the chemist and Schorlemmer the communist[24] are not easy to identify.

---

19   Letter from Engels to Bernstein, 26 July 1879, MECW 45:361.

20   Cf. for example the letter to the same Bernstein, 11 April 1884, MECW 47:125; and to Bebel, 3 December 1892, MECW 50:48.

21   On this topic, see Heinig 1974.

22   Cf. for example Partington 1962–64, p. 774 et seq; F.J. Moore 1939, p. 300 et seq.

23   Cf. for example the official East German *Geschichte*, p. 349 et seq.

24   Engels often emphasised that Schorlemmer was both a chemist and a communist or social democrat (both the latter terms had the same meaning for Engels). Cf. further below, p. 360 et seq. The literature that deals with all of Schorlemmer's opinions is limited primarily to Zimmerman 1964; Heinig 1971 and 1974; and Hager 1960 (in addition to my own paper above, Note 21).

The natural approach to the varied sources that could provide us with information about both the scientist and the politically and ideologically active friend of Engels and Marx is also a thorny one, to say the least. What he published is easily accessible enough, it is true; a great deal of it, moreover, exists in numerous editions and translations.[25] But this literature provides no information about Schorlemmer's political and ideological views, and scarcely any about his understanding of science. It is literature on chemistry – and to some extent the history of chemistry – in a strict sense

What has otherwise been preserved is almost all trifles: an incomplete manuscript for a history of chemistry[26] and a number of letters. Particularly regrettable is that the correspondence with Engels was almost entirely obliterated.[27] He was particularly close to Engels, and after Engels moved from Manchester (where Schorlemmer lived) to London, numerous messages – if only concerning external arrangements such as joint summer, Christmas and Easter holidays – must have passed between the two. In his 1892 obituary of Schorlemmer, Engels also declared that they both had exchanged many thoughts 'on natural science and party matters'[28] by letter. We do not know where all this correspondence, which likely could give us better direct insight into Engels's work on at least a dialectic of natural science, has gone. We know only that Engels looked through the papers Schorlemmer left behind before the executors of the will took possession of the property.[29] It seems reasonable to assume that he removed the letters he himself had written to Schorlemmer, and for some

25   Among the writings Schorlemmer authored on his own, this concerns in particular *Lehrbuch der Kohlenstoffverbindungen oder der organischen Chemie* (1st ed., 1871) and *The Rise and Development of Organic Chemistry* (1st ed., 1879).

26   C. Schorlemmer, *Geschichte der Chemie* I–II, Manchester University Library Special Collections. The last ever letter from Engels, dictated to his brother Hermann and addressed to the chemist Ludwig Siebold on 28 July 1895, concerns this history of chemistry which, according to Engels, was not ready for print; MECW 50:536. Siebold had informed him that a publisher in Germany was willing to publish the history; letter from Siebold to Engels, *IISG Marx-Engels Nachlass*, L 5709. Partington as well had to assure himself that Schorlemmer's history of chemistry was highly incomplete; see Partington 1962–64, Vol. IV, p. 775.

27   A single letter from Engels to Schorlemmer has been preserved; it had been forgotten in the aforementioned manuscript in Manchester. The letter provides information on a few Greek words of interest to the history of chemistry. Engels to Schorlemmer, 27 January 1891, MECW 49:111. Four letters from Schorlemmer to Engels have been preserved; *IISG Marx-Engels Nachlass*, L 5606–5609 and *IML-ZPA*, 1:5:2318. One of them contains interesting information on literature in chemistry; it is, however, from the period before 1873 (L 5607 and 1:5:2318 respectively).

28   Engels, 'Carl Schorlemmer', MECW 27:304.

29   Letter from Engels to Ludwig Schorlemmer, 30 June 1892, MECW 49:454.

reason destroyed them (he had otherwise been careful to preserve his correspondence for posterity). The only letter from Engels to Schorlemmer that has been preserved had been forgotten in the manuscript for a history of chemistry. The letters from Schorlemmer to Engels have all gone the same way but for a few exceptions.[30]

Seven brief messages from Schorlemmer to Marx have been preserved; most of them comprise responses to concrete questions.[31] In addition, there is various other, more or less inconsequential correspondence spread among libraries and collections across Europe.[32]

There is thus strikingly little material left from a life that ended more than a century ago, that moreover had a palpable literary orientation and played out within the boundaries of at least three extraordinarily dynamic fields: organic chemistry, the great victorious fashionable science of the time; socialism, embodied in its foremost leaders; and the external environment that the Manchester area, 'the cradle of the Industrial Revolution', represented. If Engels had not made a great fuss about Schorlemmer in his letters, no one would have remembered him as anything other than a successful but not exactly epoch-making chemist.

4   The Life of Schorlemmer

We do not know much about Schorlemmer's life before Manchester, or his first twenty-five years. He was born in Darmstadt in 1834 and received not too lengthy schooling. Like many other early chemists, he came in contact with the subject as an apprentice pharmacist. By degrees he managed to follow a university programme in Heidelberg, though without being able to enrol in the university,[33] and it is believed he heard the well-known Robert Wilhelm Bunsen

---

30   If Schorlemmer himself destroyed them, the letters from him to Engels would in all likelihood still exist. Naturally there is a possibility that both Schorlemmer and Engels each obliterated their respective correspondence.

31   *IISG Marx-Engels Nachlass*, 3986–3992; *IML-ZPA*, 1:5:3311. In one of the letters (25 September 1873), Schorlemmer informs Marx of the addresses for Darwin and Spencer.

32   A number of letters to Marx's daughters – Laura Lafargue in particular – are spread across Europe; in *IISG Marx-Engels Nachlass*, G 172 and 347–48; in the British Museum, Add. 45345, f. 133; and in *Colléction M.E. Bottigelli*. A number of letters on questions of chemistry from Schorlemmer are preserved at the Chemical Society in London, as are other similar letters in the Staatsbibliothek preussischer Kulturbesitz in Berlin and the Bibliothek des deutschen Museums in Munich.

33   In one preserved letter Schorlemmer – apparently on the direct request of the addressee,

lecture there. In the spring of 1859, he quit his apprenticeship at the pharmacy and went in for the study of chemistry at the most celebrated chemical laboratory of the time, the one Justus von Liebig had built at Giessen. There, he came in contact with figures such as Hermann Kopp, the great historian of chemistry.[34]

Shortly thereafter, however, by the autumn of 1859, he received an offer to become the personal assistant to Manchester professor Henry Enfield Roscoe. It was in Manchester that he would carry out his life's work. Roscoe's selection of a rather unschooled former apprentice pharmacist was bound up with his tremendous respect for the experimentally and practically oriented chemistry of the German universities, which he wanted to transplant to Manchester. The intent of Owen's College in Manchester was precisely that it should harmonise with its practical environment.[35] Roscoe was a fervent advocate of the idea.[36] It is likely that he saw in Schorlemmer a good assistant for its realisation.

We do not know how Schorlemmer reacted to the unfamiliar English industrial environment. There were plenty of Germans in the Lancashire region, and obviously he sought his countrymen out. He frequented the Schiller-Anstalt, the German cultural organisation in Manchester.[37] It was there he met Engels, who first mentioned the acquaintance in a letter from 1865.[38]

Schorlemmer's life in Manchester, however, was filled completely by scientific studies and scientific work. It can scarcely be imagined that he would have been a skilled chemist when Roscoe brought him to Manchester. After only a few years, however, he began making discoveries that attracted attention. What is remarkable is that these discoveries fell within organic chemistry, a field of chemistry where Roscoe was not a specialist. Schorlemmer had quickly chosen his own path.

The image of Schorlemmer active among his colleagues is different than the one of him in relation to Marx and Engels. Roscoe, in his obituary, said: 'He was of a retiring, most modest and unassuming disposition'.[39] It is otherwise

A. Krause – gave an account of his career (*Lebenslauf*, undated, Bibliothek des deutsches Museums). Significantly more detailed is P.J. Hartog's article 'Schorlemmer, Carl (1834–1892)' in the *Dictionary of National Biography*, Vol. L (1897). The rolls from Heidelberg say nothing about whether any Carl Schorlemmer had matriculated there.

34   Hermann Kopp's main work on the history of chemistry is *Geschichte der Chemie* (4 vols., 1843–47). Of great significance for later research is his *Die Alchemie in älterer und neuerer Zeit* (Vols. 1–2) (1866).

35   Cf. above, p. 131.

36   Roscoe 1906, p. 48 et seq. and 95 et seq.; Thorpe 1916, p. 28 et seq.

37   The documents concerning the activities of the Schiller Institute unfortunately seem to have been lost. The association disbanded at the outbreak of the First World War.

38   Letter from Engels to Marx, 6 March 1865, MECW 42:117.

39   Roscoe 1892, p. VIII; Roscoe 1895, p. 365.

remarkable that Roscoe, who himself had a lively interest in politics and was active in the liberal wing, stated that he had only limited knowledge of Schorlemmer's socialist opinions.[40]

There is another, more detailed image of Schorlemmer the man to be obtained through Engels's correspondence. Engels and Marx had a consistent nickname for Schorlemmer: Jollymayer.[41] The name indicated that Schorlemmer was cheerful company. If nothing else, it became clear when joy had left the ill and prematurely aging Schorlemmer.[42]

It thus appears that Schorlemmer had put on a different and more lively face together with Marx and Engels and other socialist acquaintances than in the circle of chemists. He was also eager to socialise with Engels as much as possible. When Engels moved to London, Schorlemmer visited him as often as opportunity allowed, or they often went on holiday trips together.[43] He also accompanied Engels in 1888 on his journey to the United States with Eleanor Marx and Edward Aveling.[44] But he could also travel on his own. He visited natural science associations in Germany numerous times,[45] he often travelled home to Darmstadt,[46] and he made a few detours to Paris and Paul and Laura Lafargue.[47]

---

40   In the obituary in *Nature*, Roscoe added that he 'knows but little of his political views, for these he did not obtrude upon his friends, though he held decided ones. He believed in popular freedom and popular rights, and was a strong supporter of the German Democratic Party (*sic*), and of the leaders of this movement, both in Germany and in England, being his intimate personal friends'. Roscoe 1895, p. 365.

41   So in innumerable letters, e.g. Marx to Engels, 24 October 1868, MECW 43:142; Engels to L. Lafargue, 2 June 1883, MECW 47:30; and Engels to Schorlemmer, 27 January 1891, MECW 49:111.

42   Letter from Engels to L. Lafargue, 20 July 1891, MECW 49:220: '... but he is getting more and more Tristymeier, you have to work very hard to get a smile out of him now'.

43   Cf. the letter from Engels to Ludwig Schorlemmer, 18 October 1892, MECW 50:14, and a large number of letters regarding Schorlemmer's visit to London and on trips taken together, e.g. Engels to P. Pauli, 25 April 1876, MECW 45:116; Engels to Marx, 7 July 1881, MECW 46:104; Engels to Jenny Longuet, 7 December 1881, MECW 46:156.

44   Letter from Engels to L. Lafargue, 6 August 1888, MECW 48:203; and Engels to F.A. Sorge, 28 August 1888, MECW 48:206, and 31 August 1888, MECW 48:207 et seq. and others. On the trip, see Tsuzuki 1967, p. 175 et seq.

45   For example, 1867 (letter from Engels to Marx, 2 September 1867, MECW 42:418) and 1869 (letter from Engels to Marx, 22 June 1869, MECW 43:296).

46   Cf. for example the letter from Engels to Pauli, 11 August 1876, MECW 45:133; and C. Schorlemmer to 'Petter' (Peter Schorlemmer), 24 March (year unknown), Staatsbibliothek preussischer Kulturbesitz.

47   Letter from Engels to L. Lafargue, 3 October 1883, MECW 47:61; letter from C. Schorlemmer to L. Lafargue, 28 June 1885, IISG *Marx-Engels Nachlass*, G 348.

Schorlemmer's life otherwise seems to have passed quite uniformly during his decades in Manchester. There were, however, changes of the slow and thorough kind. To begin with, he made his name as a conductor of experiments; the laboratory was his chief environment. But gradually he devoted a larger part of his time to writing. He began with adapting and translating Roscoe's brief textbook in chemistry,[48] and a few years later he was finished with his own textbook in organic chemistry.[49] In 1877, the first volume of his and Roscoe's *A Treatise on Chemistry* was published. According to Roscoe's own admission, Schorlemmer's share of the work was much greater. The sections dealing with organic chemistry are almost exclusively his product, and he had contributed advice and help with the earlier volumes as well.[50] It was in the 1880s that the thick volumes that had Schorlemmer as the main author were published. Schorlemmer had definitively turned his back on the laboratory by 1883.[51] He thus devoted the last years of his life exclusively to writing. But he did not manage to complete the work; others had to take over after his death.[52] At the end of his life he underwent various physical and mental changes that likely made his work more difficult.[53]

5   Schorlemmer the Chemist

Schorlemmer thus knew organic chemistry both as a successful conductor of experiments and as an even more successful author of textbooks. He reported on his experiments in a number of minor papers[54] that mostly originate

---

48   The first edition of *Kurzes Lehrbuch der Chemie* (with Roscoe alone named as author) was published in 1867.

49   *Lehrbuch der Kohlenstoffverbindungen oder der organischen Chemie*, 1871.

50   Roscoe 1892, p. viii; Roscoe 1895, p. 365.

51   Hartog 1897, p. 440.

52   Volume 5, which was published in 1896, was – as it said in the German edition – 'Continued by JW Brühl' in collaboration with Helsinki chemists E. Hjelt and O. Aschan.

53   Cf. the letter from Engels to P. Lafargue, 19 May 1892, MECW 49:424: 'You know that the latter [Schorlemmer] has been physically and mentally sick for 4 years now ...'. What Schorlemmer's physical and mental ill health consisted of is not easy to say. It can be noted that Engels, with palpable relief, announced that the autopsy showed Schorlemmer died of lung cancer, e.g. in the letter to Ludwig Schorlemmer, 39 June 1892, MECW 49:454. Judging by a letter from August Bebel of 5 June 1892 to the Austrian socialist leader Victor Adler, the rumour was circulating that 'passion and alcohol' had 'destroyed' Schorlemmer; V. Adler 1954, p. 90. It is possible that sensitive matters were hidden here that contributed to Engels not preserving the letters he received from Schorlemmer.

54   A list of Schorlemmer's papers in chemistry can be found in Dixon, p. 195. Cf. also Partington 1962–64, Vol. IV, p. 50 et seq.

from an early period in the 1860s. They deal with a number of fields in organic chemistry. It was, however, above all in one field – theoretically and practically fundamental, though limited – that Schorlemmer made a ground-breaking contribution. It is of particular interest in this context, since it was from this field that Engels took his examples of the dialectics of chemistry.

It concerns the methane series, or what in Schorlemmer's time was often called the paraffins (now called alkanes). It thus concerns simple hydrocarbons, or the compounds that are constructed in accordance with the formula C_nH_{2n+2}: methane (CH_4), ethane (C_2H_6), and so on.

Schorlemmer's discoveries had a direct connection with the great controversy over Berzelius's electrochemical theory.[55] With his meticulous experiments, Schorlemmer could add a piece of the puzzle to the new molecular theory, in which the radical could be defined in relation to the molecule: the radical was a 'remnant' of the molecule.

Schorlemmer experienced the power of resistance of the older radical theory. Edward Frankland, who in the 1860s was probably the most authoritative English chemist, defended it assiduously. Frankland started from certain problems concerning precisely the hydrocarbon radicals. He assumed, starting from the empirical knowledge available, that there existed two homologous series – the radicals (methyl, ethyl, propyl and so on) on the one hand and the methanes, or hydrides (methyl hydride, ethyl hydride and so on) on the other.

It was here that Schorlemmer made his contribution. He demonstrated that methyl and ethyl hydride were identical and traced them both back to ethane (C_2H_6). He could therefore introduce the assumption that there was a single series of hydrocarbons, and the hydrides could go the way of all flesh.[56] In a large number of reports to the Royal Society – where he rapidly became a member, the first time he was proposed[57] – he continued to report the results from his investigations into the simple hydrocarbons.[58] Through his great exactitude he could clear away Frankland's argument for a separate hydride series, namely that the boiling points for radicals and hydrides were different. Schorlemmer showed that these results were incorrect and that the mistake was due to the extraordinary difficulty in isolating hydrocarbons. Frankland wasn't easily convinced,[59] but he seems to have been quite alone in his obstinacy.

55   Above, p. 148.
56   Schorlemmer 1864.
57   Roscoe emphasised the remarkable aspects of the rapid success; Roscoe 1892, p. vii and Roscoe 1895, p. 394.
58   This concerns seven reports on the methane (or paraffin) series, published in the Royal Society's *Proceedings* between 1865 and 1871; Schorlemmer 1865.
59   For further information, see Partington 1962–64, Vol. IV, p. 508 et seq.

Schorlemmer's discoveries were thus significant for the foundations of organic chemistry. This significance was not only theoretical, however. By extension, the studies were also of extraordinary practical importance.

As is well known, petroleum (rock oil) consists to a great extent of hydrocarbons that belong to the methane, methylene and benzene series. Schorlemmer's studies of the boiling points of the methane series would be significant for the entire oil industry. Refining, namely, is built on the knowledge of the different boiling points of hydrocarbons; the earlier members of the series are gases at room temperature, and the more complex the compound the higher the boiling point. When oil is distilled, the simplest hydrocarbons thus evaporate first.

It is obvious that Schorlemmer could not have foreseen the enormous significance of oil as an energy source in the twentieth century; oil taking up the battle with coal was a preposterous idea a few decades before the emergence of the automotive industry. Schorlemmer, however, displayed a very early interest in oil. Rock oil had been extracted in small quantities for some time, it is true, but it was only in 1859 – in Pennsylvania – that real development got its start. For the time being, the most important product that was being extracted was lamp kerosene; exports of kerosene to Europe had begun in 1861.[60]

In 1862, Schorlemmer had managed to analyse 'amerikanisches Steinöl'.[61] It thus appears that analyses of this highly practical product had led him into the problem of hydrocarbons. This was nothing strange: it was how numerous chemists worked at the time. Schorlemmer's enthusiasm for petroleum, however, seems to have been prolonged: he thus carried out important analyses of naphtha, and he was the one who synthesised octane, so essential in oil.[62] In the great *Treatise*, where as we have seen he was responsible for organic chemistry, he devoted his attention to the still insignificant industrial history of oil.[63]

As noted, however, Schorlemmer's career as a conductor of experiments was a rather short one. He achieved his most brilliant results relatively early on. His contributions, in comparison to those of Frankland's, of Kolbe's, or of Wurtz's were few, and produced during a brief period of time.

---

60 The standard work on the early history of oil are Forbes 1958 and Forbes 1959. The chemists' work with oil is treated in particular in the latter work, p. 37 et seq.; Schorlemmer's contributions, p. 64 et seq.

61 Bibliotek des deutsches Museums, letter from E. Hoster to E. Erlenmeyer, 22 October and 22 November 1862, and letter from Schorlemmer to Erlenmeyer 6 November 1862. The letter from Schorlemmer, which Hoster brought to Germany, was accompanied by a sample of petroleum that Schorlemmer had analysed.

62 Schorlemmer 1868, p. 376, and Schorlemmer 1872, p. 111 et seq.

63 Roscoe and Schorlemmer 1877a, Vol. III:1, p. 141 et seq.

From our view in the present day, Schorlemmer's retreat to the writing desk and summary works may seem like a capitulation. But then we are judging him from our own time, when the theoretical construction of chemistry is relatively fixed and extremely differentiated.

In the latter half of the nineteenth century, a summary work – at least in organic chemistry, where opinions were still very divided – implied a real theoretical contribution. It should be remembered that the man who actually drew up a consistent theory of the chemistry of carbon compounds, August Kekulé, laid out his theses in a major textbook.[64] Authoring textbooks and summary works was no routine matter, which can be seen from the fact that the various works from that time mutually deviated on numerous points in their views of the foundations of chemistry.[65]

When Schorlemmer took responsibility for organic chemistry in the *Treatise*, it required him to bring order to the diversity of compounds, which was not at all a given. If further advances are a sign of success, then Schorlemmer succeeded, since the *Treatise* remained a standard work in English- and German-speaking countries for decades.

Going into the content of the thick volumes he managed to complete in more detail would be going too far. What we are interested in here is the question of the extent to which Schorlemmer influenced Engels, both directly and indirectly. We do not know the extent to which Engels acquainted himself with the *Treatise*. He refers to it only once, in the ominous manuscript of *Dialectics*, where the three dialectical laws are introduced; the reference concerns the second volume on the metals and spectral analysis (i.e. inorganic chemistry).[66] However matters stood, Schorlemmer could naturally have informed him either verbally or by letter of certain fundamental thoughts and ideas in the *Treatise*.

It is, then, in particular a very general problem that arouses our interest because it has immediate points of contact with Engels's irreductivist ideas. It concerns the question of the relation between organic and inorganic chemistry.

As is known, the older conception that there was a decisive boundary between organic and inorganic chemistry had been fought down towards the middle of the nineteenth century. As a result of it becoming possible to synthesise organic compounds, the assumption of some special vital force as the mas-

---

64   Kekulé 1859. On this famous book, see Anschütz 1929, Vol. I, p. 156 et seq.
65   The statement is based above all on a comparison between Kekulé's and Schorlemmer's reviews, and in addition on the textbooks by Erlenmeyer 1867 and Butlerow 1864–66.
66   MECW 25:361.

ter builder of these compounds was ruled out. This conclusion was not immediately drawn, of course, with the first known synthesis, Wöhler's synthesis of urea in 1828; Schorlemmer was otherwise probably one of the first to reasonably estimate the significance of Wöhler's synthesis in a historical account, and pointed out that it was only with the current of later and more complex syntheses that the idea of an insurmountable boundary between organic and inorganic died out.[67]

In that case, however, what reason was there to maintain the distinction between organic and inorganic chemistry? Those who held firmly to the older radical theory, according to which the radicals in organic compounds corresponded to the elements in inorganic compounds, could assert that the boundary lay there. But what was left for those who held to the more modern radical theory?

It was a well-known truth that all organic compounds contained carbon. August Kekulé proposed that 'organic chemistry' be used synonymously with 'the chemistry of carbon compounds'; his magnum opus was also called *Lehrbuch der organischen Chemie oder Chemie der Kohlenstoffverbindungen* (Textbook of Organic Chemistry, or Chemistry of Carbon Compounds).

Neither Kekulé nor Schorlemmer claimed that the carbon compounds could be formed in an essentially different way than other chemical compounds. Kekulé's epoch-making contribution consisted on the one hand of demonstrating that the carbon atom was quadrivalent, and on the other of explaining the infinite diversity of carbon compounds by the ability of the carbon atom to form compounds with other carbon atoms in a large number of different ways, including in saturated and unsaturated compounds.

The latter was something that gave carbon a relatively exceptional position, but according to Kekulé and a number of his followers, this did not justify marking off a specific chemistry of carbon compounds. The reason it nonetheless had to be spoken about was exclusively practical. Since there were so many carbon compounds, there also had to be specialists in them. Professorships in organic chemistry, and textbooks written in the style of Kekulé's own, were necessary solely[68] for the sake of the scientific division of labour.[69]

---

67   Roscoe and Schorlemmer 1877a, Vol. III:1, p. 7. Cf. also Schorlemmer 1889, p. 17 et seq.

68   Roscoe 1868, p. 242 et seq.: 'Chemie der Kohlenstoff-Verbindungen oder organische Chemie'.

69   Kekulé 1869, Vol. I, p. 10. See also Erlenmeyer 1867, p. 5, and Butlerow 1864–66, p. 5. Kekulé and the others of course were correct in that a division of labour between organic and inorganic chemistry took place during and after the mid-nineteenth century; cf. above, p. 158.

In his and Roscoe's great textbook, Schorlemmer had changed the understanding of what distinguished organic chemistry and what motivated its exceptional position. A number of important carbon compounds, Schorlemmer pointed out, would always be dealt with – and had to be dealt with – in inorganic chemistry. There was, however, a definite property of carbon that fundamentally – and not just practically – justified a separate organic chemistry, namely that carbon can be saturated with hydrogen. Strictly taken, organic chemistry therefore did not encompass carbon compounds in general. Schorlemmer introduced the designation 'chemistry of carbon compounds', and his portion of the great Roscoe-Schorlemmer work bore the title *'Die Kohlenwasserstoffe und ihre Derivate oder organische Chimie'* (Hydrocarbons and their Derivatives, or Organic Chemistry).[70]

Schorlemmer himself was certain that he had provided a 'correct definition' of organic chemistry.[71] It was obviously essential for him to find a theoretical justification for the difference between organic and inorganic chemistry. He said that there was a qualitative difference between organic and inorganic compounds.[72] Drawing a boundary of this kind between two disciplines immediately leads thoughts to Engels's non-reductive materialism. As far as I have been able to determine, it was none other than Engels who at that time expressed the understanding that there was a fundamental difference between two theories or two theoretical spheres in terms of a 'qualitative difference'.

If Schorlemmer's brief statement on the relation between organic and inorganic chemistry were forced, it could be made to square quite well with Engels's ideas about the different sciences and thus the different mutual relations among the levels of reality.[73] Organic chemistry could be rooted in inorganic chemistry in such a way that every organic compound could be quantitatively determined in the terms of inorganic chemistry (which would take place as soon as he could determine the composition and structure of the compound).

---

70   Roscoe and Schorlemmer 1877a, Vol. III:1, p. 27 et seq. Despite several generations of British and German students of chemistry receiving their training in Schorlemmer's textbook, his suggestion for a name never became generally accepted. Today, a normal definition of the field is as follows: 'Organic chemistry is the study of the structure, properties, composition, reactions, and preparation of carbon-containing compounds, which include not only hydrocarbons but also compounds with any number of other elements, including hydrogen (most compounds contain at least one carbon-hydrogen bond), nitrogen, oxygen, halogens, phosphorus, silicon, and sulfur'. https://www.acs.org/content/acs/en/careers/college-to-career/areas-of-chemistry/organic-chemistry.html

71   Roscoe and Schorlemmer 1877a, Vol. III:1, p. 31.

72   Ibid., p. 27.

73   Cf. below, p. 321, et seq.

On the other hand, organic chemistry would contain something qualitatively new: new qualities, new contexts.

Schorlemmer's statement, however, stands quite alone in his production. We do not have the right to conclude from it an entire conception of the relation of various theories, and thereby various spheres of reality, to one another.

6   Engels and Schorlemmer

The question that is crucial in this context, namely what the constant dealings with Schorlemmer meant for Engels's dialectic of nature, is particularly difficult to answer simply because the preserved material – including Schorlemmer's published writings – provide so little definite information. We have, for example, only one document – and that a very brief one – in which Schorlemmer commented directly on Engels's ideas. It was his laconic commentary on the letter in which Engels first expressed his intentions to work up his own dialectic of the sciences.

The comments are four in number and express thorough agreement. The thesis that the main object of study of natural science is the various 'forms of motion' of matter (mechanical motion, light, electricity, chemical force and so on) gives rise to the exclamation '*Sehr gut, meine eigne Ansicht*' (Very good, my own view). Schorlemmer also agreed with the statement that motion was always the result of the interaction of several bodies, and to Engels's admission that for the time being he did not dare to jump into the organic sphere, Schorlemmer said '*Ich auch nicht*' (Neither do I).[74]

There are a number of more or less certain conclusions we can draw from the letter and the marginal comments:

1.   Engels and Schorlemmer had hardly discussed these elevated matters previously in detail. Had they done so, it would have been meaningless for Schorlemmer to comment on Engels's opinions in this way.
2.   If we assume that Schorlemmer was being honest in his criticism – and there is no reason to believe otherwise – he had nonetheless arrived at ideas that were reminiscent of those that Engels summarised in his letter. In fact, it is highly reasonable to assume that Schorlemmer had had a decisive influence on Engels in the years prior to 1873. In his correspondence with Marx, Engels often referred to the information he had obtained from Schorlemmer on questions that were of crucial significance in his

---

74   Schorlemmer's marginal notes in MECW 44:500 et seq.

dialectic of nature. The very first time Engels mentioned Schorlemmer in a letter, it was in his capacity as an authority in natural science.[75] The same thing occurred numerous times thereafter.[76]

It thus appears quite certain that Schorlemmer had actively influenced Engels's understanding of matters that would play a role in the dialectic of nature. On the other hand, Schorlemmer himself had not drawn the general conclusions Engels would later draw, nor after 1873 did he refer to Engels's ideas more than in passing in his writings.

For his part, Engels lost no time in presenting the dialectic of nature as his own original theory. In his correspondence, there is a striking example of how he wanted to view himself as the innovator, and Schorlemmer as the one who carried the ideas out in scientific praxis. Paul Lafargue had informed Engels that Schorlemmer's conception of the relation between proteins and life had created a sensation in the French scientific press.[77] Schorlemmer had said that the mystery of life could only be solved using synthetic proteins. Engels responded to Lafargue that Schorlemmer had actually taken the idea over from him. In *Anti-Dühring*, Engels had declared, namely, that 'Life is the mode of existence of albuminous bodies'.[78] On the other hand, Engels admitted that Schorlemmer, as a professional chemist, ran greater risks than he did with such an assumption: '[I]f it falls flat, the blame will be his, whereas if it catches on, he will be the first to give me the credit'.[79]

Engels of course cannot lay claim to being the first to state that life and proteins were indissolubly connected with one another – he himself had been

---

75   Letter from Engels to Marx, 6 March 1865, MECW 42:117.
76   For example, the letter from Engels to Marx, 24 June 1867, MECW 42:387 et seq. For his part, Marx learned the basics of chemistry in Schorlemmer's German treatment of Roscoe's textbook (Roscoe 1867); cf. letter from Marx to Engels, 2 November, 27 November and 7 December 1867; MECW 42: 459, 478 and 495 respectively, as well as excerpts in *IISG Marx-Engels Nachlass*, B 145.
77   More specifically, in Grimaux 1885, p. 500.
78   MECW 25:76. The sentence in German sounds like a play on words and was perceived as such by Bertolt Brecht, for example. Cf. Lukács and Brecht 1975, pp. 220 and 223. It does not seem likely, however, that Engels would have been consciously ingenious in the formulation (*Daseinsweisse* – *Eiweisskörper*).
79   Letter from Engels to P. Lafargue, 19 May 1885, MECW 47:289. Obviously, Engels was correct in his conjecture. In his history of organic chemistry, Schorlemmer included a reference to Engels regarding the interpretation of the methane (or paraffin) series – Schorlemmer's own great specialisation. Schorlemmer says, precisely in Engels's spirit, that '*Die Paraffine zeigen, wie auch andere homologe Reihen, sehr klar, wie fortwährend "Quantität in Qualität umschlagt"* ...'. In a note, he refers to *Anti-Dühring*. Schorlemmer 1889, p. 117 et seq.

treated to such ideas long before *Anti-Dühring*[80] – but could perhaps mean here that he defined the relation in dialectical terms. The origins of life could be determined quantitatively – proteins can, in principle, be chemically analysed – but at the same time, life entails a range of new qualities or contexts of laws. It is entirely possible, to say nothing of probable, that Schorlemmer would have given Engels some of the credit if he had made any kind of groundbreaking discovery in the relation between life and proteins. But it is more difficult to define accurately how much Engels's general thoughts could actually have guided him in his work.

It is in fact much easier to see what Engels took from Schorlemmer during the years in which he was working on his dialectic of nature. As we have seen, Engels made no excerpts from works on chemistry.[81] Setting aside a popular address on chemistry that Kekulé held,[82,83] he did not cite any literature on the subject apart from the sparse references to Roscoe's and Schorlemmer's work. We can also see from the examples of dialectical processes in chemistry that Engels cited that Schorlemmer exercised a direct influence on him. The examples, namely, deal almost exclusively with Schorlemmer's area of specialisation – the hydrocarbon series and their derivatives.[84] It was an area where Engels could feel comfortable thanks to Schorlemmer.

But we thereby know extremely little, however, of Schorlemmer's own activity in the sphere of dialectical philosophy. One is tempted to draw simple psychological conclusions: the by all accounts timid chemist could scarcely have opposed the inexhaustibly dynamic, enthusiastic and dominant Engels. Nor could they both have found such pleasure in each other's company if they had irreconcilable opinions in a field that was so close to both of their hearts.

Engels made much of the fact that Schorlemmer, almost alone among natural scientists, had read Hegel.[85] We do not know how in depth these studies were, and can only assume that Engels was familiar with the circumstances. Schorlemmer owned an edition of Hegel's *Works*, which Engels purchased from his estate.[86] It is indisputable that the mere possession of such a work indicated

---

80   Even Marx called his attention to this in a letter, 18 November 1868, MECW 43:162.
81   Above, p. 333.
82   Kekulé 1878.
83   MECW 25: 530, 535 and 547.
84   Cf. for example MECW 25:117 et seq., 359 et seq. and 571.
85   E.g. MECW 25:485.
86   Letter from Siebold to Engels, 30 December 1892, *IISG Marx-Engels Nachlass*, L 5704. The work is preserved at *IML-ZPA*.

a strong interest. Tracing any influence from Hegel in Schorlemmer's, on the other hand, is difficult. In his great incomplete history of chemistry, he made use of Hegel's thinking exactly once. It concerns the division into historical periods, where Schorlemmer took Hegel's *History of Philosophy* as his starting point.[87]

Schorlemmer's works on the history of chemistry otherwise naturally raises another question, namely the extent to which he made any use of historical materialism, the central theory of Marxism. Here it can be said that his perspective was materialist in the sense that he closely and carefully placed chemistry in relation to practical and industrial developments.[88] On the other hand, he did not go into any greater perspectives here. He was, and remained, an extremely careful researcher.

One important aspect of the Engels-Schorlemmer relationship is, naturally, that Schorlemmer was an adherent of Engels's political views. He was a member of both the Royal Society and the German Social-Democratic Party. Entirely apart from his relationship with Engels, he could have been an interesting example of the meeting between science and politics in the late nineteenth century.

Even in the political sphere, however, Schorlemmer remained anonymous to a great degree. We do not know how he regarded the connection between his scientific activities and his political convictions. We do not even know how he became connected with revolutionary socialism. Engels said in a letter from 1883 that Schorlemmer was a communist even before they became acquainted twenty years earlier.[89] In the obituary, Engels repeated the statement, adding that the only thing Schorlemmer had to learn from him and Marx were 'the economic grounds for a conviction he had gained long ago'.[90]

This does not tell us much, however. How Schorlemmer's political views influenced him and his activities cannot be determined more than piecemeal from the documents that have been preserved. Engels said that he and Schorlemmer corresponded on Party matters,[91] but as noted no trace of this correspondence has been preserved. During the years of the Anti-Socialist Laws in Germany, he clearly developed a certain level of activity during his trips to

---

87   Manchester University Library Special Collections. Schorlemmer, Vol. I, p. 146 et seq.
88   This feature is also noted by Partington 1962–64, Vol. IV, p. 775. References to industrial and other practical uses are legion, e.g. in Schorlemmer 1889.
89   Letter from Engels to Bernstein, 27 February 1883, MECW 46:442.
90   MECW 27:304.
91   Above, p. 347.

visit natural science associations and his home town of Darmstadt; at one point he fell into the hands of the police in that connection.[92] His political activity, however, nonetheless cannot have been very extensive.

Engels constantly mentioned Schorlemmer in his correspondence, often with a palpable sense of pride. At one point he told Eduard Bernstein off for a lack of respect toward Schorlemmer; Bernstein had written that the editorial board of *Der Sozialdemokrat* could hardly know 'who Sch – is'.[93] Engels picked up the gauntlet in a letter that on the surface dealt with a completely different supposed injustice towards Schorlemmer; the address to Bernstein himself is nonetheless clear enough. Schorlemmer was, Engels said, 'after Marx, undoubtedly the most eminent man in the European socialist party', the foremost in the world in his specialisation and the principal figure behind the great Roscoe-Schorlemmer textbook.[94]

In these and other letters between Engels and leading German social democrats, certain differences in the assessment of Schorlemmer can be traced: Bernstein, like Bebel, looked more to the limitations in Schorlemmer's political activity while Engels placed the emphasis on his friend's scientific greatness.[95]

For Engels, the circumstance that an acknowledged scientist had joined the revolutionary workers' movement also had purely ideological significance. Schorlemmer became a kind of human argument for the ideas of scientific socialism.

---

92   Cf. the letters from Engels to Bernstein, 23 October 1884, MECW 47:209; from Engels to Charlotte Engels, 1 December 1884, MECW 47:229; and from Engels to F.A. Sorge, MECW 47:245.

93   Letter from Bernstein to Engels, 21 December 1882, Bernstein 1970, p. 173.

94   Letter from Engels to Bernstein, 21 February 1883, MECW 46:442.

95   The differences became particularly apparent during Schorlemmer's final illness and after his death. Engels informed his party comrades in Germany of their friend's decline and death as a party matter of the first order. Cf. for example the letter from Engels to Kautsky, 11 June 1892, MECW 49:436; and 27 June 1892, MECW 49:454; and from Engels to Bebel, 20 June 1892, MECW 49:448. How deeply these men were touched by the sorrowful message is difficult to determine. Bernstein, having learned from previous missteps and always anxious to keep in with Engels, expressed his bitter sorrow but was most sorry that Engels had lost a friend. Letter from Bernstein to Engels, 2 July 1892, Bernstein 1970, p. 382 et seq. Bebel expressed primarily his satisfaction that Engels had laid a wreath at Schorlemmer's funeral, since Bebel and his closest associates had apparently not thought of it: '*und ausserdem kannten wir seine Stellung zu wenig*'. Letter from Bebel to Engels, 9 July 1892, Bebel 1965, p. 563.

7   Moore

We have every right to assume that the friendship and intense exchange of ideas with Schorlemmer played an important role in Engels's philosophical work. In particular, he had gained courage and confidence in his bold enterprise.

But beyond that we know exceedingly little. Engels's direct and personal sources of inspiration are heavily obscured.

Naturally, Engels exchanged thoughts on his activities with more than just Marx and Schorlemmer. Samuel Moore ought to be mentioned as chief among them. Moore was a lawyer in Manchester and a member of the First International as well. We have already seen how Marx could regard him and Schorlemmer both as the 'authorities' in Manchester.[96] Moore's authority primarily concerned mathematics. Marx devoted greater effort to mathematics than Engels did, and Marx also exchanged a number of ideas with Moore. It was thus with him that Marx discussed the possibilities of 'mathematically determining the main laws of the crises' – one of the key problems for Marx in his mathematical work.[97] Moore was sceptical, and Marx laid the matter aside – though only temporarily.[98] Even several years later, when Marx had worked out his great mathematical manuscript, he and Moore exchanged thoughts and even papers on questions that primarily concerned differential calculus. At that point, it took place mainly through the agency of Engels. It turned out that Marx and Moore had quite different conceptions and they were unwilling to renounce their own opinions.[99]

Engels was also periodically in contact with Moore by letter. His letters to Moore have not been preserved, while on the other hand a few letters from Moore with various bits of mathematical information and ideas were found among Engels's property.

A letter from 1875[100] shows that Engels asked Moore for advice on certain mathematical questions that were directly linked to the ones he was developing in *Dialectics of Nature* at the time.[101] Since Engels's letter has not been preserved, it is difficult to see whether Moore was correcting or supplementing Engels's conceptions. The letter deals with fictive assumptions and quantities

---

96   Above, p. 13.
97   Cf. for example Endemann 1974, p. 15.
98   Letter from Marx to Engels, 31 May 1873, MECW 44:506.
99   Cf. the letters from Engels to Marx, 21 November 1882, MECW 46:378, and from Marx to Engels, 22 November 1882, MECW 46:380.
100   *IISG Marx-Engels Nachlass*, L 5041: letter from S. Moore to Engels, 2 June 1875.
101   MECW 25:536 et seq.

in higher mathematics that so greatly interested Engels. Moore showed himself to be familiar with Engels's vocabulary when he declared: 'The origin of these imaginary expressions must be sought out historically & then their dialectical nature may be found out by a strict analysis of the circumstances wh[ich] called them into existence'.

Another letter from 1879 – which was when Engels was developing his three dialectical laws[102] – shows that Engels had continued to consult Moore on various special mathematical problems.[103]

In all likelihood, the relationships with Schorlemmer and Moore gave Engels a shot in the arm when he embarked upon special problems of natural science and mathematics. Moreover, Moore had – or obtained – the advantage of having acquainted himself in detail with the Marxian world of ideas: he had translated both the *Communist Manifesto* and (together with Edward Aveling) *Capital* into English.[104]

The people schooled in natural science with whom Engels came into immediate contact all shared his political views. This also applied to the doctors whose expert knowledge in medicine and biology expertise could have played a role for him. One of them was Paul Lafargue. We have already seen how Lafargue informed Engels of certain reactions to Schorlemmer's hypothesis about proteins.[105] Much earlier, Lafargue had given Marx some information on the positions of French physiologists on spontaneous generation – an issue that by custom interested both Marx and Engels – and Marx conveyed them to Engels.[106] The rich correspondence between Engels and Paul and Laura Lafargue[107] also testifies to Engels obtaining some benefit from Lafargue's expert knowledge in biology, though it was the socialist politician far more than the physician who appeared in these letters.

Another physician with whom Marx in particular was in close contact was Ludwig Kugelmann in Hannover. He was also extremely politically active, and it was only in passing that the correspondence between him and Marx and Engels would touch on matters of natural science.[108] We thus have no possibil-

---

102 Above, p. 323.
103 *IISG Marx-Engels Nachlass*, L 5043: letter from S. Moore to Engels, 3 July 1879.
104 Marx and Engels 1888 and Marx 1887 respectively.
105 Above, p. 358 *et seq.*
106 Letter from Marx to Engels, 9 June 1866, MECW 42:284.
107 The complete correspondence has been published by Émile Bottigelli in three volumes (Engels and Lafargue).
108 See for example the letter from Engels to L. Kugelmann, 10 July 1869, MECW 43:312.

ity of determining whether Kugelmann played any role for Engels through his expert knowledge and his contacts in Germany. We can only say that it appears unlikely.

Kugelmann, however, could provide Marx and Engels with answers to a question in another matter entirely. It concerned Joseph Dietzgen, the German tanner, who was attempting to develop a philosophy – in particular an epistemology – in connection with Marxian theory. Kugelmann could provide them with some information about who this Dietzgen was.[109]

8   Other Sources of Inspiration

Joseph Dietzgen was an amateur in all scholarly contexts. When he contacted Marx by letter in 1867,[110] he immediately aroused both Marx's and Engels's curiosity: here was a worker who was trying to develop his own philosophy. At the same time, Marx's and Engels's mutual correspondence harboured a certain amount of ambivalence. In 1868, Dietzgen sent the manuscript to his first work, *The Nature of Human Brainwork*, to Marx; after reading through it he passed it on to Engels for consultation. Marx argued that Dietzgen ought to try to summarise his thoughts in two printer's sheets – in the larger format the manuscript then had, the author embarrassed himself with his lack of 'dialectical development'.[111]

For his part, Engels was slow in responding, only delivering one when Marx hurried him.[112] Dietzgen's work was difficult to assess, Engels said. The man was self-taught; he had read Feuerbach, *Capital* and sporadic popularisations of modern natural science. His terminology was '*sehr confus*' (very confused). But there were brilliant elements and ideas in the manuscript. Engels thought it was worth six or eight printer's sheets, not just two.[113] Marx answered that he certainly thought Dietzgen had made an independent impression; it was only

---

109   Cf. the letters from Marx to L. Kugelmann, 5 and 12 December 1868, MECW 43:173 and 184 respectively.

110   The letters from Dietzgen to Marx are preserved in the *IISG Marx-Engels Nachlass*, D 1030–1041; additionally, a letter from Dietzgen to Engels is also preserved (14 November 1884, L 1158). The initial letter to Marx has been published numerous times, including Dietzgen 1911, Vol. III, p. 97 et seq. The most complete edition of Dietzgen to date is Dietzgen 1961; the letters in question are in Vol. III, p. 400 et seq. There is also a selection in Dietzgen 1973, p. 119 et seq.

111   Letter from Marx to Engels, 4 October 1868, MECW 43:121.

112   Letter from Marx to Engels, 4 November 1868, MECW 43:151.

113   Letter from Engels to Marx, 6 November 1868, MECW 43: 152.

unfortunate that he had not read Hegel.[114] (It is relevant here that Dietzgen had previously confessed his unfamiliarity with Hegel in a letter to Marx.)[115]

Dietzgen played no prominent role in Marx's and Engels's continued correspondence or writings. It was only Marx who maintained somewhat closer contact with him; on one occasion he was even Dietzgen's houseguest in Sieburg.[116] The style and tone of a letter from Dietzgen to Engels after Marx's death betrayed the fact that the both of them were not more closely personally acquainted.[117] In our case, Dietzgen the man played no role in Engels's life.

But the extent to which Dietzgen in some way influenced Engels's work is another question. Engels's best-known statement about Dietzgen's philosophy indicates a marked appreciation: it was when, in *Ludwig Feuerbach*, he declared that Dietzgen had developed a materialist dialectic entirely independent of Hegel, Marx and Engels.[118] If that statement is taken entirely seriously, it would mean that Dietzgen's philosophy would be in harmony with Engels's: developing a materialist dialectic was of course Engels's primary ambition.

It is a surprising statement. For one thing, Dietzgen's main interest was different than Engels's. Dietzgen was solely on the hunt for an epistemology in the most general sense of the word (i.e. a theory of the relation between thought and reality). Engels's epistemological efforts, as we will see later, occupied a much more modest place in his work.[119] Second, and more importantly, Dietzgen's epistemological theses were in obvious conflict with Engels's. For Dietzgen, the link between thought and its object was indissoluble; reality, in other words, was immanent in thought (which of course did not mean he was an idealist). The questions of the beginning and the end of the world were not scientific problems, since the world is the precondition of thought (through the sensuously given) but not its result.[120] For Dietzgen, in other words, 'the world' was the chaotic diversity of the sensuous, whereas the abstractions that thought produces do not in and of themselves represent this 'world'. 'In itself, the world is nothing more than the sum of its phenomena', he said.[121] It is clear that Feuerbach was Dietzgen's principal philosophical mentor. Like Feuerbach, he generally equated the material with the sensuous or the empirical. The rela-

---

114   Letter from Marx to Engels, 7 November 1868, MECW 43:154 et seq.

115   Letters from Dietzgen to Marx, 22 May/3 June 1868, *IISG Marx-Engels Nachlass*, D 1032.

116   Letter from Marx to Engels, 25 September 1869, MECW 43:353.

117   Letter from Dietzgen to Engels, 14 November 1884, *IISG Marx-Engels Nachlass*, L 1158.

118   MECW 26:384.

119   Below, p. 383 *et seq.*

120   Letters from Dietzgen to Marx, 24 October/7 November 1867, *IISG Marx-Engels Nachlass*, D 1030; and Dietzgen 1973, p. 120.

121   Dietzgen 1973, p. 36.

tion between the world and thought was just as much the relation between the empirical and the theoretical, the material and the ideal, the concrete and the abstract.[122]

Dietzgen thus ruled out the possibility of an ontology of the type that comprised Engels's main goal in *Dialectics of Nature*. An absolute condition for such an ontology is that reality can, at least temporarily, be observed without reference to the subject of knowledge, and this subject of knowledge, or thought, be regarded as a part of that reality.

It is, perhaps, an indication of a certain unawareness in Engels that he could nonetheless give Dietzgen's philosophy such whole-hearted support in a work that was a summary of his own views. More likely he did not completely recall Dietzgen's epistemology when he wrote *Ludwig Feuerbach*. His most intensive contact with it lay many years behind him. At that time, in 1868, it could have made certain philosophical problems topical for him, but it was only five years later that he tackled the task of attempting to solve them. It is possible that after 1873 he would have discovered the crucial difference between his and Dietzgen's conceptions through direct contact with Dietzgen's writings.

9 Documents and Problems

The preceding has shown that Engels only had a few direct sources of inspiration for his philosophical work. Among these, it was really only Marx to whom he ascribed more than a limited authority.

That is also to say that Engels had few opportunities to discuss, test and correct his ideas. He found the scrutiny that *Anti-Dühring* was subjected to in the German Social-Democratic Party to be of no guidance whatsoever.

In these circumstances lies one of the reasons to the lack of uniformity in his works. A number of incompatible or barely compatible lines of thought run through his texts. Very few of those he was willing to listen to debated those lines of thought with him. The fact that his works could provide the opportunity for so many interpretations – and did, in reality – was not just due to their being formally incomplete. They are incomplete on an even more fundamental plane: in their very conception.

A detailed review of Engels's immediate contacts with the scientific world of his time, however, has also yielded a result of much more far-reaching essential significance for science and the history of ideas. Its breadth cannot be fully

---

122   Cf. Pannekoek 1969, p. 46 et seq., specifically page 48.

perceived until the fundamental themes of Engels's thinking are investigated, but it can already be glimpsed here. In brief, it can be summarised thus: *the predominant problems and the fundamental ideas in a scientific or philosophical work cannot be reduced to the literary and personal contacts of the author.* The questions Engels was grappling with and the answers he tested are thus neither the sum total nor a selection of the thoughts and knowledge that he came into contact with in various ways. The broad background provided in Part Two was necessary to lay bare the nerves of what Engels was doing, and that although Engels only came into direct contact with a limited and largely haphazardly selected portion of that background. The major contradictions in nineteenth-century thinking were generally not perceptible in Engels's day; they only emerged piecemeal and incompletely. Rather, they served as kinds of theoretical or intellectual agents that defined explicit questions and standpoints without being explicit themselves. They were conditions, not results. They were found in the depths, not on the surface.

No individual thinking, like Engels's, can therefore be understood simply by placing it in relation to its various origins: Hegel, Marx, certain manifestations of nineteenth-century natural science, and so on. It needs to be put in relation to the world of problems that were also incompletely expressed in these various sources. Every author is bound in their writing to a number of assumptions that they share in common with large parts of the age they live in, which neither they nor the age they live in can completely discern. These assumptions also determine the options they have; the predominant philosophical or theoretical alternatives originate from them. The well-known circumstance that people of a certain epoch grapple with similar problems and that fundamentally similar ideas emerge in different contexts, in different sciences, in aesthetics and politics, religion and ethics cannot fully be explained by direct influence from person to person or from one field to another. Tracing these influences is important not only because they are interesting in and of themselves as examples of communication and the spread of ideas, but also because they provide us with knowledge of what the fundamental problems and alternatives are. We cannot, for example, correctly define Engels's grappling with the problems of determinism if we do not trace the various influences on him.

I am thus arguing that here, we are dealing with a universal circumstance in the history of ideas and of science.[123] It is, however, a circumstance that

---

123   Similar lines of thought have lately been advanced, above all by the structuralists; among those that have gone into the problems of the history of science and of ideas, Foucault 1966, Sebag 1964 and Althusser 1965 can be mentioned. The trouble with these authors is, as far as I can tell, that they did not carry out the detailed empirical study that must form

is rather glaringly illuminated in Engels's case. Only a strikingly small part of Engels's ideas about the sciences and their mutual connections can immediately be explained by external impulses. For example, he never makes explicit the predominant controversial issue between historicists and positivists *à la* Comte and Buckle; and it is extremely unlikely that he was clear about it himself. Nonetheless, much of what he said becomes comprehensible – and interesting – in light of this conflict over the individual versus the general. He was stand-offishly unsympathetic to the system-builders of his time, and there is everything to indicate that he familiarised himself with the systems in question to only a limited extent. Nonetheless he posed problems similar to the ones they did, encountered the same difficulties they did, and in many places the solutions he arrived at were the same. The sore point of the theory of natural selection – the contradiction between the ideal of deterministic science and non-deterministic theory – was not in his field of view, but it was nonetheless noticeable as a troubling and alluring problem for him that he had not been made conscious of.

In what follows, it will be the predominant patterns of thinking and not the scattered influences that will comprise the subject of our study.

---

the basis of the conclusion (i.e. they have not troubled themselves with the tremendous amount of impulses and sources of inspiration for one or another idea or line of thought), nor have they therefore been able to *show* that the idea (problem, line of thought, etc.) is anything other than the sum of the sources of inspiration.

Theory and Empiricism: The Three Tendencies

1　The Problem

The first and most general question that Engels's philosophical writings raises is this: What did he consider himself able to accomplish with this work that could not be done in another way? And, further: What means did he argue existed for solving such an overwhelming task? How did the dialectical method he advocated relate to the methods that were being used in the specialised sciences?

Now that we are taking up these questions, we will push one aspect – namely, the ideological – into the background for the time being. In this context, we will therefore disregard the fact that he wanted to develop a socialist worldview with his work. This was without a doubt an important, crucial reason. As a temporary preliminary measure, however, we will concentrate entirely on the internal scientific aspect. Only in this way can we generally also determine the extent to which ideology, or more specifically *the battle of the competing ideologies for science* would leave their mark on his work.

2　The Tendencies

Engels was striving for a summary, in the broadest sense, of the knowledge of his time. He thus faced the same problem as Spencer, Comte, Dühring and Hartmann: what means existed to bring together knowledge that had not already been brought together in the various specialisations? Was this primarily a passive task; in other words, was this unity already given in the sciences that were flourishing in that period? Or did it require a constructive effort beyond the purely encyclopaedic; was it a matter of interpreting and re-interpreting unmanageable material, of bringing together scattered fragments, of abolishing contradictions on a higher, more philosophical plane?

The position on these questions depended on epistemological understanding. According to a strictly empirical view, this unification was a passive task. The specialised theories comprised generalisations and observations, and the syntheses of these specialised observations were in turn only generalisations of the specialised theories. In a more rationalist world of ideas, on the other hand, both the specialised theories and the syntheses stood out as the result as well of thought operations that could not be vindicated by the observations.[1]

Engels's understanding of these difficult questions is only roughly expressed in his writings. In his scattered and approximative statements, moreover, a number of different and mutually incompatible conceptions can be traced. I will distinguish *three tendencies* that I will call, respectively, the *Hegelian*, the *positivist* and the *dialectical materialist*.[2] This is not a matter of three clearly distinguished, sharply outlined tendencies. Only a small part of what Engels said can be regarded as an immediate expression of any one tendency, and thus also as incompatible with both of the others. The tendencies can thus only be identified in a number of more extreme statements. I believe, however, that the ambiguity in Engels's works can best be presented if they are regarded as the result of not one, but three different starting points. These three starting points do not have the same importance and significance for his work – the third is the most essential by far – but in their own ways they form the work that we know only in an incomplete and unfinished form.

Let us first take as our starting point Engels's direct statements on what the scientific syntheses he was striving for could and should have been. It is therefore a question of his views on a number of comprehensive questions about the relation between theory and empirical material, theory and reality, formal and real sciences. This analysis is complicated by the fact that Engels did not use any uniform terminology. It thus assumes an encirclement of an indefinite, changing vocabulary.

3   Theory and Empirical Material: The Positivist Tendency

In several places in his works, Engels distinguished between theory, or philosophy, and empirical material, or experience. He did not attempt any more

---

1 Cf. above, p. 126 *et seq.*

2 By 'positivist tendency' here I mean the concept that all theoretical statements about reality (laws, etc.) comprise only summaries of individual observations; in other words, it is a question of a highly unqualified empiricism (I understand empiricism as such as a broader concept according to which experience comprises the starting point for theoretical work; even the dialectical materialist tendency in Engels thus appears as a manifestation of empiricism). I would like to stress that this positivist tendency is not identical to Comtesian positivism, or to the neopositivism of Mach and his followers. This positivist tendency is of course found in Comte and Mach, but Comte's positivism and Mach's neopositivism contain much more than simply a positivist view of the relation between theory and empirical material.

detailed definitions. Obviously, he assumed that the content of the terms would be well known to the reader.

But the term 'theory' occurs in his texts in two different, though closely related, meanings. On the one hand, he spoke of theories in the sense of all-encompassing views or philosophies. On the other, he spoke of specialised scientific theories.

In the latter sense he could, for example, discuss Kant's nebular theory[3] or Darwinist theory.[4] At one point, he could refer to the theory of the development of species with 'Entwicklungstheorie'.[5]

These examples could be multiplied. Nonetheless, it is clear that Engels did not particularly often speak of specialised scientific theories as 'theories' but when he did, he was adopting the prevalent vocabulary.

However, he used the word 'theory' in another, broader and vaguer meaning as well. In the Preface to *Dialectics of Nature*, he distinguished between philosophical *or* theoretical development and the development of empirical knowledge. He spoke about the 'Anschauungsweise'[6] (viewpoints) of the Greek philosophers and set it against the 'Gesamtanschauung'[7] (shared experience) that had been developed in the new natural science of the time. Here, it was a question of philosophical or theoretical creations at a very high level. According to the former, the cosmos was continuously changing; according to the latter, it remained as it had been created at one point. The natural philosophy of the Greeks was nothing more than *'geniale Intuition'* (brilliant intuition; i.e. it did not have a sufficient empirical foundation). On the other hand, the modern scientific dogma of immutability had been demolished, bit by bit, by the developments in empirical natural science *as well*. The process had been initiated as a result of Kant's nebular theory: Engels, however, unhesitatingly labelled Kant a philosopher as opposed to a natural scientist, thereby certainly asserting that the breakdown had its beginnings in thought and not in empiricism.[8] But the work was continued by empiricists such as Lyell and Darwin and many others. The immutability of the world was questioned in field after field, and the time was now ripe for a philosophical summary of these various results in empirical natural science.

---

3 MECW 25:53 et seq. and 323.
4 MECW 25:63.
5 MECW 25:493.
6 MECW 25:327.
7 MECW 25:321.
8 MECW 25:323. The strict fixing of boundaries between 'philosopher' and 'scientist' may seem peculiar today but were quite natural in Engels's time. Everything Kant did – indeed, even everything Descartes did – was therefore philosophy.

Engels's argument assumed that philosophy (or theory) and experience could be developed in relatively mutual independence. The views of the Greeks had no immediate support in empiricism, and the developments of modern empiricism were taking place despite the prevalent philosophical outlook. Lyell and Darwin were as little guided by a philosophy as Heraclitus had been guided by solid experiential knowledge.

This line of thought was not fully developed, but it unambiguously implied that properly pursued, philosophy could achieve tenable results without always being supported in experience. On the other hand, it seems that tenability could only be proven with the help of experience: only with the development of modern, empirical natural science could the 'brilliant intuition' be anything more than that.

But this argument in outline provides no clear understanding of how Engels viewed the relation of theory and empirical material, and thus how he justified his own task of synthesis. One reason for this is that he was experimenting with a simple dualism and did not distinguish between theories at various levels. He spoke as if the only general theoretical contradiction concerned the issue of the changeability or immutability of the cosmos. Faced with this question, Darwin's theory, for example, seems to clearly belong to the dialectical tradition from Heraclitus to Hegel. Since Engels nonetheless did not consider it as belonging to the development of theory but to the development of empirical material, he had to assume other qualifications for the theory as well.

Engels's conception, however, of how theory relates to experience, and philosophically elaborated theory to empirically grounded theory, is vague and contradictory. In the 'old' preface to *Anti-Dühring* (which was never used) he provided justification for his philosophical activities that squares completely with the one Ernst Haeckel provided for his own.[9] Modern empirical natural science had gathered a tremendous amount of positive knowledge, and it was now a matter of tracing and showing the inner connections among all this scattered knowledge. Like Haeckel, Engels was thus arguing that the whole of science had grown more 'in breadth' than 'in depth' during its colossal expansion in the mid-nineteenth century, and that deepening it had become an increasingly pressing task. Haeckel argued that all science – even the most myopically empirical – was guided by certain philosophical assumptions and that it was time to elucidate and systematically develop these hidden assumptions. A similar conception can be seen in Engels, even if he more strongly emphasised the dualism between philosophy (or theory) and empiricism. In

---

9 Cf. above, p. 194.

the textual context in question, he declared that it was not possible to develop the complex of natural science using 'the methods of empiricism': 'here only theoretical thinking can be of assistance'.[10]

Engels therefore seems to have assumed a clear difference between theoretical thought, which makes philosophical theories possible,[11] and empirical activities, which form the basis for specialised scientific theories. On this specific point, however, he often spoke in a contradictory manner; it is here, as we soon will see, that the contradictions between the three tendencies in his presentation are expressed the most clearly. In the same 'old preface' to *Anti-Dühring* he seems also to have assumed that the results of more theoretical and more empirical scientific activities could in principle be the same. He argued, namely, that natural science could achieve a genuine natural worldview either spontaneously (*naturwüchsig*) or by giving itself over to dialectical thinking. The latter path was shorter and safer, the goal – a correct view of nature – the same.[12] According to this line of thought, natural science could thus achieve its goal without the use of theoretical thinking.

Before we continue to investigate the connections among these various statements, however, we must face another term that is of the greatest significance in this context: the term 'system'. It is easy to imagine what Engels called 'theory' or 'philosophy' as a system in the traditional sense: a compilation of current knowledge.

The word 'system', however, had an unpleasant ring for Engels. In *Anti-Dühring* he spoke dismissively about all the systems that were sprouting up out of the ground like mushrooms in Germany. In the modern state, it was assumed that every citizen was judicious in all matters they could vote on, and in modern economics it was assumed that every buyer knew the entire product line of goods by heart. In German science, Engels said, it was similarly assumed that anyone could write about anything they had not learned.[13]

This is a criticism of systems that, in the form presented here, in all likelihood also affected Engels's own attempt at bringing various scientific fields together under one dialectical theory. But by 'system', did he also mean something different, and more, than what came out in *Anti-Dühring*?

---

10   MECW 25:339. It is not known why Engels did not use this foreword in *Anti-Dühring*; perhaps he thought it had become too long and abstruse for the polemical work. He later intended to use it in *Dialectic of Nature* (MECW 25:313).

11   The phrase 'philosophical theories' conflicts with Engels's own vocabulary, according to which *theories* were in the process of replacing *philosophies* in modern science. The area that remained for philosophy was human thought (MECW 25:26).

12   MECW 25:340.

13   MECW 25:6.

A decade later, in *Ludwig Feuerbach*, he again took up the issue of the justification of systems. Here, it concerned Hegel. Engels distinguished between
'the method' (or, more precisely, 'the method of thought') and 'the system' in
Hegel. The method was the dialectic, according to which every phenomenon
was subject to change, all fixed quantities only temporary and transitory, and
every stage achieved rapidly dissolved by the contradictions it contains. Engels
drew not only theoretical conclusions from this method; in all respects, even
politically, it is a 'revolutionary' method.

Hegel's system, on the other hand, had a conservative character. By 'system',
Engels meant here a construction in thought that was upheld with a claim
to being the 'absolute truth'. Hegel constantly pointed out, Engels said, that
the truth could only be found in the process – whether a logical or historical
process, which according to Hegel were two sides of the same coin – but nonetheless his process resulted in a final stage. As regards the logical process, he
could escape the dilemma by identifying the end of the process with its beginning. For the historical process, however, he defined a terminus: the Absolute
Idea was embodied in the monarchy of Friedrich Wilhelm III.

Engels acknowledged that the passion for systems satisfied 'an everlasting
need in the human spirit ... to overcome all contradictions'. Systems, however,
were also the most transitory part of the philosophers' works. In Hegel, the fixed
system was particularly untenable, since it conflicted openly with his thesis on
the transitory character of everything.[14]

According to Engels, what qualified a system in this context was thus not
primarily its theoretical context but the claims with which it was upheld. The
polemic against Hegel's system therefore did not immediately concern its idealism but Hegel's statement that he had encircled the Absolute with his idealistic
philosophy.

Engels had expressed the same line of thought in passing back in *Anti-
Dühring*.[15] Expressing his position on Hegel in this manner in both works –
which he single-handedly sent to the printer's – is naturally worth some attention. Similar statements are found in a few letters from the 1890s, in which
Engels attempted to summarise his and Marx's theoretical outlook.[16]

That, however, is why it is not clear where Engels drew the line between
method and system. If it is imagined that Hegel developed all his thoughts and
simply avoided asserting that any of them had anything other than a relative

---

14   MECW 26:359.
15   MECW 25:26.
16   Cf. the letters to Conrad Schmidt, 1 July 1891, MECW 49:213; and 4 February 1892, MECW
      49:239.

and transitory truth, it is nonetheless highly unlikely that Engels would have asserted that they comprised genuine expressions of the dialectical method, The relation between systems in the sense of the rounded-off whole and the actual assertions about the reality that the system contains are far more intricate than that.[17]

At the same time, it is not reasonable to identify what Engels called Hegel's system with the Hegelian idealism that Engels – like Marx – often otherwise singled out as the component in Hegel's philosophy that most clearly contrasted with their own view.[18] The same distinction between system and method found in Engels is found in many accounts. Among them, Theodor W. Adorno's *Negative Dialectics* chiefly deserves mention. Adorno's main idea is that the method as such excludes idealism: it is not possible to distinguish wither the ideal or the material as the fundamental or crucial in the process of reality; both are indissolubly linked.[19] This view also excludes the materialism that Engels advocated. (I have already attempted to show, and will soon further substantiate, that this is a crucial element in Marx's and Engels's thinking that Adorno thus disqualifies, namely that in every dialectical totality – whether society, the world, or the process of knowledge – an overall or dominant moment can be distinguished: the base, matter, and the object of knowledge respectively. This is an idea that essentially has no counterpart in Hegel.)[20]

Reconstructing a clearly profiled view in Engels from the brief and scattered statements about 'system' versus 'method', however, appears impossible. Part of the problem, naturally, is that – as previously noted – the word 'system' for Engels was negatively charged: he wanted to liberate himself from the immediate accusation of being a system-builder himself.

On the other hand, what he said about systems – both Hegel's and others' – was closely connected with one of his most crucial ideas: that there are no 'fixed categories' but that everything is part of the great process of changeability. As we have seen, it was crucial for him through all the years he sought to develop his dialectic. However, during the third period of his work – the one that began when he took up *Anti-Dühring* and ended with Marx's death – it would com-

---

17   Ernst Bloch took up the issue in his paper '*Problem der Engelsschen Trennung von "Methode" und "System" bei Hegel*' in Bloch 1973, pp. 49–69.

18   Cf. Marx in *Capital*, MECW 35:19, and Engels, for example, in MECW 25:356. The metaphor 'setting on its feet what was standing on its head' is otherwise taken from Hegel, who argued it was what philosophy needed had to do with immediate (empirical) certainty; Hegel 2:25.

19   Adorno 1966, p. 293 et seq. Cf. also Lichtheim 1971, p. 22 et seq., and above, p. 324 et seq.

20   Above, p. 68 *et seq.*, below, p. 440.

pete with the idea that it was possible to draw up general dialectical laws.[21] This ambition, which had its immediate origins in a few sporadic statements by Marx, came into obvious conflict with the thesis of changeability without the contradiction becoming obvious to Engels himself. The ambition was to state something fixed about changeability, to lock the constantly evasive object into a few inflexible patterns, to state a number of general and absolutely valid truths about reality and the process of thought.

When Engels presented the three dialectical laws that he stopped at in 1879, it showed the significance his new ambition had gained for his thinking. The laws comprised generalisations of all knowledge of nature, society and human thought. They were thus 'abstracted from the history of both nature and human society'; indeed, they were 'the most general laws for both the phases of historical development and for thought itself'.[22]

This gives the impression that the dialectical laws comprised enormously comprehensive empirical generalisations from which all laws of natural and social science could be derived. In a dialectical materialism, they would play roughly the same role as the law of gravitation in the pure mechanistic worldview.

The *positivist* element in Engels's thinking can be traced in these and similar statements. This means that the dialectical summary of knowledge does not go beyond what is given in positive knowledge: thus, the dialectic is passive. It could perhaps have a heuristic value – the connections can more easily be brought to light with its help – but it could then be completely be vindicated by all the facts accumulated in the specialised sciences. Engels expressed this conception in cleartext in the 'old preface', which contains so many contradictory lines of thought, as follows:

> We all agree that in every field of science, in natural as in historical science, one must proceed from the given *facts*; ... that therefore in theoretical natural science too the inter-connections are not to be built into the facts but to be discovered in them, when discovered to be verified as far as possible by experiment.[23]

The words 'as far as possible' could possibly be interpreted as a reservation, but it rather expresses general uncertainty. It is obvious that these ideas have a problematic relation with the thesis of fluid categories. Engels tried to screen

---

21   Above, p. 322.
22   MECW 25:356.
23   MECW 25:342.

himself off from the Hegel he was simultaneously making much use of; he did not want to be suspected of following in the tracks of the speculative idealist. In his zeal, however, he professed himself an adherent of a scientific ideal that in a superficial sense seemed to vindicate his dialectical laws but obviously conflicted with his more substantial lines of thought. Broadly, it was the scientific ideal that was advocated in the nineteenth century by hordes of philosophising scientists with John Herschel and Emil du Bois-Reymond at their head and was developed in the sphere of system-building philosophy by the leading positivists such as Comte and Buckle. According to this ideal, the perfect science was distinguished by a series of harmonically linked processes of induction and deduction: a number of general statements is drawn from experiential material, and these general statements are then tested on newer and greater experiential material. Ironically enough, this was a scientific ideal that was also accepted in its essentials by the classical liberal economists. In this field, it was affected by not only Marx's, but also Engels's, criticism. Its incompatibility with the Marxian theory of society became apparent here. When the dialectical laws came up, their character was not as transparent. The very concept of law would have its consequences for Engels's thinking.

4   The Hegelian Tendency

It may seem peculiar that it is also in the development of the thesis of dialectical laws that the second, apparently contradictorily opposite *Hegelian tendency* emerges. But the relation is not a mysterious one. The dialectical laws did not apply only to the history of humanity and nature but also to the history of thought. Engels argued that Hegel had correctly grasped the dialectic of thought, and his mistake consisted in regarding this dialectic of thought as primary in relation to the dialectic of reality. As we have already seen, Engels argued that he had taken the three laws of dialectics from Hegel.[24] When he entered the sphere of logic, he also followed in Hegel's tracks, though the term 'dialectical law' is Marx's construction, not Hegel's.

The codification of three dialectical laws is also incomprehensible if it is not viewed against the background of the old conception – effectively obliterated first through Gottlob Frege[25] – that logic could be summarised in a number of *laws of thought*. These were laws for thinking, or – if you will – sum-

---

24   MECW 25:356. Cf. above, p. 323.
25   See e.g. Wedberg 1984, p. 111 et seq.

mary descriptions of how human thought comes into being. The traditional
Aristotelian logic, which Engels called 'purely formal' after Hegel, would thus
contain laws in a double sense: both rules for thinking and generalisations of
how thinking actually comes into being. The boundary between logic and the
psychology of thought (and even more so between logic and epistemology) was
thus a fluid one.

Custom distinguished three different laws of thought. These were the law of
identity ($a = a$), the law of contradiction (there cannot be both a and not-a),
and the law of double negation (a = not not-a). By being regarded as laws of
thought, they gained a kind of quasi-empirical content. The law of identity, a
being equal to a, meant not only that a could be replaced with a but also that
in correct thinking, the thought of a (any quantity whatsoever) was always the
same. It was thus not a question of a real empirical generalisation; it did not
apply to everything but only to correct human thinking. But with a traditional
and questionable concept of essence, however, it could be understood as a generalisation about human beings, of whom incorrect thinking naturally was not
a part.[26]

Hegel opposed the idea that thinking came into being this way. Again and
again, he took up the idea of laws of thought and relegated them to a 'purely
formal' sphere, devoid of content.[27] Real logic – the one that shows how thinking comes into being – cannot assume any laws of thought, he declared.[28] That
would be separating form from content, which could be done in the other sciences but not in logic.

It deserves to be pointed out that Hegel, unlike Engels, thus did not attempt
to set up any alternative laws for thought; this is yet more proof of how foreign
the idea of dialectical laws was to him.

But Hegel was not content with showing that real thinking conflicted with
laws of thought in the sense that every thought process worked with changing,
often contradictory content when attempting to find a way toward new results.
The circumstance that a is not always a in thought, no more than a dandelion
bud is the same as a dandelion in full bloom, also has consequences in formal
logic for Hegel. He demonstrates the mistake lying in the very idea of laws of
thought, but commits the opposite mistake of believing that this somehow
influences the circumstance that a bachelor is a bachelor. Traditional formal
logic thus applied to some lower, static form of thinking; dialectical logic would

26   Kusch 1995 provides a popular account on this topic.
27   See e.g. Hegel 2:233 et seq. (*Phenomenology of Spirit*).
28   Hegel 4:36 (*Science of Logic*).

not only reveal how to achieve great philosophical and scientific results but also influence the formal operations that presuppose symbols of negation and of equality.[29]

Here, Engels directly and abruptly takes over the essential aspects from Hegel. There are, he said, two different disciplines of thought: 'formal logic and the dialectic'.[30] Formal logic applies to lower, classificatory and everyday thinking; the dialectic to thinking that leads to real, comprehensive knowledge.

Engels also took over very simple errors from Hegel. For Hegel, statements of the type 'The book is red' are contrary to the law of identity, since a book is not identical with the colour red.[31] Engels repeated the mistake.[32] Here, it concerns a confusion of different meanings of 'is'. The statement 'the book is red' has nothing to do with identity; it has the form 'a is F' (or, put more simply, Fa) and not '$a = a$'.

In contrast to Hegel, however, Engels also attempted to formulate the alternate dialectical laws of thought. We can easily see that the second and third dialectical laws correspond to the second and third 'formal' laws of thought. The law of contradiction in Hegel corresponds to the old law of contradiction, and the law of the negation of the negation corresponds to the law of double negation.

The law of quality and quantity, on the other hand, occupies a more precarious position.[33] Before Engels began developing the idea of dialectical laws, he spoke about '*Identität und Unterschied*' (identity and difference) as one of the 'primary contradictions'.[34] At that time, it was not at all a question of creating any counterparts to the laws of thought – the other primary contradictions were necessity and chance, and cause and effect – but obviously '*Identität und Unterschied*' could form a counterpart to the law of identity. Now, instead, it became quantity and quality, and the reason is naturally that Marx codified precisely this law in *Capital*. On the contrary, the law as formulated emerges as a special case of the second dialectical law: the dialectical unity between quantity and quality is an example of the unity of opposites.[35] Only in a very

---

29   On this topic, cf. above all the 'Foreword' to the second edition of *Science of Logic*, Hegel 4:20–35.

30   MECW 25:26.

31   Hegel 8: § 126 et al.

32   MECW 25:496.

33   Above. p. 323.

34   MECW 25:497.

35   One person who clearly realised this and otherwise commented less formally on the three laws is Mao Zedong. One of his comments has been reproduced thus: 'The unity of oppos-

figurative sense can it be understood as a counterpart to the law of identity, namely if qualities and quantities are regarded as identical to themselves in some way (in the way that $2+2$ is identical with 4 or 'green' is identical with 'a mixture of blue and yellow'). Now, it turned out that in laying out the content of the law of quantity and quality, Engels was speaking in terms of contradiction and not of identity. It was in general the law he devoted the most study to: in *Anti-Dühring* it was explicated more sparingly than the law of the negation of the negation (9½ printed pages against 13), but in the incomplete section on 'Dialectics' in *Dialectics of Nature* it was the only one Engels commented on before he broke off his presentation, which was about five pages long. It is striking that Engels chose very few examples from the formal sciences when he attempted to explain the content of the law.[36] It appears, therefore, that it constituted a law of thought in only a secondary sense, or – as Engels said, in glaring contrast to Hegel's vocabulary[37] – a law in 'so-called *objective* dialectics'.[38]

Even if the equivalence between Engels's three dialectical laws and the old laws of thought is incomplete, it is nonetheless obvious that the laws of thought comprised the model for the enumeration he made in the manuscript from 1879. Even if the enumeration as such conflicts with Hegel's intentions, it is also clear that Engels essentially followed in Hegel's footsteps in his presentation of logic.

5   The Dialectical Materialist Tendency

It is therefore reasonable to speak of two opposing tendencies in Engels's thinking: a positivist and a Hegelian. Both emerge primarily in his development of the dialectical laws, the one in its application to nature and humanity, the other in its application to thought. Engels's chief ambition was to unite classical, mechanistic materialism with the dialectic developed by Hegel the idealist. In their own ways, both tendencies were attempts to realise that ambition. At the

---

ites is the most basic law, the transformation for quality and quantity into one another is the unity of the opposites of quality and quantity, and the negation of the negation does not exist at all'. Mao Zedong 1974, p. 226.

36   This actually occurs only in *Anti-Dühring* (MECW 25:112), where he says that it is a contradiction that a root of a should be a power of a such that $a^{\frac{1}{2}} = \sqrt{a}$ and that calculations with imaginary numbers ($\sqrt{-1}$) are possible.

37   The task of the dialectic, according to Hegel, is to overcome the contradiction between subjective and objective, between thought and reality; cf. for example Hegel 4:60 et seq.

38   MECW 20:492.

same time, however, the unity was difficult to achieve: Engels had to resort to the idea that thought, which came into being à la Hegel, 'reflected' the reality that was described in positivist generalisations of accumulations of facts. We will return to this 'reflection theory' later. As it will turn out, this would not be Engels's only idea in this context.

Both tendencies thus constituted attempts to reason with a number of large problems that were difficult to master. It concerned the general epistemological question of the relation between the subject of knowledge and its object. But it also concerned more precisely scientific problems that were linked to this question. It concerned the relation between scientific theories and the reality those theories sought to explain; it thus also concerned the relation between theory and empirical material and among various scientific theories themselves. It especially concerned the great all-reconciling dialectical theory that Engels was busy trying to develop. We have already seen how Engels, in the face of this latter task, expressed himself in a contradictory manner: now formulating his argument so that empirical study could achieve the results of the comprehensive theory on its own, now saying that theory, or 'theoretical thinking', was a necessary condition for empirical study (or, rather, for a correct interpretation of the empirical material).

I would also assert, however, that there is every reason to speak of a third, more original tendency that for the sake of simplicity I will call *dialectical materialist*. It is an outflow of what was obviously Engels's main ambition, namely to enrich traditional – or what he called 'mechanical' – materialism[39] with a dialectic that had its immediate origins in Hegel's philosophy. It scarcely needs to be added that this was also compatible with another ambition, namely setting historical materialism in a more general scientific perspective.

To get at the heart of this tendency, we must – as a preliminary measure – make a distinction that Engels himself would scarcely have been willing to make. We must distinguish between the epistemological and scientific theoretical aspect and the ontological aspect of Engels's work.[40] We recently saw that there were a number of different, though closely related, problems that Engels had posed. On the one hand, they belong to epistemology and scientific

---

39 For example MECW 25:532.

40 As is known, nor is any such distinction found in Hegel. With him, one leading thought – not to say *the* leading thought – is that at bottom the process of knowledge, or the path from pure observation to absolute knowledge, is the same path as that of ontology from pure spirit via pure material to the absolute being. He attempted to follow the former in *Phenomenology of Spirit* and the latter above all in *Science of Logic*. The problems, however, had to be completely different for Engels the materialist.

theory. On the other, they concern the connections among various scientific theories. Since Engels, by virtue of his understanding of knowledge, asserted that knowledge corresponded to its object in one sense or another, however, the question of the mutual relations of the theories will also become a question about reality – and therefore an ontological question. If it is assumed that various scientific theories – at least temporarily – correspond to reality, then an image of the various levels of reality (or 'forms of motion', as Engels said) can be constructed using these theories.

There is thus a connection between epistemology and ontology in Engels, and later it will be shown that it is more fundamental than is indicated in what has so far been presented. At the same time, however, both must be kept separate. As we have seen, Engels distinguished between a subjective and an objective dialectic, where what he called 'thought' represented the subjective dialectic. As far as I can see, however, he spoke about three different aspects of thought, namely:

a. thought as a mental process, and a process of cerebral physiology;
b. thought as a historical process (the history of thought was part of human history); and
c. thought as a true or false conception (knowledge or illusion) of reality.

Engels spoke relatively little about thought in the first sense. When he defined thought as the highest form of matter in motion, he likely had this meaning in mind,[41] and this is completely obvious when he spoke about the molecular and chemical processes in the brain that form the basis of thought.[42] The history of thought, and of science in particular, played a prominent role in Engels's philosophical writings; *Dialectics of Nature* included an unfinished section titled 'From the History of Science', and scientific historical viewpoints also predominated in the Preface.

But from both these meanings it is important to separate the one according to which thought 'corresponds'[43] or 'tallies with'[44] – or simply comprises 'reflections'[45] of – objective reality. There are, of course, always important connections between thought in this meaning and the other two, above all in that humanity's possibilities of attaining knowledge is determined by their

---

41   MECW 25:362. It should be emphasised, however, that for Engels even the history of humanity was a movement and that this 'form of movement' also includes thought as a (subordinate) part.
42   MECW 25:527.
43   MECW 25:34.
44   MECW 25:544.
45   MECW 25:24.

biological properties and by historical circumstances. But for these relations to be elucidated in general, the various links in the relations must be distinguished.[46]

Thought in the first two meanings belongs to ontology, whereas the third sense falls under epistemology. The difference between ontology and epistemology is a necessary condition for Engels's realism regarding knowledge. Positing an identity between the first and third senses presumes – provided a mystical correspondence between 'thought' and 'being' is not assumed – various auxiliary constructions; in this context, for example, Engels cited the hypothesis that acquired thought is passed on by heredity. If the second and third senses are assumed to be identical – which has actually happened in the history of Marxism[47] – realism in knowledge becomes absolutely meaningless: for something to appear as knowledge, as truth, depends entirely on the historical situation and not on the object of knowledge.

In short: false ideas, like true ideas, are biologically and historically conditioned.

6   The Dialectic of Knowledge

What we will be outlining here first of all is the dialectical materialist tendency in Engels's conception of knowledge and science. This outline would have been easier if there had been a developed mechanical materialist view in the specific questions Engels had turned to. Mechanical materialism for Engels was primarily eighteenth-century French materialism and the form of materialism that in the mid-nineteenth century would be represented by Germans such as Vogt and Büchner. Engels called the latter orientation 'vulgar materialism'.[48] The distinction between honourable materialists, who stood at the apex of the knowledge of their time, and the vulgar materialists, who went no further than their mentors despite the new scientific insights,[49] was obviously

---

46 In fact, Engels let the different meanings flow completely together. Naturally, only the true idea (objective knowledge) can be said to 'reflect' its object; but when Engels spoke about the counterpart of reality in the idea, he seems to also be asserting that since knowledge (thought) in general has its origins in objective reality, it cannot 'contradict' it either (MECW 25:34). Here it is therefore a question of both true and false ideas; both types have their origin in objective, biological or historical circumstances.

47 So it becomes almost as if truth is only determined as a 'correct class standpoint'.

48 For example MECW 25:341.

49 MECW 25:475 et seq.

modelled after Marx's distinction between classical economists such as Smith and Ricardo and the later vulgar economists.[50]

In fact, this link to Marx says more than it immediately lets on. The shortcoming in the classical liberal economists, according to Marx, was that their conceptual apparatus, and thereby their entire theoretical construction, was such that the transition from one form of production to another was *a priori* ruled out; so, for example, 'capital' was defined in such a way that capitalism appeared as an eternal and unchanging form of production. Among the classical economists, this shortcoming corresponded to one in the development of the economic reality of the time. The vulgar economists preserved this shortcoming without taking into account what was new and emerging in economic reality.[51]

According to Engels, the eighteenth-century materialists were similarly incapable of explaining how matter could assume so many different forms, since for them matter was only mechanical matter. The vulgar materialists of the time were vulgar because they did not take nineteenth-century developments in the natural sciences, which pointed beyond mechanical materialism with its 'metaphysical', or undialectical, padlocking of categories.[52]

The comparison with Marx shows that the very patterns of thought that Engels used were precisely those that Marx had developed in a different sphere entirely. On the other hand, it is clear that when Engels brought knowledge up for discussion, he often expressed himself in a way that made him a deserving target of his own criticism of mechanical materialism. When he spoke in the same breath about thought in the sense of cerebral physiological processes and the sense of knowledge of reality, he was following in the footsteps of the traditional materialists, whose main problem concerned the old issue of body and soul and whose main ambition was to show that the soul was not separate from the body but ultimately a product of the matter that comprised the body. They had also developed some epistemological ideas, however; the most representative of them was a far-reaching sensualism according to which all knowledge was 'images', or 'reflections' of external, sensuous reality.[53] Engels was one of their adherents, both when he spoke about knowledge as a reflection and when in scattered statements he asserted that all knowledge traced back to direct observations of reality. He also followed in their footsteps when he spoke about thought as a psychophysical process and knowledge in the same sentence.

---

50   Cf. above, p. 44.
51   On this topic, see also Therborn 1974.
52   MECW 25:475 et seq.
53   Cf. Wilson 1972, p. 228 et seq.

In Lenin's *Materialism and Empiriocriticism*, where general questions of epistemology were at the centre of attention to a far greater extent than in Engels, reflection theory was even more resolutely supported. Lenin consistently paid more unreserved tribute to older materialism than Engels ever did.[54]

One thing is obvious: when Engels or Lenin described knowledge as merely a reflection, they yielded to the exact mechanical, 'metaphysical', undialectical mode of thinking that Engels otherwise thoroughly polemicised against. The subjective (knowledge) and the objective (reality) were perceived literally as fixed, complete categories that stood in unchanging relation to one another.

The same mode of thinking characterises the statements by Engels where he defined correct theories as generalisations of individual facts (continuing with the metaphorical language, it could be said that Engels here regarded theories as 'reflections' of facts).

These ideas also came into obvious conflict with the central lines of thought in both Marx and Engels about the *interaction* between theory and praxis, where theory always had to be confirmed by praxis, it is true, but where praxis could not be developed without theory.[55] Engels clearly stated that he regarded empirical studies, including the experiment, as a type of praxis.[56]

The contradiction in Engels's general conception of knowledge was also expressed in his various statements about the development of knowledge. *If* knowledge is a reflection of its object, then knowledge is conclusive and complete on the day that the correct reflection is established. *If* theory absolutely comprises a summary of the observations that can be derived from it, knowledge is similarly conclusive and complete on the day that all the correct observations have been made. Both ideas thus open up the possibility of complete knowledge.

Engels also sometimes spoke as if he imagined such a terminus for scientific development. He could, for example, say that the principle of conservation of energy represented conclusive knowledge: only more substantiation and richer content could be imagined (that is, more facts cast in the same mould).[57]

---

54   Cf. in particular Lenin 14:238 et seq., where Lenin directly takes up Engels's criticism of eighteenth-century French materialists. He reproduces the three critical comments Engels has against classical materialism and draws the conclusion that Engels (like Marx) *in all other respects* agrees with it. Worthy of note is also the role Lenin gives to a number of quotes from Diderot in his own argument; ibid., p. 27 et seq.

55   Cf. below, p. 394 *et seq.*

56   The most explanatory place in the text is *Ludwig Feuerbach*, MECW 21:367.

57   MECW 25:503.

But in other contexts, he pointed out that knowledge could never be absolute or complete. He likened the development to infinite asymptotic progress.[58] Elsewhere, he declared that knowledge was biologically relative – in other words, it was always linked to the human biological constitution, the senses, the brain and so on – and even more important is his remark that knowledge is always influenced by the historical situation in which it developed.[59] All these statements thus contradict the idea of absolute, complete knowledge.

A radical and simple trick now would be to push the entire reflection theory aside and instead give oneself up to relativism.[60] If knowledge reflects anything, it does not reflect reality but human biological limitations and the limitations of the historical situation.

But that would be avoiding one evil by throwing oneself into the arms of something equally as evil.

When Engels spoke out of hand about thought in at least three different senses, he thereby naturally aroused confusion among his readers. On the other hand, it is entirely natural, based on his starting points, that he constructed various aspects of the phenomenon he indicated with the single word 'thought'. We can only regret that he did not investigate the relation among these aspects in more detail.

As I understand it, we are dealing here namely with a central example of a *dialectical relation* in a more precise meaning. We can formulate three statements:

a.   Human knowledge is entirely dependent on humanity's physical and mental constitution.
b.   Knowledge of reality is entirely dependent on the historical circumstances under which it is produced.
c.   Knowledge about reality provides a true image of reality itself.

These statements, as formulated, are incompatible: they *contradict* each other. But each of them can be perceived as immediately 'true'. The only knowledge that is accessible to us is human knowledge. As science developed, humanity was able to expand the reach of their senses through numerous instruments and apparatuses, and the tool of thought could be refined as well. But humanity is always the starting point, and just as we can naturally imagine that human-

---

58   MECW 25:515.
59   MECW 25:518 and 339, respectively.
60   Historical relativism, at least, is well represented in the Frankfurt School; cf. above, p. 45 *et seq.*

ity's image of the world is more correct and richer than that of the ant or the giraffe, we can – like Laplace – imagine an entity far more intelligent than humanity that has overcome its physical and mental limitations.

In early neo-Kantianism – the only neo-Kantianism Engels could have had any intimate knowledge of – there were ideas that opened up in that direction, though they were drawing the boundaries for human understanding. In his *Geschichte des Materialismus*, Friedrich Albert Lange – with whom Engels was well familiar[61] – concluded that science had never gotten any further than a methodical materialism; the world we can observe and measure and create theories about is a world that is arranged by human understanding but not the world in itself, the 'thing in itself'.[62] Engels mentioned neo-Kantianism in passing, and it is likely he had Lange's variant in mind. Naturally he was negatively disposed toward this total relativisation of knowledge.[63]

The thesis that knowledge is historically relative has its immediate support in the obvious circumstance that knowledge is historically changeable. From a historical materialist perspective, it becomes even more reasonable: if the history of all hitherto existing society is the history of class struggle, is the history of knowledge also not a history of class struggle? Both Engels and Marx proclaimed that the development of science had its basis in the development of production.[64] The tendency towards historical relativisation was also noticeable – if even stronger – in the historicist tradition. Hegel had said that the owl of Minerva spreads its wings only with the falling of the dusk: we know that the world changes, and we know that knowledge changes, but we cannot make any predictions.[65] Historicists of a later and less wide-embracing generation often went even further along the same path.[66]

At the same time, however, scientific development has been perceived ever since the propagation of optimism in progress as a development toward ever better knowledge of reality. An old theory has to give way to a new one because the new one better reflects reality. If this process of advance is extrapolated into the future, conclusive and complete knowledge can be imagined in the years to come. As we have seen, this idea is entirely natural to numerous materialists and many others. What stood in the way of good scientific knowledge was primarily various prejudices, and secondly lingering deficiencies in the

---

61   Cf. above, p. 15.
62   See above all Lange 1866, p. 498 et seq., and Lange 1876, Vol. II, p. 428 et seq.
63   MECW 25:341.
64   Cf. for example *The German Ideology*, MECW 5:39 et seq.; *Grundrisse*, Marx 1953, p. 439.
65   Hegel 7:37.
66   On this topic, see Iggers 1972, p. 39.

empirical means for science. Knowledge worthy of the name is only a passive reflection of reality: if the mirror is kept clean, the complete image will emerge.

A dialectical materialist conception of knowledge worthy of the name contains a combination of these three perspectives. Allowing any one of them to reign supreme puts us in an untenable position: subjectivism, historical relativism or mechanical materialism.

In their contradictoriness, however, Engels's sporadic statements show that he was not clear in his conception. When he spoke about knowledge in general, he was so anxious about ending up close to the Hegelian idealism that he repeatedly expressed himself as if he were an advocate of a pure reflection theory. Knowledge, the subjective moment, appeared as a passive element.

But there is something else to keep in mind here. What distinguished the dialectic that Marx and Engels developed from Hegel's lay not only on the level of content but also of form. It was not just – as Marx and Engels were sometimes tempted to believe[67] – that they were replacing Hegelian idealism with materialism. By imagining a dominant or overall moment – or a moment 'in the last instance', as Engels said[68] – they were breaking with a formal fundamental principle in Hegel.

When Marx and Engels introduced this dialectical innovation, they were of course talking about society and its historical development. They thus laid out their dialectical conception of history. There were, however, many good reasons to assume a fundamental *structural similarity* between the conception of history, the conception of knowledge and ontology (we will return to this last one). The reasons do not emerge in their general statements about what knowledge is but in their treatment of scientific theories, both their own and others'.

When Marx and Engels spoke about an overall moment in the dialectical totality of society, they emphasised that this moment – material production, or the base – appeared as an overall moment only in the most abstract part of the theory: the part dealing with the general context and tendency of society and social development. Going a step further in the theory, the relation among the various moments instead emerge as a relation of *reciprocal action*. We can thus distinguish two different levels: level 1, at which a moment – let us say moment a – is the overall and determinant moment in the dialectical totality $(a, b, c,$ and $d)$ and level 2, at which the various moments in the same totality mutually influence and determine each other.[69]

---

67   Cf. above, pp. 71, 93.

68   Cf. below, p. 441 *et seq.*

69   The question of various causal connections in Marxian theory was taken up for treatment in Soviet and East German literature in particular. There it was usually said that it was

We are dealing here not only with Marx's and Engels's most sweeping attempt to reveal succinctly the heart of the materialist conception of history. They were dealing not only with social reality but also the theoretical, scientific method itself of assimilating reality.

If we now look more closely at the theory they were propagandising for, we immediately find that *the specific theory is incompatible with the thesis that a correct theory reflects reality*. We would obtain different reflections at level 1 and at level 2.

The theory is also incompatible with the thesis that scientific theories can immediately be reduced to 'facts' (i.e. to empirical observations). The same observations must form the foundation for both level 1 and level 2, but they thus appear in different lights at both levels.

Marx had in fact elucidated certain fundamental features in his view of the relation between reality and theory in the preface to the *Grundrisse*, where he stressed that the result of theoretical work was a product of 'the head', not directly of reality. He objected to Hegel's thesis that reality reflected thought, but also rejected the opposite idea that thought provided a reflection of reality. He showed concretely that the development of knowledge – contrary to what Hegel had asserted – could appear entirely different than that of reality. It was thus only in developed capitalist society that the abstract category of 'labour' could be elucidated in political economy. It was therefore also only from this latter viewpoint that the previous modes of production were comprehensible.[70]

Marx thus asserted that there was a fundamental *asymmetry* between theory and the reality that the theory intended to explain. This is the same idea that recurs in the well-known distinction between method of research and method of presentation in *Capital*. In research, the diversity of material is processed,

---

important to distinguish between a 'deeper', 'more concrete' causal connection and a more superficial, more abstract one; it is possible, but not entirely a given, to interpret these statements in agreement with the interpretation cited here. Cf. for example Ilyenkov 1969, p. 87 et seq. and Zelený 1970, p. 109 et seq. The mode of expression used here goes directly back to Engels's own in the letter to Joseph Bloch, 22/22 September 1890, MECW 49:34. Between these well-known statements and Marx's own clarifications in the introduction to the *Grundrisse* on the relation between production, distribution, etc. there is a great deal of similarity; Marx 1953, p. 20 et seq. Marx also differentiates between a plane of interaction and one on which a dominant (*übergreifendes*) moment can be distinguished. the similarities between both these central statements by Marx and Engels, by all appearances formulated independently of each other and separated by 33 long years, has not previously been noted; for those who assert that there is an essential difference between Marx's and Engels's views, similar extremely central similarities must feel embarrassing.

70   Marx 1953, p. 21 et seq.

and only when this process is complete can the scientific presentation begin. In the presentation, the real process is reflected *ideally*, and it may seem that it is dealing with an '*a priori* construction'.[71] It can thus be seen here how Marx made use of the term 'reflection' in a literal manner: it is not a question of a real but of an 'ideal' reflection; reality does not have the *a priori* nature it seems to have according to the theory.

Here, Marx was dealing with a problem that had occupied philosophers for ages and had particularly influenced Kant's theoretical philosophy. The problem ultimately concerned the relation between an axiomatic theory – thus a complete '*a priori* construction' – and the reality the theory is commenting on. In Newton's mechanics (to choose the best-known example), all the assertions follow from a number of axioms and definitions, but these assertions comment on definite processes in reality. Kant's theory of the various types of judgements are essentially an attempt at overcoming the dilemma: Newtonian mechanics dealt with reality because its assertions were synthetic, but the assertions can be derived from a number of axioms and definitions and are therefore *a priori*.[72]

Marx thus touched upon the same problem. The Kantian solution was obviously foreign to him, but he sided in general with the tradition initiated, it could be said, by Kant that ascribes thought – and therefore theory – an *active* role in relation to the reality to be explained. Thought must process and transform its material to attain theories about reality, and when these theories are to be applied to that same reality, a number of transformations of a rather complex type are required. But in the view of the latter part of the process, Marx's conception differs tangibly from Kant's and lies much closer to Hegel's. Also to the point is that Kant has Newton's theory in mind, and Marx his own about capital. For Kant, the path from abstract theory to specific assertion appears as a purely formal process; for Marx, on the other hand, it is a creative process in which the more concrete assertions contain new moments that cannot be derived from the more abstract ones.

Here, Marx thus comes close to Hegel's ideas about a dialectical logic.[73] The relation between formal knowledge (mathematics and logic) and material

---

71   MECW 35:19.

72   The most explanatory account of Kant's problems to my knowledge is Popper 1972, p. 93 et seq.

73   Hegel's most pregnant comments on the dialectic can be found in *Phenomenology of Spirit* (Hegel 2:35) and in *Science of Logic* (see in particular Hegel 4:50 et seq. and 5:531 et seq.). The crucial similarity lies in Marx, like Hegel, regarding the development of a given (abstract) thesis as innovative via the dialectic (i.e. the thesis appears, when applied

knowledge is perceived as ambiguous. Material knowledge – knowledge about reality – cannot be derived from the formal as the rationalists had imagined, but at the same time it requires far-reaching mathematical formalisation for advanced knowledge of at least certain parts of this reality. In his views on mathematics, however, Marx goes far beyond Hegel and his immense *Mathematical manuscripts* (first published in 1968) have very little to do with Hegel. Hegel had viewed the mathematisation of science as a matter purely for the 'lower' sciences: with its help one could arrive only at an 'intellectual understanding' of reality in its simplest, most abstract forms of appearance.[74] Marx, on the other hand, saw it as a general problem, of urgent importance for his own theoretical work.

The general viewpoint that unites Hegel and Marx (and Engels) is that there is no established gap between the formal and the material, and thus no gap between analytical and synthetic. Using modern terminology, it could be said that they advocated a *gradualist* standpoint.[75] The more tangible similarities end there, however.

There is no justification here for going into more detail on Marx's *Mathematical manuscripts*, which otherwise has recently been the subject of a number of penetrating, if also not completely unanimous, explications.[76] Very generally it could be said that according to Marx, it is the dialectic that abolishes the contradiction between form and content. Essential processes can, of course, be elucidated in the purest mathematical terms. For Marx, a far-reaching mathematisation of his social theory was also a goal.[77] The reality to be described and explained, however, is not exhausted by exact theory. The best formula

---

to more concrete material, to have a broader content than could emerge purely formally from its abstract formulation). The difference between Marx and Hegel in their views of the dialectic can be expressed as follows: that Hegel's distinction between understanding and (dialectical) reason has no significance for Marx; in is primarily to a typical 'theory of understanding' in Hegel's meaning – political economy – that Marx applies the principles of the dialectic. In Hegel, the dialectic is primarily a philosophical matter; in Marx, it is a matter for empirical work with scientific theories.

74   Hegel deals exhaustively with mathematical issues in his *Science of Logic* (Hegel 4:293–389). His most explanatory comments on mathematics as a 'science of understanding' can be found in *System of Philosophy*; see in particular Hegel 9:84.

75   For a presentation and discussion of modern gradualist theories, see Nordenstam 1972.

76   Among the works published after the publication of the mathematical manuscripts (Marx 1968), Yanovskaya 1969 and Endemann 1974 deserve particular mention. Interesting viewpoints can also be found in Witt-Hansen 1973, above all p. 92. Among older accounts, the essay of the famous historian of mathematics Struik 1948 deserves special attention. Cf. also Colman 1931 and 1933.

77   Cf. for example the letter from Marx to Engels, 31 May 1873, MECW 44:504.

leaves something out of the calculation. If we say that $a = b$, there is nonetheless something in a that is *not* equal to b and that consequently cannot be defined through the formula. Wolfgang Endemann, one of the specialists in Marx's *Mathematical manuscripts*, calls this undefined superfluity the intensional side of the relation between a and b.[78]

Naturally, Marx was not arguing that we should be patient with this 'intensionality'. We must look further for even better mathematical aids. But the possibility of complete mathematisation is ruled out in advance.

Marx's understanding influenced his view of the use of mathematics in the material sciences. Mathematical calculations must be made 'operative' (i.e. adapted to the sphere of reality where they are to be used).[79] It is natural that he devoted particular attention to differential calculus: processes, and thus infinitely small changes, can be defined and calculated there. The numeral o here is not a symbol for 'nothing' but for 'the infinitely small' – a characteristically favourite category of the dialectic.[80]

What Engels said about mathematics in *Anti-Dühring* and *Dialectics of Nature* appears to be a pale reflection of Marx's voluminous manuscript and, moreover, a few reflections from Hegel's thoughts on mathematics.[81] Part of what he said seems completely odd – for example, that the formula $-a \times -a = a^2$ was an example of the negation of the negation. In the same investigation, another example of the negation of the negation appears, taken directly from Marx, concerning the formula $\frac{dx}{dy} = \frac{0}{0}$.[82] A significant portion of Engels's comments, however, concern the origins of mathematics: it emerged from humanity's practical needs.[83] He devoted even greater attention to the thesis that the object of mathematics had its counterpart in the sensuous world; it was that the phenomenon that so many connections in objective reality allowed themselves to be subjected to mathematical treatment and calculation that led to the conclusion that reality itself must somehow be mathematically arranged.[84] Marx's

---

78   Endemann 1974, pp. 12, 34 et seq.

79   Yanovskaya 1969, p. 26.

80   On this topic, see for example Marx 1974, p. 51 et seq.

81   Engels had plans to publish Marx's mathematical manuscripts (or at least parts of them); MECW 25:13.

82   MECW 25:127 et seq., cf. Marx 1974, p. 51 et seq.

83   MECW 25:6 et seq., 465.

84   In particular MECW 25:544 et seq., cf. also p. 37 et seq. The mistake of believing that the mathematics used in scientific theories is applied directly to reality, thereby implying that reality is mathematically ordered has a long and glorious history. It also played a role for the argument that the human sciences were not mathematisable and thus essentially separate from the (exact) natural sciences, since the world of humans could not be the

thesis was vulgarised thus: according to Marx, mathematical expressions were in no way representations, and reality could only be *approximated* in a theory, mathematical or otherwise.

7   Theory and Reality

It is clear that Marx's comments on the relation between theory and reality – and thus between theory and empirical studies – were both more comprehensive and more nuanced than Engels's. Marx naturally denied neither that theoretical tools had their origins in humanity's practical business nor that the human brain and capacity for thought were part of objective reality, but he was never tempted to summarise his findings in any statement that theory – if correct – simply reproduced objective reality. The difference, of course, depended to some extent on Engels having so many different theories in mind while in return not being busy with developing a special theory in detail, as Marx had been doing. Engels's sphere was so immensely vast that he was tempted by gross simplifications.

This does not prevent us, however, from noticing in Engels – though more a tendency than a finished programme – a dialectical view of knowledge; in fact, this unfinished dialectic is the condition for his entire enterprise with *Dialectics of Nature*.

Between this dialectical view and the understanding of the relation between base and superstructure that both Marx and Engels expressed there is a striking *structural similarity*. We can distinguish three moments that determine knowledge and the development of knowledge: humanity's physiological and mental equipment, social circumstances, and the object of knowledge. We can call them a, b, and c and say that they comprise the dialectical totality (a, b, c). In fact, we could distinguish several more moments. We could, for example, distinguish between different types of social and historical circumstances (i.e. between material and ideological). We could bring out the special relation between b and c in a study of the human sciences, since society and its devel-

---

foundation for figures and equations. See Bunge 1973, p. 131 et seq. The idea that mathematisability says something about the nature of reality (i.e. that reality must be ordered in accordance with mathematical tools) has probably more often formed the basis for religious, mystical or generally idealist discourses (e.g. God created both reality and our capacity for knowledge, and ensured that there was harmony between them) than for materialist ones. A brilliant reckoning with similar pious reflections about the mathematical nature of reality can be found in Stebbing 1958, p. 25 et seq.

opment are also the subject of knowledge there, and thus – though in different aspects – comprise both *b* and *c* in the dialectical totality. We could make these and other additions and supplement, but that is not the point here. Here, it is a matter of the very structure of the dialectical totality called 'knowledge'.

The structural similarity here consists of the fact that two levels can be distinguished here as well. On the lower, more concrete level, an interaction among the various moments can be spoken of in a figurative sense. On the higher, more abstract level, the object of knowledge – moment *c* in our example – emerges as the dominant one.

The materialistic element in this conception thus consists of knowledge ultimately being determined by its object; in other words, it is a question of a generally realist conception of knowledge. The dialectical feature is the insight that knowledge of reality is always *humanity's* knowledge and that it is always a knowledge directly or indirectly related to humanity's needs and desires as well as to the general structure of society.

The primacy of the object in knowledge means first and foremost that knowledge *can* and *must* be regarded and judged without taking into account the subjective and historical circumstances under which it came into being. This is a deep and crucial conviction in both Marx and Engels; Marx expressed it programmatically in the preface to *Capital*.[85] It is ultimately the object of knowledge that determines the quality of the knowledge. Knowledge can be revealed as an illusion only by being confronted with its object; its illusory character can then be *explained* using the historical and social circumstances under which it came into being, by the ideological interests that are satisfied by it, and so on. It is a matter of two clearly separate stages.

But we can only become familiar with the object of knowledge through experience, that is, empirical studies in the broadest sense. But the conception of the primacy of the object of knowledge follows the conception of the primacy of empirical material. This is a conviction that is fundamental for Marx's and Engels's entire intellectual conviction. When in their youth they abandoned Hegelian rationalism, they turned first to Feuerbach's philosophy. Feuerbach's materialism was only secondarily an ontological materialism (that is, a theory of the primacy of matter). Primarily it involved a general empiricism: it was in 'the sensuous' that knowledge had its origins and its governing centre.[86] When Marx and Engels criticised Feuerbach's empiricism in *The German Ideology*, their criticism did not concern empiricism as such but its narrow

---

85   MECW 35:11. See also below, p. 490 et seq.
86   Cf. above, p. 100.

delimitations. Human contact with reality, which is the foundation of knowledge, did not limit itself to serene observations. The crucial source was action:
the action that moreover changed reality. Through building society, by developing trade and industry, humanity created knowledge while changing reality
with its actions and thereby laying the foundations for new potential knowledge.[87] In the literature on Marx and Marxism, this theory of 'praxis' has often
been confused with the thesis that knowledge is determined by its external,
social circumstances.[88] In fact, it concerns two clearly separate aspects, one of
which is internal to science and the other external to it. The thesis that theory can only be corrected in praxis means that the relative *truth* of the theory
can only be tested in action, that is, in confrontation with reality. The thesis
that theoretical, scientific development always can and must be put in relation to social development means that scientific development – and thereby
the degree of truth or of likelihood of the theory, of its many-sidedness or one-
sidedness, and so on – can only conclusively be explained by taking the social
background, mode of production, class relations and thereby also the ideological conditions into account.

When Marx, in *Capital*, said that the method of research involved assimilating 'the material' in detail and that the method of presentation aimed at
presenting 'the real development' (*die wirkliche Bewegung*),[89] it was of course
the internal aspect he had in mind.

---

87   MECW 5:40.
88   The condition for such a distinction is, naturally, that a particularly internal scientific per-
      spective is generally accepted. In the tradition that began with Lukács's *History and Class
      Consciousness* and culminated in the Frankfurt School, there is a striking antipathy toward
      separating the 'internal' circumstances of science from the 'external'. Counting scientific
      observations and experiments as 'praxis' in some respects thus also appears ridiculous.
      But the ambiguity in the very pair of concepts 'theory-praxis' is serious in the tradition
      that Lukács, Habermas et al. object to; both Engels and Lenin after him (e.g. in *Material-
      ism and Empiriocriticism*, Lenin 14:132 et seq.) speak in the same breath about praxis as a
      criterion of truth and as the explanatory basis for scientific development (among other
      phenomena). Nonetheless it is obvious that in the former respect the experiment must
      be counted as praxis, whereas in the latter – since the orientation toward experiments
      in the natural science of the new age must be *explained* – this has to be explained with
      an emerging bourgeois 'praxis' (focused on quantities, tools, etc.). 'Praxis' in the former
      sense is a more sweeping term and the simplest solution would naturally be to use com-
      pletely different words. As a criterion of truth, 'praxis' thoroughly entails empirical study,
      but the emphasis is on action and not on passive observation; the phrase 'empirical study'
      would be misleading. On the complex history of the concept of praxis, see Lobkowicz
      1967.
89   MECW 35.19.

The conception of the primacy of empirical material is thus intimately bound up with the conception of the primacy of the object – of objective reality. But the category of 'experience' in Marx's and Engels's world of ideas is a very broad one. In *Ludwig Feuerbach*, where Engels referred directly back to *The German Ideology*, it says that the most striking refutation of all 'philosophical fancies' of the 'thing in itself' type – that is, the idea of an objective reality inaccessible to humanity – was 'praxis, namely the experiment and industry'. According to Engels, the thing in itself was entirely that part of reality that humanity had not learned to master or handle. Experience was thus a historically mutable category: the sphere of experience broadened along with the forces of production. Chemical compounds were things in themselves until we become familiar with their composition, a knowledge that also means that, in principle, we can synthesise them and make use of them in the chemicals industry.[90]

The fundamental principle is thus that *there is no objective reality other than the one that we – now or in future – can master in praxis*. It must be added, however, that since praxis at the same time continuously changes reality and lays the foundation for new praxis, knowledge can never reach its terminus. It must also be added that praxis in the sense of systematic, goal-oriented action presupposes theory, and that theory is something else and more than the sum of the 'actions' that it gives rise to.

I believe that this fundamental – though originally formulated – empiricism is a contributing factor to Engels being so willing to express himself as an adherent of pure positivism. It was, quite simply, difficult to find a vocabulary for the type of empiricism he and Marx represented. It was difficult to cross between Hegel's rationalist idealism and an empiricism that denied the creative significance of theory.

Some of Engels's comments that immediately seem to represent the positivist tendency in his writings could also be interpreted in the direction of a more dialectical understanding. So, for example, when speaking about various theories of electricity he could say:

> In every science, incorrect notions are, in the last resort, apart from errors of observation, incorrect notions of correct facts. The latter remain even when the former are shown to be false.[91]

---

90   MECW 26:367 et seq.
91   MECW 25:444.

This statement could be interpreted as saying that scientific development is nothing other than an accumulation of facts. This is not a necessary conclusion, however.[92] Engels could also have been arguing that empirical material – the established observations – comprise the foundation or base of the scientific process, over which the brittle superstructure of the theories forms an arch. The ambiguous word 'fact' (*Tatsache*) complicates the interpretation. But the difficulty also depends on the unfinished character of everything Engels wrote on the topic.

8   The Game of Contradictions

In a number of minor notes and drafts in *Dialectics of Nature*, Engels took up what we could call dialectical relations in epistemology and scientific theory. Most of these paragraphs were written during the first period of his work on a general dialectic, but some of them originate from the later year of 1882.[93] Throughout these studies, Engels kept very close to Hegel; direct references to Hegel's works are legion. His recurring ambition was to show, in the spirit of Hegel, that what we perceive as incompatible opposites in science and reality are actually intimately bound up, determine each other and pass into each other.

There is a motley collection of examples of similar unities of opposites that Engels cited. He took its variegated character over from his philosophical mentor. Some of the cases Engels cited seem highly trivial and pointless. No one ought to question, for example, the concept of southern and northern magnetic poles being bound together and the one having no meaning without the other.[94] If the interaction between the magnetic poles is a good example of the unity of opposites, then in that case the concept of the dialectic is so far-reaching that its fruitfulness has every reason to be questioned.

But there are also paragraphs that appear more meaningful. In a few lines, Engels provided a glimpse of his view on the relation between theory and

---

92   Calling attention to facts as the result of science is not the same as disparaging the role of theories in scientific development. The modern scientific theoretician Imre Lakatos, for example, can assert that a theory proves its superiority in relation to another by leading to the discovery of new facts; Lakatos 1970, p. 116 and *passim*. By that, of course, he does not mean that facts are independent of theories.

93   This concerns above all the note in the section titled 'Dialectics', MECW 25: 492 et seq. Cf. also 487 et seq.

94   E.g. three notes made in 1874 and 1882; MECW 25:497 et seq.

empirical material,[95] and he devoted a page and a half to laying out a concept of praxis that is entirely in line with what he and Marx developed in *The German Ideology, Ludwig Feuerbach* and so on.[96]

In a few pages, Engels also dealt with the relation between induction and deduction. His presentation does not testify to any deeper familiarity with the discussions of scientific theory of the time. He mentioned William Whewell, but was obviously unfamiliar with Whewell's leading ideas. Namely, he ascribed to Whewell the concept that Whewell vehemently attacked in his debate with John Stuart Mill.[97] In Engels's eyes, Whewell was a rabid inductivist, an unhesitating advocate of the idea that all scientific knowledge in the empirical disciplines could be achieved by the path of induction.[98]

The idea that Engels objected to is that induction and deduction comprised two clearly demarcated processes in scientific work. This can be said without doubt to have been the predominant understanding from the mid-nineteenth century for a few decades onward among those who sought the decisive norms for what science was in the natural science of the time. It was by induction from rich experiential material that general laws could be arrived at. From these laws, the individual could then be deduced. If the laws then proved untenable in the face of new empirical material, a new induction had to be tested and a path to new generalisations had to be found. The remarkable thing about this view is that it was only through induction that science could gain *new* insights: the role of deduction in the process of scientific advance was entirely passive.

This is an idea that squared with what I call the positivist tendency in Engels. When faced with the general question of induction versus deduction, however, he defended himself against the idea of the passive dependence of deduction – and thus of theory – on empirical material. He asserted that there was a constant interaction between deduction and induction. He provided in passing an example of what he meant: Traditional biological classification was a result of induction. On the basis of certain shared characteristics, plants and animals were ordered in hierarchies of species, families, classes and so on. But with the new evolutionary biology, this classification had come into a new light and a number of corrections to the earlier divisions had become necessary.[99]

---

95   MECW 25:488.
96   MECW 25:509 et seq.
97   See Whewell 1968, p. 266 et seq.
98   MECW 25:507.
99   MECW 25:493, 499 et seq., et al.

This example, which was one among many, was thus intended to show how a new theory – in the same manner as new empirical material – determined scientific knowledge itself. Engels's comments are particularly brief and incomplete, but it is nonetheless clear that here he was touching on a line of thought that was just as central for him as it was for Marx. On account of Friedrich Albert Lange's criticism of *Capital*, Marx spoke about the free motion in 'the material' that comprised the very core of the dialectical method.[100] This freedom was the freedom to change between levels of abstraction in the presentation and thus to change between inductive and deductive processes. Engels groped about for formulations that could show that the dialectic united inductivist, purely empirical conceptions of science on the one hand and deductivist, rationalist ideas on the other. In this attempt, he was obstructed – like Marx, in part – by his relative lack of familiarity with the views of science that were incompatible with the dialectical view. Like Marx, he saw in Hegel's philosophy a cure for the current dilemma of the views on science at the time, but he was also uncritical towards Hegel and freely chose from among Hegel's large and unsorted collection of examples of dialectical contradictions in science.

He came a hair's breadth closer to real clarity in these questions in a study of the relation between necessity and chance. The predominant conception entailed not only that all new scientific findings were reached through induction; it also proclaimed that deduction entailed an entirely formal inference from the general to the individual. This in turn resulted in strict determinism becoming the goal of science: theory would contain a number of generalisations that applied equally to all individual cases.

We previously saw that this was an ideal that neither Darwin's theory of natural selection nor Marx's theory of capital could fulfil. Darwin's theory could not be confirmed in every individual case, and Marx's theory had to put up with constant exceptions to the general theses on the concentration of capital.

We know that Marx was aware of this characteristic in his theory. According to the ideal of deterministic science, the theory of the primacy of the base – that is, of the mode of production – meant that every change in the base would be matched by a change, for example, in the political superstructure: every political event would be determined by the base. Marx repeatedly declared that the context was far more complicated than that. So when speaking about the Paris Commune, for example, he noted that chance played a role in the concrete historical process. The outcome of the Paris Commune was thus not only the result of the relations of production: circumstances that, viewed from the gen-

---

100   Cf. above, p. 83 et seq.

eral theory, were entirely by chance – the personalities of the leading figures, for example – also played a crucial role.[101]

Engels touched upon similar lines of thought in the unfinished section on 'Chance and Necessity' in *Dialectics of Nature*.[102] Interestingly enough, he chose Darwinism and not Marxian theory as an example of a theory that did not permit an absolute deduction from the necessary – that is, statements of law – to the chance or the individual. According to the deterministic ideal, a good theory about living beings should show how every individual feature in every living being is causally determined. It should, Engels said, explain why this specific breed of dog has a tail of such-and-such a length, or why a particular peapod should contain this many peas. A theory like Darwin's, however, did not fulfil these requirements, and generally could not do so, Engels asserted. On the contrary, Darwin had taken his starting point in chance, and his theory did not abolish these chance occurrences:

> Precisely the infinite, accidental differences between individuals within a single species ... compelled him to question the previous basis of all regularity in biology, viz., the concept of species in its previous metaphysical rigidity and unchangeability.[103]

Unfortunately, Engels broke off the more detailed investigation of this extraordinarily interesting line of thought; the manuscript ends abruptly with an unfulfilled promise to further develop the case of Darwin.[104] As a whole, however, the text scarcely provides any expectations of a more fruitful solution of the issue of a theory of Darwin's type. Engels contented himself with reproducing Hegel's equilibristic regarding the relation of necessity to chance: an equilibristic where the problem is hinted at but scarcely formulated, to say nothing of solved.

Despite his intentions, Engels's general fumbling lines of thought regarding Darwinism provide a shining example of his thesis that scientific theories can be developed and attain scientific applicability before a corresponding general scientific understanding is formulated. Darwin's theory of natural selection and Marx's theory of capital were both in conflict with the predominant scientific ideal, but it was still impossible to determine what kind of new scientific approach had seen the light of day with these and similar theories.

---

101   Cf. the letter from Marx to L. Kugelmann, 17 April 1871, MECW 44:136 et seq.
102   MECW 25:498–501 (section undated).
103   MECW 25:500.
104   MECW 25:509 et seq.

The problems of determinism can also be glimpsed in a few brief paragraphs about causality that Engels wrote down. It is characteristic of his uncertainty that in his polemic with the idea of the unambiguous cause and the unambiguous effect, he followed in Hegel's footsteps and described interaction as the solution to the dilemma.[105] He seems not to have noticed that interaction for Hegel was only a stage on the path toward 'the concept', and therefore towards the real comprehension of any totality whatsoever. Stating that the different moments in the totality influenced each other was not enough for Hegel the idealist; it was also a matter of comprehending the entity as an expression of a thought or an idea, and thus as a 'concept'.[106] Marx, as we have seen, was opposed to the idea that the totality was united in its concepts and sought instead an overall moment, a 'base' in the dialectic totality itself. Engels followed in his footsteps in several places. On one level, the relation between the moments in a totality appeared as interaction, on another – higher and more abstract – the totality was determined by one of the moments.[107] In fact, this change to the dialectical structure was connected to the materialistic conversion of Hegel: if the dialectical totality is not characterised by either an internal dominating moment or a fundamental concept in Hegel's meaning, then the interaction between the various moments can only be summarised in the uninteresting assertion that 'everything influences everything else'.[108] What Engels said about interaction in *Dialectics of Nature* in fact scarcely rises above this triviality.

Engels thus treated all the contradictory pairs that fill the entire discussion of knowledge and science with a striking awkwardness. He did not gain any new certainty with his ambition of laying out general dialectical laws. It is characteristic that both then and later he regarded antagonism itself as an example of dialectical antithesis. In the timetable from 1879 it became, as we have seen, the second of three dialectical laws. Four years previously, he had regarded 'Identity and Difference' as *one of* the main contradictions.[109] Obviously he had not subjected these statements to any logical analysis whatsoever. Otherwise, it would have become obvious to him that such expressions as 'identity and difference' and 'the unity of opposites' could only describe all the dialectical relations he

---

105   MECW 25:512. Engels asks himself where Hegel says that reciprocal action is the true *causa finalis*; the answer is *Science of Logic*.

106   See in particular Hegel 8:346 et seq. (the moment in reciprocal action must be regarded as '*eines Dritten, Höheren erkannt **werden**, welches dann eben der Begriff ist*').

107   Above, p. 388 et seq.

108   Cf. with this Lenin's highly insightful comments to Hegel's *Science of Logic*; Lenin 38:153 et seq.

109   MECW 25:496.

cited, and that at the same time they could themselves not constitute examples of pairs of opposites.

Despite this fundamental lack of clarity, in Engels's scattered statements on issues of scientific theory we can distinguish a dialectical materialist tendency that corresponds to a primary tendency in his and Marx's historical materialism. The subject of knowledge and its object, theory and empirical material, 'chance' and 'necessity' mutually determine each other, influence and define each other, but one of the moments can at the same time be characterised as the predominant one, the one that creates the connections.

To understand Engels's ambition of creating a dialectic of science and reality, we must keep this general tendency in mind. If – as some of his statements let on – he were giving himself up to positivism, the entire character of his enterprise would be different: all these dialectical investigations into the mutual dependence of theory and empirical material would appear to be nonsense. If he were adopting Hegelian idealism again, the entire foundation of his great synthesis – matter and its 'forms of motion' – would appear to be pure folly.

As we have seen, Engels called the great synthesis of knowledge 'theory', pure and simple. We have already acquainted ourselves with his general statements on what this theory is. They are the statements that can hardly be brought together into any uniform conception: Engels took up a precarious position in justifying his synthetic enterprise.

Now, however, we must go a step further down into his argument. We must find examples of the problems in which empirical material, in the sense he uses, cannot arrive at any results either *alone* or *in general*. It is thus also a question of examples of the active capability of the syntheses.

Of particular interest here is Engels's reckoning with modern spiritualism, patronised by a number of scientists with Alfred Russell Wallace at their head. In a separate chapter in *Dialectics of Nature*, Engels wrote on 'Natural Science in the Spirit World'. His conclusion was that spiritual beliefs could be supported purely empirically provided that the occurrence of similar immaterial entities could be regarded as a real possibility. 'In fact, mere empiricism is incapable of refuting the spiritualists'. Theoretical consideration is also required. There are experiments that cannot be revealed as humbug and fraud. These experiments can therefore be interpreted in the manner of the spiritualists.[110]

---

110   MECW 25:354. The article was written in 1878, at the time Engels was developing his 'dialectical laws'. The contradiction between the positivism he excels in there and the statement cited is striking.

With that, Engels hints that a materialist conception (i.e. an understanding that everything that exists is linked to various types of matter) is a prerequisite for a consistent negative attitude toward spiritualism. It is impossible to prove, purely empirically, that the spiritualists are wrong. Or, more precisely: it was not possible to do so at the stage of research at that time, and it would never be possible without being guided by a materialistic perspective in empirical research.

In this line of thought, we encounter the classic demand of the system-builders for the unity of knowledge. In Engels, as we know, this unity is relative: there are qualitative differences among different types of matter. The comprehensive viewpoint is nonetheless materialistic. All knowledge must be included in a materialistic perspective of totality.

There are a number of statements where Engels hinted at what kind of consequences this general understanding could have for empirical studies and for specialised scientific theory. One of his crucial theses was that matter is inseparable from motion: the question would otherwise arise as to where motion originated: *'Motion is the mode of existence of matter'*, it says in *Anti-Dühring*.[111] Matter and motion must be eternal: if not, material must have an immaterial origin. The amount of motion must be constant: if not, a beginning and an end can be calculated.[112]

These general starting points gave Engels some difficulties with the second law of thermodynamics on the direction of heat. As we will see in more detail in the next chapter, there is as a fundamental postulate – in his earlier notes, at least – the assumption that all non-organic forms of motion are completely reversible. This was the reason he devoted a few scathing notes to Rudolf Clausius.[113] Obviously, he imagined that the theory of entropy, or 'heat death', somehow threatened the general thesis of the eternal constancy of matter and motion.

We can therefore also suspect a split in his world of ideas between a fundamental materialism on the one hand and his similarly fundamental idea of development on the other. He denied eternal life with the same resoluteness that he asserted the eternity of matter. Organic life was an irreversible process in the utmost: life was something that arose at a definite stage in the development of matter. In *Dialectics of Nature* he attacked an idea that in different variations was advocated by such prominent secular figures as Justus von Liebig

---

111   MECW 25:56.
112   See in particular MECW 25:363 et seq.
113   See the paragraphs (from 1875); MECW 25:562.

and Hermann von Helmholtz: that the emergence of life from inorganic material did not need to be explained because living matter had existed for just as long as inorganic matter. His argument is in part empirically grounded: proteins, which form the basis of everything living, are particularly unstable and impermanent. This argument in and of itself is insufficient, however. Organisms have existed for enormous periods of time despite their unstable foundation. In itself, Engels's general thesis on the eternity of material is compatible with the idea that the various forms of motion of matter could have existed side by side for eternity.[114]

It is thus not simply the idea of matter in motion that gave Engels the right to reject Liebig's and Helmholtz's hypotheses on an *a priori* basis. He assumed not only motion but development as well: development towards ever higher (i.e. ever more complex) forms of motion. It thus concerned the idea that nature also had a history, which Engels principally developed in the preface to *Dialectics of Nature*. Like Spencer and many other of his contemporaries, and like other various development thinkers going all the way back to the Stoics of antiquity, Engels imagined that development toward increasingly complex states were succeeded by a process of dissolution. Once the development had reached its culmination, only dissolution awaited. Life on earth would be extinguished with the sun.[115]

But this exact idea about the historical undulations of nature had solid support in the specialised theories that attracted the greatest attention in the late nineteenth century: cosmology, geology, evolutionary biology, and the leading theories of history and society. In Engels's eyes, the philosophical ideas of various philosophers of antiquity on the mutability of everything were empirically confirmed in modern science.[116] The thesis of the development of matter therefore considered not to belong as much to the fundamental theoretical postulates in his theory, or general philosophy, as the theory of the priority of matter did. Materialism was more in dispute in the current natural and human sciences than the thinking on development was.

The conception of the development of matter is naturally connected with the very heart of Engels's ontology: the thesis of the qualitatively different types of matter. New stages in the process of the development of matter were constantly being achieved that could not be reduced to earlier, simpler stages. But how did this materialism relate to what Engels called mechanical materialism?

---

114   MECW 25:576 et seq.
115   MECW 25:327 et seq.
116   MECW 25:327.

What support did it have in general theory? What support did it have in empirical science?

Engels asserted at one point that mechanical materialism, with its thesis on 'the absolute qualitative identity of matter', 'can empirically neither be proven nor refuted'.[117] In this case, for the sake of consistency, the same must also be valid for the opposite conception – Engels's own. In this case, there should be other criteria for the superiority of non-reductive materialism.

From this simple statement, however, we cannot infer a consistent understanding. What is simply theory, and what for that reason is confirmed by empirical studies is, according to Engels, historically changeable. What was simply theory (or philosophy) for the ancient Greeks has become empirical truth in Engels's time.

The field of application for great comprehensive theories does not shrink with this development, however. Not only does it require that general ideas be confirmed in various specialisations; it also requires that the findings are brought together into an overall picture. The specialists do not create such pictures themselves; the pictures do not emerge spontaneously from the specialisations. Engels noted that even physicists and chemists were putting off questions that were a shared concern for them.[118] How much easier would it then have been for specialists who were working far apart from each other to disregard their mutual relations!

9   Summary

Engels's epistemological and scientific theoretical ideas are neither developed nor consistent. He shared all the difficulties of his system-building contemporaries in justifying his own synthesising activities. In Hegel's philosophy he sought a cure for the difficulties that dominated large parts of the views of his time on science. In the theory of the unity of opposites, he wanted to find the solution for all the unresolved antitheses that the scientific discussions of the time were dealing with. He often contented himself with proclaiming that unity without accounting for the connection in the unity – that is, without explaining why the antitheses were united. Sometimes he chose examples of pairs of opposites that upon closer inspection proved to be completely uninteresting in the context.

---

117   MECW 25:532.
118   MECW 25:569.

There are, however, also features and tendencies in his scattered comments that appear interesting and worth developing. Above all, this concerns the discernible idea that in epistemology and scientific theory – as in the Marxist conception of history – it was possible to speak of dominant moments. Here, it genuinely concerns a Hegel set on his feet, a Hegelian conception of totality that has been stripped of its idealism. Engels was unsuccessful in clearly and unambiguously developing this line of thought, but here in posterity we can understand its value and originality in the chaotic world of nineteenth-century science.

Next, we must now set ourselves the task of tracing the leading ideas in Engels's ontology.

CHAPTER 15

Inorganic Nature

1 The Classification

Drawing boundaries among the various sciences was a notorious problem in the nineteenth century.[1] The system-builders sought to find a natural division in which the boundaries between disciplines would coincide with the boundaries between different spheres of reality. They were thus seeking an ontological classification.

This was an ambition that Engels shared. In one of his few remarks on Comte's system, he said that Comte was guided by pedagogical considerations in his classification.[2] Engels claimed to have gotten closer to reality.

The outline of a scientific classification can be found in the letter from 1873 in which Engels first divulged his ideas on a general dialectic. The classification corresponded to what he called the various forms of motion of bodies – an idea that he would later remain faithful to. He distinguished between mechanics, physics and chemistry. In the traditional manner, he divided mechanics into terrestrial and celestial, naturally with the remark that the difference was only relative. He also distinguished a third kind of mechanics: '*Mechanik des Kontakts*', or 'ordinary' mechanics, which he exemplified with the lever and the inclined plane. It was this contact mechanics that formed the transition to true physics; the conflict or friction between bodies produces '*new*, no longer purely mechanical' forms of motion: heat, light, electricity and magnetism. These forms pass into one another under definite conditions, and under similarly definite conditions they call forth changes in the internal structure of bodies. In other words, they produce chemical changes.

Mechanics and physics, Engels explained, study inorganic bodies. The chemical nature of the most important bodies, on the other hand, appears only in substances that have emerged from the process of life, and it was increasingly becoming the primary task of chemistry to synthesise similar compounds. Chemistry thus also formed the transition to the sciences of organic life, but it was still too early to try to determine '*der dialektische Übergang*'[3] (the dialectical transition).

---

1 Cf. above, p. 296 *et seq.*
2 MECW 25:529 (undated, probably before 1876).
3 Letter from Engels to Marx, 30 May 1873, MECW 44:500 et seq. and 527 et seq.

The classification that can be discerned from these lines does not appear
to be fully consistent. Engels was of course not arguing that there were three
different mechanical forms of motion that would lead to a trisection of mechanics while on the other hand unquestioningly counted four forms of motion
in physics. Hegel's dialectical idealism had collided with his own materialism.
On the one hand, he was trying to show how the sciences were 'ideally' bound
up: the motion of the individual body – falling, for example – since this motion
is an affair between two different bodies (e.g. the falling stone and the earth).
Terrestrial mechanics thus lead into celestial mechanics. But every motion is
ultimately a question of contact between bodies: the mechanics of the heavenly bodies leads over to the mechanics of the machines.

It was thus a question of a theoretical connection, whereas the transitions
from mechanical motion to heat, light, electricity and magnetism and transitions between these phenomena are real transitions from one form of motion
to another. The transition to chemistry is of course also a real transition, even
if Engels was not speaking about any particular chemical form of motion here.

In general, the influence from Hegel is strong in all of Engels's attempts at
classifying the sciences. In a note to *Dialectics of Nature* he resolutely declared
that Hegel's original division of the natural sciences into mechanics, chemism ('*Chemismus*') and organism ('*Organismus*')[4] was still useful. Here, he thus
accepted bringing even physics and chemistry under the same heading, and he
followed the Hegelian lines of thought even further by seeing a higher unity of
mechanics, physics and chemistry in organism.[5]

At the same time, however, influences from a significantly more recent
drawing of the boundary between physics and chemistry can be traced in
this note. Even though both disciplines were thus brought into chemism in
the spirit of Hegel, it is hinted that physics is concerned with the motion of
molecules, chemistry with that of the atoms. This is a division of property
that figures such as Kekulé propagandised for, which presumed the modern
concept of the molecule and the mechanical theory of heat.[6] Engels had an

---

4 In fact, Engels here has somewhat distorted the division Hegel made in *Science of Logic*
   between 'mechanics', 'chemics' and 'teleology' (Hegel 5:179, 180–235); Engels, of course, did
   not want to concern himself with teleology. Here he did not take into account the broad,
   more elaborate division Hegel later made in *System of Philosophy*, where the triad now was
   'mechanics', 'physics' and 'organics' (Hegel 9:66 et seq.) and teleology was only mentioned in
   passing where the organic was concerned (ibid., p. 452). According to both divisions, however,
   physics and chemistry belonged to the same unit.

5 MECW 25:529.

6 Above, p. 155 *et seq.*

adherent of the same basis for classification close by, in Schorlemmer.[7] He would also hold fast to it in future. When in *Anti-Dühring* he explained the dialectical connection among the natural sciences, he described physics as 'the mechanics of molecules' and chemistry as 'the physics of atoms'.[8] In a supplement he wrote in 1885, originally with the intent of including it in the new edition of *Anti-Dühring*,[9] he stated with satisfaction that Kekulé, in a lecture,[10] drew the same boundary between physics and chemistry that he had.[11]

Engels's most ambitious attempt at classifying the sciences of inorganic nature is the chapter 'Basic Forms of Motion' in *Dialectics of Nature*. It was written in either 1880 or 1881. Here, he drew the same boundary between physics and chemistry as he did in *Anti-Dühring*. Physics was 'the theory of molecular motion', and chemistry 'the science of the motion of atoms'. He touched on the question that this basis for classification in itself provides no answer to, namely which of the disciplines is the most fundamental. Mechanics itself is naturally the fundamental materialist science, but chemistry comes 'immediately afterwards, almost alongside of ... and in some places in advance of' physics. This vague determination of position indicates that the question does not concern the theoretical connection between physics and chemistry – that is, whether the one theory presumes the other. Rather, it concerns the mutual positions of physical and chemical processes in the grand process of the development of the universe. Molecular and atomic motions are equally as fundamental and equally as primeval in this process.[12]

---

7   In Vol. I of Roscoe and Schorlemmer 1877 (for which, however, Roscoe must be regarded as primarily responsible) the division of property is not clearly defined; physics and chemistry are said to constitute a totality that is difficult to differentiate (p. 37 et seq.) while at the same time physics is associated with the concept of the molecule, and chemistry with the concept of the atom (p. 58 et seq.) Schorlemmer's support in his own writings of the strict division between physics/molecules and chemistry/atoms emerges in works such as the manuscript on the history of chemistry in the Manchester University Library, Vol. I, p. 2.

8   MECW 25:61.

9   It is worth noting that Engels later found 'much that was clumsy in my exposition' of the natural sciences in *Anti-Dühring*. He did not re-work the text, however, choosing instead to criticise and supplement his account in a long foreword to the 1885 edition; MECW 11 et seq.

10   Kekulé 1878. Also reproduced in Anzchütz 1929, Vol. II, pp. 903–16.

11   MECW 25:530.

12   MECW 25:362. Cf. the 'Introduction' (completed in 1876, before the work on *Anti-Dühring*), where Engels clearly placed physical processes *ahead of* chemical ones in the development; MECW 25:328 et seq.

A faint echo is perceptible here from the discussions on the mutual relations of chemistry and physics. Putting the 'forms of motion' of chemistry and physics in relation to each other is not easy. Engels, however, did not doubt that two distinctly different forms were concerned. The forms of motion of inorganic nature had been established once and for all, while research was just getting to grips with the corresponding motions in organic nature. It was therefore possible to comment with certainty on the former, but not on the latter.[13]

2   Motion, Force and Energy

Engels was not only trying to establish the various forms of inorganic motion. He also wanted to investigate their mutual connections, their unity.

It is characteristic of his way of treating the natural sciences that he let his philosophical imagination loose on questions where there was fundamental disagreement or uncertainty among the specialists. With fresh spirits, he entered into the old battle from the days of Descartes and Leibniz over whether force was calculated with the formula mv (mass × velocity) or with $\frac{mv^2}{2}$.[14] He devoted a great deal of attention to electricity. His authority was Gustav Wiedemann,[15] but he dwelled on questions of electricity where the experts were doubtful or divided.[16]

We have no reason to go into detail here on Engels's treatment of these controversies. His involvement in another, highly topical controversy, on the other hand, says a great deal about his ideas on the unity of the inorganic forms of motion.

Engels noted that physicists were divided over whether to speak about the constancy of force or of energy. He had also noticed that the advocates of the term 'energy' had gained ground. Helmholtz's early writings on the subject had been titled *On the Conservation of Force*. Other physicists, however – Kelvin and Tait, for example – had instead used the word 'energy' early on. At long last, even Helmholtz had adopted this usage.[17]

---

13   MECW 25:362.
14   MECW 25:379 et seq.
15   Above, p. 332.
16   Chapter on 'Electricity' (written 1882), pp. 402–51 *passim* and in particular p. 437. This 50-page section is by far the most comprehensive Engels completed for *Dialectics of Nature*. The significance of electricity in his dialectic of nature does not justify this format whatsoever.
17   Cf. Elkana 1974, p. 132 et seq.

Engels declared that there were two names for the same natural law: Helmholtz's 'conservation of *force*' and 'the newer, more precise, one of the conservation of *energy*'.[18] His investigation was based on demonstrating that the suitable
name was instead 'the conservation of motion'.

Also to the point is that the vocabulary of the leading physicists was not
only uncertain but rather inconsistent as well. In particular, this concerned
the popularisations that Engels had first been referred to. Engels sought to
bring to life Descartes' classic thesis that the quantity of motion in the universe
was constant. But 'motion' normally described only mechanical processes. In
his *Popular Scientific Lectures* – one of Engels's primary sources – Helmholtz
spoke about 'all the effects of purely mechanical, i.e. pure motive forces' and
distinguished them from the other forces of nature: 'heat, electricity, magnetism, light, chemical affinity'. There were thus different forces, and the mechanical motive force was one of them.[19] Since by 'force' Helmholtz meant active
cause,[20] his comment this meant that motive force was the cause of mechanical motion.

The term 'motion', however, had also obtained a broader meaning through
the new mechanical theory of heat. Briefly put, the theory was based on the
idea that heat was synonymous with molecular motion and thus a form of
mechanical motion. In popular contexts, at least, the theory could however be
worded in an immediately confusing manner. We can see, for example, how
John Tyndall – another of Engels's favourites in natural science – in summarising the grand topic 'The Constitution of Nature', declared: 'The whole stock
of energy or working-power in the world consists of attractions, repulsions and
motions'.[21] Motion thus became something alongside Newton's attraction and
repulsion.

The fluid and often contradictory aspects of the specialists' manner of commentary was a condition for Engels's attempt to bring a new order to the confusion. But why did he seek support in the Cartesian concept of motion? When
he put together his initial draft back in 1873, he had stopped to talk about the
forms of motion of matter.

The guess that lies closes to hand – that he took inspiration from Hegel –
turns out to be completely incorrect. For Hegel, Descartes's thesis on the quantity of motion was a manifestation of the metaphysics of understanding. It was
only a special case of a tautology whose more general formulation goes: 'Motion

18   MECW 25:363.
19   Helmholtz 1876, Vol. II, p. 108 et seq.
20   Ibid., p. 190 et seq.
21   Tyndall 1879, Vol. I, p. 24.

is motion, and rest is rest'.[22] 'Motion' for Hegel was not a conceivable name for the various processes of development.

On the other hand, there is everything to indicate that Engels got his idea from Grove's *On the Correlation of Physical Forces*. This was the work in which he first gained insights into the mysteries of the principle of conservation of energy. In many respects, it also maintained a decisive influence over his ideas. In a paragraph from 1874, Engels referred to a 'pretty passage' on the indestructibility of motion in Grove.[23] Grove was, of course, not talking about the indestructibility of any particular motion. For him, 'motion' described one of 'the forces' in nature, and like Helmholtz and most of the others he thus meant mechanical motion. At the same time, however, he added that he believed all forces 'are, and will be ultimately resolved into, modes of motion'. On the other hand, it considered it too early to identify the other forces – light, heat, magnetism, electricity and chemical affinity – with motion at that time.[24]

Engels felt himself exempted from this cautiousness of Grove's – philosophy could push empirical research on ahead.

In fact, however, Grove was only suggesting the programme of reductive mechanicism, though with reservations and with the cautious addition that science could not claim to find the causes behind phenomena but only 'facts and relations'.[25] It was a programme Engels intended to fight; nonetheless, he had resolutely chosen the word 'motion' with its multifarious usefulness.

There is nothing to indicate that there were any studies in the history of physics or philosophy that inspired Engels's concept of motion. In *Anti-Dühring* and *Dialectics of Nature*, Descartes's theory of the constancy of the quantity of movement is cited no less than seven times,[26] but neither there nor in the excerpts he made does it show that he studied Descartes. He was, however, well aware that Descartes belonged to a mechanistic tradition that he himself was foreign to.[27] This did not prevent him from preferring the term *Bewegung* (motion) to *Kraft* (force) and *Energie* (energy).

Nor was Grove's ideal unknown to him. In a note from 1874 he cites the exact passage where Grove expressed his mechanicism, and set it against his own conception.[28] In another paragraph from the same year, he declared that Grove

---

22   Hegel 9:104.
23   MECW 25:525.
24   Grove 1855, p. 8.
25   Ibid.
26   MECW 25:50, 55, 326, 339, 363, 369 and 525.
27   Cf. for example 'The merely quantitative expression of Descartes is likewise inadequate', MECW 25:525.
28   MECW 25:527.

had stopped halfway – 'he has the thing, but not the abstract thought' – which is why he failed to develop the Hegelian concept of interaction (i.e. because he regarded the reduction to a single fundamental 'motion' – mechanical motion – as the natural goal of science).[29]

We have repeatedly been able to confirm Grove's decisive significance for Engels's view of modern physics. But closer to the age in which Engels lived, there were authors as well who used of the term 'motion' to express the ideal of reductive mechanicism. So, for example, Wilhelm Wundt, in his little work *Über die physicalischen Axiome*, declared 'all causes in nature are causes of motion (*Bewegungsursachen*)'.[30] For Wundt – as for Grove and Engels – motion was thus the very fundamental concept itself, more fundamental than the concept of force. But motion was, unambiguously, mechanical motion.

Engels had at least indirect knowledge of Wundt's work, namely through Ernst Mach's printed lecture on the history of the principle of conservation of energy. As we have seen, Engels made excerpts from Mach's writings in 1873.[31] It is noteworthy – and it fires the imagination – that he came in contact so early on with a world of scientific theoretical ideas that belonged more to the early twentieth century than his own time. From Mach's writings, the new positivism – radically different from nineteenth-century Comtesian positivism – was already speaking out. The 'positive' in Comte contrasted with the 'negative', the hidden and putatively essential in speculative philosophy; Comte was striving for a series of laws of development. Mach's immediate target of attack, on the other hand, was mechanicism. Science could only comment on phenomena (*Erscheinungen*) and the relations between them. It could not reach beyond the phenomena and establish the fundamental causes. It was thus not possible, as Wundt and the others did, to name mechanical motion as the foundation for all processes in nature.[32]

It may seem peculiar that Engels could draw any lessons from writings that expressed an understanding so diametrically opposed to his own epistemological realism. There is everything to indicate, however, that he took inspiration from Mach on several points.

---

29   MECW 25:511.
30   Wundt 1866, p. 26.
31   Above, p. 332.
32   The most comprehensive biography of Mach is Blackmore 1972. Mach's monograph on the principle of conservation of energy, his first philosophical work, is mentioned there only in passing (p. 42). Blackmore takes up the question of the relation between Comte's positivism and Mach's neopositivism, but in my opinion he plays down the crucial difference in the views of the concept of scientific law and on the use of science (p. 164 et seq.).

It is true that he was not bothered by Mach ruling out all explanations of the world that were rooted in natural science. Nor did he seem to be affected by Mach proposing yet another new name for the principle of conservation of energy: Mach was not speaking about motion or force or energy but about *Erhaltung der Arbeit* (the conservation of work).

On the other hand, Mach established something that Engels could immediately use, namely that the principle of conservation of energy was not indissolubly linked with mechanicism.[33] Among the authorities Engels came in contact with during his work on *Dialectics of Nature*, Mach was the only one who disclosed such an idea. Mach of course gave no free rein to other non-mechanicistic interpretations, but for Engels the essential point was probably that Mach opposed the idea that the ultimate natural cause of every change had to be 'motion in space'.[34]

Mach seems to have met Engels halfway on another point as well. Namely, Mach asserted that the principle of conservation of energy did not originate in the mechanicistic nineteenth century; its history stretched back in time to at least the seventeenth century. Descartes certainly played no role in Mach's historical account; Galileo and Stevin, on the other hand, did.[35] A few paragraphs in *Dialectic of Nature*, written in 1873 and 1874, are extremely similar to certain viewpoints in Mach's writings.[36] In particular, it can be noted that Engels here distanced himself from Clausius's theory of heat death: in the same way, Mach declared that similar assertions about the cosmos were 'illusory'.[37] As we will soon see, Engels had his own reasons to oppose Clausius's theory. Mach had given him a shot in the arm.

The argument that Engels, though only marginally, had come under the influence of Ernst Mach – the same Mach who, a few decades later, would be singled out as the archenemy of dialectical materialism in Lenin's *Materialism and Empiriocriticism* – has its points.

But the reason that Engels used the terms 'motion' and 'forms of motion' probably also lies on a more practical plane. The various influences from Grove and Mach and the authority of a powerful tradition dating back to the seventeenth century would not have been enough. I believe that one powerful reason that he settled on the phrase 'form of movement' was that the only alternative that he knew about in 1873 was the word 'force'. By imitating figures such as

---

33   Mach 1872, p. 5.
34   Ibid., in particular p. 27.
35   Ibid., p. 5 et seq.
36   MECW 25:551.
37   Mach 1872, p. 36.

Helmholtz, he could naturally have spoken about a number of different forces in nature. But, unlike Helmholtz, he was not a reductionist. It was only for the time being that he stopped to consider biology: he would gradually also have been compelled to talk about unique 'vital forces', and he would then have found himself – verbally, at least – in a tradition that he wanted nothing to do with: vitalism. By extension he would have been compelled to talk about other, even more complex forces that acted in human societies and their development. That would have been a dangerous path.

The word 'force' had been castigated by Hegel as well. Nowhere did Engels note Hegel's criticism of the concept of motion, whereas he referred with satisfaction to the similar criticism of the concept of force.[38] When, in a text from 1874, he tried to elucidate his thoughts on these topics, however, it turned out that his inspiration was only partly Hegelian. One essential point is that force can easily be understood as distinct matter, whereas the opposite idea is scarcely possible when talking about motion. Here, he could directly cite a quote from Hegel concerning Thales, which said that it was better to say that a magnet had a soul than to assert that it possessed a force. Force was namely understood as something that did not belong to matter itself.[39] But this idea that the various forms of influence of matter could not be distinguished from matter was extraordinarily central to some older materialist traditions, above all in the orientation in eighteenth-century French materialism whose most important representative was Denis Diderot. To avoid the troublesome idea that, for example, organic life was something that was added to matter, it was instead said that manifestations of life were inherent in a certain type of matter.[40] It does not appear as if Engels was particularly well acquainted with this tradition. He boldly bundled together eighteenth-century French materialists under the category of mechanistic materialism,[41] and the only exception to the fundamental mechanistic position he found was in certain non-philosophical works such as Diderot's *Rameau's Nephew*.[42] Nonetheless, it can be assumed that the tradition was conveyed to him through figures such as Hegel.

At the same time, however, Engels took inspiration in the newest natural science. He said that motion was a more modern concept than force, and took his

---

38   E.g. 25:558, where he quotes Hegel's *System* (Hegel 9:111 et seq.).
39   Hegel, *Lectures on the Philosophy of History*; Hegel 17:223. MECW 25:558.
40   A thorough account of this tradition does not exist. For viewpoints and references to the literature, see Wilson 1972, pp. 562 and 830 et seq.
41   See e.g. 25:489.
42   MECW 25:21. It is not impossible that Engels took this assessment directly from Hegel; cf. Hegel 2:401, 20:198.

support here from the mechanical theory of heat,[43] whose close connection with a strictly mechanistic understanding troubled him as little here as it did elsewhere.

There were thus numerous reasons for him to avoid the term 'force'. But what did he have against the other main alternative in the current debate: the word 'energy'?

The solution to the question of the relationship between motion, force and energy that Engels – when he sought to summarise his views in 1880 or 1881 – arrived at was that force and energy are terms for forms of motion that are opposed to each other: more precisely, force was attraction and energy was repulsion.[44] By all appearances, this odd schematisation was the result of various chance occurrences. One of the most important was that Engels, when he was first sketching out this schema, did not know that the concept of energy had been set up as an alternative to the concept of force from Helmholtz and others. He probably became aware of it when he studied Thomson and Tait's *Natural Philosophy* in more detail. Prior to that, he had been working with the opposing pair of force and manifestation of force, following Hegel. What he said here seems trivial: force was equal to the manifestation of force, cause was equal to effect, since the magnitude and type of the force or cause could only be determined through the type and magnitude of the manifestation of force or effect. But he linked this thesis – as simple as it was saturated with tradition – with the new principle of conservation of energy, and this triviality was trivial no longer. The transition from one 'form of motion' to another (e.g. the transition from mechanical motion to heat) thus confirmed the rule of the dialectical unity of force and its manifestation. Force – in this case, mechanical motion – and its manifestation – heat – were different yet nonetheless the same.

When he later came into contact with the term 'energy' in connection with the principle of conservation of energy, it did not take the place of 'the manifestation of force' in the schema. At the same time, however, the schema was charged with new content. His interpretation of the relation between the terms '*Erhaltung der Kraft*' and '*Erhaltung der Energie*' (conservation of force and energy, respectively) seems odd, at least, but was due to his associating the word 'force' and 'energy' with more special uses. If heat *energy* is said to be released in connection with a mechanical process, energy here can be perceived as a form of repulsion. From Helmholtz, Engels took the comment that the force

---

43   MECW 25:363 et seq.
44   MECW 25:558 et seq.

that united the atoms in a chemical process was an '*Anziehungskraft*' (force of attraction). But what Helmholtz here called a force, others called energy, Engels said. Both expressions are one-sided, he argued: all talk of force was only talk of attraction, and all talk of energy was only talk of repulsion. Motion was always a game between attraction and repulsion – and thus between force and energy.[45]

We do not need to dwell on the peculiarity of this interpretation. On the other hand, we can emphasise that Engels met strict mechanicism halfway by returning the various forms of motion to the basic schema of attraction and repulsion. It may seem as if he were thus more than halfway into a reductive mechanicism. In fact, his basic ambition – the ambition of uniting mechanical materialism and the dialectic – emerges here.

3   Irreductive Materialism

When Engels said that all movement in inorganic nature (he was not speaking about anything else here) could be expressed in terms of attraction and repulsion, his argument could be expressed thus: *mechanics is the fundamental natural science and mechanical motion the fundamental form of motion* (i.e. the one in terms of which other forms of motion could be expressed). This is a very important point in his conception. Attraction and repulsion stand out as 'the two simple basic forms' to which 'a number of sub-forms' belong.[46] To put this line of thought into words that Engels preferred in other contexts, it could be said that attraction and repulsion are the two fundamental qualities. It could also be said that all forms of motion are identical, in the sense that they can be expressed here in terms of attraction and repulsion.

Engels thus went this far toward meeting reductive mechanicism. While arguing, however, that attraction and repulsion were the basic forms, or the fundamental qualities – at the same time as he asserted the uniformity or identity of the various forms of motion – he asserted that the different forms of motion were *not* exhausted with these basic forms or fundamental qualities. Heat, light, electricity, magnetism and chemical processes could be described in terms of attraction and repulsion, but at the same time they were something different and more – in other words, something that could not be reduced to attraction and repulsion. Saying – as Engels did – that heat is a form of repulsion[47] does

45   MECW 25:364–72.
46   MECW 25:370.
47   MECW 25:360.

not mean that heat is repulsion, pure and simple. There is a particular 'sub-form' or quality, heat, that distinguishes head from other forms of repulsion.

Engels found his most powerful support for this definite form of irreduction-ism in the principle of conservation of energy. As he understood this principle, it meant primarily that matter in motion under quantitatively determined and determinable conditions transitioned from one form of motion to another: it was always an issue of attraction and repulsion but in different forms; it was 'the same' and yet 'not the same' attraction and repulsion. 'Mechanical motion of masses passes into heat, into electricity, into magnetism; heat and electricity pass into chemical decomposition; chemical combination in turn again devel-ops heat and electricity and, by means of the latter, magnetism; and finally, heat and electricity produce once more mechanical movement of masses'.[48]

Engels originally took this conception of the principle of conservation of energy from Grove, and could never liberate himself from it. Every form of motion could transition into every other form of motion without quantitative changes: it was only the quality that was transformed. That is why Clausius's second law of thermodynamics would involve significant problems for him. No one has summarised the significance of this law for the understanding of the principle of conservation of energy more clearly than Gustav Wiedemann. In an article on Helmholtz, he explained:

> In connection with *Helmholtz's* principle, however, it later emerged that only certain forms of energy could be completely transformed into oth-ers – but not, on the other hand, the reverse. We only need to recall the second law of the mechanical theory of heat in *Clausius's* highly signific-ant work ...[49]

Engels quickly realised that Clausius's law threatened the interpretation of the principle of conservation of energy that he had previously brought to life. In a letter to Marx back in 1869, he announced his indignation at the new idea running rampant in Germany that 'the world is growing colder'.[50] The theory of 'heat death' had its popular breakthrough in the lecture *Über den zweiten Hauptsatz der mechanischen Wärmestheorie* (On the Second Law of the Mech-anical Theory of Heat) that Clausis gave at the meeting of the Natural Scientists' Association in Frankfurt am Main in 1867, which was then published in a sep-arate brochure. Engels was immediately informed by Schorlemmer, who had

---

48   MECW 25:370.
49   Wiedemann 1895, p. xxvii.
50   Letter from Engels to Marx, 21 March 1869, MECW 43:246.

attended the meeting.[51] In a number of early remarks in *Dialectics of Nature*, he continued his mildly bizarre polemic.[52] Obviously he was trying to defend not only his conception of the consequences of the principle of conservation of energy but his entire fundamental understanding of the eternity of the universe. In a more reasoned and reasonable remark from the same period, however, he consoled himself with the fact that the question Clausius had asked would gradually be answered: where heat came from and where it was going would have a natural explanation.[53]

In a section developed later, the name Clausius had ceased to be like a red flag to a bull for Engels. Quite the opposite; he referred several times to the latter's great main work, *The Mechanical Theory of Heat*, which was published in a second edition in 1876.[54] He even cited Clausius for the phrase 'reversible process'.[55] It was a touchy expression for Engels, since Clausius had in fact demonstrated that some processes were *not* reversible.

As we have seen,[56] there was a certain tension between Engels's obstinate insistence on the idea that all inorganic processes were reversible and his equally resolute thesis that organic life was an irreversible process with a distinct beginning in time. Clausius's law of entropy was a law of development, though, and therefore – one would think – have exerted some attraction over him. In fact, he seems to have also attempted to incorporate it into his world of ideas. In the preface to *Dialectics of Nature*, which he wrote in 1876 before he set to work on *Anti-Dühring*, he expressed the opinion that the Earth would gradually cool down to the point where life would be impossible. But history would not end with that! The heat would once again somehow be liberated and a new cycle of development would begin. Entropy would thus not have the last word.[57]

With that, the total reversibility of the inorganic forms of motion appear as support for his idea of the eternity of the universe: entropy would achieve its maximum but then decrease again.

There is a connection between belief in the eternity of matter and irreductive materialism that we cannot disregard. All the changing forms of motion that the universe can present – from mechanical motion to the development

---

51   Letter from Engels to Marx, 2 September 1867, MECW 42:418.

52   MECW 25:551 (1873) and 562 (1875).

53   MECW 25:561 et seq. (1875).

54   See the notes from 1880 or 1881, MECW 25:563 ('Conclusion for Thomson, Clausius, Loschmidt ...') as well as pages 390 and 398 from the same period.

55   MECW 25:397.

56   Above, p. 403 *et seq.*

57   MECW 25:331 et seq.

of human society – could emerge naturally from eternal matter. Matter can manifest itself in many forms without any outside influence whatsoever. The old argument against mechanical materialism, that something such as a living creature, or Roman empire, or work of poetry cannot be the result of the attraction and repulsion of non-living bodies met with opposition. Even the most basic matter can have many, qualitatively entirely different, manifestations: now mechanical motion, now heat, now electricity.

But irreductive materialism was not only a supplementary hypothesis for Engels: it also had its own key role in his attempt at a synthesis. More specifically, it represented *the dialectical element in his ontology.*

There were primarily three different places where Engels set his irreductive materialism against reductive, or mechanical, materialism. He did so in *Anti-Dühring* in his polemic with Dühring.[58] He did so in a sweeping remark from 1885, which from the start was intended as an addition to the new edition of *Anti-Dühring*.[59] And, finally, he did so in a commentary on Carl von Nägeli's lecture *Die Schranken der naturwissenschaftlichen Erkenntniss* (Opening the Gates of Scientific Knowledge), which was given at the meeting of the Scientists' Association in Munich in 1877, and which Engels learned about through the agency of Schorlemmer.[60]

Here, Engels objected to what he called 'the prevailing mechanical opinion'.[61] Briefly put, the mechanical opinion meant that physics, chemistry and ultimately biology were different types of mechanics and that the specific processes that were treated in these disciplines were in fact the kind of processes as those in mechanics. According to the mechanical opinion, speaking of particular physical properties (the properties of light, for example) or particular chemical properties (the properties of a certain element or certain compound) thus meant expressing oneself only in makeshift or practically simplified terms. Light would not be scientifically explainable until it was brought back into purely mechanical processes, and the same applied to chemical and biological phenomena. Engels objected to Dühring's manner of reducing all movement to 'mechanical forces as their given basic form'.[62] In the addition from 1885, he explained that the mechanical conception[63] was based on the idea that all change can be explained as 'locomotion' and with that all qualitative dif-

---

58   MECW 25:61.
59   MECW 25:530–35.
60   MECW 25:512 et seq. Cf. 25:678, Note 258.
61   MECW 25:513.
62   MECW 25:55.
63   MECW 25:530 et seq. ('On the "Mechanical" Conception of Nature').

ferences could be explained quantitatively.[64] With that, even chemistry, for example, was presented as 'a kind of mechanics'. The conception resulted in the theory of 'the absolute quantitative identity of matter'.[65] In his reckoning with Nägeli, Engels characterised the mechanicist view not only by the fact that qualitative differences were regarded as abolished once they could be traced back to quantitative changes; quality and quantity were also regarded as 'absolutely separate categories'.[66]

Engels's own understanding meant *on the one hand* that there was a continual, quantitatively determinable transition from one form of motion to another, from one level of nature to another. Physics could be characterised as 'the mechanics of the molecule', chemistry as 'the physics of the atom' and biology as 'the chemistry of proteins' since mechanical processes transitioned into physical processes, physical into chemical processes, chemical into biological processes.[67] With that, Engels marked off a front against all vitalist – as well as generally idealist – conceptions.

On the other hand, 'the transition from one form of motion to another always entails a leap, a decisive turning point'.[68] New qualities emerged, and even though the transition to this new quality could be quantitatively determined it did not mean that the quality had thus been eliminated. With that, Engels marked off a front against mechanicist views of various types, including mechanical materialism.

It remains now to form a more detailed conception of what he actually meant here by 'quality'. This is the concept around which his entire dialectical materialism revolves.

But first, we must state that he provided several messages about *where* the crucial qualitative boundaries between various 'forms of movement' lie. The sentence just cited about physics as the mechanics of the molecule, chemistry as the physics of the atom, and so on seems to provide a hierarchy: mechanics – physics – chemistry. On the other hand, physics encompasses several different forms of motion: heat, light and so on. In his account of the forms of motion of matter, Engels argues as if these physical forms of motion were equal to the

---

64   Here, Engels goes into a line of thought that does not square whatsoever with what he otherwise was saying. He points out that it was nowhere near possible everywhere to show the quantitative changes that led to new qualities emerging (in biology, for example). This was the usual argument of vitalism, and it conflicted with Engels's main idea that a qualitative change is always matched by a quantitative one. MECW 25:531.

65   MECW 25:532.

66   MECW 25:513.

67   MECW 25:530 et seq.

68   MECW 25:61.

chemical forms: the chemical forms are, of course, includes in the great balance sheet of the principle of conservation of energy. When he again spoke about biology, he could express himself thus: that the organic constituted a higher unity of both mechanics and physics, and chemistry.[69] The hierarchy there seems to have the following appearance:

$$\text{Physics} \nearrow \overset{\text{Mechanics}}{\underset{\text{Biology}}{\downarrow}} \searrow \text{Chemistry}$$

This diversity of classifications is due not only to the difficulty in classifying sciences but also to the ambiguity in the term 'quality'.

4   Quality and Quantity

What is a quality, according to Engels?

Regarding mechanics, he said that 'it knows only quantities; it reckons with velocities and masses, and volumes'.[70] This remark, though isolated, seems rather odd. Why would velocity and mass not be qualities? In the more or less expressly mechanistic tradition, which Engels was opposed to, the basic concepts of mechanics had often been summarised in the term 'primary qualities', set against the sensuously accessible 'secondary qualities'.[71] In Hegel, the concept of quality was fundamental to the concept of quantity[72] and, according to him, a fundamental sphere of knowledge and reality was unimaginable without qualities. 'Quantity itself is a quality', he said;[73] that is, a measurement is always a measurement of *something*, and this something, this 'determination', is a quality.

It could be assumed that Engels here was using a narrower concept of quality, in which quality meant roughly the same thing as secondary quality in the traditional philosophical terminology. In fact, he had firm support in the vocab-

---

69   See e.g. MECW 25:529.

70   MECW 25:531.

71   The distinction between properties that are assumed to belong to the object itself and properties that only an observer ascribes to the object (e.g. colour) can be traced all the way back to the materialist philosophy of antiquity, and then played a major role for figures such as Galileo, Descartes and Newton.

72   Hegel 4:219.

73   Ibid., p. 402.

ulary that was predominant among the physicists and chemists of the time and permeated the textbooks. It should not be forgotten than Engels had an author of chemistry textbooks close to hand and the literary surveys by Roscoe, Schorlemmer and others consistently spoke of *physical* and *chemical* – not mechanical – properties. Every element and compound could thus be characterised in accordance with physical properties such as hardness, colour, specific weight and temperature conditions. Their chemical properties were, again, their reactions to other elements and compounds. From these investigations, the issue of reducing the physical and chemical properties to mechanics was completely ruled out; there were no 'properties' in mechanics.[74]

Time and time again in *Anti-Dühring* and *Dialectics of Nature*, Engels revealed how closely he held to this vocabulary and thereby the world of ideas encapsulated in it. As we have seen, his prime example of the law of quantity and quality was Schorlemmer's specialty, the hydrocarbon series. The difference between methane (CH_4) and ethane (C_2H_6) is quantitatively determinable – that is, determinable in chemical quantities, in the number of atoms – but the different quantities also entail different qualities. Methane and ethane have different physical and chemical properties.[75]

It scarcely needs to be added that the concepts of physical and chemical properties are not properly demarcated, nor do they assume any lack of mechanical properties.

But is 'quality' consistently the same as any property in Engels? He provided no explicit answers himself. In later Marxist literature, there have often been attempts at distinguishing between a more general concept of properties and a concept of quality adapted to the dialectic; Russian thus distinguishes carefully between *свойство* in the former sense and *качество* in the latter.[76]

I believe a distinction of this kind squares with what was the fundamental intent of Engels's concept of quality. But in no way does that clear up the issue of their demarcation. The question of how 'quality' relates to 'property' had already placed Hegel in a certain – in his case, quite unusual – awkward situation. Quality, he said in *Science of Logic*, was a property only in an outward

---

74   Cf. for example Roscoe 1868, p. 21 et seq., 63, 93, 96 et seq., 138 et seq.; Roscoe and Schorlemmer 1877, Vol. II, pp. 821, 826; Regnault and Strecker 1853, Vol. I, p. 1 et seq., 1863, Vol. II, p. 31 et seq., 37. Even in the great Wurtz, the articles (for example, on the elements) are structured such that after a history and description of the element's natural state and method of chemically isolating and processing it, a careful review follows of first the physical and then the chemical properties.

75   MECW 25:118 et seq., 359 et seq.

76   See for example Grujić 1969, p. 37, and the words in question in Ballestrem 1964.

sense (i.e. when distinguishing one plant species from another, for example, bringing out the characteristics that differentiate the species in question from its closest relatives). It is not the species as such being asked about, but only the characteristics that separate it from other species. As regards the species itself, Hegel says, it is not the characteristics that are being spoken about; but – he added hastily – nor was it the qualities, if the subject of the determination was not being perceived as something fixed and unchangeable.[77]

Engels may have taken over Hegel's flash of uncertainty; on the other hand, the term 'quality' has a far more advanced position for him than for Hegel. For Hegel, it described a primitive concept that does not help us understand reality as a process – that is, reality in development. For Engels, it plays the key role in dialectical materialism. 'Qualitative change' has to do with 'leaps', and thus substantially to do with the transition between different forms of motion. In his polemic against mechanical materialism, Engels could assert that mechanics did not take qualities into account. When he presented his own conception, mechanical motion was one of the forms of motion, and between the different forms of motion there was a *qualitative difference*. In this context, he could also unreservedly describe 'mechanical motion' as a quality alongside heat and electricity, for example.[78]

This mode of expression, of course, squares better with his fundamental conception. Mechanics takes qualities into account as much as physics or chemistry does. 'Quality' thus becomes primarily synonymous with *essential property* or, more specifically, *property that a certain science* (mechanics, physics, chemistry, biology, and so on) *determines as decisive in its object of study*. Mechanics calculates only with mass and acceleration ('mechanical motion'); physics, moreover, with the special properties of light, heat, electricity and magnetism. The difference between physics and chemistry lies in the fact that physics only takes the molecules into account and not to the atomic composition of those molecules. By contrast, the chemist has to work with specific chemical qualities that cannot be derived from the physical ones: the qualities of the molecules reveal nothing about those of the atoms.[79] On the other hand, as we have seen, the chemist must work with the whole set of 'physical properties' of the chemical compounds. In that sense, physics is more fundamental than chemistry. If the concept of quality is taken as the outlook, the scientific hierarchy appears as an ordered series of disciplines in which the discipline higher up in the

---

77   Hegel 4:128 et seq. Cf. ibid. p. 607 et seq., where Hegel calls properties '*reflektierte Qualität*'.
78   MECW 25:357.
79   Cf. for example MECW 25:358.

hierarchy has to take into account both the specific qualities of its object of study and the qualities that the lower, more fundamental discipline takes into account. Biology thus presupposes mechanics, physics and chemistry.[80]

Once again, we must note the structural similarity between this idea, which forms the basis for Engels's ontology, and his and Marx's ideas on base and superstructure. In its way, mechanics stands out as the base of the sciences, over which the other sciences form an arch of an increasingly distant superstructure. This superstructure always presupposes the base, but this base does not determine them absolutely: in relation to the qualities of the base, the superstructure's own unique qualities appear as chance occurrences, and thus unexplainable and unpredictable. Molecules are a type of mass, and the knowledge of them presupposes the general laws of mechanics for the motion of masses; mechanics, however, cannot explain the specific qualities of the molecules. The atom also has a mass, and the atom naturally occurs only in molecular compounds; but the molecular laws of physics do not say how the atoms join and are brought together. The same applies to biology and human history.

The relation is thus analogous to what applies to the base of society and its various superstructures. To understand the Paris Commune, the development of the base in France, Europe and the world in 1871 must be known; this knowledge, however, is not sufficient to understand the history of the Commune. The fundamental qualities of the base – the relation between forces of production and conditions of production – do not, for example, determine the characters of the persons playing a part.[81]

Engels's irreductive materialism is thus closely linked with the problems of determinism that dominated nineteenth-century science to such a great degree. The law of quality and quantity was an attempt to unite chance and necessity. Quantity is the determining factor, since every transition to new qualities is quantitatively determined. Quality is the non-determining factor: the quality of molecule is not given in the quality of mass, the quality of atom is not given in the quality of molecule, and so on.

We have not, however, thereby come to full clarity on what Engels meant by 'quality'. A qualitative leap seems at times to be the genesis of new qualities (the qualities of life are not found in inorganic matter, and so on) and at times to be only changes in already existing qualities. When Engels spoke about qualitative leaps between different members of the paraffin series (methane, ethane,

---

80   E.g. MECW 25:71.
81   Above, p. 399 et seq.

etc.) he was of course referring to the latter.[82] Methane and ethane thus have the same set of qualities or essential properties, but they differ crucially from each other as regards their properties.

But how does a qualitative leap of this type *within* a form of motion or a level[83] relate to the qualitative leap *between* forms of motion or levels?

A definite difference must no doubt be taken into account, but upon closer inspection it proves to be more difficult to grasp than initially lets on. But what about – to now use the famous example from *Capital*[84] – the qualitative leap from handicraft to manufacture? Is it a question of changes within the already existing qualities or the genesis of entirely new ones?

A relativist response is possible: looking at the question from a broad perspective, if the entirety of humanity's development is kept in view, it is *not* a question of new qualities; if, on the other hand, the question is viewed from a more limited perspective, the new features in manufacture stand out as new, essential properties – and thus new qualities.

But if 'quality' is determined only as 'essential property', the determination of qualities stands out largely as a definition of an object of study. It is then that the relativity emerges most strongly: if the issue is determining what a living being is, the difference between a brown bear and a polar bear does not play a role. If, on the other hand, the characteristics of bears are under discussion, the different species of bear represent new qualities in relation to one another.

The concept of quality is thus trivialised. Engels is not innocent of this trivialisation. But at certain moments he defends himself against it; for example, when he polemicised in *Anti-Dühring* against the attempt to lay out definitions of organic life.[85]

When he spoke about different forms of motion, the different qualities of the forms of motion did not stand out as a link in defining them. They were variables in scientific theories – or, in other words, components in the context of scientific laws. The qualitative leap *de préférence* was the leap in which a new theory steps in and a new context of laws can be demonstrated. In Marxist social theory, the leap from handicraft to manufacture was just such a qualitative leap in a more qualified sense, since manufacture presents different

---

82   MECW 25:118 et seq., 359 et seq.
83   'Level' here means a theoretical area dealing with the same qualities, e.g. (according to Engels's ontology) mechanics or biology, or (to choose examples from the field of historical materialism) the base and various parts of the superstructure, respectively.
84   MECW 35:312 et seq.
85   MECW 25:77.

contexts of laws than handicraft. The leap from methane to ethane, by contrast, is no more a leap than the leap from brown bear to polar bear is.

In this sense, the law of quality and quantity means that *there is no single general theory* – the theory of mechanics, for example – *under which all other theories can be subsumed* and regarded as special cases and applications. There are, on the other hand, more or less fundamental theories where the more fundamental theory determines the framework for the less fundamental theory. This is the unique position of mechanics in relation to physics and chemistry, and the unique position of physics and chemistry in relation to biology. In the sphere of social theory, it is the unique position of the base in relation to the superstructure but also the unique position of the theory of capitalism in relation to the theory or theories of precapitalist modes of production.[86]

As we have already seen, Engels was not particularly anxious to unambiguously mark off the various theories of inorganic nature from one another. He made use of different classifications. Schorlemmer wanted to show that the boundary between organic and inorganic chemistry was not by chance and determined solely in practice.[87] He drew the boundaries entirely in the spirit of Engels, but a search of Engels's writings for an opinion on this specific issue would be in vain.

On the other hand, the question of the relation between life and lifelessness, between organic and inorganic received considerable attention in *Anti-Dühring* and *Dialectics of Nature*. There, we have one of the clearest examples of what Engels meant by a qualitative transition.

Engels thus took up the question of how life could have emerged from inorganic matter. Here, he was entirely oriented on what I have called the chemical problem:[88] his perspective was also crucially defined and influenced by Schorlemmer the chemist.

He agreed with the mechanicists that the definite qualities of life emerged from and were indissolubly bound with a definite form of matter: the protein. With his weakness for Hegelian formulations, he proclaimed: 'Life is the mode of existence of albuminous bodies'. He immediately added that chemists did not know enough about the protein: the term itself was 'unhappy'. What was certain was that the phenomenon of life was bound up with a certain type of albuminous matter.[89]

---

86 It is a central line of thought in Marx that previous modes of production are only fully comprehensible if the capitalist mode is known; cf. Marx 1953, p. 25 et seq.

87 Above, p. 356 *et seq.*

88 Above, p. 157.

89 MECW 25:75 et seq. Cf. also ibid. p. 55 et seq. and 576 et seq.

Thus far, the mechanicists were right. On the other hand, however, Engels did not accept that life could be reduced to lifeless matter, to chemistry. The genesis of life meant the genesis of a new form of movement; the transition from dead protein to living mater was a leap, '*eine entscheidende Wendung*'.[90]

It should be added that Engels had eagerly followed the chemists' and biologists' often exaggeratedly optimistic attempts to determine the point at which life had emerged from the inorganic. It was an interest that Marx shared; back in 1868 he had observed the search by Haeckel and others for the 'ur-cell'.[91] Both Marx and Engels also occupied themselves assiduously with the artificial cell of German physiologist and chemist Moritz Traube, for which Traube had given a more popular orientation at the meeting of the Scientists' Association in Breslau in 1874.[92] They obviously shared Traube's idea that a real synthesis was imminent: the detail that was still missing was the nucleus of the artificial cell.[93]

Like Marx, Engels argued that the mystery of life would conclusively be solved on the day that living matter could be synthesised. The fundamental chemical composition of life would then be known; life could then be determined *quantitatively*. But the qualities of life would not thereby be abolished.

Engels stated this basic understanding incisively:

> One day we shall certainly 'reduce' thought experimentally to molecular and chemical motion in the brain; but does that exhaust the essence of thought?[94]

90   MECW 25:61.
91   Letter from Marx to Engels, 19 November 1868, MECW 43:162. Marx's form of expression is greatly reminiscent of the one Engels used later (naturally, both may have had Schorlemmer as a shared model). 'The primaeval form must naturally be traced down to the point at which it may be produced chemically', Marx says.
92   Cf. Traube 1874. A more systematic account can be found in Traube 1867.
93   A letter from Marx to W.A. Freund, a Social-Democratic gynaecologist in Breslau, on 21 January 1877 says that Marx knew Traube and that he had been promised that Traube's works would be sent to him. The letter also revealed that Engels was thinking of using Traube's results for *Dialectics of Nature*. No correspondence between Marx and Traube (or Engels and Traube) has been preserved, and the references to Traube's research found in *Dialectics of Nature* (MECW 25:578 and 601) are older than Marx's letter. MECW 45:192.
94   MECW 25:527.

CHAPTER 16

Biology and Human Science

In *Anti-Dühring*, Engels distinguished between three classes of science. The first reached from mathematics to chemistry. The second investigated living organisms. He called the third class 'the historical sciences'. Their task was to 'study ... the conditions of human life, social relationships, forms of law and government, with their ideal superstructure in the shape of philosophy, religion, art, etc.'.[1]

The three classes thus constitute a coherent scientific hierarchy. The further down in the hierarchy one goes, the simpler the connections to be observed, and the theories correspondingly become more certain and more exact.

The opposite could be said regarding Engels's own synthesis of the sciences. The further up he went in his attempt at a synthesis, the greater his certainty and the clearer his statements. In the sphere of the human sciences he was naturally his own authority. As regards biology, Darwin and Darwinism completely dominated his field of vision.

In that sense, it is also a significantly easier task to summarise his comments on biology and human science than it is to bring clarity to his views of mechanics, physics and chemistry. At the same time, however, a summary of this kind must be of the type that, based on it, the totality and context of his entire synthesis of the sciences – and thus his ontology – can be reconstructed. In particular, it is his comments on the human sciences that reveal the paradigm in his irreductive materialism. This must therefore be brought out with great care.

1   **Biology**

There were primarily three areas of biological research that roused Engels's interest. One was the question of the origins of life and thus of the chemical foundation for the simplest forms of life. We have just acquainted ourselves with his comments on the question. Further, he was interested in the findings of cytology, or cell theory. But above all he dwelled on Darwinist evolutionary biology, which for him – as for almost everyone in his time – constituted general biological theory.

---

1   MECW 25:86 et seq.

He had intended, however, to bring cytology up for discussion in more detail. In particular, it was Rudolf Virchow's ideas that had captured his attention. In the outline for *Dialectics of Nature*, which he drew up in 1878, he promised a separate chapter titled '*Zellenstaat – Virchow*'.[2] In *Anti-Dühring*, he had gone into the foundations of cell theory.[3] In the preface to the 1885 edition of the same work, where he summarised his view of the natural sciences for the first time, he also touched on the same subject in passing.[4]

There was one aspect of cell theory that primarily occupied his thoughts: the dissolution of the fixed concept of biological individual, or organism. In *Cellular Pathology*, Rudolf Virchow declared that 'every animal presents itself as a sum of vital unities'. The organism comprises the sum of its organs, the organs of tissues, the tissues of 'cell territories'.[5] Engels commented, with a hint of irony, that Virchow had dissolved the animal individual into a federation of cell states in a more 'liberal' than scientific and dialectical manner. The taunt was obvious: Virchow was a leading representative of the national-liberal Progressive Party, which was a zealous supporter of a German federation of relatively independent states.[6] What Engels found important and interesting in Virchow's perspective, however, was the joining together of the different levels of the organism: organ, tissue and cell. The organism comprised at one and the same time the sum total and the well-arranged totality of organs, tissues and finally cells. It was obvious what he meant by a dialectic perspective of the organism. He noted that the human individual had become more problematic as well; they no longer had the unconditional 'indivisibility' that the concept itself of the individual presupposed. This line of thought hints at a continuation: on the higher, social plane there is the same relative autonomy of the individual in relation to the class and for the class in relation to the individual. There is a hierarchy of levels in which each level in relation to the next highest and next lowest levels is at once an independent unity and a passive part or sum, respectively.

The new cytology had thus dissolved some of the fixed unities in the older field of biology. It was the same merit that Engels particularly accentuated in Darwinist evolutionary biology. '*Hard and fast lines* are incompatible with the theory of evolution', he declared in 1875 in a note in *Dialectics of Nature*.[7] There

---

2 MECW 25:317.
3 MECW 25:71.
4 MECW 25:15.
5 Virchow 1871, p. 17.
6 Cf. MECW 25:648, Note 20.
7 MECW 25:493.

was thus no unbridgeable gulf established between the species. At the same time as they functioned as real unities – the species, with certain modifications, comprised the limit for potential propagation – they flowed together with neighbouring species and shared an origin with them.

Engels's comments on Darwin and Darwinism are scattered across a large number of works and letters. We have already stopped to consider some of his early comments.[8] Among his later presentations, there are two that through their fullness of detail deserve to be brought out. One is the crushing reckoning with Dühring's polemic against Darwin in *Anti-Dühring*. The other is the chapter 'The Part Played by Labour in the Transition from Ape to Man', which was written just before Engels set to work on the polemical pamphlet against Dühring and is now included in *Dialectics of Nature*. Originally, it was meant to introduce a completely different work, preliminarily titled *On the Three Basic Forms of Slavery*.[9] The chapter in question deals with the transition from the animal world to human society and will therefore be treated in the next section.

A detailed letter on Darwinism that Engels wrote to Russian anarchist Pyotr Lavrov in November 1875[10] is of special interest here. It comprises a necessary supplement to the presentation in *Anti-Dühring*, in which Engels regarded it as his main task to defend Darwin and not to demarcate his own understanding.

In addition to these three texts, which all came into being over a very short period of time, there is a wealth of more brief mentions and comments in his writings, letters and excerpts.

Playing a main role in these comments on Darwinism is the phrase 'the struggle for existence', with its complex content of strict biological selection theory, Malthusian population theory, unrestrained liberalism and elitism. A crucial question concerns whether biological selection is an essential factor of development in human history as well. But this question has to do with the transition from biology to history, and will be treated in that context.

Engels, however, also commented on the limited biological content of 'the struggle for existence'. The most important places in the text are in *Anti-Dühring* and the letter to Lavrov. At first, it may seem as if his statements are irreconcilable. In *Anti-Dühring*, he stands up in defence; in the letter, he goes on the attack. The contradiction, however, is an illusory one.

In the letter, he explains that he accepts the Darwinist theory of development itself (i.e. the thesis on the origin of species). On the other hand, he

---

8   Above, p. 107, p. 110 et seq.
9   Cf. MECW 25:671, Note 199.
10   Letter from Engels to P. Lavrov, 12 November 1875, MECW 45:106 et seq.

regards Darwin's 'method of proof' – the theory of natural selection – as an
initial makeshift attempt to explain the development of species. He remarks
ironically on the materialist champions of the 1840s and 1850s – Vogt, Büchner and Moleschott – who before Darwin emphasised cooperation in organic
nature but now only spoke about the struggle for existence. In fact, this complex biological development 'comprises harmony as well as strife, struggle as
well as cooperation'.[11]

In *Anti-Dühring* these viewpoints do not emerge: the perspective there is
entirely determined by Dühring's sharp criticism of Darwin. For the history of
Marxism, it is not insignificant that the text known to all – *Anti-Dühring* – only
contained a defence of Darwin. The modifications in the letter to Lavrov and
elsewhere remained unknown.[12]

Dühring had asserted that Darwin's theory lacked scientific value. It primarily comprised a 'natural-philosophical semi-poetry'. Darwin had borrowed the
struggle for existence – and with it, the theory of natural selection – from
Malthus; the theory actually only contained 'a piece of brutality directed
against humanity'.[13]

Marx and Engels had levelled the remarks pertaining to Darwin's dependence on Malthus much earlier.[14] This criticism, however, did not have the same
significance for them as it did for Dühring. Engels admitted than Darwin was
naive when he took over Malthus's theory sight unseen. But this did not mean
that the fact itself in the organic world that Darwin described in Malthusian
terms could be rejected. Selection is a factor of extreme significance in biological development, whatever name it is given. It could be called 'the struggle
for existence' or 'lack of conditions of life and mechanical effects'.[15]

Dühring had also levelled the often-occurring remark that Darwin had not
explained the variation among organisms within the same species, which is a
condition for selection to be able to operate.[16] Engels objected that Darwin had
not claimed to have found the causes of variation. He also argued that later Dar-

11 Ibid., p. 107. Similar viewpoints are found in the notes from 1875; MECW 25:583 et seq.
12 The uninformed literature on Engels's relation to Darwin (cf. above Chapter 4, Note 50)
    bears full witness to the fact that the bias in Engels's assessment in *Anti-Dühring* still marks
    the accounts. Part of the matter, naturally, is that a number of 'orthodox' representatives
    of Marxism from the 1890s (or late 1880s) actually sought to turn the materialist concep-
    tion of history into a type of simple application of Darwinism to human history; cf. below,
    p. 518 et seq.
13 Dühring 1875, pp. 101, 109 et seq.
14 Above, p. 111 *et seq.*
15 MECW 25:65 et seq.
16 Dühring 1875, p. 115 et seq.

winists – Ernst Haeckel in particular – had come part way with the thesis that
the development of species was the result of interplay between heredity and
adaptation, in which adaptation comprised the active and the changing, and
heredity the passive and preserving, factor.[17] It is not difficult to understand
Engels's enthusiasm over the general dialectical appearance of this thesis.[18] The
fact that it provided no enlightenment regarding the causes of variation was
another matter. It was a deficiency that not even the best Darwinist specialists
would admit.

Engels also mobilised basic biogenetic laws in the defence of Darwinism
against Dühring. The individual repeated the entire history of its species in its
development: this was the 'most secure basis' of the theory of development, he
declared.[19]

Only at the end of this reckoning with Dühring, however, does Engels arrive
at what comprises the great and decisive reason for his own acceptance of the
main features of Darwin's theory with the same fervour that Dühring rejects
it. This is the issue of *development and determinism*. Dühring was a resolute
advocate of the determinist ideal. It was impossible to speak about development without knowing about the laws of development, he said.[20] It was in
principle the same type of criticism that Nägeli, Kölliker, Jenkin and many others levelled against Darwinism.[21] A satisfactory scientific theory is a strictly
determinist theory. The theory of natural selection is not such a theory, and as
long as the sought-after theory is conspicuous in its absence, we cannot speak
of the development of a species with any scientific authority.

Engels sided resolutely with the theory of natural selection.[22] He did so
out of genuine conviction. In this specific respect, historical materialism is
the child of the same spirit as the theory. Dühring's determinist claim was
repeated in the sphere of the history of society; Engels's criticism there was

---

17   MECW 25:65 et seq.
18   It is also apostrophised in *Dialectics of Nature*; MECW 25:492, 583, Haeckel lays out his
      doctrine in such works as Haeckel 1866, p. 153 et seq.
19   MECW 25:70. Cf. also MECW 25:460.
20   Dühring 1875, p. 127. Here, Dühring uses the programme of reductive mechanicism in his
      criticism of Darwinism. He declares that '*alle Entwicklungsschematismen, soweit sie mehr
      als äusserliche Aschauungsbilder der unmittelbaren Erfahrung sein sollen, die Bearbei-
      tung eines atomistischen Materials aufweisen müssen. Nur in diesem Sinne können wir
      Entwicklungsgesetze als letzte Instanzen der Rechenschaft anerkennen, und nur in dieser
      Richtung kann es eine zergliedernde und hiermit erst wahrhafte Wissenschaft geben. Der
      reine Mechanismus hat in dieser Beziehung denselben Anspruch zu machen, und die Ent-
      wicklung muss in der rein mechanischen Composition sogar ihre erste Stelle haben*'.
21   Above, p. 187 *et seq.*
22   MECW 25:7 et seq.

of the same type. We are thus dealing here with a real theoretical antagonism between Dühring and Engels, an entirely fundamental antagonism that shows the reckoning with Dühring *was not simply an ideological struggle for influence over German social democracy but also a struggle over scientific theories and a scientific ideal.* It could be said that Engels assiduously defended Darwin's theory not only because Darwin's theory had certain formal similarities (non-determinism) with Marxist social theory but also because the theory of biological development itself in Darwinist vintage constituted the only heretofore existing theory that could constitute a foundation for Marxist social theory. The determinists' criticism of Darwinism implied a criticism of historical materialism and the theory of capital.

2   Biology and History

Engels asserted a continuity between biological development and human history. At the same time, however, he asserted a discontinuity: just as there was a qualitative leap between inorganic and organic, so was there a qualitative leap between purely biological and human.

In the sphere of biology, he was prepared to defend the theory of natural selection. At the same time, however, he defended the sphere of history against the theory of natural selection – or, more precisely, against the direct applications of Darwinist explanatory models that had become legion ever since *Origin* was published.

Relatively early on, he and Marx came into direct contact with attempts to view human history as one long 'struggle for existence' in and through Friedrich Albert Lange's *Die Arbeiterfrage* (The Labour Question). Lange regarded himself as a socialist; it was thus no social Darwinist in the spirit of Spencer who had taken up the pen. In later editions, Lange's book was full of largely approving and appreciative references to *Capital.* Marx and Engels had every reason to take up his book for serious study. Moreover, Lange had contacted Engels back when the first edition was published.[23]

But what did Lange's application of the Darwinist theory of natural selection look like? He declared that his intent was to 'derive the labour question from Darwin's principles'. In the same breath, he said that he did not regard these principles as inevitable for humanity, since humanity had raised itself above 'the ruthless and soulless mechanism through calculating purposefulness'. But

---

23   Above, p. 15

he could not liberate himself completely from the struggle for existence. Lange regarded his own book as the first, if deficient, attempt to show how both spiritual and economic development could be understood with the help of the same principles as the origin of species – that is, through the struggle for existence.[24]

It is not clear in the book, either here or elsewhere, where the boundary between blind selection and humanity's ability to plan and predict lies. The main point, in any case, was to demonstrate the significance of selection for human development. Lange interpreted the phrase 'struggle for existence' broadly. Even in nature, the struggle for existence applied not only to a struggle for mere survival: it applied to the *best* conditions of life. So it was even among humans.[25] The worker's struggle was primarily a struggle for 'the wages of labour'.[26]

The condition for selection is, naturally, overproduction. In nature, it was a question of overproduction of 'the seeds of life'. But in human society, it was instead a question of an overproduction of 'talents'. There are leadership talents scattered among the masses: in a hierarchically organised society these talents would never be put to use since leading positions were reserved for certain layers.[27]

In this and other similar arguments, Lange appears to see a more efficient 'struggle for existence' – or, more precisely, a struggle for better positions in society – as a condition for development in a socialist direction. Capitalism puts a spanner in the works by compelling workers to be simply workers. At the same time, however, this selection is a blind force that is offset by humanity's ability to calculate. Lange also put his trust in humanity's moral advances, which could take natural necessities partly out of the running.[28]

In other words, it is obvious that 'the struggle for existence' meant many different things to Lange: it functioned in both rational and irrational contexts, in a struggle on both fair and unfair terms. The derivation from Darwin's principles he spoke about was in no way of the simple, straightforward type.

Marx's and Engels's comments on Lange's book are thoroughly acid and negative. When Marx read the second edition of *Die Arbeiterfrage*, he wrote in a letter that Lange had made a great discovery, namely that all of history could be subordinated to one great *'Naturgesetz'* (natural law). But this natural law

---

24   Lange 1875, p. 29 et seq.
25   Ibid., p. 5 et seq.
26   Ibid., p. 13.
27   Ibid., p. 46 et seq.
28   Ibid., p. 15.

was nothing more than a phrase – the 'struggle for life' – and the content of that phrase was Malthus's theory of population (or, more precisely, overpopulation). Lange did not attempt to analyse the phrase, but had found in it only 'a very rewarding method – for stilted, mock-scientific, highfaluting ignorance and intellectual laziness'.[29]

In his letter, Marx pointed out that Darwin's 'struggle for existence' lost its usefulness in the sphere of history.

This was obviously also Engels's view: selection could explain essential features of biological development but not in the historical development of humanity. Lange said that humans could modify the effects of selection through their conscious, planned activities. Marx and Engels did not want to be content with seeing a modification here. Something entirely new, qualitatively speaking had arisen as a result of humanity's development.

Long before Darwin appeared with *Origin*, back in *The German Ideology*, Marx and Engels had taken up the favourite question of anthropology: the question of how humans differed from the animals. 'Men can be distinguished from animals by consciousness, by religion or anything else you like. They themselves begin to distinguish themselves from animals as soon as they begin to *produce* their means of subsistence, a step which is conditioned by their physical organisation. By producing their means of subsistence men are indirectly producing their material life'.[30]

In the main, this was a determination they held fast to. In *The German Ideology*, however, they did not yet have any biological theory on which to construct their own historical materialism: they pointed out in very general terms that production had a connection with humanity's 'bodily organisation'. Darwinism provided them with new opportunities.

Most of their comments on the boundary between biology and history, however, remained rather brief. In the letter to Lavrov about Darwinism, Engels declared that the single – but crucial – difference between human and animal societies was that 'the most animals do is *garner*, whereas humans *produce*'. The struggle for existence thus becomes a struggle not only for the means of existence but for '*socially produced* means of development'. This takes the form of class struggle. So as not to yield an inch to the 'bad naturalists', the phrase 'struggle for existence' should not be used since humanity's internal struggle was of a radically different type than that of the animals.[31] In a remark in *Dia-*

---

29   Letter from Marx to L. Kugelmann, 27 June 1870, MECW 43:527 et seq.
30   MECW 5:31.
31   MECW 45:107 et seq.

lectics of Nature, which is most likely a rough draft of the letter, the same views are found in different clothing. The conception of history as a number of shifting class struggles is 'much richer in content and deeper that merely reducing it to weakly distinguished phases of the struggle for existence', as it says there. The word 'reducing' can be emphasised. Engels regarded his own – and Marx's – term 'class struggle' as an approximate counterpart to Darwin's 'struggle for existence'.[32] The class struggle, however, cannot be reduced to the struggle for existence without losing its actual content: the class struggle is essentially not the struggle to survive but a struggle for power over production and its development.

In other contexts, Engels described the difference between animals and humans thus: that the animal merely *uses* nature, whereas humanity through its planned actions *masters* it.[33] An animal species comprises a piece of the puzzle in the context of nature, whereas humanity during its development learns to change the entirety of nature's puzzle and ensure itself ever greater space within it.

The North American anthropologist Lewis H. Morgan, who in the early 1880s – a few years after Engels provided the definition above – would come to play such a large role for both Marx and Engels, declared in his work *Ancient Society* that humans were 'the only beings who may be said to have gained an absolute control over the production of food'.[34] Morgan's line of thought is similar to Engels's but not exactly the same; what Morgan said could in other respects be easily united with the positivist tradition from Comte.[35] Engels would in no way have asserted that humanity had won 'absolute control' over the production of food; all production under capitalism is blind and uncontrolled. Morgan's statement provided Marx and Engels with a bit of a quandary. Marx commented on this in his excerpts from *Ancient Society* with an exclamation point and a question mark.[36] When Engels cited the passage in *Origin of Family, Private Property and the State*, he modified its content by letting Morgan say that humanity had *'fast unbedingte Herrschaft'*[37] (almost complete control).

---

32   MECW 25:584 et seq.

33   MECW 25:460.

34   Morgan 1877, p. 19.

35   According to Comte, humanity continually increases its domination over nature through the development of knowledge; class contradictions, for example, cannot entail an obstacle to this development.

36   Marx 1972, p. 99, and Krader 1972, p. 13.

37   MECW 26:134.

Nevertheless, this rewriting – whether intentional or not – of Morgan could only partly adapt his statement to Engels's own conception. Control over nature is not the same as control over the production of food; from a Marxist perspective, the production of food cannot be distinguished from the social conditions, from the struggle itself over control over production – class struggle. Humanity masters nature to the extent that its productive forces are developed; the conditions of production also come into play for their control of 'the production of food'.

But Engels – as we shall soon see numerous examples of – took a mildly indulgent attitude towards Morgan. He was prepared to disregard the fundamental differences in order to find authoritative support in Morgan for some of his own theses.

When Engels said that in contrast to the animals, humanity mastered nature, he intended nothing more than to say that humanity produces whereas at most animals gather. Producing something from nature presupposes mastering nature to some extent: on the basis of insights into the process of nature, something new is produced from it. In turn, production is the foundation for new insights and thus for more efficient production and a growing mastery over nature.

The only point where Engels more closely illuminated the transition from animal to man is in the chapter 'The Part Played by Labour in the Transition from Ape to Man'. The purely biological knowledge and assumptions contained in this account were taken from Darwin's *Descent*[38] and from Haeckel's *Natürliche Schöpfungsgeschichte* and *Anthropogenie*.[39] Engels's assiduous study of *Nature* certainly also provided him with information about the biological discussion.

But he was not content with providing an account of the biological assumptions. He also interpreted them using his historical materialism and his fundamental irreductionist principles. Darwin and Haeckel regarded their task as demonstrating the continual (or, to use Engels's words, the quantitative) transition from anthropoid ape to human. Their investigations also assumed certain hypotheses regarding humanity's historical development; they devoted rather absent-minded interest to similar hypotheses and were likely not aware of their significance and controversial character.

---

38   Cf. for example MECW 20:452, where Engels starts from *Descent*, Chapter VI (Darwin 1871, Vol. I).

39   Haeckel and Darwin were likely being referred to when Engels spoke about 'the most materialistic natural scientists of the Darwinian school' (MECW 25:459). Engels had pre-

Engels emphasised the crucial significance of labour, or production, for 'becoming human'. His argument took a form that deserves to be emphasised as well. It could be described as paradigmatic for his entire irreductive materialism.

First, development up until the 'qualitative leap' from animal to human stands out as a purely biological process. The distinctive features of humanity thus play no role here: they do not yet exist. The upright posture liberated the hands, and the development of the hands was accompanied by the development of the other organs including the brain. The ape that became the human was a flock animal, and therein lay a biological condition for humanity's construction of society. Another condition was the development of the organs of speech.[40]

It should not be imagined that Engels was seeking the definitive point at which ape became human and biological development transitioned into human history. As far as time is concerned, the transition can be regarded as a fully continuous process with a longer or shorter transitional stage that could be called both biological and historical. Engels, for example, emphasised that the hand was not only a condition for labour but also that typical human labour contributed to the further development of the hand.[41]

The qualitative leap is not, nor does it need to be, a crucial change in a process of development: the process itself can appear to be quite continuous. The crucial element is *the leap from one theoretical level to another.* How humans became human can be explained on a purely biological basis. But for humanity's historical development, its biological constitution is only the general fundamental condition, quite similar everywhere. The difference between feudalism and capitalism – or, for that matter, between absolute monarchy and bourgeois democracy, between Christianity and Islam, between Baroque and Empire style – cannot be explained by biology. The ultimate explanation lies in humanity's production, in its labour.

This is the same type of argument that Engels conducted with greater indecision and uncertainty when he sought to demarcate biology from mechanics, physics from chemistry, and physics and chemistry from mechanics. The chemical theory could, or would, be able to explain the composition and function of the protein clumps from which life arose. But it would never be able to explain the difference between the functions of the brain and the stomach in the living organism, or the difference between a rhinoceros and a giraffe.

---

viously read Haeckel's *Natürliche Schöpfungsgeschichte* and *Anthropogenie* and cited them both; e.g. MECW 25:488 et seq. (with notes from 1874 onward).

40   MECW 20:452 et seq.

41   MECW 20:453.

There is, however, another structure in Engels's reasoning that deserves to be pointed out. *He was seeking the crucial or determining moment in every totality*, whether it was a biological one or a historical one. In the footsteps of Darwin and Haeckel, he saw the liberation of the hand as crucial for the biological development of the anthropoid ape into a human. In accordance with historical materialism, labour – or production – was given the same role in historical development. As we have seen, the structure was characteristic for Marx's and Engels's entire theoretical formation: it was the core of their dialectic.[42]

We do not need to go into more detail on Engels's purely biological determination of the transition from ape to human. There – sensibly enough – he followed the information he was able to take from the most esteemed authorities of his time. He did, however, make a very interesting observation as regards these biologists' manner of determining the driving force of human development. Even the most materialistically inclined of them could regard thought, or ideas, as the driving force of history, he pointed out.

But this more or less latent conception of theirs was not a mystery. What makes human production, production, is its methodicalness, and this methodicalness presupposes certain ideas about how this labour is to be performed. Alongside this historical development emerge other types of ideas – political, religious and so on – and the labour of the hand increasingly stood out as the passive tool for ideas and insights. 'Man became used to explaining its activity based on its ideas instead of its needs'.

We have already encountered veins of historical idealism in Darwin's *Descent*.[43] Similar ones are found in Haeckel.[44] Engels succeeded in showing how the general materialism of scientists did not immediately imply historical materialism: it could be said that historical materialism is a specific theory and not simply a moment in a general worldview or view of science.

3   The Human Sciences

When Engels spoke about what we here – to use a neutral expression – call the human sciences, he used the word 'history'. This is a word that reveals his spiritual kinship with the historicists: he took the description immedi-

---

42   Above, p. 388 *et seq.*

43   Above, p. 245.

44   Haeckel always emphasised that everything human had a revolutionist and physiological basis, but he did not doubt for a moment than human history was a product of the human spirit. Cf. for example Haeckel 1874, pp. 7 and 3 et seq.

ately from Hegel. In this vocabulary he was not influenced by the insight that only Darwin's *Origin* awoke in him,[45] namely that nature has a history as well.

At some point, he was compelled to account for the difference between 'history' in its broader and its narrower senses. 'With man we enter *history*', he wrote in the preface to *Dialectics of Nature*. But whereas animals are subordinate to their development, humanity could influence theirs through their own activity – and this to the same extent that they distance themselves from their original animal stage.[46]

Nowhere did Engels take up other generic names for the human disciplines for discussion such as Mill's 'moral sciences' or Comte's 'sociology'. Nor did he discuss the relations among various human scientific disciplines. This was certainly bound up with the fact that he was no more interested in or concerned with the incipient specialisation in this sphere than Marx was. Naturally, like Marx, he treated political economy as a sphere in itself: the entire second part of *Anti-Dühring* has the title 'Political Economy'. As is known, however, Marx's and his demarcation of political economy was not the same as that of the classical economists: the economic relations were not isolated from social relations, and class relations were not regarded as given. Using – quite anachronistically – twentieth-century descriptions of the disciplines, it could be said that Marxist political economy was equal parts economics and sociology.

For Marx and Engels, however, political economy was primarily *the theory of the base*; and the theories of the various layers and parts of the superstructure could not be isolated from the base. Their goal was ultimately a theory of the entire sphere of the human sciences, and all of human history: this is the materialist conception of history.

Engels was thus not inquiring after the relations between different specialisations in the human sciences; he did, however, repeatedly touch on the relation between base and superstructure. His most well-known definition is that the base determines the superstructure '*in letzter Instanz*' (in the last analysis). This phrase is now primarily associated with the letter Engels wrote to Joseph Bloch in 1890, in which he exhaustively explained what he meant by it. We have already seen that this investigation squares well with what Marx, in less popular and more philosophically charged phrases, stated in the introduction to the *Grundrisse*.[47]

---

45   Above, p. 110 *et seq.*
46   MECW 25:330.
47   Above, p. 387 *et seq.*

But the phrase occurred for the first time in Engels's writings back in *Anti-Dühring*. Its origins are quite surprising and also shed light over what Engels meant by it.

Engels used it entirely in passing to describe Marx's and his own conception of history: 'We maintain on the contrary that all moral theories have been hitherto the product, in the last analysis, of the economic conditions of society obtaining at the time'.[48] It is not particularly clear what 'in the last analysis' is supposed to mean in this brief sentence.

But this chance statement is preceded and followed by a polemic against Dühring's claim to have propounded a 'final and ultimate truth'[49] in the sphere of moral philosophy and economics.

Dühring raised the same claim in the human sciences as he did in biology.[50] His moral philosophy, like his political economy, was an ambitious attempt at propounding a kind of mechanics of moral rules and economic conditions.

Even moral philosophy thus had its 'timeless principles and simple elements'. The simple elements were brought together in accordance with the same inflexible logical rules as physical theories. Ethical truths were just as unchanging as mechanical truths.[51]

Beyond the changing moral conceptions, beyond the apparent chaos of human history, there were thus certain truths in the last analysis.

At first it may seem odd that Engels polemicised with such fervour against this idea only to himself declare what the truth about history 'in the last analysis' was. But the explanation lies in that he did not actually mean the same thing with his comment. He took it over, but filled it with his own content.

Knowledge of history was not yet particularly advanced, he explained. Organisms had largely been the same since the days of Aristotle, whereas human conditions had undergone and were undergoing incessant and thorough changes. The historian was thus dealing with a changing world of experiences. The historical context becomes clearer to the observer only when an epoch moves toward its dissolution.[52] That is why knowledge in this sphere is essentially 'relative'. The hunter for truth ultimately does not have much more to

---

48   MECW 25:87 et seq.
49   Dühring 1875, p. 2, p. 14 et seq.
50   Above, p. 432 *et seq.*
51   Dühring 1875, p. 192 et seq.
52   Here, Engels's presentation is similar to the one Hegel expressed in his well-known metaphor that Minerva's owl only takes flight at dusk; Hegel 7:37.

contribute than platitudes such as 'men cannot live except by labour; that up to the present they have for the most part been divided into rulers and ruled; that Napoleon died on May 5, 1821, and so on'.[53]

Of course, Engels was commenting in a polemically incisive manner here. The fact that humans have either ruled or been ruled by each other is, as we know, not a platitude according to the materialist conception of history but the very foundation of class analysis. The target of his polemic is fully visible, however: it is the idea that historical development, and thus human conditions, can be determined using fixed, unchanging principles. The principles could of course be of many different types. It could be a system of laws and rules that are alleged to have been drawn up and established by some divine being. It could be ideas about the unchanging essence of humanity. It could be causal laws that are said to concur with laws for biological development or for the entire universe.

Dühring's 'truth in the last analysis' combines statements about essence and laws of a natural scientific type. On the one hand there are norms for human actions, and on the other general explanations for why humans do one thing or another.

Engels objects just as much to the claim of the unchangeability of these 'truths' as he does to the claim of their invariability. As regards various moral conceptions, he asserted that they had to be put in relation to the base, to material production: they changed along with the development of the base. But it was also his and Marx's opinion that the base itself underwent crucial upheavals: the capitalist mode of production could not be derived from the feudal mode. Engels repeated his criticism of Dühring's 'truths' when he took up the view of society in general.[54] It was not only morals high up in the superstructure but also the base that eluded the Dühringian scientific norms.

Two steps in Engels's criticism can thus be distinguished. First, he attacked Dühring's manner of treating morals as an independent entity. Second, he attacked the idea of eternal truths about humanity's various relations.

The first criticism was formulated thus: Dühring was pursuing ideology instead of science. 'Ideology' here has the simple fundamental meaning of 'the deduction of reality not from itself but from a concept'.[55] In his theory of

---

53   MECW 25:83.
54   MECW 25:252, 254 et seq.
55   See in particular MECW 25:89. Regarding the concept of ideology, cf. below, p. 471 *et seq.* and in particular p. 475 *et seq.*

morals, Dühring started with a number of axioms from which universal and timeless morals could be derived. Engels wanted to show that these axioms were nothing but freely floating ideas. Human equality is one such axiom: to clarify and develop it, Dühring constructed an entire history that has an extremely loose connection to actual history. It was the same type of construction that the classical liberal economists excelled at, which Marx named 'Robinsonades'.[56] Engels also repeatedly recalled the name of Robinson in his criticism of Dühring's conception of society.[57] Dühring had the same approach as Smith or Ricardo: he created an idea of what certain human relations generally entailed, and constructed a process from that idea. Greater dignity was bestowed on this process than on actual development.[58]

According to Engels, however, the fault in this approach was not only that it was ideological (i.e. it was based on certain ideas). If we conduct a thought experiment in which someone constructed a similar historical schema with on a thoroughly materialist basis, or 'axioms', they would still be subject to Engels's criticism. This is apparent from Engels's definition of historical reality, which we recently became acquainted with. In it, Engels repeated in different wording what he and Marx said in *The German Ideology* thirty years previously, namely that historical materialist 'abstractions' did not provide 'a recipe or schema ... for neatly trimming the epochs of history'.[59]

It was not his opinion, however, that the human sciences here were unique, or that in other words there was a razor-sharp boundary between what he called history and the other sciences. He explained, for example, that in essential respects economics was compelled to work 'factors known only relatively' but quickly added that even physics and chemistry in certain areas were compelled to do the same thing (his examples concerned the number of molecules in a given volume of gas and the actual, not simply relative, atomic weights).[60] The fundamental assumption of his synthesis of the sciences was that the sciences constituted a coherent hierarchy. What applied to research into history also applied, though to a lesser extent, to biology and even less so to mechanics, physics and chemistry. Approximate values had to be dealt with everywhere. In history, however, the distance between concept and reality that the concept alludes to is greatest.

---

56   Cf. above, p. 57.
57   E.g. MECW 25:147 et seq.
58   MECW 25:90 et seq.
59   MECW 5:37.
60   MECW 25:293.

We can illuminate his thinking thus: In a discipline such as Newtonian mechanics, the distance between 'abstractions' – mass and acceleration, for example – and the reality to which the abstractions are applied is extremely insignificant. Using Newton's theory, the mechanical motion of every body can be determined with extraordinary precision. Similar abstractions in the sphere of the historical sciences do not have the same simple applicability at all. If, as Engels suggests, we use abstractions such as forces of production, relations of production and class conflict, we will only succeed in very broadly determining the historical connections. We cannot determine the individual historical processes.

Dühring's mistake consisted not only of his having started out from ideas. He was also mistaken about the kind of scientific results that could be achieved in the historical disciplines. Like Smith and Ricardo (and, for that matter, Comte, Spencer and many others) he assumed that the study of history became scientific only when – like the physical sciences – it had certain fixed concepts, axioms and laws from which the individual phenomena could be derived. Engels commented ironically on Dühring's axiom for political economy, which was so banal that it said nothing about economic reality.[61] Dühring had not understood that political economy was 'essentially a *historical* science' because it had 'material which is historical, that is, constantly changing'.[62]

When Engels said that the base 'ultimately' determined the historical process, he did not mean the same thing as the Dühring who was hunting 'ultimate' truths. (Naturally one can speculate over the reasons Engels made this specific phrase his own. Was it with full awareness that the phrase could seem misleading because he had just repudiated it in the polemic with Dühring? Or did he incorporate it in pure distraction into his vocabulary? This speculation yields no results.) As far as I understand, it squares fully with Engels's vocabulary to say that mass and acceleration are 'ultimate' causes of the mechanical movement of bodies. The phrase is, however, quite pointless since there are no intermediary instances to take into account. On the other hand, it is important to use the phrase 'ultimately' when, to take one example, attempting to assert a connection between the base and Cartesian philosophy. Here the more closely neighbouring instances are legion; there is the philosophical and scientific tradition, the religious situation influenced by the offensive of the Catholic church, the legal and political conditions in Europe and so on, all of which have more immediate influence on Cartesian philosophy than on the development of the base.

---

61   MECW 25:207.
62   MECW 25:135.

According to Dühring, all these intermediate instances between the 'axiom' and the concrete historical cases can be said to be inessential in roughly the same way that Newtonian mechanics says it is inessential whether a body whose motion is to be calculated is a chunk of granite or a lump of iron. According to Engels, they continue to be significant and therefore require full attention from those who wish to elucidate 'the real historical process'.

It is now a matter of linking Engels's general dialectic and historical materialism. First, however, we must touch very briefly on Marx's and his own contacts with the new discipline of anthropology, the main problem of which was to find the link between biological development and human history.

4   Marx, Engels and Morgan

In *Anti-Dühring*, it says that all past history was the history of class struggle.[63] When Engels published a few central portions of the same work under the title *Socialism: Utopian and Scientific* in 1883, he added: 'with the exception of its primitive stages'.[64] He made a similar correction in a note to the 1888 edition of the *Communist Manifesto*. There, he remarked that 'all history' in the *Manifesto* should be interpreted as all history based on *written* testimony. The history that came before was virtually unknown in 1847, when the *Manifesto* was written. But since then, Haxthausen had discovered the common ownership of land in Russia,[65] Maurer had shown that all the Germanic tribes had originated from the same social form, and finally Morgan had laid bare the internal organisation of primitive communism.[66]

Of these names, Haxthausen's played a temporary role in both Marx's and Engels's intellectual development. But there is reason to emphasise not only Morgan's significance for their ideas about primitive society. It was Bavarian legal historian Georg Ludwig von Maurer who, so to speak, made Marx and Engels receptive to Morgan's theories. Back in 1868, Marx had expressed his

---

63   MECW 25:26.

64   MECW 25:634.

65   In all likelihood, it was Ludwig Kugelmann who drew Marx's attention to the works of Baron August von Haxthausen. The writing that Marx alluded to in his letters to Kugelmann on 4 February and 12 April 1871 (MECW 44:111 and 132 respectively) does not – as the publishers of the MECW assumed (MECW 44:132) – seem to be Haxthausen 1842 but, judging by the later letter, Haxthausen 1847, or the exact book Engels formed associations with in the 1888 edition of the *Manifesto*.

66   MECW 6:482.

enthusiasm in a few letters to Engels over Morgan's writings on the earliest developments of property and legal relations in Germany.[67] Engels shared his delight completely.[68]

What appealed to Marx and Engels in Maurer's works was certainly not their scientific orientation[69] but the theses on German prehistory that they contained. Maurer confirmed an opinion that Marx had recently put forward in the first volume of *Capital*. There, it was not yet a question of any classless society in an actual sense; it was the question of the development of products into commodities. Marx had assumed that the product did not become a commodity (i.e. the object of buying and selling) *within* primitive community but *between* the different communities.[70] He now found that Maurer's research seemed to have proven him right on that point.

But this opinion – which Marx had thus harboured before Maurer's works fell into his hands and long before Morgan became of topical interest to him – contains the very seed of the idea of a classless society. In a society where no exchange of commodities occurs, the necessities of life must be allocated in accordance with other principles. But how could this allocation occur if some class possessed power – real ownership – over the means of production and thus over the products? One simple solution was to assume that there were no classes in general but that ownership was in common.

First Maurer, and then Morgan and a number of other writers in anthropology and legal history, seem to have provided factual substantiation for this opinion. The ease with which both Marx and Engels abandoned the thesis in the *Manifesto* on the class character of all past societies shows in a nutshell how they related to this historical scientific generalisation. They did not see in it a binding statement of law from which each individual case could be derived. The generalisation in the historical sciences was certainly – to use Engels's words from *Anti-Dühring* – built on 'factors known only relatively'. The real historical process could, perhaps in some part of its course, turned out to have had a different character. In and of itself, it was not a reason to hunt for a new and better generalisation under which all historical phases could truly be arranged.

---

67   Letter from Marx to Engels, 14 March 1868, MECW 42:547 and 549; and 25 March 1868, MECW 42:557. It is above all Maurer 1854 and Maurer 1857 that Marx studied in depth.

68   Letter from Engels to Marx, 19 March 1868, MECW 42:554.

69   On the orientation of Maurer's research, which was closely bound up with his political activity, see Leiser 1967. Cf. also Brinz 1884.

70   MECW 35:98. Cf. the third volume of *Capital*, MECW 37:176, where Marx cites this 'view' and Engels adds in a note that this was a view in 1865 but now 'after the extensive research ranging from Maurer to Morgan into the nature of primitive communities', it was a fact accepted by nearly everyone.

If the general assertions – the 'axioms' in Dühring's terminology – were the main point, the historical sciences would be compelled to deal with nothing but trivialities and platitudes.

Engels also had essentially abandoned the thought of the ubiquitous presence of the class struggle in history before he came in contact with Morgan, or more precisely with Marx's excerpts of Morgan's *Ancient Society*. In the letter to Lavrov about Darwinism, which we have already come in contact with, he declared by way of conclusion that he did not believe that humanity had lived in a state of internal conflict during its earliest development.[71] He had not yet developed the idea of a classless primitive society, but he had unhesitatingly put the idea of prehistoric class struggle aside.

It was thus not the idea itself of a 'primitive state' that Marx and Engels took from Morgan. Naturally, they found in him – and in the new anthropology in general[72] – numerous new, more precise ideas about how human prehistory had taken shape. But the fundamental structure of their conception of history did not thereby change.

On the other hand, we have the right to assume that Morgan in particular influenced their view of what should be included in their own concept of *base*. It is obvious that *the family* gained a much more central position in their world of ideas. The family had played a role in their investigations of the materialist conception of history ever since *The German Ideology*.[73] But that concerned the family as an economic unit of production. Now a new aspect came in: the family as the producer of new humans.

Engels expressed the change in understanding in the preface to *Origin of the Family*. 'According to the materialist conception, the determining factor in history is, in the last resort, the production and reproduction of immediate life', he wrote; the comment does not fundamentally differ from the one he used in *Anti-Dühring*. But he now clarified the conception so that production and reproduction were of a double nature: on the one hand it concerned food, clothing, housing and so on; on the other, it concerned new humans.[74] The production of new humans thus belonged to the social base.

Engels found support for this expansion of the concept of the base in Marx's excerpts of Morgan's *Ancient Society*. In them, Marx noted with reference to Morgan that while the family was continually developing, the concept of familial relations demonstrably lagged behind: the ideas of what constituted

---

71   Letter from Engels to Lavrov, 12 November 1875, MECW 45:106.
72   Marx also excerpted from Phear, Maine and others; cf. Marx 1972.
73   Cf. for example MECW 5:31 et seq. and MECW 25:167 and 459.
74   MECW 26:131 et seq.

relatives – who were brothers, sisters, parents, uncles and so on – thus bore the traces of previous familial relations, e.g. different forms of polygamy, permitted and forbidden degrees of relationship for marriage, and so forth. Marx commented: '[T]he same applies to political, juridical, religious and philosophical systems generally',[75] and Engels quoted his comment verbatim.[76]

It was therefore obvious that the changing rules that applied in different societies for who could have children together would be attributable to the base. It may be thought that this expansion of the concept of the base could appear less significant for the theory as such: the fundamental structure remains, and the scope of the base has only expanded insignificantly.

But the change is in fact extremely significant, and in one sense it probably contributed to vulgarising and distorting the materialist conception of history during its further development around the turn of the twentieth century. We can see this by simply asking what constitutes the fundamental relations of the base.

The base, expressed in the briefest possible manner, is the relation between the force(s) of production[77] and the relations of production. If the thesis on the production of humans (i.e. having children belongs to the base) is not to be a freely floating addition to the original historical materialism, we must be able to speak about its forces of production and its relations of production. The relations of production offer no difficulties here: it is a question of monogamy or polygamy, and so on. The forces of production must be the tool with which humans make children (i.e. the genitals).

However complex the genitals may be, however linked their functions may be to intricate instinctual and hormonal conditions – their 'force of production' is a purely biological matter. In every historical discourse they stand out as given constants. However changeable the picture of sexual desire, sexual life and erotica may be, the possibilities themselves for having children are not a historical concern; there can be no talk of any development of the forces of production as there is of the development of the material forces of production.

What happened here is thus that biology invaded the sphere of the human sciences along one section of the front. Neither Marx nor Engels, it is true, took

---

75   Marx 1972, p. 112.

76   MECW 26:141.

77   The phrase 'productive force' is use in both the singular and the plural as well, for example, in *Capital*. In an exact formulation of the theory, the singular form should be used: the productive force of labour is 'a quantity that is measured by the quantum of products, which labour produces during a certain period of time in accordance with the degree of development of the determinants of production' (cf. *Capital*, MECW 35:48, 55 etc.).

the consequences into account with any particular care. Marx only provided a few comments on his excerpts, and Engels defined the new, broader scope of the base only in passing.

But the consequences themselves are in fact much greater. When Marx, and above all Engels, discussed the connection between biology and human history in earlier and other contexts – above all with regard to Darwinism – they had drawn an almost entirely consistent boundary: humans as biological creatures were the condition for all of historical development, but biology had been unable to explain this historical development itself. It had provided the framework for what humans in history could have been, but it did not determine their various social forms or worlds of ideas.

Now that having children, this thoroughly biological phenomenon, had moved into the base itself, the barrier between biology and history had been torn down. This development, in which Karl Kautsky, Edward Aveling and many others took part with gusto, and where the materialist conception of history became a conception in accordance with and in extension of Darwinist biology – where the development of the forces of production became a process entirely analogous with biological selection – gained its support (though very indirectly) from the two great authorities of Marxist theory, Marx and Engels themselves.[78] What Engels accomplished with a high degree of consistency in works such as *Anti-Dühring* was abolished in a limited but central point in *Origin of the Family*.

An example can be seen here of the impact of Darwinism – and more precisely of the new anthropology that it more or less inspired. Marx and Engels needed a more exhaustive, more detailed picture of humanity's earliest history. Above all, the new anthropology provided that picture. In Morgan's version in particular, the picture had an immediate attraction for them. But they were either unable to, or did not manage to, digest it in accordance with their own historical materialist principles.

Engels was particularly anxious to present Morgan as a historical materialist. In the preface to *Origin of the Family* he asserted that Morgan had discovered anew the materialist conception of history, independently of Marx.[79] As Krader points out, the issue of Morgan's materialism was highly controversial.[80] It can be noted that in his excerpts, Marx nowhere asserted that Morgan shared his

---

78   Kautsky provided his own picture of the fusion in Kautsky 1960, p. 214 et seq. Typical
      expressions for the same world of ideas can be found in Aveling 1884.
79   MECW 26:131.
80   Krader 1972, p. 9.

view of history. On the other hand, he put an exclamation point after the word 'ideas' when he reproduced Morgan's phrase 'the ideas of property'.[81] From Marx's perspective, it was an extremely important piece of punctuation. Morgan was looking beyond the earliest forms of property for the corresponding ideas about property.

Naturally, this idea of Morgan's does not qualify him for the label 'historical idealist'. Rather, it shows that Morgan did not have any real, carefully prepared view of history. His materialism, as Engels so emphatically pointed out, consisted of his stubbornly dwelling upon material relations in the broadest sense: biological, geographical, technological and so on. In that respect, he did not differ from all the historians of civilisation who followed Comte or Spencer and played such a large role in the nineteenth century. Above all, he was a good exponent of what I have called the new anthropology. The questions of humanity's biological and historical origins were the main issues for him. In his search, he was guided not by any fixed ideas about the relation between ideas and social reality.

The fact that Engels regarded him as a fellow thinker in historical research was due to the fact that Morgan never went into the sphere of history where Engels had fully developed views. In this sense, the consequences of Morgan's theses were compatible with both Engels's, and Comte's and Spencer's, images of historical development.

5   Theories and Processes

It is now time to summarise Engels's ontology – a summary that Engels himself never made. There are many loose threads in his writings, many unfinished beginnings and many contradictory theses. A summary will have to be a reconstruction of what stands out as fundamental beyond all these scattered comments. What is incompatible, or lacks connection with the summary, must be explained as the results of chance impulses, influences from superior authorities or a lack of clarity in Engels's ideas themselves.

First, however, a terminological remark. In traditional philosophical vocabulary, ontology is the theory of what unconditionally *is*. Modern philosophers have occasionally used the term in a narrower, more specific sense: for example, ontology could be an examination of the assumptions about reality that form the *conditions* for scientific knowledge. The idea that there is a reality that

---

81   Marx 1972, p. 127.

the various sciences have to study is itself not the result of scientific research. Examining more closely what this entails and what this means would be one example of a task for ontology.[82]

What I here call Engels's ontology contains this examination of a fundamental, pre- or extrascientific assumption as a crucial moment. Materialism is one such assumption, as is irreductionism. Spiritualism cannot be repudiated solely with empirical material, he commented at one point;[83] nor can mechanical materialism be refuted or proven via the empirical path, he said at another.[84]

But Engels's ontology did not stop there. Above all, he also wanted to show how these fundamental conditions could or would be expressed in various scientific spheres. He wanted to examine the extent to which they squared with or conflicted with current scientific theories. In this way, he was also striving for what we could call a scientifically founded worldview, which would not be a passive summary of what was held to be true by the most authoritative names and orientations in various disciplines. A summary of this kind, of already highly specialised knowledge, would not be particularly uniform. It can also be imagined that scientific orientations in circulation are incompatible with ontological principles: not all science is, for example, materialistically inclined.

The boundaries for the authority of ontology in relation to the specialised sciences were naturally a problem for Engels, as they were for all the other creators of systems of his era. In general, his principle could be said to be that the more comprehensive theories it concerns, the greater the authority of ontology and that the closer one gets to purely empirical material, the more ontology is referred to specialised knowledge. The principle as such is entirely trivial and harmless, but it encounters constant difficulties when put into practice. The difficulties culminate when there are conflicting conceptions between different scientific authorities: ontology can then rise up in judgement.

In this somewhat broader sense, ontology therefore involves not only an examination of the assumptions of science but also of its findings. The assumptions and findings are not two independent worlds: if the assumption is that

---

82   It may be pointed out that Engels himself did not use the word 'ontology'. Among the present-day authors who have carried out broader ontological studies, Bhaskar can be mentioned; he differentiates between a philosophical and a scientific ontology. The former provides the conditions for, and the latter the results of, science. The distinction may be important (1975, p. 29 et seq., p. 36); an emphasis on the interaction between conditions and results must be the essential feature of a dialectical materialist account of ontology.

83   MECW 25:354.

84   MECW 25:532.

all real science is materialist, the results will not conflict with this. The main point of Engels's investigation, however, is nonetheless the question of how these assumptions correspond to the actual situation in various sciences. For example, he put greater energy into showing that sphere after sphere of nineteenth-century science confirmed the general assumptions about the constantly changing and fluid character of reality.

For Engels, it was obvious that every science had ontological claims: they were commenting on something unconditionally real. The correspondence of thought (i.e. theories) to its object was the entire 'unconscious and unconditional premise'[85] of theoretical activity. The Kantian lines of thought that Helmholtz and Lange, for example, advocated in various ways were thus deeply foreign to him. The thought that science would comment on reality with some reservations, that there could possibly be *another* reality that science could not reach, seemed horrible to him.[86] He noted that similar reservations did not exist in scientific comments that kept close to empirical material – no one questioned whether a dog in reality had four legs – but that they befell far-reaching theoretical statements. A difference of this kind between empirical material and theory is unjustifiable, however; theory is confirmed in empirical material.[87]

If the correspondence of theory with reality is now the 'unconscious and unconditional premise' of science, this means that the idea itself of a reality where scientific statements cannot reach is an idea *about* scientific theories that conflict with the very character of scientific reality. Engels argued that we always state our opinions in the name of science *as if we possessed the absolute truth*: at every point in the development of science, the current knowledge is thus assumed to be equal to the truth. At the same time, we know that knowledge is changeable, that today's truth will not be valid tomorrow. Third, this changeability appears as a process of advancement: we know more today than we did yesterday, and if this scientific process is not interrupted, we will know more tomorrow than we did today.

At the same time, this dialectic of knowledge – which we acquainted ourselves with previously[88] – means that every ontology that comprises a summation of current knowledge must also always be a temporary arrangement. The synthesis of the sciences changes with the development of the sciences. This

---

85   MECW 25:544.
86   E.g. MECW 25:340, 501 et seq., 511 et seq.
87   MECW 25:509 et seq.
88   Cf. above, p. 386 *et seq.*

historical relativity, however, no more leads to the assumption of an inaccessible reality than biological relativity – humanity's biological and psychological limitations – does. It leads to the idea that humanity, through its historical development (which also means that it overcomes a number of its biological limitations) better understands the only reality on offer.

What I here call Engels's ontology thus presupposes an epistemology (the realist conception of knowledge), and at its base lie certain general assertions about reality (materialism, the theory of the identity of matter and motion, the theory of the 'irreducibility' of motion, the theory of reality as a constantly changing process) which – if we like – we can classify as general ontology. But its entirely dominant part is the interpretation of the current science. In a differentiated, specialised scientific culture, this means above all *an interpretation of the connection between scientific disciplines and special theories* and thus – provided that the sciences provisionally correspond to their objects – *an interpretation of the connections among the different levels of reality*.

It is Engels's often vague, often contradictory interpretations of current theories and spheres of reality that we acquainted ourselves with in the preceding chapters. But one crucial aspect has therefore been neglected. Time and time again we have been able to observe that Engels often commented in various positivist and Hegelian manners, we have seen how he spoke about knowledge as 'reflected images' of reality, and how he designated various conceptions as the definitive ones. On these points, he displayed far greater insensitivity than Marx.

At the same time, however, ever since the beginning of his efforts in the late 1850s he spoke about the fluid, changeable character of reality. He thus sought support in Hegel's philosophy, and he gladly hailed both the principle of conservation of energy and Darwinism because they abolished firm boundaries and resolved fixed contradictions and classifications.

This motif is so thoroughgoing that it is easy to ignore their significance. It is ubiquitous, and at the same time it may appear to be general lip service because in his applications, Engels often sought the fixed and the definitive instead. He achieves the culmination of this path with his three dialectical laws, which were an attempt at locking the changeable into fixed forms.

But this profession of the changeability of reality still has its crucial – if not always fully realised and actualised – significance. The fact of the matter is just that the thesis on variability and difficulty of comprehension not only comes into conflict with the highly human ambition of plucking the ripest fruits of prevailing science but also with the thesis itself of the realism of knowledge.

This realism of knowledge is most easily demonstrated and implemented if a total correspondence between theory and object is assumed: the categories of changeability then become uncomfortable.

It could be said that there is a real dialectical tension between these perspectives: the realism of knowledge and the principle of changeability. Knowledge represents its object, but the object has changed while the image was being produced.

Engels did not succeed in bringing this contradiction to a plausible, concrete conclusion: Marx had gotten farther in, for example, the *Mathematical Manuscripts*.[89] But it is both desirable and possible to realise Engels's line of thought based on the remarks we have. Only through this can we understand the rational core of his general dialectic.

When Engels wanted to bring out the evasive and difficult to grasp character of reality, he often said that reality constituted a *process*, a word whose content he took from Hegel.[90] When he asserted that *reality*, and not just our knowledge of it, was dialectic, he meant primarily the same thing as when he described reality as a process.[91] Note, however, that he would never have said that knowledge or theory constituted a process. Reality has the character of a process, at best theory could reproduce this character of a process. Reality constituting a process now entails a number of mutually closely related matters: it is complex – that is, it can never comprise a single phenomenon. It means that the more or fewer components that comprise reality are causally related to each other in multiple ways: what is cause is in turn influenced by its effect (herein lies the reason for Engels's exaggerated passion for the category of reciprocal action[92]). This in turn means that reality is in constant change and development.

Previously, we saw that there was a certain deficiency in the connection between materialism and Engels's thinking on development. In his concrete studies of, for example, the question of the eternity of organic life, they both abruptly stand side by side.[93] Only on a very abstract and general plane, where reality for Engels appears as a single coherent process, does the very foundation of his thinking on development appear. The development of the universe,

---

89   Above, p. 392 *et seq.*

90   E.g. Hegel 4:75, 5:184 et seq., 8:329 et seq., 9:67.

91   See above all the definition of process in *Anti-Dühring.*, MECW 25:24. Engels expressed similar lines of thought in *Feuerbach*, MECW 26:383.

92   E.g. MECW 25:511.

93   MECW 25:574.

which is thus the development of 'matter in motion', constitutes an ordered process: the path runs from the smaller to the more complex. The abstract starting point for the idea can be formulated thus:

> *a*. At no level of the development of the universe is there a single factor, force, or form of motion that determines the course of this development. It is always a question of a reciprocal relation among different factors. (This is a conclusion Engels drew from sources such as the principle of conservation of energy, and was directed at both the mechanistic conception and belief in creation.)
> *b*. This reciprocal relation among different factors has a tendency to produce phenomena that in further development become new operating factors in the development process. (Under precise circumstances, organic life can emerge from the interplay among mechanical, physical and chemical 'forms of motion'. Later, it will influence the process it is part of as an independent factor.)

In this sense, the process is thus spontaneously innovative: certain constellations produce new factors. A precise type of reciprocal relation among the inorganic forms of motion (a, b, c ... n) yields a living organism as a result, and once the living organism exists it will be drawn into a new, more complex type of reciprocal relation (a, b, c, L ... n), where L designates the living organism and the uppercase letter emphasises that the living organism itself is also the result of a reciprocal relation among the other forms of motion. This new type of more complex reciprocal relation gives rise to further new constellations, to new, more differentiated and complex types of organisms, and so on. The more complex the process becomes, the more the possible constellations and the more, also, the possibilities for new factors that influence the process of development. When humans enter the picture, it becomes more complicated because humans can intentionally influence a growing share of their reality.

This is the idea about development that Engels, in different words and in partly different concepts, presented in some of his comprehensive texts such as the introduction to *Dialectics of Nature*, and in a number of scattered comments in paragraphs and notes. (He also took the opposite process, a degeneration of the entire universe in which the more complex forms dissolved,[94] into account. This idea, however, does not affect our argument.)

---

94   MECW 25:331.

The essential point is now to attempt to grasp the relation between the real process of development and our knowledge of it. The goal is uniform knowledge. But how can this uniformity be attained? In science as it exists, the various parts of the process are subject to the meticulousness of the different disciplines, and the relations among these disciplines is controversial. Mechanics, physics, chemistry, biology and the human sciences comprise a hierarchy, it is true, in which the one science steps in where the other one ends. The attempt, however, to create a unity from them presupposes a number of simplifications. Mechanical materialism assumes that the simplest, most elementary part of the process is the only real one and everything else – from the qualities of chemistry and physics to human thought – is merely a phenomenon of this mechanical and material reality. Idealism, on the contrary, takes its starting point in the most complex part of the process: the part dealing with human ideas and conceptions.

Engels assumed that the starting point of materialism was reality, but he rejected the attempt by mechanical materialism to eliminate the actual differences among the various sciences. There is a crucial difference between his approach and theirs. A mechanical materialist attempts to reduce the forces of physics and chemistry to mechanical motion; the biologists, life to mechanical motion, conscious human activity to mechanical motion – it is thus a question of tracing every part of the process directly back to the simple primeval state with a few resolute operations. Engels never occupied himself with the question, for example, of whether biology could be transformed into mechanics. His attention was entirely taken up by the question of the relation between biology and organic chemistry or between human history and biology. He made no leaps across the scientific hierarchy. The goal he set for scientific development was not to anchor all the sciences in mechanics. It was to define each discipline in relation to its neighbours.

He thus assumed that the series of sciences on the whole corresponded to the real process from small to more complex states. With scientific development, the correspondence increasingly improved. The question of the relation between biology and organic chemistry and the question of the origins of life are intimately bound up. If one question can be answered approximately, then the other one can also be answered approximately: if the theoretical question of the relation between two major fields of theory can be solved, then the question of real development can also be solved.

The idea that theories provide better pictures of reality does not mean, however, that theories in any more literal sense will correspond with the reality they deal with. Not infrequently, Engels commented as if he imagined just such a total likeness of the original: this was when he spoke about knowledge as a reflected image of reality. But, for example, when he laid out the content of historical materialism, he could clearly show that in that case, a complex theory yielded different reflections: on the one hand, historical materialism ascribed the base a unique position; on the other it spoke of a reciprocal relationship.[95]

We could also ask whether the thesis on the qualitative leap actually depicts a real process. Most of Engels's examples hint that this was how matters stood throughout: water happens to boil, methane becomes ethane, and so on. But the really large, crucial leap – the leap between fields of theory – seems in and of itself not to entail corresponding sudden changes in reality. He preferred to dwell on all the intermediate forms between living and dead that contemporary science seemed to have found, and he depicted the transition from ape to human as a continual process. He obviously did not imagine that life or humanity suddenly appeared on the scene: he did, however, imagine a transition from one theory to another.

It does not appear as if this discrepancy between theory and reality was a conscious one for him, though he often emphasised the fluid character of reality and the inappropriateness of all fixed boundaries on the one hand, and the barriers between different fields of theory on the other. Here, as in many other areas, Marx appears to have been more attentive. He emphatically asserted the qualitative leap from handicraft to manufacture and from feudalism to capitalism. This did not mean, however, that he argued that the real historical process made a corresponding leap. '[E]pochs in the history of society are no more separated from each other by hard and fast lines of demarcation, than are geological epochs', he wrote in *Capital*.[96]

Another perhaps even more central question about the relation between theory and reality deserves attention as well. Engels, as we have seen, emphasised that biology – and the human sciences even more so – had not achieved the same level of exactness as mechanics, physics or chemistry. It was not clear, however, if he had though that continued scientific development would decisively reduce or obliterate this difference, or if it lay in the nature, so to speak, of the sphere of reality. (In a strict sense, the question obviously cannot be answered, since future science cannot be predicted – in other words, what is not yet known cannot be known. But here, it is a matter of the expectations

---

95   Cf. above, p. 388 *et seq.*
96   MECW 35:321. Cf. on this the explanatory account in G. Aspeling 1972, p. 109 et seq. Aspelin, of course, is correct in that Marx also had Lyell's geological theory in mind here.

for scientific development and the general assumptions about various parts of reality.) He repeatedly said that biology had *not yet* succeeded in establishing the 'forms of motion' of life, but he also declared – above all in his polemic with Dühring – that conformity to laws in biology (and in history even more so) were of a different type than that of mechanics. The conception that stands out as predominant in him, since it constituted the very condition for his attempt at a scientific synthesis, is that the differences between various sciences was one of degree, and not of type. Strict mechanicism was not valid even in the spheres of physics and chemistry, even less so in biology and least of all in the human sciences.

But with that we now come to the question that stood out as only a partially conscious condition for so many philosophical efforts – not only in Engels's writings but also throughout the nineteenth century. This is the question of determinism. Was it a shortcoming in a theory if it could not precisely determine the conformity to law in a process belonging to its sphere? Scientifically speaking, was it a failure if a given phenomenon was said to be a chance occurrence (i.e. that it could not be determined or predicted using the theory that was available)?

Marx and Engels unanimously and unambiguously answered 'no' to the questions to the extent they concerned their own theories in the sphere of the human sciences. Chance occurrences play – and must play – a role. In his brief argument on Darwinism's solution to the issue of 'chance and necessity', Engels showed that he harboured a similar understanding of biology. But he did not fully take the step: he did not take up the problem as a universal problem of scientific theory and ontology.

It is thus only possible to reconstruct in the most general terms a conception of the foundation of his general ideas about reality as a coherent process that assumes increasingly complex forms over its course. The increasing complexity means that an increasing number of factors determine the direction of this process. The number of potential phenomena grows exponentially: the determination thereby becomes smaller. The number of theoretically possible results in a purely inorganic process are fewer than in an organic or historical process.

That is not to say that the scope of *possible* results could not be determined. It could thus be said that at one or another level of biological development, the potential lines of development are thus and so. At the historical level, the class of potentialities could be even more voluminous. The thesis that the base determines the superstructure would mean that, with knowledge of the base at a given level, the approximate scope of possible lines of development in a society could be indicated. The knowledge of the superstructure would not provide a similar insight. The base does not determine the superstructure more than in the sense that it provides the boundaries for the development of the super-structure as well.

This interpretation, which in my opinion squares best with both Marx's and Engels's world of opinions, shows that theory cannot be grasped as a simple reflection of the real process. But there is one more matter to add, which emphasises the discrepancy between theory and object. The theory of the qualitative leap *in a qualified sense* – the leap from one sphere of theory to another[97] – means that the transition from inorganic to organic matter, for example, from ape to human or from one mode of production to another can be determined close to the transition itself: it is possible to demonstrate sci-entifically how the origins of life, or humanity's gradual development, or the realisation of capitalism are potential results under such and such given cir-cumstances. However, it is not a given that development can be calculated after the new 'quality' has begun to function. The most reasonable interpretation of both Marx and Engels is undoubtedly the one that says that, with knowledge of the inorganic determinations of organic life or of humanity's purely biolo-gical determinations, even the potential framework for biological and historical diversity can only be *approximately* indicated. The new quality is really new: its effects cannot be determined in any calculation. Herein also lies the reason for their well-known aversion to indicating more than the most general features of socialist society, which they regarded as qualitatively distinct from capitalist society.

6   Dialectics of Nature? A Summary

The question of the value of Engels's philosophical writings and notes from the 1870s and 1880s has been one of the largest points of contention in the political and ideological history of Marxism. It has also been one of the largest stum-bling blocks for those who have entertained Marxist theories with more or less scientific claims.

The foregoing study, in which Engels's writings have been discussed from a strictly internal scientific perspective and thus the points of comparison have exclusively been theories and lines of development in various sciences from mechanics to philosophy, have certainly shown how his theses were condi-

---

97   Cf. above, p. 425 *et seq.*

tioned by their times. It has also revealed their fragmentary – and in important
places contradictory – character.

But having said that, the question remains of the purely theoretical value of
the attempt itself.

This question can have both a relative and an absolute content. On the relative side, it concerns the value for Marx's and Engels's own theories on society
and history.

Here, the investigation just completed can provide a rather definitive response. What Engels sought to accomplish was of the greatest importance for
the materialist conception of history and for the theory of capital. There were
problems that literally cried out for solutions, concerning both the scientific
status of these theories and the relation of the sphere of history itself to the
sphere of biology. With the claims that Marx and Engels raised, they could
leave these problems aside without leaving large weak spots for criticism and
misunderstandings. When, for example, the British historian and philosopher
Gareth Stedman Jones asserted that Engels ought to have let the broad perspective wait, considering that historical materialism was still a young and
unfinished science, it should be objected: this exact earth-shaking innovation
made a confrontation with other sciences and scientific approaches that much
more necessary.[98]

The even more common opinion, that Engels's later writings lacked an
intrinsic connection with Marx's and his own studies of society and history,
can also be repudiated as immediately mistaken. The idea that Marx would
have preached some kind of historical relativism is a fundamental and fateful misunderstanding that was harboured by such prominent and renowned
figures as the young Georg Lukács, the older Karl Korsch, Theodor Adorno, Herbert Marcuse, Jürgen Habermas, Alfred Schmidt and many others. Historical
materialism does not lack, as has been asserted, a real connection with general, philosophical materialism. It is not compatible with just any materialist
conception of reality whatsoever. It is irreductionist to its very foundations: it
cannot, for example, be reconciled with an idea according to which history is
another form of biology.

It is therefore obvious that the effort itself in Engels's philosophical writings
square well with the general character of the materialist conception of history.

But the question that has been asked can also concern the substance in what
Engels began, and also completed in a few places, entirely regardless of its significance for Marxism's theory of society.

---

98   Stedman-Jones 1976, p. 24. Cf. also Colletti 1977. For interesting viewpoints on this type of
      'anti-Engelsism' see Timpanaro 1975, p. 73 et seq.

As I understand it, Engels's epistemological and scientific theoretical theses contain a number of interesting ideas, especially in the attempts to elude the iron grip of reductive mechanicism and still not end up in the morass of randomness and the disorderly accumulation of facts. His perspective is obviously limited and conditions by its times, and above all Hegel's powerful form obstructs his view. However, he gave expression to what we could call – without doing violence to the history of the word – a dialectical view of science when he sought to lay bare the play of contradictions between the claims to truth of the sciences and their historical relativity, between the subject of knowledge and its objects, and between theory and empirical material. He was essentially guided by the same open mind for the complex as when he was trying to find his way in the scientific hierarchy, attempting to show that the transition from one sphere of theory to another was at the same time continuous and discontinuous.

It thus concerns what Engels himself called the 'subjective' dialectic, the dialectic of thought. But how did it relate to its 'objective' counterpart, his ontology? His assurances that there was a dialectic in nature as well?

The answer is not a simple one. It could be said that *if* one wants to speak about a dialectic in society (and not just in social theory), one is compelled to speak about a dialectic in nature as well. The common argument, as the young Lukács, Sartre, Schmidt and others put it,[99] for limiting the dialectic to the world of humanity is that dialectical processes can only be imagined where conscious subjects are involved. But this argument is untenable before the Marxist theory of capital itself. Naturally, the capitalist mode of production was created by people, and naturally it is supported by conscious subjects. The core of Marx's theory, however, is that capitalism's fundamental and crucial development takes place regardless of human plans and desires. The culmination in *Capital* is the formulation of '*the absolute general law of capitalist accumulation*': the greater the social wealth, the greater the industrial reserve army, and so on.[100] This law certainly deals with human subjects, but it is valid regardless of the intents of these subjects. In concrete social reality, it stands out as 'the historical tendency of capitalist accumulation':[101] it is modified by any number of circumstances, including the plans and desires of the subjects. Nonetheless, however, it marks the main line of capitalist development.

---

99   See e.g. Lukács 1968, p. 42; Sartre 1960, p. 120; Sartre 1976, p. 77 et seq., A. Schmidt 1971a, p. 52. Rafoss 1974, p. 17 et seq., provides a good overview of this type of criticism.

100   MECW 35:637 et seq.

101   Ibid., p. 748 et seq.

In speaking about dialectical relations in reality, they cannot be restricted to applying solely to societies. At the most general level, the laws of social development are just as objective as the laws of nature. If class struggle is an example of the dialectic, there is a dialectic in nature as well.

A potential objection to an objective dialectic in Engels's meaning is that the phenomena it refers to can nonetheless be defined in terms of 'processes' or 'totalities'. Talking about it in society or nature would therefore be unnecessarily duplicating the content of the word 'dialectic'.

Here it is a question of a practical rather than a theoretical conclusion. For Hegel the idealist and his followers, it was obvious that the dialectic of thought was reflected in reality; reality was therefore also dialectic. From a materialist standpoint, things looked differently. The crucial reason for Marx and Engels speaking about a dialectic in reality was certainly not remaining faithful to Hegel. Rather, it was an expression of their basic realist understanding of knowledge. The dialectic of knowledge was a result of the contradictory character of reality. Laying out a theory is a very specific way of assimilating reality. But if this assimilation is to succeed, theory has to recreate certain fundamental features of the reality it is dealing with.

This, I think, is reason enough to speak of a dialectic in reality. If we are to do so, however, we cannot then let theory and reality become blurred or become a faithful reflection of each other.

Engels witnessed how the sciences of his time developed in a common direction: they all depicted reality as a process of greater or lesser complexity. The various sciences could also provide a picture of the connections among the various parts of the process: history has its origins in biological – and ultimately cosmic – development but still entailed something decisively new. This is an insight that does not seem as terrifyingly new and fascinating today as it did in the days of Clausius, Lyell and Darwin, nor can it be developed on the foundation of nineteenth-century science that Engels had at his disposal. But its importance and significance emerge once again in full glory in these latter days, when ecology is developing into a central science in the general consciousness and the question of the relation between human society, living beings and dead nature is becoming the most urgent of them all.

PART FOUR

CHAPTER 17

Ideology and Science

1   The Various Concepts of Ideology

The word 'ideology' has many airy meanings, and the literature on the concept of ideology, on ideologies and the history of ideologies is enormous.[1] The word was coined by French philosopher Destutt de Tracy in 1796, and by it he meant a 'zoology' of human ideas, a strict scientific discipline of a sensualist and naturalist type.[2] Destutt and the men around him – the 'ideologists' – gradually aroused Napoleon's displeasure. The ideologists were idea-smiths without a sense of the facts. Through Napoleon, the word 'ideology' gained a pejorative meaning alongside its general descriptive meanings. It has described many different types of systems of ideas. Swedish philosopher Christopher Jacob Boström defined ideology as 'the science of the absolute as common sense'.[3] Today, it is even possible to speak of the ideology of political parties. The only thing holding these two uses together is that they comprise neutral descriptions of contexts of ideas. Additionally, however, the term is used in a number of negative senses: false consciousness, bourgeois consciousness, mystification or – in quite general terms – an unrealistic construction.

In the history of the concept of ideology, Marx and Engels played a large, decisive role. There is complete unity on this point in even the general reference works.[4] In that respect, *The German Ideology* has particular significance among their works. But prior to the 1920s, only some minor parts of *The German Ideology* had been published. The word 'ideology', however, also played a central role in works by Marx and Engels that had exerted a greater influence much earlier: the preface to Marx's *Contribution to a Critique of Political Economy*, and Engels's *Anti-Dühring* and *Ludwig Feuerbach*.

Marx and Engels, however, did not have any clearly demarcated concept of ideology. They spoke of 'ideology' in several different senses, which meant that they did not pay particular attention to the term. It was not included in their materialist conception of history in any obvious manner.

---

1   An idea of the rapidly growing social scientific literature on the subject can be obtained from Brown 1973.
2   On the history of the concept of ideology, see above all Barth 1945.
3   Boström 1883, p. 200.
4   Here, see e.g. Braybrooke 1967 and Rejai 1973.

This has led, among other things, to the many changing orientations based on Marx's and Engels's comments on ideology using entirely different concepts of ideology. It could describe a view in the most general terms, or a summary of views on the world, society and life (with the emphasis on views of society). In this sense, it is therefore possible to speak of a Marxist ideology or a scientific ideology. What distinguishes ideology from views is principally that ideology describes the shared views of a group or class; the term is thus narrower in that respect, but at the same time it encompasses directives and programmes for actions that the view does not need to.

Lenin, for example, used the word in this sense,[5] and it was entirely predominant in Soviet Eastern Europe – a fact that the reader can assure themselves of by reading the article on 'Ideology' in the *Great Soviet Encyclopaedia*.[6] In more investigative accounts, difficulties may arise in determining the relation between philosophy (understood in the broad sense) and ideology.[7] Occasionally the meaning of 'false consciousness' may come to the fore,[8] but this is an exception.

The same broad, neutral concept of ideology dominates non-Marxist ideological debate and research in Western Europe and the US. The distance is not that great between the definition in the Soviet encyclopaedia and the following textbook definition: ideology is 'a systematic scheme or coordinated body of ideas or concepts, especially about human life or culture'.[9] It is the concept of class that makes the difference.

In Western Europe, however, a number of Marxist-inspired concepts of ideology of another orientation saw the light of day in the latter half of the twentieth century. Three main types can be distinguished: Karl Mannheim, and thus the early sociology of science; the Frankfurt School; and the Althusser school. These three were partly designed polemically and were marked off in relation

---

5   See e.g. *Materialism and Empiriocriticism*, Lenin 14:131, and *Marxism and Revisionism*, Lenin 15:27 et seq.

6   'Ideology' is defined there as a 'system of views and ideas' (*система взглядов и идей*) that describes and evaluates the relations of humans to reality and to each other, establishes goals for social development and provides directives for action. In a class society, it says further, ideology always has a class character and represents class interests. *Идеология*.

7   *Ideologie und Naturwissenschaft* offers an interesting example in which 'philosophy' is determined on page 29 and then 'ideology' is defined as follows on page 35: '*Ideologie ist eine spezifische Form des theoretischen Verhältnisses von grossen Menschengruppen zur sozialen Wirklichkeit*'. What distinguishes ideology from philosophy here is both that ideology concerns only social reality and that it is encompassed by 'large groups of people'.

8   Cf. for example Hahn 1964.

9   Reproduced according to Brown 1973, p. 9.

to one another: Frankfurt against Mannheim, Althusser against Frankfurt. In certain respects – especially through its breadth – Althusser's concept of ideology came close to the Soviet one.

Mannheim and the Frankfurt School both used the concept of ideology so that it described something that was *per se* erroneous, distorted and illusory. Mannheim regarded it as his task to demonstrate the *Seinsverbundenheit* of knowledge (i.e. its dependence on social, economic and political conditions). With that, however, he made an exception for what he called formal knowledge[10] or the exact sciences.[11] Logic, mathematics, physics and other exact disciplines were not distorted by their social origins.

For Mannheim, an ideology is a system that pretends to contain objective truth but is warped by the class or egotistical interests of its creator. External, social circumstances interest him as *false sources*, not as driving forces or stimuli.[12] To some extent, his perspective is a static one: there are always the same dangers from without that threaten knowledge of history and society. He also sees the liberation from the rule of ideologies in the liberation of intellectuals from class interests: he conjures up the image of a 'freely floating intelligence'.

It is on the latter two points that the representatives of the Frankfurt School, with Max Horkheimer and Theodor Adorno at their head, object to Mannheim and the entirety of scientific sociology.[13] Knowledge develops in a constantly changing environment of social conflict. Anyone who thinks they can create solid, universal knowledge by rising above the contradictions is setting themselves up for a truly serious ideological mistake.

For the Frankfurt School, 'ideology' is synonymous with false consciousness, and that primarily with false bourgeois consciousness. This consciousness is also expressed in bourgeois human science. The liberation from the pressure of ideology comes in the criticism of bourgeois ideology.[14]

---

10   Mannheim 1936, p. 150.

11   Mannheim 1934, reproduced also in Mannheim 1936, p. 243.

12   On this topic, see Merton 1968, p. 513. The literature on Mannheim is particularly extensive. Here Wolff and Rüschemeyer can be mentioned as well as, above all, the scarcely penetrating but worthy monograph by Remmling 1975, which also contains a particularly comprehensive bibliography.

13   One good account of how the Frankfurt School first created its concept of ideology in opposition to Mannheim's is in the anthology *Ideologienlehre und Wissensoziologie*. Especially striking is the essay by Horkheimer reproduced there, p. 505 et seq.

14   A typical, and of course also normative, text is Habermas's introduction to the 4th edition of Habermas 1971, p. 9 et seq. The discussion of ideology plays a crucial role in Habermas 1968 as well.

In the Frankfurt School, there is a strong element of historical relativism. No sharp boundaries between science and ideology are tolerated: Marxism rises above bourgeois ideology by criticising it, not by formulating scientific theories with claims to unconditional truth. Ideology is false consciousness, but this falsity is not solely theoretical in nature. Theoretical and practical, theory and value, theory and norm can never be completely separated. Bourgeois ideology is also false, perhaps above all because it does not seem liberatory for humanity.[15]

It was on points such as this that Louis Althusser put in his criticism of the Frankfurt School. Althusser made a sharp distinction between ideology and science. Ideology creates no new knowledge. An ideology that clothes itself in science only repeats its starting points in its results.[16]

Althusser's understanding could be interpreted thus: ideology, even according to his understanding, is always false. On this exact point he had the same understanding as Mannheim and the Frankfurt School. But this was not Althusser's intent. His understanding can instead be expressed thus: ideology, as a network of ideas and myths and values, create false consciousness if it is put in the place of science. Ideology, however, has its own sphere. Ideology exists, and will exist, in every type of society; it is necessary for the continued existence of every society.[17]

The battle over what an ideology is, is not simply a battle of words. In its entirety, it reflects different understandings of the relations between theory and values, and between science and society. But the debate is characterised by a fundamental uncertainty. The participants in the debate are not speaking

---

15   Here, see above all Habermas 1968. Wellmer 1974 provides a good account of the Frankfurt School's ambitions. For its history in general, see Jay 1973.

16   It may be pointed out that Althusser did not directly level his criticism against the representatives of the Frankfurt School, but against the French (and to some extent Polish: Schaff, Kołakowski) Marxists who in these respects took the standpoints that the Frankfurt School developed first and in the greatest detail. Althusser's strict boundary between ideology and science is developed above all in Althusser 1965, p. 172 et seq.

17   In Althusser 1965, p. 245, ideology is defined as 'a system (with its own logic and its own strict order) of representations (images, myths, ideas or concepts), a system that has a historical existence and a historical role in a given society'. In complete accordance with this, he explains that a communist society cannot be imagined without ideology either; p. 246. One of Althusser's 'humanist' opponents, Jean Hyppolite, also calls attention to the significance of this statement in a splendid account of Althusser's concept of ideology specifically, in *For Marx* and *Reading Capital*; cf. Hyppolite 1971, p. 368 et seq. Althusser later developed his concept of ideology without mentioning its character of universal validity, neutrality and scientific unprofitability. See above all Althusser 1968/1970.

the same language. They mark off their various standpoints by putting different meanings into the same word. Semantic differences simultaneously mark off and mask differences in approach.

2   Marx and Engels on Ideology

Studying the different meanings Marx and Engels put in the term 'ideology' in greater detail has many points of interest. First, the references to their concept of ideology play a major role in contemporary discussion. The references are often unjustifiable from a viewpoint of pure interpretation. Second, it is of interest in itself to trace their underlying conception of the relation of science to the worlds of ideas in which people think, feel and set goals for themselves. Only through this does the picture of their views of science become complete. Third, a study of this kind can form the foundation for a renewed discussion of the concept of ideology in which the result will, it is hoped, be such that it can be used for studies of the relationship between science and society. An attempt in this direction will be made in the concluding chapters. The object of study is the scientific and ideological environment in which Marx and Engels's own activities took place. It will not be a question of anything more than hints and fragments.

Now, however, it is first a question of their use of the word 'ideology' itself. Normally, it is connected with a few more developed – or more comprehensive, at least – doctrines in their writings. 'Ideology', for example, is understood to be synonymous with 'bourgeois consciousness' or – even more broadly – as 'false consciousness'.[18] We will soon see that this is an identification that has extremely feeble support in the texts. The connection of the term 'ideology' with the basic 'base – superstructure' concept pair is more reasonable; we must still be cautious, however, of being too hasty in placing ideology into this conceptual schema.

The question that could first be asked is simple enough, but still sheds some light on our subject: Where did Marx and Engels get the word 'ideology' itself from? How did it enter into their vocabulary? In all the general overviews and additionally in nearly every dictionary where the history of the word is sketched

---

18   See e.g. Lichtheim 1967, p. 18 et seq.; Reichelt 1970, p. 62 et seq. There are accounts in which identification with 'bourgeois consciousness' is not as strong, but where the pejorative content of the phrase in Marx and Engels is emphasised, e.g. Lefebvre 1957, p. 64 et seq. On the other hand, the pejorative use is rejected by Sandkühler 1973, p. 313 et seq.

out, Marx and Engels are mentioned immediately after Destutt and Napoleon as if the former had taken the word directly from the latter. There is nothing, however, to indicate that either of them, at an early stage or prior to *The German Ideology*, had obtained any direct knowledge of Destutt's writings or Napoleon's condemnation.[19] Hegel was not a likely source of inspiration. According to the *Hegel-Lexikon*, Hegel used the word only once: in the lectures on the history of philosophy where he mentioned Destutt's term in passing ('what the French call *ideology*'). He condemned ideology; it was 'abstract metaphysics', 'an enumeration and analysis of simple determinations of thought'. The determinations of thought 'are not treated dialectically; the material is taken from our reflection, from our thoughts'.[20]

There is, as we shall soon see, a clear similarity between Hegel's only comment on ideology and Marx's and Engels's later use. But this similarity is due to the similarity in their conception in general. It can almost entirely be ruled out that Marx and Engels took inspiration for their idea about German, Hegelian-inspired ideology from this obscure remark about French ideology.

There is another connection (or two, if counted carefully) between Napoleon and Marx and Engels. *Trübners Deutscher Wörterbuch*, which was published during the Nazi era and consequently took no notice of the contribution of Jews and communists to the German vocabulary, did not mention Marx or Engels, but did mention Goethe and two minor leaders: Friedrich Rohmer and Alexander Jung, both of whom are of interest in this context. Rohmer, a Swiss journalist, declared in 1835 that it was the rule of ideology (i.e. the superiority of thoughts and ideas) that also gave Napoleon power. For his part, Jung – one of the lesser-known representatives of the Young Germany movement – asserted that Napoleon had discovered that the Germans' most dangerous weapon was ideology.[21]

---

19   Marx and Engels were naturally not unaware of Napoleon's condemnation of ideology. In a newspaper article in 1842, Marx set a statement about free will as a manifestation of ideology against the Napoleons of practical politics, MECW 1:244 (MEGA² I/1:218). In this statement, however, there is nothing of the understanding of ideology that dominates in *The German Ideology*, for example. The word 'ideology' otherwise occurs in Marx's doctoral thesis on Democritean and Epicurean natural philosophy, here in a vague sentence that is difficult to interpret, MECW 1:68 (MEGA² I/1:53).

20   Hegel 19:505 et seq.

21   *Trübners deutsches Wörterbuch*, Vol. 6:1, p. 4 et seq. At that time, the word 'ideology' was used in another manner as well in German, e.g. approximately in the sense that Boström did. Geldsetzer 1968, p. 84, cites a statement by the Hegelian K. Rosenkranz which says that ideology is '*der Einheit der Metaphysik und Logik, der Begriff der Idee als solcher*'.

Rohmer was well known to Marx and Engels; he was mentioned in passing in both *The Holy Family* and *The German Ideology*.[22] But the connection with Jung is far more palpable and certainly far more significant. In 1842, Engels had demonstrated a basic knowledge of Jung's writings in a destructively negative report in *Deutsche Jahrbücher für Wissenschaft und Kunst*. He did not bring up the word 'ideology' itself, but his text constantly revolved around the ideas that Jung associated with the word.[23]

Engels was still an assiduous defender of Young Hegelianism. The idea, however, that Jung asserted and that the Young Hegelians also asserted with different words and expressions, namely, that *the Germans' most dangerous weapon was ideology* – that the philosophers and poets would liberate Germany and show the way for the rest of the world – was exactly the one that was subjected to Marx's and Engels's criticism in *The German Ideology*.

We therefore have good reason to assume that it was from Jung that Engels – and with him, Marx – took the word 'ideology'. In this case, the origins also provide a pointer regarding the fundamental meaning the word had for Marx and Engels. In its narrowest, original meaning, ideology dealt with German idealism and an idealist conception of society and history in a concrete, literal sense. The core idea of German idealism is that society will be transformed if only the correct ideas are formulated and spread.

Most of the times the word 'ideology' came up for discussion in *The German Ideology*, it was used in this sense.[24] Especially enlightening is one place where the difference between the French, English and German middle class was being discussed. Whereas the French bourgeoisie had carried out the biggest revolution up to that time, and the English had subjugated the world ocean and India, the German bourgeoisie created ideologies.[25] (The comment otherwise shows with all possible clarity that there is no necessary connection between the middle class and ideology. The middle class had also created revolutions, world markets and empires instead of ideologies.)

It thus appears here as if ideology was primarily a product of German powerlessness. German ideology became synonymous with ideology in general. But

---

22   MECW 4:211 and 5:536.
23   Engels (under the pseudonym Friedrich Oswald), 'Alexander Jung, Lectures on Modern German Literature', MECW 2:284–97. Jung answered Engels in the article *'Ein Bonbon für den kleinen Oswald, meinen Gegner in den deutschen Jarhbücher'*. Engels did not respond; cf. his letter to Arnold Ruge, 26 July 1842, MECW 2:546.
24   E.g. MECW 5:28, 37, 420 (on the latter page, the metaphor of 'putting things upside down' – *'auf den Kopf stellen'* in the original German – appears for the first time in Marx and Engels; as previously indicated, they took this image from Hegel).
25   MECW 5:455 et seq.

it seemed as if the word was thus unnecessarily limited: idealist conceptions of the type in question had germinated out of other soils than the German.

We can trace Marx's and Engels's hesitancy on this point. In their preface, they had originally written than other peoples also had their ideologies, (i.e. '[regard] the world as dominated by ideas'[26]). But they struck that part out. It would complicate their account if they presented a concept of ideology in the preface that was certainly more consistent but also lacked support in the rest of the account. Even in their later writings there was very little on any ideology other than the German. Marx would never use the word particularly often; when he did so, he did so in a single, large and notable exception in the sense of 'German idealist speculation'.[27] Even Engels, who nonetheless used the word far more often than Marx did, primarily attached the word to German speculation and philosophy.[28]

But this limitation to the German is practically determined and does not belong to the determination of the word itself in a strict sense. Carried out consistently, *ideology* becomes in what we could call *the first, narrower and negative meaning* the same as *the conception that society is steered by ideas*.

Here it is thus a question of a doctrine of society and a conception of society of a generally idealist type. This is the original meaning in Marx and Engels. We can understand its central role if we consider that we would have to look in vain for the label 'ideologue' stuck to any bourgeois economist of the classical liberal type that Marx and Engels took up for discussion. We could thus plough through the *Grundrisse*, *Capital* and *Theories of Surplus-Value* without once finding the word 'ideology'. In *Capital*, Marx spoke about 'bourgeois consciousness',[29] but he did not speak about 'ideology' even in that context. In the *Grundrisse* he had his brilliant demonstration of how the demands of the revolutionary bourgeoisie for political freedom and equality had their actual

---

26   MECW 35:9.
27   Thus in the letter to his Russian translator, N.F. Danielson, 7 October 1868. Danielson had requested a bibliographical presentation of Marx to publish in conjunction with the Russian edition of *Capital*. Speaking of *The Holy Family* and his articles in the *Deutsch-Französische Jahrbücher*, Marx said that they were 'directed against the ideological mysticism of Hegelian and, in general, speculative philosophy', MECW 43:123. See also in the well-known foreword to *A Contribution to the Critique of Political Economy*, when *The German Ideology* came up for discussion, MECW 29:264.
28   E.g. MECW 25:35 and 40; MECW 26:376 and 388. Cf. Cornu 1955–70, Vol. IV, p. 83, which says that the word 'ideology' in *The German Ideology* 'n'est pas pris dans le sens de conception du monde propre à une *classe* et à une époque, mais dans celui de mystification de la réalité par la spéculation'.
29   E.g. MECW 35:361.

basis in free and equal (i.e. unbound by privilege and restriction) exchange of goods. It may seem as if we were dealing here with a prime case of ideology in the sense that commentators have ascribed to Marx; but Marx did not use the word 'ideology' and as we have seen it was not by chance that he avoided doing so.[30] Just as little as he reproached Smith or Ricardo for neglecting praxis in their scientific activities – they had their bourgeois praxis[31] – so did he reproach them for pursuing ideology.

'Ideology', however, has more meanings here than this, the first and fundamental one. 'Ideology' thus describes not only a doctrine of society and conception of history. It also describes a related but nonetheless clearly separate *scientific* (or, if you will, quasi-scientific) *approach*, that is, a *scientific method* in a broad sense of the word. Let us call this the *second, still narrow and negative content* of the word 'ideology'.

The difference between both meanings becomes clear if we keep Marx's and Engels's view of Hegel in mind; it emerges most clearly in *Ludwig Feuerbach*. In his conception of history and society – as in general in his philosophical system – Hegel is an ideologist in that he regards ideas as the primary driving forces of development. Engels spoke of an '*ideologische Verkehrung*' in Hegel.[32] Hegel's method, however, is not ideological but 'realist'. More precisely, Engels said that while Hegel's treatment of morals is idealist in form and realist in content, the opposite applies to Feuerbach. Hegel ascribed primacy to ideas, but when he developed ethical ideas, he followed real development: family, bourgeois (or civil)[33] society, the state (i.e. he dealt with a real process and not a context of ideas). Feuerbach ascribed primacy to material conditions – he was realist in form – but he completely ignored the real conditions in these societies and preached only his abstract ethical ideal, love for humanity, and derived a range of potential social conditions from that.[34]

In both *Anti-Dühring* and *Dialectics of Nature*, 'ideology' designates primarily a scientific approach. When Engels accused Dühring of being an ideologue, he meant primarily that Dühring had applied an ideological method. When Dühring laid out his morals, he started from his *idea* of, for example, equality

---

30   Cf. Marx 1953, pp. 152–62.

31   Above, p. 48 *et seq.*

32   MECW 26:382.

33   Hegel's '*bürgerliche Gesellschaft*' has nothing to do with 'bourgeois' in the Marxist sense; it is a translation from the French '*société civile*' and can be found in every society where a division of labour prevails and where, consequently, people exchange, sell, and buy necessities, goods or services from one another.

34   MECW 26:376 et seq.

and freedom and attempted to derive a historical development from that. The opposite path was, according to Engels, the only reasonable one: deriving the changing ideas from real historical development.[35]

Two additional definitions of the word 'ideology' can be distinguished in Engels and Marx. Both are considerably much broader than the first two. Both are also related directly to the materialist conception of history.

The third meaning is found above all in a section in *Ludwig Feuerbach* and in a letter than Engels wrote to Franz Mehring in 1893. In the section in *Ludwig Feuerbach* in question, ideology stands out not only as a world of ideas or an approach that a few philosophers and scientists drifted into. Ideology is a power that leaves its mark on all human conceptions of social and political reality. 'The state', it says there, 'is the first ideological power over humanity'. The state is the instrument of power of the ruling class; with its help unity is created both outwardly and inwardly. The state creates a unity out of a society marked by class oppression and irreconcilable conflicts of interest, even in the world of ideas of its subjects. Political unity becomes more important than the fundamental social and economic split. The path to an ideology liberated from fundamental material reality lies open.

The second stage on this path is the creation of independent legal and political systems – constitutional law, civil law, and so on – through professional lawyers and professional politicians. By rewriting economic relations, for example, in legal terms, it appears as if law were the determining moment and the development of the legal statutes the essential and independent development.

The third stage comprises religions and philosophies, which are even more distant from the base. 'Here the connection between conceptions and their material conditions of existence becomes more and more complicated, more and more obscured by intermediate links. But the connection exists'.[36]

It should be noted that Engels here was not describing a historical development in an actual sense: he certainly was not arguing that the professional administration of justice preceded religion. He was rather describing three levels situated at different distances from the base.

His account constitutes a brilliant presentation of the materialist conception of history, which he accomplished using the term 'ideology'. The word here has a far broader meaning than previously, but it is entirely compatible with both the sense of 'idealist doctrine of society' and '(quasi)scientific approach'. It could be said that here, he was trying to explain how the ideological doctrine

---

35   MECW 25:89. Cf. also 25:597. See above, p. 443 *et seq.*
36   MECW 26:392 et seq.

of society and the ideological method arose. Ideology stands out in a broader perspective as a general phenomenon.

We find a similar definition in the letter to Mehring, which was written on account of Mehring's work *Die Lessing-Legende*. The letter was written in the same spirit as the earlier letter to Joseph Bloch and Conrad Schmidt: Engels wanted to emphasise that according to the materialist conception of history, ideas were not to be understood as passive impressions of material circumstances. But here he thus made use of the term 'ideology'. As I understand it, it was also the only time he equated ideology with false consciousness; nothing similar is found in Marx in general. Here, he said that '[i]deology is a process which is, it is true, carried out consciously by what we call a thinker, but with a consciousness that is spurious'. The actual driving forces remain unconscious; the process appears entirely as a matter for pure thought.

Ideology is thus regarded here as a general phenomenon in society, but its conscious designers are those that pursue ideology in the second meaning of the word, that is, those who start out only from the ideas. Engels distinguishes a particular type of 'historical ideologist', or those who regard scientific and other ideas at a given historical stage as solely having sprung from previous ideas: thought has an independent history. Engels rejects these ideas in the same way as he and Marx did nearly fifty years earlier in *The German Ideology*.[37]

We can see here the close connection between 'ideology' in the second and third meaning. Ideology in *the third meaning* is only a much broader concept. It is still a question of illusory ideas that are fostered in every society where intellectual labour is separated from material labour and where intellectual labour appears as the determinant. But ideas are what leave their mark on the views of humans, both learned and unlearned. Ideology here is a general phenomenon in every class society.

Occasionally, Engels hinted that ideological errors of judgement also had roots elsewhere than in the social structure. When he accused the materialistically inclined Darwinist biologists of going astray as regards the role of human ideas in historical development, he placed their 'ideology' in connection with the condition that what separated the human species from other species was planned activity.[38] The step from there to regarding the plan itself, in the sense of purely intellectual creation, as the real driving force of development would thus always be a short one. This viewpoint, however, does not of course rule out that the ideological view is rooted in class society. If the conception that

---

37   Letter from Engels to Franz Mehring, 14 July 1893, MECW 50:164.
38   Above, p. 440 *et seq.*

ideas play the determining role in human contexts has an immediate plausibility over it, it naturally strengthens the penetrative power of the conception in every class society.

As a result, however, of the concept of ideology being placed in connection with the concept of class, it will expand in the name of consistency beyond the limitation to illusory ideas that Engels had given it. Even the working class is a class that, if it manages to acquire a social conscience and a plan of action, will conflict with the ideologies of the other classes. But what is it that the working class asserts against these ideologies? Does it not have its own ideology? Or must a special name be coined for the working-class world of ideas?

Engels tested the latter possibility through the term 'scientific socialism'. Scientific socialism is the socialism of Marxism, and it is preceded by idealistic socialism in a limited sense, utopian socialism, which starts from ideas about a just society, good humans and so on and asserts that if only people become aware of the content of these ideas, socialism would be realised.[39]

Obviously, the idea of scientific socialism was a child of its time. Spencer crowned his synthetic philosophy with two volumes on ethics. The best programme of action would follow from real insight into the nature of reality. There is no gap between the worlds of knowing and of action. If Spencer had expressed himself in the same terms as Engels, he would have asserted that he had developed scientific liberalism.[40] Engels would have had two comments

---

39   As far as I have been able to determine, the phrase 'scientific socialism' appears for the first time in *Anti-Dühring* (MECW 25:21, 27 and specifically 189). In the chapters published separately under the title *Socialism: Scientific and Utopian* (French edition: *Socialisme utopique et socialisme scientifique*, 1880; first German edition dated 1882, published 1883) the term is given in the very title. In the foreword to the French edition, which Marx wrote after consulting with Engels and Paul Lafargue inserted over his own name, Marx also used the term 'scientific socialism'. There, he said that the selected chapters from *Anti-Dühring* constituted 'what might be termed an *introduction to scientific socialism*' (*ce qu'on pouvait appeler une Introduction au socialisme scientifique*); MECW 24:339, quote from Marx's handwritten original. It should be noted that 'scientific socialism' as Engels used it alluded primarily to Marx's theory of surplus value and thus his economic theory, and second to historical materialism in general. On the other hand, he did not seem to be alluding to Marx's entire philosophy with the phrase. Here – judging by his vocabulary – he preferred the term 'communist world outlook' (e.g. MECW 25:8, foreword to the 1885 edition of *Anti-Dühring*: '… a more or less connected exposition of the dialectical method and of the communist world outlook …').

40   Spencer was prevented from this only by his conviction that the scientific approach he advocated was universal and immediately valid for everyone who was unimpeded by prejudices. His ethics, which also contained his political theory, was aimed at 'the establishment of rules of conduct on a scientific basis'; Spencer 1862, Vol. IX, p. v. The morally correct was understood unambiguously as the biologically and sociologically advantage-

about similar claims: he would have said that Spencer's conception was not at all scientific, and he would have asserted that it was the result of a limited bourgeois class standpoint.

If Engels's epistemological realism is to be taken seriously – and in my opinion, there is every reason to do so – it is important to distinguish between both perspectives (i.e. between the question of the truth of a theory or standpoint and the question of its social origin and function). In the very phrase 'scientific socialism' lurks a danger of confusion: one could end up in class relativism, or an idea that a certain view is true only for the reason that a given class is willing to embrace it. This danger is not inevitable: historical materialism considers itself able to *explain* why the working class would find it easier than other classes to embrace a view that *for other reasons* could be described as (relatively) true. Namely, in its activities the working class is not separate from material production, which constitutes the determining moment in society. Therefore, it is easier for the working class to realise the significance of material production.

Entirely regardless of the difficulties with the phrase 'scientific socialism', however, it is obvious that a common designation is needed for all the worlds of ideas that can be described as characteristic of a class. If the word 'ideology' is thus to be reserved for worlds of illusory ideas, a collective name must be created for these ideologies and the socialism based on Marxism. The world of ideas as such does not change its character because it can be described as true in some respects. It is not a passive impression by science; it is formed and formulated so that it rebels against other worlds of ideas and can form the basis for action.

Engels did not coin any such designation, however, and moreover he was entirely a prisoner of the tremendous faith in science of his times. The gap between science and ignorance, between truth and falsehood appeared to be so unfathomable that the ideas that were compatible with the one could not have the same name as those that were compatible with the other.

Marx, on the other hand, once made use of such a collective name. It was in the preface to *A Critique of Political Economy*, where he spoke of 'ideological forms in which men become conscious of this conflict [in the base] and

---

ous: 'Not for the human race only, but for every race, there are laws of right living'; ibid., p. 132. Liberal rights and freedoms could thus be grounded in the insights into the organic and superorganic nature of humanity and human societies: for example, 'the right of property' (Vol. x, p. 94 et seq.), 'the rights of free exchange and free contract' (p. 127 et seq.), 'the rights of free belief and worship' (p. 136 et seq.), and 'the rights of free speech and publication' (p. 141 et seq).

fight it out'.[41] It should be noted that the term 'ideology' is neutral here: it designates each conscious conception that forms the basis for action regardless of the degree of insight it contains and regardless of who holds it.

We can thus find here an example of the *fourth* meaning of the term 'ideology', the broadest and the only one that does not describe something erroneous *per se*.

It would naturally be ridiculous to construct 'the truly Marxist' concept of ideology using this sole point in the text. The analysis of Marx's and Engels's use of the word 'ideology' has shown that there is no support for any strict determination in their texts. They used it in varied contexts. Certain places in the texts supported one interpretation, others supported another. The meanings changed entirely according to context. When the polemic concerned certain limited philosophical and scientific theses and theories, the word had a narrow meaning; that is why, for example, the bourgeois economists cannot be described as ideologues. On the other hand, when the whole of society enters the picture, 'ideology' gains a much broader meaning; its class character and therefore its social character is set off.

When in the subsequent sections I attempt to speak about ideologies in the fourth and broadest meaning, it is because I am arguing that it is the determination that is the most fruitful. It should be noted that I am interested above all in the relation between ideology and science. Assuming, purely terminologically speaking, that there is an entirely different relation between, for example, Marxist theory and the world of ideas associated with it than between other competing theories and their worlds of ideas is not profitable. It would complicate the study of the interaction between Marxist theory and the Marxist world of ideas, and that would generally complicate a study of Marxist theory from the perspective of the history of ideas and of science.

First, however, it is a matter of more closely determining this fourth meaning, which only faintly peeps out in Marx's text. It is then no longer a question

---

41   MECW 29:263. The use of the word 'ideology' here – like the rest of the preface – has gained extraordinary significance. It is, strictly speaking, the only place in the texts by Marx and Engels where Lenin could find support for his own use, which then became the standard for the Leninist tradition. Even Althusser's use of the word, which is now the subject of so many interpretations, has its basis there. The outstanding historian Georges Duby recently adopted Althusser's usage and sought to make it historically usable; the question, however, is whether Duby has only taken the word in the general, neutral sense it has in Marx's statement and in practice left Althusser's philosophical embellishments aside. Duby's chief ambition is to use the word '*dans le sens le plus large, et en le dégageant des intonations pejoratives*'; Duby 1974, p. 149.

of simply explicating Marx or Engels; it also becomes a question of developing a concept that can be used for studying them as well.

3   Manifest and Latent Ideology

The word 'ideology' will thus be used here in a general and neutral sense. But what does an ideology look like? Where can it be found in real life?

The possibility of identifying 'ideology' with 'world of ideas' or 'view' immediately presents itself. 'View' is the more usable of the two: it is possible to speak of a worldview as well as views on society and on life. Ideology could be defined as an amalgamation of the three. The centre of gravity in an ideology can lie in different places; the worldview can be more or less developed, the views on society (including views on history and ideas about future society) can have a more or less distinct character, and so on.

If 'ideology' only meant that, however, the word would not be particularly indispensable: a foreign synonym for 'view'.

There is an obvious difference, though. Calling something a view requires it to be relatively developed or defined. Saying 'Arthur has no views on life' would mean that Arthur could not account for his views on existence in any coherent, stringent manner. On the other hand, it would not be accusing Arthur of lacking ideology, except in an extremely vapid political vocabulary. It could be said that he lacked a *conscious* ideology. Developing and spreading a conscious, consistent ideology is a task that professional ideologues usually set for themselves.

We just saw that Marx and Engels used the word 'ideology' in several different ways. We also saw that the diversity of uses also characterises the subsequent Marxist tradition. Undoubtedly the multiple meanings of the word have to do with the difference between conscious and unconscious, or what I will here call *manifest* and *latent* ideology. A manifest ideology is a view that expresses assumptions, norms and values concerning human action, society and historical development, and nature. A manifest view is formulated in words and sentences, in books and tracts and sermons and orations. It can be more or less developed, it can deal with a larger or smaller portion of everything that could happen to humanity. It could be contradictory, vague or confused. What makes it manifest is that it is expressed in words that can be interpreted and analysed as words.

It is otherwise with a latent ideology. Latent ideology can be sought in or beyond the manifest, but it can also be traced in the actions and measures of individuals, groups, classes and institutions. It is nonsense to speak of a latent view; it is meaningful to speak of a latent ideology. Saying, for example, that a measure or action reveals contempt for women is not to say that the measure or action reveals a developed view that states that women are inferior to men. It is saying that the action, *if justified in words*, would only be compatible with a view or manifest ideology in which women in one manner or another (biologically, socially, religiously, etc.) have been defined as less capable or valuable than men.

Looking for a latent ideology in an action, a decision or a text therefore entails an interpretation of behaviours, measures or statements. The behaviours, measures or statements (or just as much a network of behaviours, measures and statements that constitute the politics of a government, a party or an institution) are translated into the terms of the manifest ideology. Inconsistencies are described as expressions of separate ideologies; lip service, for example, could conflict with the actual manner of action.

Manifest ideologies are views, latent ideologies can be explicated as views. This activity of explication constitutes a natural and central link in every political and ideological discussion. Most often, the rules for such explication are vague and unbiased. Both the one and the other can, when it is convenient, be described as manifestations of fascism, antidemocratic sentiment or contempt for humanity. If the explication is to be less random, the rules are required to be rooted in a consistent theory of society that elucidates the various relations between views and actions.

Marx and Engels strove for such a use of their theory of society. Their historical materialism would provide the very template for the analysis. According to historical materialism, latent ideology always has a determined, unchanging structure. In this context, general statements – being determines consciousness and not the other way around, for example, or the base determines social development in the last analysis – mean that the foundation of the latent ideology is to be sought in humanity's material circumstances and not in their ideas. The ideas have their origins in concrete labour (or the shortage of labour). Ideas about humanity and the world, assessments of good and evil, and norms for action have grown out of a definite type of activity that produced a definite perspective on society, on social classes, on people and by extension also on nature, on religious dogmas and rites, on form of art and so on.

But the crucial basis for ideas is not just any concrete activity whatsoever. In a guild society, it is true, the activities of the blacksmith will be the soil for ideas about existence and the world that differ somewhat from that of the shoemaker. The toil of the farmer could also, in varied societies, give him reason for similar thought about the eternal circle of nature. In a materialist analysis, however, it is not these worlds of ideas in their full breadth and width that constitute the basis of latent ideology. It is instead the role in the process of production, and therefore class affiliation. The differences between the ideas of blacksmiths and shoemakers in the same society, or the similarities between the ideas of fourteenth- and nineteenth-century farmers about nature are naturally not insignificant in a study of different concrete worlds of ideas. The fundamental analysis of ideology, however, is based on the different modes of production, the character of which is determined by the answers to questions such as: Who owns the means of production? Who has power over labour, who disposes of the surplus, the surplus labour that production generates? How are the results of production allocated? The blacksmith and the shoemaker in the same society belong to the same class, whereas the farmers of the fourteenth and nineteenth century respectively in all likelihood played different roles in production.

The starting point of latent ideology is thus classes and class contradictions in accordance with the Marxist analysis of ideology. We find an illustrative argument in Marx's *Grundrisse*, for example. There, Marx took up the bourgeoisie's slogans of freedom and equality for discussion. Here, it was thus a question of a manifest ideology, expressed in mountains of documents, speeches and proclamations. The manifest ideology had its counterpart in the political actions of the bourgeoisie, in its struggle against political and economic privileges, against customs duties, the guild system and the aristocracy. In this manifest ideology, however, Marx traced a latent one that expressed the objective interests of the bourgeois class. The basis of the proclamations of this manifest ideology about the freedom and equality of rights for all humanity was, Marx asserted, free and equal economic exchange – or, more precisely, the right of each and every one on equal terms to buy and sell anything at all, including labour power, to anyone at all.[42]

Naturally, it cannot be imagined that this simple model could be applied to all the human worlds of ideas and views. In that case, each class would have its own manifest ideology. Class affiliation would unambiguously determine the perspective on the world.

Even a child knows this is not the case. There are primarily two mutually closely related reasons for this. First, it is not a given that class affiliation itself as such fosters a world of ideas in which the actual position and potential for development of the class are evident. Second, manifest ideologies have a well-known, enormous power over the worlds of ideas.

On the first point, Marx and Engels – at least where the working class was concerned – were somewhat unclear. They often argued as if the working class

---

42   Marx 1953, p. 152 et seq.

quite simply could perceive the fundamental mechanisms of society because the class itself lacked special interests.[43] On the other hand, Marx and Engels developed a theory that they wanted to use as the basis for the actions of the working class, which on crucial points differed from the ideas that the working class up to that point had arrived at through its own ideologies. It was Lenin who first took an unambiguous position on this point: workers only had a spontaneous 'trade union' consciousness. They did not obtain knowledge of society as a whole, of their own roles and of their own possibilities in a social revolution not through their own experiences as workers; they had to obtain it elsewhere.[44]

On the other hand, Marx and Engels were particularly aware of the power of manifest ideology over the senses – regardless of the class affiliation of those senses. Their concept of the *ideology of the ruling class* must be viewed in this light.[45] The class that commands material production also places substantial portions of the production of ideas under it. It is not, however, primarily through manipulation and deliberate distortions that the ruling class commands the senses. The society itself in which it has the leading role fosters – spontaneously and through its fundamental relations between humans in production – certain ideas that, so to speak, serve the interests of the ruling class. So it is, for example, with Marx's famous commodity fetishism or the idea fostered in the capitalist production of commodities that the crucial social relations are relations between things and not between people.[46]

An ideology, however, contains much more than just conceptions that deal directly with the base and its relations. In various intricate ways, these conceptions are put in relation to ideas about political life, law, religion, diet and so on. In the final chapter, we will go into more detail in these matters in light of the attempt by Engels in particular to construct a particular Marxist or socialist

43   This is especially apparent in the plain, simple text of the *Manifesto*; see e.g. MECW 6:490 et seq. Hints of the same can also be found in the magnificent finale to the first volume of *Capital*, on the victory of the proletariat as 'the negation of negation' (MECW 35:751), which then played a crucial role in Engels's popularisations (e.g. MECW 25:122 et seq.).

44   Lenin develops this in *What Is To Be Done?*, Lenin 5:394 et seq. Johansson provides worthwhile viewpoints on this *spontaneous* ideology of the working class, in particular p. 66 et seq.

45   The concept of the ideology of the ruling class can be said to be fully developed in *The German Ideology*: 'The ideas of the ruling class are in every epoch the ruling ideas: i.e., the class which is the ruling *material* force of society is at the same time its ruling *intellectual* force'. MECW 5:59.

46   Marx develops the theory of commodity fetishism in *Capital*, MECW 35:81 et seq. One of Engels's greatest omissions is that he did not attempt to develop these lines of thought in his own interpretations of Marxism.

conception of the world: the attempt itself betrays certain definite conceptions about the relations among the various levels of ideology.

As we have seen, the crucial conception of ideology in Marx and Engels is that the foundation is to be sought in the conceptions of the base that are fostered through the fundamental relations in the base. It is there that the meeting point between material social reality and ideas lies.

Every well-developed manifest ideology has its definite hierarchy of conceptions: conceptions about a part of reality are justified by and based in conceptions about another part. In a Christian ideology of an accomplished type, the ideas of what society and the state should be are derived from ideas about God and Christ, the Creation and eternal life. The ideas about how economic life should be arranged can in turn be derived from the ideas about the state (the variations here are innumerable).

Marx and Engels imagined that such a manifest ideology could be burst asunder. The derivations proved to be illusory: beyond the manifest ideology was a latent one, and in that latent ideology the conceptions of the base form the starting point. The hierarchy of the manifest ideology is turned upside down in the latent in accordance with the following schema:

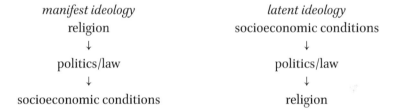

manifest ideology	*latent ideology*
religion	socioeconomic conditions
↓	↓
politics/law	politics/law
↓	↓
socioeconomic conditions	religion

This is the simple content of Marx's and Engels's metaphor in *The German Ideology* that reality in ideology appears as in a camera obscura: the furthest down appears there on top, and vice versa.[47]

A quick glance at the schema, however, also shows that the latent ideology itself could be developed into a manifest ideology. The latent ideology cannot be used only to reveal and break down already existing manifest ideologies. The latent ideology itself contains the guidelines for its own manifest ideology in which the ideas about the state, God, art and philosophy are derived from the conceptions about the base.

---

47   MECW 5:36. A particularly elegant but not so thoroughly penetrating study of the metaphors concerning ideology, especially in *The German Ideology*, has been carried out by Kofman 1973, p. 3 et seq.

According to Marx's and Engels's claim, latent ideology squares with a scientific (i.e. approximately and preliminarily true) picture of reality. Science can be mobilised not only in the struggle against ideologies; it can also create its own ideology.

Engels's philosophical efforts can be characterised as the search to develop *a manifest ideology that squares with the latent, that lies in the fundamental conception itself of historical materialism.* But for this manifest ideology of his, he did not want to use the soiled term 'ideology', speaking instead of scientific socialism. This 'scientific' socialism, however, bore all the external characteristics of a manifest ideology: it provides an ordered totality of views on society, life and the world, and it provides some general guidelines for human action. It also has the double address that distinguished nearly all manifest ideologies: while it addresses itself to all people and asserts its universal correctness and application before them, it orients itself on a particular group or class whose activity it expects and encourages (in Engels's case this applies, naturally, to the proletariat).

Historical materialism, however, is not sufficient for the attempt to create a manifest ideology. It deals with social reality: it claims to be able to explain why people under certain circumstances believe in an omnipotent god, for example, or imagine that the universe is unchanging. On the other hand, it does not claim by its own efforts to say anything about the eternity of the cosmos or the development of species. For that task, people must turn to other scientific theories. As we have seen, this is also what Engels did with inexhaustible energy and unflagging curiosity.

We have seen that this interest also had another motive. For Engels, as for Marx, the question of how historical materialism related to theories in other scientific fields was a crucial one. Only after excursions of this type into foreign disciplines could they develop and clarify the claim to the scientific character of their own theory. For that purpose, they did not need to comment on the parts of reality (molecules or heavenly bodies, light rays or biological species) that other scientific theories concerned themselves with. Methods and theorising were enough for that.

To this internal scientific need, however, an external one would be added: joining the images of reality from other sciences with the image of society that historical materialism provides in order to construct a complete manifest ideology from both.

This is a need that can scarcely be distinguished – sometimes not at all – from the internal scientific need. But it leads unconditionally to great difficulties for anyone constructing an ideology.

4   Ideology and Science

We have seen how latent ideology, according to Marx and Engels, has a definite structure that distinguishes itself from the structure of the usual ideologies.
The structure of latent ideology, however, differs just as palpably from the scientific hierarchy that Marx and Engels were adherents of. This relation can be
illustrated with a simple schema:

latent ideology	*scientific hierarchy*
cioeconomic conditions	mechanics
	physics/chemistry
	biology
politics/law	social/historical theory:
religion/philosophy/art	about the base
	about the superstructure

Latent ideology is derived from social and historical theory, and that part of
the scientific hierarchy thus offers no problems. Social and historical theory,
however, are less fundamental than the natural sciences in the scientific hierarchy. Nor, of course, is there any possibility of taking a position on the truthfulness of the theories of natural science from the perspective of social and
historical theory. At the same time, however, natural scientific theories are
indispensable for anyone wishing to replace religious and traditionally philosophical conceptions, for example, with others that are said to be in conformity
with scientific understanding.

Engels could go about this in two different ways in his presentation of scientific socialism. Either he could start from his and Marx's own social theory
and show how the conceptions of eternal law, an omnipotent god and a mechanical universe have their natural origins in different modes of production.
Against the ideas about God and nature he could have mobilised theories from
modern science as well. The starting point would nonetheless have been social
theory.

On the other hand, he could have followed the scientific hierarchy and then
enter into social theory only in the final stage of the presentation.

The second possibility is the one he consistently followed. His starting point
was ideas and theories about inorganic nature, and – as in *Anti-Dühring* – the
fields of biology and, finally, history subsequently followed.

One consequence of this approach was that the latent ideology, and thus
Marxian social theory, were completely obscured: it appeared as a derivation

from the other theories, and Engels's manifest ideology took on an appearance that conformed in a confusing manner with the many manifest ideologies produced in his time, from Comte's and Spencer's to Dühring's. Engels became one ideologically oriented system-builder among many.

Another consequence connected with this was that Engels, in order to testify to the consistency of his presentation had to attempt to persuade both himself and his readers of an indissoluble connection between the various theories in the scientific hierarchy: Marxian social theory was presented as a natural continuation of different theories of the development of the cosmos and of the biological species. The crucial differences that Engels at the same time was well aware of had to be toned down.

In my opinion, Engels's attempt to create a manifest ideology goes definitively wrong on these points. The error lies not in the fact that he wanted to use other scientific theories, or in the fact that he was striving for an ontology based in the sciences and thus not in his realist epistemology. Nor does it lie in his conception that the new workers' movement needed its own image of the world. It lies in the fact that he took the other sciences as his starting point.

For the task he set himself, a *double* use of science is necessary. The one, which is traditionally called *ideological*, entails – as we have seen – the use of social theory to reveal the latent ideology in the manifest (or in actions, decisions and so on). The other, *direct* use entails a conception in one ideology or another being defined as *erroneous* according to the prevailing scientific understanding.

In the Marxist tradition there is a widespread conception that the function of criticism of ideology should be sufficient. Revealing the social origins of the conceptions would be sufficient.[48] It is, of course, a sufficient *scientific* task but not a sufficient *ideological* task. Many of the conceptions revealed as illusory would disappear without being replaced by others. Let us take an example. The conception that an omnipotent god created the earth can be subjected to ideological criticism. It could, for example, be asserted that the latent content in a dogma of this kind is the conception of an omnipotent earthly ruler. But if we stop there, all these questions about the universe and eternity that would live on even after the conceptions of the divine creator had faded away would appear as an irritating void. For the sake of their own activity – and preferably

---

48   Cf. for example Habermas 1968, p. 84 et seq.; Wellmer year, p. 48 et seq. and 61 et seq.;
        A. Schmidt 1974, p. 104 (with a direct polemic against what Schmidt calls 'a positive theory
        of ideology'). The relation has at least become problematic in Reichelt 1970, p. 17 et seq.
        and 265 et seq.

in all modesty – ideological critics must convey the alternate answers that contemporary science perchance provides them.

It is obvious that both uses of sciences are in no way mutually exclusive. The direct use involves repudiating the truthfulness or meaningfulness of the religious statements; the critical ideological use of a definite scientific theory involves an explanation of why such statements gain credence and dissemination in a certain type of society.

The direct and the ideological uses of science can also be very closely related to each other. Let us take as an example the idea that all contradictions in a society can be resolved if every adult is given equal voting rights. The idea can be subject to direct criticism: it could be said that it is built on a misunderstanding of the relations between base and political superstructure. It is, in other words, erroneous. It could be subject to ideological criticism: its hidden content could be said to be the idea of formal equality within material production (buying and selling on equal terms of all commodities, including labour power).

It is important, however, to distinguish between direct and ideological use of science in the sphere of ideology. It is important purely for the reason that Marx and Engels (in the good company of the entire age they lived in) did not explicitly make this distinction, thereby preparing the ground for various mistakes.[49]

Engels's philosophical writings – *Anti-Dühring, Dialectics of Nature* and *Ludwig Feuerbach* – first of all provide examples of the direct use of scientific theses and theories. Engels largely mobilised all the science he had come into contact with and put his confidence in. He thus wanted to refute and change a number of ideas about the world, humanity and society. It was the same intent that Spencer, Dühring, Haeckel and the whole order of system-builders had. Using science, they wanted to change the world of humanity's (or at least *some* of humanity's, *some* social classes') ideas.

Their intent, however, was thereby not to annihilate the ideologies in general, insofar as what was meant by ideology was not that which was erroneous in itself. They wanted to change the ideology, or perhaps create a new ideology. In other words, they wanted to show that a range of assumptions that people made about reality – with which they sought to substantiate the conception of their role, their possibilities and their obligations in existence – lacked scientific support. But they also wanted to show which assumptions of this type actually *have* the blessing of current science and what consequences this would have for these ideas.

---

49   Above, p. 471 *et seq.*

A substantial difference between the direct use of science and the use of science to criticise ideology is that *the criticism of ideology in itself cannot produce any new ideology, while the direct use can.*

There are a number of difficulties, however, that must be discussed when speaking about the relation between ideology and science. They concern science as a historical and social phenomenon. A heedless use of science in ideological discussion involves treating science as a supplier of undisputable truths raised above epochs, social classes and interests. A heedless use of this kind was more the rule than the exception during the late nineteenth century with its strong faith in science.

5   A Marxist View of Science

Engels and Marx ought to have been particularly well aware of the relativity of science: it was an obvious consequence of their materialist conception of history. As we have seen, they also drew the conclusion in a number of writings from *The German Ideology* forward.[50] On the other hand, they did not develop a real theory in the fields. Their opinions are discernible in scattered comments.

These comments can be divided into two groups. On the one hand, they asserted that a particular *internal scientific sphere* had to be distinguished – a requirement that had its evident connections with epistemological realism. The truthfulness of science needed to be tested regardless of its social origins and function. This is the simple meaning of the famous quote from Dante in the preface to *Capital*.[51] Engels expressed the same understanding, including in a letter to the Darwinist zoologist Oscar Schmidt in the dispute over the relation between socialism and Darwinism, which we will soon return to.[52]

The other, more comprehensive group of comments concern the relation of the sciences to external conditions: material production, the development of material needs, class contradictions and class interests.[53] This is the group that

---

50   Above, p. 103 *et seq.*

51   'Every opinion based on scientific criticism I welcome. As to the prejudices of so-called public opinion, to which I have never made concessions, now as aforetime the maxim of the great Florentine is mine: *Segui il tuo corso, e lascia dir le genti* (Follow your own path, and let the people talk)'. MECW 35:10.

52   'With your permissions, I shall in due course and from my own standpoint subject your lecture to the kind of ruthless criticism which alone does justice to free science and which any man of science must welcome, even when applied to himself'. Letter from Engels to O. Schmidt, MECW 45:314.

53   E.g. in *The German Ideology*, MECW 5:40; the *Grundrisse*, Marx 1953, p. 438 et seq., 582

usually provided the basis for what has been regarded as the Marxist stand-point. Many Marxists have also emphatically defended it, such as Bukharin, Hessen and Bernal in the well-known feuds over science and society in the 1930s and 1940s.[54] There is no reason for us to go into the causes of this obvious simplification here: one of them, in any case, was that Marxism had its originality and its polemical strength in its emphasis on the significance of external circumstances. Marxists argued and fought in a world in which professors asserted that they spoke the truth for the simple reason that they were professors.

Nor was there any attempt in Marx and Engels to mediate both groups of arguments about science. If an understanding is to be distilled from them, a bold reconstruction must be made on the basis of their view of history and their – sporadic – epistemological understanding. The reason I am attempting such a reconstruction here is, if anything, because the result will be an interesting view on science rather than revealing a consistent and fundamental understanding in Marx or Engels. In other words, I believe that the basis for the reconstruction is quite feeble in Marx and Engels and that their writings do not justify a mediation of their comments on the independence and relativity, respectively, of science. On the other hand, I believe that if *we* carry out this mediation, we can make out the contours of a fruitful theory about the relation between science and society.

Between the thesis about the independence of science and the thesis about its dependence, there is a dialectical relation – not just in a vague, literal and decorative sense but in a qualified sense as well. It is the same relation that exists between the thesis that science is determined by its object and the thesis of its historical relativity.[55] In the latter, more general sphere, however, Marx and Engels provided a more secure basis for an interpretation. On the other hand, nowhere did they develop an understanding of the general social or specifically institutional character of science. The same could perhaps be said here as Marx said about Aristotle's economic theory,[56] namely that the reality surrounding them did not provide them with a plausible perspective on the social roots of science. In their youth, they came into contact with the German university system and fell under the influence of its most typical expression, Hegel-

---

et seq.; *Capital,* MECW 35:50, 366 et seq., 390; *Anti-Dühring* and *Dialectics of Nature,* MECW 25:6, 465 et seq., 544 et seq.

54   The Marxist contributions have been collected in *Science*; Boris Hessen's contribution: 'The social and economic roots of Newton's *Principia*'.

55   Above, p. 386 *et seq.*

56   MECW 35:70.

ian philosophy. Later in life they could follow the development of this same university system only at a distance. Their comments on it are few in number, their insights into the development of specialisation and professionalisation were obviously limited.[57] Marx, at least, would devote the greatest amount of effort to political economy, and the representatives of political economy were spread over a wide field of occupations with a mercantilist bias; only a few of them were university professors.[58] In England, Marx and Engels generally came in contact with a scientific discussion in which most of the talking was done by learned gentlemen who lacked all institutional scientific connections. In the discussion about Darwinism, for example, it was difficult to notice the purely social difference between Darwin, Wallace and Spencer on the one hand and Haeckel and Oscar Schmidt on the other. Last but not least, Marx and Engels were busy with developing a workers' movement in which they also wanted to create platforms for a learned, scientific debate beyond and independent of the traditional institutions. The picture, to say the very least, was split. What they saw as proper, real science seemed to germinate and develop in the most varied environments.

That is why there was no connection between their statements on the social bonds of science and about a scientific debate independent of all interests and side viewpoints. We could say that they actually stood for both types of statements and that *they did so with good reason*, but that they did not put the contradictory ideas they thus brought forward into relation with one another. That was a task for posterity.

I have already said that there is a dialectical relation between the thesis on freedom and the thesis on constraint. *The dialectic here consists, as elsewhere, in that incompatible statements can be made about the same phenomenon or the same sphere of reality that, in their general and abstract form are unconditionally true.*

The first statement can be formulated as follows: what we call science has its scientific character independently of the social position of its advocate, of

---

57   Among these chance statements, Marx's acrid statement that he had 'reject[ed] all the German professorial twaddle about 'use-value'' (*Notes on Wagner's* Lehrbuch der polit-ischen Oekonomie, MECW 24:545) can be mentioned, as can Engels's words in connection with Dühring's dismissal from the University of Berlin: 'And then again, a German pro-fessorship – particularly in Berlin – is the top of German petty-bourgeois philistinism and provincialism'. Neither Marx nor Engels conducted any analysis whatsoever of the scientific community, despite the good intentions in *The German Ideology* to study 'the influence of the division of labour on science', MECW 5:92.

58   Above, p. 207 *et seq.*

whose interest it is pursued in, and the use to which the results are put. Scientific truth is thus unconditional.

The second statement can be formulated as follows: science is a thoroughly social phenomenon, that without exception it has its position or positions in the social field of force, that it is pursued in definite interests and that it is continuously influenced by its use or uses. Scientific truth is relative.

There is thus no boundary between a sphere in which science is free and a sphere in which it is constrained. In discussions about modern scientific sociology, it has often seemed as if it has been assumed that somewhere – within the gates of some institution or in the face of some kind of science – that the external dependence would cease. Karl Popper has argued that the social aspect is irrelevant for the type of research that is critical (i.e. where every thesis is subjected to an unsparing test unconstrained by any authorities).[59] A number of sociologists of knowledge, on the other hand, have constructed sociological models for the same type of research; in other words, they have attempted to determine the social conditions for the freedom of science.[60]

As I understand it, the issues concerning the circumstances under which good or beneficial science is produced are being mixed up with the question of the social roots of science in general. Even a researcher whose results can only be used for meditation in closed rooms, or a research group that has total external freedom to devote its research to whatever it wants, or a science that has been liberated from a belief in authority operates in a social environment; these activities are made possible by the economic and social structure of the society, and the use to which it is put as well as its entire orientation can never be understood without taking into account the society in which it grows. Locating a boundary in real science between a free sphere and an unfree one is as feasible as trying to draw a boundary somewhere in the human body between the spheres of activity for anatomy and physiology: both study the whole, but from different perspectives.

The difference between both perspectives on science is, however, more intricate and troubling than the difference between anatomy and physiology. The perspectives conflict with each other; they seem to exclude each other. All the criteria that were developed to assess scientific content are also socially determined. Uniform criteria in a given discipline presuppose a social unity between the representatives of the discipline and, ultimately, also the approval

---

59   Popper 1962, p. 208 et seq.
60   It was a matter of showing that free science exists only in a capitalist society of free competition and voting rights; cf. for example Barber 1962, Chap. 3; Hagström 1965, p. 104 et seq. and – for a thorough criticism – Blume 1974, p. 45 et seq.

of the group's expertise by the whole of society. A group of socially identifi-
able (through their education, positions and so on) scientific authorities must
develop. In a science where there is disagreement over the basis for assessment, and where consequently different scientific orientations and traditions
can be spoken of, the disagreement can always also be defined in social terms.
No 'freely floating intelligence' ever develops.

Social constraint does not need to play any role in the usual scientific debate.
In general, things go poorly – and often unjustifiably badly – if the external
aspects become direct arguments in the discussion. We get nowhere in relation
to an idea if viewpoints such as the fact that its bearers are not members of the
Royal Society or that its character squares quite well with bourgeois intellectual life are mobilised. They can serve as *explanations* as to why one scientific
viewpoint or another is being defended and is gaining credence. These explanations can in turn always be discussed, and *that* discussion becomes exclusively
a discussion about the social bond of science.

The problems arise only if science is regarded from a broader (e.g. historical)
perspective. The external aspect can then only temporarily be isolated from
the internal aspect. Scientific changes are at one and the same time changes
to internal criteria and changes in the social position of the science. It is only
belief in scientific advance (i.e. belief that knowledge is increasing) that forms
a barrier to pure relativism. But the criteria for assessing this process of growth
is at the same time both internal and external. On the one hand, earlier science
is judged using norms that are taken from contemporary science: the scientific
advances constitute a process in the direction of the science of today.[61] On the
other hand, its social development in the broadest sense (e.g. its organisational
differentiation,[62] its practical and material usefulness, its role in the world of
individuals' and classes' ideas) is assessed.

We do not need to go further into this difficult field. General principles will
not take us far into this study of the history of science. There are any number
of relations between science and society that can be distinguished, and these

---

61   In the debates on the history of science, there has lately come a persistent criticism of
      'inductivist' or 'presentist' historical writing, in which earlier science is assessed using the
      norms taken from today; cf. in particular Agassi 1963, *passim*. The criticism is justified,
      but *on the other hand* it must be stressed that the question of scientific *advance*, which
      is entirely central to all research into the history of science, cannot be assessed without
      norms taken from later science.

62   Kuhn, who is so anxious not to see the development of science as a goal-oriented process,
      says that the advances of science 'are marked by an increase in articulation and specializ-
      ation'; Kuhn 1970, p. 172.

relations are constantly changing in content and significance from era to era, from environment to environment and from science to science.

The essential point in our context is that the same difficult-to-grasp relation between the internal and external fields of science exists when considering the relation between science and ideology. No boundary can be drawn between 'science itself' and 'the ideological use of science'. All science has ideological significance, if for no one else than its originators and practitioners. The very boundaries and limitations of the scientific occupation influences scientists' perspectives of their activities, the world and society. The line of demarcation between science and the ideological significance of science does not run between two spheres of reality; it runs between two different perspectives on science.

If by ideology we mean – as we do here – a system of beliefs that are held to be true, of norms and of values, it is obvious that the relation between beliefs held to be true and scientific theses must be particularly decisive. But care should be taken not to identify the two with each other. From the strictly internal perspective, scientific assertions about reality have no relation to values and directives for action. As we know, no norms or values follow from a statement about reality. Darwin's theory of natural selection says nothing about how society ought to be organised. From a biological perspective, however, the theory stands out as a number of beliefs held to be true that are closely associated with values and norms. The 'struggle for existence' can be regarded as a purely descriptive determination of the relation among various organisms, but the phrase is also included in an ideological context where the very word 'struggle' (or 'competition') has its emotionally charged meaning. It does not *obtain* this meaning anywhere outside any internal scientific sphere (e.g. on the path from *Origin* to popularisation). Even texts that are regarded as purely scientific can be subjected to ideological analysis. They were written by people with worldviews and social positions, and it must always be possible to seek the traces of those in the scientific presentations.

These general indications, however, are rather trivial in their abstract form. They only become interesting in a concrete context. We could say that there is always a theoretical dimension and that there is always an ideological dimension in science. But the relation between theory and ideology is constantly changing. Theory is developed in a dynamic, contradictory environment where the constellations of ideologies change along with the other changes in society. Science becomes involved in this struggle in various ways, and is engaged – and engages itself – with varying levels of strength and intensity. The type and degree of engagement continuously influences it. Sometimes it may seem like the passive party, when other worlds of ideas – political, religious, aesthetic or moral – determine its boundaries and its purposes. Sometimes it stands out as a more active force in ideological development: scientific theses are brought into the ideologies and into the trials of strength between conflicting ideologies. Sometimes it appears once again to be relatively far above the battlefield, far too subtle or far too oriented on material utilities to be able to provide arguments for conflicts of an ideological type.

When the connection of science to ideologies is a thorough one, it could be said that *the ideological determination is strong.* The ideological determination influences the dimensioning and pace of development of practical and material science just as much as its general orientation. One general assumption I made earlier[63] is that a strong ideological determination increases the tendency towards laying out comprehensive theories. The more comprehensive a theory is, the more stable it becomes as support for ideology. There is, it could be said, an ideological need for all-embracing theories in which humanity's place in the universe and the place of classes in society are labelled. But there are other relations to keep in mind as well. The issues of whether ideology steers research in the direction of defined problem areas and whether it favours certain methods and certain results at the expense of others must be studied. The extent to which science changes ideologies is also an important question.

Finally, the most general and most difficult question in this context must be asked: What makes the ideological determination of science vary in strength?

Let us attempt to formulate these questions in connection with the historical period that is the subject for the preceding investigation, namely, the late nineteenth century. This is a period that is particularly suited for a study of this kind. The ideological determination of a number of sciences was strong: scientific theories were mobilised in the struggle among ideologies, comprehensive syntheses with scientific *and* ideological claims came to light, and large numbers of scientists were themselves engaged in ideological controversies. At the same time, the resistance against this ideological use was strong enough. Scientific specialisation had reached an advanced stage, and a number of disciplines were formed to an increasing extent by their practical and material use.

The late nineteenth century could thus be regarded as an ideal field for a study of the relation between science and ideology. There is, however, another viewpoint that is more decisive here. The preceding study had Engels's philosophical writings and their relation to the science of their time in focus. The

---

63   Above, p. 26.

primary result was that what Engels achieved was not the airy fantastical construction at the heights of metaphysics that has often been assumed. But the picture is not complete if this achievement is not placed in the ideological context to which the writings also belong.

From our viewpoint, it is a happy circumstance that right at the time when Engels was developing his manifest ideology, an intense debate was being conducted about the relation between science and ideology. It was a debate that in several ways infringed on Engels's own activities. But it has more to say to us than that. It provides not only a variety of scientists' and politicians' opinions; in itself, it is also a symptom of the real changes in the relations between science and ideology that were underway and would soon place the type of activity Engels was devoting himself to in a new light.

The following chapter will thus be a review of the discussions of Darwinism and socialism, science and ideology in the 1870s.

From there, it will be a short step to the analysis in the concluding chapter of the fundamental relation between science and ideology, and Marxist science and Marxist ideology in particular.

CHAPTER 18

The Debates on Darwinism and Socialism

1   The Main Problem of the Debates

Between 3 January 1877 and 7 July 1878, *Anti-Dühring* was published as a series of articles in *Vorwärts*, the main organ of the German Social-Democratic Party. The series stirred up a certain amount of opposition in the party. The criticism culminated at the General Socialist Congress at Gotha in May of 1877, where such issues as the value of an intricate scientific discussion for the party were questioned.

At an entirely different congress that same year – namely, the fiftieth Congress of the Association of German Naturalists and Physicians, on 22 September specifically – the renowned pathologist Rudolf Virchow gave a lecture on scientific freedom in the modern state, warning the scientists against all rash judgements and in particular branding the cocksure preaching of the Darwinists. Darwinism, he argued, had a dangerous kinship with socialism. Virchow's address, which was printed in two editions that same year, aroused the indignation of several Darwinists. Both Ernst Haeckel and Oscar Schmidt replied to the charge, repudiating any dealings between Darwinism and socialism. In England, figures including John Tyndall devoted a great deal of attention to Virchow's speech. Engels followed the debate with great interest and considered devoting a special study to it in *Dialectics of Nature*. Nothing came of it, however.

There was an immediate and definite background to both of these discussions. The Paris Commune had risen and been crushed a few years earlier. Bismarck was busy forcing through his Anti-Socialist Laws in Germany. A dreadful terror for the Social-Democratic Party was being whipped up.[1]

The questions of *the ideological role of the sciences* and the ideological rights of scientists played a crucial role in these discussions. According to the former, which we can call *the idea of enlightenment*, the sphere of the ideological activities of scientists (like that of philosophers, thinkers, or journalists) was unlimited. It was their right and obligation to seek to influence everyone in every

---

1   On this topic, see above all Fricke 1964, p. 128 et seq., where the text of the Socialist Laws themselves are also reproduced. See also Auer 1913, as well as the reviews Schnabel 1964 and Geschichte.

way with the means that were on offer. The scientific discussion had to be brought forward. Common sense could not otherwise triumph, and prejudices destroyed.

According to the latter conception, which I call with some hesitation *the expert idea*,[2] the sphere of the scientists is limited to the social organisations in which they are active: universities or colleges with their institutions and governing assemblies, scientific journals and conferences, and so on. Within this limited sphere, they are free. They have the right there to bring their opinions forward without restrictions. To the world outside the sciences, they were obligated to deliver certain, indisputable knowledge that emerged from scientific activity (including the free discussion among scientists). This is why they draw wages and social prestige. On the other hand, as scientists they have nothing to do with how those scientific truths are put to use; that is a political matter, the affair of the state.

This expert idea had its counterparts outside the scientific community; it even had its advocates in the German Social-Democratic Party. Here, for natural reasons, there was less interest in the positions of scientists within the scientific community. On the contrary, it was asserted that scientific controversies ought to be limited to the sphere where they belonged. And they did not belong to the political and ideological struggle.

It could be said that the expert idea that was winning advocates within the scientific organisations was part of a much more general idea about the sciences, which we can call *the idea of the social limitation of science*. Scientific activity, including scientific discussion, has to be localised to definite spheres in society. The scientific community relates to the world outside as a supplier of indisputable truths that were useful for various purposes. The broader use – the re-melting into products of industry, criticism of religion, popular education or party programmes – falls outside the sphere of scientists' expertise and work.

The idea of the social limitation of science is therefore similar to an *idea of the de-ideologisation of science*.[3] The idea of limitation is not only broader, it

---

2   The designation 'expert' can be misleading; the scientist as expert has lately become an officious servant for various clients. The scientific expert of Virchow and his fellow thinkers has a sovereign field in which they seek the truth, whereas the expert who performs their services for state authorities and industries instead provides scientific knowledge. It could be said that the idea developed in Wilhelmine Germany stands between the traditional idea of the impartial civil servant who stands above social contradictions in their work and a newer idea about the expert in which the expert role of the scientist, for the time being, only concerns the truth.

3   Yet another de-ideologisation *outward* applies here; that is, science cannot take an ideological

also involves the scientific organisations' loss of or liberation from influence over the transformation of knowledge and proficiencies into material utilities.

It is obvious that these ideas about science here, where we are primarily dealing with the diametrically opposite ideas of enlightenment and of de-ideologisation, are part of an intricate network of social, economic and political relations and that they are also connected with different ideas, ideals and theories internal to the sciences. The idea of de-ideologisation is naturally connected with a society in which the scientific organisations have a fixed position in the social hierarchy, where their spheres of competence are carefully defined, where specialisations are well developed and where the boundaries between the formation of scientific and of general cultural political and religious opinions are clearly marked.

The idea thus found a more natural home in Germany than in England. The German scientist usually spoke *ex officio* whereas the Englishman often lacked an official capacity of any type. The boundary between scientific and popular debate was also much blurrier in England; prominent scientists wrote with gusto in the general cultural periodicals whereas the Germans appeared in scientific journals and seldom made popularised themselves in anything more than ceremonial addresses at natural scientific congresses or on the name days or birthdays of royalty. The openly ideological use of science, such as the system-builders and others like them devoted themselves to, therefore seemed much riskier in Germany than in England. Drawing ethical, political and religious conclusions from scientific positions and theories was regarded as a task for specialists other than the scientists – journalists and priests, schoolteachers and politicians. Dedicated advocates of the idea of enlightenment such as Ernst Haeckel or Oscar Schmidt stood out as entirely too reckless – and perhaps unseemly – in their attempts to extend the much-discussed academic freedom of the German universities to society as a whole.

But the connection to the ideas of either enlightenment or de-ideologisation was determined not only by the scientific organisations; Haeckel the professor and Schmidt the lecturer would otherwise never have embraced the idea of enlightenment. Rather, it was that this type of firmly organised and segmented science provided the best, but not the only, hotbed for a general scientific ideal. Despite their mutual differences, the science of the figures of the Enlightenment, the philosophers and system-builders who would storm the gates of heaven – the science of Voltaire and Hegel, Comte and Hartmann, Holbach

---

position beyond the walls of the scientific institution where it may only serve as the possessor of truth.

and Dühring, Spencer and Haeckel – was above all a science that in its very design would provide guidelines for a rational worldview, a rational social order, rational morals and aesthetics. The philosopher or system-builder could hurry empirical research – obsessed with details as it was – forward, draw lines from it, and outline the knowledge of the future.

There was another ideal as well, according to which nothing that was not *certain* knowledge could be proclaimed in the name of science. In fact, herein lay the entire scientific ideal, now usually described as 'positivism', that would dominate large parts of at least early twentieth-century science. It was a positivism that, in this respect, constituted the antithesis to Comte's classical positivism. Its philosopher above all others was not Comte but Ernst Mach, the father of neopositivism.[4] Comte and his immediate successors had wanted to draw out lines from the knowledge they considered to be certain. The neopositivists demanded not only certainty in any discipline that could be described as fundamental (e.g. mechanics) but also demanded certainty in every indi-

---

4   As we have already stated, the term 'positivism' here has a troublesome ambiguity when speaking of eighteenth-century Comtesian positivism; cf. above, p. 204. In current heated discussions of positivism, it occasionally becomes a generally pejorative term that no one wants anything to do with. The various conflicts around positivism bear witness to this; cf. above all *Positivismusstreit* with contributions from Adorno, Popper, Habermas et al. Primarily, it is important to differentiate between the legal positivism of Comte and a later neopositivism. Comte's leading idea was that all knowledge must have the character of general laws (in particular, laws of development) that were based on the 'positive' – that is, the empirical and observable. All interesting knowledge could be incorporated into these laws. For the neopositivists, *certain* knowledge became the norm superior to all else. The change was especially crucial for views of the human sciences. The certain was defined as the observable, and what could be concluded from the observable through formal rules of logic. General laws in the human sciences lay beyond the borders of the certain. It should perhaps be stressed, in general, that neopositivism here should not be understood as only the philosophical elaboration of certain more or less scattered ideas in various sciences; it should be seen as a powerful tendency in nearly all specialised disciplines, a tendency that was more or less strikingly summarised by such philosophers as Mach and his followers in the Vienna School (logical positivism or empiricism: Schlick, Carnap et al.). On Mach's relation to earlier positivism and the ambiguity of the concept itself, see Blackmore 1972, p. 164 et seq. On the ambiguity in the term 'positivism', see Wright 1971, p. 171. Here, I see Virchow as a powerful forerunner of neopositivism. Virchow's opinions were fully developed as regards his views on the use of science; here, he was clearer than most – perhaps all – of his followers. But he was not alone in his time, as shown in the discussions cited here, and there were other scientists of his era that developed early neopositivist scientific theory much more clearly than he did; first and foremost, the great French physiologist Claude Bernard should be mentioned. Cf. the major programmatic work by Bernard and – among the diversity of Bernard literature – the highly comprehensive studies by Holmes 1974 and above all Grmek 1972. See also the shorter presentation by Canguilhem 1965a.

vidual field of science. It was thus not possible in itself to suss out, in the name of science, the fundamental features of humanity's development just because these fundamental features were somehow in agreement with other, simpler and better-known forms of development. The demand for certainty applied to history as well. If the laws of development for history could not be substantiated with the same certainty in the sphere of history as, for example, the law of entropy in physics, then the laws of development would just be left alone.

This scientific ideal did not experience its great breakthrough until the decades around the turn of the twentieth century. A number of circumstances whose connections have not yet been elucidated and also fall outside the scope of this study, contributed to its success. Physics lost its firm foundation in Newtonian mechanics. Darwinism, which had developed into a worldview, was on the retreat while the materially useful but ideologically less controversial genetics – which the Darwinists either neglected or abused – became the fashionable biological science. The philosophers devoted themselves more to the boundaries and limitations of the sciences than to their contexts as regards worldviews. The human sciences did not attempt to mimic the theories of natural science as they did its methods: formulating a 'mechanics' of the human condition, as Quetelet and other sought to do,[5] or studying the 'natural laws' of history, as Marx said he was attempting to do,[6] are dubious tasks whereas greater numbers of people wanted to introduce stricter empirical – and occasionally purely experimental – methods into the human sciences.

Here, it is an issue of a rather lengthy process – or rather, perhaps, a general tendency – that did not display any total validity and had begun to be questioned more energetically towards the middle of the twentieth century. This tendency is expressed in a number of related spheres: in the whole of society, science is thus put to an increasingly limited direct ideological use while in return scientists are given more carefully defined expert tasks; in the limited scientific community, specialisation and professionalisation thereby increase; in the general view of science, the limitations and relativity of knowledge are thus emphasised and the idea of a 'scientific worldview' is questioned; in the individual disciplines, safe and certain research is prioritised over research that is of general interest and ideologically controversial.

But this tendency was nothing entirely new for the twentieth century. This is not the place to sketch out its history, whereas it is of central interest to state that it is fully discernible in the heated and hostile discussion we will now analyse.

---

5   Above, p. 251
6   MECW 35:9.

2   Virchow, Haeckel and Tyndall

It may seem as if the controversies at the socialist congress in Gotha and the steady stream of contributions that followed Virchow's speech in Munich have only an extremely superficial connection; the timing and political background were the same. The name of Dühring played a role in both: Virchow and his colleagues in Berlin sacrificed Dühring on the altar of academic freedom, and the question of Dühring's socialism was taken up in Gotha.

But there is a deeper connection as well. In both exchanges of opinion, the same fundamental contradiction about the relation between science and ideology can be traced. It is this contradiction that I will attempt to investigate here.

The issues around which both discussions primarily concentrated seem quite different. In Gotha, they fought over the suitability of letting Engels's theoretically formulated and scholarly reckoning with Dühring dominate number after number of the Social Democrats' main organ. Virchow took up the issue of the connection between Darwinism and socialism, and that issue would dominate the debate he had initiated.

But let us take our starting point in these obvious controversial questions.

Virchow did not say that Darwinism and socialism were allies; far from it. With his characteristic art of argumentation, as supremely skilful as it was insidious, he declared instead that descendance theory should not be blamed for having 'won socialism with its contact' (der Socialismus mit ihr Fühlung gewonnen hat).[7] But socialism's dangerous appetite for Darwinism was due to the fact that the theory of development had been proclaimed as an absolutely certain, scientifically indisputable doctrine. With that, it had become desirable fodder for revolutionaries, and had thus in general become dangerous to society.

Virchow's manner of bringing socialism into the picture and even conjuring up the memory of the Paris Commune certainly had a tactical basis: he knew the audience he was addressing, almost without exception, were as frightened of socialism as he himself was. He discreetly pointed out that Haeckel and other Darwinists had joined the Devil himself.

Naturally, an accusation of this kind became intolerable for supporters of empire and Greater Germany such as Ernst Haeckel and Oscar Schmidt.[8] Both put a great deal of energy into showing that on the contrary, Darwinism was

---

7   Virchow 1877, p. 12. Virchow's speech, like his entire position on Darwinism and socialism, has been treated in a scarcely penetrating matter by Ackerknecht 1953, p. 165 et seq.

8   Both responded very promptly, Haeckel in Freie Wissenschaft und freie Lehre and Schmidt in Darwinismus und Sozialdemokratie, both published in 1878.

socialism's greatest enemy: all development took place through the struggle for existence, and socialism with its ideas about equality would put an end to all such struggle. Virchow held descendance theory responsible for 'the mad teachings of social democracy' (*die verrückte Lehre der Social-Demokratie*) and for the 'atrocities' (*Gräueltaten*) of the Paris Commune, Haeckel shouted indignantly,[9] and subsequently got to grips with repelling socialism from his Darwinist viewpoints.

As I have indicated, Virchow's address also reached England. A detailed account was given in the *Times*, and the lecture in its entirety was later printed in English with a new foreword by Virchow. The comments were nearly as many and as lively as in Germany, but the ideological positions in England were not the same. The defenders of descendance theory – and in particular the defenders of its direct ideological use – were liberals, and the opposition came from religious and political conservatives. Virchow himself was a leading representative of the national-liberal party in the German Reichstag and the public debate.[10] He pleaded the cause of 'moderation': Haeckel stood to his right, Dühring to his left. Those in England who applauded Virchow were opponents of descendance theory in general, and not just of its public use; they would never have dreamed of a 'free science' in Virchow's meaning but saw all higher education and research as a stage in fostering patriotic, God-fearing and morally irreproachable gentlemen. Religious issues in particular played an incomparably greater role in the English debate over Darwinism. Even John Tyndall, who for conservative English opinion stood out as precisely the kind of corruptor of society that Virchow depicted, uttered the name of God with emotion; not only Virchow, not only Dühring but Haeckel and Schmidt as well would sooner have bitten off their tongues.

Tyndall was the one who made the weightiest contribution to the Virchow debate in England. In the sixth edition of his *Fragments of Science*, he inserted a 45-page commentary on Virchow's address and the English exchange of opinions around it.[11] Evidently, he displayed no understanding of Virchow's veiled hints of the connection between a publicly proclaimed descendance theory and socialism. Only some years later would English socialists seek to provide popular accounts of Darwinism; the pioneer was Edward Aveling, Marx's son-in-law, with writings such as *The Student's Darwin* and *The Darwinian Theory: Its Meaning, Difficulties, Evidence, History*. Tyndall showed how completely unfamiliar he was with socialist ideas by seeking support for his phobia of socialism

---

9   Haeckel 1878, pp. 4, 6.
10   On this topic, see Ackerknecht 1953, p. 134 et seq.
11   Tyndall 1879, Vol. II, pp. 375–419.

behind Friedrich Albert Lange's *Geschichte des Materialismus*; not only was he unaware of Lange's socialist preferences, he was unable to find them in Lange's writings. Despite his own socialist ambitions, what Lange said about the relation between socialist ideology and theories of various types squares quite well with Virchow's position: there was a sharp boundary, and socialism could be reconciled with many types of worldviews.[12] Tyndall, however, sought support in Lange's words for his hopes that socialism was not dangerous. He also found comfort in the fall of the Paris Commune: France had shown its capability for crushing socialists.[13]

Tyndall's comments on socialism are of interest for the reason that they illustrate his almost total ignorance of the subject. Virchow, Haeckel and Schmidt did not know much more but in any case, they had the ability to name the enemy.

It is in other respects entirely that the debate in which they took part is of more than symptomatic interest. Virchow's actual concern was not to marry Darwinism to socialism; his concerns was to communicate to his listeners and readers an image that would highlight the incorrectness of the direct ideological use of Darwinism.

The fact that his contribution touched on an extremely exhaustive discussion of the German school system in general is of relevance here. The university system was not directly involved in the discussion; a crucial question, however, concerned the extent to which new results and orientations in research justified changes in the orientation and content of education, in particular at the secondary level. Many university figures made their voices heard in the discussion. There were a number of definite ideas about how high schools and universities functioned and ought to function. At the German university there was – and ought to be – 'Lehr- und Lernfreiheit' (freedom to teach and to study). University instructors had the right to advocate any opinions and theories whatsoever in their scientific field; the students had the right to choose whichever subject and instruction from professors they thought best. In the high schools, there was not – and ought not to be – either *Lehr-* or *Lernfreiheit*. High school students were immature and could not determine what they ought to learn. Nor, therefore, could their teachers deal with the learning of any kind of knowledge whatsoever: there had to be fixed norms for what high-school students had to know before they continued on to other, higher education.

---

12   Lange 1876, Vol. II, p. 470 et seq.
13   Tyndall 1879, Vol. II, p. 411 et seq.

The image of the German university's *Lehr- und Lernfreiheit* had wide circulation internationally. It contributed to attracting students from other countries in Europe as well as the United States to Germany[14] and was fostered by the university's own spokesmen. On 15 October 1877 – shortly after Virchow's Munich address – Hermann von Helmholtz gave a speech in Berlin (*Über de akademische Freiheit der deutschen Universitäten*) in which he proudly compared German universities with their English and French counterparts. It was certainly not his intention to insult the English and the French; in their strict confessional and conservative education, the English learned to freely and correctly handle their native tongue and additionally received a splendid physical education[15] and French students received excellent occupational training through their strict examination system.[16] But the German universities were obviously the strongholds of science. Helmholtz happily quoted Ernest Renan's comment that one small and impoverished rural university produced more good science than all of rich and powerful Oxford.[17]

Helmholtz naturally meant that this German freedom had to be preserved. But freedom demanded responsibility, he said.[18] It was all well and good that 'at this moment' there were German professors who 'drew the most extreme conclusions from a materialist metaphysics', others who devoted themselves to 'the most daring speculations on the foundation of Darwin's evolutionary theory' and yet others who 'proclaimed papal infallibility in the most extreme manner'. There was not, nor should there be, any obstacles to any controversial *scientific* questions whatsoever being treated *scientifically* (the emphases are Helmholtz's own).[19]

It is not strange that the issue of the limits to the freedom of the universities was of immediate interest to Helmholtz. A few months earlier, in July 1877, he had been the driving force when Dühring was expelled from the teaching staff of the University of Berlin. The immediate reason for the expulsion was Dühring's attack on his colleagues and on the university in general. But Dühring was regarded as a socialist; and the Anti-Socialist Laws – which have already been discussed – *de facto* excluded socialists from the academic freedom of study.[20]

---

14   Cf. Herbst 1965, pp. 1–22.
15   Helmholtz 1878, p. 9 et seq.
16   Ibid., p. 13 et seq.
17   Ibid., p. 7.
18   Ibid., p. 18 et seq.
19   Ibid., p. 21.
20   Cf. above, p. 498

The image of university and scientific research that Helmholtz had conjured up essentially squared with that of Virchow. Both men also had every opportunity to influence each other. But Virchow's idea was clearer, with more preparation behind it. Virchow set the limit for the sphere of scientific freedom more clearly than Helmholtz did.

Virchow turned directly against Haeckel, who asserted that descendance theory now had to be included in schooling. The consequences of descendance theory had to be clear to every schoolboy in Germany, Haeckel argued. But this could only be so if we could say that descendance theory was beyond all doubt, Virchow objected. *Only absolutely certain knowledge could be passed on from the universities to the schools.*[21]

This applied, however, not only to the relation between university and school. It applied in general to the relations between scientific research and society beyond. Only when the scientific discussion had been concluded and all facts assured would the university transfer its knowledge to the people outside it.

Virchow illustrated his conception with a few examples that lay close to his own field of research. A theory had been developed that no fermentation could occur without yeast fungi – in other words, that fermentation was an organic process, he said (he did not mention Pasteur by name). This was a theory that was highly reasonable; it had now proven to be false, however. It was thus not certain and it thus had no business outside purely scientific discussion.[22]

As regards the question of the origin of organisms, the idea of *generatio aequivoca* – the idea that the organic originally came from inorganic material – was scientifically more plausible and fertile than belief in creation. But it was not yet beyond all doubt; it *had not yet been proven.* In scientific work we can allow ourselves to be guided by this, but to the world outside we should only say that *we know nothing* about the origins of organic nature.[23]

Virchow thus assumed a razor-sharp boundary between scientific 'facts' (among which he naturally counted certain, indisputable theories) and hypotheses and speculations that were subject to scientific discussion and had the extraordinarily crucial task of guiding new research.[24] Only that which stood on one side of the boundary could be passed on for use other than purely scientific.

---

21   Virchow 1877, p. 10 et seq.
22   Ibid., p. 16 et seq.
23   Ibid., p. 18 et seq.
24   Ibid., p. 7.

Virchow had a surer sense of the difference between practical and material, and ideological, use of science than most of those who later commented in the debates about the relations between science and society.[25] The nation had to take up the new, certain knowledge in two ways, he said. On the one hand, this knowledge promoted material advances, the development of new technologies and accomplishments. Clearly, here he was imagining that the entire actual process of research went on – and should go on – within the scientific institutions; it was only certain facts that would be put to use in the various branches of industry.

But knowledge also has a *'geistige Bedeutung'* (intellectual significance), he said. When science proclaimed some new truth, it had the right to expect that humanity's *'Anschauung von den Dinge'* (view of things) would be influenced by this truth.[26]

Undoubtedly, it is this ideological use that primarily interested him in his address: neither descendance theory nor the theory of spontaneous generation had anything to do with material welfare for the present. It was also here that his demand for absolute certainty became acute. What he asserted was nothing less than that scientists should prevent knowledge that was still debatable from being used in schools, newspapers and periodicals that did not belong to the purely scientific press, in lectures and popular educational initiatives. He wanted to screen scientific discussion off from general opinion.

3   We Scientists, and Others

Virchow's views were intimately bound up with the German university system and with the ideas that had formed around it. It never crossed his mind that his view of the role of science in society would be politically and ideologically controversial. He was truly speaking *ex cathedra*.

The objections he met with from Haeckel and Tyndall were of highly different characters. Haeckel was himself a product of the German university system, fostered by such luminaries as Johannes Müller and Virchow himself. His objec-

---

25   It seems as it the ideological use has been forgotten in the entire contemporary debate about the use and benefit of science. The whole debate, which began with Max Weber and culminated in the contradictions concerning Bernal, continuing in the 1950s and 1960s, seems to presume that science is either pursued for its own sake or for the sake of its material use; the crucial – especially from a historical perspective – ideological use is left completely out of the equation. On these debates and the literature concerning them, cf. above, p. 493 *et seq.*

26   Virchow 1877, p. 8 et seq.

tion did not concern Virchow's view of the authority of science, but rather the boundary drawn between certain and uncertain knowledge.

In his polemic against Virchow, Haeckel repeated the conception of the relation between theory and individual facts that we have already acquainted ourselves with.[27] All parts of the scientific construction were permeated by theory, by philosophy. He misconstrued – perhaps not entirely in good faith – Virchow's word *Tatsache* (fact), by which Virchow meant all certain knowledge, including certain theories. Virchow's meaning, according to Haeckel, was that science would only provide the world with certain details. Haeckel's polemic, however, was not due solely to a terminological misunderstanding. His view of science and the ideological use of science differed radically from Virchow's. Scientific discussion was a discussion between competing worldviews. No scientific results are independent of the scientists' general understanding: general philosophical starting points shone through in the details as well.[28] The consequence of Haeckel's reasoning is given. Scientific discussion cannot be isolated from other discussion, the struggle between worldviews, the struggle between godliness and godlessness, between materialism and idealism was in force in all spheres and on all planes, and scientists would fail their great task if they closed themselves off in their universities.

Haeckel did not doubt for a moment that scientists had a special place in the discussion of worldviews: their social role was *to know*. Tyndall, who lived in a country where knowing was not yet regarded as a privilege belonging to the professorial office, viewed the question from a different perspective. He advocated the idea of enlightenment as well, but in contrast to Haeckel he did not understand Virchow's argument from authority. He cited a statement by Virchow, in which he said that only when 'we' can say 'This is how things are', then 'we' can communicate our knowledge not only to the educated but even to children, and 'we' can let the knowledge become fundamental for all 'our' ideas about 'the world, society and the state'. Tyndall discreetly wondered who this 'we' was that had such power over the mediation of knowledge. Who determined that an item of knowledge was certain? Haeckel certainly would have said that descendance theory already constituted an indubitable truth, he said.

With that, he touched on an extremely weak point in Virchow's argument. Virchow's 'we' was scientific expertise, or more precisely the researchers who had attained a dominant position in the scientific community. But if this 'we' was not unanimous around what knowledge was certain, or even what the

---

27   Above, p. 193 et seq.
28   Haeckel 1878, p. 8 et seq.

certainty of knowledge could entail, an unresolvable dilemma arose. Virchow could simply leave individual people such as Eugen Dühring, the private lecturer who had been dismissed, Eduard von Hartmann, the decommissioned lieutenant, Friedrich Engels, the free-floating socialist writer, or Herbert Spencer, the independent entrepreneur in his own writings, out of the account. For consistency's sake he ought to also have excluded Charles Darwin and everyone else who lacked a fixed and respected professorial office; such peculiar consequences could only reveal the absurdity in his reasoning all too clearly. What did he do, however, with Ernst Haeckel, who without a doubt belonged to the official 'we' of German science?

Tyndall's interpretation of Virchow's statement, though benevolent, is incorrect. By 'we', Virchow could not mean scientific experts but anyone in general who was conscious of their responsibilities: the question had to concern the point in time at which society was ripe for the new truth, so that it could be conveyed – in education, for example – without risk. In that case, however, Tyndall said, society had to first be prepared so that it was receptive.[29]

Tyndall tried – on exceedingly weak grounds – to interpret Virchow's statement in this direction. Virchow could not rule out the enlightening activities of scientists. How could society otherwise be ripe for knowledge? Tyndall thus imagined that he and Virchow agreed completely that scientists should take part in the general debate and that the boundaries for the dissemination of knowledge was determined by the maturity and receptiveness of society. Naturally, he was wrong.

Nearly a century and a half after the fact, it may seem as if Haeckel and Tyndall were both advocating modern standpoints in relation to Virchow. Haeckel's thesis that conceptions of the world, theories and fact could never be isolated from one another seems to square well with essential parts of the criticism that, in later decades, was directed towards neo-positivism from widely differing directions: from Gaston Bachelard and the French structuralists, from Thomas S. Kuhn, from Mario Bunge, from the representatives of the Frankfurt School and so on.[30] Virchow's belief in the authoritative unity of the established scientific community, his confidence in the experts' sense of 'we' does not square well with the perspectives constructed by contemporary sociologists and theoreticians of science.[31] It was not he, but Tyndall, who realised that being able

---

29   Tyndall 1879, Vol. II, p. 397 et seq.
30   Here, see Althusser 1976; Kuhn 1970; Lakatos 1970, Bunge 1973, Habermas 1968; *Positivismusstreit*.
31   Here, see the splendid and original summary of the contemporary theory and sociology of science in Blume 1974, p. 2 et seq. and *passim*.

to distinguish between valuable scientific knowledge and knowledge that was prized by the scientific establishment was necessary.

Above all, Virchow's determination and delimitation of the responsibilities of scientists seems antiquated in relation to Tyndall's and Haeckel's ideas of enlightenment. According to Virchow, scientists had total responsibility in assessing the certainty of knowledge, whereas they ought to have no influence over the use of that knowledge: it was their duty to *present* that certain knowledge to the nation. Nuclear weapons, environmental destruction and the general enervation and brutalisation of the industry of consciousness has cast a light over the dangers around this limitation of responsibility in various ways.[32]

But in his time, the 1870s, it was Virchow who stood out as the modern man of the future. He was the most advanced spokesman of the scientific community up to that point. He was the neo-positivist above all neo-positivists. He propagated for the de-ideologisation of science decades before the majority of sciences more or less withdrew from the ideological struggle. Tyndall and Haeckel, by contrast, were old-fashioned. They were inspired by ideals that had previously inspired the Enlightenment thinkers, the Romantics and the wild system-builders. Voltaire read Newton and found that he immediately had to inform the educated public of Newton's significance for religion, morals and politics. The Romantics drew equally rapid conclusions from knowledge of an entirely different sort. Comte, Spencer, Dühring and Engels pursued the same tradition: they blended knowledge and knowledge, knowledge and ideology, knowledge and morals, knowledge and art and politics. In one way or another, they all wanted to be part of changing (or, occasionally, fortifying) the world, society and humanity. There was a Mephistophelian element to their activities: there were no sound, institutional limits and barriers to what knowledge could be used for.

It was Virchow who had the future before him. We cannot be blinded to the fact that that future now belongs to our past.

4   The Discussion in Gotha

The heated discussion about Dühring and *Anti-Dühring* at the socialist congress in Gotha only superficially and in an immediate sense concerns the question of how Engels's great polemical work should be published. In the background to the debate there were a number of crucial circumstances that explain

---

32   Cf. Easlea 1973, pp. 294–316.

the implacability of the exchange of opinions. First, the German Social-Democratic Party was not yet a 'Marxist party' (i.e. its programme was not unambiguously based on Marx's and Engels's theories of society). What happened a few years earlier in Gotha – in 1875, when the party was formed – was that Ferdinand Lassalle's and Karl Marx's followers united over a shared programme. Marx's criticism of the Gotha programme in the spirit of compromise was sharp and implacable. Most conscious social democrats realised in general that for the time being, the party comprised a vulnerable entity, and the immediate task was to try to dampen the internal doctrinal conflicts and to concentrate attention on the party-political actions over which a general unity prevailed.[33] It was thus in the interests of the party to tone down the contradictions between Dühring and Marx/Engels as well. In particular, it was those who harboured a more or less expressly positive interpretation of Dühring who sought to push the controversial questions into the background. 'Among us there are neither Marxists nor Dühringians', declared Julius Vahlteich back in October 1876, and with that statement roused Engels's particular annoyance.[34]

This entire exhortation to ideological caution was also bound up with another fundamental circumstance, namely that the Social Democrats were now genuinely threatened and that it might appear as if it was a matter of rescuing whatever could be rescued from the Bismarckian power apparatus. In that situation, was it wise to risk unity and the willingness to struggle over a few abstract controversial scientific issues? This was the viewpoint that August Bebel in particular advocated.

But it was against the background of these general circumstances that a number of German Social Democrats would develop an idea of the correct limitations of science and scientific controversies. We do not need to go into the question of the extent to which they thereby only made use of one tactic; the materials quite simply do not provide a basis for such an assessment. The essential point for our account is that the idea in general could be formed into an effective argument in the discussion within the Social-Democratic Party.

One question that is of natural interest in this context is Dühring's actual relations with the party. Dühring himself was not a Social-Democrat. In his later memoirs, *Sache, Leben und Feinde*, he denied any dealings whatsoever with the ideas of socialism. It was a sophisticated Jewish conspiracy (antisemitism played a large, continually growing role in Dühring's world of ideas) that on the one hand painted him as a Social Democrat and on the other calumni-

---

33   Cf. above, Note 1.
34   Cf. the letter from Engels to W. Liebknecht, 31 July 1877; MECW 45:256 et seq.

ated him in the name of Social Democracy. He couldn't help the fact that one or another Social Democrat was influenced by him. There were Social Democrats who reacted to the shameless way in which 'Herr Marx, through his manservant (House-Freddy) a former manufacturing employer by the name of Friedrich Engels' had attacked Dühring. But Dühring himself had nothing to do with the people.[35]

Much earlier, or while the battle over Dühring was still going on, Dühring had expressed essentially the same opinion. He saw a direct connection between Engels's articles in *Vorwärts* and his dismissal from the University of Berlin. In other words, Engels had helped Helmholtz and the other professors in Berlin drive out the objectionable private lecturer![36]

But was Dühring really so unfamiliar with socialist ideas? In his social scientific writings he had advocated for an egalitarian society. In that connection, he also advocated for thoroughgoing economic and social reforms. In particular, he had gotten into discussions with socialist theoreticians, primarily with Marx.[37]

Even if his understanding of society had points of contact with socialism in certain general respects, however, appearing as a socialist was totally foreign to him. He wanted to stand over all political parties and orientations; he wanted to appear solely as a scientist. It was science, not society, that he wanted to reform; it was the scientific image of society and not society itself that he subjected immediately to his criticism.[38] It was against his will that Dühring appeared as a creator of synthesis without a university and as a provider of ideological impulses. He had even given a lecture on the freedom of science in which, it is true, he did not depict Berlin and the other German universities as the seats of academic freedom, but his ideal was similar to the one Helmholtz and Virchow professed.[39]

That is why there likely were not only tactical, but internal reasons as well, for the Social-Democrats who found lessons to learn from Dühring wanting to keep the theoretical discussion outside of intimate party matters. In Dühring,

---

35   Dühring 1903, p. 165 et seq., 179 et seq., 200 et seq.
36   Dühring 1878, p. 119 et seq.
37   Cf. Dühring 1868 and Dühring 1876, p. 319 et seq. and 499 et seq.
38   This has not been taken sufficiently into consideration in the literature on Dühring, from which the comprehensive monograph by Albrecht (1927) and the fiery defence by Binder (1933) can be drawn out here. Dühring's viewpoint emerges perhaps most clearly in the introduction to Dühring 1875, p. 1 et seq.
39   The lecture dealt more specifically with women's opportunities for higher education (Dühring 1877).

they encountered a sublime science. This science was polemical enough in its own separate sphere – it even made an assault on the difficult-to-grasp dialectic in Marx's *Capital* – but it did not turn science into a political affair; rather it provided politics with knowledge and general guidelines from a safe distance.

Dühring thus represented the idea of the de-ideologisation of science in his own way, and that idea also worked its charm on German Social Democrats. In fact, this brief Dühringian influence heralded the conception that became more or less dominant in German Social Democracy around the turn of the twentieth century, that involved keeping 'theory' and 'ethics', social science and practical politics, carefully separated.[40] At the end of the 1870s the influence from Marx and Engels, those emphatic representatives of the idea of enlightenment, was still too strong for Dühring's thoughts on sublime science to catch on.

Dühring's most influential representative in the Social-Democratic Party was Johann Most. Most was not an anti-Marxist; his chief literary effort was a popular adaptation of *Capital*.[41] Devoting such attention to popularisation was typical of him. It was, he said, not a task for the scientists themselves but for those who stood nearer to practical life to convey the scientific insights to the common folk. In other words, enlightenment fell to the lot of the intermediaries.

In his popularisation, however, Most sought to bring Marx and Dühring into line with each other. This ambition found its absolute clearest expression in a lecture he gave in 1876 called *Die Lösung den socialen Frage* (The Solution to the Social Question). In it, he bound Louis Blanc, Lassalle, Marx and Dühring together. He emphasised that *Capital* was a scientific work, and that the difficulty in understanding it was purely scientifically motivated.[42] As regards Dühring, he declared that the latter had not yet created a socialist system, but that we could expect one. The crucial difference between Dühring and Marx consisted of the fact that while Dühring regarded the limited economic commune (*die Wirtschaftskommune*) as the tool for a transition to socialism, Marx

---

40   Cf. above, p. 28.

41   Most defined his brochure as '*ein populärer Auszug aus* Das Kapital *von Karl Marx*'; Most 1876 (1st ed. 1873). Most provides an interesting depiction of various selected reactions in his memoirs. While Wilhelm Liebknecht rejected the popularisation – there was not, he argued, a single unnecessary word in *Capital* – August Bebel reacted positively. This division of assessments seems likely, given Liebknecht's and Bebel's differing opinions regarding the theory of Marxism and its popularisations. Most 1903, Vol. III, p. 25 et seq. On Most's life and works, see Rocker 1924.

42   Most 1876a, p. 20 et seq.

assigned that role to the state. But this difference in understanding was insignificant on the plane where Most was moving about.[43]

For Most, a popularisation thus meant not only presenting certain scientific ideas, difficult for the common folk to understand, in a simpler fashion. It was a question of a much more thorough reprocessing. Controversial scientific issues may prove to be uninteresting on the level of popularisation, and a central idea in a theory could sink into oblivion in the popularisation.

There is an obvious, and completely natural, difference between Virchow's and Most's views on the use of science outside science itself. Most did not raise the demand that only certain knowledge be permitted to go through the mills of popularisation; socialists did not yet have any such knowledge, generally approved by the professors of science, at their disposal. However, Most largely shared Virchow's ideas of the strict categorical division between science and ideology. Most found support for his understanding not in Virchow, but in Dühring.

A series of articles by Most about Dühring was the immediate reason that Engels took up *Anti-Dühring*.[44] By that time, Wilhelm Liebknecht had already called his and Marx's attention to Dühring's growing influence in the party several times.[45] It was not at all obvious that Engels would be the one to intervene in the struggle against the Dühringians; it was more likely that Marx would take on the polemic. But both Marx and Engels hesitated. Only when Engels had Most's article in hand did he cast aside all doubt. Marx expressed his great satisfaction over Engels's decision to have a go at Dühring. It had to be *'ohne alle Rücksicht'* (with no regard whatsoever), he said. He pointed out that Dühring had earned Most's gratitude by stating in the second edition of his *Kritische Geschichte der Nationalökonomie und des Sozialismus* that with his popularisation of *Capital*, Most was the first to have done something sensible with the work. Most acknowledged this by presenting Dühring as a 'solid thinker'.[46]

---

43   Ibid., p. 21 et seq.

44   Most's *'Ein Philosoph'* (i.e., Dühring) was published in *Berliner Freie Presse* between 10 September and 21 October 1876. Engels received the manuscript to this series of articles from Liebknecht and later forwarded them to Marx. Cf. the letter from Engels to Marx, 24 May 1876, MECW 45:117 et seq.

45   Cf. Liebknecht 1963, p. 196 et seq., and MECW 25:336.

46   Cf. Dühring 1875a, p. 570. Letter from Marx to Engels, 25 May 1876; MECW 45:119 et seq.

5   Engels's and Marx's Standpoints

Engels's pamphlet against Dühring is shot through with polemical heat and
cold fury. But did the object of his polemic really have the significance that his
energy and rage seem to assume? It is difficult to correctly assess Dühring's real
influence on German Social Democracy. A number of statements and a smaller
number of writings indicate that he had his rather devoted admirers.[47] These
admirers, however – among whom Most, Vahlteich and Bebel primarily deserve
mention – did not in fact agree with Dühring's specific social scientific theories,
nor did they thereby distance themselves from Marx's theories. They appreciated Dühring because Dühring, from his still elevated academic platform,
provided them with a living example of the fact that the difference between
one theory and another was not so crucial on the plane of party politics. They
did not set Dühring against Marx in order to arouse a scientific battle within the
party; instead, Dühring became their angel of peace – or rather the person who
demonstrated with his theories that socialism could appear very different from
a scientific standpoint but that it was one and the same in political activity. In
his blistering *Critique of the Gotha Programme*, Marx brought science into the
issues of programme. Dühring, however, was another very learned man who
had entirely different theories and who, moreover, repudiated Marx's entire
dialectical method. Was that not the best proof that the goals of socialism were
one thing, and its theories another? Why should the Social-Democratic Party
risk its unity and energy on scientific disputes?

This was the conception that roused Engels's fury. Like Marx, he was an inexorable supporter of *the direct use of science* for ideology. Controversial scientific
issues had immediate practical significance, which Marx had tried to show in
the *Critique of the Gotha Programme* and Engels tried to show in *Anti-Dühring*.

The debate at the Socialist Congress of 1877 concerned exclusively the question of the significance of theory for the party. It thus did not concern for a
moment the correctness and plausibility of Marx's or Engels's (or Dühring's)
theoretical standpoints. Most, Vahlteich and Bebel wondered whether Wilhelm
Liebknecht had acted correctly when, as the editor of *Vorwärts*, he allowed

---

47   The Prussian tenant farmer and Social Democrat Abraham Enss is responsible for the
      most irascible defence of Dühring; he wrote a furious polemic titled *Engels Attentat auf
      den gesunden Menschenverstand oder Der wissenschaftliche Bankerott im marxistischen
      Sozialismus*. On this, see also Engels's ironic comments in later editions of *Anti-Dühring*,
      MECW 25:298. Many Social Democrats who were more influential than Most and Enss also
      had appreciative things to say about Dühring before Engels went on the attack; these state-
      ments have been collected in a not very penetrating paper by R. Adamiak 1974, p. 104 et
      seq.

Engels's work to fill issue after issue. Most asserted that the reckoning lacked interest for the majority of the newspaper's readers. Vahlteich asserted that Marx, Engels and Dühring had their significance for the party as providers of ideas, and that it was a mistake to play them against each other. 'The professors' dispute' did not belong in *Vorwärts*. Both Most and Vahlteich recommended that publication should be stopped (which in that case would occur before Engels managed to get to the most burning question for the party – on Dühring's social theories and socialism). Bebel went in for a compromise concerning a 'purely scientific dispute'. It did not belong in *Vorwärts*; on the other hand, the continuation of *Anti-Dühring* could be published in a special scientific supplement to the newspaper. The proposal gained an immediate hearing. Even Wilhelm Liebknecht – whose co-cooperativeness Engels often cursed – went in for it, and so it was decided.[48]

Engels's reaction to the debate and to the decision of the Congress is particularly telling. The Congress was not competent to judge on such a question, he wrote in a letter to Wilhelm Bracke.[49] In a letter to Marx, he explained himself even more clearly: science was not democratic; scientific truths could not be the subject of democratic decisions.[50] His position was thus inflexible: on the one hand, truth was truth no matter who accepted it; on the other, scientific truth had to be put to direct ideological use.

Under the influence of the decision by the Congress, Marx himself spoke warmly in a letter to Engels about a 'really scientific socialist periodical'. 'This would provide an opportunity for criticism and counter-criticism in which theoretical points could be discussed by us and the total ignorance of professors and university lecturers be exposed, thereby simultaneously disabusing the minds of the GENERAL PUBLIC – workers and bourgeois alike'.[51]

Six years later, in 1883, this periodical saw the light of day: *Die Neue Zeit* began publication. By then, Marx was dead, but his and Engels's line would dominate the periodical for at least a decade. *Die Neue Zeit* was at attempt to bridge science and ideology; likewise, it was an attempt to create a platform for a scientific debate for the workers' movement beyond and independent of the adopted, conservatively or liberally-minded scientific institutions.

---

48   *Protokoll* 1877, p. 70 et seq. Cf. also MECW 45:489.
49   Letter from Engels to Bracke, 25 June 1877, MECW 45:236. Bracke was a faithful adherent of Marx and Engels, but he still stood up in defence of Dühring and Most. Most's article on Dühring (Most 1876b), first offered to *Vorwärts*, should not have been refused, he argued. Bracke's reactions say a great deal about the somewhat confused moods in the party.
50   Letter from Engels to Marx, 25 July 1877, MECW 45:249.
51   Letter from Marx to Engels, 18 July 1877, MECW 45:241 et seq.

No one cited Dühring any longer. In the short term, Engels had won a total
victory. The idea itself, however, that had contributed to Dühring's brief successes among German Social Democrats – the idea that science was one thing,
ideology and politics another – would soon come into favour again. Paradoxically, Marxism's successes in the world of public science promoted this change.
After 1890 and the abolition of the Anti-Socialist Laws, Marxism – or, more
precisely, Marx's economic and social theories – began attracting ever greater
attention. Tomáš Masaryk, Werner Sombart and many others took them up for
serious treatment in voluminous treatises.[52] A generation of young students
greedily took Marxism for their own: student unions and student newspapers
were established in the names of Marxism and socialism.[53] Parts of Marxist
theory thereby became university affairs, and the boundary between university
and party politics was clear and indisputable.

Toward the turn of the twentieth century, Eduard Bernstein took up the old
idea, conveyed by figures like Dühring, that socialism actually was a question
of ideals and their realisation. Everything Marx said about the development
of capitalism could be incorrect; it was not crucial for socialists' success: the
essential thing was to hold on to and spread ideas about justice, equality and
so on.[54]

In the dispute that ensued – the famous battle over revisionism – Engels
was definitively prevented from commenting: he was dead. Had he been alive
he would have seen how Karl Kautsky, the person who above all defended his
positions, vulgarised and simplified his opinions – or, rather, developed the vulgarised and simplified expression that Engels himself gave to his opinions in the

---

52   There is still no study of this penetration of Marxism into the German university system.
      The difference between academic opinions of the type Treitschke 1875 and the formal
      debates of Marxism in Sombart and above all Masaryk are striking. Marxism, however,
      won its respectability at the price of a palpable theoretical smoothing out.

53   To take a single example, it was in the Social-Democratic student organ *Der sozialistische
      Akademiker* that Engels's well-known letter to Joseph Bloch was published. The letter was
      written on 21–22 September 1890 and published on 1 October. MECW 49:33 et seq.

54   It is, in other words, utopian socialism again making its voice heard; it can be stated
      without exaggeration than this utopian socialism (the word was used in the sense Marx
      and Engels had given it) at least after the First World War had become entirely predom-
      inant in the ideologies of the larger social-democratic parties. In the lengthy discussions
      that Bernstein initiated, the views on historical materialism naturally played a crucial role;
      a competent but rather unimaginative analysis of the discussion for the period from 1891
      to 1918 has been carried out by Weiss. The radical difference between ideal and statements
      about reality (theories) had support from the 1890s onward in neo-Kantian philosophy (cf.
      above, p. 28); excellent summaries of the discussion made from a decidedly neo-Kantian
      viewpoint can be found in Vorländer 1911 and 1926.

heat of polemics. For Kautsky and numerous others, Marxism was just another type of Darwinism.[55] The theory of capital accordingly became a simple theory of development. In the eyes of its interpreters, moreover, it was deterministic. Marx and Engels had turned to Hegel's dialectic in order to escape the spectre of determinism. Now, the spectre reigned over Marxism: Hegel was rejected as old rubbish. What he said about development in his clumsy German, had been said better and more elegantly by Comte and Spencer, the argument went.

If the battle over revisionism had been the terminus for Marxism, then Engels's intensive efforts from 1873 onward would have been in vain.

---

55   Cf. Kautsky's own open-hearted description of how he successfully united Darwin and Engels's *Anti-Dühring*; Kautsky 1960, p. 216 et seq. Cf. also above, p. 450, note 78. An idea of how highly regarded Darwin was in Social Democracy – the chief ideologue of which Kautsky had become – can be obtained by leafing through the annuals of *Die Neue Zeit* from its beginning in 1883 and onward. There is no end to these articles in Darwin's memory and honour, nor to the attempts to show how the materialist conception of history harmonised with the Darwinian theory of development.

CHAPTER 19

Engels and Ideology

1 The Power of Knowledge

There is an understanding in both Marx and Engels of knowledge and its power that is absolutely central to their view of society and of history: the idea that humans, before and under capitalism, were not the master of the development they were themselves part of creating because they lacked the knowledge of its determinants. They were living in 'pre-history', not in real history. They were living in an anarchy where they wanted the one – and intended to achieve it with their actions – but the result was something different. Only with knowledge of the laws of prehistory and of the possibilities in real, rational history could they create a society over which they were master.[1]

It is this idea – related yet still different from the various ideas of Enlightenment philosophers, Comtesian positivists, Romantics, Hegel, Mill and Spencer regarding the role of knowledge – that throws light upon Engels's ambitions for creating a synthesis of the knowledge that was current for him. It hastened to convey knowledge to humanity. This knowledge could not be piecemeal and divided; it could not only be techniques and operations: it had to be a living idea of nature, humanity and society. Nor could it be vague, friendly ideas about goodness and justice and love of humanity: it had to be an image of reality in all its sluggishness, contradictoriness and uncooperativeness.

Much has happened since Engels's time: wars, revolutions and counterrevolutions. Some of the world's largest countries and numerous smaller ones have been busy in various ways with trying to 'realise Marxism'. Most of the sciences in which Engels put his trust have thoroughly changed.

But how have his and Marx's ideas about knowledge held? The glories of science today are surrounded by a greater quantity of rhetoric than they were at the end of the nineteenth century. Virchow's lecture about the sole responsibility of scientists before the truth is repeated in different tongues and in various keys. Haeckel's grandiloquence echoes through this century as well. Emil du

---

1 We can find the classical expression of this idea in *Anti-Dühring*, MECW 25:254–71, in particular p. 270. Here, however, Engels is starting above all from a number of scattered comments in Volume I of *Capital*, for example, MECW 35:9 et seq., 361 and 491.

Bois-Reymond still has his tribune from which he can express his *Ignoramibus*: what, in our heart of hearts, we really want to know is something we will never learn.

On the whole, however, the views of the social role of science have also changed thoroughly. The belief in the ideological significance of science (i.e. in its power to change and orient humanity's ideas about its world) is incomparably much weaker. This is of course bound up with the fact that the actual use of science – and perhaps the natural sciences in particular – is much smaller where ideological matters are concerned. No scientific theory advanced over the last several decades has aroused a debate about worldviews, philosophies of life and political ideologies comparable to the one that Darwin's theory of selection did.

These changes have also influenced theories about the role of science in society. Not only in the general vocabulary, but also in studies of the sociology of science, has the external use of science (i.e. its benefits) been synonymous with its practical and material (and to some extent its administrative[2]) use. Both the issue of society's significance for scientific development and the issue of the role of science in the transformation of society have been limited to apply to the extent to which research is justified by, and is put to use in, material production.[3]

The entire issue of the ideological significance of science has thus been obscured. It was not so a hundred and fifty years ago. When Marx and Engels asserted that awareness of science would change humanity's world, they of course did not mean that only science would materially transform society. Nor did they mean that only their own theory of society would put certain political techniques into the hands of the working class. They also spoke about humanity's worlds of ideas: they prophesied a healthy, harmonious and rational relation among ideas, desires, norms for behaviour and actions.

---

2   By 'administrative use' I mean the use of different scientific insights to consolidate or strengthen the administration itself of the political and legal apparatus, developing techniques for administration and control based on scientific theories and empirical studies, and so on. In state-run institutions of higher education and research, this administrative use always playa a large, if not growing, role: a significant portion of scientific benefit is considered to consist of research providing tools for civil servants, social engineers, and the like.

3   The question is thus wrongly posed, that *either* science has a material (and possibly administrative) use, *or* it is 'for its own sake'. This idea distorts the ideas on the relation of science to society in Ben-David 1971, *passim* (see, for example, p. 113: eighteenth-century German humanists demanded recognition of a 'non-utilitarian science', since 'philology and history had no practical use'), in Lilley 1965, *passim*, in nearly all the participants in the debates from the 1830s to the 1860s, and in a thousand others. Cf. further above, p. 493 *et seq.*

If we are going to attempt to estimate the plausibility of Marx's and Engels's ideas about the ideological significance of science, we must move in a sphere that to a great extent lacks a developed methodology of research. Here, only by way of experiment, I will take up a few limited aspects of the problem and provide a few suggestions for solutions in outline. The most reasonable starting point will be the relation between Marxist theory and Marxist ideology.

2   Points of Intersection between Theory and Ideology

Every text can be subjected to an ideological analysis. Even the most theoretically advanced essay or book can be placed in connection with a world of ideas, with its intricate interplay between statements held as true, values and norms.[4]

Every text can also be subjected to a theoretical analysis, or more precisely: every text (except purely mathematical and logical presentations) has a connection with certain statements about reality that can be accepted or rejected using some scientific theory.[5]

But not all texts are equally accessible for an ideological or a theoretical analysis. An ideological analysis of, for example, an essay in theoretical physics assumes going far beyond the text itself and turning to the scientific organisations in which it is produced and assessed, and ultimately to the entire society that made its existence possible and in which it will be put to use in one way or another. A theoretical analysis of a prose poem similarly requires going far beyond the poem itself.

In the one case, the ideology essentially lies outside the text itself. In the other case, the theory stands at a safe distance from the presentation.

The more the ideology is located outside the text, the more ambiguous the text also is in ideological respects. A physical theory can be accepted in many different types of societies and reconciled with many types of worlds of ideas. *The fact that it can be subjected to an ideological analysis in general only means that it is not reconcilable with any world of ideas whatsoever.*

---

4 Above, p. 493.

5 Cf. above, p. 494. It is important that this is not only a question of a purely logical and semantical analysis of texts in which various types of propositions are registered (theoretical, value propositions etc.); we must dive under the surface of the text, thereby setting it in relation to the entire world of ideas for which it is an expression. It is thus possible, with a greater or lesser degree of success, to read from a text one or more – sometimes competing – theories of reality, one or more ethical systems, one or more programmes of action. It is normally a highly difficult and delicate task that continually lures us into rashness and loose constructions.

The same of course applies to texts that are not of an expressly theoretical nature.

Let us now attempt to apply this to Marx's and Engels's writings.

It is obvious that, for example, *Capital* contains more theory and less explicit ideology than, for example, the *Communist Manifesto* or *Critique of the Gotha Programme*. An ideological analysis of *Capital* therefore assumes going beyond the text itself, primarily to Marx's other writings (e.g. *Critique of the Gotha Programme*) and to his other activities. *Capital* is thus in itself more ideologically ambiguous than Marx's more ideologically-minded writings. It is entirely logical that many economists who are miles away from Marx's communist convictions can appreciate the scientific value of the theories in *Capital*. Similarly, many socialists and communists who in no way share Marx's theoretical standpoint, or have found explicit theories quite unnecessary for the cause of the revolution, have been able to accept the theoretically more ambiguous *Manifesto*.

I touched on the most striking example earlier in this account: the thesis that capitalism is a historically determined and therefore transitory mode of production.[6] It is a thesis at the centre of Marx's entire theoretical work. It marks the boundary between him and classical economics. It is, however, also at the centre of Marxist ideology. It is directed against the world of bourgeois ideas according to which all social praxis starts from the idea that the society arching over the capitalist mode of production can and should be preserved. To the same extent it is directed against various utopian socialist ideas that a new society can be constructed as soon as ideas of goodness, equality and justice have disseminated widely enough.

This does not mean, however, that the theoretical and ideological content of the thesis coincide. Theoretically, it constitutes the result of Marx's development of concepts such as value, labour power, surplus labour, surplus value and so on. There are concepts in this theoretical world of concept that are ideologically charged: exploitation, for example, which in itself is something negative to be avoided. But in Marxist theory the concept of exploitation is given a purely theoretical meaning, defined in terms of surplus value, and it thereby obtains definite theoretical (and ideological) content.[7]

Theoretically, the thesis of the transitoriness of capitalism contains no assessments of capitalism, no norms for human behaviour (this is an entirely trivial statement: no conclusions can be drawn from what is to what should

---

6   Above, p. 42 *et seq.*

7   On exploitation, see *Capital*, MECW 35:297 and 315; it is essential that *Exploitationsgrad* (degree of exploitation) can be defined in terms of Mehrwert (surplus value).

be, and vice versa). Ideologically, however, it is connected to a very definite world of ideas. It is directed at the working class, encouraging it to organise. It harbours a negative assessment of capitalism and its society; it brings out the contradictions of capitalism, its anarchy and its transitoriness as repugnant elements.

It could be asked whether there is a necessary connection between the theory and the ideology of the transitoriness of capitalism. But this question is not unambiguous. Logically, there is no connection: logically, it is possible to link the theory to any norms and values whatsoever. We can, for example, imagine a supporter of capitalism who takes everything they hold to be true about the development of the capitalist mode of production from Marxist theory and argues that it is a matter of resisting the inevitable for as long as possible, but that everything that is good and desirable in society will gradually succumb.

The interesting question, however, naturally concerns the actual connection between ideology and theory. What happens with theory and ideology when the bond between them loosens?

A solid answer to this question would require an extremely exhaustive empirical study of the historical development of Marxism. A study of this kind does not belong to this account. We can be content with stating that it was a necessary condition, for example, for the development of revisionism and for separating theory from ideology – or, more precisely, that the question of the norms and values of socialism were detached from Marx's theory of capitalism.[8] It was of course not this divorce that caused, or comprised the most important cause of, the emergence and development of revisionism. It was one moment among many. It comprised a necessary, but far from sufficient, determinant for revisionism.

Similarly, the close connection between theory and practice – and thereby between theory and ideology – is an essential feature of Leninism. It was not Lenin's struggle against revisionism that determined Leninism's appearance, but standing guard around Marx's theory and the attempt to make it the dominant element in communist ideology was an inevitable feature of Leninism.

The question of the connection between ideology and theory thus leads to another question, namely the question of the general social, ideological and theoretical circumstances that determine the relation between theory and ideology. We thus turn to the problem. It no longer concerns the effects of, but the causes behind the development of one or another connection between theory and ideology.

---

8 On this topic, cf. Bernstein 1969.

A theory cannot exclusively under its own power comprise the worthwhile material for an ideology. More is required for it to enter the ideological field of force and to influence ideology.

One necessary condition is, naturally, that the theory can be expressed as a number of statements about reality, which in ideology are closely related to its own values and norms. However, the rules for the relations between things held to be true, norms and values are particularly intricate and changing, and thus require their own comprehensive explanation.

Significantly more enlightening is another condition that is not as obvious but that adequate experience confirms, namely that the theory is *ideologically controversial*, which could mean that it is irreconcilable with theories that are cherished in other ideologies or that it is given a different ideological meaning in other ideologies. Marx's theory of capitalism is controversial because it obviously conflicts with theories cherished in other ideologies. Darwin's theory of natural selection became controversial because it was ascribed a number of different and irreconcilable ideological consequences.

The ideological controversies around theories can be disseminated to a greater or a lesser extent. They can keep within the narrow boundaries of scientific institutions or they can take entire social classes with them.

Naturally, each ideology also contains theoretical material that is *not* ideologically controversial; but this material is largely only accessible through ideological analysis: it is not an expression in the ideology's own terms and usually contains things that are regarded as self-evident at a given point in time. Here, we can ignore these essential matters – which are extremely interesting in themselves – since our question concerns the significance of theories for *manifest* ideologies.

But why do certain theories become ideologically controversial? How can it be that the same theory is more controversial at one point in time, and less so at another?

Let us assume that the core of ideology, its foundation, is always the concrete circumstances in the lives of humans, and more specifically their class roles. It is, as we have seen, Marxism's theory of the latent content in all manifest ideologies. Among other assertions, it means that thoroughgoing ideological contradictions belong to every class society. But *if* class affiliation alone determined ideology, every theory that has any connection at all with the differences between classes would be ideologically controversial. We know that this is not so. Not even class contradictions need to be conscious for the members of the classes.

According to this same Marxist view, this is due primarily to the fact that the ruling class has succeeded in imputing the other classes with its own ideology. It would mean that when a theory which – so to speak – ought to separate classes and thus be ideologically controversial nonetheless does not result in any conflicts, the explanation primarily should be sought in the fact that the ruling class has succeeded in convincing its natural opponents of the correctness of its interpretation of the theory. When, on the other hand, ideological conflicts flare up, it is a sign that the ruling class has not fully mastered the ideological field. The late nineteenth century, when the bourgeoisie and working class came to full blows over ideological matters – including matters that had a direct connection with scientific theories – would be an excellent example of a period when ideological dams had burst.

Not all ideological contradictions reveal class contradictions, however; on the contrary, ideological controversies can often mask the underlying contradictions. This is the case, for example, with the numerous battles over the right and true Christianity, the ultimate grounds for which are certainly found in class contradictions but which in the various manifest ideologies were formulated as opposing ideas about the path to eternal glory. It could thus be said that, according to Marxism, every ideological feud where ideas about class and class relations do not form the conscious starting points are feuds that mislead and blind.

Obviously, it is not in the interest of the ruling class and in general of any secure and firmly established elite holding power for society to be presented and experienced as fundamentally and at heart characterised by irreconcilable contradictions. In order to achieve any kind of stability in general, every society must create institutions that also influence people's worlds of ideas and imprint in them the image of unity and a community of interest around the most fundamental social issues. These ideas are controlled through churches, education, the administration of justice and much else.

In a society undergoing fundamental changes, however, where one class – either quickly or slowly – is outmanoeuvring another class, the institutions creating ideology are often set against one another; new institutions are created in conflict with the old, and new ideas about what constitutes the basis and unity of society compete with the old ones. This, as everyone knows, is what has been happening in Europe ever since the rise of capitalism and the bourgeoisie. Churches have changed and split, new churches have been created, new schools and types of schools have developed, and so on. Science has also been involved in this process of change. Scientific academies have been set against universities, universities against colleges, new types of universities against old ones. This institutional split has also become the foundation for ideological feuds, which have less frequently played out around fundamental class contradictions; more often they have concerned the doctrines of one

church or another, the existence or non-existence of religion, and legal and
political forms.

3   The Ideological Game

As we have seen, every manifest ideology has its main focus in what is controversial. That is the point where it must formulate itself and meet the arguments
of other ideologies. But the areas for the controversies are determined only in
the last instance by class contradictions; between class contradictions and the
ideological battles lies a broad field of religious, political, legal and scientific
orientations, movements, groups and institutions, all in alliance or in conflict
with one another, now powerful, now powerless. What seems important and
essential in the worlds of humanity's ideas is determined primarily by this
chaotic world of entities that are the creators of ideology.[9]

This is also the way in which scientific theories are brought into ideology
and become ideologically controversial. Darwinism could be of service with its
arguments in the conflict among various religious orientations and between
religion and atheism; it could equally be a weapon in the tug-of-war among
various political ideologies. It created no new ideology itself, but it could be
incorporated into ideologies, strengthening or weakening them and transforming them.

The ideological battle within and around science, however, concerns the
authority and correct use of science just as much as its theses. This is so not
only with science: a growing, but always substantial part of the ideological tug-
of-war concerns the correct use or claims of the ideological entities themselves,
their harm or their benefit, the limits of their influence. Great battles have raged
over which churches had which rights: to baptisms, to communion, to education. Great battles have raged over school forms and the relation of school to

---

9   Althusser provides interesting and essential ideas here, with his theses on 'ideological apparatuses of state', expressed in works such as Althusser 1976, p. 120 et seq. What Althusser seems
to ignore in his outline is the difficult-to-comprehend mobility – to say nothing of confusion –
in the very production of ideas. When Althusser provides examples of the need for the ruling
class to gain control over the ideological apparatus of state, he chooses Lenin (p. 123), which is
a poor choice since Lenin had a very definite, very conscious idea of the relation of ideology to
class relations in society and the political apparatus of compulsion. In a bourgeois capitalist
society, the production of ideas is, up to a certain limit (a limit that moves in accordance with
the degree of liberality and internal security in society) as blind and anarchical as material
production ever is. The essential – and difficult – task is naturally to study these limits and to
try to determine their connection with society as a whole.

church, to the state, to business; great battles have raged over the relation of the legal apparatus to the political apparatus.

These *ideological* contradictions over how *ideology* should be created are always worth a great deal of attention. They concern power over ideological production itself. They lie closer to the fundamental contradictions in society than do the feuds over various ideological theses.

Similar controversies, however, do not need to be openly ideological. The controversy over the ideological involvement of scientists, which we followed in the preceding chapter, did not play out between two openly formulated ideological positions. Only when turning to the images of society and the role of science in society, which – so to speak – are encapsulated in the arguments, do the ideologies also emerge.

The battle in question concerned two irreconcilable – and each influential – conceptions of how scientific rationality should influence and leave its mark on society. The conceptions were thus reconciled in the belief in the ability of rationality to reshape society in a favourable direction, and this belief separated them from various traditionalist, conservative or purely irrationalist views. The ideas of how rationality should influence and permeate society were irreconcilable, however.

For centuries, the older idea of enlightenment had a clear connection with the bourgeois class and thus the capitalist reshaping of society. Clear, unprejudiced calculation would change all human life. All the relations that could only be justified as the will of God or the order of tradition had to be transformed in accordance with rational principles. In this process, cold and precisely calculating science played an important role. The person who knew a great deal about science and thus recognised reason to its highest degree had to enlighten other people: reason would spread like ripples in a pond.

The idea of enlightenment appears as a clear tendency, a clearly distinguishable line in the confusion of ideological battles not only during the eighteenth century but before and after it as well. This tendency, or line, did not abolish the confusion. Reason and science had to come out now in one question, now in another. Various religious controversies incessantly broke out, and the Enlightenment professed itself an adherent of many different religions and irreligions according to circumstances and its own starting points. It was not enlightenment that created political revolutions; during those revolutions, however, enlightenment rose up and spoke its mind on the diversity of issues that emerged during the revolutionary process.

The idea of enlightenment is an idea about the relation between science and society, between science and the world of human ideas; it is not itself an ideology but one ideological element among others in many different ideologies. Even the nineteenth-century socialists were largely adherents of the idea of enlightenment. Marx and Engels were so to the greatest degree.

The idea that Rudolf Virchow was among the first to express with full clarity is not irrationalist: it did not ascribe an insignificant role to science. But it assumed that the new society in which science was active was already a largely rational society with rational institutions – creators of ideology, and others – and that science can and should leave the ideological use of science to these institutions. Bourgeois reason had gained a society to defend against socialist ideas of enlightenment. Virchow warned against the unrestrained exploitation of science. Science should not be a weapon against a society that was already sufficiently rational.

Ernst Haeckel and others who became the main opponents of Virchow in the debate around Darwinism were no subverters of society. They assessed reality differently. They saw the most powerful driving forces in society in humanity's religious ideas and in its world views in general. The German Reich could not combat errors and superstitions on its own. This required the direct involvement of the most enlightened people: the scientists.

Virchow's position was not only a consequence of his own attitude towards the society that had taken shape. It could be said that he understood far better than Haeckel the role that professional science was beginning to play in German society. Scientists had to be experts in carefully demarcated fields in a scientific organisation that was properly integrated into the diversity of institutions. They could not, as Virchow phrased it, be *Halbwisser* (dilettantes): they could not be men of enlightenment, they could not draw conclusions from the specialised knowledge they possessed in full. These conclusions were to be drawn by others, who of course did not possess any specialised knowledge but had their definite social function as educators and popularisers.

Virchow thus strove for a fixed, determined order in ideological production and reproduction. The role of science had previously been variable and temporary: now one theory or orientation, now another, was drawn into one controversy or another. Now there would be order, determined not by the sciences but by a firmly organised society.

On one point, he was unconditionally correct. The influence of knowledge over the worlds of humanity's ideas had been limited by the disorder in ideological controversies, which in turn was determined by the diversity of conflicting ideological entities. Science could not have determined the sphere of the controversies itself. It could not itself have determined what would become ideologically interesting and controversial.

Even though Marx and Engels essentially assumed a standpoint opposite to Virchow's, they shared his understanding here. But instead of writing off the idea of enlightenment, they argued that enlightenment should be given its great opportunity. The ideological confusion that obscured humanity's view and caused them to believe now that everything depended on religious faith, now that the key issue was the constitution, now that some third thing determined the welfare of the world would now be broken through. The tool for enlightenment would be the Marxist theory of society, which also contained guidelines for what was more or less fundamental in the worlds of humanity's ideas. The recipients of enlightenment would primarily be the working class, but additionally everyone who allowed themselves to be enlightened by the words of truth.

It is telling that Engels and Marx avoided, or concealed, perhaps the most comprehensive ideological controversies in which science was involved, namely religious ones. Their silence on religious matters is compact, and later led to a number of odd speculations about the relation between Marxism and religion.[10] This silence, however, is due to the fact that they saw here an ideologically superficial phenomenon, which distorted humanity's ideas about what was essential and what was not.

We will not go into the question here of the extent to which they were proven right in their optimistic thinking about a new and better enlightenment that would not be at the mercy of unknown ideological machinery but had created its own channels in the growing workers' movement. One thing is obvious: it had already immediately encountered obstacles in this workers' movement that were difficult to surmount. On the other hand, the history in this field has moved in slower turns than Marx and Engels imagined, and the enlightenment they saw as the work of a generation is perhaps a task for the centuries.

But how did Engels's philosophical works relate to the Marxist ideas of enlightenment? This is the question we must ultimately ask, since it is part of the main theme of this account to an eminent degree.

4   Ideology and Theory in Engels

When Engels was in his most positivist mood, he claimed that his statements about reality and about knowledge were extraordinarily comprehensive generalisations of the empirical material that the various sciences had gathered together.[11] We know that this was an untenable thesis. In itself, the scientific

---

10   On the 'Marxist-Christian dialogue', see Boer 2019.

11   Above, p. 472 *et seq.*

empirical material says nothing about the relations between sciences internally or between scientific theories and reality. No observation and no experiment in the world can in itself repudiate an idealistic interpretation of knowledge or confute a reduction of, for example, history to biology, or biology to chemistry or mechanics. This requires a number of interpretations of science and reality and their mutual relation. These interpretations can have a greater or lesser plausibility even in relation to scientific empirical material, and they themselves provide guidance for a great deal of purely empirical research. In themselves they are not the result of empirical study, and empirical study cannot confute or confirm them

In a number of statements, Engels showed himself to be aware of this.[12] Obviously, this understanding also squares better with the main lines of the general dialectic he sketched out, with its theses on the interaction between theory and empirical material, the general and the individual.

The contrary statements, however, cannot simply be pushed aside as temporary deviations of no interest. They are striking examples of how the ideological determination outflanks the theoretical. When Engels regarded his general statements as empirical generalisations, he showed his hand in an ongoing controversy over the status of scientific theories. His own standpoint did not comprise an alternative in this controversy; the alternatives were either pure empiricism or a speculative view of knowledge. He was forced to take a position, and he took the one that seems to have been closest to his own – namely, that of pure empiricism. It was not only lip service. His position had to be justified. The thesis on dialectical laws as a kind of super-generalisation was developed. The contrast to the general statements about knowledge and his relation to reality was sharpened.

The conflict between a purely empirical and a speculative understanding was not only, and in its pure form not primarily, a conflict internal to science. To the greatest degree it was an ideological conflict over the use and authority of science in the various spheres of life: religion, politics, ethics and aesthetics. In his youth, Engels had come into intimate contact with this conflict in connection with the battles over Hegelianism, Schelling and Feuerbach. It later played a role in the battle over materialism and in the debates about the significance of Darwinism for religious dogmas in particular. The defence of a purely speculative standpoint was thoroughly weak among scientists and philosophers; more often, it was a question of catching out an opponent with speculative inclina-

---

12   Above, p. 386 *et seq.*

tions. Engels's far too rapid and direct profession of a scientific ideal that was not his own must be viewed in this light.

The conflict was not a natural consequence of the internal developments in science: there were not two separate scientific orientations where one was clearly speculative and the other purely empirical. There were attempts at such an antagonism, but in the 1870s and 1880s they were largely obsolete from a scientific viewpoint. This antagonism found its nourishment in other fields, in the conflicts between various churches and religious conceptions, in the battles between conservative and liberal views of society, in the fight for influence over school systems, adult education, charitable organisations and political associations.

Engels was thus at the mercy of an ideological controversy that distorted his own position. He deviated from his main line. It is easy to say that he ought to have realised all the undesirable consequences that his statements could have. The audience he appealed to, who had largely been schooled in various types of educational associations and workers' associations, demanded an unambiguous response from him. He himself was plausibly a prisoner of the world of ideas in which the antagonism between pure speculation and pure empiricism – interpreted as an extreme example of the antagonisms between religion and atheism, traditionalism and rationalism, belief in authority and belief in reason – was regarded as crucial for every ideological position.

Here, we thus see how difficult it was to realise the Marxist programme of enlightenment in accordance with which Marxist social theory would constitute the basis for a new manifest ideology. The theory that was to be transformed into an ideology was immediately met by a number of ideological oppositions that were produced by unknown ideological machinery. The theory was powerful enough to reveal this machinery; but could it directly influence humanity's ideas if it did not answer, but merely pushed aside questions that had already been asked and that humanity perceived as extremely important? In that case the theory had to obtain its own ideological machinery, linked to the socialist movement. But how could people be convinced of the necessity of such machinery so long as their ideas were still influenced by completely different machinery?

It appears as if Engels in fact underestimated the difficulties. He met the opposition to *Anti-Dühring* with assurances that he himself was speaking for science. He did not go into the question of how a Most, a Vahlteich or a Bebel had arrived at their understanding. This relative lack of concern itself also made him less attentive to the consequences of his own positions.

Engels thus overestimated the ability of science to control ideology. Despite having been part of creating the theory of ideological mystification in *The Ger-*

man Ideology, when he was himself faced with the task of developing a manifest ideology, he remained uncritical in the face of much of what was presented as the crucial questions of science. Nor did he fully realise that scientific theories had varying degrees of *ideological ambiguity*.

In fact, there are crucial reasons here that his philosophical writings could be put to so many varied, and often entirely bizarre, uses in the later development of Marxism. The inconsistencies among his statements about what was scientifically important and crucial meant that the writings could fill different ideological needs.[13] The idea that a scientific theory had completely unambiguous ideological consequences paved the way for peculiar ideas that Marxism had to hold out against new scientific theories (e.g. Mendelian genetics or the theory of relativity) that gained influence after Engels's time, in conflict with the theories that Engels himself fostered.

The very backbone of Engels's works is the principle of *non-reductive materialism*. He could deviate from it, he could oppose it, but it nonetheless determined the main orientation of his activities. We have already seen that this principle here fills a crucial determinant internal to science. Using it, Engels tried to clarify the relations among various sciences (e.g. between biology and Marxist social theory). It also guided him when he clarified the relation between base and superstructure in social theory itself.

But non-reductive materialism also has an ideological significance. Or, more precisely: it *obtains* ideological significance when it is controversial on the extent to which and the manner in which various parts of science can form the basis for a worldview and understanding of society. On an ideological plane, non-reductive materialism also took up the fight with mechanistic materialism as Büchner and Vogt, for example, had developed it. According to mechanistic materialism a materialist view is possible only if every phenomenon can be related to the basic forces of mechanics. Humanity's world must thus be absolutely expressed in terms of biology, and biology in terms of physics and chemistry. The mechanistic materialists thus ignored many of the difficulties that contemporary science offered them. Achieving the desired unity required a number of gross reinterpretations and simplifications of prevalent theories.

Non-reductive materialism, however, could also be directed toward another, stricter and scientifically more established understanding of the ideological use of science, namely the one I have called reductive mechanism. The

---

13   Especially telling, naturally, is the fact that *Dialectics of Nature* could deliver arguments for both of the competing sides in the controversy between the 'mechanicists' and Deborin's adherents in the USSR in the 1920s; on this, cf. Ahlberg 1960, p. 46 et seq.

advocates of reductive mechanicism shared the conception of the mechanicist materialists that a theory gained full value as regards science and worldviews only when it became possible to reduce it to pure mechanics. Reductive mechanicism, however, was much stricter and more discriminating than mechanistic materialism. As we have already seen, its advocates claimed without exception that there were crucial boundaries for the spheres where science operates. The most mechanistic theory thus did not need to rule out a religious, or at least a generally spiritual and idealistic, view of reality. Exact science would never reach these spheres.

In relation to these conceptions, non-reductive materialism claimed that science could be put to ideological use in all spheres of life without having to regard each sphere as a kind of complicated mechanics. What was required was being able to account for the transition from one field of theory to another, and thus from one sphere of reality to another. It was futile to try to derive, for example, humanity's religious ideas from its biological nature. On the other hand, being able to create definite ideas about how the human species emerged out of biological development was important.

Here, non-reductive materialism stands out as an extremely sound principle in comparison with its competitors. Mechanistic materialism, in fact, assumed that if reality were to comprise a totality and not a split between, for example, the spiritual and the material (or living and dead, or human and non-human), it must also be homogeneous. In addition, reductive mechanicism claimed that this unity assumed that every sphere of reality, regardless of its degree of complexity, had to be treated with the same type of scientific exactness in order to be the subject of scientific criticism in general. The strict requirements could thus turn into laxity: while the mechanistic materialists reshaped and simplified biological and historical theories in order to press them into their own narrow schema, the followers of reductive mechanicism let a number of spheres – primarily religion – flourish and develop without any criticism whatsoever from scientific rationality.

Non-reductive materialism, however, was – and still is – an extremely general principle. In itself it says nothing about which theories are to be joined together; it provides very general ideas about how the merger should take place. It says only that the base and starting point must be the material and not the spiritual, the inorganic and not the organic, the simple and not the complex. It cannot determine which theory about the material or the spiritual is to apply, only that the theory of the material is and remains the basis for the theory of the spiritual.

Engels, on the other hand, imagined that a definite hierarchy of theories would forever comprise the backbone of non-reductive materialism's image of the world. In good company with almost all of his contemporaries, he believed that the more fundamental and more exact a theory was, the more inflexible and unchangeable it would also be. He could not imagine a fundamental crisis in physics. His materialism seemed to him to be indissolubly associated with Newtonian mechanics and the principle of conservation of energy. He went a step further: biology must always remain primarily Darwinist biology. That is why his hierarchy of sciences seemed to be a closed system, irreconcilable with every sweeping change to any field of theory whatsoever. It could appear as if Marxism, socialism and the workers' movement stood and fell with Newtonian mechanics or Darwin's and Haeckel's genetic theories.

In fact, a scientific theory about nature is always ideologically ambiguous. The further away from the world of humanity one goes, the greater the ambiguity and the looser the connection. Darwinism could be reconciled with a long range of conflicting ideologies, ultimately also with species of a fascistic world of ideas. No ideology can obtain a monopoly over a theory of natural science.

The ambiguity of the theories is also evident from the analysis of ideology that Engels was part of developing in *The German Ideology*: the core of ideology is humanity's practical circumstances. But when Engels himself developed a manifest ideology he abandoned his own thesis, taking his starting point not in the world of humanity but in that of mass, molecules and atoms, which appeared as the foundation not only of the scientific hierarchy but also of ideology.

Engels found himself in the company of all the system-builders of his age. But this company did not suit him. If one starts from the ideas of science about the nature of the cosmos and arrives at human relations only in the final chapter, this hints – whether intentionally or not – at an understanding that the basis of ideology and the ideological conflicts lies in various ideas about how the world came to be (eternity or God). This is not historical materialism; this is idealism.

Nowhere can the rule of ideology over Engels's own ideological activities be seen more clearly than in the composition of *Anti-Dühring* and *Dialectics of Nature*.

5   Conclusion

Separating theory from ideology is necessary: this is one of the main theses of this book. Science and philosophy, moreover, are always ideology, since science and philosophy are always part of a world of human ideas in which they are immediately associated with desires and demands, values and norms. But it is always possible, from the ideological context, to analyse the naked statements about reality, to isolate the general theses and the individual observations and their internal connections. It is possible to establish consequences in theory that are not consequences in ideology, and vice versa. It is therefore also possible to demonstrate how ideology can influence theory, and how theory can change ideology.

Engels's works appear in different lights if they are observed from an internal scientific or an ideological viewpoint. In the former, their connection with the questions of scientific theory that the materialist conception of history and Marx's theory of capital gave rise to. In the latter, it can be seen how they were influenced by more or less temporary ideological constellations and antagonisms of the age when they were written and how the fundamental ideological ambition – to provide the working class with a world view on a Marxist basis – is neglected again and again.

It is also obvious that there are antagonisms between theory and ideology in many ways; in his own ideological work, Engels breaks with the Marxist theory of what constitutes an ideology.

Anti-Dühring, *Dialectics of Nature* and *Ludwig Feuerbach* have all had an extraordinarily strong influence on posterity. In the contradictory history of Marxism, these writings have incessantly been the subject of controversies and reinterpretations. They have played a role as weapons, as authoritative accounts, as trendsetters or frightening examples in the conflicts around revisionism, in Lenin's reckoning with neo-positivism, in the debates that George Lukács and Karl Korsch brought about in the early 1920s, in the conflicts over philosophy versus positive knowledge in the young Soviet Union, and so forth. Bits and pieces of them have appeared in the endless number of more or less catechistic accounts of what is the true, real and orthodox Marxism. Mao Zedong and Chinese communism were constantly busy with re-examining their position on Engels. Philosophically influential orientations such as the Frankfurt School and the Praxis Group have used Engels's writings as a type of contrasting picture to their own Marxism.

The ideological interest in *Anti-Dühring*, *Dialectics of Nature* and *Ludwig Feuerbach* has undoubtedly been greater than the theoretical. The discussions have centred more on the possibility or impossibility of constructing a conception of the world on the basis of Marxism than on the scientific problems that Engels took up in his writings. The dominant question has been whether the lessons Engels drew from the sciences of his time and were processed in the ideological machinery of the late nineteenth century can still form the basis of a worldview.

Let me say that for my part, I find the ideological treatment of science extremely important: it is a link in the campaign for a more rational world. Ideology, however, is short-lived and linked to all the peculiar, often temporary contradictions that every era produces. The questions of ideology cannot be left to Walt Disney or the Pope. They must, however, be continually taken up anew and with awareness of the fact that the ideological factory of illusions threatens to confuse even the most unbiased gaze. The only thing in Engels's endeavour to create a manifest ideology that seems to be unconditionally of current interest today is its connection with Marx's and his own theory of the roots of all ideology being in the material circumstances of humanity. Science can take its starting point in electrons or light-years, but ideology starts with humans themselves: it is their way of creating clarity in their situation, in their society and in their world, of justifying their actions, of accounting for their desires, of setting limits for their possibilities. Engels's own manifest ideology conflicted with his own ideas about ideologies. There is no better example of the treacherous character of ideology.

Engels's ambitions for creating an ideology thus seem good, but the ideology he actually created is essentially completely out of date.

The internal scientific aspects of Engels's philosophical writings have attracted much less attention, relatively speaking. To put it more acutely, the relation can be described as such: those who ascribed decisive value to *Anti-Dühring*, *Dialectics of Nature* and *Ludwig Feuerbach* have taken their ideology as the starting point, while those who distanced themselves from these writings have themselves placed the theories of Marxism in a scientific theoretical context that is foreign not only for Engels but for Marx as well.

It may seem that the death sentence was passed on the scientific content of *Dialectics of Nature* back in 1924, when Albert Einstein wrote to Eduard Bernstein after a direct inquiry as to whether it was worth the effort to publish *Dialectics of Nature*: 'If this manuscript were to originate from an author of no interest as a historical personality, I would not advise publication; for the content is of no special interest, either from the point of view of modern physics or even for the history of physics. On the other hand, I can imagine that this text would be considered for publication as it forms an interesting contribution toward the illumination of Engels' intellectual personality'.[14]

Bernstein understood the recommendation to mean that *Dialectics of Nature* could remain unpublished. But soon thereafter, in 1925, Daniel Riazanov published the manuscript.

---

14   Quote according to Riazanov 1927, p. 141. Cf. also Deborin and Bukharin 1969, p. 94 (Deborin's statement).

At first glance, Einstein's opinion may seem crushing. But how could it be otherwise? How could the general statements about nineteenth-century physics, which Engels took from a motley collection of writings on physics, with varied orientations and content, be of interest to Einstein's physics or even for the history of physics? It would be a miraculous coincidence.

Naturally, the interest lies on another, much more general plane. The problems Engels raised about the relations among various sciences remain acutely topical; the problems concerning contexts of law and processes 'chance' and 'necessity' are similarly acutely topical. In a large part of the scientific and scientific theoretical discussion of our time, similar questions have been pushed aside or received entirely too quick, entirely too simple solutions. It is time to seriously take them on. They are significant for the sciences. They are significant for ideologies: who hasn't listened to discussions about where the boundaries between human and animals, and between social science and biology, lie? Who has not let their ideas about what can be done and achieved be controlled to some extent by ideas about what is 'necessary', in conformity with law, unchangeable or not?

The work that Engels took on at age 53 was immeasurable in scope and pretensions. But do immeasurably difficult questions not also require immeasurable effort?

Sources and Literature

Unpublished Sources

Bibliothek des deutschen Museums, Munich.
   Letters from C. Schorlemmer and E. Hoster.
British Museum, London.
   Letter from C. Schorlemmer (Add. 45345, f. 133).
Collection M.E. Bottigelli, Paris.
   Letter from C. Schorlemmer.
Russian State Archive of Socio-Political History (RGASPI), Moscow.
   Marx-Engels collections.
Internationaal Instituut voor Sociale Geschiedenis (IISG), Amsterdam.
   Marx-Engels Nachlass.
Manchester University Library. Special Collections.
   C. Schorlemmer, *Geschichte der Chemie.* I–II.
Staatsbibliothek preussischer Kulturbesitz, Berlin.
   Letter from C. Schorlemmer.
In the author's possession.
   Letter from L. Althusser.

Published Works

Abramowski, G. 1966, *Das Geschichtsbild Max Webers. Universalgeschichte am Leitfaden des okzidentalen Rationaliserungsprozess.* Stuttgart: Klett.

Acham, K. 1964, *Zum Problem des Historismus bei Wilhelm Dilthey und Martin Heidegger.* Graz.

Ackerknecht, E.H. 1953, *Rudolf Virchow: Doctor, Statesman, Anthropologist.* Madison: University of Wisconsin Press.

Adamiak, R. 1974, 'Marx, Engels and Dühring', *Journal of the History of Ideas*, 35.

Adler, M. 1908, *Marx als Denker. Zum 25. Todesjahr von Karl Marx.* Berlin: Vorwärts.

Adler, V. 1954, *Briefwechsel mit August Bebel und Karl Kautsky.* Wien: Wiener Volksbuchhandlung.

Adorno, T.W. 1966, *Negative Dialectics.* New York: Continuum.

Agassi, J. 1963, 'Toward an Historiography of Science', *History and Theory*, Beiheft 2.

Agassi, J. 1971, *Faraday as Natural Philosopher.* Chicago: University of Chicago Press.

Ahlberg, R. 1960, *Dialektische Philosophie und Gesellschaft in der Sowjetunion.* Berlin: Harrassowitz.

Albrecht, G. 1927, *Eugen Dühring: Ein Beitrag zur Geschichte der Sozialwissenschaften.* Jena: G. Fischer.

D'Alembert, J. 1743, *Traité de dynamique: dans lequel les loix de l'equilibre & du mouvement des corps sont réduits au plus petit nombre possible, & démontrées d'une maniére nouvelle: & où l'on donne un principe général pour trouver le mouvement de plusieurs corps qui agissent les uns sur les autres, d'une maniére quelconque.* Paris.

Althusser, L. 1965, *Pour Marx.* Paris: Maspero.

Althusser, L. 1968/1970, *Filosofi från proletär klasståndpunkt.*

Althusser, L. 2014, 'On the Reproduction of Capitalism', in *Ideology and Ideological State Apparatuses.* London: Verso.

Ampère, A.M. 1838, *Essai sur la philosophie des sciences, ou Exposition analytique d'une classification naturelle de toutes les connaissances humaines.* Paris: Bachelier.

Anschütz, A. 1929, *August Kekulé*, Vols. I–II. Berlin: Verlag Chemie.

Árnason, J.P. 1971, *Von Marcuse zu Marx. Prolegomena zu einer dialektischen Anthropologie.* Neuwied: Luchterhand.

Auer, I. 1913, *Nach zehn Jahren. Material und Glossen zur Geschichte des Sozialistengesetzes.* Nürnberg: Fränkische Verlagsanstalt

Austromarxism 1970, Texte zu 'Ideologie und Klasskampf', edited by H.-J. Sandkühler and R. de la Vega. Frankfurt: Europäische Verlagsanstalt.

Aveling, E. 1881, *The Student's Darwin.* London: Free Thought.

Aveling, E. 1884, *The Darwinian Theory: Its Meaning, Difficulties, Evidence, History.* London: Progressive Publising.

Babbage, C. 1829, 'Account of the Great Congress of Philosophers at Berlin', *Edinburgh Journal of Science*, 10.

Babbage, C. 1830 (new printing 1969), *Reflections on the Decline of Science in England and Some of its Causes.* Farnborough: Gregg.

Babbage, C. 1864, *Passages from the Life of a Philosopher.* London: Pickering.

Bagehot, W. 1869, *Physics and Politics.* London: Henry King.

Ballauff, T. 1971, 'Biologie', in *Historisches Wörterbuch der Philosophie*, Vol. I. Basel: Schwabe.

Ballestrem, K.G. 1964, *Russian Philosophical Terminology.* Dordrecht: Reidel.

Ballestrem, K.G. 1968, *Die sowjetische Erkenntnismetaphysik und ihr Verhältnis zu Hegel.* Dordrecht: Reidel.

Barber, B. 1962, *Science and Social Order.* New York: Collier Books.

Baron, S.H. 1963, *Plekhanov. The Father of Russian Marxism.* Stanford: Stanford University Press.

Barth, H. 1945, *Wahrheit und Ideologie.* Zurich: Manesse.

Bastian, A. 1860, *Der Mensch in der Geschichte.* Leipzig: Wigand.

Bebel, A. 1965, *August Bebels Briefwechsel mit Friedrich Engels*, edited by W. Blumenberg. The Hague: Mouton.

Beckmann, J. 1780–1805, *Beiträge zur Geschichte der Erfindungen*. Vols. I–V. Leipzig: Kummer.

de Beer, G. 1964, *Charles Darwin: A Scientific Biography*. Garden City: Doubleday.

Beiträge zur Entwicklung der Wissenschaftstheorie im 19. Jahrhundert. Vorträge und Diskussionen 1968, edited by A. Diemer. Meisenheim: Verlag Anton Hain.

Bell, W.L. 1975, *Charles Babbage: Philosopher, Reformer, Inventor*. Dissertation manuscript, Oregon State University. Microfilm 75–16808.

Ben-David, J. 1971, *The Scientist's Role in Society. A Comparative Study*. Englewood Cliffs, NJ: Prentice-Hall.

Bentham, J. 1841, *Chrestomathia. Appendix IV:* 'Essay on Nomenclature and Classification' (1816). Works, Part XV (Vol. VIII). London.

Bernal, J.D. 1953, *Science and Industry in the Nineteenth Century*. Bloomington: Indiana University Press.

Bernal, J.D. 1969 [1954], *Science in History*. Illustrated edition after 3rd edition. Vols. I–IV. London: Faber & Faber.

Bernard, C. 1865, *Introduction à l'étude de la médecine expérimentale*. Paris: Baillière.

Bernheim, E. 1901, *Entwurf eines Studienplans für das Fach der Geschichte nebst Beilage: Beispiele von Anfängerübungen*. Greifswald: Abel.

Bernstein, E. 1899, *Die Voraussetzungen und die Aufgaben der Sozialdemokratie*. Berlin: Dietz.

Bernstein, E. 1969 [1899], *Die Voraussetzungen und die Aufgaben der Sozialdemokratie*, edited by G. Hillman. Berlin: Dietz.

Bernstein, E. 1970, *Eduard Bernsteins Briefwechsel mit Friedrich Engels*, edited by H. Hirsch. Assen: Van Gorcum.

von Bertalanffy, L. 1936, 'Eduard von Hartmann und die moderne Biologie', *Archiv für Geschichte der Philosophie und Soziologie*, 38, nos. 3–4.

von Bertalanffy, L. 1952, *Problems of Life. An Evaluation of Modern Biological and Scientific Thought*. Ann Arbor: University Microfilms International.

Beuchelt, E. 1974, *Ideengeschichte der Völkerpsychologie*. Meisenheim: Hain.

Bhaskar, R. 1975, *A Realist Theory of Science*. Leeds: Leeds Books.

Biermann, K-R. 1973, *Die Mathematik und ihre Dozenten an der Berliner Universität 1810–1920*. Berlin: Akademie-Verlag.

Binder, H. 1933, *Das socialitäre System Eugen Dührings*. Jena.

Blackmore, J.T. 1972, *Ernst Mach: His Work, Life and Influence*. Berkeley: University of California Press.

Bladen, V.W. 1965, 'Introduction' to Mill 1965, Vol. I.

Bloch, E. 1973, *Über Methode und System bei Hegel*. Frankfurt: Suhrkamp.

Blume, S.S. 1974, *Toward a Political Sociology of Science*. New York: The Free Press.

Blumenbach, J.F. 1788, *Handbuch der Naturgeschichte*. 3rd edition. Göttingen: Bey Johann Christian Dieterich.

Boer, R. 2019, *Red Theology: On the Christian Communist Tradition*. Leiden: Brill.

Bochenski, I.M. 1956, *Der sowjetrussische dialektische Materialismus*. Bern: Francke.

Boeckh, A. 1817, *Die Staatsaushaltung der Athener*, Vols I–II. Berlin.

Bollnow, H. 1954, 'Untersuchung über Engels' Auffassung von Revolution und Entwicklung', in *Marxismusstudien I*. Tübingen.

Bollnow, O.F. 1955, *Dilthey. Eine Einführung in seine Philosophie*. 2nd edition. Stuttgart: Kohlhammer.

Bölsche, W. 1920, *Ernst Haeckel. Ein Lebensbild*. Berlin: Seeman.

Bonar, J. 1924, *Malthus and his Work*. 2nd edition. London.

Boström, C.J. 1883, *Skrifter. Utgifvna af H Edfeldt*. Vols. 1–2. Uppsala: Victor Roos.

Braun, O. 1909, *Eduard von Hartmann*. Stuttgart: F. Frommanns.

Braybrooke, D. 1967, 'Ideology', in *The Encyclopaedia of Philosophy*, Vol. IV. London: Macmillan.

Brazill, W.J. 1970, *The Young Hegelians*. New Haven: Yale University Press.

Brinz, M. 1884, 'Maurer, Georg Ludwig v', *Allgemeine Deutsche Biographie*, 20.

Broberg, G. 1975, *Homo Sapiens, l. Studier i Carl von Linnés naturuppfattning och människoskolära*. Uppsala: Almqvist och Wiksell.

Brooke, C. 1872, 'Force and Energy. The Conservation of Energy a Fact, not a Heresy of Science', *Nature*, 6, 13 June.

Brown, L.B. 1973, *Ideology*. Harmondsworth: Penguin.

Bruhat, J. 1972–74, 'La place du *Capital* dans l'histoire du socialisme', in *Histoire générale du socialisme*, edited by J. Droz. Vols. I–II. Paris: PUF.

Büchner, L. 1855, *Kraft und Stoff. Empirisch-naturphilosophische Studien. In allgemeinverständlicher Darstellung*. Leipzig.

Büchner, L. 1868, *Sechs Vorlesungen über die Darwin'sche Theorie*. Leipzig.

Büchner, L. 1876, *Kraft und Stoff. Empirisch-naturphilosophische Studien. In allgemeinverständlicher Darstellung* (14th edition with subtitle *Naturphilosophische Untersuchungen auf thatsächliche Grundlage*). Leipzig.

Buckle, H.T. 1857–61, *History of Civilisation in England*, Vols. 1–5. London: Longman.

Bukharin, see Deborin and Bukharin.

Bunge, M. 1973, *Method, Model and Matter*. Dordrecht: Reidel.

Burrow, J.W. 1966, *Evolution and Society. A Study in Victorian Social Theory*. Cambridge: Cambridge University Press.

Butlerow, A.M. 1864–66, *Lehrbuch der organischen Chemie*, Vols. II–III. Leipzig.

Butterfield, H. 1955, *Man on His Past. The Study of the History of Historical Scholarship*. Cambridge: Cambridge University Press.

Butts, R.E. 1968, 'Introduction' to Whewell 1968.

Caldwell, J.W. 1893, 'The Epistemology of Eduard von Hartmann', *Mind*, 2.

Calvez, J-Y. 1956, *La Pensée de Karl Marx*. Paris: Bordas.

Canguilhem, G. 1959, 'Les concepts de "Lutte pour existence" et de "Sélection naturelle" en 1858: Charles Darwin et Alfred Russel Wallace', in *Les Conférences du Palais de la Découverte* 61.

Canguilhem, G. 1965a, 'Le théorie cellulaire', in ibid., *La connaissance de la vie*, 2nd edition. Paris.

Canguilhem, G. 1965b, 'L'idée de médecine expérimentale selon Claude Bernard', in *Les Conférences du Palais de la Découverte* 101.

Cannan, E. 1950, 'Editor's Introduction' to Smith 1950.

Cardwell, D.S.L. 1968, 'John Dalton and the Manchester School of Science', in Dalton 1968.

Cardwell, D.S.L. 1971, *From Watt to Clausius. The Rise of Thermodynamics in the Early Industrial Age*. London: Heinemann.

Cardwell, D.S.L. 1972, *The Organisation of Science in England*. 2nd edition. London: Heinemann.

Carew Hunt, R.N. 1955, *Marxism. Past and Present*. London: Macmillan.

Carpenter, W.D. 1860, 'Darwin and the Origin of Species', *Natural Review*, January.

Carpenter, W.D. 1872, 'Inaugural Address' at the meeting of the British Association at Brighton, in *Nature*, 6, 15 August.

Chambers, R. 1844, *Vestiges of Creation*. London.

Charlton, D.G. 1959, *Positivist Thought in France During the Second Empire 1852–1870*. Westport, CT: Greenwood Press.

Chartier, R., and Roche, D. 1974, 'Le livre. Un changement de perspective', in *Faire de l'histoire*, edited by Le Goff-Nora, Vol. III. Paris: Gallimard.

Clausius, R. 1867, *Über den zweiten Hauptsatz der mechanischen Wärmetheorie. Ein Vortrag*. Braunschweig: Vieweg.

Clausius, R. 1876, *Die mechanische Wärmetheorie*, 2nd edition, Vol. I. Braunschweig: Vieweg.

Clow, A. 'The Industrial Background to John Dalton', in Dalton 1968.

Cole, G.D.H. 1953–56, *A History of Socialist Thought*, Vols. I–III. Basingstoke: Macmillan.

Colman, E. 1931, 'Short Communication on the Unpublished Writings of Karl Marx dealing with Mathematics, the Natural Sciences and Technology', in *Science at the Crossroads* 1931.

Colman, E. 1933, 'Eine neue Grundlegung der Differentialrechnung durch Karl Marx', *Archeion*, 15.

Colp Jr., R. 1974, 'The Contacts between Karl Marx and Charles Darwin', *Journal of the History of Ideas*, 35.

Comte, A. 1968–69 [1830–42], *Oeuvres d'Auguste Comte*, Vols. 1–6.

1. *Les préliminaires généraux et la philosophie mathématique.*

2. *La philosophie chimique et la philosophie biologique.*

3. *Partie dogmatique de la philosophie sociale.*

4. *La partie historique de la philosophie sociale.*

5.   *Complément de la philosophie sociale et contributions générales.*

6.   *Cours de philosophie positive.*

Conry, Y. 1974, *L'introduction du Darwinisme en France au XIXe siècle.* Paris: Vrin.

Cornelius, A. 1958, *Die Geschichtslehre Victor Cousins unter besonderer Berücksichtigung des Hegelschen Einflusses.* Paris: Librairie Minard.

Cornu, A. 1955–70, *Karl Marx et Friedrich Engels*, Vols. 1–4. Paris: PUF.

Coulter, J. 1971, 'Marxism and the Engels Paradox', *The Socialist Register*, 8.

Cournot, A.A. 1851, *Essai sur les fondements de nos connaissances et sur les caractères de la critique philosophique.* Roma: Bizzarri.

Cournot, A.A. 1969, *Essai sur les fondements de nos connaissances et sur les caractères de la critique philosophique*, edited by J-C. Pariente. Roma: Bizzarri.

Crosland, M. 1975, 'The Development of a Professional Career in Science in France', *Minerva*, 13.

Crump, C.G. 1928, *History and Historical Research.* London: Routledge.

Dagognet, F. 1967, *Méthode et doctrines dans l'oeuvre de Pasteur.* Paris.

Dalton 1968, *John Dalton & the Progress of Science. Papers presented to a conference of historians of science held in Manchester*, edited by D.S.L. Cardwell. Manchester: Manchester University Press.

Darlington, C.D. 1959, *Darwin's Place in History.* Oxford: Blackwell.

Darwin, C. 1859, *The Origin of Species by Means of Natural Selection or the Preservation of Favoured Races in the Struggle for Life.* London: John Murray.

Darwin, C. 1871, *The Descent of Man, and Selection in Relation to Sex.* London: John Murray.

Darwin, C. 1872, *The Origin of Species by Means of Natural Selection or the Preservation of Favoured Races in the Struggle for Life*, 6th edition. London: John Murray.

Darwin, C. 1872, *The Origin of Species by Means of Natural Selection or the Preservation of Favoured Races in the Struggle for Life, 1872, The Expression of the Emotions of Man and Animals.* London: John Murray.

Darwin, C. 1887, *The Life and Letters of Charles Darwin. Including an Autobiographical Chapter*, edited by Francis Darwin, Vols. I–III. London: John Murray.

Darwin, C. 1903, *More Letters of Charles Darwin: A Record of his Work in a Series of Hitherto Unpublished Letters*, edited by F. Darwin, A.C. Seward. Vols. I–II. London: John Murray.

Darwin, C. 1958, *The Autobiography of Charles Darwin*, edited by Nora Barlow. London: Collins.

Deborin, A.M. 1924, 'Lukács und seine Kritik des Marxismus', *Arbeiterlitteratur*, 10.

Deborin, A.M., and Bukharin, N. 1969, *Kontroversen über dialektischen und mechanistischen Materialismus. Einleitung von O Negt.* Frankfurt.

Deiters, H. 1960, 'Wilhelm von Humboldt als Gründer der Universität Berlin', in *Forschen und Wirken. Festschrift zur 150-Jahr Feier.* Vol. I. Berlin.

Dewey, J. 1910, *The Influence of Darwin on Philosophy and Other Essays*. New York: H. Holt.

Dicke, G. 1960, *Der Identitätsgedanke bei Feuerbach und Marx*. Köln: Westdeutscher Verlag.

Diderot, D. 1950, *Le neveu de Rameau*, edited by E. Fabre. Genève: Droz.

Diemer, A. 1968a, 'Die Differenzierung der Wissenschaften in die Natur- und Geisteswissenschaften und die Begründung der Gesiteswissenschaften als Wissenschaft', in *Beiträge zur Entwicklung der Wissenschaftstheorie im 19. Jahrhundert. Vorträge und Diskussionen*, edited by A. Diemer. Meisenheim: Verlag Anton Hain.

Diemer, A. 1968b, 'Die Begründung des Wissenschaftscharakters', in *Beiträge zur Entwicklung der Wissenschaftstheorie im 19. Jahrhundert. Vorträge und Diskussionen*, edited by A. Diemer. Meisenheim: Verlag Anton Hain.

Dietzgen, J. 1869, *Das Wesen der menschlichen Kopfarbeit. Dargestellt von einem Handarbeiter*. Hamburg: Meissner.

Dietzgen, J. 1911, *Joseph Dietzgens Sämmtliche Schriften*, edited by E. Dietzgen, Vols. I–III. Berlin: Dietz.

Dietzgen, J. 1961–65, *Schriften in drei Bänden*, edited by Der Arbetsgruppe für Philosophie an der Deutschen Akademie der Wissenschaften zu Berlin. Berlin: Akademie-Verlag.

Dietzgen, J. 1973, *Das Wesen der menschlichen Kopfarbeit und andere Schriften*, edited by H.G. Haasis. Neuwied: Luchterhand.

Dilthey, W. 1911, 'Die Typen der Weltanschauung und ihre Ausbildung in den metaphysischen Systemen', in *Weltanschauung, Philosophie und Religion*. Berlin: Teubner.

Dilthey, W. 1922, *Gesammelte Schriften*, Vol. I: *Einleitung in die Geistwissenschaften*. Leipzig: Teubner.

Dilthey, W. 1924a, *Gesammelte Schriften*, Vol. V: *Ideen über eine beschreibende und zergliedernde Psychologie*. Leipzig: Teubner.

Dilthey, W. 1924b, *Beiträge zum Studium der Individualität*. Leipzig: Teubner.

Dilthey, W. 1960, *Der Junge Dilthey: Ein Lebensbild in Briefe und Tagebüchern 1852–1870*, edited by Clara (Dilthey) Misch, 2nd edition. Leipzig: Teubner.

Dixon, H.B. 1893, 'Memoirs of the late Carl Schorlemmer, LLD, FRS, FCS', in *Memoirs and Proceedings of the Manchester Literary and Philosophical Society*, Fourth Series, Vol. VII. Manchester.

Dobb, M. 1973, *Theories of Values and Distribution since Adam Smith. Ideology and Economic Theory*. Cambridge: Cambridge University Press.

van Dooren, W. 1965, *Het Totalitetsbegrip bij Hegel en zijn Voorgangers*. Dissertation, Assen.

Dorpladen, A. 1965, *Heinrich von Treitschke*. Princeton: Princeton University Press.

Drews, A. 1902, *Eduard von Hartmanns philosophisches System im Grundriss*. Heidelberg: Winter.

Driesch, H. 1905, *Der Vitalismus als Geschichte und als Lehre*. Leipzig: Barth.

Droysen, J.G. 1863, 'Die Erhebung der Geschichte zum Rang einer Wissenschaft', *Historische Zeitschrift*, 9 (also in Droysen 1868 and 1937).

Droysen, J.G. 1868, *Grundriss der Historik*. Leipzig.

Droysen, J.G. 1937, *Historik. Vorlesungen über Enzyklopädie und Methodologie der Geschichte*, edited by R. Hübner. Berlin.

Du Bois-Reymond, E. 1848, *Untersuchungen über thierische Elektrizität*, Vol. I. Berlin.

Du Bois-Reymond, E. 1872, *Über de Grenzen des Naturerkennens. Ein Vortrag in der zweiten öffentlichen Sitzung der 45. Versammlung deutscher Naturforscher und Aerzte zu Leipzig am 14. August 1872* (also in Du Bois-Reymond 1886). Leipzig.

Du Bois-Reymond, E. 1886–87, *Reden*, Vols. I–II. Leipzig.

Duby, G. 1974, 'Histoire sociale et ideologies de societés', in *Faire de l'histoire*, edited by Le Goff-Nora. Vol. I. Paris: Gallimard.

Duchesneau, F. 1975, 'Organisme et théorie cellulaire', *Revue philosophique de la France et de l'étranger*, 2.

Dühring, E. 1865, *Natürliche Dialektik. Neue logische Grundlegungen der Wissenschaft und Philosophie*. Berlin.

Dühring, E. 1867, 'Marx, *Das Kapital*', *Ergänzungsblätter zur Kenntniss der Gegenwart*, 3.

Dühring, E. 1875, *Cursus der Philosophie als streng wissenschaftlichen Weltanschauung und Lebensgestaltung*. Leipzig: Koschny.

Dühring, E. 1875, *Kritische Geschichte der Nationalökonomie und des Socialismus*, 2nd edition. Leipzig.

Dühring, E. 1876, *Cursus der National- und Socialökonomie*, 2nd edition. Leipzig: Koschny.

Dühring, E. 1877, *Der Weg zur höheren Berufsbildung der Frau und die Lehrweise der Universität*. Leipzig.

Dühring, E. 1878, *Neue Grundgesetze zur rationellen Physik und Chemie. Erste Folge*. Leipzig.

Dühring, E. 1903, *Sache, Leben und Feinde. Als Hauptwerk und Schlüssel zu seinen sämmtlichen Schriften*, 2nd edition. Leipzig.

Easlea, B. 1973, *Liberation and the Aims of Science. An Essay on Obstacles to the Building of a Beautiful World*. London: Chatto and Windus.

Eco. U. 1984, *Semiotics and the Philosophy of Language*. Indiana: Bloomington.

Eisler, R. 1910, 'Historismus', in *Wörterbuch der philosophischen Begriffe*, Vol. I. Berlin: Mitter & Sohn.

Elkana, Y. 1974, *The Discovery of the Conservation of Energy*. Cambridge, MA: Harvard University Press.

Ellegård, A. 1957, 'The Darwinian Revolution and Nineteenth-Century Philosophy of Science', *Journal of the History of Ideas*, 18.

Ellegård, A. 1958, *Darwin and the General Reader*. New York: Scribner.

Elzinga, A. 1972, *The Growth of Knowledge. Some notes on possible historiographical novels*. Göteborg.

Elzinga, A. 1973, *Objectivity and Partisanship in Science*. Göteborg: Stencil.

Endemann, W. 1974, 'Einleitung' to Marx 1974.

Engel-Janosi, F. 1944, *The Growth of German Historicism*. Baltimore: Johns Hopkins University Press.

Engels, F. 1900, Letter to F.A. Lange, 2 March 1865; reproduced in *Die Neue Zeit*, 28.

Engels, F. 1927, 'Dialektik und Natur', in *Marx-Engels Archiv*, Vol. II, edited by D. Riazanov. Frankfurt.

In MECW, works by Engels:

Vol. 2:	'Schelling on Hegel', 1841.
	'Schelling and Revelation', 1842.
	'Schelling, Philosopher in Christ', 1842.
	'Alexander Jung. Lectures on Modern German Literature', 1842.
	Letters, 1838–42.
Vol. 3:	'Outlines of a Critique of Political Economy', 1844.
Vol. 4:	*The Condition of the Working-Class in England*, 1845.
Vol. 6:	'Principles of Communism', 1847.
Vol. 10:	*The Peasant War in Germany*, 1850.
Vol. 11:	'Revolution and Counter-Revolution in Germany', 1851–52.
Vol. 16:	'Karl Marx, A Contribution to the Critique of Political Economy, I–II', 1859.
Vol. 20:	Articles and Review written in connection with the publication of Volume I of *Capital*, 1867–68.
	'Karl Marx', 1869.
Vol. 24:	'Karl Marx', 1878.
	Socialism: Utopian and Scientific, 1880.
	'On the Death of Karl Marx', 1883.
Vol. 25:	*Herr Eugen Dühring's Revolution in Science (Anti-Dühring)*, 1877–78.
	Dialectics of Nature, 1873–86.
Vol. 26:	*The Origins of Family, Private Property, and the State*, 1884.
	Ludwig Feuerbach and the End of Classical German Philosophy, 1886.
Vol. 27:	'Carl Schorlemmer', 1892.
	'To the International Congress of Socialist Students', 1894.
Vols. 38–50	Letters, 1844–1895.

Engels, F., Lafargue, P., and Lafargue, L. *Corréspondence*, edited by É. Bottigelli, Vols. I–III, 1956–59.

Engels, F. See also Gemkow.

Engels, F. See also Marx and Engels.

Enss, A. 1877, *Engels Attentat auf den gesunden Menschenverstand oder Der wissenschaftliche Bankerott im Marxistischen Sozialismus. Ein offener Brief an meine Freunde in Berlin*. Grand-Sacconer: Selbstverlag.

Erlenmeyer, F. 1867, *Lehrbuch der organischen Chemie*. Leipzig: Winter.

Fairchild, H.N. 1928, *The Noble Savage*. New York: Columbia University Press.

Falkenheim, H. 1892, *Kuno Fischer und die litteraturhistorische Methode*. Berlin: Verlag Speyer & Peters.

Farley, J. 1974, 'The Initial Reactions of French Biologists to Darwin's *Origin of Species*', *History of Biology*, 7.

Farr, W. 1885, *Vital Statistics, a Memorial Volume of Selections from the Reports and Writings of William Farr*, edited by N.A. Humphreys. London: Sanitary Institute.

Fawcett, H. 1860, 'A Popular Exposition of Mr. Darwin on the "Origin of Species"', *MacMillan's Magazine*, 3.

Fetscher, I. 1967, *Karl Marx und der Marxismus*. München: Piper.

Feuerbach, L. *Sämtliche Werke. Neu herausgegeben von W Bolin und F Jodl. 2 undveränderte Auflage*. Stuttgart: Bad Cannstatt.

Vol. 2: *Philosophische Kritiken und Grundsätz*, 1843.

Vol. 6: *Das Wesen des Christenthums*, 1841.

Vol. 7: *Erläuterungen und Ergänzungen zum Wesen des Christenthums*, 1846.

Fichte, J.G. *Sämmtliche Werke*, edited by I.H. Fichte. Berlin: De Gruyter.

Vol. I/1: *Erste Einleitung in die Wissenschaftslehre* (1797), 1845.

Fichte, J.G. 1910, 'Deducirter Plan einer zu erreichenden höheren Lehranstalt', in Spranger 1910.

Fichte, J.G. 1960 [1910], in *Idee und Wirklichkeit einer Universität. Dokumente zur Geschichte der Friedrich-Wilhelm-Universität zu Berlin*, edited by W. Weischedel. Berlin: De Gruyter.

Fischer, K. 1854–77, *Geschichte der neueren Philosophie*, Vols. I–IX. Mannheim: Bassermann.

Flexner, A. 1968 [1930], *Universities. American, English, German*. London: Oxford University Press.

Forbes, R.J. 1958, *Studies in Early Petroleum History*. Westport, CT: Hyperion Press.

Forbes, R.J. 1959, *More Studies in Early Petroleum History 1860–1880*. Westport, CT: Hyperion Press.

Fortlage, K. 1955, *System der Psychologie als empirischer Wissenschaft aus der Betrachtung des innern Sinnes*, Vols. I–II. Leipzig: Brockhaus.

Foucault, M. 1966, *Les mots et les choses. Une archéologie des science humaines*. Paris: France Loisirs.

Fraas, C. 1847, *Klima und Pflanzenwelt in der Zeit. Ein Beitrag zur Geschichte beider*. Landshut.

Frankland, E. 1902, *Autobiographical Sketches from the Life of Sir Edward Frankland (1825–1899)*. London.

Frazer, J.G. 1905, *Lectures on the Early History of the Kingship*. London: Macmillan.

Freudenthal, H. 1975, 'Quetelet, Lambert-Adolphe-Jacques', in *Dictionary of Scientific Biography*, edited by C.G. Gillispie, Vol. XI. New York: Scribner.

Fricke, D. 1964, *Die deutsche Arbeiterbewegung. Ihre Organisation und Tätigkeit 1965– 1890*. Leipzig: VEB Verlag Enzyklopädie.

Galton, F. 1869, *Hereditary Genius. An Inquiry into its Laws and Consequences*. London: Macmillan.

Gasking, E. 1959, 'Why was Mendel's Work Ignored?' *Journal of the History of Ideas*, 20.

Gay, P. 1967–70, *Enlightenment: An Interpretation*, Vols. I–II. New York: Knopf.

Gedö, A. 1960, 'Zu einigen theoretischen Problemen der ideologischen Klassenkampfes der Gegenwart', in *Georg Lukács und der Revisionismus*. Berlin.

Geldsetzer, L. 1968, *Die Philosophie der Philosophiegeschichte im 19. Jahrhundert. Zur Wissenschaftstheorie der Philosophiegeschichtsschreibung und -behandlung*. Meisenheim am Glan: Hain.

Gemkow, H. et al. 1970, *Friedrich Engels. Eine Biographie*. Berlin: Dietz.

Gerratana, V. 1973, 'Marx and Darwin', *New Left Review*, 82.

Geschichte der deutschen Arbeiterbewegung 1966, Vol. I. Berlin: Institute for Marxism-Leninism.

Ghiselin, M. 1969, *The Triumph of Darwinian Method*. Berkeley: University of California Press.

Gilbert, F. 'European and American Historiography', in Higham 1965.

Gillet, C. 2016, *Reduction and Emergence in Science and Philosophy*. Cambridge: Cambridge University Press.

Gillispie, C.F. 1951, *Genesis and Geology*. New York: Harper.

Gooch, C.P. 1959 [1913], *History and Historians in the Nineteenth Century*. Boston: Beacon Press.

Goyard-Fabre, S. 1972, *La philosophie des lumières en France*. Paris: Librairie Klinksieck.

Greene, J.C. 1959, *The Death of Adam*. New York: Mentor Books.

Greene, J.C. 1963, *Darwin and the Modern World View*. Louisiana: New American Library.

Greene, J.C. 1975, 'Reflections on the Progress of Darwinian Studies', *Journal of the History of Biology*, 8.

Grimaux, L-E. 1885, 'Les substances colloïdales et la coagulation', *Revue scientifique*. 3me série, LX.

Grimm, J. 1821, *Deutsche Grammatik*, Vol. I, 2nd edition. Berlin.

Grmek, M.D. 1972, *Raisonnement experimentale et recherches toxicologiques chez Claude Bernard*. Lille.

Grove, W.R. 1855, *On the Correlation of Physical Forces*, 3rd edition. London.

Grujić, P.M. 1969, *Hegel und die Sowjetphilosophie der Gegenwart*. Bern: Francke.

Habermas, J. 1968, *Erkenntnis und Interesse*. Frankfurt: Suhrkamp.

Habermas, J. 1968, *Technik und Wissenschaft als 'Ideologie'*. Frankfurt: Suhrkamp.

Habermas, J. 1971, *Theorie und Praxis. Sozialphilosophische Studien*, 4th edition. Frankfurt: Suhrkamp.

Hacking, I. 1970, 'Bayes, Thomas', in *Dictionary of Scientific Biography*, Vol. I. New York: Scribner.

Haeckel, E. 1866, *Allgemeine Morphologie der Organismen. Allgemeine Grundzüge der Formen-Wissenschaft, mechanisch begründet durch die von Charles Darwin reformierte Deszendenz-Theorie*, Vols. I–II. Berlin: De Gruyter.

Haeckel, E. 1868, *Natürliche Schöpfungsgeschichte. Gemeinverständliche wissenschaftliche Vorträge über die Entwicklungslehre im Allgemeinen und diejenige von Darwin, Goethe und Lamarck im Besonderen*. Berlin: Reimer.

Haeckel, E. 1868, *Über die Entstehung und den Stammbaum des Menschengeschlechts*. Berlin.

Haeckel, E. 1873, 4th edition of *Natürliche Schöpfungsgeschichte*. Berlin.

Haeckel, E. 1874, *Anthropogenie oder Entwicklungsgeschichte des Mensch. Gemeinverständliche wissenschaftliche Vorträge*. Leipzig: Engelmann.

Haeckel, E. 1878, *Freie Wissenschaft und freie Lehre. Eine Entgegnung auf Rudolf Virchows Münchener Rede über 'Die Freiheit der Wissenschaft im modernen Staat'*. Stuttgart.

Haeckel, E. 1902, 10th edition of *Natürliche Schöpfungsgeschichte*. Berlin.

Haeckel, E. 1905, *Der Kampf um den Entwicklungsgedanken*. Berlin.

Hager, K. 1960, 'Die Weltanschauung Carl Schorlemmers', in *Forschen und Wirken. Festschrift zur 150-Jahrfeier der Humboldt-Universität zu Berlin*, Vol. III. Berlin.

Hagstrom, W.O. 1965, *The Scientific Community*. New York: Basic Books.

Hahn, E. 1964, 'Marxismus und Ideologie', *Deutsche Zeitschrift für Philosophie*, 12.

Haines IV, G. 1957, *German Influence on Education and Science, 1810–1866*. New London: Conneticut College.

Halbfass, W. 1968, *Descartes' Frage nach der Existenz der Welt*. Meisenheim am Glan: Hain.

Haller, H.R. 1968, *Gustav Wolff (1865–1941) und sein Beitrag zur Lehre vom Vitalismus*. Basel.

von Hartmann, E. 1868, *Über die dialektische Methode*. Berlin: Duncker.

von Hartmann, E. 1869, *Philosophie des Unbewussten. Versuch einer Weltanschauung*. Berlin: Duncker.

von Hartmann, E. 1872, *Das Unbewusste vom Standpunkt der Physiologie und Deszendenztheorie*. Berlin: Duncker.

von Hartmann, E. 1875, *Wahrheit und Irrthum im Darwinismus*. Berlin: Duncker.

von Hartmann, E. 1876, *Gesammelte Studien und Aufsätze gemeinverständlichen Inhalts*. Berlin: Duncker.

von Hartmann, E. 1877, *Das Unbewusste vom Standpunkt der Physiologie und Deszendenztheorie*, 2nd edition, signed by the author. Berlin: Duncker.

von Hartmann, E. 1885, *Philosophische Fragen der Gegenwart*. Leipzig: Friedrich.

von Hartmann, E. 1888, *Lotzes Philosophie*. Leipzig: Friedrich.

von Hartmann, E. 1896, *Kategorienlehre*. Leipzig: Haacke.

von Hartmann, E. 1906, *Das Problem des Lebens*. Bad Sachs im Harz: Hermann Haacke.

von Hartmann, E. 1907, *System der Philosophie im Grundriss*. Vol II: *Grundriss der Naturphilosophie*. Bad Sachs im Harz: Hermann Haacke.

von Hartmann, E. 1910 [1877], *Neukantianismus, Schopenhauerianismus und Hegelianismus*, 3rd edition. Bad Sachs im Harz: Hermann Haacke.

Hartmann, K. 1970, *Die Marxsche Theorie. Eine philosophische Untersuchung zu den Hauptschriften*. Berlin: De Gruyter.

Hartog, P.J. 1897, 'Schorlemmer, Carl', in *Dictionary of Scientific Biography*, Vol. L. New York: Scribner.

von Haxthausen, A. 1842, *Über den Ursprung und die Grundlagen der Verfassung in den ehemals slavischen Ländern Deutschlands im Allgemeinen und des Herzogthums Pommern in Besonderen*. Berlin: Krause.

von Haxthausen, A. 1847–52, *Studien über die inneren Zustände, das Volksleben und insbesondere de ländlichen Einrichtungen Russlands*, Vols. I–III. Hannover.

Häusser, L. 1859, 'Macaulay's *Friedrich der Grosse*. Mit einem Nachtrag über Carlyle', *Historische Zeitschrift*, 1.

Hayek, F.A. 1952, *The Counter-Revolution of Science. Studies on the Abuse of Reason*. New York: The Free Press.

Hegel, G.W.F. 1929–41, *Sämtliche Werke. Jubiläumsausgabe in zwanzig Bänden. Neu herausgegeben von Hermann Glockner*. Stuttgart: Frommann.
Vol. 2: *Phänomenologie des Geistes*, 1807.
Vol. 3: *Philosophische Propädeutik*, 1810.
Vols. 4–5: *Wissenschaft der Logik I–II*, 1812–16.
Vol. 6: *Heidelberger Enzyklopädie*, 1817.
Vol. 7: *Rechtsphilosophie*, 1821.
Vols. 8–10: *System der Philosophie I–III*, 1841.
Vol. 11: *Geschichtsphilosophie*, 1837.
Vols. 17–19: *Geschichte der Philosophie*, 1837.

Hegel-Lexikon 1957, H. Glockner (also Vols. 23–25 of Hegel 1929–41).

Hegel, K. 1861, Review of G. Waitz, *Deutsche Verfassungsgeschichte*, Vol. 3 (1860), *Historische Zeitschrift*, 5.

Heinig, K. 1971, 'Über das Verhältnis der deutschen Chemiker des 19. Jahrhunderts zur Hegelschen Philosophie', in *Wissenschaftliche Zeitschrift der Humboldt-Universität zu Berlin. Mathematik/Naturwissenschaften*, K XX.

Heinig, K. 1974, *Carl Schorlemmer, Chemiker und Kommunist ersten Ranges*. Leipzig: Teubner.

Heintel, P. 1967, *System und Ideologie. Der Austromarxismus im Spiegel der Philosophie Max Adlers*. Wien: Oldenbourg.

von Hellwald, F. 1883, *Kulturgeschichte in ihrer natürlichen Entwicklung bis zum Gegenwart*, Vols. I–II (1874), 3rd edition. Augsburg: Lampart & Comp.

Helmholtz, H. 1847, *Über die Erhaltung der Kraft* (also in Helmholtz 1882). Berlin: Reimer.

Helmholtz, H. 1876, *Populäre wissenschaftliche Vorträge*, Vols I–II (1865), 2nd edition. Braunschweig: Vieweg.

Helmholtz, H. 1878, *Über die akademische Freiheit der deutschen Universitäten. Rede, etc*. Berlin.

Helmholtz, H. 1882–95, *Wissenschaftliche Abhandlungen*, Vols I–III. Berlin.

Helmholtz, H. 1976, *Epistemological Writings*, edited by R.S. Cohen and Y. Elkana. Boston.

Henderson, W.O. 1976, *The Life of Friedrich Engels*, Vols. I–II. London: Cass.

Henle, J. 1844, *Allgemeine Anatomie*. Leipzig.

Herbst, J. 1965, *The German Historical School in American Scholarship. A Study in the Transfer of Culture*. Ithaca: Cornell University Press.

Herder, J.G. 1784–91, *Ideen zur Philosophie der Geschichte der Menschheit*, Vols. I–IV. Riga/Leipzig.

Herneck, F. 1960, 'Emil du Bois-Reymond und die Grenzen der mechanistischen Naturauffassung', *Forschen und Wirken. Festschrift zur 150-Jahrfeier der Humboldt-Universität zu Berlin*, I.

Herschel, J. 1830, *Preliminary Discourse on the Study of Natural Philosophy*. London.

Herschel, J. 1850, Review of Quetelet 1846, in *Edinburgh Review*, 185, and in French translation in Quetelet 1869, Vol. I.

Herschel, J. 1966, Facsimile edition of Herschel 1830 with a new 'Introduction' by M. Partridge. New York: Johnson.

Hesse, M.B. 1961, *Forces and Fields. The Concept of Action at a Distance in the History of Physics*. London: Thomas Nelson & Sons.

Heussi, K. 1932, *Die Krisis des Historismus*. Tübingen.

Heyer, P. 1975, *Marx and Darwin: A Related Legacy on Man, Nature and Society*, Dissertation manuscript, Rutgers University, Microfilm 75–24695.

Hiebert, E.N. 1962, *The Historical Roots of the Principle of the Conservation of Energy*. Madison: The State Historical Society of Wisconsin.

Higham, J., with Krieger, L. and Gilbert, F. 1965, *History*. Englewood Cliffs, NJ: Prentice-Hall.

Himmelfarb, G. 1959, *Darwin and the Darwinian Revolution*. Garden City: Doubleday.

Histoire générale du socialisme 1972–74, edited by J. Droz, Vols. I–II. Paris: PUF.

Hodges, H.A. 1952, *The Philosophy of Wilhelm Dilthey*. London: Routledge.

Hofmeister, W. 1867, *Handbuch der physiologischen Botanik*, Vol. I. Leipzig: Engelmann.

Hofstadter, R. 1955 [1944], *Social Darwinism in American Thought, 1860–1915*. Philadelphia: University of Pennsylvania Press.

Holmes, F.L. 1974, *Claude Bernard and Animal Chemistry. The Emergence of a Scientist.* Cambridge, MA: Harvard University Press.

Hook, S. 1933, *Towards the Understanding of Karl Marx: A Revolutionary Interpretation.* New York: The John Day Company.

Hook, S. 1958 [1950], *From Hegel to Marx. Studies in the Intellectual Development of Karl Marx.* Ann Arbor: University of Michigan Press.

Hopkins, W. 1860, 'Physical Theories of the Phenomena of Life', *Fraser's Magazine*, 61.

Horkheimer, M. 1974 [1930], 'Ein neuer Ideologibegriff', reprinted in *Ideologienlehre und Wissenssoziologie. Die Diskussion um das Ideologieproblem in den zwanzigen Jahren*, edited by H-J. Lieber. Darmstadt.

Horowitz, I.L. 1961, *Philosophy, Society and the Sociology of Science.* Springfield, IL: Charles C. Thomas.

Howrath, O.J.R. 1931, *The British Association for the Advancement of Science 1831–1931.* London.

Hull, D.L. (ed.) 1973, *Darwin and His Critics. The Reception of Darwin's Theory of Evolution by the Scientific Community.* Cambridge, MA: Harvard University Press.

von Humboldt, W. 1822, 'Über die Aufgabe des Geschichtsschreibers', in *Abhandlungen der Historisch-philosophischen Klasse der Königlichen Preussischen Akademie der Wissenschaften zu Berlin 1820–21*, 4.

Huxley, J. 1924, 'The Outlook in Biology', *The Rice Institute Pamphlets*, 11.

Huxley, J. 1942, *Evolution. The Modern Synthesis.* New York: Harper.

Huxley, L. 1903 [1900], *Life and Letters of Thomas Henry Huxley*, Vols. I–III. New York: Appleton.

Huxley, T.H. 1863, *Man's Place in Nature.* New York: Hurst & Co.

Huxley, T.H. 1874, 'On the Hypothesis that Animals are Automats, and Its History', *Nature*, 10.

Huxley, T.H. 1887, 'On the Reception of *Origin of Species*', in Darwin 1887, Vol. II.

Huxley, T.H. 1897, *Hume: With Helps to the Study of Berkeley. Collected Essays*, Vol. VI. New York: Appleton.

Hyppolite, J. 1971, 'Le "scientifique" et "l'idéologique" dans une perspective marxiste', *Fiogures de la pensée philosophique*, I.

Idee und Wirklichkeit einer Universität. Dokumente zur Geschichte der Friedrich-Wilhelm-Universität zu Berlin 1960, edited by W. Weischedel. Berlin: De Gruyter.

Ideologie. Ideologiekritik und Wissenssoziologie 1967, edited by K. Lenk, 3rd edition. Neuwied: Luchterhand.

Ideologie und Naturwissenschaft 1969, edited by G. Domin and R. Mocek. Berlin.

Ideologienlehre und Wissenssoziologie. Die Diskussion um das Ideologie-problem in den zwanzigen Jahren 1974, edited by H-J. Lieber. Darmstadt.

'Ideologiia' 1972, in *Bol'shaia Sovietskaia Entsiklopediia*, Vol. 10.

Ideology in Social Science. Readings in Critical Social Theory 1972, edited by R. Blackburn. London: Fontana.

Iggers, G.G. 1972, *Deutsche Geschichtswissenschaft. Eine Kritik der traditionellen Ge-schichtsauffassung von Herder bis zu Gegenwart*. Munich: Deutscher Taschenbuch Verlag.

Ilyenkov, E.V. 1969, 'Die Dialektik des Abstrakten und Konkreten im *Kapital* von Marx', in *Beiträge zur marxistischen Erkenntnistheorie*, edited by A. Schmidt. Frankfurt: Suhrkamp.

Ineichen, H. 1975, 'Von der ontologischen Diltheyinterpretation zur Wissenschaftsthe-orie in praktischer Arbeit. Neue Dilthey-litteratur', *Philosophische Rundschau*, 22.

Interpretations of Life and Mind: Essays Around the Problem of Reduction 1971, edited by M. Greene. London.

d'Irsay, S. 1932, *Histoire des universités françaises et etrangères*, Vol. II. Paris: Picard.

Jay, M. 1973, *The Dialectical Imagination. A History of the Frankfurt School and the Insti-tute of Social Research*. Berkeley: University of California Press.

Jenkin, F. 1867, 'The Origin of Species', *The North British Review*, 46.

Jenkins, M. 1951, *Frederick Engels in Manchester*. Manchester.

Jensen, J.V. 1970, 'The X Club. Fraternity of Victorian Scientists', *British Journal for the History of Science*, 5.

Johach, H. 1974, *Handelnder Mensch und objektiver Geist. Zur Theorie der Geistes- und Sozialwissenschaften bei Wilhelm Dilthey*. Meisenheim am Glan: Hain.

Johnston, J.F.W. 1847, *Lectures on Agricultural Chemistry and Geology*. New York: Wiley & Putnam.

Jones, B. 1971, *The Royal Institution*. London.

Jones, M. 1974, *Darwinism and Social Thought: A Study of the Relationship between a Science and the Development of Social Thought in England, 1860–1914*.

Jordan, Z.A. 1967, *The Evolution of Dialectical Materialism. A Philosophical and Sociolo-gical Analysis*. London: Macmillan.

Jorpes, E. 1970, *Jöns Jacob Berzelius: His Life and Work*. Stockholm: Almqvist & Wiksell.

Jukes, J.B. 1862, *The Student's Manual of Geology*. Edinburgh.

Jung, A. 1842, 'Ein Bonbon für den kleinen Oswald, meinen Gegner in den deutschen Jarhbücher', *Königsberger Literatur-Blatt*, 42.

Kamenka, E. 1970, *The Philosophy of Ludwig Feuerbach*. London: Routledge.

Kant, I. *Gesammelte Schriften. Herausgegeben von der Königlichen Preussischen Akade-mie der Wissenschaften*. Berlin: Reimer.

  Vol. 4: *Metaphysische Anfangsgründe der Naturwissenschaft* (1786), 1903.

  Vol. 5: *Kritik der Urteilskraft* (1790), 1908.

Kautsky, K. 1960, *Erinnerungen und Erörterungen von Karl Kautsky*, edited by B. Kautsky. The Hague: Mouton.

Kedrov, B.M. 1971, *Engel's o khimii*. Moscow.

Keeling, S. 1968, *Descartes*. Oxford: Oxford University Press.

Kekulé, A. 1859–87, *Lehrbuch der organischen Chemie oder Chemie der Kohlenstoffver-bindungen*, Vols. I–IV. Erlangen: Enke.

Kekulé, A. 1878, *Die wissenschaftliche Ziele und Leistungen der Chemie. Rede gehalten beim Antritt des Rectorats der Rheinischen Friedrich-Wilhelms-Universität am 18. Oktober 1877*. Leipzig.

Kerr, C. 1961, 'Remembering Flexner', in Flexner 1961.

Kessel, E. 1955, 'Wilhelm von Humboldt und die deutsche Universität', *Studium generale*, VIII.

Kessel, E. 1963, 'Zur Geschichte der philosophischen Fakultät', *Studium generale*, XVI.

Kirchhoff, G. 1877 [1874], *Vorlesungen über mathematische Physik. Mechanik*, 2nd edition. Leipzig: Teubner.

Kirchhoff, G. 1968, *Die Klassifikation der Wissenschaften als philosophisches Problem*, Autorenkollektiv, edited by R. Rochhausen. Berlin: Deutscher Verlag der Wissenschaften.

Klaus, G. 1966, *Kybernetik und Erkenntnistheorie*. Berlin: Deutscher Verlag der Wissenschaften.

Klaus, G. 1972 [1965], *Moderne Logik. Abriss der formalen Logik*, 6th edition. Berlin: Deutscher Verlag der Wissenschaften.

Klein, M. 1936, *Histoire des origines de la théorie cellulaire*. Paris: Hermann & Co.

Knowles, D. 1963, *Great Historical Enterprises*. London: Nelson.

Koch, H. 1960, 'Theorie und Politik bei Georg Lukács', in *Georg Lukács und der Revisionismus*. Berlin: Verlag für Kultur und Politik.

Koeber, S. 1884, *Das philosophische System Eduard von Hartmanns*. Breslau: Koebner.

Kofman, S. 1973, *Camera obscura de l'idéologie*. Paris: Gililée.

Kołakowski, L. 1968 [1966], *Positivist Philosophy. From Hume to the Vienna Circle*. Harmondsworth: Penguin.

Kölliker, A. 1861, *Entwicklungsgeschichte der Menschen und der höheren Thiere. Akademische Vorlesungen*. Leipzig.

Kölliker, A. 1864, *Über de Darwinsche Schöpfungstheorie. Ein ... Vortrag*. Leipzig.

Kölliker, A. 1872, *Morphologie und Entwicklungsgeschichte des Pennatudilenstammes nebst allgemeinen Betrachtungen zur Deszendenzlehre*. Leipzig: Teubner.

Kölliker, A. 1861, *Entwicklungsgeschichte der Menschen und der höheren Thiere. Akademische Vorlesungen*, 2nd edition. Leipzig.

König, G. 1968, 'Der Wissenschaftsbegriff bei Helmholtz und Mach', in *Beiträge zur Entwicklung der Wissenschaftstheorie im 19. Jahrhundert. Vorträge und Diskussionen*, edited by A. Diemer. Meisenheim: Verlag Anton Hain.

König, R. 1935, *Vom Wesen der deutschen Universität*. Leipzig: Quelle & Meyer.

Kopp, H. 1843–47, *Geschichte der Chemie*, Vols. I–IV. Braunschweig: Vieweg.

Kopp, H. 1866, *Die Alchemie in älterer und neuerer Zeit*, Vols. I–II. Heidelberg: Winter.

Korsch, K. 1963 [1938], *Karl Marx*. New York: Russell & Russell.

Krader, L. 1972, 'Introduction' to Marx 1972.

Krieger, L. 1975, 'Elements in Early Historicism: Experience, Theory, and History in Ranke', *History and Theory*, 14.

Kuhn, T.S. 1955, 'Energy Conservation as an Example of Simultaneous Discovery', in *Critical Problems in the History of Science*, edited by M. Clagett. Madison: University of Wisconsin Press.

Kuhn, T.S. 1970 [1962], *The Structure of Scientific Revolutions*, 2nd edition. Chicago: University of Chicago Press.

Kusch, M. 1995, *Psychologism: A Case Study in the Sociology of Philosophical Knowledge*. London: Routledge.

Lakatos, I. 1970, 'Falsification and the Methodology of Scientific Research Programmes', in *Criticism and the Growth of Knowledge*, edited by I. Lakatos and A. Musgrave. Cambridge: Cambridge University Press.

Lamprecht, K.L. 1902 [1896], *Alte und neue Richtungen in der Geschichtswissenschaft*. Berlin: Heyfelder.

Lamprecht, K.L. 1891, *Deutsche Geschichte*, Vol. I, 3rd edition. Berlin: Gärtner.

Landauer, G. 1959, *European Socialism. A History of Ideas and Movements*, Vol. I. Berkeley: University of California Press.

Landes, D.S. 1965, 'Technological Change and Development in Western Europe', *The Cambridge History of Europe*, 6, no. 1.

Landgrebe, L. 1965, 'Das Problem der Dialektik', *Marxismus-Studien*, 3.

Lange, F.A. 1865, *Die Arbeiterfrage in ihrer Bedeutung für Gegenwart und Zukunft*. Duisburg.

Lange, F.A. 1866, *Geschichte des Materialismus und Kritik seiner Bedeutung in der Gegenwart*. Leipzig.

Lange, F.A. 1876, *Geschichte des Materialismus und Kritik seiner Bedeutung in der Gegenwart*, 3rd edition, Vols. I–II. Leipzig.

Lange, F.A. 1968, *Über Politik und Philosophie. Briefe und Leitartikel 1862 bis 1875*, edited by G. Eckert. Duisburg: Braun.

Langlois, V. and Seignobos, C. 1898, *Introduction aux études historiques*. Paris: Hachette.

de Laplace, P.S. 1920, *Essai philosophique sur les probabilités. Éd. nouvelle avec une introduction par XT Bayle*. Paris: Chiron.

de Laplace, P.S. 1969, 'Om sannolikhet'. Swedish translation of Laplace 1920.

von Laue, T. 1950, *Leopold Ranke. The Formative Years*. Princeton: Princeton University Press.

Laurent, A. 1854, *Méthode de Chimie*. Paris: Mallet-Bachelier.

Lefebvre, H. 1957 [1939], *Le matérialisme dialectique*, 4th edition. Paris: PUF.

Lefebvre, H. 1968 [1966], *Marx sociologi*, Swedish translation of Lefebvre 1957.

Leiser, W. 1967, *Geschichte als politische Wissenschaft. GL von Maurer*.

Lenin, V.I. 1961–64, *Sochineniia*, 4th edition, Moscow; German translation: *Werke*, 1961–64. Berlin.

Vol. 5: *What Is To Be Done?* (1902).

Vol. 14: *Materialism and Empiriocriticism* (1908).

Vol. 25: *State and Revolution* (1917).

Vol. 38: *Philosophical Notebooks*.

Lenzen, V.F. 1947, 'Helmholtz's Theory of Knowledge', in *Studies and Essays in the History of Science and Learning Offered to George Sarton*, edited by A. Montagu. New York: Schuman.

Leontiev, L.A. 1970, *Engels und die ökonomische Lehre des Marxismus*. Translated from the Russian. Berlin: Akademie Verlag.

Levere, T.H. 1971, *Affinity and Matter. Elements of Chemical Philosophy 1800–1865*. Oxford: Clarendon Press.

Levine, N. 1975, *The Tragic Deception: Marx Contra Engels*. Oxford: Clio Press.

Lichtheim, G. 1961, *Marxism. A Historical and Critical Study*. New York: Praeger.

Lichtheim, G. 1967, *The Concept of Ideology and Other Essays*. New York: Vintage.

Lichtheim, G. 1970, *A Short History of Socialism*. New York: Praeger.

Lichtheim, G. 1971, *From Marx to Hegel and Other Essays*. New York: Herder and Herder.

Liebig, J. 1840, *Die organische Chemie in ihrer Anwendung auf Agricultur und Physiologie*. Braunschweig.

Liebig, J. 1842, *Die organische Chemie in ihrer Anwendung auf Physiologie und Pathologie*. Braunschweig: Vieweg.

Liebig, J. 1844, *Chemische Briefe*. Leipzig: Winter.

Liebig, J. 1859, *Chemische Briefe*, 4th edition, Vols. I–II. Leipzig: Winter.

Liebknecht, W. 1963, *Briefwechsel mit Karl Marx und Friedrich Engels. Herausgegeben G Eckert*. Berlin: Dietz.

Liedman, S-E. 1966, *Det organiska livet i tysk debatt 1795–1845*. Lund: Berlingska Boktryckeriet.

Liedman, S-E. 1986, *Den synliga handen: Anders Birch och ekonomiämnena vid 1700-talets universitet*. Stockholm: Dialogos.

Lilley, S. 1965 [1962], *Machines and History. The Story of Tools and Machines in Relation to Social Progress*, 2nd edition. London: Lawrence and Wishart.

Lindborg, R. 1965, *Descartes i Uppsala: Striden om "nya filosofin" 1663–1689*. Uppsala: Lychnos-bibliotek.

Littré, E. 1863, *Auguste Comte et la philosophie positive*. Paris: Hachette.

Lobkowicz, N. 1967, *Theory and Practice: History of a Concept from Aristotle to Marx*. Notre Dame: University of Notre Dame Press.

Lottin, J. 1912, *Quetelet Statisticien et Sociologue*. Paris: Alcan.

Lotze, R.H. 1842, *Allgemeine Pathologie und Therapie als mechanische Naturwissenschaft*. Leipzig: Wiedmann.

Lotze, R.H. 1842–53, 'Leben. Lebenskraft', in R. Wagner 1842–53, Vol. I.

Lotze, R.H. 1852, *Medicinische Psychologie oder Physiologie der Seele*. Leipzig: Wiedmann.

Lotze, R.H. 1856–64, *Mikrokosmus. Ideen zur Naturgeschichte und Geschichte der Menschheit*, Vols. I–III. Leipzig: Hirzel.

Lubbock, J. 1865, *Prehistoric Times*. London: Williams and Norgate.

Lubbock, J. 1870, *The Origin of Civilisation*. London: Longmans, Green.

Lukács, G. 1923, *Geschichte und Klassenbewusstsein*. Berlin.

Lukács, G. 1954, *Die Zerstörung der Vernunft*. Berlin.

Lukács, G. 1960, *Die Zerstörung der Vernunft*, 2nd edition. Berlin.

Lukács, G. 1968, *Historia och klassmedvetande*. Swedish translation of Lukács 1923.

Lukács, G. and Brecht, B. 1975, *'Det gäller realismen'. En 30-talsdebatt rekonstruerad av Lars Bjurman*. Staffanstorp: Cavefors.

Lukas, E. 1964, 'Marx' und Engels' Auseinandersetzung mit Darwin: Zur Differenz zwischen Marx und Engels', *International Review of Social History*, 9, no. 3.

McConnaughey, G. 1950, 'Darwin and Social Darwinism', *Osiris*, 9.

McCormmach, R. 1976, 'On Academic Scientists in Wilhelmine Germany', in *Science and Its Public: The Changing Relationship*, edited by G.J. Holton. Dordrecht: Reidel.

MacDonagh, O. 1975, 'Government, Industry and Science in Nineteenth-Century Britain: A Particular Study', *Historical Studies*, 16.

Mach, E. 1872, *Die Geschichte und die Würzel des Satzes von der Erhaltung der Arbeit. Ein Vortrag ....* Prag: Calve.

McKinney, H.L. 1972, *Wallace and Natural Selection*. New Haven: Yale University Press.

McLellan, D. 1971, 'Introduction' to Marx 1971.

McLellan, D. 1973, *Karl Marx. His Life and Thought*. Basingstoke: Macmillan.

MacLeod, R.M. 1970, 'The X Club. A Social Network of Science in Late Victorian England', *Notes and Records of the Royal Society*, 24.

Maine, H.S. 1861, *Ancient Law*. London: John Murray.

Maine, H.S. 1875, *The Effects of the Observation of India on Modern European Thought*. London: John Murray.

Makreel, R. 1975, *Dilthey: Philosopher of the Human Studies*. Princeton: Princeton University Press.

Mandelbaum, M. 1967, 'Historicism', in *Encyclopedia of Philosophy*, edited by P. Edwards. New York: Macmillan.

Mandelbaum, M. 1971, *History, Man & Reason. A Study in Nineteenth-Century Thought*. Baltimore: Johns Hopkins University Press.

Mannheim, K. 1934, 'Wissenssociologie', in *Handwörterbuch der Soziologie*, edited by A. Vierkandt. Stuttgart.

Mannheim, K. 1936 [1929], *Ideology and Utopia*. London: Routledge & Kegan Paul.

Mannheim, K. 1964, *Wissensoziologie. Auswahl aus dem Werk*, edited by K.H. Wolff. Berlin: Luchterland.

Mao, Z. 1974, *Mao Tse-tung Unrehearsed. Talks and Letters: 1956–71*, edited and introduced by Stuart Schram. Harmondsworth: Penguin.

Marcuse, H. 1941, *Reason and Revolution*. London: Milford.

Marcuse, H. 1960, *Reason and Revolution*, 2nd edition. London: Routledge & Kegan Paul.

Marshall, A. 1890, *The Principles of Economy*. London: Macmillan.

Marshall, A. 1897, 'The Old Generation of Economists and the New', *Quarterly Journal of Economics*, 11.

Marshall, A. 1925, *Memorials of Alfred Marshall*, edited by A.C. Pigou. London: Macmillan.

Martin, T. 1941, *The Royal Institution*. London: Longmans, Green and Co.

Marwick, A. 1970, *The Nature of History*. London: Macmillan.

Marx, K. 1887, *Capital: A Critical Analysis of Capitalist Production*, translated from the Third German Edition by Samuel Moore and Edward Aveling, and edited by Frederick Engels, Vols. I–II. London: Sonnenschein, Lowrey & Co.

Marx, K. 1903, 'Einleitung zur Kritik der politischen Ökonomie' ('Einleitung' to Marx 1953), *Die Neue Zeit*, 31.

Marx, K. 1927–35, *Karl Marx-Friedrich Engels Gesamtausgabe* [MEGA1], editors in chief D. Riazanov and W.W. Adoratski, 12 vols (cf. MECW below).

Marx, K. 1939–41, *Grundrisse der Kritik der politischen Ökonomie*, Vols I–II. Corrected reprinting in one volume, 1953. Berlin: Dietz.

Marx, K. 1968, *Mathematische Manuskripte*. German and Russian parallel text, edited by S.A. Yanovskaia. Kronberg: Scriptor.

Marx, K. 1971, *The Grundrisse*, edited by D. McLellan. New York: Harper & Row.

Marx, K. 1972, *The Ethnological Notebooks of Karl Marx*, edited by L. Krader. Assen: Van Gorcum.

Marx, K. 1973, *Grundrisse. Foundations of the Critique of Political Economy*. English translation of Marx 1953, edited by M. Nicolaus. Harmondsworth: Penguin.

Marx, K. 1974, *Mathematische Manuskripte*, edited by W. Endemann. Kronberg: Scriptor.

Marx, K. (MECW) *Marx & Engels Collected Works*. London: Lawrence and Wishart.

By Marx:

Vol. 1:	Letter from Marx to His Father. 10 November 1837.
	Doctoral dissertation: *On the Difference between the Democritean and Epicurean Philosophy of Nature*, 1841.
Vol. 3:	*Economic and Philosophical Manuscripts of 1844*.
Vol. 5:	*Theses on Feuerbach*, 1845.
Vol. 6:	*The Poverty of Philosophy. An Answer to* The Philosophy of Poverty *by M Proudhon*, 1847.
Vol. 10:	*The Class Struggles in France, 1848 to 1850*, 1850.
Vol. 11:	*The Eighteenth Brumaire of Louis Bonaparte*, 1852.
Vol. 17:	*Herr Vogt*, 1860.
Vol. 20:	*Value, Price and Profit*, 1865.
Vol. 22:	*The Civil War in France*, 1871.
Vol. 24:	*Critique of the Gotha Programme*, 1875.
	'Introduction' to the French edition of *Socialism: Utopian and Scientific*, 1880.

Vol. 28:   *A Contribution to the Critique of Political Economy*. Part One, 1859.

Vol. 31:   *Theories of Surplus Value*, 1861–63.

Vol. 35:   *Capital. A Critique of Political Economy*, Vol. I, 1867.

Vol. 36:   *Capital*, Vol. II, 1885.

Vol. 37:   *Capital*, Vol. III, 1894.

Vols. 28–50: *Letters, 1844–1883*.

By Marx and Engels:

Vol. 4:   *The Holy Family, or Critique of Critical Criticism*, 1845.

Vol. 5:   *The German Ideology. The Critique of Modern German Philosophy*, 1845–46.

Vol. 6:   *Manifesto of the Communist Party*, 1848.

Marx, K. 1975, *Karl Marx Friedrich Engels Gesamtausgabe* (MEGA2; new edition of MEGA1), editors in chief Günter Heyden and Anatoli Egorov, Vol. I/1: Karl Marx, Werke, Artikel, literarische Versuche bis März 1843.

Marx, K., and Engels, F. 1888, *Manifesto of the Communist Party*. Authorised English Translation (by Samuel Moore), edited and annotated by Frederick Engels. London: William Reeves.

Marx, K. 1954, *Briefe über Das Kapital*. Berlin: Dietz.

Masaryk, T. 1899, *Die philosophischen und sociologischen Grundlagen des Marxismus. Studien zur socialen Frage*. Wien: Carl Konegen.

von Maurer, C.L. 1854, *Einleitung zur Geschichte der Mark-, Hof-, Dorf- und Stadt-Verfassung und der öffentlichen Gewalt*. München: C. Kaiser.

von Maurer, C.L. 1865–66, *Geschichte der Dorfverfassung in Deutschland*, Vols. I–II. Erlangen: F. Enke.

Maxwell, J.C. 1875 [1870], *Theory of Heat*, 4th edition. London: Longmans, Green and Co.

Mayer, G. 1934, *Friedrich Engels*, Vols. I–II. Den Haag: Nijhoff.

Mayer, J.R. 1842, 'Bemerkungen über die Kräfte der unbelebten Natur', *Annalen der Chemie und Pharmacie*, 42, 233–40.

Mehring, F. 1875, *Herr von Treitschke, der Sozialistentödter und die Endziele des Liberalismus. Eine sozialistische Replik*. Leipzig.

Mehring, F. 1893, *Die Lessing-Legende, Eine Rettung … Nebst einem anhange über den historischen Materialismus*. Stuttgart: J.H.W. Dietz.

Meier, G., and Baldwin, R.E. 1957, *Economic Development. Theory, History, Policy*. New York: Wiley.

Meinecke, F. 1929, 'Johann Gustav Droysen. Sein Briefwechsel und seine Geschichtsschreibung', *Historische Zeitschrift*, 141.

Meinecke, F. 1936, *Die Entstehung des Historismus*, Vols. I–II. Berlin: Oldenburg.

Merton, R.K. 1949, *Social Theory and Social Structure*. Glencoe: Free Press.

Merton, R.K. 1968, *Social Theory and Social Structure*, 3rd edition. New York: Free Press.

von Meyer, E. 1899, *Geschichte der Chemie von den Ältesten Zeiten bis zur Gegenwart: Zugleich Einführung in das Studium der Chemie*. Leipzig.

von Meyer, E. 1905, *Geschichte der Chemie von den Ältesten Zeiten bis zur Gegenwart: Zugleich Einführung in das Studium der Chemie*, 3rd edition. Leipzig.

Michelet, K.L. 1876–81, *Das System der Philosophie als exacter Wissenschaft*, Vols. I–IV. Berlin: Nicolai.

Mill, J.S. 1843, *A System of Logic*. Cambridge: Cambridge University Press.

Mill, J.S. 1851, *A System of Logic*, 3rd edition, Vols. I–II. London: Parker.

Mill, J.S. 1859, *On Liberty*. London: Parker.

Mill, J.S. 1865, *Auguste Comte and Positivism*. London: John Chapman.

Mill, J.S. 1965, *Collected Works of John Stuart Mill*, Vols. II–III: *Principles of Political Economy with Some of its Applications to Social Philosophy*, Vols. I–II (1848). London: Routledge.

Mill, J.S. 1973–74, *Collected Works, Vols. VII–VIII: A System of Logic*. Toronto: University of Toronto Press.

Mirzoyan, E.N. 1961, 'Evolutsiia vzgliadov Ch. Darwina na sootnosheniii individual'- nogo i istoricheskogo razvitiia', *Trudy Instituta Istorii Estestvoznaniia i Tekhniki*, 36.

Misch, G. 1947, *Vom Lebens- und Gedankenkreis Wilhelm Diltheys*. Frankfurt: Gerhard Schulte-Bulmke.

Moleschott, J. 1852, *Der Kreislauf des Lebens*. Mainz.

Moleschott, J. 1855, *Der Kreislauf des Lebens*, 2nd edition. Mainz.

Monod, G. 1923, *La vie et la pensée de Jules Michelet*. Paris: H. Champion.

Montgomery, W.M. 1975, *Evolution and Darwinism in German Biology, 1800–1887*, Dissertation manuscript, University of Texas. Microfilm 75–4427.

Moore, F.J. 1939 [1918], *A History of Chemistry*, 3rd edition. New York: McGraw-Hill.

Moore, J. 1872, 'The Conservation of Energy not a Fact, but a Heresy of Science', *Nature*, 6.

Morgan, L.H. 1877, *Ancient Society, or, Researches in the Life of Human Progress from Savagery, through Barbarism to Civilization*. New York: H. Holt.

Mosse, G.L. 1966, *The Crisis of German Ideology. Intellectual Origins of the Third Reich*. London: Weidenfeld and Nicolson.

Most, J.M. 1873, *Kapital und Arbeit. Ein populärer Auszug aus 'Das Kapital' von Karl Marx*. Chemnitz: G. Rübner & Co.

Most, J.M. 1876a, *Die Lösung der socialen Frage. Ein Vortrag*. Berlin.

Most, J.M. 1876b, 'Ein Philosoph', *Berliner Freie Presse*.

Most, J.M. 1903–07, *Memoiren. Erlebtes, Erforschtes und Erdachtes*, Vols. I–IV. London: Slienger.

Motteler, J. 1876, 'Congress der Sozialisten Deutschlands', *Der Volksstaat*.

Müller, J. 1834, 'Jahresbericht über die Fortschritte der anatomisch-physiologischen Wissenschaften im Jahre 1833', in Müllers Archiv.

Müller, J. 1838, *Handbuch der Physiologie des Menschen*, Vol. I. Coblenz.

Müller-Markus, S. 1966, *Einstein und die Sowjetphilosophie*, Vols. I–II. Dordrecht: Reidel.

Mullin, N.C. 1972, 'The Development of a Scientific Speciality', *Minerva*, 10.

von Nägeli, C. 1865 [1861], *Entstehung und Begriff der naturhistorischen Art*, 2nd edition. München.

von Nägeli, C. 1877, 'Die Schranken der naturwissenschaftlichen Erkenntniss', in *Tageblatt der 50. Versammlung deutscher Naturforscher und Aerzte in München 1877*, Beilage.

Negt, O. 1964, *Strukturbeziehungen zwischen den Gesellschaftslehren Comtes und Hegels*. Frankfurt: Europäge Verlagsanstalt.

Negt, O. 1969, 'Marxismus als Legitimationswissenschaft. Zur Genese der stalinistischen Philosophie', in Deborin and Bukharin 1969.

Negt, O. 1975, *Der späte Engels*. Frankfurt: Suhrkamp.

Newman, J.H. 1947 [1852], *The Idea of a University*. New York: Longmans, Green.

Nicolaus, M. 1972, 'The Unknown Marx', in *Ideology in Social Science. Readings in Critical Social Theory*, edited by R. Blackburn. New York: Vintage.

Nicolaus, M. 1973, 'Foreword' to Marx 1973.

Nordenstam, T. 1972, *Empiricism and the Analytic-Synthetic Distinction*. Oslo: Universitetsforlaget.

Oestreich, G. 1969, 'Die Fachhistorie und die Anfänge der sozialgeschichtlichen Forschung in Deutschland', *Historische Zeitschrift*, 208.

Oiserman, T.I. 1965 [1962], *Die Entstehung der marxistischen Philosophie*. Translated from the Russian. Berlin: Dietz.

Oken, L. 1833–41, *Allgemeine Naturgeschichte für alle Stände*, Vols. I–VII. Stuttgart: Hoffmann.

Orsini, G.N. 1969, *Coleridge and German Idealism. A Study in the History of Philosophy with Unpublished Materials from Coleridge's Manuscripts*. Carbondale: Southern Illinois University Press.

Osnovy marksizma-leninizma 1963, also in English, German and French translations. 2nd edition. Dordrecht: Reidel.

Ostwald, W. 1908, *Die Energie*. Leipzig.

Ostwald, W. 1909, *Energetische Grundlagen der Kulturwissenschaft*. Leipzig.

Paley, W. 1803, *Natural Theology or Evidences of the Existence and Attributes of the Deity*. London: Wilks and Taylor.

Pannekoek, A. 1969 [1938], *Lenin als Philosoph*, edited by A. Schmidt. Frankfurt: Europäische Verlagsanstalt.

Partington, J.R. 1962–64, *A History of Chemistry*, Vols. III–IV. London: Macmillan.

Partridge, M.F. 1966, 'Introduction' to Herschel 1966.

Passmore, J. 1957, *A Hundred Years of Philosophy*. London: Penguin.

Passmore, J. 1959, 'Darwin's Impact on British Metaphysics', *Victorian Studies*, 3.

Paulsen, F. 1902, *Die deutsche Universitäten und das Universitätsstudium*. Berlin: A. Asher.

Peel, J.D.Y. 1971, *Herbert Spencer. The Evolution of a Sociologist*. New York: Basic Books.

Peirce, C.S. 1877, 'The Fixation of Belief', *Popular Science Monthly*, 12.

Pfetsch, F.R. 1860, Review of Darwin's *Origin*, in *Archives des Sciences de la Bibliothèque Universelle*, III.

Plamenatz, J. 1975, *Karl Marx's Philosophy of Man*. Oxford: Clarendon Press.

Plekhanov, G. 1891/92, 'Zu Hegel's sechzigstem Todesdag', *Die Neue Zeit*, I.

Plümacher, O. 1881, *Der Kampf um's Unbewusste*. Berlin: Duncker.

Poppe, J.H.M. 1807–11, *Geschichte der Technologie*, Vols. I–II. Göttingen.

Poppe, J.H.M. 1807–09, *Geschichte der Technologie*, Vols. I–II. Göttingen.

Poppe, J.H.M. 1830, *Die Physik vorzüglich in Anwendung auf Künste*. Tübingen: Fues.

Popper, K.R. 1957, *The Poverty of Historicism*. London: Routledge & Kegan Paul.

Popper, K.R. 1962 [1945], *The Open Society and Its Enemies*, Vol. II, 2nd edition. London: Routledge & Kegan Paul.

Popper, K.R. 1968 [1935], *The Logic of Scientific Discovery*, 2nd edition. London: Hutchinson.

Popper, K.R. 1972 [1963], *Conjectures and Refutations. The Growth of Scientific Knowledge*, 4th edition. London: Routledge & Kegan Paul.

Positivismus im 19. Jahrhundert. Beiträge zu seiner geschichtlichen und systematischen Bedeutung 1971, edited by J. Ritter. Frankfurt: Klostermann.

Der Positivismusstreit in der deutschen Soziologie 1969, with contributions by T.W. Adorno, R. Dahrendorf et al. Berlin: Luchterhand.

Protokoll des Sozialistenkongress zu Gotha vom 27–29 Mai 1877 1877.

Quetelet, A. 1846, *Lettres à S.A.R. le duc regnant de Saxe-Coburg et Gotha, sur la théorie des probabilités, appliquée aux sciences morales et politiques*. Bruxelles.

Quetelet, A. 1869 [1835], *Physique sociale ou essai sur le développement des facultés de l'homme*, 2nd edition, Vols. I–II. Bruxelles.

Rand, C.G. 1964, 'Two Meanings of Historicism in the Writings of Dilthey, Troeltsch, and Meinecke', *Journal of the History of Ideas*, 25.

Randall, J.H. 1961, 'The Changing Impact of Darwin on Philosophy', *Journal of the History of Ideas*, 22.

von Ranke, L. 1824, *Zur Kritik neuerer Geschichtsschreiber*. Leipzig: Reimer.

Regnault, V. and Strecker, A. 1853, *Kurzes Lehrbuch der Chemie*, Vol. I, 4th edition. Braunschweig.

Regnault, V. and Strecker, A. 1863, *Kurzes Lehrbuch der Chemie*, Vol. II. Braunschweig.

Reichelt, H. 1970, *Zur logischen Struktur des Kapitalbegriffs bei Karl Marx*. Frankfurt: Europäische Verlagsanstalt.

Reiprich, K. 1969, *Die philosophisch-naturwissenschaftlichen Arbeiten von Karl Marx och Friedrich Engels*. Berlin: Dietz.

Rejai, M. 1973, 'Ideology', in *Dictionary of the History of Ideas*, Vol. II. New York: Scribner.

Remmling, G.W. 1975, *The Sociology of Karl Mannheim*. London: Routledge & Kegan Paul.

Reports of the Third Meeting of the British Association for the Advancement of Science Held at Canterbury in 1833 1834.

Riazanov, D. 1927, 'Einleitung des Herausgebers' to Engels 1927.

Riazanov, D. 1973 [1927], *Karl Marx and Friedrich Engels. An Introduction to their Lives and Works*. New York: Monthly Review Press.

Ricardo, D. 1817, *Principles of Political Economy and Taxation*. London: John Murray.

Ricardo, D. 1903, *Principles of Political Economy and Taxation*, new edition, edited by C.K. Gonner. London: George Bell.

Rickert, H. 1902, *Die Grenzen der naturwissenschaftlichen Begriffsbildung*. Tübingen: J.C.B. Mohr.

Ringer, F.K. 1969, *The Decline of the German Mandarins: The German Academic Community, 1890–1933*. Cambridge, MA: Harvard University Press.

Ritter, C. 1852, *Einleitungd zur allgemeinen vergleichenden Geographie und Abhandlungen zur Begründung einer mehr wissenschaftlichen Behandlund der Erdkunde*. Berlin: Reimer.

Rodinson, M. 1966, *Islam et capitalisme*. Paris: Seuil.

Rockhausen. See *Classification*.

Rocker, R. 1924, *Johann Most. Das Leben eines Rebellen*. Berlin: F. Kater.

Roll, E. 1973 [1938], *A History of Economic Thought*, 4th edition. London: Faber & Faber.

Roscoe, H.E. 1867 [1866], *Kurzes Lehrbuch der Chemie nach der neuesten Ansichten der Wissenschaft*, translated from English and revised by Carl Schorlemmer. Braunschweig: Vieweg.

Roscoe, H.E. 1892, 'Carl Schorlemmer', *Proceedings of the Royal Society of London*, LII.

Roscoe, H.E. 1895, 'Carl Schorlemmer, LLD, FRS', *Nature*, XLVI.

Roscoe, H.E. 1906, *The Life and Experiences of Sir Henry Enfield Roscoe, Written by Himself*. London: Macmillan.

Roscoe, H.E. and Schorlemmer, C. 1877–84, *Ausführliches Lehrbuch der Chemie*, Vols. I–III. Braunschweig: Vieweg.

Rosdolsky, R. 1969 [1968], *Zur Entstehungsgeschichte des Marxschen 'Kapital'*, Vols. I–II, 2nd edition. Frankfurt: Europäische Verlagsanstalt.

Ross, R. 1949 [1923], *Aristotle*, 5th edition. London: Oxford University Press.

Rossi, P. 1960, *Storia e Storicismo nella Filosofia Contemporanea*. Milano: Lerici.

Rothacker, E. 1960, 'Das Wort "Historicismus"', *Zeitschrift für deutsche Wortforschung*, 16.

Roux, W. 1881, *Der Kampf der Teile im Organismus*. Leipzig: Engelmann.

Rosental, M.M. 1969 [1962], *Die dialektische Methode der politischen Ökonomie von Karl Marx*, translated from the Russian. Berlin: Dietz.

Rüschemeyer, D. 1968, *Probleme der Wissenssoziologie. Ein Kritik der Arbeiten Karl Mannheims und Max Schelers.* Köln.

Rüsen, J. 1969, *Begriffene Geschichte. Genesis und Begründung der Geschichtstheorie J.G. Droysens.* Köln.

Salet, G. 1874–76, 'Affinité', in Wurtz (ed.) 1874–76, Vol. I:1.

Salet, G. 1874–76, 'Chaleur', in Wurtz (ed.) 1874–76, Vol. I:2.

Sandkühler, H.J. 1973, *Praxis und Geschichtsbewusstsein. Studien zur materialistischen Dialektik, Erkenntnistheorie und Hermeneutik.* Frankfurt: Suhrkamp.

Sartre, J-P. 1960, *Critique de la raison dialectique,* Vol. I. Paris: Gallimard.

von Savigny, K. 1814, *Vom Beruf unserer Zeit für Gesetzgebung und Rechtswissenschaft.* Heidelberg: Mohr und Zimmer.

Schaxel, J. 1918, *Grundzüge der Theorienbildung in der Biologie.* Jena: Fischer.

Schelling, F.W.J. 1857–58, *Sämmtliche Werke,* edited by F.K.J. Schelling. Stuttgart.
- Vol. I/2:   *Ideen zu einer Philosophie der Natur,* 1797.
              Von der Weltseele, 1798.
- Vol. I/3:   *Erster Entwurf eines Systems der Naturphilosophie,* 1799.
- Vol. I/4:   *Bruno oder über das göttliche und natürliche Prinzip der Dinge,* 1802.
  Vorlesungen üuber die Methode des akademischen Studiums, 1803.

Schelling, F.W.J. 1962, *Briefe und Dokumente, Vol. I: 1775–1809,* edited by H. Fuhrmanns. Bonn.

Schleiden, M.J. 1838, 'Beiträge zur Phytogenesis', *Archiv für Anatomie, Physiologie und wissenschaftl. Medicin.*

Schleier, H. 1965, *Sybel und Treitschke. Antidemokratismus und Militarismus im historisch-politischen Denken grossbourgeoiser Ideologien.* Berlin: Akademie Verlag.

Schleiermacher, F. 1867, *Werke. Auswahl in vier Bänden,* Vol. 4. Stuttgart.

Schleiermacher, F. 1910, 'Gelegentliche Gedanken über Universitäten im deutschen Sinn', in Spranger 1910.

Schmid, G. 1935, 'Über die Herkunft der Ausdrücke Morphologie und Biologie', *Nova Acta Leopoldina,* 2, H. 3/4, No. 8.

Schmidt, A. 1971a [1962], *Der Begriff der Natur in der Lehre von Marx.* 2nd edition. Frankfurt: Europäische Verlag.

Schmidt, A. 1971b, *Geschichte und Struktur. Fragen einer marxistischen Historik.* München: Carl Hanser Verlag.

Schmidt, A. 1973, *Emanzipatorische Sinnlichkeit. Ludwig Feuerbachs anthropologischer Materialismus.* München: Carl Hanser Verlag.

Schmidt, A. 1974 [1969], 'Det strukturalistiska angreppet på historien', in *Vetenskap som kritik. En introduktion till Frankfurtskolans aktuella positioner,* edited by K. Aspelin and T. Gerholm. Stockholm: PAN.

Schmidt, O. 1877, *Die naturiwissenschaftlichen Grundlagen der Philosophie des Unbewussten.* Leipzig: F.A. Brockhaus.

Schmidt, O. 1878, *Darwinismus und Sozialdemokratie*. Bonn: Strauss.

Schmitt, M. 1918, 'Die Behandlung des erkenntnistheoretischen Idealismus bei Eduard von Hartmann', *Kantstudien*, 41.

Schnabel, F. 1964, *Deutsche Geschichte im neunzehnten Jahrhundert*, Vol. II. München: Deutscher Taschenbuch Verlag.

Schopenhauer, A. 1922 [1819], *Schopenhauers sämmtliche Werke*, Vol. 3: *Die Welt als Wille und Vorstellung, Vol. II*, 2nd edition, edited by J. Frauenstädt. Leipzig: Reclam.

Schorlemmer, C. 1864, 'On the Action of Chlorine upon Methyl', *Proceedings of the Royal Society of London*, 12.

Schorlemmer, C. 1865–71, 'Researches on the Hydrocarbons of the Series C_nH_{2n+2}', Parts 1–7, *Proceedings of the Royal Society of London*, 14–19.

Schorlemmer, C. 1871, *Lehrbuch der Kohlenstoffverbindungen oder der organischen Chemie*. Braunschweig: Vieweg.

Schorlemmer, C. 1872, 'On the Normal Paraffine', *Philosophical Transactions*, CLXII.

Schorlemmer, C. 1879, *The Rise and Development of Organic Chemistry*. Manchester: J.E. Cornish.

Schorlemmer, C. 1889, *Der Ursprung und die Entwickelung der organischen Chemie*. Braunschweig: Vieweg.

Schorlemmer, C. See also Roscoe and Schorlemmer.

Schraepler, E. 1966, *August Bebel. Sozialdemokrat im Kaiserreich*. Zurich: Musterschmidt.

Schramm, C.A. 1872, 'Der Tauschwert', *Volkstaat*.

Schumacher, H. 1883 [1875], *J.H. von Thünen. Ein Forscherleben*, 2nd edition. Forbach: R. Hupfer.

Schumpeter, J.A. 1954, *History of Economic Analysis*, edited from manuscript by E.B. Schumpeter. Cambridge, MA: Harvard University Press.

Schuon, K.T. 1975, *Bürgerlicher Gesellschaftswissenschaft der Gegenwart. Einführung und Kritik*. Köln: Keipenheuer und Witsch.

Schwann, T. 1839, *Mikroskopische Untersuchungen über die Übereinstimmung in der Struktur und dem Wachsthum der Thiere und Pflanzen*. Berlin.

Schönebaum, H. 1961, 'Karl Lamprechst und Ernst Bernheim', *Archiv für Kulturgeschichte*, 43.

Science at the Crossroads: Papers presented to the International Congress of the History of Science and Technology held in London from June 29th to July 3rd, 1931 by the delegates of the USSR 1931, London: Kniga.

Sebag, L. 1964, *Marxisme et structuralisme*. Paris: Payot.

Seignobos. See Langlois and Seignobos.

Simon, E. 1928, 'Ranke und Hegel', *Historische Zeitschrift*, Supplement 15.

Simon, J. 1887, *Victor Cousin*. Paris: Hachette.

Simon, W.M. 1963, *European Positivism in the Nineteenth Century. An Essay in Intellectual History*. Port Washington, NY: Kennikat Press.

Simonsson, T. 1958, *Face to Face with Darwinism*. Lund.

Simpson, C.G. 1949, *The Meaning of Evolution. A Study of the History of Life and of Its Significance for Man*. New Haven: Yale University Press.

Smith, A. 1896 [1763], *Lectures on Justice, Police, Revenue and Arms, Delivered in the University of Glasgow*, edited by A. Cannan. Oxford: Clarendon Press.

Smith, A. 1950 [1776], *An Inquiry into the Nature and Causes of the Wealth of Nations*, edited by A. Cannan, 6th edition. London: Methuen.

Sombart, W. 1894, 'Zur Kritik des ökonomischen Systems von Karl Marx', *Archiv für sociale Gesetzgebung und Statistik*, 7.

Southern, R.W. 1961, *The Shape and Substance of Academic History*. Oxford: Clarendon Press.

Spencer, H. 1862–93, *A System of Synthetic Philosophy*. London: Williams and Norgate.

   Vol. I: *First Principles*, 1862.

   Vols. II–III: *The Principles of Biology*, 1864–67.

   Vols. IV–V: *The Principles of Psychology*, 1855; 2nd edition 1870–72.

   Vols. VI–VIII: *The Principles of Sociology*, 1876–97.

   Vols. IX–X: *The Principles of Ethics*, 1879–93.

Spencer, H. 1869 [1864], *Classification of the Sciences*, 2nd edition. London: Williams and Norgate.

Spencer, H. 1872, 'Survival of the Fittest', *Nature*, V.

Spencer, H. 1873, *The Study of Sociology*. London: Kegan Paul.

Spencer, H. 1880, *The Study of Sociology*, 8th edition. London: Williams and Norgate.

Spencer, H. 1904, *An Autobiography*, Vols. I–II. London: Williams and Norgate.

Spencer, H. 1966 [1891], *The Works of Herbert Spencer*, Vol. XIV, *Essays: Scientific, Political & Speculative, Vol. II*. Osnabrück: O. Zeller.

Spranger, E. 1910, *Fichte, Schleiermacher, Steffens über das Wesen der Universität*. Leipzig: Durr.

Stadler, P. 1958, *Geschichtsschreibung und historische Denken in Frankreich 1789–1871*. Zurich: Verlag Berichthaus.

Stebbing, L.S. 1958, *Philosophy and the Physicists*. New York: Dover.

Steffens, H. 1822, *Anthropologie*, Vol. I. Breslau: J. Max.

Stepanova, E.A. 1958 [1956], *Friedrich Engels. Sein Leben und Werk*, translated from the Russian. Berlin: Dietz.

Stewart, B. 1872, Review of J. Clerk Maxwell, 'Theory of Heat', *Nature*, V.

Strecker, see Regnault and Strecker.

Struik, D.J. 1948, 'Marx and Mathematics', *Science and Society*, 12.

Suter, J.F. 1960, *Philosophie et histoire chez Wilhelm Dilthey. Essai sur le problème de l'historicisme*. Bâle: Verlag für Recht und Gesellschaft.

von Sybel, H. 1859, 'Vorwort', *Historische Zeitschrift*, I.

von Sybel, H. 1885 [1874], *Vorträge und Aufsätze*, 3rd edition. Berlin: Hoffmann.

Tait, P.G. 1876, 'Force. Evening Lecture at the Glasgow Meeting of the British Association for the Advancement of Science', *Nature*, 14.

Tait, P.G. See also Thomson and Tait.

Therborn, G. 1974, *Science, Class and Society. On the Formation of Sociology and Historical Materialism*. Göteborg: Revo Press.

Their, E. 1954, 'Etappen der Marxinterpretation', *Marxismusstudien*, I.

Thackeray, A. and Merton, R.K. 1972, 'On Discipline Building: The Paradoxes of George Sarton', *Isis*, 63.

Thomas Aquinas 1967, *Utvalg. Innledning og oversettelse vid K-E Tranøy*. Oslo: Pax.

Thompson, J. 1886, *The Owen's College, Its Foundation and Growth*. Manchester.

Thomson, W. and Tait, P.G. 1867, *Treatise on Natural Philosophy*, Vol. I. Oxford: Clarendon Press.

Thorpe, E. 1916, *The Right Honourable Sir Henry Enfield Roscoe. A Biographical Sketch*. London: Longmans, Green and Co.

von Thünen, J.H. 1826–63, *Der isolierte Staat in Beziehung auf Landwirtschaft und Nationalökonomie*, Vols. I–III. Berlin.

Tiedemann, F. 1830, *Physiologie der Menschen*, Vol. I. Darmstadt.

Timpanaro, S. 1975 [1970–73], *On Materialism*, translated from the Italian. London: NLB.

Traube, M. 1867, 'Experimente zur Theorie der Zellenbildung und Endosmose', in *Archiv für Anatomie, Physiologie und wissenschaftliche Medicin*, edited by C.B. Riecherts and E. Du Bois-Reymonds. Berlin.

Traube, M. 1874, 'Über Zellenbildung', in *Tageblatt der 47. Versammlung deutscher Naturforscher und Aerzte in Breslau 1874*.

von Treitschke, H. 1859, *Die Gesellschaftswissenschaft. Ein kritischer Versuch*. Leipzig.

von Treitschke, H. 1875, *Der Sozialismus und seine Gönner*. Berlin: Reimer.

Trémaux, P. 1865, *Origine et transformations de l'homme et des autres êtres*, Vol. I. Paris: Hachette.

Treviranus, G.R. 1831, *Die Erscheinungen und Gesetze des organischen Lebens*, Vol. I. Bremen: Heyse.

Troeltsch, E. 1922, *Gesammelte Schriften*, Vol. III: *Der Historismus und seine Probleme. Erstes Buch*. Aalen: Scientia Verlag.

Trübners deutsches Wörterbuch 1939, 6, no. 1.

Tsuzuki, C. 1967, *The Life of Eleanor Marx 1855–1898. A Socialist Tragedy*. Oxford: Clarendon Press.

Turner, F.M. 1974, *Between Science and Religion. The Reaction to Scientific Naturalism in Late Victorian England*. New Haven: Yale University Press.

Tylor, E.B. 1865, *Researches in the Early History of Mankind and the Development of Civilization*. London: John Murray.

Tylor, E.B. 1871, *Primitive Culture*, Vols. I–II. London: John Murray.

Tyndall, J. 1870 [1862], *Heat a Mode of Motion*, 4th edition. London: Longman, Green and Co.

Tyndall, J. 1876, 'Professor Tyndall on Germs', *Nature*, 13.

Tyndall, J. 1879 [1871], *Fragments of Science*, 6th edition, Vols. I–II. New York: D. Appleton.

Überweg, F. 1863–66, *Grundriss der Geschichte der Philosophie*, Vols. I–III. Leipzig.

Ulrici, H. 1873, *Gott und der Mensch*, Vol. I. Leipzig.

Ure, A. 1843–44 [1839], *Technisches Wörterbuch*, Vols. I–III, translated from the English. Prag.

Vaihinger, H. 1876, *Hartmann, Dühring und Lange. Zur Geschichte der deutschen Philosophie im XIX. Jahrhundert. Ein kritischer Essay.* Iserlohn: J. Baedeker.

Veblen, T. 1923, *Absentee Ownership*. New York: A.M. Kelley.

Virchow, R. 1856, 'Alter und neuer Vitalismus', *Archiv für pathologische Anatomie und Physiologie und für klinische Medicin*, 9.

Virchow, R. 1871 [1858], *Die Cellularpathologie in ihrer Begründung auf psychologische und pathologische Gewebelehre*, 4th edition. Berlin: August Hirschwald.

Virchow, R. 1877, *Die Freiheit der Wissenschaft im modernen Staat. Rede gehalten in der dritten allgemeinen Sitzung der fünfzigsten Versammlung deutscher Naturforscher und Aerzte zu München.* Berlin.

Vogt, C. 1854, *Köhlerglaube und Wissenschaft*. Giessen.

Vogt, C. 1859, *Mein Prozess gegen die Allgemeine Zeitung*. Genf.

Vorländer, K. 1911, *Kant und Marx. Ein Beitrag zur Philosophie des Sozialismus*. Tübingen: J.C.B. Mohr.

Vorländer, K. 1926, *Von Machiavelli bis Lenin*. Leipzig.

Vorzimmer, P. 1963, 'Charles Darwin and Blending Inheritance', *Isis*, 54.

Vorzimmer, P. 1970, *Charles Darwin. The Years of Controversy*. London: University of London Press.

Vranicki, P. 1972 [1970], *Geschichte des Marxismus*, Vol. I, translated from the 2nd Croatian edition. Frankfurt: Suhrkamp.

Wagner, F. 1951, *Geschichtswissenschaft*. Freiburg: Alber.

Wagner, R. (ed.) 1842–53, *Handwörterbuch der Physiologie mit Rücksicht auf physiologischen Pathologie*, Vols. I–IV. Braunschweig: Vieweg.

Wagner, R. (ed.) 1854, *Über Wissen und Glauben*. Göttingen.

Waitz, G. 1859a, 'Falsche Richtungen. Schreiben an den Herausgeber von Georg Waitz', *Historische Zeitschrift*, I.

Waitz, G. 1859b, 'Preussen und die erste polnische Theilung', *Historische Zeitschrift*, III.

Waitz, G. 1867, *Die historischen Übungen zu Göttingen. Glückwunschschreiben an Leopold von Ranke.* Göttingen.

Waitz, T. 1861, 'Über die Einheit des Menschengeschlechts', *Historische Zeitschrift*, V.

Wall, K.A. 1966, *The Doctrine of Relation in Hegel*. Düsseldorf.

Wallace, A.R. 1872a, 'The Last Attack on Darwinism', *Nature*, 6.

Wallace, A.R. 1872b, 'The Beginnings of Life', *Nature*, 6.

Watermann, R. 1960, *Theodor Schwann: Leben und Werk*. Düsseldorf: L. Schwann.

Wedberg, A. 1984, *The History of Philosophy*, Vol. III. Oxford: Clarendon Press.

Weigand-Abendroth, F. 1959, *Max Adlers transzendentale Grundlegung des Sozialismus*. Doctoral dissertation, University of Vienna.

Weischedel, W. 1960, 'Einleitung' to *Idee und Wirklichkeit einer Universität. Dokumente zur Geschichte der Friedrich-Wilhelm-Universität zu Berlin* 1960, edited by W. Weischedel. Berlin: De Gruyter.

Weismann, A. 1876, *Studien zur Deszendenztheorie, Vol. II: Über die letzten Ursachen der Transmutation*. Leipzig.

Weismann, A. 1902, *Vorträge über Deszendenztheorie*, Vols. I–II. Jena.

von Weiss, A. 1965, *Die Diskussion über den historischen Materialismus in der deutschen Sozialdemokratie 1891–1918*. Wiesbaden: O. Harrassowitz.

Wetter, G.A. 1960, *Der dialektische Materialismus*. Kaidenkirchen: Steyler.

Whewell, W. 1838 [1837], *On the Principles of English University Education*, 2nd edition. London: Parker.

Whewell, W. 1967 [1840], *The Historical and Philosophical Works of William Whewell*, photographic reproduction, *Vol. V: Philosophy of the Inductive Sciences*. London: Cass.

Whewell, W. 1968, *William Whewell's Theory of Scientific Method*, edited by R.E. Butts. Pittsburgh: University of Pittsburgh Press.

White, H.V. 1975, 'Historicism, History, and the Figurative Imagination', *History and Theory*, 14.

Wideqvist, S. 1963, *Organisk kemi*. Stockholm.

Wiedemann, G. 1872–74 [1861], *Die Lehre vom Galvanismus und Elektromagnetismus*, 2nd edition, Vols. I–II. Braunschweig: Vieweg.

Wiedemann, G. 1882, 'Vorwort' to Helmholtz 1882–95, Vol. III.

Wigand, A. 1874–75, *Der Darwinismus und die Naturforschung Newtons und Cuviers*, Vols. I–III. Braunschweig: Vieweg.

Williams-Ellis, A. 1966, *Darwin's Moon. A Biography of Alfred Russel Wallace*. London: Blackie.

Wilson, A.M. 1972, *Diderot*. New York: Oxford University Press.

Windelband, W. 1894, *Geschichte und Naturwissenschaft*. Strassbourg.

Wolff, H.H. 1964, 'Karl Mannheim in seinen Abhandlungen bis 1933', in Mannheim 1964.

von Wright, G.H. 1971, *Explanation and Understanding*. London: Routledge & Kegan Paul.

Wright-Mills, C. 1962, *The Marxists*. Harmondsworth: Penguin.

Wundt, W. 1866, *Über die physikalischen Axiome und ihre Beziehung zum Causalprincip*. Erlangen: F. Enke.

Wurtz, A. (ed.) 1874–76, *Dictionnaire de chimie pure et appliquée*, Vols. I–III. Paris: Hachette.

Wurtz, A. (ed.) 1874–76, 'Atomicité', in Wurtz (ed.) 1874–76, Vol. I:1.

Wygodski, W.S. 1967, *Die Geschichte einer grossen Entdeckung*. Berlin.

von Wyss, W. 1958, *Charles Darwin. Ein Forscherleben*. Zürich.

Yanovskaya, S.A. 1969, 'Karl Marx, "Mathematische Manuskripte"', *Sowjetwissenschaft, Gesellschaftswiss. Beiträge. I Halbjahr*.

Zelený, J. 1970 [1962], *Die Wissenschaftslogik bei Marx und* Das Kapital, translated from the Czech. Wien: Europa Verlag.

Ziegler, L. 1910, *Das Weltbild Hartmanns. Eine Beurteilung*. Leipzig.

Zimmermann, H. 1964, *Carl Schorlemmer – Chemist und Kommunist, Freund und Kampfgefährte som Karl Marx und Friedrich Engels*. Merseburg.

Zloczower, A. 1966, *Career Opportunities and the Growth of Scientific Discovery in 19th-Century Germany*. New York: Arno Press.

Zuppinger, H. 1974, *Albert Kölliker und die mikroskopische Anatomie*. Zürich: Juris Druck + Verlag.

Index of Subjects

Note: A large number of definitions have been incorporated into the index. If words are used in a special manner in the text, the definition is marked with an asterisk (*). References to passages that provide a more detailed investigation of the use of the word are *italicised*.

Printed in the United States
by Baker & Taylor Publisher Services